CONTEMPORARY'S

ESSENTIAL GED

Coordinating Editor
Patricia Mulcrone, Ed.D.
Professor *Emerita*
Adult Educational Development
William Rainey Harper College
Palatine, Illinois

McGraw-Hill Contemporary

Contributing Authors
Critical Thinking Skills—Patricia Mulcrone
Language Arts, Writing—Linda W. Nelson, Associate Professor/Co-Chair
Social Studies—Kathleen D. Millin and Suzanne E. Rausch, Instructors
Science—Suzanne E. Rausch and Kathleen D. Millin
Language Arts, Reading—Patricia Mulcrone and Linda W. Nelson
Mathematics—Janice S. Phillips, Associate Professor

Special thanks to: LeRoy T. Mulcrone, Schaumburg, IL,
consultant for Language Arts, Reading and Social Studies

McGraw-Hill
Contemporary

Send all inquiries to:
McGraw-Hill/Contemporary
130 E. Randolph, Suite 400
Chicago, IL 60601

ISBN: 0-07-252754-4

Printed in the United States of America.

1 2 3 4 5 6 7 8 9 10 QPD 08 07 06 05 04 03 02

CONTENTS

SOCIAL STUDIES   127

ACKNOWLEDGMENTS

The editors have made every effort to trace the ownership of all copyrighted material, and necessary permissions have been secured in most cases. Upon notification of any oversight, proper acknowledgment will be made in future editions.

Excerpt on page 3 is adapted from "Select Batteries According to How They Will Be Used," *Daily Herald*, November 26, 2000.

Excerpt on page 9 is from "I Have a Dream" speech by Martin Luther King, Jr. Reprinted by arrangement with the Estate of Martin Luther King Jr., c/o Writers House as agent for the proprietor. Copyright 1963 Martin Luther King Jr., renewed 1991 by Coretta Scott King.

Graphic and text on page 17 is from "How Cells Divide," as appeared in *Daily Herald*, March 31, 2000. Reprinted with permission of AP/Wide World Photos.

Photo and caption on page 20 are reprinted from *How in the World?* copyright © 1990 The Reader's Digest Association Limited. Used by permission of The Reader's Digest Association, Inc., Pleasantville, NY, www.rd.com.

Excerpt on page 22 is from *Message in a Bottle* by Nicholas Sparks. Copyright © 1998 by Nicholas Sparks. By permission of Little, Brown and Company (Inc.).

Excerpt on pages 24–25 is from *Saint Joan* by George Bernard Shaw. Reprinted by permission of The Society of Authors on behalf of the Bernard Shaw Estate.

Excerpts on page 26 are from *The Diary of Anne Frank: The Critical Edition* by Anne Frank, copyright © 1986 by Anne Frank-Fonds, Basle/Switzerland, for all texts of Anne Frank. Used by permission of Doubleday, a division of Random House, Inc.

Excerpt on page 41 from "Stem Cells Opening Path to Brain Repair," *Chicago Tribune*, June 27, 1999. Copyright © 1999, Chicago Tribune Company. All rights reserved. Used with permission.

Excerpt on page 44 is from "When you need help climbing out of debt," by Jean Sherman Chatzky, *USA Weekend*, Feb. 18–20, 2000. Reprinted by permission of Jane Sherman Chatzky, contributing editor, *USA Weekend*.

Excerpt on page 45 adapted from *Revolution From Within* by Gloria Steinem (New York: Little Brown and Company, 1992).

Excerpt on page 46 is from "Discoveries: Don't Cut it Out," *Chicago Tribune*, October 31, 1999. Copyright © 1999, Chicago Tribune Company. All rights reserved. Used with permission.

Excerpt on page 54 is abridged from "7 Habits 11 Years Later" by Stephen Covey as appeared in *USA Weekend*, July 7–9, 2000. Used with permission from Franklin Covey Co., All rights reserved. www.franklincovey.com.

Excerpt on page 55 is from "Business," by Steven L. Kent as appeared in *Sky* magazine, April 2000. Reprinted by permission of the author.

Standards on page 123 are permission granted from GEDTS (General Educational Development Testing Service) A program of ACE (American Council on Education).

Essays and scores on pages 124 and 125 are permission granted from GEDTS (General Educational Development Testing Service) A program of ACE (American Council on Education).

Excerpt on page 172 is adapted from *How the United States Government Works* by Nancy Gendron Hofmann, Ziff-Davis Press, 1995. Reprinted by permission.

Figure on page 187 is from *Consumer Economics in Action*, 1st edition, by Roger LeRoy Miller and Alan D. Stafford, © 1993. Reprinted with permission of South-Western College Publishing a division of Thomson Learning. Fax 800 730-2215.

Table on page 202 is from *World Population: Challenges for the 21st Century* by Leon F. Bouvier and Jane T. Bertrand. © 1999 by Leon F. Bouvier and Jane T. Bertrand. Reprinted by permission of Seven Locks Press.

Figure on page 214 is from "A Brave, New World Emerging at Biopharms," *Chicago Tribune*, February 8, 1998. Copyrighted 1998, Chicago Tribune Company. All rights reserved. Used with permission.

Excerpt on page 290 is from Eudora Welty, *A Curtain of Green and Other Stories*, (Orlando: Harcourt Brace and Company,1941).

Excerpt on page 292 is from "Winter Dreams." Reprinted with permission of Scribner, a Division of Simon & Schuster, from *The Short Stories of F. Scott Fitzgerald*, edited by Matthew J. Bruccoli. Copyright 1922 by Metropolitan Publications, Inc. Copyright renewed 1950 by Frances Scott Fitzgerald Lavahan.

Excerpt on page 297 reprinted with permission of Scribner, a Division of Simon & Schuster, from *The Old Man And The Sea* by Ernest Hemingway. Copyright © 1952 by Ernest Hemingway. Copyright renewed © 1980 by Mary Hemingway.

Excerpt on pages 298 is from *The Newman Assignment* by Kurt Haberl (Los Altos Hills: May Davenport, Publishers, 1996).

Excerpt on pages 301 is from "A Canary for One." Excerpted with permission of Scribner, a Division of Simon & Schuster, from *Men Without Women* by Ernest Hemingway. Copyright 1927 by Charles Scribner's Sons. Copyright renewed 1955 by Ernest Hemingway.

Excerpt on page 302 is from *Upon the Sweeping Flood and Other Stories* by Joyce Carol Oates (New York: Random House, 1966), p. 100.

Poem on page 306 is from *The Collected Poems of Langston Hughes* by Langston Hughes, copyright © 1994 by The Estate of Langston Hughes. Used by permission of Alfred A. Knopf, a division of Random House, Inc.

Poem on page 307 "Child of the Americas" is from *Getting Home Alive*, Aurora Levins Morales, Firebrand Books, Ithaca, New York. © Copyright 1986 by Aurora Levins Morales. Used by permission.

Poem on page 308 "Dawn Over the Mountains" by Kenneth Rexroth, is from *One Hundred Poems from the Chinese*, copyright © 1971 by Kenneth Rexroth. Reprinted by permission of New Directions Publishing Corp.

Poem on page 309 is "Poem in Three Parts" by Robert Bly from *Silence in the Snowy Fields*, Wesleyan University Press, Middletown, CT, 1962. Reprinted by permission of the author.

Poem on page 310 is "Hope" by Emily Dickinson. Reprinted by permission of the publishers and the Trustees of Amherst College from *The Poems of Emily Dickinson*, Thomas H. Johnson, ed., Cambridge, Mass.: The Belknap Press of Harvard University Press, Copyright © 1951, 1955, 1979 by the President and Fellows of Harvard College.

Excerpt on page 312 is from "Memory" in *Cats* music by Andrew Lloyd Webber, words by T.S. Eliot. Reprinted by permission of Faber and Faber Ltd.

Poem on page 316 is "Leisure" by W. H. Davies. Reprinted by permission of Dee & Griffin of Gloucester, on behalf of The Trustees of Mrs. H.M. Davies Will Trust.

Footnotes on page 318 are from "Hamlet," pp. 1074–1075, from *The Complete Works of Shakespeare* 4th ed. by David Bevington. Copyright © 1992 by HarperCollins Publishers. Reprinted by permission of Pearson Education, Inc.

Excerpt on pages 322 is from *Born Yesterday* by Garson Kanin. Reprint permission granted by Estate of Garson Kanin. Copyright renewed 1973 Garson Kanin.

Excerpt on page 325 is from *Men Are From Mars, Women Are From Venus* by John Gray, Ph.D. (New York: HarperCollins Publishers, 1992), p.10.

Excerpt on page 327 is from "Look Who's Talking With Their Hands," by Diane Brady. Reprinted from the August 14, 2000 issue of *Business Week* by special permission, copyright © 2000 by The McGraw-Hill Companies, Inc.

Excerpt on page 328 is from "Brady Law Still Makes Sense." Reprinted from *Daily Herald*, August 7, 2000.

Excerpt on page 331 is from Tom Browkaw, *The Greatest Generation*. (New York: Random House, 1998), pp 165, 169.

Excerpt on page 333 is from "Parents Shouldn't Be on Call All the Time" by Nicole Wise. *Newsweek*, August 7, 2000, © 2000 Newsweek, Inc. All rights reserved. Reprinted by permission.

Excerpt on page 337 is from *The Geography of the Imagination* by Guy Davenport. Reprinted by permission of David R. Godine, Publisher, Inc. Copyright ©1981 by Guy Davenport.

Excerpt on page 459 is adapted from "Cleaning House Can Reduce Impact of Allergens in the Air" as appeared in *Daily Herald*, October 29, 2000. Reprinted by permission of The Carpet and Rug Institute.

Excerpt on page 476 from "Ellis Island," National Monument New York, U.S. Department of the Interior National Park Service by Brian Fenney.

Excerpt on page 477 from *The Greatest Generation* by Tom Browkaw (New York: Random House, 1998).

Chart on page 487 is from *American Medical Association Family Medical Guide* by American Medical Association, copyright © 1982 by The American Medical Association. Used by permission of Random House, Inc.

Excerpt on page 492 is from *Arsenic and Old Lace* by Joseph Kesselring, copyright 1941 and renewed 1969 by Charlotte Kesselring. Used by permission of Random House, Inc.

Excerpt on page 494 is from *Being There*, copyright © 1970 by Jerzy Kosinski, reprinted by permission of Harcourt, Inc.

Excerpt on page 496 is "Passage One" and "Passage Two" from *Divine Secrets of the Ya-Ya Sisterhood* by Rebecca Wells. Copyright © 1996 by Rebecca Wells. Reprinted by permission of HarperCollins Publishers, Inc.

Excerpt on page 498 is from "Leave 'em Laughing," *Newsweek Extra*, Summer. © 1998 Newsweek, Inc. All rights reserved. Reprinted by permission.

TO THE STUDENT

If you're studying to pass the GED Tests, you're in good company. In 1999 the American Council on Education GED Testing Service reported that over 750,700 adults took the GED Test battery worldwide. Of this number, more than 526,400 (70 percent) actually received their certificates. One in seven (14 percent) of those who have high school credentials has a GED diploma. One in twenty students (5 percent) in their first year of college study is a GED graduate.

The average age of GED test-takers in the United States was over 24 (and over 30 in Canada) in 1999, but nearly three quarters (70 percent) of GED test-takers were 19 years of age or older. Two out of three GED test-takers report having completed the tenth grade or higher, and more than a third report having completed the eleventh grade before leaving high school.

Why do so many people choose to take the GED Tests? What difference does passing the GED make? Some do so to get a job, to advance in a present job, to go to college, or to qualify for military service. Some have been home schooled and use the GED to document their learning and qualify for college scholarships and financial aid. More than two out of every three GED graduates work toward college degrees or further trade, technical, or business schools. A study in Colorado showed that some GED graduates reported the following: improvements in educational and employment status and in personal finances; greater participation in the community or in cultural activities; and increased awareness of psychological benefits and health strategies.

The GED diploma has been recognized throughout North America by employers and colleges, and more than 14 million adults earned the GED diploma between 1942 and 1999. You probably recognize some of these famous GED graduates: country music singers Waylon Jennings and John Michael Montgomery, comedian Bill Cosby, Olympic gold medalist Mary Lou Retton, former New Jersey Governor James J. Florio, Delaware Lieutenant Governor Ruth Ann Minner, U.S. Senator Ben Nighthorse Campbell, Wendy's founder Dave Thomas, movie actor Kelly McGillis, Famous Amos Cookies creator Wally Amos, and Triple Crown winner jockey Ron Turcotte.

What does GED stand for?

GED stands for the Tests of **General Educational Development.** The GED Test battery is a national examination developed by the GED Testing Service of the American Council on Education. The credential (certificate) earned for passing the test is widely recognized by colleges, training schools, and employers as equivalent to a high school diploma. The American Council reports that almost all (more than 95 percent) of employers in the nation employ GED graduates and offer them the same salaries and opportunities for advancement as high school graduates.

The GED Test reflects the major and lasting outcomes normally acquired in a four-year high school program. Since the passing rate for the GED is normed (based) on the performance of graduating high school seniors, you can rest assured that your skills are comparable. In fact, those who pass the GED Test actually do better than one-third of those graduating seniors. Throughout the test, your skills in communication (both reading and viewing text), information processing, critical thinking, and problem solving are keys to success. There is also special emphasis in the questions on preparation for entering the workplace or entering higher education. Much that you have learned informally or through other types of training can help you pass the test.

What is the test like overall?

The GED Tests

Tests	Minutes	Questions	Content/Percentages
Language Arts, Writing Part I (65%) (Editing) Part II (35%) (Essay)	75 45	50 1 topic	Organization 15% Sentence Structure 30% Usage 30% Mechanics 25%
Social Studies	70	50	World History 15% U.S. History 25% Civics and Government 25% Economics 20% Geography 15%
Science	80	50	Life Science 45% Earth and Space Science 20% Physical Science 35% (Physics and Chemistry)
Language Arts, Reading	65	40	Literary Text (75%) Poetry [15%] Drama [15%] Fiction [45%] Nonfiction Prose (25%) Informational Text Literary Nonfiction Viewing Component Business Documents
Mathematics Booklet One: Calculator Booklet Two: No Calculator	90	25 25	Number Operations and Numbers Sense 20–30% Measurement and Geometry 20–30% Data Analysis, Statistics, and Probability 20–30% Algebra, Functions, and Patterns 20–30%
Totals:	425 minutes (about 7 hours)	240 questions + Essay	

On all five tests, you can expect subject matter to be *interdisciplinary*. All five subjects will be interrelated. For example, a mathematics question might include a social studies chart. A science question might require the use of mathematics computation skills. You are expected to demonstrate the ability to think about many issues.

Special editions of the GED Test include the Canadian French-language, Spanish-language, Braille, large print, and audiocassette formats. Many adult education programs or test centers can assist you if you need accommodations such as special reading or marking devices.

What should I know to pass the test?

You are tested on knowledge and skills you have acquired from life experiences, work experiences, television, radio, books, magazines, newspapers, consumer products, and advertising. Many questions will involve the roles that adults play: citizen and community member, worker, and/or family member. Many documents will be "how to" documents especially found in business settings.

In particular, keep these facts in mind about the specific tests:

A. Part I of the **Language Arts, Writing Test** requires you to recognize or correct errors, revise sentences or passages, or shift constructions in the four areas of organization, sentence structure, usage, and mechanics (capitalization, punctuation, and spelling). The types of letters and memos you would normally write are likely to be included. Informational texts from business-related documents will be used.

In Part II you will have to write a well-developed essay on a topic familiar to most adults. You will be asked to have an *audience* and a *purpose* in mind for the essay. You will write in a *real life context* and *adopt a role*. You will be asked to generate (produce) ideas, express them clearly, organize the ideas, and connect them appropriately.

B. Three of the five tests—Social Studies, Science, and Language Arts, Reading—require that you answer questions based on reading passages or interpret graphs, charts, maps, cartoons, or diagrams. Developing strong reading and thinking skills is the key to succeeding on these tests.

The **Social Studies Test** looks at history in terms of critical points in time and clusters (groups) of historical periods. Psychology, the science of behavior, is not a separate content area, but it is included in other social studies areas. More emphasis is placed on U.S. and world history and civics and government.

The **Science Test** is based on the National Science Education Standards (NSES). It emphasizes scientific understandings and places special emphasis on the environment and on health questions. Science education focuses on the activities or ways in which people use science in their daily lives.

As expected, the **Language Arts, Reading Test** asks you to read literary text and to show that you can comprehend, apply, analyze, synthesize, and evaluate concepts. In addition, the test asks you to read and comprehend nonfiction prose including informational texts (such as job benefits or letters to the editor typical in daily living), literary nonfiction, texts based on viewing components, and business documents.

C. The **Mathematics Test** consists mainly of word problems to be solved. Therefore, you must be able to combine your ability to perform computations with problem-solving skills. Fifty percent of the problems will require the use of a calculator provided at the test site, and fifty percent of the questions will not permit the use of a calculator. Alternate formats are especially important on this test.

The calculator use is intended to eliminate the tediousness of making complex calculations in realistic, everyday settings. Thus, two separate booklets are used. Booklet One, Mathematical Understanding and Application, permits the use of the calculator provided by the GED Testing Service. Booklet Two, Estimation and Mental Math, does not permit calculator use. Twenty percent (20%) of the questions will include alternate formats of bubble-in grids or graphs (coordinate plane graphs with number lines).

This book has been designed to help you, too, succeed on the test. It will provide you with instruction in the skills you need to pass, background information on key concepts in the five subject areas of language arts/writing, social studies, science, language arts/reading, and mathematics. The book will provide you with plenty of practice through pretests, exercises in each instructional section, and posttests in all areas.

Who may take the tests?

Some 3,500 GED Testing Centers are available in all fifty United States, the District of Columbia, eleven Canadian provinces and territories, U.S. and overseas military bases, correctional institutions, Veterans Administration hospitals, and certain learning centers. People who have not graduated from high school and who meet specific eligibility requirements (age, residency, etc.) may take the tests. Since eligibility requirements vary, it would be useful to contact your local GED testing center or the director of adult education in your state, province, or territory for specific information.

May I retake the test?

You are allowed to retake some or all of the tests. Again, the regulations governing the number of times that you may retake the tests and the time you must wait before retaking them are set by your state, province, or territory. Some states require you to take a review class or to study on your own for a certain amount of time before taking the test again.

How can I best prepare for the test?

Many community colleges, public schools, adult education centers, libraries, churches, community-based organizations, and other institutions offer GED preparation classes. While your state may not require you to take part in a preparation program, it's a good idea if you've been out of school for some time, if you had academic difficulty when you were in school, or if you left before completing the eleventh grade. Some television stations broadcast classes to prepare people for the test. If you cannot find a GED preparation class locally, contact the director of adult education in your state, province, or territory.

If I study on my own, how much time should I allow?

The amount of time you should allow for studying depends on your readiness in each of the five subject areas; however, you should probably allow three to six months to do the following:

1. Read the introductory section of the book.

2. Take and score the five Pretests. Decide which areas you need to focus on the most.

3. Complete the Critical Thinking Skills for the GED Test section of the book.

4. Read and complete the exercises in those areas on which you decided to focus.

5. Take the Posttests to determine how much improvement you've made.

6. Review the test-taking tips on the following page.

7. Contact the GED administrator of your preparation program or the director of adult education in your state, province, or territory and arrange to take the GED.

What are some test-taking tips?

1. **Prepare physically.** Get plenty of rest and eat a well-balanced meal before the test so that you will have energy and will be able to think clearly. Intense studying at the last minute probably will not help as much as having a relaxed and rested mind.

2. **Arrive early.** Be at the testing center at least 15 to 20 minutes before the starting time. Make sure you have time to find the room and to get situated. Keep in mind that many testing centers refuse to admit those who come once the test has started. Some testing centers operate on a first come, first served basis; so you want to be sure that there is an available slot for you on the day that you're ready to test.

3. **Think positively.** Tell yourself you will do well. If you have studied and prepared for the test, you should succeed.

4. **Relax during the test.** Take half a minute several times during the test to stretch and breathe deeply, especially if you are feeling anxious or confused.

5. **Read the test directions carefully.** Be sure you understand how to answer the questions. If you have any questions about the test or about filling in the answer form, ask before the test begins.

6. **Know the time limit for each test.** Some testing centers allow extra time, while others do not. You may be able to find out the policy of your testing center before you take the test, but always work according to the official time limit. If you have extra time, go back and check your answers.

7. **Have a strategy for answering questions.** You should read through the reading passages or look over the materials once and then answer the questions that follow. Read each question two or three times to make sure you understand it. It is best to refer back to the passage or graphic in order to confirm your answer choice. Don't try to depend on your memory of what you have just read or seen. Some people like to guide their reading by skimming the questions before reading a passage. Use the method that works best for you.

8. **Don't spend a lot of time on difficult questions.** If you're not sure of an answer, go on to the next question. Answer easier questions first and then go back to the harder questions. However, when you skip a question, be sure that you have skipped the same number on your answer sheet. Although skipping difficult questions is a good strategy for making the most of your time, it is very easy to get confused and throw off your whole answer key.

   Lightly mark the margin of your answer sheet next to the numbers of the questions you did not answer so that you know what to go back to. To prevent confusion when your test is graded, be sure to erase these marks completely after you answer the questions.

9. **Answer every question on the test.** If you're not sure of an answer, take an educated guess. When you leave a question unanswered, you will always lose points, but you can possibly gain points if you make a correct guess.

   If you must guess, try to eliminate one or more answers that you are sure are not correct. Then choose from the remaining answers. Remember that you greatly increase your chances if you can eliminate one or two answers before guessing. Of course, guessing should be used only when all else has failed.

10. **Clearly fill in the circle for each answer choice.** If you erase something, erase it completely. Be sure that you give only one answer per question; otherwise, no answer will count.

11. **Practice test-taking.** Use the exercises, reviews, and especially the Posttests in this book to better understand your test-taking habits and weaknesses. Use them to practice different strategies such as skimming questions first or skipping hard questions until the end. Knowing your own personal test-taking style is important to your success on the GED Test.

How do I use this book?

1. You do not have to work through all of the five sections in this book. In some areas you are likely to have stronger skills than in others. However, before you begin this book you should take the Pretests. These will give you a preview of what the five tests include, but more important, they will help you to identify which areas you need to concentrate on most. Use the **Evaluation Charts** at the end of the Pretests to pinpoint the types of questions you answered incorrectly and to determine the skills in which you need extra work.

2. Complete the sections of the book that the Pretests indicate you need to review. However, to prepare yourself best for the test, work through the entire book.

3. After you have worked through the subject areas that needed strengthening as indicated by the Pretest scores, you should take the half-length Posttests at the end of this book. These tests will help you determine whether you are ready for the actual GED Test and, if not, what areas of the book you need to review. The Evaluation Charts are especially helpful in making this decision.

4. If you determine that you need still more practice at the GED level in answering the kinds of questions to be found on the GED Test, we recommend that you work through McGraw-Hill/Contemporary's satellite series, available for each of the five GED subject areas:

   Language Arts, Writing
   Social Studies
   Science
   Language Arts, Reading
   Mathematics

   Additional titles that McGraw-Hill/Contemporary offers for effective test preparation in mathematics and writing include *The GED Math Problem Solver* and *The GED Essay.*

5. This book has a number of features designed to help make the task of preparing for the actual GED Test easier as well as effective and enjoyable:
   - A special essay section helps to prepare you for the Part II of the Language Arts, Writing portion of the GED Test.
   - A critical thinking skills section that explains all six levels of thinking skills and provides practice in using the skills of the five levels represented on the test—comprehension, application, analysis, synthesis, and evaluation.
   - Skill builders, hints, and tips help you increase your proficiency in all sections.
   - A variety of exercise types including multiple-choice, fill-in-the-blank, true-false, matching, and short essay questions help to maintain interest.

- Half-length Posttests that are simulated GED Tests present questions in the format, level of difficulty, and percentages you will find on the actual tests.
- Answer keys (coded by skill level) for each section explain the correct answers for the exercises.
- Evaluation charts for the Pretests and Posttests help pinpoint weaknesses and refer you to specific pages for review.
- Hundreds of questions are provided to strengthen your reading, writing, and thinking skills.

McGraw-Hill/Contemporary prints a wide range of materials to help you prepare for the tests. These books are designed for home study or classroom use. Our GED preparation books are available through schools and bookstores and directly from the publisher. For the visually impaired, a large-print version is available. For further information, call Library Reproduction Service (LRS) at 1-800-255-5002.

- Review the test-taking tips on pages xv and xvi.

- Relax. Don't study.

- Get a good night's sleep.

Finally, we'd like to hear from you. If our materials have helped you to pass the test or if you feel that we can do a better job preparing you, write to us at the address on the copyright page of this book to let us know. We hope you enjoy studying for the GED Test with our materials and wish you the greatest success.

The Editors

<u>PRETESTS</u>

How do I use the Pretests?

The Pretests will help you determine what you need to study in this book. They are tests in the *format* and *level of difficulty* of the real GED Test, **one-quarter-length.** The results of these tests will help you map out a plan of study. We recommend the following approach to the Pretests.

1. **Take only one Pretest at a time.** Don't attempt to do all of the tests at one sitting. Read the directions before you start a test. Except for the essay and the Mathematics Pretest, observe the time guidelines for taking the tests to know whether the time you are spending on the Pretests is reasonable. Use the answer sheets at the beginning of each test to mark your choices.

2. **Check the answers in the Answer Key and fill in the Evaluation Chart.** A Pretest Answer Key and an Evaluation Chart for each test can be found at the back of this book. For all of the questions that you miss, read explanations of the correct answers.

3. **Based on the information in the Evaluation Charts, you may choose to do one of two things.** If you miss half or more of the questions in a Pretest, you should work through the entire subject area. If you miss fewer than half of the questions, focus on particular areas of the test that gave you difficulty.

4. **For best results you will want to review the section on Critical Thinking Skills, beginning on page 31.** The order of the Pretests and the time allotted for each is listed below. One-fourth the time of the full-length tests is indicated for all tests except Mathematics. Mathematics is a *skills test* and not timed.

5. **Although these are Pretests, you should give them your best effort.** If an item seems difficult, mark it and come back later. Always answer every question— even if you have to make an "educated guess." Sometimes you may know more than you give yourself credit for. Also, on the actual GED Tests an item left blank counts as a wrong answer. It's always wise to answer every question as best you can.

Good Luck on the Pretests!

Time Allowed for Each Test		
Language Arts, Writing	Part I: Editing	19 minutes
	Part II: Essay	45 minutes (full length)
Social Studies		18 minutes
Science		20 minutes
Language Arts, Reading		16 minutes
Mathematics		not timed

LANGUAGE ARTS, WRITING PRETEST

Part I: Editing

Directions: Part I of the Language Arts, Writing Pretest consists of 13 multiple-choice questions and should take approximately 19 minutes. The questions are based on documents of several paragraphs marked by letters. Each paragraph contains numbered sentences. Most sentences contain errors, but a few may be correct as written. Read the documents, and then answer the questions based on them. For each item, choose the answer that would result in the best rewriting of the sentence or sentences. The best answer must be consistent with the meaning and tone of the rest of the document.

When you have completed this Pretest, check your answers with the Answer Key on page 510.

LANGUAGE ARTS, WRITING PRETEST ANSWER GRID

1 ① ② ③ ④ ⑤   8 ① ② ③ ④ ⑤

2 ① ② ③ ④ ⑤   9 ① ② ③ ④ ⑤

3 ① ② ③ ④ ⑤   10 ① ② ③ ④ ⑤

4 ① ② ③ ④ ⑤   11 ① ② ③ ④ ⑤

5 ① ② ③ ④ ⑤   12 ① ② ③ ④ ⑤

6 ① ② ③ ④ ⑤   13 ① ② ③ ④ ⑤

7 ① ② ③ ④ ⑤

Directions: Choose the best answer to each question that follows.

Questions 1–5 refer to the following document.

BATTERIES

(A)

(1) Many of the gadgets we use regularly require batteries to power them. **(2)** Flashlights, smoke alarms, toys, and portable CD players are a few examples. **(3)** When replacing the batteries that these devices require, we should understand the types of batteries available.

(B)

(4) First of all, some batteries are rechargeable, and some are not. **(5)** Rechargeable batteries are not good choices for devices that are seldom used. **(6)** Rechargeable batteries are best for high-drain devices. **(7)** Which are used fairly regularly. **(8)** There is a disadvantage to these batteries due to the fact that they require frequent recharging.

(C)

(9) Three kinds of primary-cell batteries are general-purpose, heavy-duty, or alkaline. **(10)** General-purpose batteries are low priced but usually won't last very long. **(11)** Heavy-duty batteries cost more and represent a good choice for low to medium-drain devices. **(12)** These batteries are very good choices for smoke, alarms or flashlights.

(D)

(13) Lastly, alkaline batteries work best for high-drain devices that are used often, such as a CD player. **(14)** These batteries are the most expensive.

(E)

(15) Knowing the choices of batteries that are available helps us save money and frustration. **(16)** In this case, education can truly translate into power.

—Source: *Daily Herald.* "Select batteries according to how they will be used" November 26, 2000

1. Sentences 6 and 7:
   Rechargeable batteries are best for high-drain <u>devices. Which are used fairly regularly.</u>

   Which is the best way to write the underlined portion of the text? If the original is the best way, choose option (1).

   (1) devices. Which
   (2) devices, and which
   (3) devices. That
   (4) devices those which
   (5) devices that

2. Sentence 8: **There is a disadvantage to these batteries due to the fact that they require frequent charging.**

   If you rewrote sentence 8 beginning with *One disadvantage to these batteries is* the next words should be

   (1) recharging due
   (2) that they
   (3) besides the fact
   (4) even though they
   (5) resulting in

3. Which revision would make this document more effective?

   (1) move sentence 2 to follow sentence 3
   (2) remove sentence 3
   (3) move sentence 10 to follow sentence 11
   (4) combine paragraphs C and D
   (5) combine paragraphs D and E

4. Which sentence below would be most effective at the beginning of paragraph C?

(1) We use batteries very often in household devices.

(2) The disposal of batteries can be a problem.

(3) Batteries in cars keep rising in cost.

(4) Not all batteries are rechargeable as explained earlier.

(5) Batteries that are not rechargeable are called primary cells.

5. Sentence 12: **These batteries are very good choices for smoke, alarms or flashlights.**

What correction should be made to sentence 12?

(1) change <u>are</u> to <u>were</u>

(2) change <u>very</u> to <u>vary</u>

(3) change <u>for</u> to <u>fore</u>

(4) remove the comma after <u>smoke</u>

(5) insert a comma after <u>alarms</u>

Questions 5–9 refer to the following document.

Memo: To All Employees

From: Gregory Bolsho, Human Resources

Subject: Direct Deposit

(A)

(1) I am pleased to announce that beginning March 1, all employees will have the option of using direct deposit. **(2)** Direct deposit provides for the automatic deposit of salary into the financial institution of your choice. **(3)** Many financial institutions also offer credit cards. **(4)** Using direct deposit should reduce the incidence of lost or stolen payroll checks.

(B)

(5) You will need to follow several steps if you sign up for this option. **(6)** First, you will need to contact your financial institution to confirm that it participates in the direct deposit plan. **(7)** Attached to this memo, you will need to complete a form. **(8)** Be sure that you have signed the form. **(9)** After the form is completed, return them to the business office. **(10)** Direct deposit will go into effect at the end of the pay period after which the form is returned. **(11)** Direct deposit may be an option that you elect for as your choice at any time during the next six months. **(12)** If you choose to use direct deposit, a record of the deposit and copy of your deductions will continue to be issued to you each week on Friday.

(C)

(13) Our company hopes that offering this option will benefit you by providing greater convenience. **(14)** If you have any questions in this matter, you may call the business office.

6. Sentence 3: **Many financial institutions also offer credit cards.**

Which revision should be made to sentence 3?

(1) move sentence 3 to follow sentence 5
(2) move sentence 3 to the end of paragraph B
(3) move sentence 3 to the end of paragraph C
(4) remove sentence 3
(5) no revision is necessary

7. Sentence 7: **Attached to this memo, <u>you will need to complete a form.</u>**

Which is the best way to write the underlined portion of the text? If the original is the best way, choose option (1).

(1) you will need to complete a form.
(2) is a form to complete.
(3) a complete form is required.
(4) a form is to be completed.
(5) you complete the given form.

8. Sentence 9: **After the form <u>is completed, return them</u> to the business office.**

Which is the best way to write the underlined portion of the text? If the original is the best way, choose option (1).

(1) is completed, return them
(2) was completed, return them
(3) is completing, return them
(4) is completed, returned them
(5) is completed, return it

9. Sentence 11: **Direct deposit may be an option that you elect for as your choice at any time during the next six months.**

The most effective revision of sentence 11 would begin with which group of words?

(1) You having the next six months
(2) To elect direct deposit because
(3) Six months of direct deposit
(4) You may elect to change
(5) For as long as six months later

Questions 10–13 refer to the following document.

FIRE SAFETY

(A)

(1) Most fire-related deaths result from fires in the home, fire is a frightening event. (2) Smoke from a fire is especially deadly because it reduces visibility and can impair breathing within minutes. (3) To help guard against fire, every person should have a working smoke alarm and fire extinguisher in the home.

(B)

(4) Smoke detectors serve to warn residents of fire. (5) Change the batteries of smoke alarms once a year or more to ensure that they are in working order. (6) In most cases when a fire has started or with the smoke alarm sounding, everyone should evacuate a home. (7) Be sure to have a plan of evacuation prepared, and be sure that every member of the household knows that plan. (8) Establish a designated meeting place outside the home for all members of the household. (9) Someone outside the home should

call the fire department. **(10)** In some instances, when a fire is very limited and immediately located, a fire extinguisher can actually help people fight fires. **(11)** Several kinds of fire extinguishers are available, and each is suitable for a particular type of fire. **(12)** These extinguishers generally come with instructions. **(13)** Fire departments may offer training in the use and operation of extinguishers to people in various areas of the country. **(14)** Keeping the extinguisher in an easily accessible location is extremely important.

(C)

(15) Smoke alarms and fire extinguishers served as important tools for protection against fire. **(16)** The cost of these tools is minimal compared to their value.

10. Sentence 1: **Most fire-related deaths result from fires in the home, fire is a frightening event.**

    Which is the best way to write the underlined portion of the text? If the original is the best way, choose option (1).

    (1) home, fire is
    (2) home, or fire is
    (3) home fire is
    (4) home, and fire is
    (5) home so, fire is

11. Sentence 6: **In most cases when a fire has started or <u>with the smoke alarm sounding</u>, everyone should evacuate a home.**

    Which is the best way to write the underlined portion of the text? If the original is the best way, choose option (1).

    (1) with the smoke alarm sounding
    (2) alarms sound from the smoke alarm
    (3) the sounding of the smoke alarm
    (4) there is an alarm sounded that you hear
    (5) the smoke alarm sounds

12. Sentence 10: **In some instances, when a fire is very limited and immediately located, a fire extinguisher can actually help people fight fires.**

    Which revision to sentence 10 would make the document more effective?

    (1) begin a new paragraph with sentence 10
    (2) move sentence 10 to follow sentence 3
    (3) remove sentence 10
    (4) move sentence 10 to follow sentence 15
    (5) no revision is necessary

13. Sentence 15: **Smoke alarms and fire extinguishers <u>served as important</u> tools for protection against fire.**

    Which is the best way to write the underlined portion of the text? If the original is the best way, choose option (1).

    (1) served as important
    (2) serving as important
    (3) serves as important
    (4) serve as important
    (5) has been serving as important

Part II: The Essay

Directions: This part of the test is designed to find out how well you write. The test has one question that asks you to present an opinion and explain your ideas. Your essay should be long enough to develop the topic adequately. In preparing your essay, you should take the following steps:

1. Read the directions and topic carefully.

2. Think about your ideas and plan your essay before you write.

3. Use scratch paper to make notes of your ideas.

4. Write your essay in ink on two other pages of paper.

5. After finishing your writing, read your paper carefully and make appropriate changes.

Topic

What is one day that you will always remember?

In your essay, identify the day and the events that occurred. Explain the reasons that the day is so memorable for you.

Information on evaluating your essay is on page 511.

SOCIAL STUDIES PRETEST

Directions: This Social Studies Pretest consists of 13 questions. Some of the questions are based on short reading passages, and some of them require you to interpret a graph, chart or table, map, or an editorial cartoon. You should take approximately 18 minutes to complete this test.

When you have completed this Pretest, check your answers with the Answer Key on page 512.

SOCIAL STUDIES PRETEST ANSWER GRID

1 ① ② ③ ④ ⑤	8 ① ② ③ ④ ⑤
2 ① ② ③ ④ ⑤	9 ① ② ③ ④ ⑤
3 ① ② ③ ④ ⑤	10 ① ② ③ ④ ⑤
4 ① ② ③ ④ ⑤	11 ① ② ③ ④ ⑤
5 ① ② ③ ④ ⑤	12 ① ② ③ ④ ⑤
6 ① ② ③ ④ ⑤	13 ① ② ③ ④ ⑤
7 ① ② ③ ④ ⑤	

Questions 1 and 2 are based upon the following passage.

I HAVE A DREAM

Delivered on the steps at the Lincoln Memorial in Washington, D.C., on August 28, 1963

Five score years ago, a great American, in whose symbolic shadow we stand, signed the Emancipation Proclamation. This momentous decree came as a great beacon light of hope to millions of Negro slaves who had been seared in the flames of withering injustice. It came as a joyous daybreak to end the long night of captivity.

But one hundred years later, we must face the tragic fact that the Negro is still not free. One hundred years later, the life of the Negro is still sadly crippled by the manacles of segregation and the chains of discrimination. One hundred years later, the Negro lives on a lonely island of poverty in the midst of a vast ocean of material prosperity. One hundred years later, the Negro is still languishing in the corners of American society and finds himself an exile in his own land. So we have come here today to dramatize an appalling condition.

In a sense we have come to our nation's capital to cash a check. When the architects of our republic wrote the magnificent words of the Constitution and the Declaration of Independence, they were signing a promissory note to which every American was to fall heir. This note was a promise that all men would be guaranteed the inalienable rights of life, liberty, and the pursuit of happiness.

—Martin Luther King, Jr.

1. A year after Dr. King's speech in Washington, D.C., Congress passed the Civil Rights Act in 1964. Which of the following is reasonable to infer?
   (1) All Americans supported the Civil Rights Act.
   (2) Dr. King believed in Congress, the president, and the American people.
   (3) This Act supported only African American citizens.
   (4) Dr. King was responsible for drafting the Civil Rights Act.
   (5) This act passed unanimously in the House of Representatives and the Senate.

2. What position does Dr. Martin Luther King, Jr., hold in his speech, *I Have a Dream*?
   (1) The Constitution of the United States gives too little power to the states.
   (2) The Declaration of Independence was completely ineffective in freeing African Americans from all forms of segregation.
   (3) The Emancipation Proclamation was very effective in freeing African Americans from all forms of segregation.
   (4) By 1963, African Americans should have been free from all forms of segregation.
   (5) By 1963, African Americans were finally free from all forms of segregation.

Questions 3 and 4 are based on the circle graphs below.

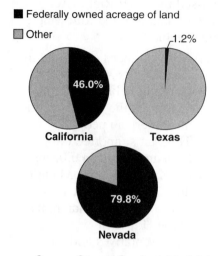

■ Federally owned acreage of land

□ Other

California — 46.0%

Texas — 1.2%

Nevada — 79.8%

Source: General Services Administration

3. What conclusion can be drawn from the above data on federally owned land acreage by individual states?

(1) California has more acreage than Texas.
(2) Nevada has more national parks than Texas.
(3) The federal government controls the greatest percentage of all land in Nevada.
(4) The percentage of federally owned acreage is similar in Texas and in California.
(5) Nevada has a larger population than California.

4. What type of information is included in the circle graphs?

(1) the names of all fifty states
(2) the percentage of federally owned land
(3) the population of three states
(4) a list of national parks
(5) an explanation of other land ownership

Questions 5 and 6 are based on the following chart.

The Relationship Between Income and Education for Men, 1997

Level of Education	Median Income
Elementary 9th grade or less	$19,291
High School (9th–12th grade)	
no diploma	$24,726
graduate with diploma	$31,215
College	
no degree	$35,945
associate's degree	$38,022
bachelor's degree or higher	$53,450

Source: U.S. Department of Commerce, Bureau of the Census Reports

5. Which of the following conclusions is supported by the chart?

(1) No relationship exists between education level and median income.
(2) Men with an elementary education will earn at least $19,291 per year.
(3) A college education is required to earn over $35,945 per year.
(4) Education is the sole factor that determines a person's income.
(5) Men who have more education are more likely to earn a higher income.

6. On the basis of the data in the chart, what advice might a high school counselor offer a young male client in 1997?

(1) To prepare for the 21st century, you need to major in business at college.

(2) To increase your income, you must get a bachelor's degree from a private university.

(3) To raise your income, you should get your high school diploma.

(4) To make more than $19,000 a year, you must finish high school.

(5) To raise your income, you must complete four years of college.

Questions 7 and 8 are based on the following passage.

The great rule of conduct for us in regard to foreign nations is, in extending our commercial relations, to have with them as little political connection as possible. So far as we have already formed engagements, let them be fulfilled with perfect good faith. Here let us stop.

Europe has a set of primary interests which to us have none or a very remote relation. Hence she must be engaged in frequent controversies, the causes of which are essentially foreign to our concerns. Hence, therefore, it must be unwise in us to implicate ourselves by artificial ties in the ordinary vicissitudes (changes) of her politics or the ordinary combinations and collisions of her friendships or enmities . . .

It is our true policy to steer clear of permanent alliances with any portion of the foreign world . . .

—Excerpted from
George Washington's Farewell Address

7. Which one of the following statements reflects George Washington's attitude as expressed in this address?

The United States should

(1) offer its assistance wherever needed in the world

(2) avoid becoming involved in world political affairs

(3) withdraw from European affairs while assisting other areas of the world

(4) become as politically connected with Europe as possible

(5) support policies that would increase the territory under its control

8. Based on his address, what would George Washington think of America's position today as a world power?

He would think that the United States

(1) has been successful in leaving other nations alone

(2) has achieved its primary goal of being a world power

(3) has continued to control the other nations of the world

(4) has become too involved in other nations' affairs

(5) has not changed much from the time when he was president

Questions 9 and 10 are based on the following graph and passage.

Percentage of Married Women Who Hold Full-Time Jobs and Have Children Under 18 and Husbands Who Work

Year	Percentage
1955	27.0%
1965	35.0%
1975	47.3%
1985	62.1%
1995	69.7%
1998	72.3%

Source: U.S. Department of Labor, Bureau of Labor Statistics

The way a male or female acts or is expected to act in society is called a role. In the past the traditional role in the American family for the husband was as breadwinner while the wife's role was homemaker. According to the bar graph above, however, family roles are changing.

9. Which of the following is *least likely* to be considered a cause of the changing role of married women in the family?

(1) additional expenses requiring second incomes in many families

(2) increased numbers of women with careers and families

(3) decreased respect for the role of homemaker

(4) greater availability of child care options

(5) more opportunities for women

10. Between 1935 and 1957, a period that included World War II, the birth rate rose from 16.9 to 25 per 1000 people. What was the most likely cause of this "baby boom"?

(1) the return of young American soldiers from war

(2) the growth of the urban/suburban areas after World War II

(3) the mobility of the American family of the 1950s

(4) the expansion of the middle class and its new wealth

(5) the change in view toward artificial birth control methods

Question 11 is based on the following cartoon.

James Grasdal–Edmonton Journal

11. Which plan would *best* guarantee a strong financial future for a baby boomer?

(1) investing in high-risk stocks
(2) graduating from a business college
(3) participating in a savings plan at work
(4) creating one's own business
(5) opening multiple credit accounts

Questions 12 and 13 are based on the following passage.

The Great Depression seemingly began with the crash of the stock market in 1929. On the floor of the New York Stock Exchange, the scene was one of complete chaos as investors panicked on "Black Tuesday." Thousands gathered in the streets and police both on foot and mounted on horses tried valiantly to control the crowds. In desperation, investors who had thought they could make a lot of money in the stock market now began a tremendous sell-off of stock. Some of the most desperate of bankrupt investors even took their own lives that day as they feared the loss of their life savings.

12. What was one consequence of the sudden fall in stock prices?

(1) Confident bankers bought more stock.
(2) Indifferent shareholders ignored the collapse of the market.
(3) Worried investors frantically sold stock shares.
(4) Pleased factory workers experienced wage increases.
(5) Concerned shareholders bought more stock.

13. Which one of the following expressions best illustrates a value that played a role in the stock market crash of 1929?

(1) "A penny saved is a penny earned."
(2) "Honesty is the best policy."
(3) "Health is everything."
(4) "You can never be too rich. . . ."
(5) "The early bird catches the worm."

SCIENCE PRETEST

Directions: The Science Pretest consists of 13 multiple-choice questions. Some of the questions are based on graphs, maps, tables, diagrams, editorial cartoons, and reading passages. You should take approximately 20 minutes to complete this test.

When you have completed this Pretest, check your answers with the Answer Key on page 514.

SCIENCE PRETEST ANSWER GRID

1 ① ② ③ ④ ⑤   8 ① ② ③ ④ ⑤

2 ① ② ③ ④ ⑤   9 ① ② ③ ④ ⑤

3 ① ② ③ ④ ⑤   10 ① ② ③ ④ ⑤

4 ① ② ③ ④ ⑤   11 ① ② ③ ④ ⑤

5 ① ② ③ ④ ⑤   12 ① ② ③ ④ ⑤

6 ① ② ③ ④ ⑤   13 ① ② ③ ④ ⑤

7 ① ② ③ ④ ⑤

Choose the best answer to each question that follows.

Question 1 is based upon the following cartoon.

Steve Kelley, Copley News Service

1. Which of these statements provides the **best** support for the opinion of this cartoonist?

   (1) The cost of a pack of cigarettes is too high and should be lowered.
   (2) Mothers who smoke during pregnancy could have children who suffer learning disabilities.
   (3) As many as 53,000 nonsmoking Americans die annually from inhaling second-hand smoke.
   (4) Adolescents who do not smoke before age 20 are not likely to ever start smoking.
   (5) Smoking is the number one preventable cause of death in America today.

2. Physicians say that chewing on an aspirin (acetylsalicylic acid) thins the blood and helps prevent the blood from clotting. What is one positive application of this knowledge?

   Aspirin may be used to

   (1) relieve muscle pain
   (2) reduce inflammation
   (3) lessen the possibility of heart attack
   (4) act as a stimulant
   (5) stop heavy bleeding

Question 3 is based on the chart below.

Transfusion Relationship		
Blood type	Can receive blood from	Acts as donor to
O	O	O, A, B, AB
A	O, A	A, AB
B	B, O	B, AB
AB	O, A, B, AB	AB

3. If a person with blood type AB wishes to donate blood, those with which blood type(s) may receive the blood?

   (1) only type O
   (2) only types O and B
   (3) only types B and AB
   (4) only type AB
   (5) all types of blood

Question 4 is based on the following information.

The most common organic acids are **formic acid** and **acetic acid**. Formic acid occurs naturally in red ants and in pine needles. In concentrated form it can burn the skin; however, diluted formic acid is used for its germicidal properties. Acetic acid is responsible for the sour taste of pickles and sharp odors that can burn the nostrils. Cider vinegar contains 3 to 6 percent acetic acid and is made by the natural oxidation of apple cider.

4. Which of the following organic acids occurring in low concentrations is essential to humans but is highly dangerous in high concentrations of exposure to humans?

   (1) citric acid found in citrus fruits
   (2) lactic acid found in milk products
   (3) hydrochloric acid found in the stomach's gastric juices
   (4) oxalic acid found in rhubarb leaves
   (5) folic acid, a form of vitamin B used to treat anemia

Question 5 is based on the following weather map.

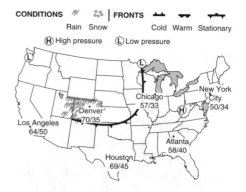

5. Which of the following generalizations would be made by a weather forecaster given the information on this weather map?

   (1) Most of the nation is experiencing a drought.
   (2) No state should encounter temperatures below 50°.
   (3) Denver, Colorado, will probably have a record amount of snow.
   (4) Travelers on vacation in Florida should not have to worry about rain.
   (5) Laredo, Texas, continues to battle high winds and severe weather.

Question 6 is based on the following diagram.

HOW CELLS DIVIDE

A new study suggests that aging may be caused by mistakes in the transfer of genes and chromosomes during cell division. Here is an illustration of how cells divide.

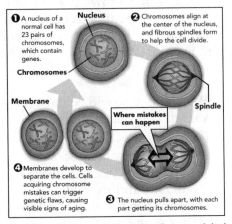

Source: Associated Press article in *Daily Herald,* March 31, 2000

6. According to this study, aging may be the effect of cells losing their capacity to reproduce properly. Which of the following conditions would probably **not** be the result of cellular degeneration or mutation?
   (1) arthritis—a chronic disorder that affects the joints and muscles
   (2) Alzheimer's disease—a degenerative disease of the central nervous system
   (3) osteoporosis—the deterioration of bone
   (4) kidney stone—a solid object that is usually caused by an excessive amount of calcium in the urine
   (5) cancer—a malignant tumor that tends to spread uncontrollably in the body

Question 7 is based on the following passage.

There is, perhaps, no part of the world where the early geological periods can be studied with so much ease and precision as in the United States. Along the northern border between Canada and the United States, there runs a low line of hills known as the Laurentian Hills. Insignificant in height, nowhere rising more than two thousand feet above the level of the sea, these are nevertheless the first mountains that broke the uniform level of Earth's surface and lifted themselves above the waters. Their low stature, as compared with that of other, loftier mountain ranges, is in accordance with an invariable rule by which the relative age of mountains may be estimated. The oldest mountains are the lowest, while the younger and more recent ones tower above their elders and are usually more jagged and dislocated.

7. The Appalachian Mountains are lower than the Rocky Mountains. What conclusion can you draw from this?
   The Appalachian Mountains are
   (1) younger than the Rocky Mountains
   (2) older than the Rocky Mountains
   (3) the same age as the Rocky Mountains
   (4) more scenic than the Rocky Mountains
   (5) more torn and dislocated than the Rocky Mountains

Question 8 is based on the following information.

Dentistry Predictions for the Twenty-first Century

• "smart fillings" that prevent further tooth decay

• toothpastes that restore tooth minerals and strengthen teeth

• chewing gums and mouthwashes that reverse early tooth decay

• gene transfer and tissue engineering used for repair of damaged or diseased tissues

• tooth regeneration technology

Source: *Newsweek* October 2000

8. Many people are reluctant to visit the dentist. How do you think the average dental patient will be affected by these predictions for the twenty-first century?

   The patient will experience

   (1) no need to practice oral hygiene
   (2) less pain and more natural results
   (3) fewer visits to the dentist for fillings
   (4) an increase in cavities
   (5) more approved dental plans by HMOs

Question 9 is based on the following information.

The Fathometer is a device used for determining ocean depths. It operates by sending sound waves under water. A sudden pulse of sound is transmitted by a ship and then picked up again after it has been reflected, or echoed, from the sea bottom, and the elapsed time is recorded. If one knows the time and the speed of sound waves through water, the depth of the sea at any point may be computed, often to the nearest foot.

9. Which point would be most relevant to the central idea of this passage?

   (1) The depth of the ocean is already known and doesn't require further studying.
   (2) The speed at which underwater sound waves travel from the ocean's surface to the bottom remains constant.
   (3) Fathometers show only approximate depths and are extremely reliable.
   (4) Fathometers work best in shallow waters and shouldn't be used to determine the depth of the ocean.
   (5) Fathometers should operate on scientific and not mathematical principles.

Question 10 is based on the information and table below.

Heat is able to pass from one molecule to another through **heat conduction**. In the table that follows, the numbers (called coefficients) indicate the relative rates of heat transfer in the materials listed.

Heat Conduction Coefficients

Material	Coefficient
silver	100
copper	92
aluminum	50
iron	11
glass	0.20
water	0.12
wood	0.03
air	0.006
perfect vacuum	0

10. According to the information in the table, which are the best conductors?

(1) gases
(2) natural materials
(3) metals
(4) liquids
(5) compounds

Question 11 is based on the following information.

The International Space Station is planned as the largest collaborative scientific project in history. Sixteen nations are making plans to take part: United States, Russia, Canada, Belgium, Denmark, France, Germany, Italy, Netherlands, Norway, Spain, Sweden, Switzerland, United Kingdom, Japan, and Brazil. The station will be made up of six laboratories with enough living space for up to seven people. Scientists have planned to conduct research on the growth of living cells and the effects on the human body in an environment with reduced or zero gravity. They will also examine the long-term changes in Earth's environment by observing Earth from orbit. The projected completion date for the International Space Station project is 2004.

11. According to the passage, which of the studies below would be best conducted in the International Space Station?

(1) analysis of fossil fuel samples
(2) development of new surgical procedures
(3) examination of tree samples from a rain forest
(4) measurement of greenhouse gasses in the atmosphere
(5) exploration of occupational hazards in the twenty-first century

Question 12 is based on the following information.

DETERMINING DISTANCE BY PARALLAX

Since astronomers cannot use radar to work out the distance of a star, they use the parallax method. Photographs are taken of the sky from the same position on Earth all through the year, and these reveal that some stars remain 'fixed,' whereas others seem to 'move.' Those stars that show visible movement are closer to Earth than those which do not. To find the distance of a star which 'moves,' astronomers look at two photographs taken six months apart, from the same observatory. (It takes six months for Earth to reach the far points in its orbit.) Using the diameter of Earth's orbit around the sun as a baseline, two lines are drawn from each end of the baseline to the star, one to each shifted position. Where the two lines intersect, they form the apparent angle of motion. Knowing the diameter of Earth's orbit and the size of the angle of motion, astronomers can calculate the distance to the star.

—Excerpted from *Readers Digest*
How in the World?

12. Which component would **not** be important to an astronomer when calculating the distance of a star?
    (1) the exact diameter of Earth's orbit
    (2) an observatory outfitted with modern technology
    (3) the size of the angle of motion
    (4) a clear and accurate photograph of the sky
    (5) measurements of the gravitational pull

Question 13 is based on the following information.

13. Pediatrics professor Samuel Katz said, "Immunization is the single intervention that has most dramatically reduced childhood morbidity and mortality." Which of the following arguments would Professor Katz include in support of his theory on immunizations?
    (1) Vaccines could cause severe side effects in inoculated children.
    (2) Smallpox has been eliminated, and many other life-threatening diseases are seldom found.
    (3) The Food and Drug Administration should continue to monitor results of inoculations and complications resulting from them.
    (4) Parents should question the need for vaccinations for their infants and toddlers.
    (5) The government needs to be involved in policies regarding vaccinations.

LANGUAGE ARTS, READING
<u>PRETEST</u>

Directions: The Language Arts, Reading Pretest Reading Test consists of 10 questions. The questions are based on excerpts from fiction (a novel), poetry, drama, and nonfiction prose (a diary). You should take approximately 16 minutes to complete this test.

When you have completed this Pretest, check your answers with the Answer Key on page 515.

LANGUAGE ARTS, READING PRETEST ANSWER GRID

1 ① ② ③ ④ ⑤		**6** ① ② ③ ④ ⑤	
2 ① ② ③ ④ ⑤		**7** ① ② ③ ④ ⑤	
3 ① ② ③ ④ ⑤		**8** ① ② ③ ④ ⑤	
4 ① ② ③ ④ ⑤		**9** ① ② ③ ④ ⑤	
5 ① ② ③ ④ ⑤		**10** ① ② ③ ④ ⑤	

Questions 1–3 deal with the following passage.

WHAT CONFLICTS DOES THERESA FEEL?

Deanna leaned across the table. "Just what I said—I think we should run this letter in your column this week. I'm sure other people would love to read it. ***

"We don't even know who they are. Don't you think we should get their permission first?"

"That's just the point. We can't. I can talk to the attorney at the paper, but I'm sure it's legal. ***

"I know it's probably legal, but I'm not sure if it's right. I mean this is a very personal letter. I'm not sure it should be spread around so that everyone can read it."

"It's a human interest story, Theresa. People love those sorts of things. Besides, there's nothing in there that might be embarrassing to someone. This is a beautiful letter. And remember, this Garrett person sent it in a bottle in the ocean. He had to know that it would wash up somewhere."

Theresa shook her head. "I don't know, Deanna. . . "

"Well, think about it. Sleep on it if you have to. I think it's a great idea."

Theresa did think about the letter. . . . She found herself wondering about the man who wrote it—Garrett, if that was his real name. And who, if anyone, was Catherine? His lover or his wife, obviously, but she wasn't around anymore. Was she dead, she wondered, or did something else happen that forced them apart? And why was it sealed in a bottle and set adrift? The whole thing was strange. Her reporter's instincts took over then, and she suddenly thought that the message might not mean anything. It could be someone who wanted to write a love letter but didn't have anyone to send it to. It could even have been sent by someone who got some sort of vicarious thrill by making lonely women cry on distant beaches. But as the words rolled through her head again, she realized that those possibilities were unlikely. The letter obviously came from the heart. And to think that a man wrote it! In all her years, she had never received a letter even close to that. Touching sentiments sent her way had always been emblazoned with Hallmark greeting card logos. David had never been much of a writer, nor had anyone else she had dated. What would such a man be like? She wondered. Would he be as caring in person as the letter seemed to imply?

—Excerpted from *Message in a Bottle*
by Nicholas Sparks

1. Based on Theresa's thoughts about the letter, what are her next actions likely to be?
   (1) She will expose the writer of the love letter in her column.
   (2) She will discover why the writer made women cry.
   (3) She will determine whether she could care for the writer.
   (4) She will sue Garrett for plagiarism.
   (5) She will offer Garrett a job working for the newspaper.

2. What techniques are most in contrast in the passage?
   (1) dialogue versus mental questions
   (2) facts versus opinions
   (3) hypotheses versus conclusions
   (4) chronological events versus flashback
   (5) narrator versus author comments

3. What is the likely overall purpose or intent of the passage?
   (1) to give Theresa a reason to determine the identity of the man who wrote the letter
   (2) to provide Theresa with an excuse to take a trip to the ocean to look for other bottles
   (3) to enable Theresa to have a chance to get a scoop for her column at the newspaper
   (4) to allow Theresa to make up her mind about whether to marry David after all
   (5) to help Theresa decide whether she would prefer writing Hallmark greeting cards

Questions 4–6 refer to the following poem.

WHERE IS THE SPEAKER OF THE POEM?

The Road Not Taken

Two roads diverged in a yellow wood,
And sorry I could not travel both
And be one traveler, long I stood
And looked down one as far as I could

5 To where it bent in the undergrowth;
Then took the other, as just as fair,
And having perhaps the better claim,
Because it was grassy and wanted wear;
Though as for that the passing there
10 Had worn them really about the same,

And both that morning equally lay
In leaves no step had trodden black.
Oh, I kept the first for another day!
Yet knowing how way leads on to way,
15 I doubted if I should ever come back

I shall be telling this with a sigh
Somewhere ages and ages hence:
Two roads diverged in a wood, and I—
I took the one less traveled by,
20 And that has made all the difference.

—by Robert Frost

4. What do the lines "long I stood/And looked down one as far as I could" (lines 3–4) reveal about the speaker's feelings?
   (1) uncertainty about a decision
   (2) confidence in what lies ahead
   (3) distaste for what must be done
   (4) sorrow about the future
   (5) excitement over the unknown

5. Which of the following lines best demonstrates that the speaker feels regret?

 (1) Then took the other, as just as fair (line 6)
 (2) And having perhaps the better claim (line 7)
 (3) And both that morning equally lay (line 11)
 (4) Oh, I kept the first for another day! (line 13)
 (5) I shall be telling this with a sigh (line 16)

6. Which statement best expresses the overall theme of the poem?

 (1) Life prepares individuals for any new situation.
 (2) Life confuses individuals with threatening circumstances.
 (3) Life offers different possibilities but rarely second chances.
 (4) Life prevents creative exploration or discovery.
 (5) Life requires change for the sake of change.

Questions 7–8 refer to the following excerpt.

WHAT DOES DUNOIS BELIEVE ABOUT JOAN?

Scene 5

Dunois. Come, Joan! you have had enough praying. After that fit of crying you will catch a chill if you stay here any longer. It
5 is all over: the cathedral is empty; and the streets are full. They are calling for The Maid. We have told them you are staying here alone to pray; but they want to see you
10 again.

Joan. No: let the king have all the glory.

Dunois. He only spoils the show, poor devil. No, Joan: you
15 have crowned him; and you must go through with it.

Joan. [shakes her head reluctantly].

Dunois. [raising her] Come
20 come! It will be over in a couple of hours. It's better than the bridge at Orleans: eh?

Joan. Oh, dear Dunois, how I wish it were the bridge at Orleans
25 again! We lived at that bridge.

Dunois. Yes, faith, and died too: some of us.

Joan. Isn't it strange, Jack? I am such a coward: I am fright-
30 ened beyond words before a battle; but it is so dull afterwards when there is no danger: oh, so dull! dull! dull!

Dunois. You must learn to be
35 abstemious in war, just as you are
in your food and drink, my little
saint.

Joan. Dear Jack: I think you
like me as a soldier likes his com-
40 rade.

Dunois. You need it, poor inno-
cent child of God. You have not
many friends at court.

Joan. Why do all these
45 courtiers and knights and church-
men hate me? What have I done
to them? I have asked nothing for
myself except that my village shall
not be taxed; for we cannot afford
50 war taxes. I have brought them
luck and victory: I have set them
right when they were doing all
sorts of stupid things: I have
crowned Charles and made him a
55 real king; and all the honors he is
handing out have gone to them.
Then why do they not love me?

Dunois. [rallying her] Sim-ple-
ton! Do you expect stupid people
60 to love you for shewing them up?
Do blundering old military dug-
outs love the successful young
captains who supersede them?
Do ambitious politicians love the
65 climbers who take the front seats
from them? Do archbishops enjoy
being played off their own altars,
even by saints? Why, I should be
jealous of you myself if I were
70 ambitious enough.

—Excerpted from *Saint Joan* by
George Bernard Shaw

7. What effect is produced by the
series of questions Dunois asks
in lines 59–70?

They serve as comparisons to
illustrate the relationship between

(1) Joan and the king's court
(2) Joan and Dunois
(3) Dunois and the king
(4) the king and the people
(5) the king and the church

8. During the time period in which
the play is set, the role of women
in military service or government
leadership was very limited.
How does this information relate
to the portrayal of Joan in this
passage?

(1) Joan appears more criminal
and devious.
(2) It makes the play seem quite
absurd and strange.
(3) The king appears very open-
minded.
(4) Joan seems even more extraordinary.
(5) Joan appears very representative of her time.

Questions 9–10 refer to the following excerpts.

WHY DOES ANNE FRANK KEEP A DIARY IN THE "SECRET ANNEXE" FOR THREE YEARS DURING WW II?

PASSAGE ONE

Friday, 9 October, 1942

Dear Kitty,

I've only got dismal and depressing news for you today. Our many Jewish friends are being taken away by the dozen. These people are treated by the Gestapo without a shred of decency, being loaded into cattle trucks and sent to Westerbork, the big Jewish camp in Drente. Westerbork sounds terrible: only one washing cubicle for a hundred people and not nearly enough lavatories. There is no separate accommodation. Men, women, and children all sleep together. . . .

PASSAGE TWO

Tuesday, 7 March, 1944

Dear Kitty,

If I think now of my life in 1942, it all seems so unreal. It was quite a different Anne who enjoyed that heavenly existence from the Anne who has grown wise within these walls. Yes, it was a heavenly life. Boy friends at every turn, about twenty friends and acquaintances of my own age, the darling of nearly all the teachers, spoiled from top to toe by Mummy and Daddy, lots of sweets, enough pocket money, what more could one want?

—Excerpted from *Anne Frank: The Diary of a Young Girl*

9. In the diary entry selected from October 9, 1942, Anne Frank explains what is happening in Holland during the early years of World War II. The events as paraphrased in relation to the Jewish community would include which of the following emotions?

(1) oppression
(2) celebration
(3) ceremony
(4) glorification
(5) toleration

10. In the introduction to the book, former First Lady Eleanor Roosevelt wrote, "Anne herself . . . matured very rapidly in these two years, the crucial years from thirteen to fifteen in which change is so swift and so difficult for every young girl." What evidence in Passage Two supports the idea of Anne's growing maturity?

(1) Anne's continuing interest in boyfriends
(2) Anne's ability to get along with her teachers
(3) Anne's being spoiled by both her parents
(4) Anne's continuing supply of sweets and money
(5) Anne's realization of her life in 1942 as different

MATHEMATICS PRETEST

Directions: The Mathematics Pretest consists of 15 items. It offers you the opportunity to test both your computational and problem-solving skills. These are not multiple-choice items, so you will have to work as accurately and carefully as possible. Try the test without using a calculator. Later, go back and try it again using the calculator when necessary. Be sure to use any diagrams or charts that are provided with the problems. Use the formula page 456 as needed.

When you have completed this Pretest, check your answers with the Answer Key on page 516.

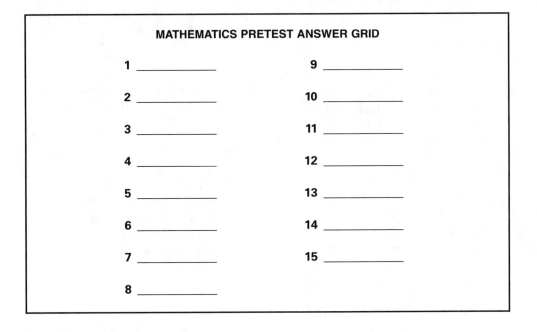

MATHEMATICS PRETEST ANSWER GRID

1 _____	9 _____
2 _____	10 _____
3 _____	11 _____
4 _____	12 _____
5 _____	13 _____
6 _____	14 _____
7 _____	15 _____
8 _____	

Directions: Solve each problem.

1. Find 1.43 plus .5.

2. Martha had $12\frac{2}{3}$ yards of drapery material. She used $\frac{3}{4}$ of it to make the drapes for her family room. How much does she have left to make matching throw pillows?

3. During the last winter carnival, the local college students built a 30-foot snowman out of 100 tons of snow. How much snow will be needed to build a 36-foot snow-man this year?

4. Find 72% of $350.

5. Nick's time card shows his hours for one week. If he works 8 hours per day before earning overtime, find Nick's gross pay before deductions for the week of July 8–12.

Phillips Corporation Time Card

Name: Nick Acino

SS#: 002-00-0021

Date	From	To
7/8	8:30 A.M.	4:30 P.M.
7/9	8:30 A.M.	5:15 P.M.
7/10	8:00 A.M.	4:30 P.M.
7/11	8:30 A.M.	6:00 P.M.
7/12	8:30 A.M.	4:45 P.M.

Regular Hours @ $10.40/hour

Overtime Hours @ $15.60/hour over 40

6. The diameter (d) of a circle is twice as long as the radius (r). If $r = 3$ m and π is equal to approximately 3.14, write the expression that could be used to find the circumference of the circle.

7. There were many increases in gasohol sales over a nine-year period. What is the percent of increase from year 3 to year 5?

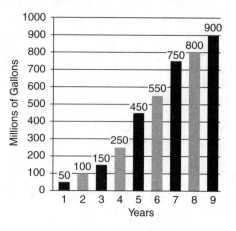

8. How much sand is needed to fill a sandbox 8 feet by 6 feet to a depth of 18 inches?

9. Main Street and Union Avenue are parallel roads as shown below. The railroad tracks cut across both streets. What is the angle measure of the land on which the station rests, based on the information given in the diagram?

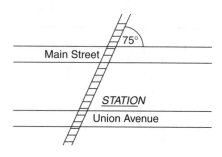

10. Solve for x: $4x - 9 = 7$.

11. Evaluate $-4 + (-3) - (-2)$.

12. Find the average temperature of most of Illinois for the frigid day reported on this weather map.

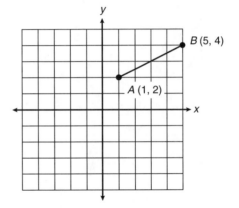

13. Miguel has fourteen coins in his pocket. He has one more dime than quarters and three more nickels than dimes. How many of each coin does he have?

Question 14 is based on this drawing.

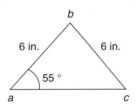

14. Find the length of the line segment from point A to point B.

15. Look at the triangle below. What is the measure of $\angle b$?

b

6 in.   6 in.

55°

a   c

CRITICAL THINKING SKILLS

Developing strong reading and thinking (reasoning) skills is key to your success on the GED. This section focuses on skills you will use in taking all of the GED Tests, particularly the writing, reading, and social studies tests. Knowledge is the basis for reading and thinking skills. The skills you will develop to build on knowledge include comprehension, application, analysis, synthesis, and evaluation.

You can picture thinking skills as layers of a pyramid. Each skill is a stepping-stone to one at the next level. The pyramid of thinking skills is shown below.

Pyramid of Thinking Skills

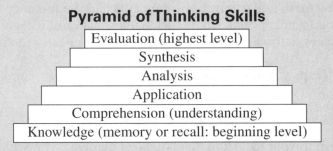

Evaluation (highest level)
Synthesis
Analysis
Application
Comprehension (understanding)
Knowledge (memory or recall: beginning level)

Knowledge: also known as concepts or memory or recall. You acquire basic concepts and use memory techniques. In a biology example, this would mean memorizing the major systems of the human body.

Comprehension: show your understanding by interpreting or explaining in your own words what something means. In a biology example, you might demonstrate comprehension of the major systems of the human body by restating in your own words how the digestive system works.

Application: transfer your understanding of concepts or principles from one context to another. In a biology example, you might apply what you know about cardiovascular systems to designing an exercise program for someone who needs to build endurance.

Analysis: examine the pieces to understand better what makes up the whole, and clarify the relationships among ideas or elements. In a biology example, you might compare and contrast the functions of the large and small intestines.

Synthesis: put many elements together to form something new. In a biology example, you might use the scientific method to conduct an experiment breeding fruit flies and then write a paper describing your findings.

Evaluation: judge how well or how poorly an idea or object meets certain criteria, which can be either objective or subjective. In a biology example, you might read about cloning theory and use your own criteria to decide if it should be explored.

1
<u>KNOWLEDGE</u>

<u>FORMING, ATTAINING, OR RECALLING CONCEPTS</u>

What Is Knowledge?

Knowledge, sometimes referred to as concepts or memory or recall, is the foundation of the thinking pyramid. You gain knowledge through words, numbers, objects, and so on. At the knowledge level—the base of the thinking pyramid—you **form and attain basic concepts** and use **memory techniques**.

When you form concepts, you notice names, patterns, categories, examples or instances, attributes (characteristics), values, or rules (definitions or statements).

Memory helps you answer the questions *who, what, when, where,* and *how.*

Practice Assignment

Take a trip to your local zoo, the botanical gardens, a museum of natural history, or anywhere else where there is obvious organization. Make notes of the names, patterns, categories, examples, attributes, values, or rules you find there. Form your own concepts. Then practice memory techniques using the following approach: developing awareness (underlining, listing, reflecting); developing associations (key words, substitute words, links to other words or ideas); expanding sensory images; recognizing ideas; and practicing recall.

2
COMPREHENSION
UNDERSTANDING WHAT YOU READ

What Is Comprehension?

Comprehension is the second level of the thinking pyramid. Light bulbs are a symbol for understanding because many people associate comprehension or understanding with "a light going on" or an "Aha!" expression. You achieve comprehension by translating words into meaning, interpreting meaning, or extrapolating meaning. You show your understanding by interpreting or explaining in your own words what something means.

When you **translate words into meaning**, you follow directions, read literally (that is, word-for-word), reword a message, translate expressions from one language to another, or convert a message into other forms of communication.

When you **interpret meaning**, you explain clearly what the text means or you paraphrase ideas. You think about the importance of ideas and how the ideas relate. You make inferences on your own from unstated main ideas or assumptions. (The ideas or assumptions are not stated directly, so you are really **reading between the lines**.) You also make generalizations or produce summaries.

When you **extrapolate meaning**, you try to understand general trends, tendencies, or conditions in given information. Then you apply your understanding to make estimates or predictions.

Interpreting Meaning

Explaining Implications of Text

In order to explain what the text means, you must first think about the meaning of words, phrases, and sentences that make up the text. You can ask yourself any of the *who*, *what*, *when*, *where*, *why*, and *how* questions that are relevant. This helps you to understand the context and arrive at an overall impression and explanation of the text. You show your understanding by being able to explain the text in written, verbal, or graphic form.

Example

When the Wright brothers finally realized their vision of powered human flight in 1903 at Kitty Hawk, NC, they made the world a forever smaller place.

Who was involved? <u>the Wright brothers</u>

What did they do? <u>finally realized their vision of powered human flight </u>[finally invented the airplane]

When? <u>in 1903</u>

Where did it take place? <u>Kitty Hawk, NC</u> [North Carolina]

Why was this important? <u>They made the world a forever smaller place.</u> [They made it possible for people to travel by airplane all over the world, thereby "shrinking" the world forever.]

Paraphrasing or Restating Ideas

On the GED Tests you may be required to show how well you comprehend the text by recognizing a restatement of a phrase, a sentence, or an idea. When you paraphrase (restate) information, you use different words and phrases to express the same idea. The following are two examples of restated information.

1. <u>Original</u>. During the last four decades, family life has become more complicated, less locked in to traditional roles.

2. <u>Restatement</u>. In the last forty years, family life has become harder to define.

Making Inferences from Unstated Main Ideas

Read the following biographical family sketch and compose a main idea from the information given.

A FAMILY PORTRAIT

The mother was born in the United States, but was taken to Sicily at a young age; she lived half her life there and had all but the last two of eight children there. As an American citizen she was able to emigrate to the United States, taking one daughter with her. Later, other family members came to the United States a few at a time between 1947 and 1949 and settled in Chicago. On a rare day in 1952, all ten family members were home at the same time when a photographer came to the door. He was going door to door and asking whether families wanted to pose for portraits. Someone rounded up everyone in the family and lined them up. The father and the oldest boy found suits to wear. All six daughters wore rather ordinary clothes, but someone arranged bows in the hair of the three youngest girls to help them "dress up." The strap was missing on the shoe of the eight-year-old, but she beamed anyway. Little did they know that this impromptu portrait would be the only complete family portrait they would ever take.

Hint: Think about the past, present, and future.
Your expression of the main idea is:_____

_____

The main idea could be: *Take advantage of the present because the future is unknown.* The reader must infer this from the details provided: *she [the mother] was able to emigrate to the United States; On a rare day in 1952, all ten family members were home; a photographer came to the door; this impromptu portrait would be the only complete family portrait . . . ever.*

Producing Summaries

Does this happen to you? You answer the phone at work for a coworker, and the caller gives you a long story about the reason for the call. You generally won't write down every word the caller says. You summarize the message, writing down the key thought or purpose of the call. Another time you might jot down key words or summarize main ideas is when you take class notes.

Here's an example of a message one teacher took for another teacher. Summarized message:

To: Mike

From: Lee

Mrs. Kim called. Daughter Anita upset about book report grade. Computer down. Quoted department policy. Call mother at work: 555-5555.

Full message represented by the summary:

To: Mike

From: Lee

Mrs. Kim is upset that her daughter received a grade of "0" on her book report. She said that the report was late because the computer crashed in the middle of typing the report. I asked her how long her daughter had been given to do the assignment, and she said three weeks. I asked why Anita had waited so long to do the assignment and why she hadn't just done the assignment longhand. I reminded Mrs. Kim that department policy does not permit late papers unless there are extenuating circumstances. Please call her at work: 555-5555.

SKILL BUILDER: SUMMARIZING THE MAIN IDEA

1. Circle key words in a sentence. Which words are absolutely necessary to get the message across?

2. Identify key ideas (groups of key words) contained in a paragraph. List what these ideas have in common. This is the main idea.

3. Notice headlines and titles; they usually contain key ideas.

EXERCISE 1: SUMMARIZING THE MAIN IDEA

Directions: Practice summarizing the following message. Use a separate page to write your summary.

Full message (to Christopher from his roommate at college):

Christopher, your mother called from Paris! She said you can't use your family credit cards. She was very upset, but everyone is all right. She lost her wallet while getting on a subway train. She thinks that a young boy and girl who bumped her reached into her purse and stole her wallet. Then they jumped off the train just before the train pulled away. Your mom and dad and aunt and uncle got off at the next stop and immediately went back to the same train stop. The kids were gone, so your mom and the others went to ask the clerk at the station for help. Your aunt did the best she could to try to speak French to the clerk to say what happened. The clerk advised them to to report it to the police.

They had a hard time asking people on the street for directions to the police station. They found it about 45 minutes later and found a very sympathetic English-speaking police officer who took their report. The officer says this happens all the time, and he let your mom use the phone to call the international credit card bureau. She can't get her French francs back, but she reported her credit cards as stolen. The credit card companies closed those accounts immediately, but the young thieves (probably working with their parents) managed to charge over $800 in drapery fabric (of all things) in the time it took to get to the station. Your family is not liable for unauthorized charges, but it will be a few days before cards with new numbers are issued and sent to all of you. Chris, in the meantime, if you need to buy something, I'll put it on my credit card and you can pay me back later.

Possible answers are on page 518.

Extrapolating or Interpolating Meaning

Another way to improve your comprehension is to extrapolate or interpolate ideas. To **extrapolate** is to predict from past experience or known data. To **interpolate** is to insert words or values between known text or values.

To extrapolate or interpolate meaning, you try to understand general **trends**, **tendencies**, or **conditions** in information that you have already. Sometimes you have to make **estimates** or **predictions** when the information is not complete.

Consider the following example. A young couple, Jeff and Jennifer, decided to move with Maggie, their chocolate Labrador Retriever dog, from an apartment in one city to a house in another. How can they decide the method of moving? What arrangements would you make if you were to move?

What information is given?	What information is extrapolated?

• who is to be relocated
  family members
  pets
	• the 750-mile distance between cities
	• the time of year
	• what is to be relocated
	  cars or other vehicles
	  furniture, appliances, and so on
	  household goods

• method of moving:
  nonbinding estimate (depends on weight of goods; difficult to budget)
  "binding" (set) price (fair price may be above or below that)
  "not to exceed" price (price can go down but not up)

3
APPLICATION

APPLYING WHAT YOU READ

What Is Application?

One of the most important outcomes of education is the ability to apply what you have learned, to make a "leap" (a mental one) from one situation to another. Using the skill of **application**, you show that you can transfer your understanding of concepts or principles from one situation to a new context or situation. For example, apprentice painters must be able to apply principles of color and texture before they can be awarded their journeyman status and actually work on homes.

In solving problems on the GED Tests, you will have to apply knowledge that you have gained. You may be given information in the form of a definition, theory, or principle. You will encounter application questions primarily in the areas of science and social studies; however, the Language Arts, Reading Test will include some application questions as well.

EXERCISE 2: APPLYING APPROPRIATE DEFINITIONS OR PRINCIPLES

Directions: To practice your skill in applying definitions, read the following passage about forms of drama and answer the questions that follow.

The major forms of drama are the comedy and the tragedy. Comedies generally are light and amusing. They usually begin in humorously difficult situations and always end happily. Not all comedies are funny and lighthearted, although the majority are. One type of comedy is slapstick, a form of physical comedy that includes pratfalls (embarrassing mishaps) and pie-in-the-face acts. Farce is another type of comedy that features exaggerated circumstances, improbable plots, and foolish action and dialogue.

In contrast to comedies, tragedies often begin happily but always end in disaster. The main character is usually good, but loses to an opponent in a conflict and is either ruined or killed. The major reason for the main character's failure is his or her tragic flaw—the human weakness that has made the tragic hero or heroine vulnerable.

Somewhere between comedy and tragedy lies melodrama, a type of drama that emphasizes the plot and provides thrilling action.

1. In the 1990s *Friends* was a popular television program. It portrayed the activities of six young women and men who lived across the hall from each other. What is the best description for this humorous, easygoing look at friendships?

   (1) comedy
   (2) slapstick
   (3) farce
   (4) tragedy
   (5) melodrama

2. The movie *Titanic* and the book *A Night to Remember* were based on the sinking of a passenger ship. The ship was on its first voyage, and many lives were lost. What is this an example of?

   (1) comedy
   (2) slapstick
   (3) farce
   (4) tragedy
   (5) melodrama

3. *Third Rock from the Sun* is a comedy whose main characters are aliens who try to have relationships with humans. What is this an example of?

   (1) comedy
   (2) slapstick
   (3) farce
   (4) tragedy
   (5) melodrama

Answers are on page 518.

EXERCISE 3: USING APPLICATION IN SCIENCE

Directions: Read the definitions below and apply the information to answer the following questions.

The human body is composed of several systems that keep it functioning. Though each system may be viewed separately, it is closely related to the others in the body. A problem in one system invariably affects another. Defined below are five of at least ten systems that make up the human body.

excretory system—the system that excretes or expels water and salts from the body; it includes the urinary system, in which the kidneys, ureters, urethra, and bladder play vital roles

endocrine system—the system made up of glands such as the pituitary, thyroid, and adrenal, which secrete body fluids, stimulating cells and regulating the body's development

lymphatic system—the system that circulates lymph (a pale fluid) to the body's tissues, bathing the cells; lymphocytes found in the system produce antibodies that help fight bacterial infections

digestive system—the system that processes and distributes nutrients from food; composed chiefly of the esophagus, stomach, liver, and large and small intestines

muscular system—the system composed of the three types of tissue that enable the body and its parts to move

1. AIDS (acquired immunodeficiency syndrome) is a disease that inhibits the body's ability to fight off infections. AIDS would interfere mainly with the proper functioning of which system?
   - **(1)** excretory
   - **(2)** endocrine
   - **(3)** lymphatic
   - **(4)** digestive
   - **(5)** muscular

2. A new "super aspirin" pain reliever (Cox-2 inhibitor), available only by prescription, is said to work especially well with inflammation of joints and muscles. This drug would help with pain in which system?
   - **(1)** excretory
   - **(2)** endocrine
   - **(3)** lymphatic
   - **(4)** digestive
   - **(5)** muscular

3. A number of foods including apples, berries, broccoli, fish, nuts, brown rice, and tomatoes are said to inhibit the growth of cancerous tumors. The processing of foods in the body is through which system?
   - **(1)** excretory
   - **(2)** endocrine
   - **(3)** lymphatic
   - **(4)** digestive
   - **(5)** muscular

Answers are on page 518.

4
ANALYSIS

EXAMINING WHAT YOU READ

What Is Analysis?

When you analyze something, you take it apart. You examine the content to understand better what makes up the whole. A symbol for analysis can be the magnifying glass because in **analysis** you look closely at individual elements when you examine content. When you analyze, you do one of several things. You identify, classify, or distinguish elements. You make explicit (fully clear) the relationships among ideas or elements. Lastly, you recognize organizational or structural patterns.

Recognizing the Main Idea

One way to show that you can analyze material is to recognize the main idea(s). The **main idea** sums up what the writer is saying. In a paragraph the main idea often is stated first. **Details** (or subordinate ideas) that support the main idea are included in the sentences that follow.

Hint: Sometimes articles that appear as a passage (several paragraphs) in a newspaper or magazine are really one cohesive paragraph.

Read the following paragraph to identify the main idea. Where is the main idea stated in the paragraph?

New research is overturning old notions about how the brain works. Once thought to be unchangeable, unrepairable, and constantly losing neurons, the brain is now seen to be always changing, eminently repairable, and constantly making new cells. One of the new findings, which has enormous implications, involves brain stem cells, a newly discovered cell that has the almost magical ability to make every other type of brain cell, including more of itself. Preliminary experiments in animals suggest it may be possible to inject brain stem cells into patients with a wide range of mental disorders to cure diseases such as Alzheimer's disease and multiple sclerosis.

—Excerpted from "Stem cells opening path to brain repair,"
Chicago Tribune, June 27, 1999

1. Which of the following sentences states the main idea of this passage?

(1) The older one gets, the more brain cells are lost.
(2) Research is changing ideas about brain repair.
(3) The brain remains unchangeable and unrepairable.
(4) Animal experiments involving brain cells are promising.
(5) Stem cells may cure mental disorders such as Alzheimer's.

The correct answer is (2). The main idea of the passage is stated in the introductory sentence: *New research is overturning old notions about how the brain works.* The passage goes on to explain how the brain can change, repair itself, and make new cells.

Choice (1) is not expressed in the passage. Choice (3) is contradicted by the statement *the brain is now seen to be always changing.* . . . Choice (4) agrees with the statement, *Preliminary experiments in animals suggest it may be possible . . . to cure diseases.* . . , but does not tell what the whole paragraph is about. Choice (5) agrees with the last sentence in the paragraph which once again states *it may be possible to inject brain stem cells.* . . , but the whole paragraph is not about stem cells.

Read the passage below. Where is the main idea placed in the paragraph?

In 1932 the Museum of Modern Art conducted an exhibit that introduced American architects to European "modernism," with emphasis on glass and steel. In 1966 architect Robert Venturi affirmed the right of designers to use "ornament" in their buildings. Both events emphasized that ideas definitely influence the buildings that influence our lives. It was in 1909, however, that Frank Lloyd Wright introduced the "modernist" Robie House, while Daniel Burnham and Edward Bennett set up the "classical" Plan of Chicago. These two strands capture opposite trends that continue to this day. Thus, 1909 was thought of as the top year for architecture in the twentieth century.

Source: "The Best Years of the Century," *Chicago Tribune,* September 26, 1999

The main idea is stated in the last sentence of the paragraph: *Thus, 1909 was thought of as the top year for architecture in the twentieth century.* The main idea is stated only after supporting details have built a case for it: *In 1932 the Museum of Modern Art, In 1966 architect Robert Venturi, In 1909 . . . Frank Lloyd Wright, . . . Daniel Burnham and Edward Bennett . . .*

If the main idea is not the first sentence in the paragraph, it will most likely be the last sentence in the paragraph.

Distinguishing Facts from Opinions and Hypotheses

Some of the material you will read on the GED Tests will be based on facts, opinions, or hypotheses. **Facts** can be proved by using one or more of the five senses. Newspapers and magazine articles are based largely on facts.

Opinions are beliefs that may or may not be supported by facts. Opinions express feelings or ideas and are influenced greatly by one's background, values, and outlook on life. For example, editorials and columns in newspapers generally present a writer's opinions along with the facts.

Hypotheses are educated guesses that are made to explain a phenomenon or an event. Hypotheses may be proved or disproved by the passage of time or the acquiring of additional information. The statements below show how facts, opinions, and hypotheses differ.

EXERCISE 4: RECOGNIZING FACTS, OPINIONS, AND HYPOTHESES

Directions: Read each group of statements below. Write **F** for the statements that express a fact, **O** for those that express an opinion, and **H** for those that express a hypothesis.

1. _____ Our city is a great place to live because of the housing, schools, parks, and businesses.

2. _____ The population of our city in the year 2000 was 73,500.

3. _____ Newer "megamovie" theaters that have 25 or more movie screens will cause older, smaller theaters to close in the future.

4. _____ The United States Department of Labor reported that each year 10 percent of the work force switches occupations.

Answers are on page 518.

Adequacy of Facts

When you don't have all the facts, you can't draw a conclusion or make an informed decision. Suppose you were interested in an issue in your community, such as "Should a new community center be built to provide services for lower-income residents?" To be able to determine how you feel about the issue, you need to know all the facts. You need to know the following:

1. How many people could be served at the center (each day, week, month, or year)?

2. What will the services be (adult education classes, medical services, counseling, recreation, child care, and so on)?

3. Will the services be free to residents, on sliding scale, or at full charge?

4. Who will pay for the construction project? Will local taxes be increased to support the center?

Knowing these facts (and others) will help you decide where you stand on the community center issue. Similarly, when you answer questions on the GED Tests, you may need to determine whether there is enough information to support the writer's conclusion or point of view.

EXERCISE 5: DETERMINING ADEQUACY OF FACTS

Directions: Read the passage from *MoneySmart* by weekend magazine columnist Jean Sherman Chatzky. The passage is a commentary about serious debt reduction. Put **F** next to the charges that the commentator has supported with facts, **CS** next to those supported with credible sources, and **N** next to comments for which the author has not cited any evidence.

> If you're far behind on payments, look into joining a program, says Gerri Detweiler, co-author of *Slash Your Debt* (Financial Literacy Center, $10.95). If you're just having trouble making ends meet, you probably don't need a formal program. Instead, talk to a financial planner or take a course in debt management. Either way, you'll have to learn to live on less than you earn. (Your credit cards may not be the problem, says Steve Rhode, co-founder of Debt Counselors of America: Look at things like premium cable, advanced phone services, or your car lease.) You also can try to negotiate with creditors yourself; explain why you're having trouble and ask for a lower interest rate. Many will work with you.
>
> It should take six to seven years, at most, to get out of debt if you're in a counseling program (typically, it takes four to six years). If that looks out of reach, bankruptcy might make more sense for you than counseling. But because counseling services get a "fair share" rebate from your creditors (8–12% of what you pay on your debts), you can't count on them to tell you this.

> —Excerpted from "When you need help climbing out of debt,"
> *USA Weekend,* February 18–20, 2000

1. _____ Is counseling right for you? If you're far behind on payments, look into joining a program, says Gerri Detweiler, co-author of *Slash Your Debt* (Financial Literacy Center, $10.95).

2. _____ It should take six to seven years, at most, to get out of debt if you're in a counseling program (typically, it takes four to six years).

3. _____ But because counseling services get a "fair share" rebate from your creditors (8–12% of what you pay on your debts), you can't count on them to tell you this.

Answers are on page 518.

Distinguishing Conclusions from Supporting Statements

A **conclusion** is something you arrive at after considering the statements that are offered in support as "evidence." If the statements are given first, it is a natural progression to lead into the conclusion. As you read the conclusion, think about the number and strength of the supporting statements that came before the conclusion. Decide whether you are convinced and, indeed, whether you accept the conclusion. If the conclusion comes first in the paragraph, you need to withhold judgment until you have read the supporting statements.

The author of a passage usually gives clues that point to the conclusion. Consider the following example.

EXERCISE 6: DISTINGUISHING CONCLUSIONS FROM SUPPORTING STATEMENTS

Directions: Read the passage below. Then determine whether the numbered sentences (or parts of sentences) are supporting statements or conclusions.

(1) As infants and small children, we cannot possibly earn our welcome in the world; **(2)** yet we sense very soon whether we are in fact welcome. **(3)** The comfort of having someone respond to our cries and needs, **(4)** the sensuousness of being cuddled and held, **(5)** the reassurance of seeing ourselves intensely "mirrored" in the faces of caregivers, **(6)** the sheer pleasure of hearing sounds and, a little later, **(7)** words of love and encouragement—**(8)** all these things confirm (or their absence denies) our welcome. **(9)** Perhaps that's why the most child-loving cultures, **(10)** and those childrearing practices that seem to produce the most secure children, share a belief: **(11)** it is not possible to "spoil" a child before the age of two or three. **(12)** Total dependence on the world creates a corresponding right to feel that it is totally dependable, **(13)** and that we are the center of it.

> —Source: "It's Never Too Late for a Happy Childhood"
> in *Revolution from Within* by Gloria Steinem

1. Which sentence (or part of a sentence) suggests the strongest, most definite belief (the conclusion)?
   (1) sentence 1: As infants and small children, we cannot possibly earn our welcome in the world;
   (2) sentence 5: the reassurance of seeing ourselves intensely "mirrored" in the faces of caregivers,
   (3) sentence 7: words of love and encouragement—
   (4) sentence 8: all these things confirm (or their absence denies) our welcome.
   (5) sentence 11: it is not possible to "spoil" a child before the age of two or three.

2. Which of the following sentences is a <u>secondary conclusion</u> rather than a supporting statement?

   (1) sentence 2: yet we sense very soon whether we are in fact welcome.
   (2) sentence 3: The comfort of having someone respond to our cries and needs,
   (3) sentence 6: the sheer pleasure of hearing sounds
   (4) sentence 10: and those childrearing practices that seem to produce the most secure children,
   (5) sentence 13: and that we are the center of it.

3. What is the purpose of the words *a corresponding right* in Sentence 12?

   (1) a link between *dependence on the world* and *it is totally dependable*
   (2) an explanation of the author's feeling about childhood
   (3) a statement of the childhood "bill of rights" document
   (4) a contrast between childhood and adulthood views
   (5) a summary of different means to spoil a young child

Answers are on page 518.

Drawing Conclusions through Inductive and Deductive Reasoning

The **scientific method** is based on logical reasoning. When you draw conclusions that support evidence gathered in an investigation, you are following logic. Two methods of reasoning that are involved in logic are inductive reasoning and deductive reasoning.

Inductive reasoning involves drawing a conclusion by moving from the specific to the general. In following induction, you observe the behavior or characteristics of members of a class or group and then apply this information to the unobserved members of the group. In other words, you **generalize** about the other members of the group.

EXERCISE 7: DRAWING CONCLUSIONS THROUGH INDUCTIVE REASONING

Directions: To see how a doctor follows inductive reasoning, read the following passage; then answer the questions that follow on a separate piece of paper.

> **Don't cut it out.** It may be time to stop most of the adenoidectomies and adenotonsillectomies that more than 425,000 children under the age of 15 undergo each year.
>
> A study of 461 children with persistent middle ear infections, the most common reason for these operations, found that those who had their adenoids removed or who had both adenoids and tonsils removed fared little better than those who did not undergo surgery, said Dr. Jack L. Paradise of the Children's Hospital of Pittsburgh.
>
> The average number of ear infections in children who had an adenotonsillectomy was 1.4 per year compared to 2.1 per year for

children who did not have surgery, he reported in the *Journal of the American Medical Association*.

"Given that we found both operations to have limited efficacy, and in view of their not inconsiderable risks, morbidity, and costs, we believe that neither operation ordinarily should be considered as an initial intervention in such children," Paradise said. Medical treatment followed by ear tubes should be tried first, he added.

—Excerpted from "Discoveries: Don't Cut It Out,"
Chicago Tribune, October 31, 1999

1. Which population was studied?
2. What groups were studied?
3. What were the finding(s) of the study?
4. What conclusion was drawn from the study?
5. What generalization can be made as a result of this study?

Answers are on page 518.

Deductive reasoning involves drawing a conclusion by applying a generalization to a specific example or case. For a valid conclusion to be drawn, the generalization must be known, accepted, and true. In the case above, medical researchers will use their generalizations (arrived at through inductive means) to treat future cases. If a generalization is faulty, however, it cannot be applied to a specific example.

EXERCISE 8: DRAWING CONCLUSIONS THROUGH DEDUCTIVE REASONING

Directions: Read the generalization. Then write **yes** for each conclusion that is valid based on the generalization and **no** for each conclusion that is not valid.

Generalization: A stroke is a condition in which there is lessening or loss of consciousness, sensation, and motion caused by the rupture or obstruction of an artery of the brain.

1. _____ An embolism is the sudden blockage of a blood vessel by a mass or an air bubble in the blood; therefore, an embolism in the brain can lead to a stroke.

2. _____ A tumor is a mass of tissue that does not swell and that rises from tissue that already exists; therefore, brain tumors generally lead to a stroke.

3. _____ An aneurysm is a permanent, abnormal, blood-filled swelling of a vessel; therefore, the rupture of an aneurysm can cause a stroke.

Answers are on page 518.

Recognizing Organizational Patterns

Writings in social studies and science are organized according to certain patterns. Likewise, literary works such as novels, short stories, plays, and forms of nonfiction also are based on organizational patterns. Three common patterns used in writing are sequence or time order, comparison and contrast, and cause and effect. These organizational patterns can be the framework for a single paragraph or entire books. There may be a mixing of these three patterns within both single paragraphs and longer selections. Generally, however, you can see a predominant pattern within paragraphs of longer selections.

Recognizing Sequence

Often writers organize their works on the basis of **sequence**, sometimes known as **time order**. With this pattern of organization, events follow a series. Sequence is an organizational pattern that is especially common in social studies for describing historical events. It also is used widely in science writing to outline the steps in an experiment. Sequence is used as a pattern of organization in literature as well. In novels, short stories, and plays, plot events must follow a sequence.

SKILL BUILDER: RECOGNIZING SEQUENCE IN A PASSAGE

Some words and phrases that signal sequence include *on* (a certain date—e.g., January 1), *not long after, now, before, next, then, when, first, second,* and *third.*

Using Comparison and Contrast

A writer uses the comparison/contrast pattern of organization to explain or show the similarities and differences among ideas, people, or things. A writer who points out how two or more ideas, things, or people are alike is making a **comparison**. Likewise, a writer who points out how they are different is using **contrast**. Comparisons and contrasts are made with words, phrases, sentences, paragraphs, or whole passages.

SKILL BUILDER: IDENTIFYING COMPARISON
AND CONTRAST PATTERNS

Words and phrases that signal comparisons include *like, likewise, also, similarly, on the one hand, in the same way or fashion,* and *compared to.* Words and phrases that signal contrasts include *however, but, on the other hand, differently, on the contrary, while, although, yet, conversely, on the other side of the coin, versus, in contrast to,* and *either . . . or.*

EXERCISE 9: IDENTIFYING COMPARISON AND CONTRAST PATTERNS

Directions: Read the following passage in which the writer compares and contrasts major interests of our first ladies since the 1960s. Then fill in the blanks with the appropriate comparison and contrast phrases or names.

*Hint: In this exercise, comparison words have been indicated in <u>underlined type</u> and contrast words have been indicated in **boldface type**.*

In the history of the United States there had been forty-three first ladies up until the end of the previous century. All the first ladies were (by definition) wives, and all <u>also</u> were mothers. In that time period, of course, some were married to Democratic presidents **while** others were married to Republican presidents. Since the 1960s, Democratic first ladies included Jacqueline Lee Bouvier Kennedy, Claudia Taylor Johnson, Rosalynn Smith Carter, and Hillary Rodham Clinton; **conversely,** Republican first ladies included Patricia Ryan Nixon, Elizabeth Bloomer Ford, Nancy Davis Reagan, and Barbara Pierce Bush. Several first ladies were known to the nation by nicknames: "Jackie" Kennedy, "Lady Bird" Johnson, "Pat" Nixon, and "Betty" Ford.

Each of the nation's first ladies has been identified with particular special interests, causes, or projects. <u>On the one hand</u>, some first ladies concentrated their efforts on causes that developed during the time their husbands were governors of various states. **On the other hand,** other first ladies pursued personal interests. **In contrast to** those who pursued personal interests and those who followed their husbands' agendas, some first ladies pursued both types of programs.

<u>Both</u> Pat Nixon and Barbara Bush promoted volunteer service. Pat Nixon, Rosalynn Carter, and Hillary Clinton <u>all</u> encouraged support for the performing arts. Betty Ford and Nancy Reagan <u>similarly</u> supported the campaign against alcohol and drug dependency.

Some causes were **different** with each first lady. Lady Bird Johnson worked for the environment and beautification and for the "War on Poverty." Pat Nixon worked to increase the White House art collection. Betty Ford's special cause was support for women's rights and the Equal Rights Amendment (ERA). Rosalynn Carter devoted efforts toward peace and human rights and better mental health care. Nancy Reagan helped charitable groups and renovated the White House. Barbara Bush showed great interest in literacy and established a literacy foundation. Finally, Hillary Clinton concentrated her efforts on children and families and on health care reform.

The nation owes a debt of gratitude to all the first ladies. They supported their husbands as presidents; <u>likewise,</u> they helped pursue the presidents' agendas. Sometimes, **however,** they earned our respect by working toward national causes of their own.

Source: *A Glimpse into the Past, the National First Ladies' Library,* the White House

Comparative Words and Phrases (Similarities)

Name two of the first ladies who belonged to the Democratic Party.

1. _____

2. _____

Name two of the first ladies who belonged to the Republican Party.

1. _____

2. _____

Compare the causes that were similar and identify the first ladies associated with those causes.

Volunteer Service

1. _____

2. _____

Promotion of the Performing Arts

1. _____

2. _____

Campaign Against Alcohol or Drug Dependency

1. _____

2. _____

Contrasting Words and Phrases (Differences)

Contrast the causes that were different by naming the first lady associated with each cause.

1. Mental health care _____

2. Literacy _____

3. Equal Rights Amendment _____

4. Health care reform _____

Answers are on page 519.

Identifying Cause-and-Effect Relationships

The **cause and effect** pattern of organization shows a relationship between events. We connect causes with effects every day. Sometimes the cause is listed first, and it is easy to see the effect that results. Other times the effect is stated first, and you have to trace back to its cause. Several effects can come from a single cause, or a number of causes can result in a single effect.

SKILL BUILDER: RECOGNIZING CAUSE-AND-EFFECT RELATIONSHIPS

The cause-and-effect relationship is frequently signaled by key words such as *because, since, therefore, as a result, consequently, accordingly, if . . . then, led to, brought about, the outcome was, the result was,* and *was responsible for.*

First, let's practice recognizing causes and effects by noticing some of the **signal words** listed.

Example:

The National Fire Protection Association reports that the top five causes of fatal home fires are smoking, arson, heaters, electrical systems, and children's playing with lighters, matches, or candles.

What are the *signal words* used above?   causes . . . are

What are the five **causes** mentioned above?

1) smoking, 2) arson, 3) heaters, 4) electrical systems, 5) children's playing with lighters, matches, or candles

What is the **effect** of those causes?   fatal home fires

Now, let's work with a longer passage.

EXERCISE 10: IDENTIFYING CAUSE-AND-EFFECT RELATIONSHIPS

Directions: Read the passage below, noting cause-and-effect signal words. Write each **effect** that resulted from the stated **cause**. Or, trace each **cause** from the stated **effect**. The first one is done for you.

A home builder specializing in retirement housing nationwide was very successful in designing homes for seniors aged fifty-five years of age and older in the Southwest and Southeast parts of the United States. The builder promoted a particular community lifestyle that included an emphasis on recreation. Accordingly, the corporation researched a colder, Midwestern climate and believed it would be successful there as well. The builder decided to build a similar community with thousands of homes. In order to find enough land, it chose a location some 45 miles from a major city.

Many seniors took advantage of the development because they could have the community lifestyle without moving away from their families and lifelong friends. The construction of thousands of new homes brought about the need for a number of community services. The closest hospital was fifteen miles away; consequently, there was an increase in the demand for emergency health services. Other outcomes included the need for additional grocery stores, pharmacies, movie theaters, restaurants, and other facilities.

The building of stores, pharmacies, theatres, and restaurants led to general development of the whole town, and other age groups were attracted to the area. Many young families moved in, and this led to the need for more schools and more taxes to support the schools. The younger families, especially, supported the schools because they had children in the school system, but many seniors did not want their taxes to be raised for the schools. The result was a division between the two groups. At last word, local governmental leaders still were trying to resolve the issue.

Example

Cause: The builder promoted a particular community lifestyle that included an emphasis on recreation.

Effect: A home builder specializing in retirement housing nationwide was very successful in designing homes for seniors aged fifty-five years of age and older in the Southwest and Southeast parts of the United States.

1. **Cause:** Seniors could have the community lifestyle without moving away from their families and lifelong friends.
   Effect: _____

2. **Cause:** _____
   Effect #1: This brought about the need for a number of community services.
   Effect #2: Other outcomes included the need for additional grocery stores, pharmacies, movie theatres, restaurants, and other facilities.

3. **Cause:** _____
   Effect #1: This led to general development of the whole town.
   Effect #2: Other age groups were attracted to the area.

Answers are on page 519.

5
SYNTHESIS

PUTTING ELEMENTS TOGETHER
TO FORM A NEW WHOLE

What Is Synthesis?

Synthesis involves putting many elements together to form one new whole. This is what you do when you write an essay based on facts from various sources or based on your personal knowledge and experience. Synthesis can involve drawing inferences from multiple parts of a single text, such as when you read an entire literary selection in poetry, prose (fiction or nonfiction), or drama (plays).

As you would expect, there are many writing activities in the Language Arts, Writing section of the book. It is said that clear writing is clear thinking, so additional writing activities are included in three other sections: Science; Social Studies; and Language Arts, Reading. By writing paragraphs to answer the variety of questions asked, you strengthen your synthesis skills.

To use synthesis, for example, let's say that four relatives decide to take a four-day trip for a long weekend in a major city. To share the experience with family members who didn't go, the four agree that each one will take notes for one aspect of the trip. They decide that the major categories are *getting there* (transportation), *seeing the sights* (attractions), *eating out* (restaurants), and *adapting to local ways* (customs). Thus, they will be able to answer the expected questions comparing the city visited with their home city. They will be able to form an overall impression of the trip.

Another skill of synthesis involves the study of two or more pieces of writing that are related in terms of subject matter. You may read two or more articles, essays, speeches, biographies, or other texts on the same subject. You may study one piece in prose form and another in poetry or drama form. You may derive additional information on the same subject from another form such as a graph, map, table or chart, or cartoon. You may combine information from written text and from some other visual component such as a painting, film, photograph, computer image, or other visual means.

Classics—that is, works that have withstood the test of time—invite a variety of opinions and interpretations of the original works. Even works that are not considered classics but have attracted a good deal of attention are often analyzed by many writers. Sometimes the original writer will "revisit" his own work and talk about it later. Your task as the reader is to read two or more versions of or opinions about the original work and form your own opinions. Again, synthesis involves studying two or more sources to form a new whole—a *new understanding* of the text.

Let's practice this skill with two sources, one from a well-known author and one from another writer. *The 7 Habits of Highly Successful People* by Stephen Covey was published in 1989, and it was included on *The New York Times* Bestsellers List for more than a decade.

EXERCISE 11: USING SYNTHESIS

Directions: Read the passage below and answer the following questions.

WHAT IS THE AUTHOR SAYING ABOUT HIS ORIGINAL WORK?

In my book *The 7 Habits of Highly Effective People*, I laid out what I believe are the seven basic principles of effective living, based on such immutable [unchangeable] qualities as responsibility, integrity, respect, mutual understanding, patience and purpose. These principles are as true today as they were in 1989, when *7 Habits* was published.

But technology has changed our world profoundly. Today we are under even more pressure in our professional and personal lives than we were a decade ago. I attribute this in part to technology, because it often has served to quicken the pace, and to separate us rather than bring us closer together.

Technology can be a great tool to help us become more effective—in our work and our relationships. Remember this and you are already a step ahead: Technology is a good servant but a bad master.

Now for the seven habits, revisited here to reflect the new challenges of life in a technological world:

1 BE PROACTIVE.® Ask yourself, "Are my actions based on self-chosen values or on my moods, feelings and circumstances?"

2 BEGIN WITH THE END IN MIND.® Ask yourself, "What would I want written on my tombstone? Have I written a personal mission statement that provides meaning, purpose and direction to my life? Do my actions flow from my mission?"

3 PUT FIRST THINGS FIRST.® Ask yourself, "Am I able to say no to the unimportant, no matter how urgent, and yes to the important?"

4 THINK WIN-WIN.® "Do I seek mutual benefit in all of my relationships?"

5 SEEK FIRST TO UNDERSTAND, THEN TO BE UNDERSTOOD.® Ask yourself, "Do I avoid talking initially about my concerns and instead express my understanding of the other person and his or her point of view?

6 SYNERGIZE.® Ask yourself, "Do I seek and value opinions, viewpoints and perspectives from others to create solutions that are better than I would have created on my own?"

7 SHARPEN THE SAW.® Ask yourself, "Am I continually improving the physical, mental, spiritual and social dimensions of my life?"

—Excerpted from "7 Habits 11 Years Later" by Stephen Covey in *USA Weekend*, July 7–9, 2000. Used with permission.

Part A—*Directions:* Read the following statements and put the number of the author's seven habits with which each statement agrees.

a. _____ You decide when to do routine things such as return phone or e-mail messages.

b. _____ Ignore interruptions, especially during "family time"; organize life activities and commitments.

c. _____ Keep promises, be kind and courteous, make your expectations clear, make apologies, accept feedback, and remain loyal to others.

d. _____ Listen effectively to other persons, carrying on relationships through technology if necessary.

e. _____ Take a long walk, learn a new software program, or send an inspirational message to friends.

Part B—*Directions:* Read a second passage and answer the questions.

WHAT PERSPECTIVE DOES A SECOND AUTHOR PROVIDE?

Ten years later, Covey's book—still on the New York Times bestsellers list and published by Simon & Schuster—has become an icon of a generation obsessed with self-help. Covey was already a highly sought-after speaker when he published *The 7 Habits*; he has gone on to become a counselor to political leaders, chief executives and ordinary people the world over and the vice chairman of Franklin Covey, a global professional-services company and publishers of the Franklin Planner products.

Although his seven habits are now recognized as a tried-and-true short course in leadership, Covey is as self-effacing as ever. "I shouldn't get credit for creating any of the principles," he says. "I just packaged and sequenced timeless principles that transcend culture and never change."

***

In fact, Covey wants to make sure people focus on the seven habits and not on him. Sometimes he worries about having become, in effect, a guru.

—Excerpted from "Business" by Steven L. Kent, *Sky*, April 2000

1. What information does Kent reveal about what Covey has become in the decade since *The 7 Habits* was published?

_____

2. What attitude do you think Kent has about Covey and his book?

_____

Possible answers are on page 519.

6
EVALUATION

JUDGING WHAT YOU READ

Judging Information against Criteria

When you **evaluate** something, you make a judgment. The scales of justice are a good symbol for evaluation because you "weigh" how well or how poorly an idea or object meets certain standards. For example, when you evaluate a movie, you judge it according to the quality of its acting, directing, cinematography, sound track, and other standards. Standards used in making a judgment are called **criteria**.

Criteria may be either subjective or objective. **Objective** criteria are standards that are not affected by an individual's personal tastes, beliefs, or opinions. In contrast, **subjective** criteria are standards that are affected by an individual's personal tastes, beliefs, or opinions.

EXERCISE 12: EVALUATING OBJECTIVE AND SUBJECTIVE CRITERIA

Directions: In the space provided write **O** if the standard is objective and **S** if it is subjective.

1. _____ The Bureau of the Census reported in 2000 that more than $170 billion in federal funds is allocated each year based on population data for each state.

2. _____ The number of United States representatives and senators for each state is determined by Census data every ten years.

3. _____ Voting materials should be translated into as many languages as are spoken by United States citizens.

4. _____ Community services must be available for senior citizen programs, mental health support, and job skills training for young adults.

Answers are on page 519.

The Roles of Values and Beliefs

When people make decisions, they are, in part, influenced by facts. But we all have deeply held values and personal beliefs that also influence our decision-making. Some of the literature selections that you read on the GED Tests will consist of commentaries—writers' opinions of various literary and artistic works. These commentaries are based on the writers' own values. In social studies and science-related issues, you will see that personal values have a big impact on decision making.

EXERCISE 13: UNDERSTANDING THE ROLE OF VALUES AND BELIEFS

Directions: Here is a summary of a real case reported in the media (including accounts from *Time*, *Newsweek*, and many newspapers) at the end of the previous century. Read the passage and identify the value or belief represented by each statement listed.

THE ROPE BECAME LONGER AND LONGER

At first it seemed extraordinarily simple. A mother had bound her only child to an inner tube when the sea was swallowing her boatmates one by one. In the end, only the six-year-old boy survived the attempt to reach the promised land of freedom. Some reasoned that the boy should stay in the country his mother had so desperately tried to reach. The mother had perished in the attempt, but the boy should have freedom as his mother's last will and testament.

The boy's natural father, however, disagreed. The father lived in a dictatorship and supported its ideals. Though he was divorced from the boy's mother, back home in his country he was, by all accounts, a loving father. He even passed the Immigration and Naturalization Service (INS) "test" showing a right to custody. He knew his son's shoe size, his teachers, his friends. With the death of the boy's mother, the father insisted on his parental right to raise his son.

On one side of the rope was freedom (and a bicycle, toys, Disney World, Barney at Universal Studios, and birthday parties). Congress moved toward offering him "honorary citizenship" so he wouldn't be an "alien," and presidential candidates argued that the boy should be allowed to stay in the United States to avoid communist oppression.

On the other side of the rope was dictatorship (and a loving father, a stepmother, a baby half-brother, and two sets of loving grandparents). The INS ruled that the boy should be returned to his father, and the president and attorney general said he should go back to his father. Presidential candidates campaigned that child custody cases should be settled by the courts. The human tug of war continued. And the rope became longer and longer.

1. **Statement:** "In the end, only the six-year-old survived the desperate attempt to reach the promised land of freedom."
   Value: _____

2. **Statement:** "the father insisted on his parental right to raise his son."
   Value: _____

3. **Statement:** "and a bicycle, toys, Disney World, Barney at Universal Studios, and birthday parties . . ."
   Value: _____

4. **Statement:** "The INS ruled that the boy should be returned to his father, and the president and attorney general said he should go back to his father."
   Value: _____

Answers are on page 519.

LANGUAGE ARTS, WRITING

The GED Language Arts, Writing Test consists of two parts. You must take both Parts I and II at the same time, but you may work back and forth between the two parts. The total time for both parts is 120 minutes.
What does Part I of the Test contain?

Part I: Editing (65% of the test)

Part I contains 50 multiple-choice questions that require the skill of **application**. You will have 75 minutes to answer these questions. In this part several documents of 200 to 300 words each will be followed by questions about the sentences within the documents. Some questions will ask you to edit or correct errors in the document while other questions may ask you to restate an idea in different words. The questions will test your knowledge of **sentence structure**, **usage**, **mechanics** (capitalization and punctuation), and **spelling** (possessives, contractions, and homonyms).

Mastering your editing skills is important so that you can demonstrate the ability to **proofread** and to correct writing in a realistic setting. There will be up to ten errors per document.

What are the content areas of Part I?

Part I of the Test can be broken down into the following **content areas**. The percentages are approximate.

Organization	15%	(7 questions)
Sentence Structure	30%	(15 questions)
Usage	30%	(15 questions)
Mechanics	25%	(13 questions)

What types of documents are used on the test?

Most (80%) of the documents used on the test are **instructional** (how-to) or **informational** texts. Instructional documents consist of instructions or directions using technology, utilizing leisure, increasing personal effectiveness, improving family life, or preparing for the business world. The remainder (20%) of the documents are **business documents** including memos, letters, notices, editorials, reports, executive summaries, applications, or meeting notes.

What types of questions are on the test?

Three types of questions will appear on the Language Arts, Writing Test:

Correction	45%	(22–23 questions)
Revision	35%	(17–18 questions)
Construction Shift	20%	(10 questions)

In the **correction** type, you'll see a sentence followed by a question, "What correction should be made to this sentence?" The five answer choices will focus on different parts of the sentence and test your knowledge on any of the four content areas.

In the **sentence revision** type, you may be asked to correct one sentence, a number of sentences, a paragraph, the text as a whole, or a heading. A sentence from the passage will be given with a part underlined. You will need to choose the best way to correct that underlined portion. The first answer choice in this question type is always the original version of the sentence, and this version is sometimes the correct answer!

In the **construction shift** type, you are asked to choose the best way to rewrite a sentence or combine two sentences. In this type of question, the original sentences contain no error. Your job is to understand how the ideas are related in a sentence and which of the answer choices has the same meaning as the original sentence.

Part II: The Essay (35% of the test)

You will be given 45 minutes to complete Part II of the Language Arts, Writing Test. In this part you will be given a topic and asked to write a well-developed essay. You will not be given a choice of topics, but you will not need any special information or knowledge in order to write the essay. The topic will draw on your general knowledge and ask you to explain something about a common issue or problem. In this part of the Language Arts, Writing Test, you should be able to plan, organize your thinking, and communicate your thoughts clearly on paper.

1
BASIC ENGLISH USAGE

What Is Standard English?

We often communicate without using a single word. Our facial expressions, body posture, gestures, or tone of voice can express our feelings and thoughts to others. Using words, however, increases our ability to explain our ideas more fully and better enables us to achieve our purposes.

Have you ever wondered who makes these rules? In the United States, no government agency dictates laws regarding the use of standard English. Rather, the faculty at large, prestigious universities identify and develop usage rules. Knowledge of standard English indicates education. This knowledge is a tool that can be helpful not only in school, but in business as well.

Writing in Complete Sentences

One major difference between spoken and written English is that we do not always speak in complete sentences. For example, in a conversation you might mix complete sentences with **fragments**, groups of words that are not complete sentences.

Characteristics of a Complete Sentence
1. A complete sentence must have a subject that tells whom or what the sentence is about.
2. A complete sentence must have a predicate that tells what the subject is or does.
3. A complete sentence contains a complete thought. It does not leave the reader hanging and waiting for more.

Although we often speak in incomplete sentences without subjects or predicates, generally we must use complete sentences when we write. This is because in writing we cannot use facial expressions, gestures, or tone of voice to communicate our meaning. When writing, use sentences that contain both subjects and predicates. Complete sentences are a feature of standard written English that will be important on the Language Arts, Writing Test and the Essay.

For practice in working with subjects and predicates, try matching a subject from the left column with a predicate from the right. Notice that you are connecting *whom* or *what* the sentence is about with what this subject *is* or *does*.

Subject	Predicate
The leaves of the rhubarb plant	is 186,282 miles per second.
About 70% of Earth's surface	is made up of water.
The speed of light	visit the Grand Canyon each year.
Thousands of tourists	are poisonous if eaten.

Parts of Speech

Subjects and predicates are built from the **parts of speech.** You will not have to define or explain these terms on the Language Arts, Writing Test, but knowledge of these major parts of speech and their functions will help you understand how standard English sentences are built. You will be studying the following parts of speech closely.

Basic Parts of Speech

Part of Speech	Function	Examples
noun	names person, place, thing, or idea	**Tony** went to a **bookstore** to buy a **book** on **politics**.
pronoun	replaces a noun	**Someone** recommended a book to **him**, so **he** bought **it**.
verb	shows action or state of being (is, are, was, were, being, be, been)	Elizabeth **plays** cello and piano. She **enjoys** music very much. She **is** very talented.
conjunction	joins words and groups of words	Sasha is a cute dog, **but** she sometimes gets into trouble. The garden **and** deck look nice.
adjective	describes nouns and tells what kind or how many	Bill, who is a **good** fisherman, caught **five** fish in Canada.
adverb	describes verbs, adjectives, or adverbs	Debbie cooks **well** and **often** prepares wonderful crab legs.

What Is a Noun?

Noun as a Subject

A noun can be the **subject** of a sentence. Think of the subject as the main noun or the *actor* in the sentence. To find the subject of a sentence, ask yourself: Who or what is doing something or being described in this sentence?

The following sentence contains several nouns, but only one is the subject. Which one?

A <u>sign</u> warned <u>drivers</u> about falling <u>rocks</u> along the <u>road</u>.

All of the nouns in the sentence are underlined. If you ask yourself, "What is this sentence about?" you might answer, "falling rocks." But if you ask, "Who or what is doing something?" your answer will be "sign." The noun *sign* is the subject of the sentence.

Singular and Plural Nouns: Spelling Tips

Singular means "one" (single). **Plural** means "more than one." Rules for forming plurals often depend on combinations of **vowels** and **consonants** at the ends of words. The most common rule to form a plural noun is to add -*s* (book-books). Other rules for forming plurals involve the vowels (*a, e, i, o, u,* and sometimes *y*) and consonants (all the other letters of the alphabet).

If you're not sure how to form a plural, look up the singular word in the dictionary. The plural will sometimes be listed there.

Possessive Nouns

Many people confuse possessive nouns and plural nouns. Look at *friends* and *friend's* in the following sentences. Which shows ownership or possession?

His **friends** came for a visit Saturday.

His **friend's** mother called on Friday.

In the second sentence *friend's* shows possession—the friend has a mother. Notice the possessive ending: *'s*.

Study the following rules for forming possessive nouns.

Rules for Forming Possessive Nouns

1. Add *'s* to form most singular possessive nouns.

    benefits of the company → the company's benefits

    music of the orchestra → the orchestra's music

2. Add *s'* to plural nouns to form most plural possessive nouns.

    team of several employees → several employees' team

    books of all the students → all the students' books

3. Add *'s* to plural nouns that do not end in *s*.

    health care for women → women's health care

    wool of the sheep → sheep's wool

EXERCISE 1: POSSESSIVE NOUNS

Directions: Insert apostrophes wherever they belong in the following sentences. Remember, not all nouns ending in *-s* are possessive.

Example: Animals have always played a big part in people's lives and history all over the world.

1. Years ago Australians bought weasels to hunt rabbits, but instead the weasels attacked the Australians chickens.

2. Today in the United States animals such as dogs, birds, and cats are popular childrens pets.

3. Japans scientists have been investigating to see if cows and worms can predict earthquakes.

Answers are on page 520.

What Is a Verb?

Our world is interested in action. We tell our friends what we've been doing. We tell potential employers what we can do. We turn on news to learn what is happening. **Verbs** are the words that show action. Which of these verbs describe actions that you do everyday?

breathe	eat	talk
cook	think	sleep
work	drive	study

Every sentence in English must contain a predicate, and every predicate must have a verb. Sometimes, however, we communicate an idea that does not involve action. When an idea does not involve action, we use another kind of verb—the **linking verb**. Linking verbs link the subject to words that describe the subject. They work much like an equal sign does in mathematics. No action is shown in the following sentences, but the subjects, *name* and *chair,* are connected to words that describe them, *Buddy* and *blue*.

His name is Buddy.   His name = Buddy.

The chair is blue.   The chair = blue.

Is and *are* are forms of the most common linking verb, *to be*. Forms of *to be,* as well as some other common linking verbs, are shown in the box on the next page.

Common Linking Verbs
to be: is, am, are, was, were, be, being, been
other linking verbs: appear, seem, become

Fill in the blanks in the sentences below for practice. Use forms of the linking verbs in the box.

Inge _____ an excellent gardener.

Every summer the garden _____ beautiful.

The projects Roland completes _____ usually very impressive.

Function of Verbs

Verbs can tell about the action or what is true. They can explain what has already happened, is happening now, or will happen in the future. We can learn about the time of an event as well as the action of an event from verbs. The tense of a verb changes in order to specify *when* something happens. Information about the time of an event is given through the tense of a verb.

To form different tenses, verbs must be changed using one word or several words.

Past: Yesterday we **hoped** for the best.

Present: Today we **hope** for the best.

Future: Tomorrow we **will hope** for the best.

Some verb tenses are formed using a single word, such as *hope*. Other tenses require a verb phrase, such as *will hope*. In the verb phrase *will hope, hope* is the **base verb** and *will* is a **helping verb**. To form all verb tenses, you need the base verb. For some you also need to use helping verbs, as you will see as you review the verb tenses.

Regular Verbs

Knowing how to form different verb tenses correctly is very important for the Language Arts, Writing Test. **Regular verbs** are verbs that form the simple past tense and the **past participle** (used to form the perfect tenses) by adding *-ed* to the base verb. The tenses of regular verbs are the easiest to master. However, knowing some spelling rules for regular verbs is helpful.

Spelling Regular Verb Forms

So far you have been writing different forms of verbs by adding *-ed* or *-ing* to the base verb. However, not all verbs change form so simply. Following are three rules for adding *-ed* and *-ing* that cover regular verbs. Study each rule.

1. If the base verb ends in -y preceded by a consonant, change the y to i when adding -ed, but keep the y when adding -ing.

    apply → applied, applying

    try → tried, trying

2. If the base verb ends with a silent e, drop the e before adding -ed or -ing.

    love → loved, loving

    receive → received, receiving

3. If the base verb ends in a single vowel and a single consonant other than h, w, or x, and if the accent falls on the last (or only) syllable of the verb, double the final consonant of the base verb when adding -ed or -ing.

    prefer → preferred, preferring

    allow → allowed, allowing

Irregular Verbs

Many English verbs are irregular—they do not change according to these regular patterns. When you study irregular verbs, you need to learn the simple present, the simple past, and the past participle, which is used to form the perfect tenses.

Have, Do, and Be

Make sure you know the three most common irregular verbs: *have, do,* and *be.*

	Present	Simple Past	Past Participle
I, you, we, they (friends)**	have	had	had
he, she, it (dog)*	has	had	had
I, you, we, they (coworkers)**	do	did	done
he, she, it (horse)*	does	did	done
I	am	was	been
he, she, it (train)*	is	was	been
you, we, they (airplanes)**	are	were	been

*or any singular noun   **or any plural noun

The most common mistake people make with irregular verbs is confusing the past participle with the simple past tense. Remember, the past participle is used to form the perfect tenses, so a helping verb (*has, have,* or *had*) must always be used with a past participle.

INCORRECT: She done her work.

CORRECT: She did her work. (or) She has done her work.

Other Common Irregular Verbs

For other common irregular verbs, keep a list of the simple present, simple past, and past participle forms. Some examples are *catch-caught-caught*, *fall-fell-fallen*, and *lie-lay-lain*.

The Simple Tenses

The **simple present** tense is used for something that happens regularly or something that is always true. The simple present tense is sometimes used for something that is happening now, especially when explaining what a writer or speaker thinks, feels, or believes. The base form of the verb forms the simple present tense unless the subject is *he, she, it,* or a singular noun. For these subjects add *-s* (or *-es* if the verb ends in *s, sh, ch, x* and *z*).

> The moon **is** full tonight.
>
> I **drink** orange juice every day.
>
> Samuel **feels** sick.

The **simple past** tense shows action that occurred in the past. To form the simple past of any regular verb, add *-ed* to the base verb. To form the past tense of any irregular verb, consult a dictionary.

> The driver **stopped** for gas a while ago.
>
> Judy **took** a cruise last month.

The **simple future** tense shows action that will happen in the future. Form the simple future for any subject by using *will* with the base verb.

> Next January a new year **will begin.**

EXERCISE 2: THE SIMPLE TENSES

Directions: Fill in the correct simple tense form of the verb indicated in the parentheses. Time clues such as *yesterday*, *today*, and *tomorrow* in the sentences will help you decide whether to use the past, present, or future tense.

1. (drink)   Every morning Barb _____ two cups of coffee.

2. (try)   He _____ to use the computer for the first time a few hours ago.

3. (vote)   I _____ in the next presidential election.

Answers are on page 520.

The Continuous Tenses

The **continuous tenses** show action continuing in the past, present, or future, as in the following examples.

> PAST: Columbus **was looking** for a passage to India when he discovered America.

> PRESENT: He can't come to the phone right now because he **is taking** a shower.

> FUTURE: We **will be discussing** the essay in the next section of this book.

As you can see, the continuous tenses are formed by combining helping verbs with the base form of the verb plus -*ing*. The following chart shows how to form all the continuous tenses.

	Present Continuous	Past Continuous	Future Continuous
I	am thinking	was thinking	will be thinking
he, she, it (the computer)*	is thinking	was thinking	will be thinking
we, you, they (students)**	are thinking	were thinking	will be thinking

*or any singular noun   **or any plural noun

EXERCISE 3: THE CONTINUOUS TENSES

Directions: Fill in the correct continuing tense form of the verb indicated in parentheses. Time clues such as *yesterday, today,* and *tomorrow* in the sentences will help you decide whether to use the past, present, or future tense.

1. (walk) We _____ out the door when Latisha became sick yesterday.

2. (begin) One week from today I _____ a new job in another state.

3. (shine) The sun _____ right now, but the weather forecast calls for rain.

Answers are on page 520.

The Perfect Tenses

The **perfect tenses** show action completed before or continuing to a specific time. These tenses are used to show more specific time relationships than the simple or continuous tenses. Certain words or expressions often serve as clue words for the perfect tenses. These include *since, already, yet, up to now, so far* and *for*.

The **present perfect** tense shows that an action started in the past and either continues into the present or has just been completed.

> They **have lived** there since 1998.

> Surfing the Internet **has grown** increasingly popular.

The **past perfect** tense shows that an action was completed before a specific time in the past.

> Up until yesterday, he **had** never **seen** a camel.

The **future perfect** tense shows that an action will be completed by a specific time in the future.

> By next month, all the leaves **will have fallen** from those trees.

	Present Perfect	Past Perfect	Future Perfect
I, you, we, they (the parents)**	have thought	had thought	will have thought
he, she, it (a repairman) *	has thought	had thought	will have thought

*or any singular noun   **or any plural noun

EXERCISE 4: THE PERFECT TENSES

Directions: Fill in the correct perfect tense form of the verb indicated in parentheses. Pay careful attention to the meaning of each sentence before you decide whether to use the past, present, or future perfect.

Example: (start) My car ___ has started ___ every morning up until now.

1. (leave)   By 6:00 A.M. tomorrow morning, Juan _____ for Texas already.

2. (save)   So far Gwendolyn _____ enough money for the down payment on a new car.

3. (have)   The Johnsons _____ no chance to meet their new neighbors yet.

4. (perform) Up until the development of anesthetics, doctors

    _____ surgery with the patient awake.

Answers are on page 520.

Using the Correct Verb Tense in a Passage

On the Language Arts, Writing Test, you will have to be able to correct verb tense in the context of a whole passage. Not every sentence in a passage will contain clues such as *a few nights ago* or *tomorrow* to tell you what tense to use.

In the following GED practice exercise make sure that you choose consistent verb tenses to correct the passage. First, identify verbs. Then, identify the tenses used in the paragraph. Pay attention to any clue words that help clarify the time. Next, determine which verb tense is needed and make any required changes.

EXERCISE 5: VERBS

Directions: Read the following passage and answer the questions. Be sure that all verb tenses are correct and that verb forms are spelled correctly.

(1) Penicillin is an antibiotic drug that will be used widely today in medical treatments. (2) However, in 1942, Anne Sheafe Miller made medical history as the first patient to be saved by penicillin. (3) She was near death as a result of an infection and temperature of almost 107 degrees. (4) Before doctors gave her the experimental drug, they should try sulfa drugs, blood transfusions, and surgery. (5) Once Anne Sheafe Miller has received penicillin, her temperature dropped overnight. (6) She began to recover and lived more than fifty years longer. (7) Since that first successful use of penicillin, we have called antibiotics our miracle drugs. (8) We hope these antibiotic drugs will continue to be effective against disease in the future.

1. Sentence 1: **Penicillin is an antibiotic drug that <u>will be used</u> widely today in medical treatments.**

   Which of the following is the best way to write the underlined portion of this sentence? If you think the original is the best way to write the sentence, choose option (1).

   (1) will be used
   (2) is using
   (3) had been used
   (4) is used
   (5) was used

2. Sentence 4: **Before doctors gave her the experimental drug, they <u>should try</u> sulfa drugs, blood transfusions, and surgery.**

   Which of the following is the best way to write the underlined portion of this sentence? If you think the original is the best way to write the sentence, choose option (1).

   (1) should try
   (2) had tried
   (3) are trying
   (4) try
   (5) will be trying

3. Sentence 5: **Once Anne Sheafe Miller <u>has received</u> penicillin, her temperature dropped overnight.**

    Which of the following is the best way to write the underlined portion of this sentence? If you think the original is the best way to write the sentence, choose option (1).

    (1) has received
    (2) will receive
    (3) receives
    (4) is receiving
    (5) received

4. Sentence 7: **Since that first successful use of penicillin, we <u>have called</u> antibiotics our miracle drugs.**

    Which of the following is the best way to write the underlined portion of this sentence? If you think the original is the best way to write the sentence, choose option (1).

    (1) have called
    (2) had called
    (3) are calling
    (4) will have called
    (5) will be calling

Answers are on page 520.

Subject-Verb Agreement

Agreement makes the English language easier to understand. **Subject-verb agreement** means that you have chosen the correct verb form to match the number and person of the subject. In grammar, the subject and verb of a sentence are like a right and left shoe. We expect them to match. Language is easier for everyone to understand when the grammar follows what is expected. When you are writing, it is important to make subjects match, or agree, with verbs.

The Basic Pattern

If the subject of a present-tense verb is *he, she, it,* or any singular noun, the verb must end in *-s* or *-es*. Verbs ending in *s, sh, ch, x,* and *z* require *-es* as an ending.

Notice that even the forms of irregular verbs end in *-s* or *-es* when the subject is *he, she,* or *it.*

In the following examples, identify each subject. Fill in the correct form of the verb *fall* to agree with each subject.

Snow _____ silently on the earth every winter.

Snowflakes _____ silently on the earth every winter.

You should have written *falls* in the first sentence because the subject, *snow,* is a singular noun. The subject of the second sentence, *snowflakes,* is a plural noun, so the correct verb is *fall.*

Subject-Verb Agreement Problems

Subject-verb agreement is only a problem in the present tense, with one exception. In the past tense the irregular verb *be* changes form for different subjects. (See page 65).

Keep subject-verb agreement in mind when you see contractions. If you have trouble figuring out the correct form, take the contraction apart. For example, *doesn't* means *does not,* and *don't* means *do not.*

INCORRECT: He don't (do not) want any more.

CORRECT: He doesn't (does not) want any more.

Compound Subjects

If the parts of a compound subject are connected by *and,* the subject is usually plural and the verb does not end in *-s.*

The rolls and the bread **seem** very fresh.

If the parts of a compound subject are connected by *or* or *nor,* the verb agrees with the part of the subject closer to it.

Neither the rolls nor the bread (seems, seem) very fresh.

Neither the bread nor the rolls (seems, seem) very fresh.

In the first sentence the verb must agree with *bread.* You should have chosen *seems.* In the second sentence the verb must agree with *rolls.* You should have chosen *seem.*

Inverted Order

In three common types of sentences, the verb comes before the subject. Underline the subject of each of the following sentences; then circle the correct verb.

(Is, Are) my keys on the table?

There (goes, go) Pat and Jan before anyone else.

Over the fireplace (hangs, hang) two pictures.

If you have trouble finding the subject of these sentences, mentally rearrange the word order:

My keys (is, are) on the table.

Pat and Jan (goes, go) there before anyone else.

Two pictures (hangs, hang) over the fireplace.

You should have chosen *keys are* for the first example, *Pat and Jan go* for the second, and *pictures hang* for the third.

EXERCISE 6: SUBJECT-VERB AGREEMENT

Directions: Underline the subject; then circle the correct verb in parentheses.

1. The employees and the boss (was, were) busy yesterday.

2. Neither the employees nor the boss (was, were) busy on Tuesday.

3. The bread or the crackers (comes, come) with the soup.

4. In the drawer (is, are) a serving spoon and butter knife.

5. There (seem, seems) to be many problems with this plan.

Answers are on page 520.

Interrupting Phrases

The subject and verb of a sentence often are separated by **prepositional phrases** and phrases that add information to the subject. Neither type of phrase affects agreement between subject and verb.

Some of the most common prepositions are *of, in, for, to, from, with, on,* and *by*. The prepositional phrases in the following example sentences are in *italics*. They are not part of the subject. The subject and the verb are in **bold type**.

Every **player** *in the Olympic Games* **trains** very hard.

A **deck** *of cards* **has** fifty-two cards.

Other **interrupting phrases** may seem to make the subject plural, but they do not. They do not change the main subject of the sentence. They often start with words such as *as well as, in addition to,* and *like*. These phrases are set off by commas. The subject and verb are in **bold type**.

That roller **coaster**, like all the others, **is** very scary.

Chuck, unlike his friends, **likes** all roller coasters.

Indefinite Pronouns as Subjects

Indefinite pronouns are pronouns that do not specify a distinct noun. There are three groups of **indefinite pronouns**. Sometimes these are used as subjects in sentences. Some indefinite pronouns are always singular, some are always plural, and some can be either singular or plural, depending on their antecedents (see page 74). Singular indefinite pronouns almost always end in *-one* or *-body*.

Singular		Plural	Singular or plural (depending upon their use)
everyone	everybody	both	some
someone	somebody	few	any
no one	nobody	many	more
anyone	anybody	several	most
one	each (one)		all
either (one)	neither (one)		none

What Is a Pronoun?

A **pronoun** is a word that replaces and refers to a noun. Using a pronoun allows us to avoid repeating the same words over and over again.

Personal Pronouns

Personal pronouns are divided into three groups, or cases. Each group has different functions.

	Subjective Case (These pronouns act as subjects. They often do the action.)		Objective Case (These pronouns do not act as subjects. They often get the action.)		Possessive Case (These pronouns show ownership. They do not need an apostrophe to do that.)	
First Person (might be used when you're writing a diary or journal)	I	we	me	us	my* our*	mine ours
Second Person (might be used when you're writing advice to somebody else)	you	you	you	you	your*	yours
Third Person (might be used when you're writing about the actions of somebody else)	he she it	they	him her it	them	his* her* its* their*	his hers its theirs
Relative	who		whom		whose	

Note that the starred * possessive pronouns are used with another noun, as in *my car*. The possessive pronouns without stars are used alone: *The car is mine.*

Subject and Object Pronouns

Hint 1: Is the pronoun the subject of a verb, or is the pronoun getting the action?

In the following sentence what is the verb? Will the pronoun be the subject of that verb?

> A bee stung (he, him) on the arm.

In the sentence above, the verb is *stung*. The subject of *stung* is *bee,* so the pronoun will not be the subject. The object pronoun *him* is correct.

Hint 2: Cross out any nouns connected to the pronoun with *and*. Then look at the pronoun alone to see if it is the subject of a verb.

Which pronoun is correct in the following example?

> (She, Her) and Peter will be here soon.

Cross out *and Peter.* The correct pronoun is *She.*

EXERCISE 7: PRONOUN FORMS

Directions: Replace the words in **bold type** in each sentence with the correct pronoun. Read the sentence carefully to determine whether to use a subject, object, or possessive pronoun. Remember that there are two types of possessive pronouns.

1. **Juan** drove to work with **Kevin and Kelly**.

2. **The men's** shirts cost the same as **Sharon's** hat.

3. The invitation said that children were invited, so I brought **my children**.

5. Yesterday Mike and **Mike's** family left to go camping.

Answers are on page 520.

Possessives and Contractions

To show ownership, we might use possessive nouns such as *Jay's* or *Mary Kim's.* Notice that we use an apostrophe to form the possessive of nouns. However, if we use **possessive pronouns** such as *his* or *hers* to show ownership, we do not use an apostrophe. It is easy to confuse some possessive pronouns with **contractions**. The meaning is the key to knowing whether an apostrophe is needed. Look at the two sentences below and note the difference in meaning and punctuation.

> The car lost **its** muffler. (ownership)

> She is glad that **it's** snowing. (contraction)

Possessive Pronoun	Sound-alike Contraction
its	it's (it is)
theirs	there's (there is)
their	they're (they are)
your	you're (you are)
whose	who's (who is)

When you're deciding whether to use a contraction in a sentence, substitute the two words for which the contraction stands.

They told us that (their, they're) leaving on Saturday.

Test the sentence with *they are,* the two words that the contraction *they're* stands for: *They told us that they are leaving on Saturday.*

EXERCISE 8: POSSESSIVE PRONOUNS AND CONTRACTIONS

Directions: Underline the correct word to complete each sentence.

1. The earth is mostly water, so only about 30% of (it's, its) surface is land.

2. Seven of the planets in our solar system have moons, and all (they're, their) moons have names.

3. If you think (you're, your) uncomfortable on a hot day in summer, just consider that the temperature in the center of the sun is about 27,000,000 degrees Farenheit.

4. Stephen Hawking, (who's, whose) contributions to science include knowledge about black holes and the evolution of the universe, may be one of the greatest physicists of the twentieth century.

Answers are on page 520.

Identifying Antecedents

The noun that a pronoun replaces and refers to is called its **antecedent.** The relationship between a pronoun and its antecedent must be clear so that the reader can comprehend the meaning. There are several specific pronoun problems that you are likely to find on the Language Arts, Writing Test.

Example: **William Shakespeare** became famous for the plays **he** wrote.

Pronouns often refer to antecedents in other sentences.

Example: **John F. Kennedy** was president during the sixties. **He** gave a famous speech to **Americans. He** told **them they** should ask what **they** could do for **their** country, not what **their** country could do for **them.**

EXERCISE 9: IDENTIFYING ANTECEDENTS

Directions: In the following paragraph, some pronouns are numbered. Fill in the correct antecedent for each pronoun.

When people read the newspaper one morning, **they** found that **it** contained a story about a farmer in Elburn, Illinois. The farmer had received a bill from ComEd for $544,450.11, and **he** was quite stunned. **His** average monthly electric bill was normally about $120 to $130. The highest electric bill **that** the farmer ever received was $1,500. A ComEd spokesperson **who** spoke to reporters claimed that the bill was a mistake, and **she** said **it** should never have been sent. Many people feel **their** electric bills are too high, but few people receive bills **that** cost half a million dollars in a month.

Pronoun	Antecedent
1. His	_____
2. that	_____
3. who	_____
4. she	_____
5. it	_____
6. their	_____

Answers are on page 520.

Agreement in Number

Pronouns and antecedents must agree in number. The pronoun *they* is used in the sentence below because its antecedent, *plants,* is plural.

Tiny **plants** called phytoplankton make the food **they** need from sunlight and minerals from water.

The antecedent of a pronoun is not always in the same sentence as the pronoun. In the following passage, find the pronoun that does not agree in number with the rest of the passage and correct it.

Today tomatoes are popular and used in many dishes. Years ago, however, no one ate tomatoes because they were believed to be poisonous. The first person to cultivate tomato plants in North America was Thomas Jefferson. He grew it hundreds of years ago in his garden. Today people know tomatoes are safe to eat although their leaves are toxic.

[Answer: *it* should be replaced with *them.*]

Compound Antecedents

The antecedent of a pronoun is not always a single noun. Sometimes the antecedent is made up of two nouns connected by *and, or,* or *nor.* In this example, the two nouns in the antecedent are connected by *and.* The pronoun is plural.

Tony and Elizabeth watched **their** favorite show Sunday night.

And makes a **compound antecedent** (an antecedent of more than one noun) plural. Use a plural pronoun to refer to a compound antecedent joined by *and.* When a compound antecedent is joined by *or* or *nor,* the rule is different. *Or* and *nor* separate the nouns in a compound antecedent. The pronoun must agree with the closest noun in the antecedent.

Either **Lisa or the kids** will share **their** fruit.

Either **the kids or Lisa** will share **her** fruit.

In the first example above, *the kids* is closest to the pronoun, so the pronoun is plural, *their.* In the second example, *Lisa* is closest to the pronoun, so the pronoun is singular, *her.*

EXERCISE 10: AGREEMENT IN NUMBER

Directions: Cross out incorrect pronouns in this passage and write in correct ones, making sure the pronouns agree in number.

Each company has certain expectations of their employees. Its expectations often include work practices, dress code, and safety procedures that workers need to follow during their employment. Employees, in turn, have certain expectations about a company and their treatment of personnel. Their expectations often include salary schedules, benefit provisions, and working conditions.

Answers are on page 521.

More than One Antecedent

The meaning of a pronoun is unclear if the pronoun can refer to more than one antecedent. Remember that the reader should not have to guess at the intended meaning.

CONFUSING: When the car crashed into the wall, it was damaged.

CLEAR: When the car crashed into the wall, the car was damaged.

Sometimes replacing a noun with a pronoun is not the best way to keep the meaning clear.

CONFUSING: I was holding the eggs in one hand and the tomatoes in the other when I stumbled and dropped them.

CLEAR: I was holding the eggs in one hand and the tomatoes in the other when I stumbled and dropped everything I was holding.

No Antecedent

Some pronouns are used without any antecedent at all. The pronouns *it*, *this*, and *they* commonly appear without an antecedent. Here's an example:

VAGUE: When she registered to take the test, she learned they required two pieces of identification.

CLEAR: When she registered to take the test, she learned that the testing service required two pieces of identification.

EXERCISE 11: CLARIFYING ANTECEDENTS

Directions: Read the following sentences carefully, looking for confusing pronoun references. If a sentence or group of sentences is written clearly and does not need to be revised, write **C** in the blank. If revision is needed, write **X** in the blank and revise on a separate sheet of paper.

Example: ___X___ The pet stores had rabbits and hamsters for sale, and they were very cute.

The pet store had rabbits and hamsters for sale, and all were very cute.

1. _____ Wendy gave Bonnie her car keys.

2. _____ The man followed Mr. Reynolds in his new car.

3. _____ We heard on the news that they are trying to find a cure for diabetes.

4. _____ Obesity and malnutrition are growing concerns in the United States. This continues to be a threat to the health of many people.

5. _____ Children need to be raised with love and patience. This child-rearing advice is very well-known.

Possible answers are on page 521.

Keeping Track of Person

To enable a reader to comprehend clearly what you write, you need to be consistent in the way you use pronouns. Read this paragraph and try to keep track of the pronouns.

If a person wants to increase your earning power, you might want to consider increasing his education. One report from the U.S. Department of Education showed that male high school or GED graduates between ages 25 and 34 earned 41 percent more than those males who had no high school credentials. For females, the difference was 58 percent higher. Very often a person can get a better-paying job if you have greater education.

The pronouns in this paragraph are mixed between *he* and *you*. All of the pronouns in the paragraph are singular, so they agree in number, but they shift in **person** (from *you* to *he* and back again). Within a passage, the pronouns should not shift from one person to another.

FIRST PERSON: I, me, my, mine, we, us, our, ours

SECOND PERSON: you, your, yours

THIRD PERSON: he, she, it, him, her, his, hers, its, them, they, theirs

EXERCISE 12: AGREEMENT IN PERSON

Directions: Circle the pronouns in **bold type** that need to be corrected in the following passage.

One survey report states that 66 percent of **us** just want some time for ourselves. In general, **we** are working more than ever, so **you** have less and less free time. Two strategies **you** can use to save some of that valuable time are helpful. **We** need to learn to combine **your** errands, and **we** need to buy time rather than things.

Answers are on page 521.

EXERCISE 13: USAGE

Directions: Read the passage below and then answer the items based on it. For each item, choose the answer that would result in the most effective writing of the sentence or sentences. The best answer must be consistent with the meaning and tone of the rest of the passage.

(A)

(1) The modern world offers many opportunities for living happy and meaningful lives. **(2)** However, it's not a world without conflict. **(3)** Work disputes, social disagreements, and family problems sometimes causes feelings of confusion or helplessness. **(4)** Fortunately, when a conflict arises between you and another person, there are some useful tips that can help.

(B)

(5) First of all, it is important to recognize your own point of view, including whatever biases and judgments we may have. **(6)** Next, you should try to consider the other person's point of view. **(7)** As you talked with the other person, use sentences that begin with the word "I" to explain your feelings. **(8)** At the same time, avoid using sentences such as "You never" or "You always." **(9)** When the other person will talk, listen and try not to interrupt. **(10)** It is important for real communication. **(11)** Also, don't hesitate to give an apology when one is appropriate.

(C)

(12) Perhaps most meaningfully, a code of civility and respect are important to follow. **(13)** Treat others with respect, and in turn, others will respect you. **(14)** The philosopher William James once said, "I will act as if what I do makes a difference."

1. Sentence 3: **Work disputes, social disagreements, and family problems sometimes causes feelings of confusion or helplessness.**

   What correction should be made to sentence 3?

   (1) change <u>causes</u> to <u>caused</u>
   (2) change <u>causes</u> to <u>cause</u>
   (3) change <u>causes</u> to <u>will cause</u>
   (4) replace <u>of</u> with <u>or</u>
   (5) no correction is necessary

2. Sentence 5: **First of all, it is important to recognize your own point of view, including whatever biases and judgments we may have.**

   What correction should be made to sentence 5?

   (1) replace <u>we</u> with <u>you</u>
   (2) replace <u>it is</u> with <u>its</u>
   (3) replace <u>your</u> with <u>you're</u>
   (4) change <u>is</u> to <u>will be</u>
   (5) change <u>is</u> to <u>was</u>

3. Sentence 7: **As you talked with the other person, use sentences that begin with the word "I" to explain your feelings.**

   What correction should be made to sentence 7?

   (1) replace <u>you</u> with <u>I</u>
   (2) replace <u>your</u> with <u>his</u>
   (3) change <u>talked</u> to <u>talk</u>
   (4) change <u>begin</u> to <u>begins</u>
   (5) change <u>begin</u> to <u>began</u>

4. Sentence 9: **When the other person <u>will talk, listen and try</u> not to interrupt.**

   Which is the best way to write the underlined portion of the text? If the original is the best way, choose option (1).

   (1) will talk, listen and try
   (2) will talk, listen and tried
   (3) talk, listen and try
   (4) was talking, listen and try
   (5) is talking, listen and try

5. Sentence 10: **It is important for real communication.**

Which is the best way to write the underlined portion of the text? If the original is the best way, choose option (1).

(1) It is
(2) There is
(3) Listening is
(4) It's
(5) It will be

6. Sentence 12: **Perhaps most meaningfully, a code of civility and respect are important to follow.**

What correction should be made to sentence 12?

(1) change are to were
(2) change are to has been
(3) change are to is
(4) replace respect with honor
(5) change are to being

Answers are on page 521.

2
SENTENCE STRUCTURE

A subject and predicate together must express a complete thought. A group of words that does not meet these requirements is a **fragment**. Fragments often occur in speech because a speaker has additional ways, such as facial expressions, gestures, or tone of voice, to communicate his or her meaning more fully. A writer such as a novelist may use fragments to imitate speech or to create an effect. However, general communication, such as business documents, instructions, or letters, will be more understandable when written in complete sentences.

In a certain type of sentence, the subject is clearly understood, but it may not be printed in the sentence. In the following sentences, who is supposed to do the action?

Study hard for the GED Test.

Enjoy your success once you've passed.

The person who is supposed to study is *you*. The person who should enjoy success is also *you*. These two sentences are complete, not fragments.

A sentence fragment may occur because a writer has failed to attach it to the previous sentence where the fragment actually belongs. Sometimes a fragment has been separated from the sentence that follows it.

EXERCISE 1: REWRITING FRAGMENTS

Directions: Rewrite the following paragraph, fixing all of the sentence fragments. You can fix these fragments by adding a missing subject or predicate, or by joining two fragments.

The most successful people often are those who are willing to experience failure. Without letting it stop them. One such person was Abraham Lincoln. Lincoln failed in business, failed to get into law school in 1832, and failed to win in more than six elections. He also suffered severe hardship in his life. For example, the deaths of his mother and fiancée. Nevertheless, he became president of the United States and still is respected for many of his efforts.

Answers are on page 521.

Run-ons and Comma Splices

A run-on or comma splice attempts to put together too much information. A **run-on** actually has within it two or more sentences that should be separated or combined in a more appropriate way.

RUN-ON: The Appalachian Trail, or AT, is over 2,000 miles long it runs through woods from Georgia to Maine.

Another type of error, a **comma splice**, results when two complete sentences are joined only by a comma. If you use only a comma to try to correct the run-on above, you will create a comma splice.

COMMA SPLICE: The Appalachian Trail, or AT, is over 2,000 miles long, it runs through woods from Georgia to Maine.

Two punctuation marks that will correct run-ons are a period and a semicolon:

The Appalachian Trail, or AT, is over 2,000 miles <u>long. It</u> runs through woods from Georgia to Maine.

The Appalachian Trail, or AT, is over 2,000 miles <u>long; it</u> runs through woods from Georgia to Maine.

EXERCISE 2: RUN-ONS AND COMMA SPLICES

Directions: On a separate sheet of paper, rewrite the following paragraph, correcting all the run-ons and comma splices. Either separate the incorrect sentences into two sentences, or combine them using a comma with *and, but, or, for, nor, so,* or *yet.*

We tend to take our feet for granted, they are actually quite remarkable. Our feet have 52 bones, one quarter of all the bones in the body. Each foot has 33 joints, 107 ligaments, and 19 muscles. Every year approximately 19 percent of people in the United States suffer from foot problems including corns, calluses, fallen arches, fungal infections, and injuries. Women suffer from foot problems about four times as often as men do some of those problems are directly related to the wearing of high heels. We do need to care for our feet, they will be used to carry us thousands and thousands of miles during our lifetimes.

Source: "10 Facts about Feet" *Chicago Tribune,* April 11, 1999

Answers are on page 521.

Sentence Combining

Run-ons or comma splices can also be revised effectively by using connecting words to combine sentences. To make one sentence out of the two sentences below, use the joining word *and.*

The left front tire of the car is flat.

The car window has a hole in it.

In the combined sentence that follows, notice that a comma is necessary before the connecting word—where the period was in the first sentence.

> The left front tire of the car is flat, and the car window has a hole in it.

The combined sentences you have just seen are made up of two independent clauses joined by a comma plus *and*. A **clause** is a group of words that contains a subject and a verb. An **independent clause** can stand on its own as a complete sentence: it has a subject and a predicate, and it expresses a complete thought.

The following joining words, or **coordinating conjunctions**, are used with a comma to combine independent clauses: *and, but, or, nor, for, so, yet.* As a writer, you should select the most appropriate connective to explain to the reader the relationship between the two ideas that you are combining. The following chart shows coordinating conjunctions and their meanings.

Coordinating Conjunction	Meaning
and	adds information
but	shows contrast
or	provides alternative
nor	rejects both alternatives
for	gives reason
so	shows result
yet	shows contrast

EXERCISE 3: CONJUNCTIONS

Directions: Choose a logical conjunction from the chart above to connect each pair of sentences. Then, on a separate sheet of paper, rewrite each pair as one sentence. Be sure to punctuate each new sentence correctly.

> *Example:* I can't imagine how people wrapped gifts without cellophane tape. I can't imagine how people watered a garden without a rubber hose.
>
> I can't imagine how people wrapped gifts without cellophane tape, nor can I imagine how people watered a garden without a rubber hose.

1. The first compact microwave ovens were sold in the 1960s. They didn't become widely used until the 1980s.

2. People ate with their hands for centuries. A big change finally occurred in the 1100s when people used forks, knives, and spoons.

3. It seems silly to say we will dial a telephone number. Push button phones are used everywhere.

Answers are on page 521.

Clues about Commas

Don't use a comma every time you see a coordinating conjunction such as *and* or *but*. If a coordinating conjunction does not connect two complete sentences, do not use a comma.

NO COMMA NEEDED: Our family and friends celebrated Thanksgiving together. We ate everything but the dessert.

COMMA NEEDED: Our family celebrated Thanksgiving, and
(TWO COMPLETE SENTENCES) our friends joined us. We ate everything, but we didn't eat any dessert.

EXERCISE 4: USING COMMAS CORRECTLY

Directions: Place commas where they are needed in the following sentences, according to the rule you have just learned.

1. Jessica won the first game and Elizabeth asked for a rematch.

2. They started a third game but they were interrupted by the doorbell.

3. Games are inexpensive and entertaining so they are popular to play.

4. A game such as chess has been played for hundreds of years so it is very well known in the world.

Answers are on page 522.

Joining Dependent and Independent Clauses

A second type of conjunction makes one clause "dependent" on the other and shows the relationship between the two clauses. Look at the two short sentences and the combined sentence in the following example.

Sally is a vegetarian. She doesn't eat meat.

Since Sally is a vegetarian, she doesn't eat meat.

The **dependent clause** *Since Sally is a vegetarian* is not a complete thought on its own—it needs the independent clause that follows it. The conjunction *since* makes the clause dependent and shows the relationship between the two ideas.

Following is a list of some common **subordinating conjunctions**, grouped according to meaning.

Subordinating Conjunction	Meaning
before, after, while, when, whenever, until	shows time relationship
because, since, so that	shows cause or effect
if, unless	shows the condition under which something will happen
though, although, even though	shows a contrast
as though, as if	shows similarity
where, wherever	shows place

The clauses in a sentence using one of these conjunctions can be moved around. When the dependent clause comes first, a comma separates the two clauses. When the independent clause comes first, no comma is needed.

When all applications have been reviewed, three applicants will be brought in for interviews.

Three applicants will be brought in for interviews when all applications have been reviewed.

EXERCISE 5: DEPENDENT CLAUSES

Directions: Using the list of subordinating conjunctions above, fill in the blank with an appropriate word. There are several possible answers in each case.

1. Books were made more cheaply and quickly _____ Gutenberg invented moveable type to use in printing in 1450.

2. _____ the invention of a process to produce paper in China, the Chinese used clay or wood blocks to make books in the 10th century.

3. In early Egypt, scribes would write needed documents on scrolls in a library _____ the documents were stored in jars.

4. _____ information is stored electronically in the modern world, a lot of paper is still used.

Answers are on page 522.

Using Active and Passive Voice

The **voice** of a sentence is determined by the relationship between the subject and verb. When the subject does the action, the sentence is in the **active voice**. When the subject receives the action, the sentence is in the **passive voice**.

ACTIVE VOICE: The man **drove** to work.

PASSIVE VOICE: The man **was driven** to work.

In the first example, the man *does* the driving. He does the action. In the second example, the man *receives* the action.

Usually the active voice is more effective in writing because the active voice is stronger, more emphatic, and less wordy.

EXAMPLE: Their house **was robbed.** (by someone)

This sentence is in passive voice because the agent who did the action is unknown.

Abraham Lincoln **was elected** president. (by the people)

This sentence is in passive voice because *the people* belong to a vague group which is less important to the author than Abraham Lincoln.

EXERCISE 6: PASSIVE OR ACTIVE VOICE

Directions: Read each sentence below. Mark the sentence as **P** for passive voice or **A** for active voice.

1. _____ The man was bitten by the dog.

2. _____ The dog bit the man.

3. _____ Last week the driver was given a ticket.

4. _____ Last week a police officer gave the driver a ticket.

Answers are on page 522.

To make sentences more effective, you should also avoid wordiness. Empty or repetitious words that add little to the meaning do not create effective sentences. Read the two example sentences below.

POOR SENTENCE: Dinner was eaten with a lot of hunger and talking was done with a great deal of cheerfulness by all the various, different members of the family on Friday.

IMPROVED VERSION: All the family ate hungrily and talked cheerfully at dinner on Friday.

Sentence Structure and Types of Questions on the GED Test

The construction shift question on the Language Arts, Writing Test will require you to change the structure of a sentence or to combine two sentences without changing the meaning. Approximately 15 percent of the questions on the test will be this type.

The original sentence or sentences will contain no error. You will have to figure out which of the answer choices will result in a new sentence that has the same meaning as the original.

There are two types of these questions. Think about the answers to the two questions below as you read the example below.

What ideas from the original sentence are given already?

What ideas from the original sentence does this answer still have to supply?

Example Sentence 1: **Many years ago, for the purpose of helping to preserve some natural regions of the United States, lands were declared to be national parks by Teddy Roosevelt.**

If you rewrote Sentence 1 beginning with

Teddy Roosevelt declared some lands to be national parks

the next words should be

(1) in order to (help preserve some natural regions many years ago).
(2) on the other hand (help preserve some natural regions many years ago).
(3) as though (help preserve some natural regions many years ago).
(4) for instance (help preserve some natural regions many years ago).
(5) as soon as (help preserve some natural regions many years ago).

Notice that the *only* choice that provides the same meaning as the original sentence is **(1)** *in order to.* On the GED Test the choices will not be followed by the part of each answer in parentheses. You must supply the rest of the sentence mentally so that you can choose the right answer.

Example Sentence 2: **Despite the fact that we do not find any possibility of accommodating you at the present time, in the future, there is every hope that such a possibility will exist.**

The most effective revision of sentence 3 would include which group of words?

(1) there is no future possibility
(2) we hope to accommodate
(3) your request is a matter of fact
(4) a past possibility that
(5) because of the hope

The general meaning of Sentence 2 is this: Although we cannot help you now, we hope to accommodate you in the future.

The only answer choice that provides for this meaning is (2) *we hope to accommodate*. Notice the word *include* in the question. Sometimes the question will ask which words begin a sentence or which words combine sentences. Always read the question carefully.

EXERCISE 7: STRUCTURE AND USAGE

Directions: Read the following paragraphs and look for errors in sentence structure and usage. The questions that follow will require you to correct errors as well as choose correct ways of rewriting portions of the paragraph.

(A)

(1) How important is the ability to read for an individual today in American society? (2) It is a belief of most people that in our contemporary times, reading skills are very necessary. (3) Nevertheless, according to the U.S. Department of Education, illiteracy continued to rise in the U.S. (4) Indeed one study estimated that one out of every four adults in the U.S. are functionally illiterate. (5) There is another estimate that is disturbing which made the claim that the level of reading of more than one third of elementary and high school students is below grade level.

(B)

(6) Some constructive advice to counter this problem suggests that a family can read together to succeed together. (7) Parents should read to their children, parents also need to read themselves. (8) Parents who read set an example for their children and underscore the value of the activity. (9) Any kind of reading material is helpful. (10) A variety of different kinds of newspapers, magazines, and books can all serve the purpose of the building of skills and the establishment of the habit of reading.

—Source: "Want your child to be a reader?" *Chicago Tribune.* February 27, 2000

1. Sentence 4: **Indeed, one study estimated that one out of every four adults in the United States are functionally illiterate.**

   What correction should be made to sentence 4?
   (1) change <u>estimated</u> to <u>will estimate</u>
   (2) change <u>are</u> to <u>is</u>
   (3) change <u>are</u> to <u>have been</u>
   (4) replace <u>every</u> with <u>each</u>
   (5) no correction is necessary

2. Sentence 5: **There is another estimate that is disturbing which made the claim that the level of reading of more than one third of elementary and high school students is below grade level.**

If you rewrote sentence 5 beginning with

Another disturbing estimate

the next word should be

   (1) since
   (2) reading
   (3) than
   (4) claimed
   (5) so

3. Sentence 7: **Parents should read to their <u>children, parents</u> also need to read themselves.**

Which of the following is the best way to write the underlined portion of this sentence? If the original is the best way, choose option (1).

   (1) children, parents
   (2) children parents
   (3) children so parents
   (4) children but, parents
   (5) children, but parents

4. Sentence 10: **A variety of different kinds of newspapers, magazines, and books can all serve the purpose of the building of skills and the establishment of the habit of reading.**

The most effective revision of sentence 10 would begin with which group of words?

   (1) Newspapers, magazines, and books help build
   (2) In order to serve the habit of reading
   (3) The establishment of newspapers, magazines, and books
   (4) Because reading is an established habit
   (5) As soon as different newspapers, magazines, and books

Answers are on page 522.

Dangling and Misplaced Modifiers

Another way to combine sentences is to use **modifying phrases**—phrases that describe or add information. A correct sentence will always make clear exactly what a modifying phrase modifies and place the modifying phrase as close as possible to the word it modifies. A reader should not have to guess at the meaning.

Look at the two sentences below. How is the meaning changed by the placement of the modifying phrases?

> 1. We gave a gift with a bright red bow to the girl.

> 2. We gave a gift to the girl with a bright red bow.

Notice that in sentence 1 the gift has the bright red bow. In sentence 2 the girl is wearing the bright red bow. The placement of the modifying phrase can make a significant difference.

In addition to being misplaced, modifiers also may "dangle." A sentence with a **dangling modifier** contains no word for the modifier to modify.

> INCORRECT: Eating the buttery popcorn, my hands became greasy.

> CORRECT: As I was eating the buttery popcorn, my hands became greasy.

The incorrect sentence contains a dangling modifier, *Eating the buttery popcorn*. The sentence does not tell you *who* was eating the popcorn. In the correct sentence, the dangling modifier has been changed to a dependent clause containing the subject *I*.

EXERCISE 8: DANGLING AND MISPLACED MODIFIERS

Directions: Underline the modifying phrase in each of the following sentences. Rewrite each sentence that contains a dangling or misplaced modifier.

Example: Her cousin sent them an engraved invitation to the party <u>with gold lettering</u>.
Her cousin sent them an engraved party invitation with gold lettering.

1. Slowly sinking beneath the horizon, we watched the sunset.

2. He bought an instruction book from the bookstore for training dogs on Saturday.

3. A cold drink tasted refreshing after working outside in the heat for several hours.

4. After listening to the music for an hour, the radio program was interrupted by a weather bulletin.

5. Our neighbors took their dog to the groomer with fleas.

Answers are on page 522.

Parallel Structure

In geometry parallel lines are lines that are the same form. They are always the same distance apart, and they go in the same direction. In sentences, two or more elements that have the same function must be written in the same form to have **parallel structure**.

> NOT PARALLEL: They enjoy hiking, swimming, and to fish.

> PARALLEL: They enjoy hiking, swimming, and fishing.

Do you see the difference? In the first sentence *to fish* is not the same form as the two *-ing* words that make up the series. To make the form parallel, change *to fish* to *fishing*.

The first sentence below is incorrect, but it has been rewritten using parallel structure.

> NOT PARALLEL: She said that she wanted to be beautiful, happy, and have a lot of money.

> PARALLEL: She said that she wanted to be beautiful, happy, and rich.

EXERCISE 9: PARALLEL STRUCTURE

Directions: Circle the letter of the correct sentence from each pair.

1. **(a)** To be loved, respected, and appreciated were three goals she hoped to attain.
   (b) To be loved, respected, and the appreciation of others were three goals she hoped to attain.

2. **(a)** Thomas Alva Edison invented the light bulb, a doll that could talk, and the musical phonograph.
   (b) Thomas Alva Edison invented the light bulb, a talking doll, and the musical phonograph.

3. **(a)** Time pressure, boring work, and when there is too much work are factors that can affect health.
   (b) Time pressure, boring work, and too much work are factors that can affect health.

4. **(a)** People using computers have complained of eye irritation, difficulty focusing, and eye strain.
   (b) People using computers have complained of eye irritation, that they had difficulty focusing, and eye strain.

Answers are on page 522.

3
MECHANICS

The English language can be compared to a car. Parts that fit and work together on a car are like the grammar and usage of English. The design or the body structure of a car is like the sentence structure of language. Language also has mechanics that help it operate. **Capitalization, punctuation**, and **spelling** make up the mechanics of English. When we read, we rely on the signals of capitalization and punctuation to help us understand the writing. We also must be able to recognize the words by accurate spelling. We have all read, or tried to read, writing that contains so many mistakes that it fails in its purpose to communicate.

Capitalization

Always capitalize **proper nouns,** or names. The naming process is similar for all nouns. We name our children, our boats, our artwork, and our businesses. All these particular people, places, and things have names that need capital letters.

In each blank write a proper noun and be sure to capitalize it.

Common Nouns (General)	Proper Nouns (Specific)
author	*Mark Twain*
river	
person	
city	
language	
store	

Other Capitalization Rules

1. **Capitalize a word used as a person's title.**

    She was scheduled to see **Doctor** Garvey on Saturday.

    Don't capitalize a word used as an occupation.

    The **judge** ruled on the case in traffic court.

2. **Capitalize the names of specific places. Also capitalize words derived from the names of specific places.**

    Mesa Verde is an ancient site of the Anasazi Indians.

    Don't capitalize general geographical terms.

    They hiked **west** on the trail.

3. **Capitalize names of holidays, months, and days of the week.**

> Flowers and candy are popular on **Valentine's Day.**

> We are planning to leave on **Friday, October 17.**

Don't capitalize the names of seasons unless they are part of the name of a specific event or place.

> If **winter** is here, **spring** cannot be far behind.

4. **Capitalize the names of historic events and documents.**

> Abraham Lincoln issued the **Emancipation Proclamation** in 1863.

> During the **Industrial Revolution,** people moved from the countryside to the cities.

EXERCISE 1: CAPITALIZATION RULES

Directions: Rewrite the following sentences, putting in capital letters where they belong and taking out those capitals that are incorrect. The number of errors in each sentence is in parentheses.

1. Our friends went to a Concert last monday on Labor day and listened to music from an opera called *The Magic flute* by mozart. (5 errors)

2. Not only did Thomas Jefferson write the declaration of independence for the Country, but he also served as a Governor of Virginia. (4 errors)

3. If you take interstate 80 and travel West, you will see many National Parks such as yellowstone or Grand Teton, that have been preserved because of the efforts of John Muir and John Rockefeller. (5 errors)

4. The ceiling of the sistine chapel in rome contains a painting 133 feet long and 45 feet wide that was painted by michelangelo for pope Paul III. (5 errors)

> **Answers are on page 522.**

Punctuation

As you know from all your work in writing, every sentence ends with a **period** [.], a **question mark** [?], or an **exclamation point** [!]. Watch out for end punctuation that is missing or incorrect. As you learned in the sections about sentence fragments, the fact that a group of words ends with a period or a question mark does not mean it is a complete sentence.

> INCORRECT: In a minute.

> CORRECT: Elmo will quiet down in a minute.

The Comma

A **comma** instructs a reader to pause when reading. It is used to separate units of meaning in language. As a writer, you need to understand the uses of the comma so that you can give appropriate instructions to the reader. Remember that *extra* commas, which interrupt reading comprehension, are just as incorrect as missing ones.

Comma Rules

1. Use a comma with a coordinating conjunction to join two independent clauses.

> Kate wanted to dive into the pool, but her dog Charlie wanted her to throw his ball.

Remember that an independent clause is a complete thought. If the second part of the sentence is not a complete thought, do not separate it from the first part with a comma.

> INCORRECT: Chrissy finished lunch, and ate a chocolate brownie.

> CORRECT: Chrissy finished lunch and ate a chocolate brownie.

2. Put a comma after an introductory dependent clause.

> **While Joan was lying by the pool,** Tim was at work.

Remember that if the dependent clause follows the independent clause, no comma is needed.

> INCORRECT: They put on sunscreen, because the day was sunny.

> CORRECT: They put on sunscreen because the day was sunny.

3. Use commas to set off transitional or parenthetical expressions.

Transitional expressions provide a smooth movement from one idea to another. Many expressions such as *however, therefore, furthermore,* or *for example* work this way.

Parenthetical expressions add comments, explanations, or interruptions to the sentence. Expressions such as *of course, quite honestly, amazingly,* or *unfortunately* are examples of parenthetical expressions. Because both transitional and parenthetical expressions interrupt or introduce the main sentence, these expressions must be set off with commas.

> **Indeed,** what we do comes back to us.

> Chicken soup, **as you probably know,** is good for a cold.

The phrases in **bold type** above introduce or interrupt the main flow of the sentence. Notice that these phrases never contain the subject or verb of a sentence. They simply add an extra thought to the sentence.

4. **Use commas to set off modifying phrases.**

> **Tired and hot,** the man sat down under the shady tree to rest.

> The hostess served an appetizer with mushrooms, **the one food to which I am allergic.**

Notice that each of the above phrases in **bold type** describes or modifies another word in the sentence.

5. **Use commas to separate items in a series** (a list of three or more items, actions, or descriptions). Notice that each of the following series is in **parallel structure.**

> Underground hot springs in Iceland supply hot water to **public buildings, swimming pools,** and **hothouse gardens.**

> **Chinese, English,** and **Spanish** are spoken by more people than any other languages today.

No comma comes before the first item in a series or after the last item.

> INCORRECT: The path looked, silent, dark, and forbidding.

> CORRECT: The path looked silent, dark, and forbidding.

Do not use commas to separate only two items.

> INCORRECT: Liz reads mysteries, and writes textbooks.

> CORRECT: Liz reads mysteries and writes textbooks.

EXERCISE 2: USING COMMAS

Directions: Insert commas wherever they are needed in the body of the following memo. (You should insert a total of nine commas.)

To: All Employees
Subject: Insurance

The new insurance plan will go into effect in the next month so all company employees need to attend an information session. After hearing the information each employee must of course select a plan option. In addition each employee will need to indicate whether family members are to be covered. An employee may opt for coverage for a spouse dependents or just the employee. Registration for an information session can be completed by dialing extension 608. Six sessions have been scheduled and each will last approximately one hour. If there are any immediate questions please call the director of personnel at extension 442.

Answers are on page 523.

The Apostrophe

1. **Use an apostrophe to show possession.**

   add *'s*   *to all singular nouns*
   Some of Sharon's talents include fundraising and needlepoint.

   to all plural nouns not ending in s
   The men's golf game was disrupted by rain.

   add *'*   *to plural nouns ending in s*
   Judy maintains three labs' computers very carefully.

2. **Use an apostrophe to replace missing letters in contractions.**

   Erinn was wearing hot pink pants that we hadn't seen before.

Other Punctuation Marks

The punctuation marks in the box below will not be explicitly tested on the multiple-choice section of the Language Arts, Writing Test. However, you may wish to use some of these marks as you write your essay.

semicolon	;	used to join two complete sentences that are related in meaning
colon	:	used to introduce a list or concluding explanation
quotation marks	" "	used to indicate the exact words someone has said
dash	—	used to interrupt a thought with a shift in tone or idea
hyphen	-	used to separate syllables or some compound adjectives
parentheses	( )	used to include examples, explanation, or facts that may be useful or interesting but not necessary to the meaning
ellipsis	...	used to indicate that some of the text has been left out
brackets	[ ]	used to indicate a comment or change that an author wishes to make in the middle of quoting material by someone else

EXERCISE 3: PUNCTUATION REVIEW

Directions: Find and correct one error in each sentence below.

1. We can learn a lot from other peoples experiences and ideas.

2. Charles Kingsley, said that people shouldn't ever go to sleep at night without having added to another person's happiness that day.

3. If you look in the library you will find many great writers' books.

4. Many famous artists masterpieces hang in the Louvre in Paris.

Answers are on page 523.

4
ORGANIZATION

If you have a closet at home, how you arrange all of the items greatly affects your ability to find something. The more items you put into the closet, the more important it is to organize them. The same can be said about writing. Once you begin writing text that is more than one sentence long, you need to organize the writing so that a reader can find the meaning easily and understand your ideas. Skills such as composing paragraphs, organizing sentences into paragraphs, dividing text into paragraphs, and maintaining unified, coherent ideas will all be tested in the editing section of the Language Arts, Writing Test. In addition, these same skills will be helpful to you on the essay portion of the test.

Paragraph Composition

Writing is generally organized into paragraphs. A **paragraph** consists of several related, unified sentences that develop an idea. Paragraphs can be short or lengthy, depending on their purposes. Generally, a paragraph requires at least four to six sentences to develop an idea. Of those sentences, the **topic sentence** should include the **topic** and a **controlling idea** to limit the topic.

> Topic Sentence = topic + controlling idea

Example: Training a puppy takes patience and repetition.
       topic   controlling idea

In the example topic sentence above, the topic you can expect to read about is *Training a puppy*. The controlling idea that narrows the topic is *patience and repetition*. Notice that the controlling idea narrows the general topic to more specific content. You would not expect to read about the expense and equipment needed for puppy training in this paragraph.

EXERCISE 1: TOPIC SENTENCES

Directions: Underline the topic and circle the controlling idea in each of the topic sentences below.

1. A linguist is more interested in describing how language is used rather than in prescribing how it should be used.

2. The movie we saw last weekend was the worst we had seen in years.

3. Some studies suggest that belief in a treatment or medicine may be more important than previously thought.

Answers are on page 523.

A good topic sentence has a clear focus and is neither wordy nor vague. Compare the two examples below.

A. There are a couple of different reasons that were the rationale for our decision about why we chose the car that we bought.

B. We bought the car because of its cost and reliability record.

Sentence A is very repetitious and vague. Sentence B provides a definite focus and prepares the reader for the explanation to come.

EXERCISE 2: EFFECTIVE TOPIC SENTENCES

Directions: Read the topic sentences below. Circle the letter of the more effective one in each pair.

1. **(a)** One positive thing about music is that it can be good to listen to.
   (b) Classical sonatas are relaxing after a stressful day at work.

2. **(a)** The leaves of some ordinary garden-variety plants are quite toxic.
   (b) Various plants found all over in the world and environment around us can be extremely bad.

3. **(a)** There are several things about smoking that are negatives.
   (b) The health risks, the costs, and the smell make smoking undesirable.

Answers are on page 523.

Placement of Topic Sentences

Most of the time, a topic sentence is placed at the **beginning** of the paragraph. However, a topic sentence can also appear at the **end**, at both the **beginning and end** of a paragraph, or even in the **middle**. In certain limited instances, such as in a description, the topic sentence may be **implied**. The primary purpose of a topic sentence is to help organize the writing by providing a focused central idea on which other sentences build.

EXERCISE 3: TOPIC SENTENCES IN PARAGRAPHS

Directions: Read the paragraphs below. Underline the topic sentence or write a sentence giving the main idea that you have inferred.

1. I walk through the two automatic doors to enter the immense, fluorescent-lit store, reaching for one of the steel carts jammed into the area on my left. Loudly colored posters glare at me, hanging over my head as I make my way through the crowded aisles of cans, bottles, and boxes. From the shelves, as I approach, metallic boxes flash out at me and shoot slick rectangles of paper, screaming in thin electronic voices, "Fifty cents off." Clerks behind demonstration counters thrust foam cups of food samples at me, cajoling me to taste and buy. Overhead, somewhere through a scratchy PA system, a tinny recording urges customers to gather quickly at the head of aisle 12. I pause for a moment and take a deep breath.

2. As she entered the dimly lit room, a soft squish that seemed to come from underfoot made her pause. Carefully, she reached out for the light switch, flipping it on and looking about the room. Outside, the wind had subsided, and she knew that finally the storm that had brought strong winds and a violent downpour of rain had ended. As she moved away from the light switch, she heard the noise again. Her heart sank in dismay. She realized upon hearing the noise that she had a problem; water had flooded the basement.

Answers are on page 523.

Text Division

Once you understand what the composition of a paragraph should be, you will be better prepared to divide text into effective paragraphs. You will need to divide text into paragraphs as you write your essay for the Language Arts, Writing Test, but you will also be tested on paragraph division in the editing section. Although three solid pages of unbroken text might alert you that some text division is needed, length alone is not the determining factor in paragraphing. You will want to identify each topic sentence and the relevant sentences that support it. Then, create a new paragraph each time a new idea with another topic sentence and supporting sentences appears. The standard method of beginning a new paragraph requires indenting the first sentence in the paragraph about five spaces from the left margin. In some documents leaving a line between the paragraphs in a text indicates paragraph division.

The passage below is an example of text that should be divided into two paragraphs. Where do you think the passage should be divided? What idea is presented in the first paragraph? What idea is discussed in the second paragraph?

Getting organized is sometimes a matter of simplifying life. One way to simplify your life involves setting limits. To begin with, don't buy more than you need or keep items in the hope that someday they will be valuable. Get rid of possessions that you don't need rather than add new space. When you travel, don't bring back lots of souvenirs. Forget the spoon rests and t-shirts and come back with good memories. Another way to simplify your life involves changing your habits. Slow down and don't rush. You'll lose more time if something isn't done right and you have to do it over again. Next, learn to schedule tasks and follow through on what you plan. Also, give your kids the responsibility of organizing themselves. Serve as a good example to them, and you will all benefit.

—Source: "Getting Started" *Chicago Tribune,* April 7, 2000

The text should be divided so that the second paragraph begins with this sentence: *Another way to simplify your life involves changing your habits.* Note the way the ideas change. The first paragraph in this text discusses setting limits as a way to simplify life. The second paragraph discusses changing habits as a way to simplify life. Additionally, the wording serves as a signal for a change of ideas. The topic sentence of the second paragraph begins with the expression *Another way* in contrast to the first paragraph, which used the expression *One way.* Good writers try to provide textual devices and transitional expressions that prepare readers for a change of ideas.

EXERCISE 4: TEXT DIVISION

Directions: Read the passages below and divide them into effective paragraphs.

1. Who is the greatest writer in English? In answer to that question, many people would name William Shakespeare. Shakespeare lived in England from 1564 to 1616. He was an actor and playwright in London, but he also wrote poems about nature, love, and change. His plays are divided into three categories: comedies, tragedies, and histories. Probably his greatest play is the tragedy *Hamlet*, but many of his other plays are well-known and appreciated. Before Shakespeare, the most famous writer of English literature was Geoffrey Chaucer. Chaucer lived from 1340 to 1400. He was a military man and later a member of the king's court. He was very influenced by Italian writers. Like Shakespeare, Chaucer also wrote poems, but his poems were much longer. His greatest work is the *Canterbury Tales*, which was never finished.

2. Many great scientific advances occurred in the 20th century. In the early 1900s Albert Einstein proposed his famous theories of relativity and strongly impacted the field of physics. In the 1930s blood banking began because of the initiative of Dr. Bernard Francis. Approximately twenty years later Watson and Crick discovered the double-helix structure of DNA. In 1977 the world's last naturally occurring case of smallpox was recorded, and the disease was finally vanquished. Many notable scientific achievements occurred before the 20th century as well. In the early 1500s the Polish astronomer Copernicus suggested that the planets moved around the sun. Later, in 1543 Vesalius described human anatomy in one of the most significant medical books ever written. The laws of gravity, motion, and optics that Sir Isaac Newton developed at the end of the 17th century influenced the world for more than 200 years.

Answers are on page 523.

Text divided into too many paragraphs is just as confusing as text that has not been divided enough. The paragraph needs to express a main idea and its support, which should be organized properly. Read the paragraphs below. What is the most effective way to reorganize them?

Offers that seem to be too good to be true usually are. Each year smooth operators, who seemingly offer a good deal, cheat hundreds of people in scams. The U.S. government attempts to investigate and prosecute con artists and frauds, but a consumer needs to act with a little smart caution as well.

Don't hesitate to check into the background of a person or organization before sending money. Read all contracts carefully, checking the terms. Be especially careful about believing everything you read on the Web. Remember, an unbelievably good deal is often a deal you should not believe.

The two paragraphs should be combined into one. The main idea of the paragraph is stated in the first sentence: *Offers that seem to be too good to be true usually are.* The last sentence restates the topic sentence: *Remember, an unbelievably good deal is often a deal you should not believe.* All the other sentences provide explanation and advice about avoiding fraud.

EXERCISE 5: ORGANIZING TEXT

Directions: Read the seven paragraphs below. On a separate piece of paper, organize and combine the sentences into more effective paragraphs.

(1) It's important to store food carefully to maintain the quality and safety. Improperly stored food can cause health problems.

(2) Furthermore, food that is not stored properly will not taste very good. Eggs are very perishable and require careful storage practices. Buy refrigerated grade A or AA eggs with uncracked, clean shells and keep them refrigerated at 40 degrees or lower.

(3) Do not store eggs in the door of the refrigerator. Egg dishes can be left at room temperature for a maximum of two hours. These guidelines for egg storage will help ensure safety and quality.

(4) Ice cream is another example of a food that benefits from proper storage.

(5) Keep ice cream stored at 0 degrees or lower. Once a carton of ice cream has been opened and used, put plastic wrap over the surface of the remaining ice cream before replacing the carton's lid and storing in the freezer.

(6) The plastic wrap will help prevent a skin from forming and help control the formation of ice crystals.

(7) Be careful to wrap other foods in the freezer tightly so that the odors do not taint the ice cream. A little effort can ensure some good results.

—Source: "Top Ten Egg Safety Tips" *Chicago Tribune,* January 12, 2000

Answers are on page 523.

Paragraph Unity

Imagine having a conversation with a friend when suddenly another person who has been listening interrupts your conversation. Written communication, even more so than speech, obligates the author to stay on the subject. Effective **paragraph unity** requires that all the sentences in the paragraph develop the central idea. Sentences that are unnecessary or irrelevant can cause a reader to lose interest or confidence.

Read the letter below. Which sentences are irrelevant?

Alex Robertson, Supervisor
Stanton Corporation
3535 Belvidere Blvd.
Los Angeles, CA 90217

Dear Mr. Robertson:

I have been employed by Stanton Corporation for eighteen months now. During that time, I have been evaluated in my position of technical assistant twice, and both times I received very high ratings in all categories. I showed my wife one of those evaluations. Since I began this position more than a year ago, my knowledge and experience in the job have increased substantially. As a result, I would like to request a raise in my salary because I believe that my contribution to the company has grown. I have not received a raise since I began. Two of my friends got raises last week at the companies where they work, and I would like one as well. Would you please review my personnel record and consider my request?

Sincerely,

Vincent Lowes

Two sentences in this letter are irrelevant: *I showed my wife one of those evaluations,* and *Two of my friends got raises last week at the companies where they work, and I would like one as well.* This information would not matter to a supervisor, and including those sentences weakens the persuasive appeal of the letter.

EXERCISE 6: IRRELEVANT SENTENCES

Directions: Read the paragraph and cross out irrelevant sentences.

It sometimes takes a lot of courage to make a change for the better in our world. One example of that kind of courage is found in the story of a priest named Damien and his attempt to help the sick. Many years ago, a disease known as leprosy caused people to develop terrible sores on their bodies and eventually die. That was even before the development of computers. The disease was highly contagious, so people were extremely afraid of contracting leprosy. People were also afraid of other diseases as well. In Hawaii those people who became afflicted with leprosy were taken to an island and left there without any medical care. Damien learned of the situation and went to the island to tend the sick. Not only did he tend the sick, but he also drew world attention to the suffering caused by this illness. His efforts inspired research that ultimately led to treatment and a cure. Unfortunately, Father Damien contracted the disease himself and died from it. He should be remembered as a courageous man.

Answers are on page 524.

Paragraph Coherence

Paragraph unity and paragraph coherence are comparable to a jigsaw puzzle. **Paragraph unity** means that all the right pieces for the puzzle are here. **Paragraph coherence** means that the puzzle pieces fit smoothly together.

For paragraph coherence, first check the placement of sentences in the paragraph. Second, make sure to provide smooth movement from one thought or sentence to the next. The three methods below can help you achieve that smooth movement.

1. Use effective grammar, especially pronoun reference.   *Example:* Language is always changing. **It** is a product of the culture.   (see Chapter 1)
2. Repeat words or sentence patterns such as parallel structures.   *Example:* **Not all men** like sports. **Not all women** like shopping.   (see Chapter 2)
3. Use appropriate transitional expressions. (see next page)   *Example:* A tomato is technically a fruit. **However**, most people think it is a vegetable.

Transitional Words and Expressions

Transitional expressions clarify the relationships that exist between ideas; as a result, the reader's understanding of a text improves. Smooth coherence increases comprehension.

To Contrast	To Compare	To Provide Example or Emphasis
however, nevertheless, although, even though, on the other hand, in spite of, despite, on the contrary, yet, regardless, though	in the same way, likewise, similarly, also, just as, like	for example, that is, for instance, indeed, in fact, specifically, of course
To Add to an Idea	**Show Order or Cause**	**To Show Result or Time**
additionally, besides, furthermore, also, moreover, in addition	therefore, as a result, consequently, thus, hence, because, since	meanwhile, so far, at last, then, first, lastly, when, next

EXERCISE 7: TRANSITIONAL EXPRESSIONS

Part A—*Directions:* Read the sentences below. Choose words to complete the sentences appropriately. More than one choice is possible.

1. Mexico City is a very large city. _____, it is the largest city in the world.

2. Modern doctors scrub and sterilize their equipment and hands. _____, fewer people die from infections after operations.

3. My neighbor was a careless driver who was always in a hurry. _____, one day he received a ticket.

Part B—*Directions:* Complete the second sentence in each pair so that the sentences make sense.

1. Judy ate a cheeseburger, salad, baked potato, taco, and ice cream cone for lunch. As a result,

   _____

2. As we get older, we grow more experienced. Furthermore,

   _____

3. We would love to travel to many places in the world. For example,

   _____

Answers are on page 524.

EXERCISE 8: WRITING ERRORS

Directions: Read the following paragraphs. Answer the multiple-choice questions, correcting errors in paragraphing, sentence structure, usage, and mechanics.

COINS

(A)

(1) Collecting coins has been a popular hobby for years, but the U.S. Mint's program to honor each of the 50 states with its own quarter has increased interest in coin collecting. **(2)** Stamp collecting is another popular hobby in the United States. **(3)** It is a fact that the first state quarters were issued by the mint in the year 1999. **(4)** The quarters are minted and issued according to the order in which states ratified the Constitution or were admitted into the United States. **(5)** On the front of each quarter being the silhouette of George Washington. **(6)** On the back of each quarter is a unique design for each state.

(B)

(7) In addition to minting the state quarters, the responsibility is the mint's for production of all other U.S. coins. **(8)** All coins minted for general circulation are made in Denver and Philadelphia. **(9)** Commemorative coins and regular proof sets are made in San Francisco.

(C)

(10) Some commemorative coins are produced at West Point. **(11)** The location of the actual headquarters of the U.S. Mint that oversees all of the various sites is in Washington, D.C.

1. Sentence 2: **Stamp collecting is another popular hobby in the United States.**

   Which revision should be made to Sentence 2 to make Paragraph A more effective?

   (1) move sentence 2 to follow sentence 6
   (2) move sentence 2 to follow sentence 11
   (3) remove sentence 2
   (4) begin a new paragraph with sentence 2
   (5) no revision is necessary

2. **Sentence 3: It is a fact that the first state quarters were issued by the mint in the year 1999.**

   The most effective revision of sentence 3 would include which group of words?

   (1) despite the mint issuing
   (2) although the state quarters
   (3) the very first quarters because
   (4) quarters before 1999
   (5) the mint began issuing the first

3. **Sentence 5: On the front of each quarter being the silhouette of George Washington.**

   What correction should be made to sentence 5?

   (1) insert a comma after <u>quarter</u>
   (2) replace <u>each</u> with <u>every</u>
   (3) change <u>being</u> to <u>is</u>
   (4) insert <u>side</u> after <u>front</u>
   (5) replace <u>silhouette</u> with <u>head</u>

4. **Sentence 7: In addition to minting the state quarters, <u>the responsibility is the mint's</u> for production of all other U.S. coins.**

   What is the best way to write the underlined portion of the text? If the original is the best way, choose option (1).

   (1) the responsibility is the mint's
   (2) the responsibility of the mint's
   (3) the mint having responsibility
   (4) the mint is responsible
   (5) the mint and the responsibility

5. Which revision would make the document "Coins" more effective?

   (1) remove sentence 4
   (2) combine paragraphs B and C
   (3) remove sentence 8
   (4) move sentence 11 to the end of paragraph B
   (5) no revision is necessary

Answers are on page 524.

5
PREPARING FOR THE GED ESSAY

Writing involves **content** as well as **form**. Your opinions, explanations, stories, and observations provide the content for your writing. Developing writing that is meaningful to read involves some careful thought, but the way you think differs from the way you need to write. You may think with pictures, images, fragmented sentences, or even feelings. Thus, it takes some work to transform thoughts and ideas into written communication that will be understood by someone else. Writing consists not only of a **product** but also a **process** by which that product is created.

The Writing Process

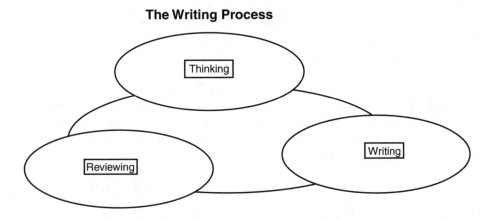

The Writing Process

EXERCISE 1: MAKING A LIST

Directions: Choose one of the options below and make a list. Remember to think about what should be on your list. After writing the list, review it to see whether you have forgotten anything or wish to change anything.

1. List of things to do for the week

2. List of your goals for the next year

3. List of the features you really want on your next car

Answers will vary.

Topic, Purpose, and Audience

The first stage of the writing process is thinking. As you begin thinking and before you start to write, you need to consider the **topic**, **purpose**, and **audience** for your writing.

The **topic** is the subject of your writing—what you are writing about. In a letter to a landlord, the topic may be high rent or faulty air conditioning. In an essay about stress, the topic may be causes of stress on individuals today or ways to cope with stress today.

You need to identify your **purpose**. Why are you writing? What point do you wish to make? Are you writing to tell a story, to voice a complaint, to describe an accident, or to persuade an employer to hire you? What are the best strategies for achieving that purpose?

You also need to consider the **audience**—who will be reading what you write. Sometimes you're writing in a journal intended for your eyes alone. More often, however, you are writing to communicate with other people in a general or a specific group or person. How would you summarize your life experiences to a potential employer compared to the way you would explain them to your best friend?

On the Language Arts Writing Test, Part II, you will be writing an essay on a topic that has been already selected for you. Although you do not have a choice of topics, you will have some choice regarding the approach to the topic. You will also need to determine the purpose of your writing and assume that your audience is general readership.

EXERCISE 2: PRACTICE WITH TOPIC, PURPOSE, AND AUDIENCE

Directions: Write a short letter on one of the choices given.

Topic	Purpose	Audience
1. An issue you feel government should address	You want a change.	a government leader
2. The qualities you really like in someone	You wish to express your admiration.	a famous writer, athlete, star, or leader
3. A problem or inconvenience you've encountered	You would like a refund or restitution.	customer service department of a company

Answers will vary.

Thinking and Generating Ideas for Writing: Stage One

Writing down ideas as you are thinking is called **brainstorming**. Brainstorming is especially valuable for two main reasons. First of all, by writing down ideas as they come to you, you will reduce the possibility of forgetting them. As adults, we have a lot of things on our minds: family issues, work responsibilities, car problems, and many more. Writing down your ideas as you think of them helps prevent their being lost.

Second, when you have brainstormed and written down some ideas, you can easily organize them. Once you have developed a list of ideas, you can select those that seem best, and you can organize them to provide a basic framework from which you can develop your writing.

Seven Steps for Highly Effective Brainstorming

Step 1: Adopt an attitude. Give yourself permission to be silly, stupid, obvious. Don't judge yourself.

Step 2: Consider the topic carefully.

Step 3: List some ideas on the topic.

Step 4: Make choices.

Step 5: Develop associations.

Step 6: Use the five W's (who, what, where, when, why) and organize.

Step 7: Write a main idea sentence.

Now let's apply these steps to a sample topic.

TOPIC: A Place I'll Never Forget

Step 1: **Adopt an attitude.** Give yourself permission to put down any idea that comes to mind without worrying about whether it is silly, stupid, or obvious. You can help prevent writer's block by turning off the voice in your head that criticizes your ideas before you have even written them down.

Example: OK, I've got it! As Shakespeare said: *The readiness is all!* I'm ready to try Step 2.

Step 2: **Consider the topic carefully.** Be sure you understand what you should write about. If the topic is not in question form, turn it into a question that you can address.

Example: What is a place I'll never forget? Why does this place hold such a strong memory for me? What would I like my readers to understand about this place?

Step 3: **List some ideas on the topic.**

Example:

Kauai	Lake in the Woods	My Backyard
wonderful—I'd write to make readers wish they could go there	miserable—I'd write to make readers hope they never go there	special—I'd write to share my memories and evoke the reader's sense of home

Step 4: **Make choices.** Select one idea to develop.

Example: the lake in the woods

Step 5: **Develop associations.** Write down any words or phrases that come into your mind as you are thinking.

Example: cold water–leeches; clouds of mosquitoes

Step 6: **Use the five Ws and organize.** Use the five question words, *who*, *what*, *where*, *when*, and *why* to make questions appropriate to the topic; then answer them.

Example: The Lake in the Woods

Who was there?	**What** happened?	**Where** was the place?
grandparents	**What** was true?	in the country
parents	biting insects	rural area
uncle	nasty plants	north woods
brother	frightening leeches	lake retreat

When did this happen?	**Why** will I never forget?
15 years ago	made me very miserable
in childhood	made me itch and ache
one week visit	made me distrustful of woods

Step 7: **Write a main idea sentence.** In a paragraph, the sentence that states the main idea is called the topic sentence (see Chapter 4.) A topic sentence should contain a topic and a controlling idea.

Example: A place I will never forget is the lake in the woods where one long week of misery created a memory that has lasted more than 15 years.

EXERCISE 3: BRAINSTORMING PRACTICE

Directions: Select one of the topics below. Develop the topic by applying the seven steps for brainstorming. Keep your notes. You will need them to do Exercise 4.

1. A place I'll never forget

2. A person I'll never forget

3. An object that has meaning for me

Answers will vary.

Writing a Draft: Stage Two

Once you've done some thinking, you'll be ready to write a draft. This is a first version of writing that you will change later. As you are writing, which of the following should you do?

1. Pause to think carefully about the rules for commas, apostrophes, and grammar so that everything is correct.   **Yes   No**

2. Stop often to check your spelling.   **Yes   No**

3. Start over every time you make a mistake.   **Yes   No**

4. Focus on transforming your notes and thoughts into developed, extended written form.   **Yes   No**

The only statement that you should have answered *yes* to is number four, the last one. The most important thing to do when writing a draft is to focus on putting your ideas into written form. Use the ideas that you have generated during brainstorming. Don't interrupt the flow of writing to agonize over corrections. If you're aware that something isn't quite right, *underline* the text in question. You can make changes and improvements later.

EXERCISE 4: WRITING A DRAFT

Directions: Use your notes on the topic you chose for Exercise 3. Write a draft on the ideas you have developed. Save the draft to use in Exercise 5.

Answers will vary.

Reviewing and Editing: Stage Three

The third stage of the writing process involves reviewing what you've written. It's a good idea to review your writing at least twice. At the first reading, consider the content you have written. Are all the ideas you wanted to include actually there? Use the checklist below to help you.

Checklist for Revision

1. Is there a sentence that clearly states the main idea?

2. Does the rest of the writing support the main idea?

3. Are enough details and examples included?

4. Has the writing been organized effectively? Should any sentences be moved or removed?

5. Does the writing appear unified and coherent? How smooth is the transition between sentences and paragraphs?

6. Does the writing have a satisfactory conclusion?

After you have reviewed your text and made one set of revisions, read it again. In this second reading you can concentrate on proofing the writing for mechanical, usage, and structural errors. This is the time to think back to the usage rules and practices you have learned.

Proofreading Checklist

1. Does the sentence structure need editing? Are there any fragments or run-ons? Is there any problem in parallelism or modification?

2. Is the grammar correct? Check verb tenses, subject-verb agreement, and pronoun use.

3. Are there spelling, punctuation, or capitalization errors to be corrected?

4. Is the vocabulary effective and appropriate? Has the same word been used too many times?

5. Does the writing all make sense?

EXERCISE 5: REVIEWING AND EDITING A DRAFT

Directions: Read the draft you wrote for Exercise 4. Review and edit the draft, using the checklists given above.

Answers will vary.

Types of Writing

Depending on your purpose and your topic, you may use a particular type of writing or a combination of different types. These are the four most commonly used types of writing:

Type of Writing	Purpose
Narrative	tell a story or experience
Descriptive	create a picture or show something
Informative	instruct or explain facts
Persuasive	influence or convince the reader to agree

Whatever type of writing you use, it will still need to be organized and unified. Remember to organize your writing into paragraphs that contain topic sentences that give the main idea. You also need supporting sentences that develop those main ideas. To review paragraph organization, see Chapter 4.

EXERCISE 6: TYPES OF WRITING

Directions: Read the start of the story below. What two types of writing can you find?

> Everything happened so quickly that now it's almost a blur in my mind. I will tell you, to the best of my abilities, what happened on those fateful days, when King Tutankhamen, still alive and unaware he was destined to die, paid a visit to the House of Life, where I worked as an apprentice scribe.
>
> It was a boiling hot day. Egypt's blazing sun beat down upon the broiling earth without mercy. Even the shade of the palm trees couldn't provide relief from the scorching heat. All was quiet, except for the cries and shouts of the poor boys, happily playing in the cool waters of the Nile. I paused for a moment, stopping my writing in mid-sentence, to gaze longingly at the cheerful sight in the river. That's why I didn't notice . . .

Selection used with permission of Elizabeth Nelson

Answers are on page 524.

Narrative Writing

The purpose of **narrative writing** is to tell a story or relate an experience. Very often, the writing is organized by time order. For this reason the sequencing of events, as well as the verb tenses, is very important. Read the following paragraph. What problem has occurred in the writing?

> The clock outside the depot told him he was late before he even entered the station. As he rushed over to the window to buy a ticket, he saw the train pulling in. He reached into his jacket pocket to take out his wallet. To his great dismay, the pocket was empty. At once he remembers the man bumping into him on the crowded street. He curses inwardly. Then he heard the whistle of the train.

The problem is that the verb tense is not consistent with the time order of the story. Most stories are told in the past tense. This story begins in the past tense, but the writer slips into the present tense with the verbs *remembers* and *curses*. Those verbs should have been *remembered* and *cursed* to remain consistent with the time span used in the narrative.

Notice also that certain transitional words such as *before, At once,* and *Then* in the paragraph help order the events. Listed on the next page are some transitional words that may be helpful in narrative writing because they indicate time order.

Time-Order Transitional Words			
after	at once	at last	later
during	as soon as	prior to	meanwhile
first	before	eventually	at the same time
next	finally	for some time	in the end
simultaneously	second	then	before too long
while	now	when	again

Descriptive Writing

Writing that creates a picture in a reader's mind is **descriptive writing**. Good descriptive writing draws not only on what we see, but also on our other senses, describing how something smells, feels, tastes, and sounds. Including specific details in descriptive writing enables a reader to picture what the writer is trying to show.

When you read the paragraph below, why doesn't it seem to be very effective as a description?

The forest seemed very big as we drove through it. It was filled with all different things everywhere. There were various plants and things growing near the sides of the road. We drove slowly along, gazing at everything in our path, wishing we had the time to stop.

This paragraph is too general and too vague. The vocabulary isn't very specific. The writing hasn't supplied enough details to create a picture. To visualize the forest a reader would have to make up his or her own picture, but that might not be the one the writer intended to portray.

Now compare the paragraph below to the one you just read. Notice the differences in the vocabulary. Does the description appeal to more than one of the senses?

The green forest seemed immense as we drove the old, red Chevy through the deserted woods. The woods were filled with tall oaks, graceful beeches, and fragrant pine. Rays of warm sun, welcome in the cool air, caught the leaves of the trees and turned them gold. Purple and white flowers grew in low clusters along the roadside. We heard the crunch of leaves under the tires and the chirping of red-winged blackbirds nearby. Slowly we drove along, gazing in wonder at this evidence of nature's beauty, wishing we had the time to stop.

In the paragraph above details of sight, smell, touch, and sound are described. Did you note the words *red*, *fragrant*, *warm*, and *crunch*, for instance?

Informative Writing

Informative writing is often used to instruct or present facts. The writer's opinion should not be included. A factual story from the newspaper is supposed to be informative. Other common examples of informative writing are recipes and instructions on how to do something.

Informative writing requires clear explanation in order for a reader to follow directions or comprehend the content. Some transitional expressions that help when comparing and contrasting points of information include the following:

Transitional Expressions	
For Comparison	**For Contrast**
not only, but also	however
in the same way	nevertheless
similarly	on the other hand
just as	while
both	whereas
likewise	still

Read the informative paragraph below. What transitional expressions are used to clarify the comparison and contrast that is made?

A garden may consist of annuals, perennials, or a combination of both. Annuals are plants that only live for one season. Perennials, on the other hand, last for many years. Flowers of annuals stay in bloom for the entire season they live. However, perennials only flower for a short time each year. While annuals require replanting every spring, perennials need division or replanting only after several years. Both annuals and perennials contribute beauty and color in their different ways.

You should have found *on the other hand, However, While, Both*, and *different*.

Persuasive Writing

Persuasive writing expresses an opinion. The writer wants to influence the reader to accept the validity of a point of view. A persuasive writer must be able to state an opinion, then focus on clear, logical reasons that support that opinion. In other words, as a persuasive writer, you must be prepared to tell what you think and why you think that.

EXERCISE 7: IDENTIFYING SUPPORTING REASONS

Directions: Read the statements below. Which ones are persuasive? Which ones do not give real reasons to support the statement?

1. Prolonged exposure to sun should be avoided in order to prevent sunburn and the risk of skin cancer.

2. Winter is the most unpopular season of the year because people just don't like it.

3. Summer is very popular because people can participate in more outdoor activities and enjoy the green lushness of nature.

Answers are on page 524.

An example of a persuasive paragraph is given below. Notice that the topic sentence states the writer's opinion. The rest of the paragraph attempts to persuade the reader of the validity of that opinion by providing reasons and examples.

> Every person in American society today needs to become educated on the use of computers. The widespread introduction of computers during the last two decades has greatly affected American life. The computer has become an integral part of every aspect of society—business, home, community, and even recreation. Some immediate examples of the prevalence of computers are obvious from my own daily life. When I go to work five days a week, I spend several hours working on a computer using information that others have obtained through computers. When I go to the grocery store to buy my family's food, my check has to be cleared through a computer. When I take my car to be repaired, the mechanic hooks it up to a computer. Even when I take a vacation, my plane tickets and reservations are made through a computer. What does this mean? It means that I and others have to keep educated and learn about computers. Thus, we all have to change some of the ways we do things in order to keep up with this change in the world.

Sometimes when you are giving reasons for your opinion, you may be citing the causes or the effects of a situation. Certain transitional expressions help identify those relationships.

Cause-and-Effect Transitional Expressions			
as a result	then	hence	if . . . then
therefore	because	since	for
thus	for this reason	consequently	

EXERCISE 8: NARRATIVE, DESCRIPTIVE, INFORMATIVE AND PERSUASIVE WRITING

Directions: Choose one of the following topics to write a narrative, descriptive, informative, or persuasive paragraph.

Narrative
1. Tell about the events that happened on a day you will never forget.
2. Write out the story of a good movie you have seen.

Descriptive
1. Describe your favorite shopping mall.
2. Describe someone you know very well.

Informative
1. Explain how to prepare a recipe you have.
2. Explain how to put gas into a car.

Persuasive
1. Does a man need an education more than a woman?
2. Has technology made life better or worse for you?

Answers will vary.

Review of the Writing Process

Examine the topic, brainstorm, and write down some ideas.

State a sentence that gives your main idea on the topic.

Structure your paper into three parts: introduction, body, and conclusion.

Add detail, examples, and support in the body.

You're finished after you read over your work and edit it.

The Written Product

A look at the product created through this writing process shows an essay organized into three major parts: introduction, body, and conclusion.

The Introduction

An **introduction** to an essay has two main functions. First, it introduces the topic and attempts to interest the reader in the text. Second, and even more important for an essay test, the introduction generally includes a **thesis statement**, a sentence that gives the main idea for the whole essay.

Do	Don't
Interest the reader	Apologize
Ask a question	Be too general
State a statistic or fact	Be too wordy
Tell a short story	
Disagree with accepted wisdom	
Give a quotation	
State a thesis	

A good thesis statement is more than just the topic. Many writers will write about the same topic, yet each writer will have a different approach and different focus on the topic. A thesis statement should be more specific than the topic, and it should provide a focus that the rest of the paper supports. Look at the example thesis statements given below.

WEAK: There are several different things I do if I feel stressed out by something.

STRONGER: In order to cope with stress, I read a good book, talk to a friend, or listen to music.

EXERCISE 9: THESIS STATEMENTS

Directions: Read the pairs of statements below. Which one makes the better thesis statement for an essay?

1. **(a)** In my opinion, I think something should be done to help people get some kind of medical care that they can afford.

   (b) A universal health care plan is needed in the U.S.

2. **(a)** The purpose of this essay is to discuss three major events in my life.

   (b) Three major events that influenced my life were moving to another state, marrying the one I love, and becoming a parent.

Answers are on page 524.

The Body

The **body** of an essay contains the support for the thesis statement. This is the part where you should be explaining why you think what you do. To develop that explanation well, give examples, cite reasons, retell an experience, or give facts and figures.

Do	Don't
Include details	Assume the reader knows what you mean
Give examples, description, reasons	Keep repeating the opinion that you stated in the introduction
Keep focused	Wander off the thesis

EXERCISE 10: DEVELOPMENT AND SUPPORT FOR AN ESSAY

Directions: Read the essay that has been started below. Note that the thesis statement is in **bold type** and prepares for a discussion of three issues. The first issue, destruction of the environment, has been developed with reasons and examples for support. Complete the essay by writing two more paragraphs so that each of the remaining two problems stated in the thesis has a paragraph of support.

BE HAPPY, BUT BE CONCERNED

Although I generally agree with advice telling us, "Don't worry. Be happy," I do have some concerns about American life today. **Specifically, the destruction of the environment, the continuing increase of crime, and the lack of affordable medical care for all are problems that we as a country need to address.**

The destruction of our environment continues as we pollute the air, water, and land. Pollution to the atmosphere from car exhaust, manufacturing, and chemical use has caused the death of thousands of plants and animals all over the earth. A well-known example is that of frogs, which are vanishing from the earth. Biologists have suggested that their disappearance may be due to pollution. Furthermore, a study conducted by the United Nations predicted that the threat of global warming brought on from pollution will most likely be even worse than earlier believed. An astounding increase in cases of asthma and allergies has also been linked to environmental pollution. Although we have taken some measures to protect the environment, these are still inadequate, and we need to do more.

The increase in crime is another . . .

Answers will vary.

The Conclusion

The **conclusion** for an essay on an exam can be brief. Most important, you want to end the essay so that there is a sense of closure. The writing should not just stop. To close an essay, you could simply restate or emphasize the thesis statement. Other strategies for concluding include calling for some action, giving a quotation, or answering a question that you raised in the introduction.

Do	Don't
Restate or emphasize your opinion	Disagree with what you have already written
Create a sense of closure	Throw in something you have not discussed
	Use *In conclusion*

EXERCISE 11: ESSAY ANALYSIS

Directions: Read the essay below. This essay has two major problems. What are they?

Stress is a problem for many of us today. Life is full of lots of changes, and even good change causes stress. When I feel very stressed out, I often go for a walk through the park near my home. Sometimes I just call a friend to talk for awhile. A long, hot bath is another way in which I relax.

At other times, I just eat a box of chocolate candy with lots of toffee and chocolate-covered nuts. I might just retreat for a time and sit in the garden to watch birds and butterflies. In the winter that doesn't work, so I might deal with my stress by exercising and working it off. Sometimes I go shopping, and sometimes I go to a movie. Another good way to deal with stress is to listen to music. Just doing nothing is good too.

Stress is not something anyone seeks out, but like it or not, we have to cope with stress as a part of life.

Answers are on page 524.

What You Should Know about the GED Test Essay

Some Common Questions

1. How much time will I have? How long should the essay be?

You will be given 45 minutes to write a well-developed essay. Keep in mind that the development of your idea is very important to the quality of your essay. You will be given scratch paper for prewriting and brainstorming as well as two pages of lined paper on which to write your essay. Your paper must be written in ink, and your handwriting is not judged unless it makes your paper illegible.

2. What is the essay topic like?

You will be asked to write an opinion or explanation on a single topic. No specialized knowledge will be necessary. You will be evaluated on how well you have presented the opinion you state.

3. How will the essay be scored?

Two readers will read and score your essay on a scale of 1–4. If your score is not 2 or higher, you must retake the Language Arts, Writing Test. To score well, your essay must effectively support a focused idea. A paper can contain some errors and still receive a high score.

Language Arts, Writing, Part II Essay Scoring Guide

	1 Inadequate	2 Marginal	3 Adequate	4 Effective
	Reader has difficulty identifying or following the writer's ideas.	Reader occasionally has difficulty understanding or following the writer's ideas.	Reader understands the writer's ideas.	Reader understands and easily follows the writer's expression of ideas.
Response to the Prompt	Attempts to address the prompt but with little or no success in establishing a focus.	Addresses the prompt, though the focus may shift.	Uses the prompt to establish a main idea.	Presents a clearly focused main idea that addresses the prompt.
Organization	Fails to organize ideas.	Shows some evidence of an organizational plan.	Uses an identifiable organizational plan.	Establishes a clear and logical organization.
Development and Details	Demonstrates little or no development; usually lacks details or examples or presents irrelevant information.	Has some development but lacks specific details; may be limited to a listing, repetitions, or generalizations.	Has focused but occasionally uneven development; incorporates some specific detail.	Achieves coherent development with specific and relevant details and examples.
Conventions of EAE (Edited American English)	Exhibits minimal or no control of sentence structure and the conventions of EAE.	Demonstrates inconsistent control of sentence structure and the conventions of EAE.	Generally controls sentence structure and the conventions of EAE.	Consistently controls sentence structure and the conventions of EAE.
Word Choice	Exhibits weak and/or inappropriate words.	Exhibits a narrow range of word choice, often including inappropriate selections.	Exhibits appropriate word choice.	Exhibits varied and precise word choice.

EXERCISE 12: SCORING AND EVALUATING ESSAYS

Directions: Below you will find a topic and two essays that were written on it. The essays come directly from the GED Testing Service. Read each essay and assign a score. Remember that a score of 4 is high and a score of 1 is low. The answers will reveal how the GED Testing Service actually scored each paper.

Topic: If you could make one positive change to your daily life, what would that change be? In your essay, identify the change you would make. Explain the reasons for your choice.

ESSAY A

If I could make one positive change in my life, the change would be in my attitude. I would change my attitude toward people and life. My attitude toward certain people I think is outrageous, those certain people are those people who think they're god's gift to the world and I would also change my attitude toward people who are of my age but, act so child like. I would change my attitude toward these people because in the future I may need some of these people that I've treated so negatively. If I continued to treat these people badly, I may not amount to anything in the future. My attitude toward life would also have to change I think because I'm doing so well at this point in my life. Life I think is just a game that everyone has to play in order to survive. I'm not playing to survive I playing only to get by. I feel if my attitude doesn't change at this point, I will never be able to survive the game. The above things about my attitude have to be my positive change in my daily life.

Score _____

ESSAY B

If I could make one positive change in my life it would be to stop being such a procrastinator. I will put things off until when the angels in heaven above start biting their nails! Putting things off until the next day or when I have more time has really become a problem in the past few years. Recently in my senior English class, I turned in my final research paper of my high school career. It looked really good. All of the words were spelled correctly and form was perfect. I expect an A paper. But what few people knew is that I just barely finished that paper, which was assigned two and a half months prior, at 5:30 that morning. I came to school worn-out and grumpy because I had not had any sleep and because as usual I waited until the last minute to work on my paper. The effect of my procrastination was felt all through the day by my teachers and friends who had to suffer through my sour attitude.

The funny thing about my procrastination is that I can't figure out where I could have possibly picked up such a bad habit. My mother and sister always get their work done on time without running themselves ragged and most of my friends start on long term assignments weeks before the due date.

Lately, I have really been bothered by my lack of attention to time because I will start college in the fall. No one will be there to make me get started on my projects. I want to learn before I leave home how to pace myself and how to force myself to make time for long term projects. If I can't learn the basic steps of time management in the next few months, I can't be sure of what the future holds for me. I'm not sure I could handle the stress of last minute work anymore.

Still, I know that any changes in my daily habits must be made by me. I realize that I must begin with the small things, such as cleaning my room on a scheduled basis rather than putting it off until the weekend or an even later date. I believe even that small of a change would help me with my school, church, and community projects.

I know that my life is in my hands and what I make of it depends on how I spend my time. A procrastinator holds himself back and I must move forward. The only way I can do that is to get up and "Just Do It."

Score _____

Source: GED Testing Service

Answers are on page 524.

Making the Most of Your Time

One of the steps you should take in preparing for the GED essay is learning to adapt the writing process to the testing situation. You have practiced all the steps in the writing process before, but you need to have a strategy for using your time well when you take the test. Study the following description of how you might approach the essay. Think about how you could adapt this strategy to suit your own writing style.

Prewrite (5–10 minutes): Study the topic and think about the choices you have. Write down some ideas, make a choice, then jot down some notes. Write a main idea sentence to use as a thesis statement. Be sure you have a clear plan of how your ideas will be organized before you begin drafting your essay.

Draft (25–30 minutes): Neatly write a rough copy of your essay in ink, keeping in mind that you won't have time to recopy the paper. Leave wide margins so that you can go back to add ideas and make corrections. As you write, be sure to refer to the overall organizational plan that you have prepared.

Revise and edit (5–10 Minutes): Read over your essay. Look for changes you can make that will improve the writing and clarify the ideas. Check the structure of the sentences, paragraphs, and whole essay. Make sure you have included a clear thesis statement in your introduction and provided some detailed development for your opinion. Correct any problems in grammar, mechanics, or wording.

Sample Topics for Practice

The best way to study for the essay section of the Language Arts, Writing Test is to practice writing. Here are some essay topics that are similar to ones that may be used on the test. Practice using the skills that you have learned. Time yourself to grow accustomed to writing under a time constraint. Remember that you should spend about 45 minutes on an essay.

1. Who is someone you admire? Explain the reasons why you admire that person.

2. What were three major events in your life? Describe each one and explain its significance to you.

3. What makes a good parent? Support your opinion with specific examples and reasons.

4. What are three qualities that you value in a friend? Be specific and use examples to support your views.

5. What can be done to help with the problem of road rage? Give suggestions and examples that support your opinion.

6. If you could have any three jobs during your lifetime, what three jobs would you want? Explain why you would want each one.

SOCIAL STUDIES

The GED Social Studies Test requires you to know basic social studies concepts. You will not have to recall facts, but you will have to draw upon your **prior knowledge** of important social studies concepts, principles, events, and skills. The test includes clusters of historical time periods and critical historical points.

The context of the test is that of daily life settings that show you as an individual, acquirer, organizer, and user of information. It depicts common roles of adults, including that of citizen, family member, worker, and consumer. The test studies relationships between science, technology, and society and acknowledges local and global problems, issues, and events. You might say that the test has a world view. The test integrates research, communications, and the workplace and shows the diverse population of the United States.

Some of the skills you will need to demonstrate include information processing and technical skills, problem solving skills, interpersonal and social participation skills, and critical and creative thinking skills. To answer successfully, you will need to be able to show that you can comprehend (understand) what you read, apply information to a new situation, analyze relationships among ideas or concepts, and make judgments about the material presented.

How many questions are on the test?

There are 50 multiple-choice questions, and you will be given 70 minutes to complete the test.

- Approximately 40% based on reading passages of up to 250 words each

- Approximately 40% based on visuals—graphs, maps, charts, photos, pictures, diagrams, advertisements, political cartoons, or practical documents (voters' handbooks or registration forms, tax forms, driver's manuals, insurance forms, bank statements, workplace benefits packages or contracts, almanacs, atlases, political speeches, and local, state, or national budgets)

- The remaining 20% are reading passages and visuals together.

What's on the test?

The GED Social Studies Test can be broken down into these content areas:

United States History	25%
World History	15%
Geography	15%
Civics and Government	25%
Economics	20%

A given question may draw from a number of these subjects. In discussing society or people, it is natural to touch on a number of topics. For example, a question on the U.S. Constitution may draw from material covered in both political science and history. The test acknowledges the interdisciplinary nature of social studies.

Some particular documents that are helpful for you to study are fundamental U.S. documents: excerpts from the Declaration of Independence, U.S. Constitution, Federalist Papers, Bill of Rights, Supreme Court landmark cases. Don't forget to review newspapers and magazines.

What are the thinking skills needed for the test?

Thinking skills that you will be tested on include the following:

Understanding Ideas	20%
Applying Ideas	30%
Analyzing Ideas	30%
Evaluating Ideas	20%

Of the thinking skills listed above, the skill of **analysis** is especially important. Questions of this type might involve looking for main ideas, drawing conclusions, identifying supporting details, comparing and contrasting views, or tracing causes or effects of events.

1
WORLD HISTORY

To study world history is to read about the origins of the human race and its cultural development from primitive times to ancient civilizations to the present. The world's social, religious, industrial, agricultural, political, and economic traditions can all be traced to early humanity.

Early Humanity

The study of the earliest humans is considered prehistory because there is no written account of their lifestyles. From archeologists' discoveries of primitive dwellings, cave drawings, skeletal remains, and artifacts, we know where the earliest human communities existed. **Anthropologists** have examined these **artifacts**—items such as tools, weapons, and pottery—and have intensely researched bone fragments and **fossil** remains to uncover evidence about different periods of human development.

The earliest stage of cultural development has been classified as the **Stone Age** because of the evidence that early humans used stone tools. These early people were **nomadic**—they had no permanent shelters and followed the herds of animals that they hunted for survival. Over time many groups of early humans ceased their nomadic lifestyle to become hunters and gatherers in areas of abundant game, fresh water, and fertile soil. Scientific study of these sites has shown that these early farmers were able to determine which crops would grow best for their soil and climate. With such developing knowledge of agriculture, these people learned to work the land and to domesticate animals. Many of these early groups built more permanent shelters. Gradually communities developed, and societal organization became necessary for survival.

Individuals practiced special skills or trades. Commerce developed through **bartering** goods (e.g., food, cloth, or pottery) or services (e.g., medicinal, labor). As the basic communities grew, a need for rules and organization also grew; so the early forms of government were created. A unifying factor in these early settlements was fear and lack of knowledge about the surrounding world. The ways early humans explained these natural phenomena led to the early forms of religion and to the development of traditions and beliefs.

EXERCISE 1: EARLY HUMANITY

Directions: Select the *best* answer to each question based on what you learned from the passage.

1. Which of the following would be considered a fossil?
   (1) a clay pot used for cooking
   (2) a club used for defense
   (3) the ancient remains of a bird
   (4) the spear of a hunter
   (5) a basket made for gathering food

2. Identify the skill or trade that did not have its beginnings with early humans.

   (1) banker
   (2) tailor
   (3) farmer
   (4) doctor
   (5) carpenter

Answers are on page 526.

Early Civilization

Evidence of much of humanity's early technological advancement has been found in ancient Egyptian civilization. Beginning about 5000 B.C., the Nile River Valley in northeast Africa provided the agricultural conditions for many permanent settlements to develop. The abundance of good harvests allowed for thriving communities that continued to expand. With the support and influence of the rulers and religious leaders, cultural advancement took place in art, music, entertainment, technology, and science.

The ancient **Egyptians** are considered one of the most advanced of the early civilizations. Evidence of their contributions to the world can be seen in the magnificent statues of their gods, in pottery and jewelry, in the ruins of their colossal pyramids and tombs, and within their written language known as **hieroglyphics**. They also perfected the mummification process for rulers, wealthy citizens, and religious leaders.

Ordinary citizens and slaves did not have such a burial. In fact, servants were often sealed into the grave with their dead masters to serve them when they reached the other side. The rulers of Egypt, the **pharaohs**, thought to be gods among men, had pyramids or tombs erected for their eventual placement after death. Their earthly treasures of jewelry, statues, weapons, and furniture were buried with them to insure their wealth in the hereafter. Although many of these precious artifacts were stolen or destroyed over the centuries, researchers have learned valuable information about this early civilization through the treasures that remained.

We learned much about the early Egyptian culture after we were able to translate the symbols and pictures found on the walls of the tombs. Symbolic picture writing, hieroglyphics, presented accounts of the tomb's occupant and the society in which he or she lived. In the early 1800s a French scholar, Jean Champollion, deciphered a slab of black stone. Known as the **Rosetta Stone**, it has two hieroglyphic scripts and one ancient Greek script written on it. By 1822 Champollion was able to translate from the Greek back through the two sets of hieroglyphic scripts. Since that discovery, archaeologists and scholars have been able to translate the written language of ancient Egypt.

EXERCISE 2: EARLY CIVILIZATION

Directions: Read the following questions and select the *best* response.

1. Which of the following statements is true based on the information about the early Egyptians?

   (1) The Egyptians had an advanced language with a lettered alphabet.
   (2) The Egyptians did not understand written language.
   (3) The Egyptians recorded their history with a symbolic language.
   (4) The Egyptians did not record their early history.
   (5) The Egyptians had only a few people who could write.

2. Which of the following descriptions of the Egyptian culture is *not* true?

   (1) The Egyptians were a strong civilization that conquered other tribes.
   (2) Art and music were very important in the Egyptian culture.
   (3) Wealthy Egyptians were preserved after their deaths.
   (4) Egyptians were successful farmers because of the fertile Nile Valley.
   (5) Treasures and servants were often buried with the Egyptian dead.

Answers are on page 526.

Civilizations Begin to Interact

The Fertile Crescent

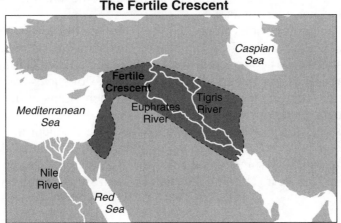

The Middle East and the coastal regions of the Mediterranean Sea, as well as the Nile Delta, were the locations for the beginnings of many early civilizations, including Babylonian, Sumerian, Phoenician, Persian, and Greek. This close proximity allowed for trade and also created competition for land and resources. The interaction among various cultures created changes in and exchanges of traditions and technology.

The classical civilizations that had the largest impact on the world's cultural development are the **Greek** and **Roman Empires**. Greek civilization continued the Egyptian priorities of art, literature, music, theater, architecture, and the sciences. The first major citizen participation in government occurred in ancient **Athens**, a powerful Greek city-state. All male citizens participated in the assembly, which determined laws and policies.

During the golden age of ancient Greece (500 B.C. to 300 B.C.), many great philosophers and educators such as **Socrates**, **Plato**, and **Aristotle** shared their wisdom with the world. For the first time, the improvement of the mind and the body was viewed as an important priority for society. The challenge of improved physical fitness was the reason the **Olympic Games** were begun in ancient Greece.

Eventually, the Romans conquered the Greeks, copying their architecture, art forms, poetry, and even some of their mythological gods. Both the Greeks and the Romans had maintained early people's practice of using myth to explain natural phenomenon like seasonal changes, flooding and severe weather, and success in agriculture. To make the myths easier to understand and appreciate, the Greeks and Romans both had gods with human attributes. Greek and Roman mythology has continued to exist even after our under-standing of the universe has outgrown the need for story-like explanations. Many of the planets including Jupiter, Neptune, Mars, Venus, and Mercury were named for Roman gods.

The Romans were interested in military strength and acquiring land for the empire. Thus, athletic competition and training for combat as a form of entertainment developed in Rome. The Roman government differed from the Athenian model as well. One, two, or sometimes three consuls were chosen by the Roman senate, a group of the wealthiest landholders, or **patricians**. The vast majority of the citizens were **plebeians**—the small farmers, trades-men, artisans, and merchants.

Wealth and connections among family members thus determined position in the social classes within Roman culture. This status determined if a mem-ber of the society was considered worthy of having a vote. This system of government was called a **republic**. The lower class of slaves and the common class of farmers and tradesmen were limited in their rights of marriage part-ners and land ownership.

One lasting contribution of the Romans was the calendar introduced by **Julius Caesar** in 46 B.C.E. (before the common era). Caesar made the months of unequal days and added leap years to make the reckoning more equal to an actual year. This Julian calendar, with some modifications, is still in use today.

EXERCISE 3: CIVILIZATIONS BEGIN TO INTERACT

Directions: Read the following questions and choose the *best* response.

1. Which of the following is a feature only of the Roman civilization and not the Greek civilization?

    (1) athletic competition and training
    (2) military strength to fight off invaders
    (3) interest in art and music as entertainment
    (4) citizen participation in government
    (5) belief in mythological gods

2. Which of the following activities would not be an example of the Greek philosophy of improvement of mind and body?

(1) going to an educational movie
(2) taking a yoga stretching class
(3) playing a computer strategy game
(4) watching a football game
(5) enrolling in a math class

Answers are on page 526.

The Middle Ages and the Feudal System

With the fall of the Roman Empire in C.E. 476 (year 476 in the common era), western Europe was thrown into chaos. Tribal chiefs and kings of small regions took control for local protection. Most of the population, except for royalty and clergy, was illiterate. It was a time when art and literature and architecture no longer flourished. This period was called the **Dark Ages**.

During the Dark Ages in Europe, the **feudal system** was instituted. This was a well-defined system of classes within society. It was based on the belief that if everyone had a place in society, there would be less conflict. The feudal system had top-ranking nobles: the king, the lords, the lesser lords, and the knights. The peasants and the townspeople made up 90 percent of the population. The lord was responsible to the king and managed the estate that the peasants worked in return for protection from invading enemies.

In the early 13th century, battles for land were being fought in England. Invasions by the Vikings and ongoing conflicts with the Roman Church kept England constantly fighting. The split that finally divided the church in England started with **Henry II**, when he and **Thomas Becket**, the Archbishop of Canterbury, argued over the supreme authority of the king and the church. Henry's son, John, made an attempt to settle the conflict after his father's death. This required the barons of England to pay heavy taxes to the church. When the barons complained, the **Magna Carta** was written in 1215 to protect their rights. This document served to establish rights of even those who were not nobles. It limited the powers of the monarchy, forcing even the king to obey the laws.

The economic structure of the feudal system was very weak. Poor harvests led to famines. A weakened population was not able to fight off infectious diseases, which had spread throughout the trade routes. During the 14th century, a terrifying **bubonic plague** (the **Black Death**) hit Europe. This plague is said to have killed one-third of all Europeans; no class, from peasants to royalty, escaped. Without farming, trading, and craft working, the economy collapsed even further. Western Europe took more than 100 years to recover.

EXERCISE 4: THE MIDDLE AGES AND THE FEUDAL SYSTEM

Directions: Choose the *best* response to each of the following questions.

1. What was the main idea of feudalism in the Middle Ages?
   (1) protection of the lower classes
   (2) transition of wealth
   (3) education of the nobles
   (4) preservation of the middle class
   (5) suppression of the peasants

2. The *Magna Carta* states:

   > In the first place we have granted to God, and by this our present charter confirmed for us and our heirs forever that the English church shall be free, and shall have her rights entire, and her liberties inviolate; and we will that it be thus observed; which is apparent from this that the freedom of elections, which is reckoned most important and very essential to the English church. . .

   What is the main idea of this section of the *Magna Carta*?
   (1) Liberties are only granted by the Pope.
   (2) The church in England will be free from the king's rule.
   (3) Elections should not be free so that a king will always be in power.
   (4) God created the *Magna Carta* because the people deserved it.
   (5) Church members only have freedom in England.

Answers are on page 526.

The Renaissance

In the late Middle Ages, about C.E. 1400, Western Europe was becoming more stable, both politically and economically. Many wealthy Europeans were in positions of power and were able to fund cultural pursuits such as music, art, and literature. This period of time is known as the **Renaissance**, from a French word meaning "rebirth." Not since the fall of the Roman Empire had there been such a revitalized interest in and support of arts, crafts, and architecture. This was a time when wealthy patrons supported great French and Italian artists. **Michelangelo** created the sculpture of David; and other artists, such as Donatello, **Leonardo da Vinci**, and Raphael Sanzio, completed their timeless masterpieces during the golden years of the fifteenth and early sixteenth centuries. Great poets, writers, and inventors also flourished at this time.

One invention that greatly advanced culture in Europe and eventually the world was the **printing press**. In the 1440s a German engraver, **Johannes Gutenberg**, created the first printing press that used movable pieces of type. His invention started a revolution in printing, which made books available to all classes of people.

EXERCISE 5: THE RENAISSANCE

Directions: Read the following questions and select the *best* answer based on the passage.

1. Which of the following statements about the Renaissance is opinion?

   (1) The arts were a significant aspect of the Renaissance.
   (2) Wealthy patrons supported many French and Italian artists.
   (3) Many wealthy Europeans were in powerful positions during the Renaissance.
   (4) The best poetry was created during the Renaissance.
   (5) The Gutenberg Bible is a historical literary work.

2. Which was the most important factor in beginning the Renaissance?

   (1) French and Italian artists were creating masterpieces.
   (2) Gutenberg invented the printing press.
   (3) Western Europe had stabilized.
   (4) Poets and other writers flourished during this time.
   (5) Michelangelo sculpted his David.

Answers are on page 526.

America Is Discovered

In 1492, while Spain was under the rule of King Ferdinand and Queen Isabella, the Italian navigator **Christopher Columbus** received permission and support to find a faster trade route to China and the East Indies. He believed that by sailing directly west, instead of south around the Cape of Good Hope as other explorers had done, he would discover a more direct route. It is because of this historic journey, during which he landed in an unknown hemisphere, that we celebrate the discovery of America.

Explorers of the New World

Year	Explorer	Region
1000	Leif Ericson	Newfoundland
1492	Christopher Columbus	the Caribbean
1497	John Cabot	the east coast of Canada
1497	Amerigo Vespucci	the northeast coast of South America
1513	Juan Ponce de Leon	Florida and Mexico

The Reformation Divides Christianity

The Catholic Church suffered a great upheaval in 1517, when a German monk named **Martin Luther** made a list of complaints against the church. These 95 complaints sparked another split in Christianity. The new group was called **Protestants**; their split from the Catholic Church started a **Reformation** throughout Europe.

The royal family of England also had quarrels with the Roman Catholic Church. **King Henry VIII** wanted to annul his marriage to Catherine of Aragon, since after 18 years of marriage she had not produced a son to be the next heir to the English throne. The Pope refused to give the king an annulment of this marriage so he would be free to marry Anne Boleyn. In 1529, Henry VIII took control of the church in England, and by 1534 the Act of Supremacy had given the king power over the English church.

After Henry VIII's death, his first daughter, **Mary Tudor**, inherited the throne. She was raised as a Catholic and attempted to return England to Catholicism. Because of her persecutions of those who did not follow her lead back to the Roman church, she was given the nickname Bloody Mary. When Mary died, her Protestant half-sister, **Elizabeth I**, became queen.

In the 1500s, **Philip II** of Spain attempted to centralize power over all Europe. The Netherlands in northern Europe had long been establishing itself as a center of trade and banking. Philip II sent many troops to reassert Catholic theology over the Dutch who, with the help of **Calvinist** preachers, were becoming increasingly Protestant. The Dutch revolt won their independence in 1581 with some support from the English, who did not want to see Catholic rule spread to their own shores. The Spanish sent a fleet of ships called an **armada** to England, only to have them sink in a terrible storm as they approached the English Channel.

EXERCISE 6: THE REFORMATION DIVIDES CHRISTIANITY

Directions: Select the *best* answer based on the information provided.

1. What conclusion can you draw about the Reformation?
   The Reformation was about
   (1) a variety of religious freedoms
   (2) the beginning of Protestantism
   (3) European economic expansion
   (4) the combining of many religions
   (5) additional taxation of noblemen

2. Which of the following people encouraged Catholicism during the Reformation?
   (1) Elizabeth I
   (2) Mary Tudor
   (3) Calvinist preachers
   (4) Catherine of Aragon
   (5) Henry VIII

Answers are on page 526.

The Enlightenment

The period known as the **Enlightenment** saw a new focus on science and technology. From the late 1500s and into the 1600s, scholars and early scientists began questioning humanity's place in nature as taught by the Roman

Catholic Church. It was at this time that **Copernicus, Galileo,** and **Sir Isaac Newton** proposed new ideas about astronomy and physics. Medical science rose to a new level of prominence, in part because **Anton van Leeuwenhoek** and his microscope gave new understanding of microbes and diseases. **William Harvey** discovered and demonstrated the circulation of blood.

Later, in the late seventeenth and eighteenth centuries, philosophers and statesmen began questioning people's role in society in addition to the study of the physical world. **John Locke** became a very influential author who wrote about the role that the individual played in society. Others, such as the writers **Voltaire** and **Jean-Jacques Rousseau**, argued that common sense, tolerance, and a natural belief that human beings were good were needed to make a great society work.

EXERCISE 7: THE ENLIGHTENMENT

Directions: Read the following question and select the *best* answer.

1. What is one consequence of the Enlightenment?
    (1) Doctors could cure all diseases in people.
    (2) Influential authors changed how people understood diseases.
    (3) The church supported scientific discoveries.
    (4) New discoveries made scientists wealthy.
    (5) The microscope helped to identify causes of diseases.

Answer is on page 526.

The French Revolution and Napoleon

In late eighteenth-century France, social unrest existed between the aristocracy and the impoverished citizenry. The citizens were angry and frustrated at the excessive lifestyle of **King Louis XVI** and his wife, **Marie Antoinette.** The people were also being exposed to the openness of thought expressed by Voltaire and Rousseau. The Americans had successfully rebelled against the British monarchy to win their independence, proving that monarchies could be resisted. In 1788 the king called for a meeting of the Estates-General, an assembly that had not been called for nearly 175 years. Three hundred of the deputies represented the monarchy, three hundred represented the church, and the other 600 represented the masses. The last group called for a vote by head and created the National Assembly, which voted to limit the powers of both the monarchy and the church.

Ongoing struggles between the National Assembly and the French king led to some people challenging the king's loyalty to France. Eventually the French peasants revolted in 1789, beginning with storming the **Bastille**, a Paris prison that symbolized oppression to the people. Both the king and the queen, as well as hundreds of aristocrats, were later beheaded.

Years of unrest continued because France lacked effective leadership. The people required a strong leader because the new governing body, the Directorate, was weak and disorganized. The people were eager to follow **Napoleon Bonaparte**, whom they considered a war hero. With the support of the armies and the people, he easily overthrew the Directorate. He established a new government, later known as the First Empire. Napoleon introduced a new system of laws that became known as the **Napoleonic Code**. The code recognized that all male citizens were equal under the law. It also allowed the people of France to participate in the religion of their choice and to work in the occupation of their choice.

That same year Napoleon declared himself emperor of France. He wanted to conquer Europe, and his armies engaged the British in the west and in the Mediterranean, in addition to the Austrians, Prussians, and Russians in the east. His downfall came in 1815 at the hands of the British and their allies at the **Battle of Waterloo**, near Brussels, Belgium. Following this disastrous defeat, the British banished Napoleon to the island of St. Helena, where he died in 1821.

The Industrial Revolution

In nineteenth-century Europe and the United States, changes continued to occur in technology and the social order. During the **Industrial Revolution**, factories were built in the larger cities, with mechanized assembly lines for mass production of goods. For the first time, a new working class was earning wages in factory jobs.

As the people in the United States and throughout most of Europe had achieved independence from foreign rulers, each nation now had to face its own economic problems and deal with the changes caused by the Industrial Revolution. Populations moved from a mostly rural existence to crowded cities where workers formed a large part of the community. The telegraph and telephone provided means of long distance communication, which brought people and communities closer together.

While the business leaders gained great wealth, they often did so at the expense of poorly paid factory workers. German author **Karl Marx** wrote about the terrible working conditions of the period and the flaws he saw in the capitalist system that created them. He believed that capitalism would drag more workers into poverty. Marx explained his ideas in a book called *The Communist Manifesto*, which influenced Vladimir Lenin and helped bring about the overthrow of the Russian czar in 1917 (see page 140).

EXERCISE 8: THE INDUSTRIAL REVOLUTION

Directions: Label each statement as true (**T**) or false (**F**).

1. _____ The telegraph and the telephone were not important inventions.

2. _____ Many people moved to the cities to get jobs in factories.

3. _____ Marx thought that the factories were a good idea.

Answers are on page 526.

The World Enters World War I

After the **Napoleonic Wars**, many European nations formed alliances for mutual protection and economic reasons. One family, the **Hapsburgs**, sat on many of the European thrones. Some Central European nations had been formed as a result of previous wars and still felt the domination of certain powers. This consolidation of power in the monarchies was seen by some as an organized effort to take freedoms away from the new working class.

In the Balkans, various national alliances engaged in warfare for economic reasons. Austria had created the new state of Albania to keep Serbia from becoming too powerful. Many people in the Austrian province of Bosnia felt aligned to Serbia and wanted to be free from Austrian control. When **Archduke Francis Ferdinand**, the heir to the Austrian throne, and his wife, Sophie, visited Sarajevo, Bosnia, in June 1914, the couple was assassinated.

This attack caused the **Austro-Hungarian Empire** to declare war on Serbia, which looked to its Russian allies to provide aid. Germany, allied to Austria-Hungary, insisted that Russia cease its mobilization of troops. When Russia refused, Germany declared war on both Russia and its ally France. In order to get a first-strike position on France, Germany moved its forces through the neutral country of Belgium.

This act of aggression brought Great Britain into the war as it acted to defend Belgium. Eventually, in 1918, a weakened Germany agreed to an armistice. The **Treaty of Versailles** ended the war and required Germany to dissolve its standing army.

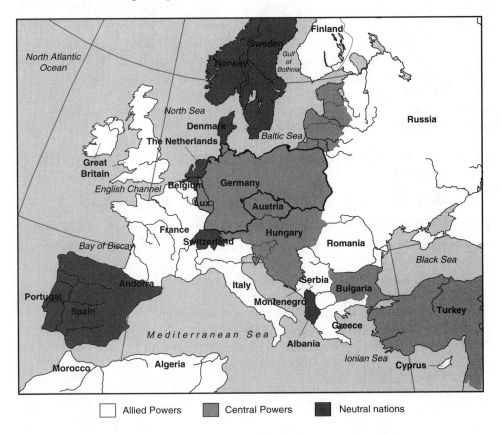

EXERCISE 9: WORLD WAR I

Directions: Place an **X** next to the countries that were allies of Germany in World War I according to the map on the previous page.

1. _____ Russia   3. _____ Belgium

2. _____ England   4. _____ Austria-Hungary

Answers are on page 527.

The Russian Revolution and the Rise of Communism

In 1917, one year before the end of World War I, Russia's resources had been depleted. The working class was in poverty, food shortages existed, and the people no longer believed in the rule of **Czar Nicholas II** of the Romanov Dynasty. New leaders were able to generate support from the desperate citizens. At this time, **Vladimir Lenin** led the **Bolsheviks** into a position of power. Czar Nicholas was forced to give up the throne, and he and his family were killed.

Lenin followed the beliefs of Karl Marx, forming a **Communist** government and a classless society, the **Soviet Union**. Lenin and his followers killed anyone who disagreed with their policies, giving the leadership of the Communist Party total control of the government. In March 1918 the Soviet Union signed a treaty with Germany, taking itself out of the war and dissolving the Soviet army. After Lenin's death in 1924, **Josef Stalin** and his supporters climbed to power to try to industrialize the poverty-stricken nation. Stalin continued Lenin's policies and became sole dictator of the Soviet Union. He and his immediate supporters had absolute control in this **totalitarian** government until his death in 1953.

EXERCISE 10: THE RUSSIAN REVOLUTION AND THE RISE OF COMMUNISM

Directions: Read the following questions and select the *best* answer.

1. Based on the information on the Russian Revolution, which of the following is a likely assumption as to why the Communist Party rose to power?

   (1) The citizens resisted the Industrial Revolution.
   (2) Russia signed a treaty with Germany.
   (3) Czar Nicholas II and his family were executed.
   (4) The working class lost faith in their ruler.
   (5) The totalitarian government had absolute control.

2. Match the leader with what he is best known for.

_____ Vladimir Lenin   **a.** wrote *The Communist Manifesto*

_____ Josef Stalin   **b.** brought industrialization

_____ Karl Marx   **c.** gave the Communist Party total control

Answers are on page 527.

World War II

The treaty ending World War I dealt harshly with Germany, throwing the country into financial chaos. **Adolf Hitler** did not have trouble focusing the nation's attention on national pride and economic recovery through conquest. The **Nazi Party**'s strength increased as it provided Germany with scapegoats, blaming the poor economic conditions mainly on the Jews. In addition to this propaganda campaign, the Nazi intimidation tactics forced other Germans to focus hatred against those selected as traitors. The genocide of millions of Europeans at the direction of Hitler, the **Holocaust**, was not entirely under-stood until after World War II.

World War II brought an alliance among Italy, Germany, and Japan. Each of these nations sought expansion of its territories. In the 1920s **Benito Mussolini** became dictator of Italy, and in 1936 he invaded Ethiopia. In the 1930s Hitler had gained control of Germany, annexed Austria, and invaded Czechoslovakia. He then signed a nonaggression treaty with Russia. Great Britain entered the war when Germany invaded Poland, but it could not stop Hitler.

By 1940 Britain was the last holdout against the Nazis until Germany attacked the Soviet Union in 1941. The Soviets then entered the war in sup-port of the British. During this time the United States had been providing medical and military supplies to Britain and the Soviet Union, known as the **Allies**, but had stayed out of the fighting. On December 7, 1941, Japan bombed **Pearl Harbor**, a major U.S. naval base in Hawaii. Within three days of this attack, Germany and Italy declared war on the United States. Now the United States was fighting on two fronts: Europe and the Pacific.

The United States and the Allied forces, mainly Britain and the Soviet Union, broke all German resistance. In May of 1945, Germany surrendered. It wasn't until August 1945, after the United States dropped atomic bombs on **Hiroshima** and **Nagasaki**, that the war with Japan ended. At the end of the war in Europe, the Soviet Union, under Stalin, gained control of the same middle European countries that Hitler had invaded. This Soviet dominance began a period of time known as the **Cold War**.

EXERCISE 11: WORLD WAR II

Directions: Fill in the blank with a word that would correctly complete the sentence.

1. _____ is a campaign of giving false or biased information to influence the attitudes of groups of people.

2. The Holocaust is considered an act of _____ when millions of people were killed because they were not accepted as valuable citizens.

3. World War II brought an alliance among Italy, _____ , and _____ .

4. The United States dropped atomic bombs on _____ and _____ , bringing an end to the war.

Answers are on page 527.

Technology as a Future

Since World War II, world history has been deeply connected to advancements in science and technology. Space exploration, such as the Soviet launching of **Sputnik** (1957), followed by the NASA program that put Americans on the moon in 1969, has led technological development. One obvious benefit of the technology that has dominated world history is the beginning of the computer age. Computers have allowed the space program to have remote control of a vehicle in orbit around the earth or in deep space, and to make calculations quickly and accurately. Gradually, this technology has been made available to the civilian population and heavily used in communication, research, and commerce.

Technology has come to determine wealth and power. No longer is the acquisition of land the determining factor for power among nations. The world has seen a shift in focus to global commerce. Smaller countries such as Japan and South Korea are major factors in the electronic marketplace. The **Internet**, originally intended to be a computer network for the U.S. Department of Defense, has developed into a global research, commerce, and communication tool. It and other forms of instant electronic communication have connected every part of the world into a global economy.

2
U.S. HISTORY

This chapter will highlight some of the most important events in U.S. history from the discovery of North America to the present.

A New Nation Is Born

Although it is commonly assumed that **Christopher Columbus** discovered the Americas, many argue that they were really discovered by **Leif Ericson.** The Norwegian Vikings traveled to the New World 400 years before Columbus and landed on North America's shores at what is now Newfoundland. They were actually the first Europeans to reach North America.

When Columbus sailed from Spain in 1492, he was searching for a shorter route to the treasures of the East. The "shortcut" Columbus took by sailing west landed him on a small island in what is now the Bahamas. Thinking he was in India, he called the native Americans "Indians," a name that remains today. Columbus died in 1506, never knowing that he had actually landed in North America.

Columbus's error, however, opened the doors for later exploration of the New World. A partial listing of explorers demonstrates the multicultural influences on the foundation of the United States: Italian explorer **Amerigo Vespucci**, for whom the Americas are named; **Hernando de Soto** (Spain), who discovered the Mississippi River; **Francisco Vasquez de Coronado** (Spain), who explored what would become the southwestern United States; as well as **John Cabot** (England) and **Henry Hudson** (The Netherlands). As Spain grew in wealth and power because of settlements in what is now Central and South America, the French ventured north to Canada. The English settled on the coastland between the areas claimed by Spain and France.

EXERCISE 1: A NEW NATION IS BORN

Directions: Using the map, choose the *best* answer for each question.

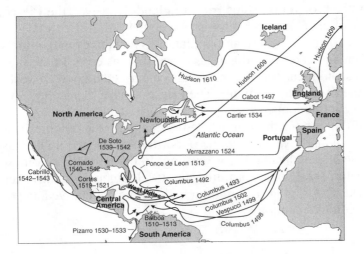

1. From the map of European explorations in the Americas, which of the following conclusions can be drawn?

   (1) Most explorers were from France.
   (2) Columbus was the only explorer from Spain.
   (3) John Cabot explored the east coast of America.
   (4) Many countries sent explorers to the New World.
   (5) Henry Hudson explored the Gulf of Mexico.

2. What is the purpose of this map?

   (1) show resources in the New World
   (2) compare the financing of each exploration
   (3) highlight slave routes to America
   (4) distinguish African and Asian explorers
   (5) illustrate the routes taken by explorers

Answers are on page 527.

The Original Thirteen Colonies

As the population of English colonies grew, some people looked to settle in the land beyond the Appalachian Mountains, which had been claimed by France. In the mid-1700s, England and France fought over the land in the northern and central parts of North America. This became known as the **French and Indian War**. England won the war in 1763. The Treaty of Paris gave England total control over the land from the east coast of North America all the way to the Mississippi River. The land from Georgia to Maine became known as the **thirteen colonies**. (See the map on page 145.)

A council or governor appointed by the king of England governed each of the thirteen colonies. These leaders were to control the colonies in the name of the king. Because colonists came from many areas, they brought with them different customs, religious beliefs, and dialects. This diversity of people made each colony unique and difficult to govern.

Coming to a strange land and trying to make a new start was difficult for the colonists, who were often poor and had to begin life there using only what could be brought on ships from England. However, the **Pilgrims** at Plymouth Colony (Massachusetts) survived the first difficult year with help from the local Native American population. The natives taught the settlers how to plant and care for indigenous crops such as corn. In the fall of 1621, the Pilgrims and local Native Americans celebrated a good harvest and observed the first **Thanksgiving**. The Pilgrims gave thanks for new opportunities and new freedoms.

One of the reasons the English settlers came to the colonies was the chance to own land. New economic opportunities opened up because of the vast expanse of land available for farming. In the northern colonies, the abundance of natural resources permitted the development of trades such as shipbuilding and iron mining. Fur trading and fishing also played a significant role in the colonial economy.

EXERCISE 2: THE ORIGINAL THIRTEEN COLONIES

Directions: Using the map, choose the *best* answer for the following questions.

Colonial America 1763

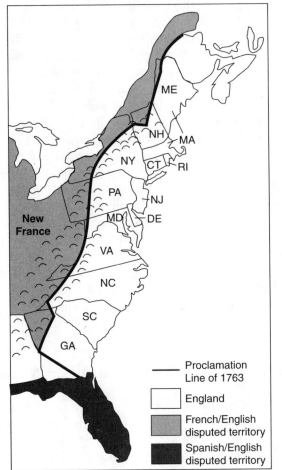

1. From the details in the map, what can we tell about the New England state of Maine?

   (1) It was not discovered by the English.
   (2) It was owned and controlled by the French.
   (3) It was governed and subdivided by Spain.
   (4) It was considered a part of Canada.
   (5) It was originally part of Massachusetts.

2. Which of the following can be proved by the map to be *false*?

   (1) Georgia was the last colony to become a state.
   (2) Pennsylvania was the most powerful colony.
   (3) By the 1700s, France gave up all interest in the New World.
   (4) England controlled much of the eastern seaboard.
   (5) The first colonists in New York were Dutch.

Answers are on page 527.

The Declaration of Independence

After the **French and Indian War**, England needed to finance a huge war debt. **King George III** decided that the colonists would pay for the war because they were the ones who benefited from the victory. As a result, the king and the English Parliament passed the Stamp Act of 1765 and the Townshend Acts of 1767. The **Stamp Act** required all official documents in the colonies to bear a British stamp paid for with a new tax. The **Townshend Acts** placed large import taxes on glass, lead, and tea. The colonists were outraged by these taxes and protested. The English Parliament punished the colonies for these protests by passing laws known as the **Intolerable Acts**, which sought to further establish the authority of the king.

The colonists were quick to respond. In September 1774, at the **First Continental Congress**, representatives from all thirteen colonies demanded that the Intolerable Acts be repealed. Moreover, the colonists demanded to be treated fairly and given the same rights as all other English citizens. However, the king and Parliament refused.

Battles between British soldiers and colonists had already taken place by May 1775 when the **Second Continental Congress** began. Inspired by colonist **Thomas Paine**'s pamphlet "Common Sense," in which he explained why separation from England was necessary, **Thomas Jefferson** drafted the **Declaration of Independence**. This important document justified the need for a revolution by listing grievances that the colonists had against King George III. The Second Continental Congress approved the declaration on July 4, 1776.

AN EXCERPT FROM THE DECLARATION OF INDEPENDENCE

When in the Course of human events, it becomes necessary for one people to dissolve the political bands which have connected them with another, and to assume among the Powers of the earth, the separate and equal station to which the Laws of Nature and of Nature's God entitle them, a decent respect to the opinions of mankind requires that they should declare the causes which impel them to the separation.

We hold these truths to be self-evident, that all men are created equal, that they are endowed by their Creator with certain unalienable Rights, that among these are Life, Liberty, and the pursuit of Happiness.

EXERCISE 3: THE DECLARATION OF INDEPENDENCE

Directions: Use information from the passage and the excerpt from the Declaration of Independence to answer the following questions.

1. Which of the following led directly to the Boston Tea Party?
    (1) the French and Indian War
    (2) the Stamp Act
    (3) the Townshend Acts
    (4) the Intolerable Acts
    (5) the Declaration of Independence

2. What was the main idea of the excerpt from the Declaration of Independence?

    (1) Colonists wanted to pay less in taxes to England.
    (2) All men are created equal and have inalienable rights.
    (3) The king needs to reside in the colonies to govern.
    (4) A member of Parliament should be from the colonies.
    (5) The colonies demanded stronger ties to England.

Answers are on page 527.

The Revolutionary War

The **Revolutionary War** was a long and costly conflict for both sides. The fighting ended in 1781 when the British army under General Charles Cornwallis was surrounded by American troops and their ally, the French fleet, at Yorktown. Finally, in 1783, the **Treaty of Paris** was signed. In addition to granting U.S. independence, the treaty gave the new nation all the land that England had won in the French and Indian War: west to the Mississippi River, north to the Great Lakes, and south to Florida.

EXERCISE 4: THE REVOLUTIONARY WAR

Directions: Complete the cause-and-effect chart below.

Causes

1. _____

2. The Declaration of Independence

3. King's refusal to compromise

4. _____

Effects

a. First Continental Congress

b. _____

c. _____

d. Signing of the Treaty of Paris

Answers are on page 527.

The Beginnings of American Government

The first U.S. central government, under the **Articles of Confederation,** was deliberately made weak in order to prevent the abuses the colonies suffered under the king. Within the framework of this new system of government, each of the thirteen states was determined to maintain its sovereignty. This posed a serious problem for the new nation because it limited the powers of the central government in dealing with major issues.

Government leaders called a convention to amend the Articles of Confederation in Philadelphia in May 1787. This convention eventually created the **Constitution**—the document by which the United States has been governed for more than 200 years.

The Beginnings of American Government

Powers of the States	Powers of the Central Government
The thirteen states had the power to • levy taxes • regulate business and commerce • decide whether to support the decisions of the central government	The central government had the power to • make treaties with other nations • govern Indian affairs • declare war • develop a postal service

Weaknesses of the Articles of Confederation
The Articles of Confederation limited the powers of • trade regulation • currency • defense of new nation

EXERCISE 5: THE BEGINNINGS OF AMERICAN GOVERNMENT

Directions: Read the following questions and select the *best* answer.

1. Why would the states want to maintain their sovereignty under the Articles of Confederation?
   (1) They wanted to remain independent from the other states.
   (2) Some states wanted to be English colonies again.
   (3) They wanted the country to collapse.
   (4) Some states wanted to have their own armies.
   (5) They were concerned about central government abuses.

2. Which was *not* a consideration in creating the new Constitution?
   (1) There was no specific outline for the powers of the central government.
   (2) The Articles of Confederation allowed the king to have power in the colonies.
   (3) The new government could not issue powers to the individual states.
   (4) With the Constitution, there would be no army to defend the nation.
   (5) It was illegal for the nation to print money without states' approval.

Answers are on page 527.

The U.S. Constitution and Federalism

The challenge facing the Constitutional Convention was to develop a written document that would give the central government more power while allowing the states to retain their sovereignty. To accomplish this, the Constitution was written to create a federal system of government. Under **federalism**, a union is formed by the states. A central government is given final authority over certain clearly defined areas, such as national defense and the ability to regulate trade. All other powers are left to the individual states.

The Constitution established the framework for American democracy, but several disputes arose. The **Federalists** wanted a strong central government with authoritative control over the states, but the **Anti-Federalists** feared that the individual states would lose their freedom under a strong central government. The Federalists (including **Alexander Hamilton**) were largely members of the merchant class who favored commercial and industrial expansion. The Anti-Federalists (including **Thomas Jefferson**) were largely farmers who favored individual liberties and did not believe strongly in territorial expansion.

The disputes that arose out of the Constitutional Convention and their compromises are illustrated in the following chart.

Dispute	Compromise
Should the states be governed by a strong central government (Federalists' view) or should the new government be based on the sovereignty of the states (Anti-Federalists' view)?	1. The president was to be elected by electoral college; the Senate, by the state legislatures (this was later changed by the Seventeenth Amendment, adopted in 1913); and House of Representatives, by the people. 2. The Bill of Rights—the first ten amendments—was added to the Constitution later to guarantee individual rights.
Should the makeup of Congress be based on each state's population (large states' view) or should all states have equal representation (small states' view)?	Bicameral legislature (two houses in Congress) 1. Members of the House of Representatives were based on each state's population. 2. Senate would have two delegates from each state. (This was called the **"Great Compromise."**)
Should slaves be counted in the population (southern states' view) or should slaves be excluded from the population count (northern states' view)?	1. Slave importation would be allowed until at least 1808. 2. Slaves would be counted as three-fifths of a person only for purposes of representation and for assessing taxes; however, they were not permitted to vote.

EXERCISE 6: THE U.S. CONSTITUTION AND FEDERALISM

Directions: Based on the preceding chart, choose the *best* answer for each of the following questions.

1. Why was counting slaves as only three-fifths of a person favorable to the northern states?

    (1) It limited the number of senators representing the South.
    (2) It limited the South's number of seats in the House of Representatives.
    (3) It was based on the amount of property for taxing purposes.
    (4) It kept slavery from spreading from the South to the North.
    (5) It equalized the number of representatives for the North and the South.

2. Today, many Southern conservatives—Democrats and Republicans alike—are strong supporters of states' rights. Which philosophy would these Americans likely have supported in the 1780s?

(1) antifederalism
(2) federalism
(3) colonialism
(4) democracy
(5) monarchy

Answers are on page 527.

Early Domestic and Foreign Policy

The years between 1791 and 1803 saw the United States expand geographically. Between 1791 and 1796, Vermont, Kentucky, and Tennessee were admitted to the Union under the administration of **George Washington**, the first U.S. president. In 1803, under President **Thomas Jefferson**, Ohio was admitted to the Union, and the largest acquisition of land for the United States occurred with the **Louisiana Purchase**. By paying France $15 million for the territory, Jefferson doubled the size of the country. He subsequently appointed **Lewis and Clark** to explore the acquired territory.

The United States in 1803

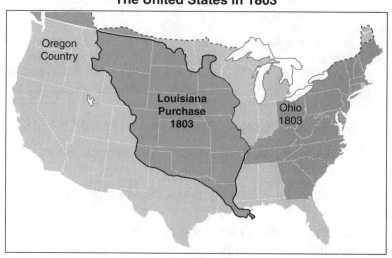

The Monroe Doctrine

A strong sense of nationalism developed after the War of 1812. For the first time the United States could afford to look inward and pay less attention to European affairs. As a result, U.S. westward expansion continued, with victories over several Native American tribes.

In 1823, President **James Monroe** proclaimed to the world that European powers would no longer be allowed to colonize the Americas. He indicated that the United States would remain neutral in European conflicts as long as the European powers left the emerging republics in North and South America alone. Known as the **Monroe Doctrine**, this foreign policy statement marked the appearance of the United States on the world political stage.

Jacksonian Democracy and the Mexican War

After Monroe left office, sectionalism became a problem for the United States. **Sectionalism** refers to the political, cultural, and economic differences among regions of the country—in this case the agricultural South and West and the industrial Northeast. The conflicting demands that each section put upon the government caused great political turmoil.

The first U.S. president elected to office as a result of these factional differences was **Andrew Jackson** in 1828. A Southerner and hero in the War of 1812, Jackson was considered to be a **populist**, a man who represented the interests of the common people. He believed that *all* people, not just the propertied few, should have a voice in deciding how the government should be run.

As the champion of the common people, Jackson opposed the establishment of a national bank because he believed that it would only benefit the wealthy and because he feared the Eastern merchants and industrialists would control it. Under Jacksonian democracy, farmers and craftspeople gained a louder voice in government than they had had under previous administrations. Despite pressure to annex Texas during his second term, Jackson refused, fearing a war with Mexico.

President **James Polk**, Jackson's successor, had no such fear. Congress, agreeing to the demands of the Texans, annexed the Texas Republic in 1845. Thus, the expansionist fervor in the United States was renewed. **Manifest Destiny**—the drive to extend the U.S. borders to the Pacific Ocean—became a rallying cry. When President Polk was unable to purchase the territory that included New Mexico and California, the United States declared war on Mexico in 1846 as a result of a territorial dispute between the two countries.

The **Treaty of Guadalupe Hidalgo** that ended the war in 1848 resulted in the United States gain of the land that would later become California, Utah, Nevada, and parts of Colorado, New Mexico, Arizona, and Wyoming. Thus, the United States had set its continental boundaries. The following map shows the boundaries of the United States by 1853.

Expansion of the United States, 1783–1853

Oregon Country 1819

Missouri R

Louisiana Purchase 1803

Mississippi R

Mexican Cession 1848

Ohio

THE UNITED STATES IN 1783

Gadsden Purchase 1853

Texas Annexation 1845

1810

1813

Florida 1846

EXERCISE 7: JACKSONIAN DEMOCRACY AND THE MEXICAN WAR

Directions: Choose the *best* answer for each of the following questions.

1. Which word below best describes Jackson's attitude toward the people of the United States?

   (1) racist
   (2) populist
   (3) colonialist
   (4) sectionalist
   (5) federalist

2. What does the above map of the expansion of the United States illustrate?

   (1) the boundaries of the newest colonies
   (2) the population centers in the new territories
   (3) the agricultural and industrial centers in the territories
   (4) the boundaries of the new expansion territories
   (5) the regions of war that allowed the expansion of territories

Answers are on page 528.

Prelude to War

By the 1850s, all the continental United States land was under the control of the federal government. Sectionalism persisted, however, as citizens seemed more loyal to their own region than to the Union as a whole. **Tariffs** (taxes imposed on goods imported into a country) were viewed by certain regions as unequal and unfair. The people of the South and West thought the tariffs were harder on them than on the North because of the South's lack of manufacturing. Expansion laws were also seen by different sections of the country as unjust; however, it was the issue of slavery that ultimately pitted one region against the other.

One central question was whether new territories admitted to the Union would become free states or slave states. Some Americans supported the concept of **popular sovereignty,** which meant that the people who were affected should determine what was best for their own state. Others believed that slavery should not be permitted in the new territories and states, but they did not advocate banning slavery from regions where it already existed. **Abolitionists,** however, believed that slavery was evil and demanded that it be banned throughout the country.

The **Dred Scott decision** of 1857 only worsened the strained relations between the North and the South. The case involved Dred Scott, a slave who sued for his freedom because his master had taken him to a free territory. The Supreme Court ruled that a slave was property and could not sue in federal court. The South applauded the court's decision, but the North opposed it bitterly. The division between the regions became more evident and more hostile; war became inevitable.

EXERCISE 8: PRELUDE TO WAR

Directions: Choose the *best* answer for each question.

1. A referendum is a political procedure that allows voters to approve or disapprove a measure proposed by the voters themselves or by the legislature. This method is most similar to which of the following proposed solutions to the issue of slavery?

   (1) abolitionism
   (2) compromise
   (3) popular sovereignty
   (4) secession
   (5) territorial balance

2. The passage cites the Dred Scott decision as a decisive event leading to the Civil War. Which value was upheld by the Supreme Court's decision?

   (1) Slavery was inhuman.
   (2) States had more rights than people.
   (3) New states could permit slavery.
   (4) Slavery could only be maintained in the South.
   (5) Human beings could be treated as property.

Answers are on page 528.

Secession

Abraham Lincoln, elected president in 1860, promised to restrict slavery to the states where it already existed. The Southern states, feeling that they were being treated unfairly, feared that the North would eventually dominate them. They voted to secede from the United States and to form their own government—the **Confederate States of America**.

South Carolina was first to secede in 1860; by February 1861 Georgia, Florida, Alabama, Mississippi, Louisiana, and Texas had seceded. **Jefferson Davis** was elected president of the Confederacy. In response, President Lincoln determined that the only way to preserve the Union was through the use of force. The South was disobeying the laws of the land. Lincoln believed that if the South did not follow the law, any state that chose to disagree with a national decision would feel that it could simply ignore the law. The Confederacy's firing on **Fort Sumter** in April 1861 opened the bloodiest war in the nation's history.

EXERCISE 9: SECESSION

Directions: Based on the following map, match the state in the left column with its description in the right column.

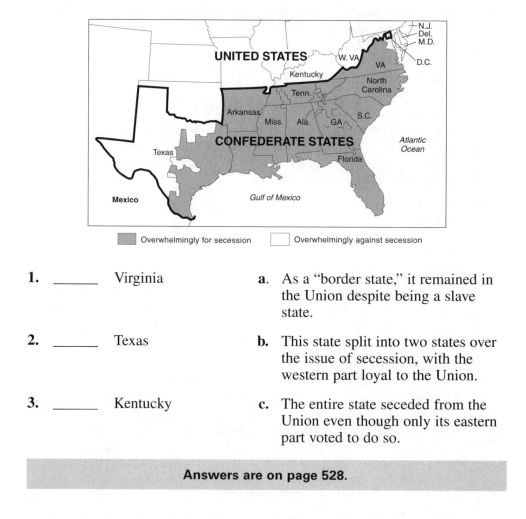

Overwhelmingly for secession   Overwhelmingly against secession

1. _____ Virginia

   a. As a "border state," it remained in the Union despite being a slave state.

2. _____ Texas

   b. This state split into two states over the issue of secession, with the western part loyal to the Union.

3. _____ Kentucky

   c. The entire state seceded from the Union even though only its eastern part voted to do so.

Answers are on page 528.

The Civil War and Reconstruction

The nation could not exist half slave and half free, and the war that settled the question lasted four years. Most of the war was fought in the South. The North had the advantage of a larger army because of its greater population, an ability to manufacture goods needed for the war effort because of its mechanization, an excellent transportation system, and an abundance of natural resources. The South, on the other hand, had the advantage of a greater familiarity with battle sites, as the war was fought on its soil, and great confidence in its outstanding military leaders.

In 1862, President Lincoln issued the **Emancipation Proclamation**. The document ordered the freeing of slaves in those slave states that were in rebellion against the Union. As a result, the Union army's ranks grew by 180,000 former slaves who then fought against the South.

The war ended on April 9, 1865, when the Confederate general **Robert E. Lee** surrendered. However, the task ahead for President Lincoln and the citizens of the Union was enormous. The division between the North and the South had to be mended, and the devastated South had to be rebuilt.

Reconstruction

Lincoln's plan for reuniting the nation included allowing the South to regain citizenship rights and statehood. However, he did not live to see the plan, known as **Reconstruction**, carried out. Abraham Lincoln was assassinated by a Confederate sympathizer. Lincoln was succeeded by a Tennesseean, **Andrew Johnson**. During his presidency, the passage of the **Thirteenth Amendment** in December 1865 abolished slavery in the U.S.

Though he supported the Union, Johnson was mistrusted by Congress as being pro-South. This mistrust contributed to Johnson's becoming the first U.S. president to be impeached—charged with official misconduct; however, the Senate failed to convict Johnson.

By 1870, the **Fourteenth Amendment** was ratified, guaranteeing citizenship to blacks, and the **Fifteenth Amendment**, passed the same year, gave blacks the right to vote. Despite these gains, racial issues and their resulting problems would plague the South for years.

EXERCISE 10: THE CIVIL WAR

Directions: Choose the *best* answer for the following question.

1. What effect did the Emancipation Proclamation have on the war?
   - **(1)** The South was more determined to win the war, winning most of the battles following the Proclamation.
   - **(2)** The South gained a reliable source of soldiers in the freed slaves.
   - **(3)** It officially ended the war since slavery was no longer an issue.
   - **(4)** It made President Lincoln one of the most popular presidents.
   - **(5)** It gave the Union army additional troops because many former slaves fought on the side of the North.

Answer is on page 528.

Growth of Big Business and Urbanization

Rapid and widespread **industrialization** (production by mechanical means) led directly to the development of big business. As one company bought another related company, large corporations began to control the marketplace. This was true especially in the steel, railroad, and oil industries. Working conditions for employees deteriorated as businesses ran unchecked by the government, and power became concentrated in the hands of a few powerful industrialists. The government practice of noninterference in the affairs of business is termed *laissez-faire* business policy.

Urbanization is the shift of the population away from rural areas and to cities where people could be close to jobs. Before industrialization, only one out of every six Americans lived in the cities. By 1890, one-third of the population lived in the cities. Cities such as New York, Chicago, and Philadelphia had populations of more than one million people. These cities were railway centers that provided transportation for people, supplies, and manufactured goods.

Businesses and factories found an abundant labor supply in the cities. The tremendous number of immigrants who entered the United States from 1870 to 1900 flooded the job market. People from Ireland, Germany, Italy, Russia, and the Scandinavian countries fled poverty at home and came to the United States in search of a better life. Their willingness to work long hours for little money forced other workers to accept the same conditions. Immigrants were often prevented from living in certain areas or from applying for certain jobs. Yet people continued to come to the cities, bringing with them different cultures and backgrounds.

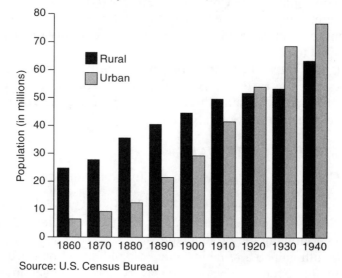

U.S. Population Shift, 1860–1940

Source: U.S. Census Bureau

EXERCISE 11: GROWTH OF BIG BUSINESS AND URBANIZATION

Directions: Choose the answer that *best* completes the statements below.

1. The 2000 census estimated the U.S. population at more than 275 million. Figures in the bar graph support the fact that the United States reached *nearly half* this population by what year?
   (1) 1900
   (2) 1910
   (3) 1920
   (4) 1930
   (5) 1940

2. The urban population increased dramatically from 1860 to 1930. What happened to the rural population?
   (1) It stayed the same.
   (2) It increased rapidly.
   (3) It increased slowly.
   (4) It decreased rapidly.
   (5) It first increased, then decreased.

Answers are on page 528.

Labor and Progressivism

Health, safety, and comfort for laborers were largely ignored during the period of rapid industrialization. In response to these conditions, **labor unions** were organized to represent the needs of the workers when dealing with employers. The Knights of Labor, formed in 1869, was the first attempt at a nationwide labor union. The American Federation of Labor (AFL) followed in 1881. By 1904, more than a million laborers had joined the AFL, led by **Samuel Gompers**.

In addition to labor, other groups and individuals emerged to fight the abuses of industrialization. The **Progressive Era** arose out of a reform movement whose goal was to eliminate political corruption and improve the quality of life for Americans. One great supporter of **Progressivism** was the U.S. president with whom the movement was closely associated—**Theodore Roosevelt**. During the Progressive Era, the government abandoned its hands-off policy toward big business and initiated reforms that affect Americans today. Some of these reforms are highlighted in the following chart.

Progressive Reforms	
Sherman Anti-Trust Act	Outlawed monopolies
Hepburn Act	Gave Interstate Commerce Commission increased authority to regulate the nation's railroads
Pure Food and Drug Act	Set standards for production and sale of food and drugs
United States Department of Agriculture (USDA)	Began inspecting meat
Child Labor Laws	Prohibited child labor
Minimum wage and worker's compensation laws	Improved working conditions and wages

EXERCISE 12: LABOR AND PROGRESSIVISM

Directions: Read the passage below and choose the *best* answer to each of the questions that follow.

The Sherman Anti-Trust Act outlawed price-fixing, under-production of goods, market sharing, and any other form of monopolizing among producers of a similar product. However, public utilities such as gas, electric power, and water companies are exempted from these restraints. These government-sanctioned monopolies are permitted to exist so that essential services are not duplicated and natural resources are not wasted.

1. According to the Sherman Anti-Trust Act, which of the following is an example of an illegal monopoly?
   (1) the existence of only one power company in a city, giving consumers no choice of service provider
   (2) a large commercial bank that has branches located throughout the city in direct competition with other banks
   (3) a hamburger chain's restaurants, all of which belong to the same system of franchises
   (4) oil manufacturers in a state that agree on a minimum price to set for gasoline
   (5) a local telephone company that sets minimum and maximum rates for customers in a particular service area

2. Why did the Sherman Anti-Trust Act allow government-sanctioned monopolies?
   (1) to give consumers a choice of service provider
   (2) to promote competition
   (3) to conserve resources
   (4) to set prices for goods and services
   (5) to allow new businesses to grow

Answers are on page 528.

The United States as a World Power

From the time it achieved its independence from England, the United States stayed out of the affairs of other countries. This policy of **isolationism** prevented the United States from forming alliances.

In 1867, the secretary of state for the United States (**William Henry Seward**) bought the territory of Alaska from Russia. The purchase turned out to be a good investment because of Alaska's many natural resources. Also, because Alaska was the first land acquired outside the boundaries of the continental United States, the purchase marked the beginning of a new foreign policy. The United States was no longer an isolationist country.

Another motive for the United States to become less isolationist was the need to develop more markets for its manufactured goods. U.S. ships sailed the Pacific Ocean carrying goods to Japan and China. These ships often docked in the many island ports along the way to buy supplies and to make repairs. By the late 1890s, the U.S. government had taken possession of a number of Pacific islands for their convenient locations and available resources. This marked America's emergence as an **imperialist** country—a nation that controls other territories or nations.

EXERCISE 13: THE UNITED STATES AS A WORLD POWER

Directions: Choose the *best* answer to each of the following questions.

1. Which of the following current foreign policy actions is a direct result of early American imperialist policy?

   (1) America's military support of Israel in the Middle East
   (2) the support of Taiwan's status as independent from China
   (3) America's establishment of military bases in the Philippines' Subic Bay
   (4) the stationing of American troops in western Germany
   (5) America's patrolling of waters off the Libyan coast

2. From the end of the American Civil War until the Spanish-American War in 1898, most Americans were isolationists. Which is the most likely cause of such widespread desire for withdrawal from international concerns?

   (1) the lack of information about events taking place in foreign lands
   (2) the desire to expand U.S. boundaries farther across the continent into Canada and Mexico
   (3) the disillusionment with foreign allies who had refused to take sides during the Civil War
   (4) the nation's preoccupation with reconstruction and industrialization after the Civil War
   (5) the resentment toward the new immigrants flooding the country

Answers are on page 528.

World War I

After 1910, conflicts over boundary lines and power struggles among European countries resulted in a war that, by its end, involved twenty-seven nations. For this reason, it was called a world war. The nations divided themselves into two rival groups—the **Central Powers** and the **Allied Powers**. The Central Powers included Germany, Austria-Hungary, Bulgaria, and Turkey. The Allied Powers included Great Britain, France, Russia, Belgium, and Italy.

The United States tried to remain neutral during the early years of the war, which had begun in 1914. In 1917, however, in response to German attacks on ships carrying American citizens, the United States declared war. Factories shifted their production to the manufacture of needed military weapons and supplies. Women and older children replaced draftees as factory workers. Shipyards built only naval vessels. To conserve food for the soldiers, the U.S. government asked that the consumption of meat and bread be restricted to particular days.

Strengthened by the United States' entrance in the war on their side, the Allies drove the Central Powers back to their own boundaries. When the Allies broke through the German lines, the Germans conceded defeat.

The **Treaty of Versailles**, signed in early 1919, officially ended the war. One condition of the treaty was that the **League of Nations** be established to maintain peace throughout the world. Although the idea of the League of Nations was conceived by U.S. president **Woodrow Wilson**, Congress did not want the United States to become involved in European affairs again, so the country did not join the League of Nations. This was a major factor in the organization's decline. After the war, the United States returned to a policy of isolationism and a focus on domestic issues.

The Suffrage Movement

Both before and after the war, women's participation in politics was highly controversial even though high numbers of middle-class women held jobs. Women were encouraged to take on social or community service, but participation in politics or public meetings was deemed "unladylike."

Women in many parts of the United States were not allowed to own property or to have a will. Change in these restrictions was difficult because women did not enjoy **suffrage**, the right to vote. Despite not being able to vote in many states, women played an important role in many of the reform movements in the 19th and early 20th centuries. In fact, many historians credit women's vocal support of the **temperence movement** with the delay in their getting the national right to vote. In the early 20th century, women banded together to force the government to add a constitutional amendment guaranteeing women's right to vote. This amendment, the **Nineteenth**, was ratified in 1920. The **Eighteenth Amendment** outlawing alcohol, commonly referred to as **Prohibition**, had already been ratified in 1919.

From the Roaring Twenties to the Stock Market Crash

During the 1920s, the Immigration Acts of 1921 and 1924 were enacted to preserve jobs for American workers. These acts strictly limited the number of immigrants who could enter the United States. The government at this time enacted few regulations as well as lowering taxes to the individual. As a result, the people had more money to spend, and businesses were able to expand. This period in U.S. history was called the **Roaring Twenties** because of the prosperity the nation enjoyed. The period was characterized by speculation (taking unwise risks in investments hoping to increase gains), bootlegging (the manufacture and purchase of illegal liquor, the sale of which was banned by the Eighteenth Amendment), and an emphasis on materialism.

Unfortunately, by the end of the decade, the Roaring Twenties became quiet, as the stock market fell in 1929. Businesses failed and the unemployment rate soared. By 1932, however, the number of unemployed workers reached 11 million, nearly 10 percent of the nation's 123 million people. The U.S. economy required drastic measures in order to recover.

The New Deal

In 1932, the voters overwhelmingly elected Democrat **Franklin D. Roosevelt** president on his campaign promise to give Americans a "New Deal." The goals of the **New Deal** were to bring relief to people who were in need, to direct the recovery of the economic system, and to establish reforms that would prevent another depression from occurring.

Roosevelt's programs radically changed governmental policy. Many of the agencies created during the New Deal remain today. Most notable are the Social Security system and the Federal Housing Administration. The Federal Deposit Insurance Corporation ensured that bank deposits up to $100,000 would be insured by the government if the banks failed, and the Agricultural Adjustment Act paid farmers to cut back on crops so that food prices would remain stable.

Roosevelt instituted the National Industrial Recovery Act, which provided unlimited workers for public projects, and the Civilian Conservation Corps, a program that recruited young unmarried men to work in U.S. forests and national parks. Roosevelt's actions reversed the economic and emotional climate of the country. Voters reelected him by the largest margin (up to that time) in U.S. history.

EXERCISE 14: THE NEW DEAL

Directions: Match the group in the left column with the New Deal legislation it would have most likely supported in the right column.

1. _____ sharecroppers   **a.** National Industrial Recovery Act

2. _____ unemployed laborers   **b.** Federal Deposit Insurance Corporation

3. _____ the elderly   **c.** Agricultural Adjustment Act

4. _____ bankers   **d.** Social Security Act

Answers are on page 528.

World War II

Although World War II began in Europe in 1939, the United States did not officially join the fighting for more than two years. On December 7, 1941, the Japanese Air Force attacked **Pearl Harbor**, an American naval base on the Hawaiian island of Oahu. After the attack, the United States declared war on Japan and its **Axis** allies, Germany and Italy. The United States joined Great Britain, the Soviet Union, France, and others as the **Allied Forces**.

World War II was truly a global war. Battles were fought in Europe, North Africa, Asia, and on many Pacific Ocean islands. Although the Axis powers won the early battles, the Allied invasion at Normandy on June 6, 1944, turned the tide of the war in favor of the United States and the Allies.

In February 1945 President Roosevelt, Great Britain's **Winston Churchill**, and the Soviet Union's Joseph Stalin met in the Soviet city of Yalta to prepare for the Axis surrender. Under the **Yalta** agreement, Germany was divided into four zones, each under the control of one of the major Allied powers.

In April of that year, one month before massive Allied military efforts forced Germany to surrender, President Roosevelt died. Vice President **Harry Truman** succeeded him. Truman was determined to end the war with Japan. The dropping of atomic bombs on **Hiroshima** and **Nagasaki** brought a quick surrender from Japan on September 2, 1945. Soon after, the **United Nations** was established as an organization to maintain world peace.

Although the war ended many years ago, its scars remain. In addition to the death of thousands of people and the radioactive fallout from the dropping of the atomic bombs in Japan, the Nazi extermination of six million Jews—now known as the **Holocaust**—is a continual reminder of the war's atrocities.

EXERCISE 15: WORLD WAR II

Directions: Read the following questions and select the *best* answers.

1. World War II was the first technical war. Which of the following military items does not support that statement?
   - **(1)** amphibious airplanes
   - **(2)** aircraft carriers
   - **(3)** the atomic bomb
   - **(4)** fuel-efficient aircrafts
   - **(5)** dark green army fatigues

2. Which of the following conclusions can you draw based on the information about World War II?
   - **(1)** The formation of the United Nations ended the war.
   - **(2)** Italy was the last country to join the Allied forces.
   - **(3)** Japan caused the United States to enter the war in 1941.
   - **(4)** Adolf Hitler wanted an alliance with the United States.
   - **(5)** President Roosevelt welcomed troops after the war was over.

Answers are on page 528.

The Korean Conflict

At the end of World War II, the Soviet Union and the United States (allies at the time) agreed that the nation of Korea should be free from Japanese control. To protect this freedom, the Soviet Union occupied the northern half, while the United States occupied the southern half. By 1950, however, a "cold war" had developed between the United States and the Soviet Union. Each feared that the other would try to take control of Korea.

South Korea held public elections to determine its leadership, while a Communist government was established in North Korea. Armies representing the North and the South were stationed along the border. When a North Korean army crossed the border into the South, President Truman committed U.S. troops and asked for troop support from the United Nations.

President Truman claimed that the **Korean Conflict** was a "UN" action and never asked Congress for a formal declaration of war. Despite this, the United States suffered 137,000 casualties; the UN's losses were 263,000. It was not until 1953, under newly-elected president **Dwight D. Eisenhower**, that a treaty was signed, maintaining the separation of North and South Korea at the **38th parallel**.

The end of the Korean Conflict marked only the end of armed conflict. The United States and the Soviet Union did not trust each other. Each increased its military forces, and both developed the hydrogen bomb. This nuclear weapon was far more powerful than the atomic bomb. The mistrust between the two superpowers continued the **Cold War**—a war of words and beliefs—the Soviet Union pushing communism and the United States spreading its capitalist influence.

EXERCISE 16: THE KOREAN CONFLICT

Directions: Choose the *best* answer for each of the following questions.

1. Which of the following is an opinion about the Korean Conflict?
   (1) Dwight Eisenhower finally ended American military action in Korea.
   (2) The Soviet Union and the United States mistrusted each other's intentions in Korea.
   (3) The Korean conflict was an extension of American policy to contain communism.
   (4) Our government has no right to make soldiers fight in an undeclared war.
   (5) After the war, the boundary between the two countries was reinstated.

2. Which of the following is a direct cause of the Korean Conflict?
   (1) different customs in North and South Korea
   (2) the alliance of the Soviet Union and the United States in World War II
   (3) public elections in South Korea
   (4) United Nations troops in North Korea
   (5) North Korean troops crossing the border

Answers are on page 529.

The Eisenhower Years

In the 1950s, during Dwight D. Eisenhower's first term as president, **Senator Joseph McCarthy** used the country's hatred and fear of communism to his political advantage. He accused hundreds of government officials, prominent businesspeople, and entertainers of being part of a Communist plot to take over the country. Although his charges were never proven, they ruined many people. However, his reputation was so badly damaged that he soon lost his influence and power.

President Eisenhower's second term was marked by economic development and social change. Important technological advances encouraged America's involvement in the exploration of space. In 1957, the launching of the first artificial satellite (**Sputnik**) by the Soviet Union precipitated the entry of the United States into the space race.

Also during the Eisenhower administration, the modern civil rights movement began as a direct result of the famous U.S. Supreme Court decision *Brown v. Topeka Board of Education*. In the case, the court ruled that "separate educational facilities are inherently unequal." This ruling was resisted in many school districts throughout the South. Later, the **Civil Rights Act of 1957** established the Civil Rights Commission to investigate illegal voting requirements based on race, national origin, or religion.

EXERCISE 17: THE EISENHOWER YEARS

Directions: Choose the *best* answer to the following questions.

1. McCarthyism has often been compared to the Salem witch trials in colonial Massachusetts. What did the two events have in common?

   (1) People were burned at the stake.
   (2) Accusations were made with little evidence.
   (3) Congress held hearings.
   (4) Federal troops were used.
   (5) Mostly women were convicted.

2. Why is the *Brown v. Topeka Board of Education* decision significant today?

   (1) It sanctioned schools segregated on the basis of race.
   (2) It allowed Eisenhower to set a precedent by sending out federal troops.
   (3) It served as the legal basis for school busing to achieve desegregation.
   (4) It permitted blacks to attend private schools.
   (5) It helped to increase Eisenhower's personal popularity.

Answers are on page 529.

The Kennedy Administration

John F. Kennedy, the first Catholic and the youngest man to be elected president, brought great promise to the office. Kennedy's challenge to America at his inauguration was service to the country. Youth rallied to his call when Kennedy established the **Peace Corps** to share America's wealth and knowledge with developing nations.

The U.S. space program helped symbolize Kennedy's vision of a "new frontier" as the Mercury 7 astronauts ushered in the era of U.S. manned space flights. In 1961, the Soviet Union began supplying nuclear missiles to pro-Soviet **Cuba**, located some 90 miles off the Florida coast. President Kennedy established a naval blockade to prevent any Soviet ships from reaching Cuba. He demanded that the missile site already established be dismantled and the missiles be removed. Soviet Premier **Nikita Khrushchev**, not wanting to risk war, agreed to withdraw all of the missiles from Cuba.

On the domestic front, Kennedy continued Eisenhower's policy of guaranteeing civil rights to the nation's black minority. In 1963, a civil rights commission found that voting rights of blacks were still being denied. Also that year, the **Reverend Martin Luther King, Jr.**, led a series of nonviolent protests throughout the South, culminating in a historic march on Washington that August.

President Kennedy's death by an assassin's bullet in November 1963 prevented many of his social programs from becoming realities. In 1964, his successor, **Lyndon B. Johnson** pushed through Congress the most significant achievement of his career—the **Civil Rights Act**. The law forbade racial discrimination in circumstances where federal funds were used.

EXERCISE 18: THE KENNEDY ADMINISTRATION

Directions: Choose the statement that *best* answers each question below.

1. The Soviet Union's attempt to establish a missile base in Cuba may be interpreted as a direct violation of which important policy?

   (1) the Declaration of Independence
   (2) the Truman Doctrine
   (3) the Monroe Doctrine
   (4) the Treaty of Paris
   (5) the U.S. Constitution

2. Based on the information in the passage, what can you conclude?

   (1) The Soviet Union sought to control Cuba.
   (2) The Soviet Union planned an attack on the United States from Cuba.
   (3) Cuba and the United States enjoyed friendly relations.
   (4) Cuba, a Communist country, was an ally of the Soviet Union.
   (5) Cuba planned to attack the United States.

Answers are on page 529.

The Vietnam War

Despite President Johnson's domestic achievements in the area of civil rights, his foreign policy—particularly with regard to the **Vietnam War**—proved to be his undoing. Under Johnson, the Vietnam War was escalated in 1965. The number of American soldiers fighting in the undeclared war grew from approximately 25,000 in 1963 to more than 500,000 by 1968. In the United States, public controversy over the war painfully divided the country. Supporters maintained that the war was necessary to contain communism and protect democracy in the Far East. Critics maintained that the war was essentially a civil war in which outsiders did not belong.

President Johnson continued to seek a military end to the war, but because of the division within the country, he chose not to seek reelection to the presidency in 1968. His decision not to run opened the door to new leadership and a new direction for the American people.

Détente and Watergate

Richard M. Nixon, elected president in 1968, continued Johnson's earlier bombing strategy to force surrender in Vietnam. He ordered troops into Cambodia, a military move that was unpopular with the American people. Nixon did, however, gradually withdraw troops and negotiate a pullout by March 1973. The agreement to end the war included a cease-fire, U.S. withdrawal of all military troops, and a release of all prisoners captured during the war.

His policy of **détente** (the easing of tensions between nations) helped to establish the first **SALT** (Strategic Arms Limitation Talks) agreement. The United States and the Soviet Union agreed to limit the number of missiles each could have. Nixon was the first American president ever to visit the People's Republic of China, to which he traveled in 1972.

Overshadowing all of these achievements in Nixon's career, however, was his involvement in the **Watergate** scandal that began in June 1972, during his reelection campaign. Nixon's part in the attempted cover-up led to his resignation in 1974. To spare the country the difficulties of impeachment proceedings, he became the first U.S. president ever to resign from office.

EXERCISE 19: DÉTENTE AND WATERGATE

Directions: Label each statement below as fact (**F**) or opinion (**O**).

1. _____ Nixon's involvement in Watergate ruined his presidency.

2. _____ Nixon wanted the United States to be involved with China.

3. _____ The SALT treaty limited the number of missiles the United States could have.

4. _____ The agreement to end the Vietnam War included complete U.S. withdrawal.

Answers are on page 529.

EXERCISE 20: ENDING THE TWENTIETH CENTURY

Directions: Use the chart on page 168 to answer these questions.

1. Considering the events that occurred between 1977 and 2000, which of the following was not a challenge for one of the presidents?
   (1) hostage situations
   (2) moral character issues
   (3) foreign affairs
   (4) an economic depression
   (5) military defense issues

2. During which years did the United States witness the disbanding of the Soviet Union?
   (1) 1977–1981
   (2) 1981–1989
   (3) 1989–1993
   (4) 1993–1999
   (5) 1999–2001

Answers are on page 529.

Ending the Twentieth and Beginning the Twenty-First Century

Significant Events in Presidential Administrations

President	Significant Events in Administration
Jimmy Carter 1977–1981 Democrat	• encouragement of peace treaty between Egypt and Israel • establishment of full diplomatic relations with China • signing of second SALT (Strategic Arms Limitation Talks) treaty with Soviet Union • return of Panama Canal to Panama • takeover of American Embassy in Teheran, Iran in which more than sixty Americans were held hostage
Ronald Reagan 1981–1989 Republican	• supporting hard-line defense policies • joining with France and Italy to maintain peacekeeping force in Beirut, Lebanon • holding of four summit meetings with Mikhail Gorbachev • development of Iran Contra Scandal • elimination of short-and-medium range missiles from Europe
George Bush 1989–1993 Republican	• collapse of communism in Eastern Europe • invasion of Kuwait by U.S. forces resulting in a quick victory • end of "Cold War" • U.S. economy going into recession
Bill Clinton 1993–2000 Democrat	• approval of North American Free Trade Agreement (NAFTA) • impeachment of a second president of the United States on issues of perjury and obstruction of justice • joining of United States North Atlantic Treaty Organization (NATO) nations in aerial bombing campaign • strength of economy • military intervention in Bosnian Civil War
George W. Bush 2001– Republican	• terrorist attacks on World Trade Center and Pentagon • war on terrorism through military, economic, political, and intelligence means • dispute over accuracy of popular vote

3
CIVICS AND GOVERNMENT

To maintain order in a society, governments with rules and laws are established to meet the needs of individuals in society. The main goals of local, state, and federal governments in the United States are to maintain order, provide necessary services, and protect basic freedoms and liberties. In turn, U.S. citizens have the responsibility to get involved and participate in their government through voting and other methods.

Types of Political Systems

Several types of political systems exist in the world. The differences among political systems chiefly concern the way the government acquires and uses its authority.

Types of Political Systems	
Democracy	• head of government is chosen by the people to be governed • pure democracy allows the people to make decisions directly • representative democracy includes election of representatives by the people
Dictatorship	• one leader completely controls the political, social, and economic aspects of life in a country • official is not elected by the people
Monarchy	• power to rule is held by a royal family • power is passed within the family from generation to generation
Oligarchy	• government by a few leaders who form a group, usually from upper classes • officials are not elected by the people

EXERCISE 1: POLITICAL SYSTEMS

Directions: Listed below are applications of political systems in the world. Choose the appropriate response for each question.

1. Adolf Hitler's rise to power in Germany is an example of what type of political system?

   (1) pure democracy
   (2) monarchy
   (3) dictatorship
   (4) representative democracy
   (5) oligarchy

2. What type of political system is headed by Queen Elizabeth II of England?

   (1) dictatorship
   (2) oligarchy
   (3) pure democracy
   (4) representative democracy
   (5) monarchy

3. The president of the United States is elected by the electoral college. What type of system is this?

   (1) dictatorship
   (2) monarchy
   (3) pure democracy
   (4) oligarchy
   (5) representative democracy

Answers are on page 529.

The U.S. Federal Government

The U.S. Constitution is based on **federalism** whereby the authority of the government is divided between the states and a central government. The central government is further divided into three branches: the **legislative**, which makes the laws; the **executive**, which carries out the laws; and the **judicial**, which interprets the laws. Under this separation of powers, no one part of government is able to dominate another. Each branch of government is able to exert its authority to prevent another branch from becoming too powerful.

The Legislative Branch: Maker of Laws

The legislative branch of the government is outlined in Article One of the Constitution. The U.S. legislature, called the **U.S. Congress**, is made up of two houses—the **House of Representatives**, (the lower house), and the **Senate**, (the upper house). Each of the houses has equal power in Congress.

In the House of Representatives, each state's number of representatives is based on its population in relationship to the population of the entire country. To determine the correct number of representatives for each state, a **census**, or counting of the population, occurs every 10 years. In the Senate, states are equally represented, with two senators each.

Representatives are chosen by popular election and serve for two years. Senators, also chosen by popular election, serve six-year terms. The number of terms that members of the Congress may serve is not limited by the Constitution.

EXERCISE 2: LEGISLATIVE REPRESENTATION

Directions: Choose the *best* answer for each of the questions below.

1. Although New Jersey is smaller in area than Wyoming or Nevada, it has a larger number of representatives. Based on this fact, which of the following can you infer to be true?
    (1) New Jersey has a dwindling population.
    (2) New Jersey is primarily an urban, industrial state.
    (3) New Jersey is a densely populated state.
    (4) New Jersey is an urban state with a dwindling population.
    (5) New Jersey is densely populated but dwindling in population.

2. Arizona, one of the fastest-growing Sunbelt states, is attracting residents from the industrial Northeast. Based on this fact, which of the following hypotheses could be true?
    (1) The number of senators for Arizona will need to be increased.
    (2) The number of representatives for Arizona will need to be adjusted.
    (3) The number of representatives for the Northeast states that are losing residents will need to be adjusted.
    (4) Both (1) and (2)
    (5) Both (2) and (3)

Answers are on page 529.

The U.S. Congress has the power to	
• levy and collect taxes	• introduce a revenue or tax bill (House only)
• approve treaties (Senate only)	• declare war
• borrow money	• approve presidential appointments (Senate only)
• impeach the president (House only)	• provide and maintain an army and navy
• regulate commerce	• admit new states to the Union
• introduce bills other than tax bills	• coin money

These **enumerated** powers are listed in Article One of the U.S. Constitution. In addition, the Constitution provides for powers that are not listed. The **elastic clause** enables the legislative branch to "stretch" its authority to meet the needs of unforeseen specific situations.

EXERCISE 3: THE LEGISLATIVE BRANCH

Directions: Write **C** in the space if the action listed is an example of a power stated in the U.S. Constitution and listed in the table on the previous page. Write **E** in the space if it is an example of an application of the elastic clause.

1. _____ Congress approved economic sanctions against Iraq following the Gulf War.

2. _____ Congress approved the North American Free Trade Agreement (NAFTA) in 1993.

3. _____ The Senate approved President Clinton's appointment of Ruth Bader Ginsburg to the U.S. Supreme Court.

Answers are on page 529.

The Executive Branch: Enforcer of the Laws

Article Two of the U.S. Constitution outlines the powers of the executive branch of the U.S. government. The executive branch consists of the president, the vice president, and various agencies and departments. The **president** serves for four years and is limited to serving a maximum of two terms. The **vice president** serves if the president becomes disabled or dies in office before completing the term.

As described in Article Two of the U.S. Constitution, the president has the following responsibilities:

- serves as commander in chief of the armed forces

- grants reprieves and pardons for offenses against the United States

- appoints judges to the U.S. Supreme Court and ambassadors, with the approval of the Senate

- nominates and appoints major executive officers

- vetoes (refuses to approve) some bills sent by Congress

The President serves as both our symbolic and political leader. In many countries this dual leadership role is held by separate individuals. The power of office, combined with the considerable economic, political, and military might of the United States, makes our President one of the world's most visible and powerful leaders.

—Source: *How the United States Government Works* by Nancy Gendron Hofmann

EXERCISE 4: PRESIDENTIAL POWERS

Directions: Place an **X** next to each responsibility that is one of four specific powers of the president as defined in the U.S. Constitution.

1. _____ serves as commander in chief

2. _____ grants reprieves and pardons

3. _____ appoints Supreme Court judges

4. _____ declares war

Answers are on page 529.

EXERCISE 5: THE EXECUTIVE BRANCH

Directions: Choose the *best* answer for the question below.

1. The Twenty-second Amendment to the Constitution limits a president to serving no more than two full terms. Which of the following could be a result of this decision?
  (1) creation of a third party
  (2) unconstrained presidential power
  (3) institution of new policy ideas
  (4) reduction of the president's pension
  (5) weakened image of the president

Answer is on page 529.

The Judicial Branch: Interpreter of the Laws

Article Three of the U.S. Constitution describes the Supreme Court of the United States. The purpose of the **Supreme Court** is to rule on the constitutionality of certain laws passed by Congress, the president, and the states themselves. The authority to decide whether or not a law is in keeping with the spirit of the Constitution is called **judicial review**.

The Supreme Court is composed of nine justices appointed for life by the president and is headed by the **chief justice**. The judicial branch of the federal government consists of the U.S. Supreme Court, the 11 circuit courts of appeals distributed throughout the country, and approximately 90 federal district courts. The Supreme Court is the most powerful court in the United States.

The Supreme Court has the powers to rule on

- cases involving a state and citizens of another state

- controversies among two or more states

- cases between citizens of different states

- conflicts over patents and copyrights

In Supreme Court rulings, a decision is reached when a majority of the justices agree. When all nine justices are present and vote, a majority decision requires at least five votes.

EXERCISE 6: THE JUDICIAL BRANCH

Directions: Choose the *best* answer to complete each of the following statements.

1. Chief Justice Charles Evans Hughes wrote in 1907, "The Constitution is what the Judges say it is." Which Supreme Court power does this quotation best define?
   (1) checks and balances
   (2) ignoring legislative decisions
   (3) being "above the law"
   (4) judicial review
   (5) judicial restraint

2. What is the purpose of the statement in Question 1?
   (1) define the role of the Supreme Court
   (2) show that the Supreme Court is the final authority
   (3) show the attitude of Chief Justice Hughes
   (4) both (1) and (2)
   (5) (1), (2), and (3)

Answers are on page 530.

System of Checks and Balances

The powers of the three branches of the federal government had to be balanced so that no one center of power dominated the other two. To prevent any one branch from imposing its will on the others, the U.S. Constitution allows for certain actions by one branch to restrain the activities of another. One such restraint is the ability of the president to refuse approval of (**veto**) a bill sent from Congress.

However, Congress could still pass the bill into law by a two-thirds majority vote of its members by **overriding a veto**. Finally, if the issue is brought to the Supreme Court, the Court can still declare the law unconstitutional. Compromises within the three branches of government assure citizens of the United States that changes in laws will occur with great consideration among the lawmakers.

EXERCISE 7: SYSTEM OF CHECKS AND BALANCES

Directions: In column I, write the branch of government that exercises the power described on the left. In column II, write the branch of government that is checked by the use of that power.

	I	**II**
Power	**Who exercises power?**	**Who is checked?**
1. to appoint federal judges	**(a)** _____	**(b)** _____
2. to override a veto	**(a)** _____	**(b)** _____
3. to rule a law unconstitutional	**(a)** _____	**(b)** _____
4. to veto a bill	**(a)** _____	**(b)** _____

Answers are on page 530.

The Enactment of a Law

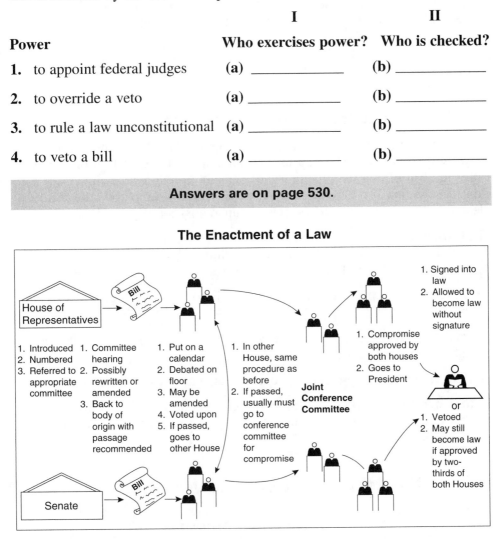

EXERCISE 8: THE ENACTMENT OF A LAW

Directions: Choose the *best* answer for each of the following questions.

1. Which statement is best supported by the preceding chart?
   (1) Bills justified by the elastic clause in the Constitution must be introduced directly by the president.
   (2) Before being sent to the president, a bill must be approved in identical form by both houses of Congress.
   (3) A filibuster on certain bills may not take place in either house.
   (4) A bill introduced in the Senate may be changed by the House, but not vice versa.
   (5) The president must sign all bills for them to become law.

2. Which of the following is *not* true according to the preceding chart?

    (1) Vetoed bills cannot become law.
    (2) Bills passed in the Senate go to the House.
    (3) Bills can become law without the president's signature.
    (4) Bills can be amended after they come out of committee.
    (5) All bills are debated on the floor of the House and Senate.

Answers are on page 530.

Amending the Constitution

There have been only 27 changes (amendments) to the Constitution since it was written in 1787. The first ten amendments to the Constitution are called the **Bill of Rights**, guarantees of personal freedoms for citizens. Consider the first five amendments stated below and summarize the main idea of each in your own words. (Use a separate sheet of paper.)

First Amendment: establishment of a specific, government-approved religion is prohibited; freedom of speech, freedom of the press, right to assemble, and right to petition the government to address grievances

Second Amendment: a well-regulated militia for security; right to keep and bear arms

Third Amendment: restriction of quartering soldiers in private homes only allowed under specific conditions

Fourth Amendment: protection from unreasonable search and seizure

Fifth Amendment: provisions concerning prosecution and due process of law double jeopardy restriction; private property not to be taken without compensation

State and Local Governments

State Government

Article Four of the U.S. Constitution defines the role of state governments. The structure of the state government resembles that of the federal government. The executive authority of the state is the **governor**. Like the president, the governor has veto power.

The **legislative branch**, which makes the laws, is composed of two houses in 49 of the 50 states (except for Nebraska). Each state has its own **court system**, which includes trial courts, appellate courts, and a state supreme court.

Each state has its own written constitution that outlines the powers and duties of various state officials and agencies. Like the federal governmental system on which they are based, the 50 state governments have a system of checks and balances among the three branches of government. In addition, the state constitutions cannot conflict with the U.S. Constitution.

Most criminal codes and civil laws, such as a legal drinking age, are established by state law. The state also establishes laws for contracts, business charters, and marriage and divorce. Another responsibility of state government is to charter local governments. The powers of municipalities—villages, towns, and cities—are outlined and defined in charters approved by the state. State legislatures create local governments, which are usually of three types: mayor-council, council-manager, or commission.

EXERCISE 9: POWERS OF STATE GOVERNMENT

Directions: In the spaces provided, write **S** if the power belongs to the states, **F** if it belongs to the federal government, and **B** if it belongs to both.

1. _____ vetoing a bill by the chief executive

2. _____ declaring war against a foreign country

3. _____ setting import quotas and duties

4. _____ establishing a legal age for drinking alcoholic beverages

Answers are on page 530.

The U.S. Political System

The voting public holds a range of positions on political issues. These political positions can be illustrated as occupying one of five segments (**political labels**) of a spectrum. To win an election, each political party must obtain a majority of the votes cast. Since most U.S. voters occupy the middle three parts of the spectrum, both political parties must appeal to this group of voters to win.

The following illustration shows the five political positions.

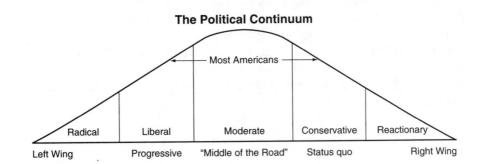

The Political Continuum

Most Americans

| Radical | Liberal | Moderate | Conservative | Reactionary |

| Left Wing | Progressive | "Middle of the Road" | Status quo | Right Wing |

radical: one who advocates sweeping changes in laws and methods of government with little delay

liberal: one who advocates political change in the name of progress, especially social improvement through governmental action

moderate: one who believes in avoiding extreme changes and measures in laws and government

conservative: one who advocates maintaining the existing social order and believes that change, if any, should be gradual

reactionary: one who resists change and usually advocates a return to an earlier social order or policy

Political Parties

A **political party** is a group whose goal is to influence public policy by getting its candidates elected to office. Although the U.S. Constitution makes no provision for political parties, they serve a useful function in our democracy. Political parties

- define the issues and propose possible solutions for governmental problems

- act as another check in our governmental system of checks and balances by monitoring the policies of the party in power

- enable citizens to become involved in the governmental apparatus

- help to keep the number of candidates running for public office manageable

The differences between the Democratic and Republican parties tend to center on domestic, economic, and social issues as well as foreign policy. Most fundamentally, however, the two parties differ in their views of the role of government in solving problems.

In general, the **Democratic Party** favors a strong federal government at the expense of the sovereign rights of the states. This party advocates government regulation of business, endorses labor unions, and champions federal programs for the disadvantaged and minorities.

The **Republican Party** favors stronger state authority at the expense of the federal government. This party advocates individual free enterprise, supports a strong national defense, and believes in keeping any government social programs to a minimum.

EXERCISE 10: POLITICAL PARTIES

Directions: Write **D** in the space provided if the statement generally applies to the Democratic Party philosophy and **R** if it generally applies to the Republican Party philosophy.

1. _____ favors having state and local governments solve their own problems

2. _____ supports labor unions and the right of their members to strike

3. _____ advocates spending large amounts of money for welfare and other social services

Answers are on page 530.

The Electoral Process and Voting

Both the Democratic and Republican parties maintain national party headquarters and staffs. Every four years, each party holds a national convention to nominate a presidential candidate who must have won a majority of delegates in the primaries that precede the nominating convention. A political **primary** enables members of a party to express their preference for a candidate to run in the general election. In most primary elections, the candidate must receive a **plurality** (more votes than any other candidate) to win. Primaries may be open or closed. In an **open primary** voters need not declare their party affiliations but must do so in a **closed primary**.

At the nominating convention, each state sends a designated number of delegates to help select the party's nominee. At the end of a forum, the delegates vote to choose the party's nominee and to approve the party's **platform** (a formal declaration of party principles).

After the candidates from each party campaign for office, the general election is held. In the general election, the winner must receive a **majority** of the votes cast in each state to earn that state's electoral votes. The president and vice president are chosen by popular vote within each state, but the electoral college later officially elects the president based on the winner of the popular vote in each state. The number of electoral votes for each state is equal to the number of U.S. representatives from that state plus its two senators. Once elected, public officials are responsible to a **constituency**— the people who elected them to office.

EXERCISE 11: THE ELECTORAL PROCESS AND VOTING

Directions: Match each definition on the right with the correct term on the left.

1. _____ plurality

2. _____ primary

3. _____ platform

a. declaration of a party's stand on the issues

b. a party election to select a candidate to run in the general election

c. more votes than any other candidate (but not more than half)

Answers are on page 530.

The Electoral College

The **electoral college** consists of a group of electors from each state who cast votes for the president and vice president according to who won the popular vote in their state. To be officially elected president, a candidate must receive 270 electoral votes. The electoral college was originally established to serve as a check and balance against an unsound decision made by the voters and to preserve the voice of the less populated states. Recently, however, the electoral college has been the target of great criticism.

Critics of the electoral college were very vocal during the presidential election of 2000. For the first time since the election of 1888, a candidate was elected president without receiving the majority of the popular vote. Candidate Albert Gore narrowly won the **popular vote** but still lost the presidency to George W. Bush because of the electoral college. Of the 538 possible electoral votes, 271 were pledged to Bush and 267 were pledged to Gore. Later the American people learned of great numbers of disputed ballots and of the need to update election technology, increase training of poll workers, and further educate voters.

EXERCISE 12: VOTER RULES

Directions: Write fact (**F**) or opinion (**O**) for each of the following statements about voting in the United States.

1. _____ The most serious offense a citizen can commit is voter fraud.

2. _____ The Voting Rights Act of 1965 abolished literacy tests.

3. _____ The Twenty-sixth Amendment gave 18-year-olds the right to vote.

4. _____ Non-citizens should be allowed to vote in elections.

Answers are on page 530.

4
ECONOMICS

Economists study how a society meets its unlimited material needs with its limited resources. The fact that resources are limited requires people to make choices about what needs to satisfy.

Factors of Production

Every society must answer three basic questions when determining the type of economic system under which it will operate. These questions are:

- **What should be produced?** What do members of a society need and want?

- **How should it be produced?** Should each person make his or her own goods, or should businesses or the government manufacture them for the entire society?

- **How should the products be distributed?** Should the products be given to everyone equally or only to those who can afford to buy them?

To answer these questions, each government must first identify its goals and values and then determine what resources are available to produce what the society needs.

The following chart identifies three vital **factors of production: natural resources**, **capital**, and **labor.**

Factors of Production	Definition	Examples
1. natural resources	• raw materials	• ore to make steel • trees
2. capital	• equipment, factories, or machines • money invested in enterprises	• sewing machines used to manufacture clothes • lumber to build a building
3. labor	• people who do the work	• seamstresses who cut and sew • construction workers to build buildings

Despite careful and efficient management, the factors of production (natural resources, capital, and labor) remain limited. The demands society makes upon them, however, are continually increasing. All countries are concerned about environmental protection and awareness, but natural resources such as coal, air, water, and virgin timber are in great demand around the world. A continued supply of natural resources depends on reasonable economic growth and cooperation among all nations.

EXERCISE 1: FACTORS OF PRODUCTION

Directions: In each example, write **N** if the factor of production refers to natural resources, **C** if it refers to capital, and **L** if it refers to labor.

1. _____ gemstones imported by the United States from India

2. _____ computers and printers used in a publishing firm

3. _____ carpenters who help build new shopping malls

Answers are on page 530.

Economics and Government

A nation's system of government often determines the type of economic system under which the nation will operate. Recent history has shown that changing economic systems often brings political changes as well. Political leaders around the world assemble to exchange views and examine economic issues in order to keep the world economy as stable as possible.

Capitalism

Capitalism is an economic system based on the private ownership of the resources of production. Investment decisions are made by the individual or corporation rather than by the government. The production, distribution, and prices of goods and services are determined by competition in a free market. The government intervenes only when necessary to protect the public interest. Capitalism is the predominant economic system under which the American economy operates.

Socialism

Under **socialism**, the most important industries and services are publicly and cooperatively owned. These industries, which may include steel production, banking and finance, public transportation, or healthcare, are controlled by the government with the intent of providing equal opportunity for all.

In socialist economies, ownership of private property is permitted; however, owners of businesses together with the government decide what goods and services are produced, how they are produced, and who should get them. The economy of Sweden is a socialist economy.

Communism

A third economic order does not permit private ownership of property and the means of production. Under **communism**, the government, described as the community, owns the property and distributes the society's merchandise in accordance with the "common good." The government decides what goods and services are produced and who should get them. Examples are the economies of the People's Republic of China, Cuba, and the former Soviet Union.

None of these three economic systems exists in pure form. That is, no completely capitalist, socialist, or communist economy exists in the modern world. In its operation, each of the economic systems incorporates some aspect of another.

The term **mixed economy** is used to describe the U.S. economy since some government regulation of private enterprise exists. For example, the Food and Drug Administration ensures that any new medicine or drug that is marketed in the United States has been properly tested before it is sold to the public.

EXERCISE 2: ECONOMIC SYSTEMS AND GOVERNMENTS

Directions: Choose the *best* answer for each question below.

1. The quotation "In the area of economics, the government that governs least governs best" best describes which type of economic system?

   (1) capitalism
   (2) socialism
   (3) communism
   (4) mixed economy
   (5) none of the above

The Continuum of Economic Systems

Market Capitalism   Socialism   Communism Command

2. According to the continuum of economic systems, which of the following conclusions may be drawn?

   (1) Communism is the best example of the market system.
   (2) Capitalism is the best example of the command system.
   (3) Socialism is the opposite of capitalism.
   (4) Capitalism is the opposite of communism.
   (5) Capitalism is better than any other system represented.

3. Which of the following situations *best* supports the statement "Each of the economic systems incorporates some aspect of the other"?

   (1) In socialist Sweden, SAAB, the automobile manufacturer, is owned and run by the government.

   (2) In Cuba, the government-controlled media schedules the broadcasting for all television and radio programs.

   (3) In the United States, a dairy manufacturer is told by a government agency the percentages of milk and cream a product sold as ice cream must contain.

   (4) In the People's Republic of China, all of the nation's farms are nationalized, and young people are forced to work them.

   (5) In the United States, major air carriers engage in "price wars" to attract passengers during the vacation seasons.

Answers are on page 530.

Supply and Demand

The foundation of American capitalism is supply and demand. **Supply** is the quantity of goods and services available for sale at all possible prices. **Demand** is the desire to buy the product or service and the ability to pay for it.

Producers or suppliers are in business to make a profit; therefore, they supply goods and services at a price. They must charge prices high enough to cover their costs for production and earn a profit for themselves. Consumers who are willing and able to buy these goods and services create demand.

The amount of production (supply) of an item and its price depend on the cost of production and the demand in the marketplace. In general, producers seek the highest possible prices to maximize their profits. Consumers seek the lowest possible prices to keep money in their pockets. These opposing goals of producers and consumers significantly affect prices.

In general, the higher the price, the greater the number of companies that wish to supply a product or service. A high-priced item or service that yields a large profit will attract many producers, who will compete with one another for a share of the market. This applies chiefly to manufactured goods and to services. Precious minerals and metals such as diamonds and gold, which are scarce, command higher prices than more common minerals and metals.

A good example of the relationship between price and supply is the running shoes phenomenon. When they were introduced to the buying public, running shoes bearing the trademarks of such companies as Nike and Reebok created great demand. Consumers—adults and teens—paid higher prices for the labels than they ordinarily might have for other brands. As a result, several competitors entered the market (increasing the supply) seeking to make money on the product. Each running shoe manufacturer fought to capture a share of the market.

When too many producers compete in the marketplace, however, supply exceeds demand because buyers cannot or will not buy all of the goods offered for sale. As a result, a surplus occurs and prices fall. Producers no longer reap the profits necessary for them to compete successfully. Some businesses streamline their operations, and others are forced out of business.

From the consumer's viewpoint, the higher the price, the lower the demand; the lower the price, the greater the demand. If prices for running shoes became too high, consumers might stop buying them and revert to wearing off-brands. On the other hand, when prices for an item fall too low and consumer demand exceeds the producer's ability to provide the product, a shortage in supply occurs. As a result, prices rise higher, and in extreme cases, the product is rationed. Under **rationing**, the quantity of the item sold is restricted.

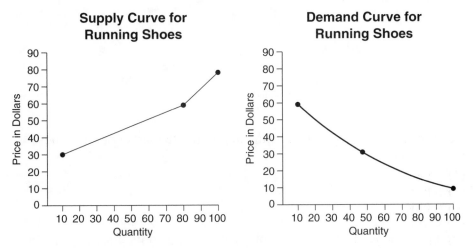

As shown in the graph on the left, as the price of running shoes goes up, the quantity supplied increases. In this graph, producers cannot supply running shoes at a price of $5. However, as the price increases to $30, about ten pairs of running shoes are available for purchase. According to this graph, if the price were $60, there would be about 80 pairs of running shoes available for purchase.

As shown in the graph on the right, as the price of running shoes goes down, the quantity demanded rises. At $60 each, the demand would be for ten pairs. If the price were lowered to $30, the demand would increase to about 45 pairs. According to this graph, if the price rose to $70 per pair, you could infer that there would be no demand for running shoes at this price.

Supply and Equilibrium

To produce exactly the amount that consumers are willing to buy, producers must determine at what point supply equals demand. Economists call this point the **equilibrium** where the supply and demand curves intersect. This establishes the market price for a product or service.

When the price is greater than the equilibrium, demand falls and there is more of a product or service than people want to buy. This is called a **surplus**. When the price falls below the equilibrium, demand increases, exceeding supply, and a **shortage** in the product or service occurs.

EXERCISE 3: SUPPLY, DEMAND, AND EQUILIBRIUM

Directions: Study the graph and answer the following questions.

Supply, Demand, and Equilibrium: Digital Cameras

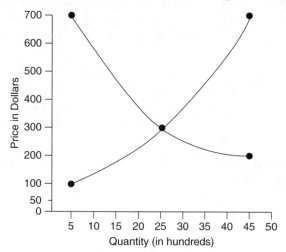

1. According to the graph, what is the approximate market price of these digital cameras?

   (1) $500
   (2) $400
   (3) $300
   (4) $200
   (5) $100

2. In recent years, the Asian economies have developed the technology to manufacture and export to the United States electronic equipment such as digital cameras. If demand for digital cameras were low, what impact would Asia's entrance into the market have on the sale of digital cameras in the United States?

   (1) Prices for digital cameras would increase because the supply would be greater.
   (2) Prices for digital cameras would decrease because the supply would be lesser.
   (3) A surplus of digital cameras might occur as a result of lower prices.
   (4) Stores would cease ordering and stocking digital cameras.
   (5) Prices for digital cameras would not be affected.

Answers are on page 530.

Economic Growth

In a growing economy, there is an increasing capacity to produce more goods and services. During periods of great economic growth, consumers are increasingly able to buy these goods and services. However, the best type of growth is steady and controllable.

The world economy must grow evenly, or problems will occur. There have been several periods in our country's history when the economy has increased rapidly. During those periods, citizens experience positive economic times and many new businesses are created. When the rate of growth slows down, workers can be laid off and businesses are closed.

EXERCISE 4: ECONOMIC GROWTH

Directions: Study the graph and answer the following questions.

The Business Cycle

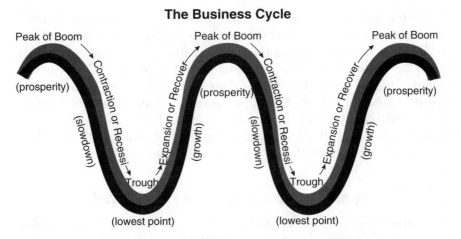

Source: *Consumer Economics in Action* by Roger LeRoy Miller and Alan D. Stafford

1. According to the graph, which of the following is not a stage in the business cycle?

   (1) peak
   (2) depression
   (3) unemployment
   (4) recession
   (5) recovery

2. During which of the following business cycle stages would you assume that the economy is functioning poorly and the *most* people are suffering economically?

   (1) peak
   (2) depression
   (3) unemployment
   (4) recession
   (5) recovery

Answers are on page 530.

Inflation and Its Effects

When too much money and credit are available and too few goods are available to satisfy demand, the dollar loses its value and the prices of goods increase. The country begins a period of **inflation**.

For consumers to be able to keep pace with the rise in the cost of goods, their wages must increase. For producers to pay the increased wages, they must produce more goods and charge higher prices for them. This circular pattern in which wage increases feed on price increases is called an **inflationary spiral**. An "inflation psychology" sets in as consumers rush to make major purchases because they believe that prices will only increase. For inflation to fall, demand must be decreased and credit restricted. However, one result of curbing high inflation is an economic recession.

Deflation and Its Effects

When too little money and credit are available, and more goods are available than necessary to satisfy demand, the dollar gains value and the prices of goods decrease. Under these circumstances, the economy enters a period of **deflation**. Because goods remain unsold, producers' profits fall. Falling profits lead to layoffs. Unless the situation is corrected, a recession occurs; if the recession is prolonged, a depression can result. The United States has not experienced a depression since the 1930s, but the U.S. economy has been affected by varying levels of economic challenges in other countries throughout the 20th century and into the 21st century.

Measurement of Economic Growth

Econometrics is the use of statistical methods to study economic and financial data. These data are then interpreted by economic experts to show how the economy is performing. Among the more commonly used economic statistics are stock market trading, unemployment percentages, number of housing starts, and the gross domestic product (**GDP**).

The GDP represents the total amount of all goods and services produced in one year within a country's borders. The gross national product (**GNP**) measures international activities and is more of a global measure of economic enterprises.

Top Countries with the Highest Gross Domestic Product

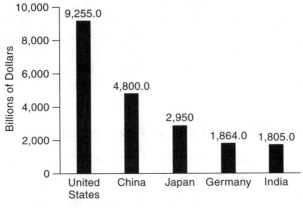

Source: CIA, *The World Factbook 2000*

The Consumer Price Index

The **Consumer Price Index (CPI)** is the measure of change in prices of a group of goods or services that an average consumer would purchase. As stated in the graph below, the CPI in the United States has increased steadily since World War II.

Consumer Price Index 1915–1999

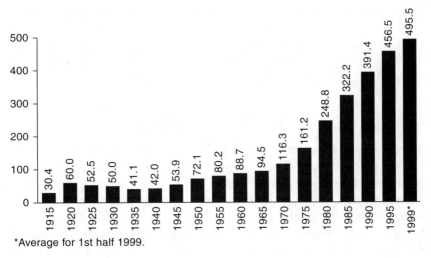

*Average for 1st half 1999.

Money and Monetary Policy

Money is the medium of exchange accepted by a society in payment for goods and services. A nation's money supply consists mainly of coins, bills, and checking and savings deposits.

The increased power of computers and the other advancements in technology have led to increased use of "electronic money" or digital representation of currency in the United States. In 2002, eleven European nations launched the **euro** as their shared currency. The euro can make it easier to transfer funds from country to country.

The U.S. **Federal Reserve Board** is responsible for setting the nation's monetary policy—the regulation of the nation's supply of money and credit in order to keep the economy in balance. Through the national banking system, the Federal Reserve Board controls the availability of credit to consumers in two ways—by determining the reserve ratio and setting the discount rate.

EXERCISE 5: MONEY AND MONETARY POLICY

Directions: Using the information provided on money, decide whether each of the following statements is a fact (**F**) or an opinion (**O**).

1. _____ The dollar is the most widely used unit of money.

2. _____ Money makes trade among countries convenient.

3. _____ The peso is a unit used in many Latin American countries.

Answers are on page 530.

The Reserve Ratio

Every lending institution—banks and savings and loan associations—must hold onto a certain amount of its deposits. This amount that cannot be lent out is called the **reserve ratio**. Most banks are members of the nation's Federal Reserve System (the Fed). By controlling the reserve ratio, the Fed determines the amount of money banks are able to lend.

The Discount Rate

A second way in which the Fed influences the nation's economy is through the discount rate. The **discount rate** is the rate of interest the Fed charges member banks to borrow money. Banks make money by charging a higher interest rate on loans than they pay to those who deposit money into checking and savings accounts.

To have more money to meet demand, banks often borrow from the Federal Reserve System. The bank then lends the money to its customers (borrowers) at a higher rate.

The Fed adjusts the discount rate to affect the supply of money. For example, if the discount rate is 5 percent, consumer banks might lend money out for 10 percent. If the discount rate were raised to 15 percent, consumer banks might charge 20 percent. Thus, you can see the impact a changing discount rate has on the availability of credit in the U.S. economy.

Government and Fiscal Policy

While the U.S. Federal Reserve Board directly influences the supply of money and credit in the economy, the government, through its fiscal policy, also indirectly affects the nation's economic condition.

In establishing **fiscal policy**, the president proposes an annual budget to the Congress. As Congress determines what programs are needed, it must also consider how these programs will be funded. Raising taxes is the simplest and most common answer.

Consumers and businesses pay these taxes to the government. The government, in turn, spends the money on programs designed to benefit the citizens and the country, such as education, interstate highways, and the military. By deciding whether to raise or lower taxes and whether to increase or decrease spending, the government is controlling a major part of the money supply.

If the government spends less than it collects in taxes, a **budget surplus** results. If the government spends more than it collects, the condition is called **deficit spending**. A **balanced budget** results when the income from taxes equals the money spent on programs.

EXERCISE 6: GOVERNMENT AND FISCAL POLICY

Directions: Circle the correct answer choice in parentheses for each statement.

1. During a recession, to put more money in circulation, the president and Congress should (increase/decrease) government spending while (raising/lowering) taxes.

2. During an inflationary period, the Fed should (increase/decrease) the money in circulation by (raising/lowering) the discount rate while (increasing/decreasing) the reserve ratio.

3. When the government spends more money than it receives in taxes, there is a (budget surplus/budget deficit).

Answers are on page 530.

Technology and the Worker

The workplace for many Americans is the office. As a result of increased technology, many workers **telecommute**. They are able to work out of their homes with personal computers and fax machines. According to the Bureau of Labor Statistics, in 1997 more than 25 million American workers had flexible work schedules, largely because of technology and worker demand. Businesses utilize mobile communications to assist employees with time management and efficiency.

The advancement of technology allows workers to communicate with companies in different countries. Managers from every country are required to deal effectively with employees of many nationalities. In *The Evolving Global Economy* Kenichi Ohmae states, "Today's global economy is genuinely borderless. Information, capital, and innovation flow all over the world at top speed, enabled by technology and fueled by consumers' desires for access to the best and least expensive products."

The Technology Revolution, like the Industrial Revolution, has transformed the U.S. workplace. At the close of the 20th century, there had been an elimination of 42 million jobs and the creation of 67 million jobs. Many jobs were eliminated as quickly as new jobs were created. As jobs became more technical, more workers went back to school in order to be competitive in the workplace. The trend for higher education increased; however, so did the costs for college tuition.

The Baby Boom Generation

American citizens born between 1946 and 1964 are called **baby boomers.** These 76 million people have unmistakably affected the economy of the United States, and economists predict that they will continue to affect the economy through 2030.

Cause	Effect
baby boomers were born 1946–1964	• strong sales of baby food
baby boomers entered school	• increase in elementary-school construction • shortage of teachers
baby boomers became teenagers	• national focus on parenting techniques and family values
baby boomers entered job market	• overcrowded job market • depressed wages
baby boomers bought first homes, cars, furniture	• real estate surge • prices of homes at new heights • acquired substantial debt from loans
baby boomers retire 2010–2030	• possible employment opportunities • possible exhaustion of Social Security and strain on Medicare
baby boomers downsize homes and liquidate investments	• possible fall in housing prices • possible market decline

Source: *Boomeromics* by William Sterling and Stephen Waite

5
GEOGRAPHY

Geography is the study of the landform features of the surface layer of the earth. The physical features of the land's surface have been studied and recorded by many specially trained experts. **Geologists** study the rock layers and composition of the earth, **cartographers** make maps to represent the landform features, and **geophysicists** explain the forces that create those landforms.

Mapping

Mapping of the earth's surface can be difficult because of the earth's spherical shape. When flat maps are created, sizes and shapes of the continents are distorted. The mapping of a sphere is called a **map projection**. There are several map projection types that try to correct for this distortion. Some examples are

- **Mercator** (which is accurate for the equatorial areas but distorts at the poles)

- **Gnomic** (which identifies a single area on the globe but distorts around the edges)

- **Conic** (which maps a small triangular section, but not much of the planet at a time)

Maps are also created to identify specific features of the earth. These topics include

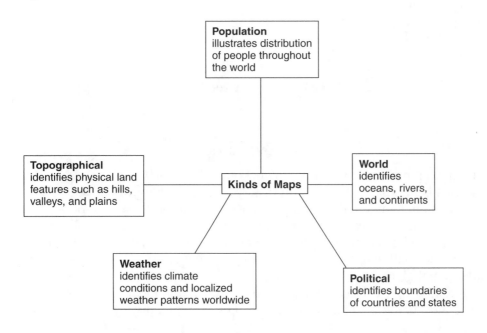

Population
illustrates distribution of people throughout the world

Topographical
identifies physical land features such as hills, valleys, and plains

Kinds of Maps

World
identifies oceans, rivers, and continents

Weather
identifies climate conditions and localized weather patterns worldwide

Political
identifies boundaries of countries and states

A very common type of map is a **topographical map**. These maps show relief features, or surface configurations, of an area. Traditionally, these maps were made by physically measuring an area; this is called **surveying**. More recently, mapmakers are relying on aerial photographs to assist in creating maps that give true accuracy of ground detail. These views especially help in creating urban maps that are designed to show roadways and direction.

EXERCISE 1: STYLES OF MAPS

Directions: Complete the following statements about different types of maps.

1. What assumption can be made about mapping the earth?
   (1) It is not difficult to map the earth accurately using the Mercator method.
   (2) Mapping any spherical shape is impossible.
   (3) Aerial maps can only be used to map urban areas.
   (4) A three-dimensional sphere always gets distorted on a flat map.
   (5) Mapmakers do not try to correct for the distortion of a sphere.

2. Which of the following is the best map to show the boundaries for the 50 states in the United States?
   (1) topographical map
   (2) population map
   (3) world map
   (4) political map
   (5) weather map

3. Which type of map would show the highest elevation of the Cascade Mountains?
   (1) topographical map
   (2) population map
   (3) world map
   (4) political map
   (5) aerial map

Answers are on page 531.

Map Symbols

In making maps, mapmakers provide symbols to show important features of the area being mapped. A **legend** or **key** tells what the symbols mean.

For example, on a political map, a star usually indicates a state or nation's capital. On a population map, the number of people that live in a given city is indicated by the size of the dot that locates the city. Larger dots indicate cities with large populations, while smaller dots indicate cities with smaller populations.

On road maps, a scale of miles is often provided in the legend. A scale of miles is most commonly shown in inches. For example, the legend on a map scale might read "one inch equals 50 miles." An example of a scale is shown on the map below. Maps are also drawn to align with compass point directions. The compass point will indicate which direction is north, usually toward the top of the page or screen. You can measure distance with a ruler or with a strip of paper that has a straight edge.

EXERCISE 2: MEASURING DISTANCES

Directions: Study the map and answer the questions that follow.

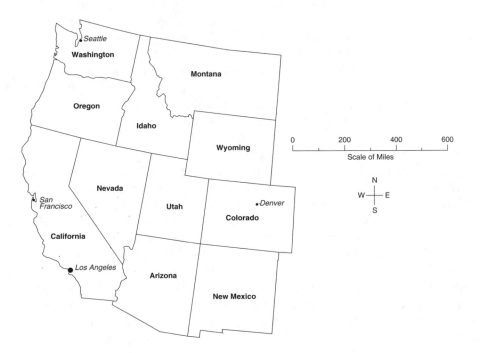

1. According the map shown here, approximately how far is Denver from San Francisco?

    _____

2. Which of the following cities shows the greatest population:
    Los Angeles, Seattle, or Denver?

    _____

3. In what direction would you travel if you were heading to California from Colorado?

    _____

Answers are on page 531.

Latitude and Longitude

The **equator,** an imaginary line that circles the earth's center, divides the earth into two **hemispheres,** or halves. The land and the water above the equator lie in the **Northern Hemisphere**; the area of land and water below the equator is known as the **Southern Hemisphere**. Canada, the United States, and Mexico, as well as Europe, Russia, and Asia are all in the Northern Hemisphere. Most of South America and Africa, as well as all of Australia, are in the Southern Hemisphere.

The distance from the equator is measured on maps and globes by degrees of latitude. Lines of **latitude** are parallel lines that measure distance north and south of the equator in degrees. These lines are often marked on maps and globes in 20-degree increments. The equator is located at 0 degrees latitude, the North Pole at 90 degrees north latitude, and the South Pole at 90 degrees south latitude. Most of the continental United States lies between 25 and 50 degrees north latitude. Hawaii is at about 21 degrees north latitude, and Alaska is between 61 and 72 degrees north latitude.

Lines of **longitude** are lines that measure distances in degrees east and west of the **prime meridian**, an imaginary line running through Greenwich, England. Lines of longitude divide the world into the Eastern and Western Hemispheres. The prime meridian is located at 0 degrees longitude. There are 180 degrees east of the prime meridian and 180 degrees west of it, for a total of 360 degrees around the earth. Most of the United States, including Alaska and Hawaii, lies between 65 and 125 degrees west longitude.

The lines of latitude and longitude cross each other to form what is called a grid. To locate a particular place on a globe or map, you must find the point where two lines intersect. The number of degrees latitude and longitude indicate the location. For example, in the grid diagram below, the island of Madagascar, located off the southeast coast of Africa, is located at approximately 20 degrees south latitude and 45 degrees east longitude.

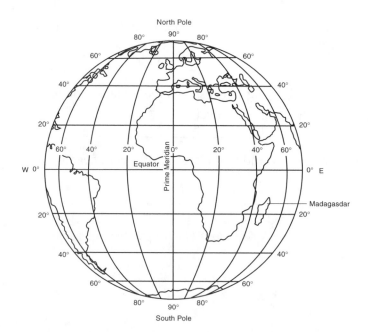

Based on the grid, which continent is found at 50 degrees north latitude and 0 degrees longitude? If you answered *Europe,* you would be correct. The point where the 50-degree-north line of latitude meets the 0-degree line of longitude is on the continent of Europe.

EXERCISE 3: LATITUDE AND LONGITUDE

Directions: Choose the *best* answer for each of the following questions, which are based on the information in the grid.

1. Which of the following is at 15 degrees north latitude and 20 degrees east longitude?
   (1) northern Europe
   (2) eastern South America
   (3) western Africa
   (4) southern Asia
   (5) central Africa

2. What country is located nearest 30 degrees south latitude and 20 degrees east longitude?
   (1) Italy
   (2) Chile
   (3) Egypt
   (4) South Africa
   (5) England

Answers are on page 531.

Time Zones

There are 24 standard time zones, divided according to lines of longitude. The earth rotates 15 degrees in one hour, so each time zone covers 15 degrees of latitude. The 24 time zones equal 360 degrees of latitude, or one complete rotation of the earth.

In the continental United States, there are four **time zones:** eastern, central, mountain, and pacific. As people travel west, they move into an earlier time zone for every 15 degrees of latitude they travel. For example, people completing a journey west through the eastern time zone at 5:00 P.M. would have to change their watches to 4:00 P.M. as they entered the next time zone (central). The four time zones for the continental United States are shown on the following map.

EXERCISE 4: TIME ZONES

Directions: Use the map below to choose the *best* answer for each question.

Time Zones Across North America

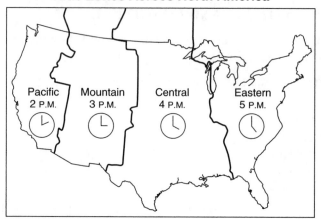

1. According to the map, what time is it in Los Angeles when it is midnight in Philadelphia?
   (1) 9:00 A.M.
   (2) 9:00 P.M.
   (3) 3:00 P.M
   (4) 3:00 A.M.
   (5) 2:00 A.M.

2. The lines marking the four time zones are irregular. All of Indiana (except a tiny section of northwest Indiana) lies in the eastern time zone. Which of the following is the most reasonable explanation for why northwest Indiana lies in a central time zone?
   (1) The people in northwest Indiana voted to be included in the central time zone.
   (2) The time zone must be evenly divided; in order to obtain an even division, part of Indiana was put in the central time zone.
   (3) Since part of Kentucky was in the central time zone, Indiana had to have its borders stay in line with the state directly to the south.
   (4) Northwest Indiana was once part of Illinois but kept the same time after becoming part of Indiana.
   (5) Northwest Indiana is connected to the Chicago area for economic and business reasons, so it makes sense to be on the same time.

Answers are on page 531.

Topography

Topographical maps can show land features anywhere in the world because in spite of regional differences, there are a few standard features that appear everywhere. Generally, geographers divide the earth into flatlands (plains) and highlands (hills, plateaus, and mountains).

Plains are typically areas with little or no land elevation and few trees. **Hills** are elevations of less than 1000 feet that have sides sloping up to flat or rounded tops. **Plateaus** rise sharply above the level of the neighboring areas and have elevations less than 500 feet and broad, flat tops. **Mountains** are elevations of over 1000 feet, usually with steep, rocky inclines on all sides and pointed or rounded tops.

Mapmakers illustrate the varying heights and shapes of landmasses by using **contour lines**, lines that connect points of the same elevation in feet or meters. The closer together the contour lines, the steeper the incline. The base line for determining the height of the highland elevations is **sea level**. The following is an example of a contour map.

Contour Map

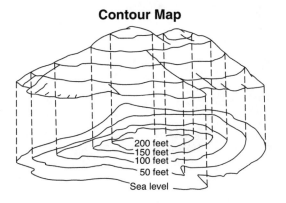

200 feet
150 feet
100 feet
50 feet
Sea level

What would this land form be classified as—a plain, a hill, a plateau, or a mountain?

Because the landmass is lower than 1000 feet and has a rounded top, it would be classified as a hill.

Contour Map

Elevation

Feet		Meters
9000		2743
5000		1524
2000		610
1000		305
500		152
< 0		< 0

Source: U.S. Geological Survey

EXERCISE 5: U.S. TOPOGRAPHY

Directions: Choose the *best* answer for the question below.

1. Based on its location, which of the following cities in the United States is at the highest altitude?
   (1) Detroit
   (2) Boston
   (3) Denver
   (4) Los Angeles
   (5) New Orleans

Answer is on page 531.

Climate

The physical features of the earth can also affect a region's climate. **Climatologists**, scientists who study weather patterns and conditions, are also geographers because of the close cause-and-effect relationship between landforms and weather patterns.

Plains regions have a uniform climate characterized by hot, dry weather during the summer and very cold temperatures during the winter. Because plains are frequently treeless, there are no barriers against the cold air that sweeps across them during the winter. Hills and plateaus generally share the same climate characteristics of the plains near which they are located. Mountains often act as boundaries between different climate regions. The lower slopes of the mountains usually share the climate of the surrounding area, but the higher elevations have colder temperatures. Also, mountains are often snowcapped because the colder air is unable to hold moisture. This moisture falls to earth as snow.

EXERCISE 6: CLIMATE

Directions: Choose the *best* answer for each question below.

1. Based on the information in the passage, what conclusion can you draw?

   During the winter it is likely to be colder in the
   - (1) mountains than the plains
   - (2) plains than the hills
   - (3) plateaus than the mountains
   - (4) hills than the mountains
   - (5) plains than the plateaus

2. According to the passage, colder air is unable to hold moisture. Based on this information, what conclusion can you draw?

   In summer,
   - (1) the mountains have less precipitation than the plains
   - (2) the mountains have more precipitation than the plains
   - (3) the mountains and plains have the same amount of precipitation
   - (4) the mountains and the hills have the same amount of precipitation
   - (5) the mountains have less precipitation than the hills

Answers are on page 531.

Population Distribution

Climate and topography are two factors that affect where people live in the world. **Population demographics** is the study of the numbers and locations of people in a region. Most of the world's population lives in the temperate zones because humans cannot survive very long in regions with extreme cold or intense heat. Also, regions with plains allow for a greater and more even distribution of population than regions that are mountainous. In mountainous regions, people tend to inhabit the land at the foot of the mountains or in the valleys.

EXERCISE 7: POPULATION DISTRIBUTION

Directions: Choose the *best* answer for each question below.

1. According to the passage, which of the following factors would *not* affect population distribution?
   - (1) high elevations
   - (2) cultivated plains
   - (3) grassy valleys
   - (4) subzero temperatures
   - (5) rapid waterways

2. Of the following states, which would most likely have the *least* even distribution of population because of its land features?

(1) the farm fields of Georgia
(2) the rolling hills of New Jersey
(3) the grassy plains of Kansas
(4) the mountains of West Virginia
(5) the small lakes of Minnesota

Answers are on page 531.

Population Growth

A serious problem facing the human race in the twenty-first century is population growth. Currently 95 million people are added to the world population every year. By the middle of the twenty-first century, the world population could exceed nine billion people! Two factors that contribute to population growth are an increase in fertility (live births) and a decline in mortality (death) rates.

Selected Country Populations (in thousands)

Country	1960	1995	2000	2010	2025	2050
France	45,684	58,104	59,061	59,944	60,393	59,883
Germany	72,673	81,594	82,688	82,483	80,877	73,303
Italy	50,200	57,204	57,194	55,828	53,237	41,197
United Kingdom	52,372	58,079	58,336	58,727	59,535	56,667
United States	180,671	267,115	277,325	298,885	332,481	349,318
Canada	17,909	29,402	30,678	33,010	36,385	42,311
Japan	94,096	125,068	126,428	127,044	121,348	104,921
Australia	10,315	17,866	18,838	20,853	23,931	25,761
Algeria	10,800	28,109	31,599	38,636	47,332	57,731
Nigeria	42,305	111,721	128,786	168,369	238,397	244,311
Pakistan	49,995	136,257	156,007	200,621	268,904	345,484
Philippines	27,561	67,839	75,037	88,813	105,194	130,893
Turkey	27,509	60,838	65,732	74,624	85,791	100,664
Haiti	3,804	7,124	7,817	9,416	12,513	15,174
Mexico	36,530	91,145	98,881	112,891	130,196	146,645

Source: *World Population: Challenges for the 21st Century* by Borwier and Bertrand

SCIENCE

What is the GED Science Test like overall?

The GED Science Test requires you to know some basic science concepts. You will not have to recall specific facts or formulas, but you will have to draw upon your prior science knowledge. You will need the skill of distinguishing a science fact, name, or term from a principle, concept, or law.

The context of the Science Test is that of daily living or workplace settings and shows you as an individual acquirer, organizer, and user of information in a lifelong process. It depicts your common roles as an adult, including that of citizen, family member, worker, or consumer. The test includes studies of relationships between science and technology, research, communications, and society. The test acknowledges local and global problems, issues, events; frequently, the test requires problem-solving skills.

You will need to comprehend (understand) what you read, apply information to a new situation, analyze relationships between ideas or concepts, and synthesize information from two or more sources. You will need to demonstrate that you have the general reading competency of a high school graduate.

What's on the test?

The GED Science Test is based on the National Science Education Standards (NSES) Scientific Understanding Strands and is divided into these content areas:

Life Science (Biology)	45%
Earth and Space Science	20%
Physical Science (Chemistry and Physics)	35%

How many and what type of questions are on the test?

There are 50 multiple-choice questions, and you will be given 80 minutes to complete the test.

Passage sets versus stand-alone questions

- Approximately 25% (12–13) of the questions are based on passage sets. This means that two or more questions are based on the same passage or the same graphic.

- Approximately 75% (37–38) of the questions will be single, stand-alone questions. This type of question could, for example, state the scientific theory and then ask a question based on using the theory in a real-life situation.

Reading text versus graphics

- Approximately 50% (25) of the questions will be based on text material.

- Approximately 50% (25) of the questions will be based on visuals—graphs, maps, charts or tables, photos, pictures, diagrams, advertisements, or political cartoons.

What else do I need to know to prepare?

A given question may draw from a number of these subjects and topics. The test acknowledges the interdisciplinary nature of science. For example, a question could involve a daily living situation of moving furniture, could use the physics principle of the lever (a simple machine), and could draw on the skill of multiplication from mathematics in order to arrive at pounds of force necessary.

You can also prepare by reviewing the health sections of newspapers and magazines or health newsletters provided by some employers. Also, you need to prepare in mathematics because the test assumes that you have proficiency through beginning algebra.

1
LIFE SCIENCE
BIOLOGY—THE STUDY OF LIVING THINGS

Biology is the scientific study of all life forms. Biologists are interested in how living things grow, how they change over time, and how they interact with one another and with their environment. Of particular interest are the characteristics that all living things have in common. All living things react to stimuli, take in food and use it to grow, eliminate wastes, and reproduce. The starting point is an examination of the basic unit of life, the cell.

The Cell, the Basic Unit of Life

The **cell** is the smallest unit of living material capable of carrying on the activities of life. Like the bricks of a building, cells are the "building blocks" of an organism. Cells were first observed in 1665 by Robert Hooke with the aid of a crudely made microscope. Cells vary widely in size and appearance. The number of cells in an organism, and not the size of cells, determines the size of an organism. The cells of a human being and a whale are of equal size. The whale is larger because its genetic pattern dictates that a larger number of cells be produced.

Types of Cells

Two kinds of cells are known to exist—**plant cells** and **animal cells**. Cells are responsible for the exchange of food and wastes within the organism. Inside of all cells are the structures that provide the specific jobs needed for these exchanges. One difference between the two is that a plant cell has a **cell wall** that protects it and an animal cell does not. Also, plant cells contain **chloroplasts**, structures active in the food-making process, while animal cells do not.

Both plant and animal cells are surrounded by a delicate boundary, the **cell membrane**. The cell membrane

- preserves the cell by acting as a barrier between it and the outside environment

- helps the cell maintain its shape

- regulates molecular traffic passing into and out of the cell

The following illustration shows the differences between the plant cell and the animal cell:

Cell Structure

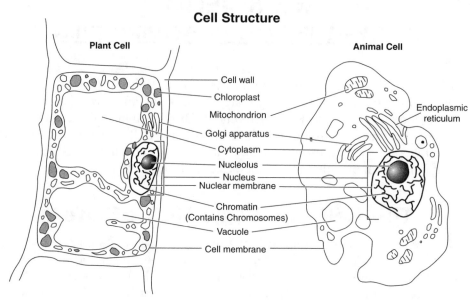

A highly specialized and complex structure, the cell has its own control center, transportation system, power plants, factories for making needed materials, and even a reproductive blueprint, or chemical recipe.

Cytoplasm: protoplasm found between the nuclear membrane and the cell membrane

Endoplasmic reticulum: a tubular transport system within the cell or to the outside

Mitochondrion: power plant inside cell which produces energy for cellular function; plural is mitochondria

Golgi apparatus: the packaging plant, which gathers proteins and carbohydrates in membraneous sacs; in gland cells it releases hormones to the rest of the body

Nucleus: the control center for the cell, surrounded by a double nuclear membrane; it contains the chromosome or genetic blueprint for the cell

Chromosome: the genetic blueprint found in the nucleus; it contains DNA that makes up the genes, which are the genetic code for the cells, organs, and structure of the body

Nucleolus: the holding tank for RNA, the essential acid for the chemical activity of the cell and the chromosome information that permits the manufacture of protein

EXERCISE 1: CELL STRUCTURE

Directions: Match each term on the right with the mechanical function it performs on the left. Write the letter of the correct term in the space provided.

1. ___c___ regulator of traffic passing into and out of the cell

   a. nucleus

2. ___A___ control center for the cell

   b. endoplasmic reticulum

3. ___B___ means of transportation for material within the cell

   c. cell membrane

4. ___d___ factory in which RNA ingredients are assembled and stored

   d. nucleolus

Answers are on page 532.

EXERCISE 2: CELLS

Directions: Choose the *best* answer for each of the following questions.

1. What is the main idea of the informational text on pages 205–206?

   (1) All living things are made of cells.
   (2) The nucleus is the control center of the cell.
   (3) There are differences between plant and animal cells.
   (4) The cell is an organized structure with subsystems.
   (5) The Golgi apparatus functions as a packaging plant in the cell.

2. In plant cells, chloroplasts are active in the chemical processes required to make food. Animal cells have no chloroplasts. On this basis, what can we conclude?

   (1) Plant cells are more complex than animal cells.
   (2) Plant cells and not animal cells generate chemical reactions.
   (3) Animal cells prey upon plant cells as a food source.
   (4) Animal cells are more complex than plant cells.
   (5) Animals must obtain food from outside sources.

3. According to the text, mitochondria are the power plants that produce energy for important life processes in the animal cell and are responsible for cellular respiration. What part of a plant cell serves a similar function?

   (1) the cell wall
   (2) the nucleus
   (3) the nucleolus
   (4) the chromosome
   (5) the chloroplast

Answers are on page 532.

Cells and Active Transport

Every cell has a membrane that selectively permits the passage of certain molecules in and out of the cell. The movement of molecules through the cell membrane without any effort on the cell's part is achieved by diffusion. **Diffusion** is the movement of molecules from an area of high concentration to an area of low concentration. Vibrating molecules are propelled away from one another after they collide. It is through this process that odors can fill a large room in a short period of time. Diffusion is important in higher organisms. In the human body, for example, oxygen moves from the air sacs in the lungs through cell membranes and into the blood through diffusion.

A cell's cytoplasm contains many substances in varying degrees of concentration. These concentrations differ sharply from those in the fluid surrounding the cell. Such differences are so essential that the cell can die if the differences are not maintained. Given the opportunity, diffusion would quickly eliminate these critical differences. Therefore, the cell must be able to negate, and sometimes even reverse, the process of diffusion. This is accomplished by active transport. During **active transport**, the cell moves materials from an area of low concentration to an area of high concentration. This work requires energy.

EXERCISE 3: CELLS AND ACTIVE TRANSPORT

Directions: In the blank spaces below, write the words that correctly complete each of the following statements.

1. Diffusion is the movement of molecules from an area of ___H___ concentration to an area of ___L___ concentration.

2. In active transport, materials are moved from an area of ___L___ concentration to an area of ___H___ concentration.

Answers are on page 532.

EXERCISE 4: DIFFUSION AND OSMOSIS

Directions: Choose the *best* answer for each of the following questions.

1. How does the process of diffusion function in the human body?
   (1) It allows for concentrations of materials, where needed in the body, through stockpiling.
   (2) It regulates blood flow between organs through veins and arteries.
   (3) It allows an even distribution of substances throughout all cells of the body.
   (4) It comes into play in times of extreme illness and stress.
   (5) It plays an insignificant role in the body's functioning.

2. **Osmosis** may be described as a process through which water in a solution is able to move through the cell membrane from a *higher* concentration to a *lower* one in order to maintain balance on either side of the membrane. If the salt solution in blood plasma surrounding red blood cells is higher than the solution inside the cells, which is most likely to occur?

(1) Water will leave the cell and pass into the blood plasma.
(2) Water will leave the blood plasma and pass into the cell.
(3) The cell will expand because of a gain in water.
(4) The cell will carry on respiration at a slower rate.
(5) Cellular division starts to try to save the cell.

Answers are on page 532.

Mitosis—Cell Division

Active cell transport requires energy. Energy is also needed for the growth of an organism. As a cell grows, its cell membrane becomes less able to provide oxygen and nutrients for the interior of the cell, and wastes become unable to leave the cell. In addition, a nucleus can control only so much cytoplasm. Therefore, when a cell reaches its limit in size, it must divide or undergo a process called mitosis.

Mitosis is the process through which cells reproduce themselves by division. In a multicellular organism mitosis leads to tissue growth and maintenance. In a single-celled organism mitosis results in two new genetically identical independent organisms. Mitosis can be divided into four stages or phases, as shown in the diagrams.

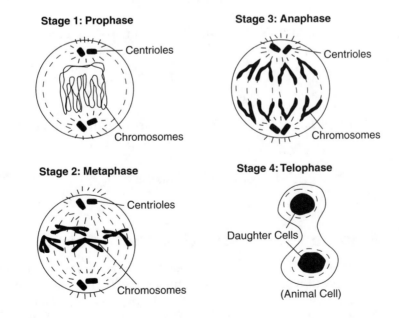

Stage 1: Prophase — Centrioles, Chromosomes

Stage 2: Metaphase — Centrioles, Chromosomes

Stage 3: Anaphase — Centrioles, Chromosomes

Stage 4: Telophase — Daughter Cells (Animal Cell)

Stage 1: Prophase: Just before prophase begins, genetic material in the nucleus is duplicated (doubled). Then the nuclear membrane and nucleolus disappear. The chromosomes (genetic material) shorten, visible centrioles appear at opposite ends of the cells, and small fibers start to form between them.

Stage 2: Metaphase: The spindle fibers attach themselves to the center of the chromosomes (centromeres). The chromosomes are now quite thick and visible. They begin to line up at the equator of the cell.

Stage 3: Anaphase: The centromeres divide, and the duplicate pairs of chromosomes separate. The separate pairs then move toward the poles of the cell.

Stage 4: Telophase: The nuclei re-form, the chromosomes gradually become less visible, and the cell separates to form two new cells. The daughter cells are genetically and physically identical to the parent cell except for size.

In single-cell organisms cell division results in the creation of two new individuals. In complex organisms (made of more than one cell) the new daughter cells form a subsystem of the parent cell. In many organisms, cell reproduction is at its peak while the organism grows. As the organism ages, the process is limited to the replacement of old and damaged cells.

EXERCISE 5: MITOSIS

Directions: Match each phase of mitosis on the left with its description on the right.

1. _____ Prophase

    a. The chromosomes become easily visible.

2. _____ Metaphase

    b. The chromosomal material lines up at the center of the cell.

3. _____ Anaphase

    c. The cell divides to form two new cells.

4. _____ Telophase

    d. The pairs of chromosomes move to opposite poles.

Answers are on page 532.

Meiosis—Reproductive Cell Division

A special type of cell division for reproductive purposes is called meiosis. **Meiosis** is a process in which a parent cell undergoes two special types of cell division that result in the production of four **gametes** (reproductive cells). Each gamete has half the number of chromosomes of the original parent cell. Each organism has a chromosome number that is characteristic of that organism. For example, all of the cells in the human body contain 46 chromosomes except for the gametes (the reproductive cells). The reproductive cells (sperm and egg) cannot carry the same number of chromosomes as those of other parts of the body. If they did, the offspring that would result from the union of the egg and sperm would have twice the normal amount of genetic material after cell division. In animals this doubling would result in the termination of the embryo early in development. To prevent termination, the sex cells undergo meiosis.

The following illustrations show the two stages of meiosis.

Meiosis I

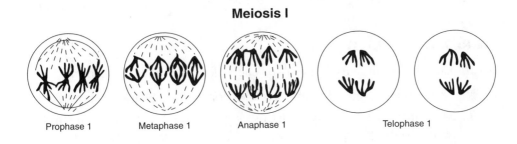

Prophase 1   Metaphase 1   Anaphase 1   Telophase 1

The chromosome pairs come together to exchange genes. This process is called **crossing over**. Crossing over ensures a recombination of genetic material. Later the pairs separate, and one chromosome of each pair moves to a new cell. During telophase 1, the cytoplasm divides, and two daughter cells are formed. Each daughter cell is called a **haploid** cell, a cell that contains half the number of chromosomes of the original parent cell.

Meiosis II

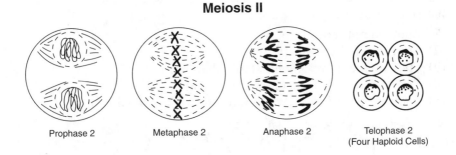

Prophase 2   Metaphase 2   Anaphase 2   Telophase 2 (Four Haploid Cells)

(Note: Only one daughter cell from Meiosis I is shown here.)

In Meiosis II the chromosomal material combines, separates, and moves to new cells, resulting in four reproductive cells. In human beings, when two haploid cells (a sperm and an egg, each containing 23 chromosomes) unite in fertilization, they form a **diploid** cell, a cell containing 46 chromosomes. The fertilized cell contains 46 chromosomes, or 23 pairs—half from the mother and half from the father.

EXERCISE 6: MEIOSIS

Directions: Number the steps in meiosis in the order in which they occur.

_____ Two new cells divide, resulting in four reproductive cells.

_____ Chromosomes come together in pairs.

_____ Chromosome pairs separate, and each chromosome moves to a new cell.

_____ Chromosomes exchange genes.

Answers are on page 532.

EXERCISE 7: CELL DIVISION

Directions: Choose the *best* answer for each of the following questions.

1. Which method of reproduction provides for the most variety in offspring?
   (1) asexual (nonsexual) reproduction: genetic information from a single parent to offspring
   (2) mutative reproduction: occasional mutation of a cell changing the organism's appearance
   (3) sexual reproduction: exchange of genetic information from two parents
   (4) cloning: duplication of genetic information of a single organism
   (5) cellular reproduction: cell division into two cells

2. Cancer is a condition in which cells that serve no function in the body invade healthy ones. On this basis, what can we conclude about malignant cancer cells?
   (1) They do not reproduce by mitosis.
   (2) They divide by meiosis.
   (3) They divide more unpredictably than normal cells.
   (4) They divide less frequently than benign cells.
   (5) They are parasites and do not reproduce by division at all.

Answers are on page 532.

Genetics and Heredity

Heredity is the term used to describe the passing of traits from parents to children. Every species has its own set of traits that it transmits to its offspring. **Genetics** is the study of how traits are passed on. **Geneticists**, the scientists who study heredity, have found that hereditary information of an organism is carried by the chromosomes of the cell nucleus.

Genes determine all of our inherited traits. Every human being receives two genes for each trait—one from the mother and one from the father. Genes may be **dominant** or **recessive**. The dominant gene, if present, will always appear in an offspring. For example, because brown eye color is a dominant trait, 90 percent of human beings have brown eyes. If two dominant genes are inherited, the resulting trait will be a combination of the two inherited characteristics.

Sexual reproduction ensures that the offspring has genetic material from both parents. This genetic material is thoroughly remixed with every fertilization so that, with the exception of identical twins, no two offspring of the same parents are exactly alike genetically.

Sex and Mutations

Whether a mother gives birth to a boy or girl is determined by the X and Y chromosomes. A person receives two sex chromosomes—one from the father's **sperm cell** and one from the mother's **egg cell**. Egg cells contain a single X chromosome. Male sperm cells may contain either an X or a Y chromosome. If two X chromosomes unite, a female will be created. If the sperm reaching the egg has a Y chromosome, a male will be produced. The sperm cells, then, carry the chromosome that determines the **sex (gender)** of offspring.

Sometimes a mistake occurs in the genetic makeup of a chromosome during cell duplication. This change in the genes, called a **mutation**, may be passed on to offspring. Two mutations in humans are **Down's Syndrome**, which results in brain damage, and **muscular dystrophy**, a disease that causes muscles to waste away.

Cloning

Until the mid-1990s, reproduction involved the contribution of genetic material from two parent organisms. In 1996 in Scotland, a sheep named Dolly was created by a process that is called **cloning**. The egg cell (whose nucleus had been removed) from an adult sheep was "fertilized" with the nucleus of a mature female mammary cell. The developing embryo had the full genetic information from a single adult and was considered a clone of the adult from which the mammary nucleus had come.

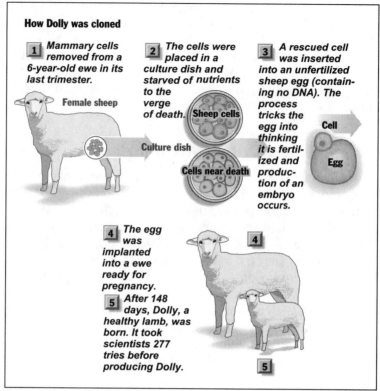

How Dolly was cloned

1 *Mammary cells removed from a 6-year-old ewe in its last trimester.*

Female sheep

Culture dish

2 *The cells were placed in a culture dish and starved of nutrients to the verge of death.*

Sheep cells

Cells near death

3 *A rescued cell was inserted into an unfertilized sheep egg (containing no DNA). The process tricks the egg into thinking it is fertilized and production of an embryo occurs.*

Cell

Egg

4 *The egg was implanted into a ewe ready for pregnancy.*

5 *After 148 days, Dolly, a healthy lamb, was born. It took scientists 277 tries before producing Dolly.*

Source: *Chicago Tribune*, February 8, 1998

EXERCISE 8: CLONING

Directions: Mark the following statements about cloning as being true (**T**) or false (**F**).

1. _____ Scientists are working on ways to clone a deceased child.

2. _____ A clone has two parents but looks like only one of them.

3. _____ The first sheep to be cloned was created in the United States.

4. _____ A cloned organism still must go through the development of an embryo.

5. _____ The egg cell that is used for a clone must have the original nucleus removed.

Answers are on page 532.

Organ Systems

The human body is made up of several **organ systems** that specialize in functions that are necessary for an organism to thrive. The nervous system is made up of the brain, the spinal cord, and nerve cells. The circulatory system is in charge of circulating the blood from the heart through a series of arteries, veins, and capillaries (small connecting vessels).

The circulatory system works very closely with the respiratory system, using blood cells to exchange oxygen and carbon dioxide through the lungs. Nutrients are distributed and wastes are removed from the human body by the digestive and excretory systems. All of these systems are able to maintain their form and position in the human body because of the skeletal and muscular systems.

EXERCISE 9: ORGAN SYSTEMS

Directions: Match each health concern on the left with the correct system on the right.

1. _____ ulcer   **a.** nervous system

2. _____ cough   **b.** circulatory system

3. _____ broken arm   **c.** muscular system

4. _____ heart attack   **d.** digestive system

5. _____ migraine headache   **e.** respiratory system

6. _____ muscle cramp   **f.** skeletal system

Answers are on page 532.

The Nervous System

The **nervous system** is the means of communication of the body and contains the brain, the spinal cord, and specialized neurons. The brain is divided into two hemispheres, each of which is responsible for different but overlapping functions. If a portion of the brain is injured in an accident, another region can often be trained to compensate for the nonfunctioning area.

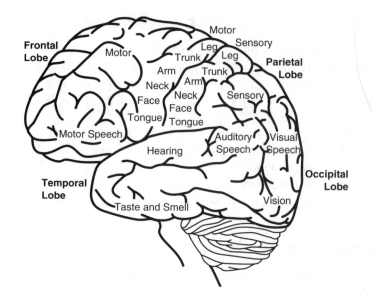

Speech, Sight, and Visual Memory

People who have had strokes or severe concussions may lose the ability to use the speech center in the brain located in the area called the **temporal lobe**, found near the temples. Another lobe is called the **occipital**. This lobe is located in the back of the brain and is in charge of sight. The **optic nerve** in the eye connects to the occipital lobe of the brain, where images projected on the **retina** are recorded and evaluated. This part of the brain also is in charge of visual memory.

Voluntary and Involuntary Functions

The brain has both voluntary and involuntary levels of function. The portion of the brain that controls voluntary functions is referred to as the **cerebrum**. It controls all motor coordination and intrepetation of sensory information from inside and outside the body.

The **cerebellum** is the large part of the brain that coordinates the actual movements of the muscles. The cerebellum is in charge of involuntary muscle action including coordinating sports movements, personality, and decision making. If the cerebellum is injured, the personality of the victim may be dramatically altered. Passive or shy people have been known to become very hostile and verbal, while people with outgoing personalities have become withdrawn and introverted.

Another subconcious portion of the brain is the **medulla oblongata**, located in the back of the brain. It governs involuntary body functions like breathing and digestion. The neurons are located everywhere throughout the body and are responsible for taking messages to and from the brain to the organs and the muscles. The motion of your diaphragm, which draws in air, and the **peristalsis** or movement of food through the digestive tract are both examples of medulla regulation.

Spinal Cord and Message Transport

The **spinal cord** is the long system of nerves that travels down the spine from the brain. At times the spinal cord acts as a body defense system that prevents injury by immediately acting on an emergency nerve-cell message. This immediate response, called a **reflex**, is used when the message going to the brain and out to the trauma area would take too long (such as touching a hot material or blinking).

In the case of spinal injury, the messages relayed from the brain might not be able to travel the spinal cord to the muscle site. This injury is referred to as **paralysis**. The muscles do not act if they cannot receive the message from the brain. As a person ages, the bones lose strength. In the case of the spinal column, the individual vertebrae may move and pinch the spinal cord. This action can be very painful and may cause temporary paralysis. Doctors may advise surgery for the patient to fuse vertebrae together to prevent slippage.

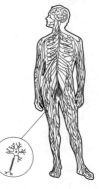

EXERCISE 10: THE NERVOUS SYSTEM

Directions: Answer the following questions based on what you have learned about the nervous system.

1. Which region of the brain would be in control of the following activities in the human body?

   a. _____ muscle coordination and skill in playing sports

   b. _____ a reflex to put hands up to block an object from hitting the face

   c. _____ automatic increased heart rate while doing exercises

   d. _____ thinking of what tasks need to be done at work

2. Identify the following statements as true (**T**) or false (**F**).

   _____ The cerebrum controls reflex response.

   _____ Photographic memory relies on memory in the occipital lobe.

   _____ Voluntary functions such as walking are controlled by the cerebrum.

   _____ There are four hemispheres in the brain.

Answers are on page 532.

The Circulatory and Respiratory Systems

The **circulatory system** transports nutrients to the cells and removes the cell's waste through a system of vessels called arteries, veins, and capillaries. These vessels provide the pathway for the carriers of the nutrients and waste: the blood cells. When the blood cells are pumped out of the heart through **arteries**, they are rich with oxygen, having just returned from the lungs. These blood cells are squeezed tightly in single file through the **capillaries** where the actual exchange of gases into and out of the cells occurs. The route back to the heart takes the blood cells by way of the **veins**.

When in the heart, the blood receives an extra push to get it to the lungs, where it releases the carbon dioxide from the cell and receives new oxygen. The heart is the main pump for this flow of cells. There are four chambers in the heart with two smaller chambers to receive blood (the **atria**) and two lower chambers (the **ventricles**) to send the blood to the next location. The heart has a complex series of valves at the opening of each chamber in the heart. These valves are one-way doors to prevent blood from flowing backwards into the previous chamber. The heart itself has many small capillaries that feed its own muscular walls.

The **respiratory system** involves the exchange of the outgoing carbon dioxide from the cells with the incoming air. This exchange takes place in the lungs, which are able to exchange gases through small spongelike sacs called **alveoli**. Carbon dioxide and oxygen diffuse in and out of the cells to the alveoli and are transported inside and outside the body through the branchlike system of **bronchiole**. The bronchiole connect to the **trachea** or wind pipe and release breath through the mouth and nose.

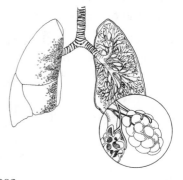

EXERCISE 11: THE CIRCULATORY AND RESPIRATORY SYSTEMS

Directions: For each of the following questions, choose the *best* answer based on the information above.

1. Which part of the respiratory system is responsible for the actual exchange of oxygen and carbon dioxide?
   - **(1)** the trachea
   - **(2)** the alveoli
   - **(3)** the windpipe
   - **(4)** the lungs
   - **(5)** the bronchiole

2. Which of the following are parts of the heart (**H**) and which are vessels (**V**)?

_____ atria

_____ capillaries

_____ veins

_____ ventricles

_____ arteries

Answers are on page 532.

The Digestive and Excretory Systems

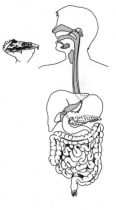

Digestion is the breakdown of food into simple molecules so it can be absorbed into the cells. Digestion begins when food enters the mouth, and chewing mixed with saliva starts the breakdown. The stomach continues the chemical breakdown using gastric acids. The food then travels to the **small intestine**, which is in charge of absorbing the digested nutrients. The **pancreas**, the **gall bladder**, and the **liver** each focus its digestive enzyme on specific food chemicals. The small intestine connects the stomach to the **large intestine** (the **colon**) which absorbs water remaining in the digested food. It also stores the waste material until it is expelled from the body.

The digestive system uses **enzymes** which are chemically very acidic. These acids are produced when a stimulus (such as food) is present or can be produced in response to stress (and may have a digestive effect on the stomach's protective mucous lining). The area damaged by the acids is called an **ulcer**, with several common regions in the digestive tract susceptible to this condition, including the sensitive connection from the stomach to the **esophagus** (the tube from the mouth to the stomach). A person with this condition is said to be suffering from **acid reflux**.

EXERCISE 12: THE DIGESTIVE AND EXCRETORY SYSTEMS

Directions: Match the definitions on the left with the terms on the right.

1. _____ chemicals used to digest   **a.** large intestine

2. _____ tube from mouth to stomach   **b.** enzymes

3. _____ portion of digestive path   **c.** ulcer

4. _____ also known as the colon   **d.** esophagus

5. _____ damaged section of stomach lining   **e.** small intestine

Answers are on page 533.

The Skeletal and Muscular Systems

The human body depends on the **skeletal** and **muscular** 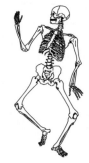 **systems** for motion and protection. The human skeleton contains 206 bones, made mostly of the minerals calcium and phosphorus. The inner section of a bone has soft tissue called **marrow**, where blood cells are created. Bones are connected at places called **joints**. Some joints, such as the plates of the skull, are fixed. Some, such as the vertebrae, are slightly movable, and some are quite movable such as the elbow or the shoulder. **Ligaments** are attached to bones and help hold them together. If the bones lose density, they become brittle and break easily. This is called **osteoporosis**.

The muscular system includes three types of muscles—skeletal, smooth, and cardiac muscles—which allow the skeleton of the human body to move and support itself. **Skeletal muscles** are responsible for voluntary movement. **Smooth muscles** are found in the organs. Their contractions move food along the digestive tract and help blood move through the vessels. The **cardiac muscles** are found only in the heart; when they contract, the heart is "beating," the rhythm that pumps blood through the heart to the lungs and then out through the body.

EXERCISE 13: THE SKELETAL AND MUSCULAR SYSTEMS

Directions: Based on the reading, fill in the blanks below.

1. There are three types of muscles: _____,
   _____ and _____.

2. The medical condition for having very brittle bones is called

   _____.

3. Blood cells are actually created in the _____ of the
   long bones.

4. The complete adult human body has _____ bones that
   make up the skeleton.

5. _____ are attached to bones to help hold them together.

Answers are on page 533.

Growth, Energy, and Living Things

Some of the characteristics that distinguish living things from nonliving things are the capacities for growth, food consumption, and release of energy for cellular work. Important biological processes involved in these functions for plants are the **nitrogen cycle, photosynthesis**, and **cellular respiration**.

The Nitrogen Cycle

Nitrogen, which makes up nearly 80 percent of Earth's atmosphere, is an essential ingredient for living tissues. Human beings and other animals depend on plants as a source of nitrogen. Plants cannot manufacture nitrogen themselves, so to obtain it they must depend on other organisms. Free nitrogen, however, cannot be used by organisms, so it must combine with other elements to form nitrates that can be used. Plants absorb these **nitrates** to manufacture **amino acids**, which are essential components of protein needed by living cells. Amino acids are used to manufacture both proteins and nucleic acids that are absorbed by human beings and other animals.

The conversion of free nitrogen into a combined form is called **nitrogen fixing**. This is best achieved by certain bacteria—microorganisms and decomposers—that live in the soil. These microorganisms live in special sacs, called **nodules**, on the roots of legumes—plants such as alfalfa, peas, and beans. The microorganisms produce **nitrogenase**, an enzyme that is essential to nitrogen fixing. Scientists believe that all of the nitrogen in Earth's atmosphere has been fixed and liberated many times. At any one time probably only a few pounds of nitrogenase exist on our planet. This small amount, however, is enough to sustain all life on Earth.

EXERCISE 14: THE NITROGEN CYCLE

Directions: Choose the *best* answer for each of the following questions.

1. Symbiosis describes the relationship between two organisms that are different but that live together for their mutual benefit. The microorganisms that live in the nodules attached to legumes may be described as symbiotic. What would be another example of a symbiotic relationship?

   (1) bacteria that can live only in the stomachs of hoofed animals and that help the animals digest food
   (2) bees that make their hives in caves, thereby providing a ready source of food for bears
   (3) soldier ants that live and work together in colonies
   (4) tapeworms that live in the intestines of human beings
   (5) scavengers such as vultures that feed on the carcasses of dead animals

2. Which of the following farming procedures best illustrates the process of increasing soil nutrients by assisting in nitrogen fixing?

   (1) rotating a crop of cotton one year with a crop of beets
   (2) irrigating the land with more modern methods
   (3) using more advanced equipment to plow the land
   (4) rotating planting in alternating years with crops of soybeans or peas
   (5) using airplanes to spray the crops with insecticides

Answers are on page 533.

Photosynthesis

Plants provide the oxygen we need to breathe and the nutrients we need to thrive. Green plants are self-sufficient because they are able to make their own food, whereas human beings and lower animals must obtain their food to live. **Photosynthesis** is the food-making process by which green plants convert the light from the sun into usable chemical energy. The process of photosynthesis involves several steps.

The first step is the capture of energy by the plant. In most plants the process of photosynthesis takes place within the **chloroplasts**, where chlorophyll molecules absorb light. **Chlorophyll** is the substance that gives plants their green color. Using the energy that chlorophyll releases from sunlight, the plant splits water into its two components—oxygen and hydrogen. The oxygen is released to the atmosphere, and the hydrogen recombines with carbon dioxide to produce carbohydrate molecules (a form of starch) in the plant.

Two other chemicals inside the leaves do the same job as chlorophyll. **Xanthophyll** and **carotene** appear as yellow- and orange-colored pigments that are masked during the summer by the chlorophyll. Eventually the shorter daylight hours of fall cause the plant to stop the production of chorophyll, allowing us to see the other pigments.

The food that is created by photosynthesis is transported through the plant by the **phloem**. This cellular transport system carries the newly created food down the stem of the plant to the storage center called the **root**. Water is transported by a similar system called the **xylem**. This cellular system allows the roots to take in water from the soil and transport it up to the leaves through the stem for the process of photosynthesis.

EXERCISE 15: PHOTOSYNTHESIS

Directions: Choose the *best* answer for each of the following questions.

1. Indicate whether the following statements are true (**T**) or false (**F**) about plants and the process of photosynthesis.

    _____   Plants that do not possess chlorophyll must use a process other than photosynthesis to produce the energy they need.

    _____   Photosynthesis is used by flowering plants to make energy by converting the sun's energy.

    _____   Plants that do not use the process of photosynthesis must obtain food from another source.

    Question 2 is based on the information in the following passage.

    The leaves of certain plants have some areas that lack chlorophyll and some areas containing chlorophyll. A coleus plant, with its brightly colored leaves, is one example. In an experiment in which the pigment (color) of the coleus leaf is removed, an iodine solution will identify places where starch is present by turning that part of the leaf brown.

2. Which of the following would you predict will happen to a coleus leaf in such an experiment?
    (1) The areas that were green originally would turn brown.
    (2) The leaf would not turn brown at all.
    (3) The leaf would turn yellow and red.
    (4) The entire leaf would turn brown.
    (5) Only half the leaf would turn brown.

Answers are on page 533.

Cellular Respiration

Cellular respiration is the complex series of chemical reactions through which a cell releases the energy trapped inside glucose molecules. **Glucose**, a form of sugar, is the end product of the process of photosynthesis. The process of cellular respiration, then, is the reverse of photosynthesis. During cellular respiration, cells (plant or animal) break down the glucose so that energy is released for cellular work. Because it cannot float freely in the cell, the energy is repackaged and stored. Cellular respiration occurs in three stages, beginning with the breakdown of a molecule of glucose and ending with the energy needed for the cell to perform its work. Energy that is not used is released in the form of heat.

EXERCISE 16: CELLULAR RESPIRATION

Directions: Choose the *best* answer for each of the following questions.

1. From the information about cellular respiration, what can we infer?

   (1) Photosynthesis in plants must always precede cellular respiration.
   (2) No relationship exists between photosynthesis and cellular respiration.
   (3) Photosynthesis and respiration share many processes.
   (4) Cellular respiration occurs only in animal cells.
   (5) Plants do not perform cellular work.

2. The rate of cellular respiration in humans can be measured by the amount of carbon dioxide exhaled. Which of the following would you expect to be true about the rate of cellular respiration for a group of students who are the same age, height, and weight?

   (1) Africans would have a higher rate of cellular respiration than Asians.
   (2) Boys would have a higher rate of cellular respiration than girls.
   (3) Girls would have higher rates of cellular respiration than boys.
   (4) Physically active people would have higher rates of cellular respiration than nonphysically active people.
   (5) Nonathletes would have higher rates of cellular respiration than athletes.

3. Gas exchange that occurs in the large forested areas on our planet helps keep the balance with all the carbon dioxide produced in human processes. In some areas large tracts of forests are being cut down by the logging industry. These areas are necessary to maintain the balance between the carbon dioxide and oxygen cycles. Which of the following suggestions would contribute most to maintaining these large forests?

   (1) Pump out large amounts of oxygen to make up for the missing gas.
   (2) Have loggers replace the quantity of trees logged with new trees.
   (3) Make machines that would absorb the extra carbon dioxide.
   (4) Stop all logging all over the planet and stop using wood products.
   (5) Remove residents from populated areas and start new forests.

Answers are on page 533.

Classification of Organisms

We relate and group organisms by similarities with a classification system which moves from the general to the specific. Each downward step in the classification system provides more details about the organism that is classified. The **kingdom** is the broadest grouping. Within each kingdom the organisms with the greatest similarities are grouped further into a **phylum**, followed by a **class**. The class is followed by an **order**, a **family**, a **genus**, and a **species**. The human classification (Homo sapiens) is illustrated in the following chart.

Taxonomy of Human Classification

Category	Taxon	Characteristics
Kingdom	Animalia	Is multicellular, cannot make its own food, is able to move
Phylum	Chordata	Has a notochord (skeletal rod) and hollow nerve cord
Class	Mammalia	Has hair or fur, female secretes milk to nourish young
Order	Primate	Has flattened fingers for grasping, keen vision, poor sense of smell
Family	Hominidae	Walks on two feet, has flat face, eyes facing forward, color vision
Genus	Homo	Has long childhood, large brain, speech ability
Species	Sapiens	Has reduced body hair, high forehead, prominent chin

EXERCISE 17: CLASSIFICATION OF ORGANISMS

Directions: Read the definitions of the five kingdoms, from lowest to highest, into which all living organisms are classified. Then choose the *best* answer for each of the questions that follow.

Kingdoms of Living Organisms

Monera: simple one-celled, mobile organisms lacking organelles, some of which can produce their own food (Example: bacteria)

Protista: single-celled, mobile organisms having a more complex cell structure than monera (Example: paramecia)

Fungi: multicellular, lacks chlorophyll, cannot move, obtains food from other organisms (Example: mushroom)

Plantae: multicellular, has chlorophyll, produces its own food, has no mobility (Example: moss)

Animalia: multicellular, capable of moving and obtaining its own food (Example: bird)

1. Streptococcus is a single-celled organism that has no organelles and that occurs in a sequence of chains. It causes strep throat when it invades that area. In which kingdom would it be classified?
   (1) Monera
   (2) Protista
   (3) Fungi
   (4) Plantae
   (5) Animalia

2. Mold is a parasite that grows on bread, cheese, or other foods. It lacks chlorophyll and obtains nutrients from the host. In which kingdom would it be classified?

(1) Monera
(2) Protista
(3) Fungi
(4) Plantae
(5) Animalia

Answers are on page 533.

Evolution and Natural Selection

Organisms are assigned classifications, but very often their characteristics are altered over generations. Organisms that go through such change are said to evolve. One explanation for these changes that has scientific support is the **theory of evolution**. Proposed in 1859 by **Charles Darwin** in his book *On the Origin of Species,* the theory holds that all forms of life developed gradually (over 600 million years) from different and often much simpler ancestors. With weaker or less adaptable strains dying out, these forms of life adapted over the years to meet the demands of their environment. Thus, all lines of descent can be traced back to a common ancestral organism.

As offspring differed from their parents, generations with characteristics that were less and less alike resulted. Ultimately, new species were formed from the diverse offspring because these new characteristics were inheritable. The new characteristics of the offspring are explained by a process called natural selection. According to the theory of **natural selection**, the species that are best adapted to their living conditions survive, and those that do not adapt die out. This theory is also known as the "survival of the fittest." The **creationist theory** holds that all species have been created and remained unchanged since the beginning of time. In the Galapagos Islands Darwin studied populations of finches, and several groups of birds showed specific beak adaptations that allowed them to live together without competing for food. Darwin demonstrated that evolution is an ongoing process whose final outcome has not yet been determined.

EXERCISE 18: EVOLUTION AND NATURAL SELECTION

Directions: Choose the *best* answer for each question below.

1. An unusual member of the animal kingdom is the duckbill platypus—an animal that has many characteristics of birds, mammals, and reptiles. The animal, found in Australia and Tasmania, has a ducklike bill, has webbed and clawed feet, is covered with thick fur, and reproduces by laying eggs. Which of the following hypotheses related to Darwin's theory of evolution could be applied to the platypus?

(1) The platypus is the result of the interbreeding of three distinct animal classes.
(2) The platypus is the earliest living member of the mammalian family.
(3) The platypus developed independently in a closed environment during the early history of mammals.
(4) The platypus was not subject to the influences described in Darwin's theory.
(5) Mammal life originated in Australia and Tasmania hundreds of millions of years ago.

Question 2 refers to the following passage.

Mammals are classified in two groups—**placental** (having a placenta that nourishes the fetus) and **marsupial** (having a pouch in which the young are nourished and carried). Most of the world's marsupials are found on the continent of Australia and the islands nearby, where few placental mammals lived during the early history of the continents.

2. What can we infer based on the preceding information about how marsupials differ from placental mammals?

(1) Marsupials are less biologically advanced than placental mammals.
(2) Placental mammals are more primitive than marsupials.
(3) Marsupials cannot survive in areas other than Australia and North America.
(4) Marsupials are the oldest forms of life on Earth.
(5) Marsupials descended from the reptiles.

3. Which of the following mammals does *not* exhibit a physical adaptation to environmental conditions?

(1) a bird's migration south
(2) an eagle's keen eyesight
(3) a mouse's sensitive ears
(4) a seal's flippers
(5) a bear's dense fur

Answers are on page 533.

Ecology and Ecosystems

The science of **ecology** involves the interrelationship of a living organism with its nonliving environment. Ecology is the study of how we live on the planet Earth. The ecologist studies the relationships among the component organisms and their environments. A self-supporting environment is called an **ecosystem**. The photosynthetic producers, the consumers, the decomposers, and their environment constitute an ecosystem.

In a typical ecosystem the **primary producers** are the green plants that derive their energy from the sun. A **primary consumer** is a rabbit that feeds on the leaves of the green plant. A **secondary consumer** is a fox that preys on the rabbit. A **tertiary**, or **third-level**, **consumer** is the buzzard that feeds on the carcass that the fox leaves behind. Finally, **decomposers**—the bacteria and fungi that feed on the scraps left by the buzzard—provide the nitrates necessary for the green plants.

Environmentalists study the natural cycles and begin to understand the impact of human intervention. Yellowstone (the first U.S. National Park), located in the northwest corner of Wyoming, was once the home to the gray wolf, but the wolf was a threat to herds of deer and cattle. Ranchers eliminated the wolves. The increased numbers of grazing animals ate all the food and starved or died of diseases. The government has stepped in and started a reintroduction program for the gray wolf and has guaranteed financial reimbursement for any animals killed by wolves. The ecological balance of a community is delicate. The removal of one key element can destroy a system, sometimes permanently.

EXERCISE 19: ECOLOGY AND ECOSYSTEMS

Directions: The following passage describes an imbalance in a particular ecosystem. Read the passage and fill in the blanks below with the correct element in the ecosystem.

At the turn of the century, ranchers moved onto the grassy Kaibab Plateau in northern Arizona. They were attracted by the fine grazing areas and large numbers of deer for hunting. Fearing that the mountain lion, another inhabitant of the region, would prey on the cattle and deer, the ranchers waged a campaign to eliminate the cat from the plateau. They were successful in their effort, and mountain lions disappeared within a few years.

Their success produced terrible ecological results, however. Increased numbers of deer, along with herds of grazing cattle, stripped the land of all grasses. Soon, heavy rains caused major erosion, and the land was reduced to a fraction of its usefulness. This problem has occurred repeatedly where humans have changed an ecosystem without considering the possible consequences.

1. primary producer _____

2. primary consumers_____ and _____

3. tertiary consumer _____

4. The destruction of the_____ led to the increase of grazing by

_____ and_____ , which led to_____

of the land and its eventual _____ by heavy rains.

Answers are on page 533.

2
EARTH AND SPACE SCIENCE

Earth science is the study of the planet Earth—its origin and the forces at work that are constantly changing the surface of the planet. Earth science differs from the life sciences in that it focuses on nonliving rather than living things. Earth science is a very broad field that covers the subjects of astronomy, geology, meteorology, paleontology, and oceanography.

Astronomy: The Study of Space

One of the oldest fields of study in science deals with how Earth was created and how this planet fits into the design of the universe. **Astronomy** is the study of the size, movements, and composition of the planets, stars, and other deep-space objects. By observing the stars, planets, comets, and other objects in space, astronomers hope to understand how our planet was created and how it evolved. A number of important theories have been advanced to explain the beginning of Earth and the universe in which it lies.

The Beginning of the Universe

According to the leading theory, the **big bang theory**, "a cosmic egg," made up of dust and gas containing all the matter in the universe, exploded. This explosion occurred 15 to 20 billion years ago, creating the basic atoms of our lightest gases from which the stars formed. The big bang theory accounts for the measured expansion of the universe and the background radiation found in all directions in outer space. Scientists theorize, according to the **open universe theory**, that the universe will either continue the expansion indefinitely or begin a collapse. If enough mass can be identified in the universe, calculations show that the universe will gravitationally collapse at some point in the distant future; this is referred to as the **closed universe theory**. This collapse, also referred to as the "big crunch," predicts that the total mass of the universe is large enough to gather up all matter into a concentrated central point.

The most distant (but unknown) objects detected by science are known as **quasars** (quasi-stellar radio sources). The light and energy that has arrived from these objects is about 16 billion years old. It is likely that the energy that we receive now came from these objects during their formation. Every time science investigates deep-space objects, scientists must remember that information we receive now took time to get to Earth. Even the light from the Sun takes eight minutes to reach Earth. The nearest star to the Sun is Alpha Centauri, which is more than four light years away.

Stars and Galaxies

The big bang theory also explains how stars are formed. According to supporters of the theory, the energy from the bang was so powerful that matter lighter than air remained suspended in space. Eventually, the force of gravity exerted itself, and the matter was drawn, along with helium and hydrogen gases, into dark, cloudlike formations called **nebulae**. The gaseous matter became compressed, and the colliding of the compressed particles produced heat. A star developed when the temperature reached 15 million degrees centigrade—the temperature at which the nuclear reaction called **fusion** begins.

The lifetime of a star ranges from a few hundred thousand years to billions of years. Most stars eventually use up their supply of hydrogen, which ends the fusion reaction and leaves only gravity. The compaction without the energy source at the center forces the outer layers to swell as they become cooler. This is said to be the **red giant stage**, which marks the beginning of the death of a star. The outer layers are cast off in a process called a **nova** (with the explosive release of these outer layers called a **supernova**).

The explosion results in clouds of dust and gas, referred to as a **nebula**, with the star's core being left after the release of the outer layers. The core collapses under remaining gravity into a **dwarf star**. If the collapse is more significant (from a more massive star), a very dense star called a **neutron star** will be created. These stars spin at a very fast rate and are nicknamed **pulsars** as a result of energy released from their poles as they spin. The most massive stars, which are said to be **black holes**—remains of the giant stars that have gravitational fields so strong that not even light escapes from them—contract indefinitely.

Stars exist within a very large formation called a **galaxy**. Hundreds of millions of galaxies are believed to exist in the universe. The universe is a very organized system of grouped objects separated by great expanses of space. Our galaxy, **the Milky Way**, is a spiral galaxy. The other galaxy shapes include barred spirals, ellipticals, and irregulars. The Milky Way is composed of at least 100 billion stars and enough matter, in the form of dust and gas, to create millions of additional suns. The following illustration shows the heart of the Milky Way galaxy.

The Milky Way Galaxy

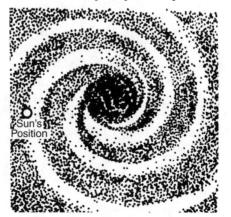

Sun's Position

EXERCISE 1: STARS AND GALAXIES

Directions: Answer the following questions based on the information in the previous passages.

1. Number the steps in star formation in the correct sequence.

_____ Heat is produced by the colliding of molecules.

_____ Fifteen million degrees centigrade is reached, and visible light is emitted.

_____ Dust and gas move throughout the universe.

_____ Gas and dust become compressed because of gravitational forces.

2. Identify the following statements as either true (**T**) or false (**F**).

_____ The most massive stars become pulsars.

_____ The first visible sign of a star's death is a red giant.

_____ An open universe would expand until gravity stops it.

_____ The light from all stars takes eight minutes to reach Earth.

Answers are on page 533.

The Sun and the Solar System

The Sun is the star at the center of our **solar system** but of "average" mass and age. The Sun is 4 to 5 billion years old and 860,000 miles in diameter (about 100 times Earth's diameter). Other members of the solar system include the nine **planets**, seven of which have one or more **satellites** (moons), 1,600 large **asteroids**, and an ever increasing number of identified **comets**.

The following illustration shows our solar system.

Our Solar System

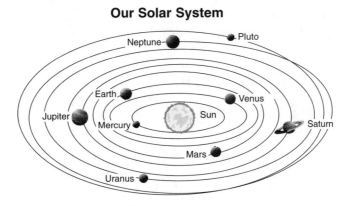

The inner planets (**Mercury, Venus, Earth**, and **Mars**) are small, with high densities and few satellites. Venus, once nicknamed our twin or sister planet, has been found to be a remarkably hostile world. Russians sent probes called *venera* to the surface, and they were able to send photographs of the surface and climate readings. The surface is dry, and it is far too hot for water to exist. Moisture that does occur in the heavy cloud cover is sulfuric acid. The cloud cover is also mainly carbon dioxide, the greenhouse gas. The runaway greenhouse effect on the surface makes the temperature hot enough to melt metal on the surface. The atmosphere is so dense that it makes the atmospheric pressure one hundred times greater than it is on Earth.

Mars is more likely to be a place that people may explore. Early probes have determined that there is water in a permafrost form under the Martian soil. Early views of Mars led people to believe that Mars had civilization that had created water canals or an irrigation system. Closer views have revealed that the surface has evidence of stream beds that contained water when the planet was warmer. U.S. probes have sent back photos and information about the surface features and climate conditions.

Two distinct landform features include *Mons Olympus* (the highest mountain in the solar system at three times the height of Mt. Everest) and *Vallis Marineris* (a canyon that would stretch from New York to Los Angeles). Colonization of Mars would depend on our ability to **terreform** the surface of the planet. Terreforming is climatic changing of a planet to fit the needs of the life forms creating the change.

The outer planets (**Jupiter**, **Saturn**, **Uranus**, and **Neptune**) are large gas giants and have many moons. **Pluto** is so far from the Sun that it is an icy world that sees our sun as only a faint star. Galileo was the first to see the four large moons that orbit Jupiter. The "Galilean moons" are visible as small points of light near Jupiter through binoculars or a telescope. The colorful bands on Jupiter's gaseous surface travel in opposite directions. These wind belts also cause great hurricane-like storms on the surface.

Saturn is known for its extensive ring system. All the outer gaseous planets have some ring system, but the small moons around Saturn actually keep the rings distinct by clearing up any loose particles. The density of Saturn is less than that of water.

The planets are believed to have begun as clumps of matter within the dust cloud that formed the Sun. They were too small to achieve the conditions needed to become stars. Instead, they cooled and became the planets as we know them. Our space probes have reached all except the most distant outer planets, and it appears that Earth is the only inhabited body in our solar system.

EXERCISE 2: THE SUN AND THE SOLAR SYSTEM

Directions: Choose the *best* answer for each of the following items.

1. Match each planet on the left with the correct characteristic on the right.

_____	Jupiter	**a.**	most extensive ring system
_____	Mars	**b.**	Galilean Moons
_____	Saturn	**c.**	hottest surface temperature
_____	Venus	**d.**	highest mountain

2. Identify the following planetary facts as true (**T**) or false (**F**).

     _____   Jupiter has huge dust storms on the surface.

     _____   From early views, Mars seemed to have irrigation canals.

     _____   Jupiter has bands of winds that blow in opposite directions.

     _____   The Sun is between four and five billion years old.

     _____   Venus has a thick cloud that produces rain every day.

Answers are on page 534.

EXERCISE 3: SPACE TRAVEL

Directions: Read the following passage and choose the *best* answers.

People have pursued travel into space in order to collect information without the use of probes. Space capsules built to support human life during space travel started with the NASA (National Aeronautics and Space Administration) flights to the moon in the 1960s. The next generation of spacecraft started the concept of space stations (such as Skylab and the Russian station Mir) to test the long-term effects of space and microgravity.

Currently, the United States has a small fleet of space shuttle-craft called **orbiters.** These ships were created to reenter the atmosphere and land like an airplane. These shuttles are also part of the construction and maintenance of the new International Space Station. This station is a construction and research effort from many countries interested in advancing knowledge about the future of humanity in space.

1. Number the following spacecraft in order of their creation.

     _____   international space station

     _____   probes

     _____   orbiters

     _____   capsules

     _____   space station (Skylab)

2. Finish the following sentences based on information provided in the above reading.

Orbiter space crafts are made to re-enter the atmosphere and _____.

The Space Station is being constructed by _____.

Previous space stations were called _____ and _____.

N.A.S.A. stands for _____.

Answers are on page 534.

EXERCISE 4: THE PLANETS

Directions: Use the information in the table to complete each of the statements that follow. Write the name of the correct planet in the blank.

	Mercury	**Venus**	**Earth**	**Mars**
Length of Year	88 days	225 days	365.26 days	686.98 days
Rotates on Its Axis Every Day	58 days	243 days	23.9 hours	24.6 hours
Number of Satellites	0	0	1	2
Distance from Sun (miles)	36 million	67 million	93 million	142 million

1. The length of the day is approximately the same on _____ and _____.

2. Of the planets listed, based on Earth years, you would age at the fastest rate on _____.

3. Mars takes a little more than three times longer to revolve around the Sun than does _____.

Answers are on page 534.

Geology: The Forces That Shape Our Earth

Planetary surface conditions identify each planet as a unique world. Historically, the Earth's crust has been referred to as rock solid. Only recently have geologists been able to measure and record the motion of the crust. The surface is constantly changing because of forces such as volcanoes and earthquakes. **Geology** is the study of the features of Earth and how they affect its development. In the last century alone, geologists made significant discoveries that revolutionized the entire field of earth science. Probably the most significant of all recent findings has been the formulation of the **Plate Tectonics Theory**, which explains the development of mountains and ocean trenches and the occurrence of earthquakes and volcanic eruptions.

Continental Drift and Plate Tectonics

Scientists have long observed that accurately drawn maps of Africa and South America suggest that the two continents once fit together. Using **jigsaw fit**, geologists formulated the **Theory of Continental Drift**: the formation of all seven continents into a supercontinent millions of years ago called **Pangaea**. It broke apart and split into the land masses that are recognized today as the seven continents.

Despite the fact that the continents appear to interlock like pieces of a puzzle, scientists could not explain why the continents drifted apart. The **Plate Tectonics Theory**, advanced in the 1960s, provided an explanation of the phenomenon. According to the theory, Earth is made up of the crust, mantle, outer core, and inner core, as depicted in the following illustration.

Earth's Structure

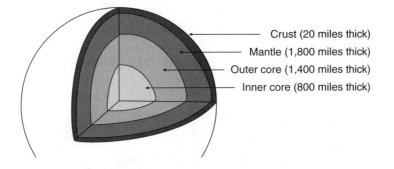

Crust (20 miles thick)
Mantle (1,800 miles thick)
Outer core (1,400 miles thick)
Inner core (800 miles thick)

Earth's Structure

The crust and upper mantle are made up of about twenty plates. These plates may be likened to plates floating on the surface of water in a vast sink. They move very slowly—approximately one-half inch to four inches per year. Attached to the surface of these plates are the continents and the ocean floor. As the plates slowly move, they carry the continents with them. Geologists explain that the plates move because currents of partially-molten rock in the mantle carry them.

This motion can be demonstrated when a saucepan of liquid is placed on a stove burner. As the liquid near the bottom of the pan gets hot, it rises to the surface and moves out of the way for the newer, hotter material that is rising right behind it. Earth's mantle is like liquid, heated by the core. As it rises to the surface (the crust), it moves over to make room for the newer, hotter mantle rising right behind it. The older cooler material is denser and, therefore, sinks back to near the core, where it is heated again. This circulation pattern is called a **convection current**, and it is responsible for the motion experienced at the crust.

EXERCISE 5: PLATE TECTONICS

Directions: Choose the *best* answer for the following question.

1. According to the passage, the Theory of Plate Tectonics helps explain which of the following?

   (1) Earth's gravitational pull
   (2) earthquakes, volcanoes, and mountains
   (3) the theory of continental drift
   (4) seasonal changes
   (5) magnetic north and south poles

2. Which of the following could *not* be the result of plate tectonics as described in the reading on the previous page?

   (1) mid-oceanic ridges where the seafloor is splitting open
   (2) large volcanic mountain ranges along crustal boundaries
   (3) the movement of the western portion of California in a northern direction
   (4) a deep glacier valley region found in mountain ranges of the far North
   (5) earthquakes that occur near mountain boundary regions as in South America

Answers are on page 534.

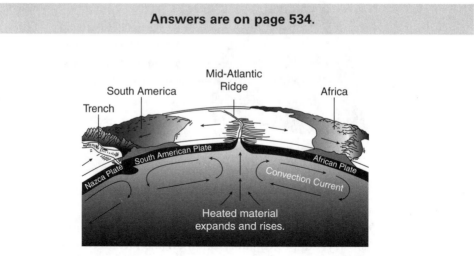

Mountain Formation and Earthquakes

This motion of the plates appears to explain the formation of mountains and ocean trenches and the occurrence of earthquakes and volcanoes. For example, when two plates collide, one plate piles atop another, forming a mountain. This action is known as **buckling**. Some mountains that have been created in this manner are the Himalayas of Tibet and the Alps in southern Europe, near Italy.

When one plate is forced down into the mantle of another, a **trench** is created. A **volcano** occurs when the heat beneath the surface of Earth melts the plate material that was forced into the trench and sends the molten rock to the surface. This type of plate boundary action, called **subduction**, occurs all along the North and South American continents. The Cascade Mountains in

Oregon and Washington are a volcanic chain created by subduction. The Andes of Peru are also volcanic as a result of the Pacific Plate's being melted under the South American Plate. Islands called **island arcs** are also created in this manner. Japan and the Philippines, as well as the Aleutian Islands off Alaska's coast, have frequent volcanic eruptions as a result of their origins by subduction.

An **earthquake** is formed by the shifting and breaking of the surface rocks when two plates slide past each other. This plate boundary action is called **translocation** or **transform faulting**. The best example of two plate boundaries that are slowly grinding past each other occurs in the San Andreas Fault in California. The San Andreas system passes through San Francisco and travels southward past San Diego out through the Gulf of California. The Pacific Plate is slowly moving in a northwesterly direction. This movement will eventually carry the coast of California north to the Alaskan shore.

The vibrations caused by the slippage of plates, called **seismic waves**, are measured by a device called a **seismograph** and rated on the **Richter Scale**. Earthquakes measuring more than 4.5 on the Richter Scale are considered potentially dangerous.

EXERCISE 6: CONTINENTAL DRIFT

Directions: Read the passage and choose the *best* answer for the question.

Ascension Island is a small volcanic island located in the South Atlantic halfway between Africa and South America. It is a famous breeding ground for sea turtles. Giant green turtles each year swim more than 2,000 miles from the coast of South America to lay their eggs on Ascension Island. This phenomenon has puzzled scientists for years.

1. Which of the following geological hypotheses best explains the behavior of the giant sea turtles?
   (1) Ascension Island is the only place where turtle eggs can survive.
   (2) Predators, such as alligators that live on the coast of South America, eat turtle eggs, forcing the sea turtles to migrate.
   (3) The turtles laid their eggs on Ascension Island millions of years ago before the continents of Africa and South America became separated.
   (4) The turtles have found that the climate on Ascension Island is the best for turtle eggs.
   (5) Ascension Island authorities have passed laws to protect the turtles by creating a nature sanctuary.

Answer is on page 534.

EXERCISE 7: EARTHQUAKES

Directions: Choose the *best* answer for the questions that follow.

U.S. Earthquake Zones and Seismic Risk

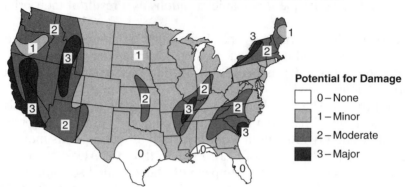

1. Which of these statements about earthquakes is supported by the map?
   (1) California is the only state in which residents might expect major earthquake damage.
   (2) Texas and Florida are the only areas that do not have to worry about earthquakes.
   (3) The greatest potential for moderate to major earthquake damage is in the Western United States.
   (4) Most of the continental United States is not affected by earthquakes.
   (5) Earthquakes are the most dangerous phenomenon on Earth.

2. Identify which of the following statements are true (**T**) and which are false (**F**).

   _____ Seismic waves can also be called vibrations.

   _____ Seismic waves are measured by a seismograph.

   _____ All earthquakes occur along plate boundaries.

   _____ One plate forced under another plate is called subduction.

Answers are on page 534.

Geologic Time

The drifting of continents and the formation of mountains are very gradual events that occur over a long period of time (possibly millions of years!). **Geologic time** extends back nearly five billion years, when geologists believe Earth was formed. We owe our concept of **absolute time**— time not influenced by man's arbitrary reference points—to geology. Geologists are able to fix periods of time by studying the rocks found in Earth's crust.

The rocks found in Earth's crust are of three types, described according to their origins. These rocks are igneous, metamorphic, and sedimentary. **Igneous rocks** are formed when molten rock (**magma**) hardens. **Metamorphic rocks** are those that have been changed by high pressure and temperature within the crust. **Sedimentary rocks** are made of pieces or sediments that were weathered or broken up, then cemented and compacted together. In sedimentary rock, the oldest layers are on the bottom and the youngest are on the top.

The Rock Cycle

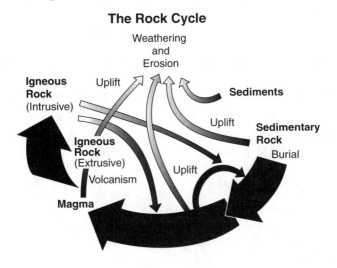

Instruments for Measuring Time

How do we determine which rocks are older than others? **Radiometric measurement** is one tool that scientists use to measure absolute time. Geologists measure the rate of radioactive decay in the minerals found in the rock. Over the last century, scientists have learned that radioactive substances will change, or decay, into nonradioactive substances over a period of time. This method is valid for matter up to 50,000 years old. Radiometric dating works well with samples of igneous and sedimentary rocks because it measures the radioactivity of minerals created when the rocks were formed. For metamorphic rock, however, the age of the original rock and the age of metamorphism are difficult to pinpoint.

Geologists also can examine the types of animal fossils found in layers of sedimentary rock to give an estimation of the rock's age. Igneous and metamorphic rock rarely contain fossils. Scientists have found that certain layers of sedimentary rock contain certain kinds of fossils, no matter where in the world the rock is located. Moreover, scientists have found that certain fossils are always found at lower layers than others, indicating that a sequence exists to the evolution of organisms.

EXERCISE 8: MEASURING GEOLOGIC TIME

Directions: Choose the *best* answer for each of the following questions.

1. According to the information in the preceding passage, which correctly describes the placement of the three types of rocks?

   (1) Igneous rock is located at the surface, metamorphic in the middle, and sedimentary on the bottom.

   (2) Sedimentary rock is located at the surface, metamorphic in the middle, and igneous at the bottom.

   (3) Metamorphic rock is located at the surface, sedimentary in the middle, and igneous at the bottom.

   (4) Igneous rock is located at the surface, sedimentary in the middle, and metamorphic at the bottom.

   (5) Sedimentary rock is located at the surface, igneous in the middle, and metamorphic at the bottom.

2. Trilobite fossils are found at a depth of 18 meters in a rock bed, and coral fossils are found at 14 meters. Which of the following is likely to be true about each organism?

   (1) Coral is older than trilobites.

   (2) Coral and trilobites are the same age.

   (3) Coral and trilobites share a common ancestry.

   (4) Trilobites are more advanced than corals.

   (5) Trilobites are older than corals.

Answers are on page 534.

Minerals and Rocks

Minerals are the building blocks of rocks. A **mineral** is a natural, inorganic solid with a specific composition and structure. All specimens of a given mineral share certain physical properties: crystalline form, hardness, color, and cleavage (splitting along planes). More than 95 percent of Earth's crust is made up of the minerals formed from the elements oxygen and silicon. The following chart shows the eight main elements, including the percentage of the crust's weight and volume that they occupy.

Element	Percentage of Crust's Mass (weight)	Percentage of Crust's Volume (space)
Oxygen	46.71	94.24
Silicon	27.69	0.51
Aluminum	8.07	0.44
Iron	5.05	0.37
Calcium	3.65	1.04
Sodium	2.75	1.21
Potassium	2.58	1.85
Magnesium	2.08	0.27

EXERCISE 9: MINERALS AND ROCKS

Directions: Choose the *best* answer for each of the following questions.

1. According to the information in the table, which element represents less of the crust's weight but occupies more than three times the space of silicon, a major component of the crust?

   (1) sodium
   (2) calcium
   (3) potassium
   (4) magnesium
   (5) iron

2. Which of the following best explains why oxygen, a gas, is the largest component of Earth's crust?

   (1) Oxygen gives Earth's crust its lightness.
   (2) Oxygen is the most abundant element in the world.
   (3) Oxygen is found in plants, which occupy large parts of Earth's crust.
   (4) Oxygen is needed to sustain all life on Earth.
   (5) Oxygen can be combined with most of the elements in Earth's crust.

Answers are on page 534.

The Changing Earth

Erosion is the transportation of weathered pieces of bedrock through the agents of wind, water (rivers and ice), and gravity. As mountains are built up by tectonic forces, they are also broken down and carried away by weathering and erosion.

The pull of **gravity** makes surface material move downward. Downslope movements may be rapid or very slow. They may involve only the surface material, or they may involve the bedrock underneath. Houses built on hills can contribute to soil movements because the weight of the homes may add to the gravitational force. Wind contributes to the erosional process by carrying surface material from one location to another. **Glaciers**, huge sheets of ice that can move slowly over land, pick up and carry rocks and soil with them. When they pass through river valleys, the glaciers deepen those valleys. Mountain glaciers, coupled with the downward force of gravity, create avalanches that can cause great erosional damage.

Of all the erosional agents, running water is the most powerful. Rivers, working with the force of gravity, have a devastating erosional impact. The action of rivers flowing against the land has formed gorges as large as the Grand Canyon. As rivers erode land, they carry deposits with them. **Deltas** are formed at the mouths of rivers that empty into a lake or an ocean. The soil that is carried along a river and deposited at its mouth is the richest and most fertile of all soils. The Nile and Mississippi Rivers have deltas noted for their rich soil, making these regions highly desirable for agriculture.

Soil Conservation

Erosion has proven to be one of farmers' worst fears. In the 1930s many farmers of the central plains of the United States overused their land; this meant that the nutrient content had no time to recover. The crops grown in such soil were weak; thus, when an extended drought struck, crops quickly died. With no plant roots to hold the soil, high winds blew much of the top-soil away from this farming region, which became known as the **Dust Bowl**.

The U.S. government started programs to assist farmers financially and to teach soil conservation techniques that would prevent this crisis from happening in the future. Some techniques used to prevent erosion include planting trees for windbreak barricades, using contour plowing so the wind and water cannot pick up speed to carry soil away, or terracing or making flat fields along hillsides to create more growing land. Other techniques are resting and revitalizing soil with nutrients from plants or fertilizers or letting the land have some resting time to recover.

Natural processes to create even an inch of topsoil are very slow. The process begins with the breakdown of the bedrock material. This action is called **weathering**. Eventually the bedrock is broken down into small particles and mixed with water and minerals to form the new layer called **subsoil**. Subsoil does not have the organic material necessary to provide nutrients to assist with growing plants. This organic material comes from the decomposition and decay of dead plant and animal tissue with organic material referred to as **humus**. Humus is a necessary part of any fully developed soil layer called **topsoil**. This creation of layers takes hundreds of years to finish what is called a mature soil profile.

EXERCISE 10: THE CHANGING EARTH

Directions: Choose the *best* answer for each of the following items.

1. Name the agent of erosion most likely responsible for the following.

    _____ large boulders that tumble down the slope of a hill or cliff

    _____ sand dunes that move and change location in the desert

    _____ a wide valley that used to be as narrow as the river that cut the valley

    _____ a flood plain area that has the top soil layer removed during heavy rains

2. Which of the following procedures followed by a farmer is not related directly to preventing erosion?

    (1) planting grass in gullies to act as a filler
    (2) planting crops in alternate rows (strip farming)
    (3) contour plowing around a hill
    (4) planting new trees to replace those that die
    (5) planting more seeds than are necessary to yield a bountiful crop

Answers are on page 534.

Paleontology: The Study of Past Life

Paleontology is the study of the evidence of Earth's past. Rock layers hold fossils that can be identified and connected to a long history of life-form changes for planet Earth. Some of the fossil remains are of large dinosaurs that once roamed the land. These dinosaurs are extinct now, and only a few distant descendants, such as the alligator and the crocodile, remain. Scientists study how the conditions of the Earth might have changed to have had quite an impact on extremely successful organisms such as the dinosaurs. By understanding the conditions of Earth and examining the changes, we hope to learn and prevent future changes that might affect human existence.

©The Field Museum

Sue, the most complete skeleton of a Tyrannosaurus Rex ever found, is on display at the Field Museum in Chicago.

Paleontologists have had great success in studying the past through rock layers in the Grand Canyon. Without having to drill down through the crust, the Colorado River created the way for us to examine the Earth's layers over the millions of years that it has cut throught the sedimentary layers. These ordered layers hold information about the changes of climate and weather conditions that have affected Earth.

A specialized field within paleontology is **archaeology**, the study of historic and prehistoric peoples and their cultures. Archaeologists study past civilizations by examining the remaining artifacts (tools and pottery), structures (monuments and dwellings), and recorded inscriptions (writing and drawings).

Oceanography: The Study of Earth's Oceans

Earth's surface is 71 percent covered by oceans. The study of large bodies of water is called **oceanography**. From their studies of the oceans, oceanographers have made many discoveries that help them to understand and explain phenomena they observe on Earth. For example, the theory of plate tectonics was further substantiated by the finding that a ridge encircling the globe lies under the ocean—the **oceanic ridge**.

This ridge circles the globe like the seam of a baseball. Numerous openings have been photographed along the crest of this ridge. Evidence from the pictures provided the basis for the theory that magma forces itself up from the ridges, pushes the ocean plates apart, cools, and forms new rock that becomes part of the ocean plate. Inventions such as **sonar** (an underwater ranging device), deep-diving submarines, and remote-control cameras have aided in our exploration of the oceans.

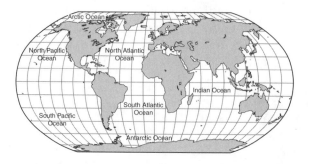

The Beginning of the Oceans

Oceanographers are not sure how Earth's oceans began. Many believe that the oceans were formed by the release of gases (hydrogen and oxygen) trapped in the magma in the Earth's interior. These gases were released, cooled, and condensed into the water that covers most of our planet's surface. Scientists know that the volume of water covering Earth is affected by the formation of glaciers and the melting of huge blocks of ice covering Earth's surface. (Glaciers covered much of Earth 20,000 years ago.)

EXERCISE 11: THE BEGINNING OF THE OCEANS

Directions: Choose the *best* answer for each of the following questions.

Distribution of Water on Earth

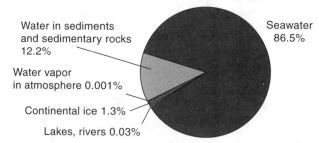

1. To which theory does the presence of 12 percent of water in sediments and in sedimentary rocks lend support?
   (1) continental drift
   (2) plate tectonics
   (3) the rise of Earth's sea level over time
   (4) the origin of the oceans
   (5) evolution

2. What percent of the water on Earth is available for us as drinking water?

   (1) .001 percent
   (2) .03 percent
   (3) 1.3 percent
   (4) 12.2 percent
   (5) 86.5 percent

Answers are on page 534.

Ocean Tides

One phenomenon of oceans that can be easily observed is the occurrence of tides. **Tides** result from the rising and falling of the ocean's surface caused by the gravitational pull of the Sun and the Moon on Earth. The Moon is the dominant factor in causing tides because of its closeness to Earth.

When the Moon is directly overhead, the ocean beneath it tends to bulge up, causing a tide. On the opposite side of Earth, the oceans experience a lesser bulge. As Earth rotates once every twenty-four hours, it experiences two high tides and two low tides. The position of the Moon in relation to the Sun and Earth determines the period and height of the tides. **Spring tides** are tides of greater-than-average range. **Neap tides** are tides of smaller-than-average range. The illustration in the exercise below shows a spring tide and a neap tide.

EXERCISE 12: OCEAN TIDES

Directions: Choose the *best* answer for each of the following questions.

Spring and Neap Tides

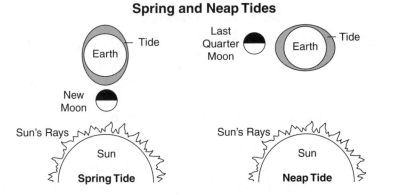

1. Spring tides are tides of greater-than-average range. During which phase of the Moon is the gravitational pull of the Moon together with that of the Sun likely to be greatest, causing a spring tide?

   (1) first quarter—when the Moon is to the right side of Earth
   (2) full moon—when Earth is between the Sun and the Moon
   (3) last quarter—when the Moon is to the left side of Earth, as shown
   (4) new moon—when the Moon is between Earth and the Sun
   (5) crescent moon—when the moon is between new and first quarter

Question 2 is based on the following explanation.

Syzygy (siz'-e-je) is a rare alignment of the Sun, the Moon, and Earth that causes extraordinarily high tides. This phenomenon occurred during the period from December 30, 1986, to January 4, 1987. It aggravated the severe storms that occurred along the U.S. Atlantic Coast. Three coinciding events occurred during this five-day period.

A. The Moon's orbit was closest to Earth—about 223,000 miles instead of 240,000 miles.

B. The Moon was directly between Earth and the Sun, causing a new moon.

C. Earth's orbit was the closest to the Sun—91 million miles, instead of the normal 93 million miles.

2. Imagine these conditions: the Moon's orbit is farthest from Earth, Earth is between the Sun and Moon, and Earth's orbit is farthest from the Sun. These conditions would likely result in which of the following situations?
   (1) the same effect as syzygy
   (2) the least effect on tide levels
   (3) higher high tides
   (4) spring tides
   (5) unusually low tides

Answers are on page 535.

Meteorology:
The Study of Earth's Atmosphere

The **atmosphere** is the invisible layer of air that envelops Earth. Scientists believe that it is primarily because of our atmosphere that life exists on Earth and not on neighboring planets such as Mars and Venus.

Meteorology is the study of Earth's atmosphere to understand and predict the weather. The atmosphere is not one distinct air mass that surrounds Earth; it is composed of several layers of air that begin at specific altitude ranges. Meteorologists have identified four layers of Earth's atmosphere. In ascending order (from lowest to highest) they are the troposphere, stratosphere, ionosphere, and exosphere.

Atmosphere Layer	Altitude	Conditions
Troposphere	Earth's surface to seven to ten miles	• Earth weather-occurrence • cloud formation
(Tropopause is the area between the Troposphere and the Stratosphere.)		
Stratosphere	begins at seven to ten miles; extends to 30 miles	• little vertical air motion • airplane travel
Ionosphere	30 to 300 miles	• thin air with electrified particles • radio-wave transmission
Exosphere	over 300 miles	• the highest layer • extreme heat from the sun during the day • extreme cold at night

EXERCISE 13: LAYERS OF EARTH'S ATMOSPHERE

Directions: Use the table above and the diagram below to answer the following questions.

Atmosphere Phenomena and Observation Tools

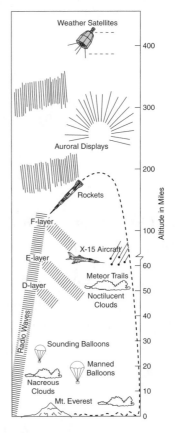

1. Noctilucent clouds, spectacular clouds that can be seen only at dusk, appear shortly after sunset. At which atmospheric level are these clouds visible?

   (1) the exosphere
   (2) the troposphere
   (3) the stratosphere
   (4) the ionosphere
   (5) the tropopause

2. At what layer may "D" layer radio waves that are transmitted around the world be found?

   (1) the lower range of the stratosphere
   (2) the upper range of the stratosphere
   (3) the lower range of the ionosphere
   (4) the upper range of the ionosphere
   (5) the upper range of the troposphere

3. What does the illustration suggest about the peak of Mt. Everest?

   (1) It is at times hidden by clouds.
   (2) It extends beyond the tropopause.
   (3) It reaches 15 miles in height.
   (4) It touches the stratosphere.
   (5) It is not high enough to touch these layers.

Answers are on page 535.

The Water Cycle

In predicting the weather, meteorologists must consider not just the air surrounding us but also how it interacts with the water that covers Earth's surface. The atmosphere and the **hydrosphere** (the watery portion of Earth) create the **water cycle**. This cycle helps to explain precipitation, an important element in our weather.

The Sun is a key link in the chain of events that makes up the water cycle. The Sun radiates heat, which daily **evaporates** millions of tons of water from Earth's oceans, lakes, rivers, and streams into the air. As moist air rises, it slowly cools. Finally, it cools so much that the humidity (the amount of water vapor the air is holding) reaches 100 percent. At this point the water vapor **condenses**, and clouds form. Depending on the temperature and other conditions, either rain or snow falls as **precipitation** when the clouds cannot hold all of the water. The rain or melted snow eventually flows to the ocean, and the cycle is completed again. The illustration that follows shows the water cycle.

The Water Cycle

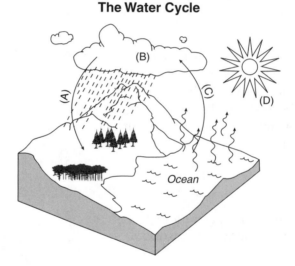

EXERCISE 14: THE WATER CYCLE

Directions: Identify the letters in the illustration that correspond to each process below.

1. _____   Condensation occurs, forming clouds.
2. _____   The Sun radiates heat.
3. _____   Precipitation in the form of rain or snow falls.
4. _____   Water evaporates into the atmosphere.

Answers are on page 535.

EXERCISE 15: HUMIDITY

Directions: Read the following passage and answer the questions below.

Humidity is the amount of water vapor in the air at a given time. At warm temperatures, air can hold more moisture than it can at cold temperatures. Relative humidity is the amount of vapor the air is holding expressed as a percentage of the amount the air is capable of holding. For example, at 86 degrees Fahrenheit, air can hold a maximum of 30.4 grams of water per cubic meter. If the air at the same temperature is holding only 15.2 grams of water, the relative humidity is 50 percent. At the point at which the air becomes saturated (exceeds the level of water vapor it can hold), it releases water vapor in the form of dew or condensation.

1. If the air at 75 degrees is holding the maximum amount of moisture that it can, and the temperature suddenly drops to 60 degrees, what is likely to be the result?

    (1) The humidity will remain unchanged.
    (2) The relative humidity will decrease.
    (3) Precipitation will be released in the form of rain.
    (4) Precipitation will be released in the form of hail.
    (5) Precipitation will be released in the form of snow.

2. During subfreezing days in many parts of the country, the indoor relative humidity decreases when homes are heated. Furniture and skin dry out, and static electricity increases. For health reasons, doctors recommend the use of humidifiers. Which of the following best explains the lack of humidity in the air indoors?

    (1) The amount of water vapor in the air goes down.
    (2) The water vapor in the air evaporates.
    (3) The humidity in winter is lower.
    (4) The cold temperatures prevent humidity.
    (5) Dry air can only occur in warm air.

Answers are on page 535.

Warm and Cold Air Masses

Humidity and temperature affect how an air mass or body of air interacts in the atmosphere. Air masses are created when a body of air takes on the characteristics from the land or water over which it forms. The central region of Canada usually creates cold and dry air masses. Air masses that form over the Gulf of Mexico are warm and have high humidity. The Pacific Northwest creates air masses that are cool but also humid. The air masses that begin over the southwestern region of the United States are often dry but warm. Meteorologists track these air masses to help them make weather forecasts. The air masses that move across the United States from west to east help meteorologists predict the weather.

Cold air masses tend to be unstable and turbulent and move faster than warm air masses. When a cold air mass comes into contact with a warm air mass, it forces the warmer air upwards. This forces any moisture in that air to condense quickly. The clouds that are formed by quick vertical air movements are **cumulus clouds**—puffy, cottonlike clouds. If the air is holding a great deal of moisture, the instant vertical draft creates a **cumulonimbus** or thunderhead. These are the storm clouds that drop a heavy load of precipitation quickly. Very often the quick rush of moist air will create a separation of electric charges within the cloud. This is how **lightning** is created. The release of the charged particles through the air superheats the individual air particles. They expand so fast that small sonic booms, or **thunder**, are heard.

Warm air masses are usually stable, and the wind that accompanies them is steady. Clouds that are formed by warm air masses are **stratus clouds**—low-lying, level clouds that in warm weather bring precipitation in the form of drizzle. As the warm air continues over the cooler air mass, the cloud formation becomes higher and thinner. The highest wispy clouds are **cirrus clouds** and do not contain enough moisture to bring precipitation.

Air Masses Cause Fronts

A **front** occurs when two air masses collide and a boundary between the two masses forms. The weather for the land below is affected. Fronts may be either weak or strong. Strong fronts generally bring precipitation. When cold air acts like a plow and pushes warm air back, a **cold front** forms. If the cold air retreats, and the warm air pushes it away, a **warm front** occurs. Sometimes, the boundary between the two air masses does not move, and the front becomes stationary. **Stationary fronts** bring conditions similar to those brought by warm fronts. The precipitation that results, however, is usually milder and lasts longer.

More commonly, these collisions of fronts take place at the change of seasons. In the central part of the United States, spring means collisions of the newly arriving warm, moist air from the Gulf of Mexico with the retreating dry and cold air from central Canada. This annual springtime tradition generates the conditions that cause tornadoes. **Tornadoes** are the result of a very isolated strong updraft of warm, moist air. The rotation of the planet puts the circulation pattern of a counterclockwise spin into the updraft. (This is known as the **Coriolis Effect** and is demonstrated by all wind and water currents in both hemispheres. It is the reason the trade vessels in the Atlantic Ocean coming from Europe to North America must travel south to the equator instead of straight across the Atlantic.) Tornadoes may have wind speeds of up to 300 miles per hour, and they travel across the ground at around 30 miles per hour. Most tornadoes are produced in a region known as Tornado Alley: an area starting in the northern sections of Texas, through Oklahoma, Kansas, Missouri, and parts of Iowa and Illinois.

Hurricanes are also seasonal storms. As the energy from the Sun leaves the northern hemisphere in the late summer, the oceans near the equator develop air mass and water-current low pressure systems. Hurricane season is August through October, when the conditions are right for the start of these large circulation patterns that are fueled by the warm ocean waters near the equator.

EXERCISE 16: AIR MASSES, FRONTS, AND WEATHER

Directions: Choose the *best* answer for the following questions.

1. Which of the following changes in the weather can occur when a strong warm air mass displaces a cold air mass?
   (1) Cumulus clouds may form, winds may become gusty, and thunderstorms may result.
   (2) Stratus clouds may form, winds may become steady, and drizzling may occur.
   (3) Stratus clouds may form, winds may become turbulent, and thunderstorms may result.
   (4) Cumulus clouds may form, winds may become steady, and thunderstorms may result.
   (5) The sky may remain cloudless, and no winds or precipitation may occur.

2. Based on the passage, what causes an air mass to form?
   (1) air taking on the characteristics of the land or water over which it forms
   (2) cold air overcoming weaker warm air over a large area
   (3) the Coriolis Effect from the rotation of the planet
   (4) the stability of the winds that cause weather patterns
   (5) the collision of moist air and dry air that generates storms

3. Identify the following statements as true for a tornado (**T**), a hurricane (**H**), or both (**B**).

   _____ Wind speeds are sometimes measured at three hundred miles per hour.

   _____ Winds spin around a low pressure center in a counterclockwise direction.

   _____ The low pressure is fueled by the heat from the ocean waters near the equator.

   _____ These storms generally occur during the spring and very often in the Midwest.

Answers are on page 535.

3
PHYSICAL SCIENCE
CHEMISTRY—THE STUDY OF MATTER

Chemistry is the branch of science that deals with the composition, structure, and properties of matter as well as the changes it undergoes. **Matter** is any substance that occupies space and has mass. Your chair, desk, and table are composed of matter. Even the air you breathe is composed of matter. Matter exists in four states—**solid**, **liquid**, **gas**, and **plasma** (an ionized gas of which the Sun is made).

The Atom, the Basis of Matter

In chemistry, atoms are the building blocks for matter. The **atom** is the smallest particle of an element that has the properties of that element. An **element** is a substance that occurs in nature and that cannot be broken down into a simpler substance. Nearly 100 fundamental substances known as elements are known to occur in nature. A few elements have been produced synthetically by man. Atoms also form molecules. A **molecule** is the smallest part of a compound that can exist by itself. A molecule consists of two or more atoms joined together chemically.

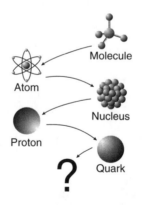

In the early 19th century, only a few elements were known to exist. According to the theory of John Dalton, an atom cannot be made, destroyed, or divided; and atoms of the same element are alike. This concept became known as **atomic theory.** Later physicists discovered that the nucleus of an atom can be split by bombarding it with neutrons, a process known as **nuclear fission.**

A Russian chemist, **Dmitri Mendeleyev**, constructed the **periodic table**, by which he calculated the atomic weights of the different elements. Hydrogen, the lightest known element with only one proton, was assigned the atomic number 1. An atom of oxygen has a mass 16 times that of a hydrogen atom; therefore, oxygen was given an atomic mass of 16. Oxygen is the eighth lightest element and is assigned the atomic number 8. Dalton's and Mendeleyev's discoveries were most significant in the field of chemistry since that of Antoine-Laurent Lavoisier, a French chemist who identified oxygen as the key element that supports combustion. The periodic table appears on page 259.

Atomic Structure

Scientists have learned a great deal about atoms since Dalton's time. For example, an atom is composed of a nucleus with electrons that surround it. The **nucleus**, located in the center of the atom, is made up of protons and neutrons. A **proton** is a positively charged particle. An element's atomic number is determined by the number of protons it has. Because hydrogen has only one proton in its nucleus, it has an atomic number of 1. A **neutron** has a mass nearly equal to that of a proton but has no charge at all. The nucleus has a positive charge, determined by the number of protons it contains. The nucleus provides the mass number for an element.

An **electron** is a negatively charged particle. Electrons occupy an orbit, or shell, that surrounds the nucleus. Each shell can hold only a fixed number of electrons. It is the number of shells that distinguishes one element from another. The greater the number of shells with orbiting electrons that an element has, the greater its atomic number. The following illustration shows the structure of an atom.

The Helium Atom

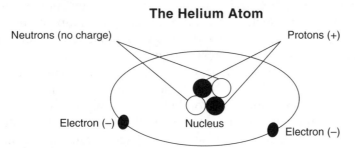

EXERCISE 1: ATOMIC STRUCTURE

Directions: Match each term on the right with its description on the left.

1. _____ the second lightest element; contains two protons in its nucleus

    a. oxygen

2. _____ a negatively charged particle

    b. neutron

3. _____ the part of an atom that determines an element's mass

    c. proton

4. _____ a particle that has no charge

    d. helium

5. _____ a positively charged particle

    e. electron

6. _____ an element containing eight protons in its nucleus

    f. nucleus

Answers are on page 535.

Nuclear Energy

The nucleus of every atom contains an almost unimaginable amount of potential energy. The protons that are locked together are all positive and naturally repel each other. It takes the strongest force in the universe, **nuclear force**, to keep those subatomic particles locked together. Science has been able to unlock and capture this energy by splitting larger atoms (those with the greatest number of protons) by firing a neutral neutron at the atom. This process of splitting the larger atoms is **nuclear fission**. The fuel for this reaction is uranium because of the great size of its nucleus and its unstable qualities. When a material is unstable and able to release radiation, it is said to be **radioactive**. This radioactive material is made into pellets that are held by fuel rods placed in a heavily shielded nuclear reactor. The process of regulating the release of the nuclear energy requires that the fuel rods remain partially covered with control rods. These control rods prevent free neutrons from splitting too many uranium atoms in an uncontrolled explosion.

Radioactivity and Environmental Protection

One of the dangers of nuclear energy is that such an explosion could release radioactive materials into the environment, causing serious and extensive contamination of radioactivity to any living organisms, plants, and animals in the vicinity. One such explosion occurred at a Ukranian nuclear power plant, Chernobyl, in the early 1980s with radioactive particles and gases sent outside to the nearby forest and town.

The United States also experienced the fear of a near disaster at a nuclear power plant at Three Mile Island, New Jersey. A leak of cooling water allowed the reactor to become very hot, but it was equipped with an automatic shut-off system that was activated when the recorded temperature exceeded maximum capacity. There was no leakage of radioactive materials, and nuclear-energy advocates explain that this fact proves that the automatic system keeps nuclear power safe. These advocates still do not have an answer to the biggest concern nuclear-energy opponents have: the safe disposal of radioactive wastes. Currently, these wastes are sealed in large barrels and are transported to empty underground mines that are reinforced with a lining to protect the environment.

EXERCISE 2: NUCLEAR ENERGY

Directions: Read the passage below and choose the *best* answer for each of the following items. You may need to refer to the periodic table shown on page 259.

Nuclear energy may be released in two ways: by fission and by fusion. Nuclear *fission* involves the splitting of the nucleus of a heavy chemical element by bombardment with neutrons. Nuclear *fusion* involves the uniting of two nuclei of an element at high temperatures and pressure to form the nucleus of a new, heavier element. In each process, nuclear energy is released.

1. According to the information in the passage and the atomic masses shown in the periodic table, when would energy from nuclear fusion be released?
   (1) when uranium nuclei are fused to make plutonium
   (2) when hydrogen nuclei are fused to make oxygen
   (3) when oxygen nuclei are fused to make helium
   (4) when hydrogen nuclei are fused to make helium
   (5) when helium nuclei are fused to make hydrogen

2. Energy from nuclear fission would be released in the splitting of the nucleus of which element?
   (1) plutonium
   (2) hydrogen
   (3) oxygen
   (4) helium
   (5) carbon

3. Identify the following statements as true (**T**) or false (**F**).
   _____ The Three Mile Island accident contaminated a nearby forest.
   _____ Nuclear waste is safe to dispose of in landfills.
   _____ Fuel rods must also have control rods to control the reaction.

Answers are on page 535.

Radioactivity That Is Useful

Not all radioactivity is harmful. Particles of **radioactive carbon** are in the air and inhaled by animals and people every day. It is this radioactive carbon that allows paleontologists to calculate how long an organism has been dead. Once the organism dies, it no longer takes in additional radioactive C_{14}, and the amount of radioactive carbon that is present in the organism starts to decay or lose some of its radioactivity in the form of subatomic particles called alpha or beta particles. The release of alpha and beta particles would contaminate nearby objects with radioactivity. This process of **radiocarbon dating** has given scientists a tool to examine and date fossils from once-living organisms including early man.

Smoke detectors also have a small, safe amount of material that gives off alpha particles. Some smoke detectors contain small amounts of Am_{241} (Americium) that releases a steady stream of alpha particles between two electrodes. When smoke particles interrupt the current between the two electrodes, an alarm sounds.

Radioactive materials are also used in the treatment of some cancers. An entire branch of medicine, called **nuclear medicine**, researches and uses radioactive materials to treat the human body.

One of the most popular forms of radiology involves the use of Xrays to detect broken bones. While having Xrays at the doctor's or dentist's office, the patient is also given a protective lead cover to prevent overexposure of the other parts of the body. **CAT** (computerized axial tomography) **scans** use computers to monitor the body's reaction to Xrays from a variety of angles. Doctors use CAT scans as well as **MRI** (magnetic resonance imaging) screens to help in diagnosis of internal problems.

EXERCISE 3: ISOTOPIC ELEMENTS

Directions: Use the passage and table below to answer the questions.

Sometimes the number of neutrons in the atom of an element varies. This can affect the mass number of an element. For example, the element carbon has six protons in its nucleus, but it can also have six or seven neutrons in its nucleus. An element whose number of neutrons can vary in its nucleus is described as **isotopic**. Thus, two isotopes of carbon exist—carbon 12 and carbon 13—and they have different chemical properties. Of the two, carbon 12 is the more common.

Element	Atomic Number	Mass number
Hydrogen	1	1.01
Helium	2	4.00
Lithium	3	6.94
Beryllium	4	9.01
Boron	5	10.81

1. The only element in the chart that could have an isotope of mass number 6 and whose two nuclei might be fused to form carbon 12 would be which of the following?

   (1) hydrogen
   (2) helium
   (3) lithium
   (4) beryllium
   (5) boron

2. Deuterium and tritium are two isotopes that have mass numbers of 2 and 3, respectively. Of the two isotopes, tritium is especially radioactive. Based on the preceding chart, to which element would these two isotopes belong, knowing that they both have only one proton?

(1) hydrogen
(2) helium
(3) lithium
(4) beryllium
(5) boron

3. Identify the following statements as either fact (**F**) or opinion (**O**).

_____ Radioactivity is very dangerous, and people should not use it.

_____ Radiation can be used to treat certain medical problems.

_____ Lead is used as a screen to protect internal organs when using Xrays.

_____ CAT scans and MRIs are the best ways to diagnose disease.

_____ Radioactive wastes need to be securely protected from contaminating the environment.

Answers are on page 535.

Elements and Periodicity

In the periodic table, elements are organized according to their atomic and physical properties. The table relates the properties of the elements to their atomic numbers. Elements in the same row (across) have the same number of shells containing a varying number of electrons. Elements in the same column (down) have the same number of electrons in their outermost shell.

In classifying elements according to physical properties, scientists consider color, odor, taste, density, boiling point, solubility (ability to dissolve), malleability (capability of being shaped by beating), and hardness. Out of these properties arose the three broad groupings that chemists have used to categorize all of the elements—**metals**, **nonmetals**, and **metalloids**.

	Features	Examples
Metals	conduct heat and electricity well melt at high temperatures have high density and brilliant luster	sodium gold aluminum
Nonmetals	melt at low temperatures have low luster are less dense than metals are poor conductors of heat and electricity	carbon sulfur oxygen
Metalloids	have properties of metals and nonmetals	antimony arsenic

According to **periodic law**, as the atomic number increases for elements in a column, similar properties occur regularly and to a greater degree. For example, the metals with the atomic numbers 3, 11, and 19—lithium, sodium, and potassium, respectively—are all chemically active metals. In many cases, the greater the atomic number, the higher the degree of certain physical or chemical properties. Whereas the second member of this group, sodium, is chemically active, the fourth member, rubidium, is so highly active that it bursts into flame upon exposure to air.

The periodic table appears on the next page.

EXERCISE 4: ELEMENTS AND PERIODICITY

Directions: Choose the *best* answer for each of the following questions.

1. The metals copper, silver, and gold are in the same family (column), having atomic numbers of 29, 47, and 79 respectively. According to the principle of periodic law, of the three metals, gold would have the highest degree of which physical property?

   (1) value
   (2) rarity
   (3) volatility
   (4) malleability
   (5) scarcity

2. Radon is in the same family as helium, neon, argon, krypton, and xenon. Which of the following facts would help you to determine that radon has a greater density than the other elements in the same family?

   (1) Radon is found in the ground whereas other elements are not.
   (2) Radon has a higher atomic number than the other elements in its family.
   (3) Radon poses potential health problems where great concentrations are found in the ground.
   (4) Radon is used in many medical treatments that require chemical reactions in the body.
   (5) Radon is atomically very unstable and is dangerous to use.

Answers are on page 536.

Periodic Table Key

- Atomic Number: ②
- Symbol: **He** (* man made)
- Name: Helium
- Mass Number (number of protons and neutrons): 4

Period	1	2	3	4	5	6	7	8	9	10	11	12	13	14	15	16	17	18
1	① H Hydrogen 1																	② He Helium 4
2	③ Li Lithium 7	④ Be Beryllium 9											⑤ B Boron 11	⑥ C Carbon 12	⑦ N Nitrogen 14	⑧ O Oxygen 16	⑨ F Fluorine 19	⑩ Ne Neon 20
3	⑪ Na Sodium 23	⑫ Mg Magnesium 24											⑬ Al Aluminum 27	⑭ Si Silicon 28	⑮ P Phosphorus 31	⑯ S Sulfur 32	⑰ Cl Chlorine 35	⑱ Ar Argon 40
4	⑲ K Potassium 39	⑳ Ca Calcium 40	㉑ Sc Scandium 45	㉒ Ti Titanium 48	㉓ V Vanadium 51	㉔ Cr Chromium 52	㉕ Mn Manganese 55	㉖ Fe Iron 56	㉗ Co Cobalt 59	㉘ Ni Nickel 59	㉙ Cu Copper 64	㉚ Zn Zinc 65	㉛ Ga Gallium 70	㉜ Ge Germanium 73	㉝ As Arsenic 75	㉞ Se Selenium 79	㉟ Br Bromine 80	㊱ Kr Krypton 84
5	㊲ Rb Rubidium 85	㊳ Sr Strontium 88	㊴ Y Yttrium 89	㊵ Zr Zirconium 91	㊶ Nb Niobium 93	㊷ Mo Molybdenum 96	㊸ Tc* Technetium 98	㊹ Ru Ruthenium 101	㊺ Rh Rhodium 103	㊻ Pd Palladium 106	㊼ Ag Silver 108	㊽ Cd Cadmium 112	㊾ In Indium 115	㊿ Sn Tin 119	﹙51﹚ Sb Antimony 122	﹙52﹚ Te Tellurium 128	﹙53﹚ I Iodine 127	﹙54﹚ Xe Xenon 131
6	﹙55﹚ Cs Cesium 133	﹙56﹚ Ba Barium 137	﹙57﹚ La Lanthanum 139	﹙72﹚ Hf Hafnium 178	﹙73﹚ Ta Tantalum 181	﹙74﹚ W Tungsten 184	﹙75﹚ Re Rhenium 186	﹙76﹚ Os Osmium 190	﹙77﹚ Ir Iridium 192	﹙78﹚ Pt Platinum 195	﹙79﹚ Au Gold 197	﹙80﹚ Hg Mercury 201	﹙81﹚ Tl Thallium 204	﹙82﹚ Pb Lead 207	﹙83﹚ Bi Bismuth 209	﹙84﹚ Po Polonium 209	﹙85﹚ At Astatine 210	﹙86﹚ Rn Radon 222
7	﹙87﹚ Fr Francium 223	﹙88﹚ Ra Radium 226	﹙89﹚ Ac Actinium 227	﹙104﹚ Rf Rutherfordium 261	﹙105﹚ Db Dubnium 262	﹙106﹚ Sg Seaborgium 263	﹙107﹚ Bh Bohrium 262	﹙108﹚ Hs Hassium 265	﹙109﹚ Mt Meitnerium 266	﹙110﹚ Uun* Unnilennium 269	﹙111﹚ Uuu* Unununium 272	﹙112﹚ Uub* Ununbium 277		﹙114﹚ Uuq* Ununquadium 285		﹙116﹚ Uuh* Ununhexium 289		﹙118﹚ Uuo* Ununoctium 293

Rare Earth Elements

Lanthanide series:

﹙58﹚ Ce Cerium 140	﹙59﹚ Pr Praseodymium 141	﹙60﹚ Nd Neodymium 144	﹙61﹚ Pm* Promethium 145	﹙62﹚ Sm Samarium 150	﹙63﹚ Eu Europium 152	﹙64﹚ Gd Gadolinium 157	﹙65﹚ Tb Terbium 159	﹙66﹚ Dy Dysprosium 163	﹙67﹚ Ho Holmium 165	﹙68﹚ Er Erbium 167	﹙69﹚ Tm Thulium 169	﹙70﹚ Yb Ytterbium 173	﹙71﹚ Lu Lutetium 175

Actinide series:

﹙90﹚ Th Thorium 232	﹙91﹚ Pa Protactinium 231	﹙92﹚ U Uranium 238	﹙93﹚ Np* Neptunium 237	﹙94﹚ Pu* Plutonium 244	﹙95﹚ Am* Americium 243	﹙96﹚ Cm* Curium 247	﹙97﹚ Bk* Berkelium 247	﹙98﹚ Cf* Californium 251	﹙99﹚ Es* Einsteinium 252	﹙100﹚ Fm* Fermium 257	﹙101﹚ Md* Mendelevium 258	﹙102﹚ No* Nobelium 259	﹙103﹚ Lr* Lawrencium 262

Elements and Chemical Reactions

Each chemical reaction has two components: a reactant and a product. A **reactant** is the substance or substances that enter into the reaction. The **product** is the substance or substances that result from the reaction. A chemical reaction may be either a **combination reaction**, in which two elements or substances are combined, or a **decomposition reaction**, in which an element or substance is broken down.

A chemical reaction is written in a shorthand called a **chemical equation**. A chemical formula uses symbols for elements and shows the number of atoms for each element of a substance. For example, the chemical reaction that produces water would be written this way:

$$2H_2 + O_2 \rightarrow 2H_2O$$

When you read a chemical equation, the large number tells how many **molecules** (structures containing more than one atom) are present. When only a single molecule or atom is present, the number 1 is not written. The smaller subscript number tells how many atoms of an element are present in each molecule.

The equation for water says that two molecules of hydrogen gas ($2H_2$) plus one molecule of oxygen gas (O_2) combine to form two molecules of water ($2H_2O$). Notice that one molecule of hydrogen gas (H_2) contains two atoms of hydrogen, and one molecule of oxygen gas (O_2) contains two atoms of oxygen. Each molecule of water (H_2O) contains two atoms of hydrogen and one atom of oxygen.

The chemical reaction in which one atom of carbon unites with two atoms of oxygen to form carbon dioxide would be written this way:

$$C + O_2 \rightarrow CO_2$$

This equation says that one molecule of carbon plus one molecule of oxygen (two atoms of oxygen) combine to form one molecule of carbon dioxide (CO_2).

All chemical reactions are governed by the **Law of Conservation of Matter**. This law holds that matter can neither be created nor destroyed in a chemical reaction. A chemical equation adheres to this law; it shows the same number of atoms on both sides of the arrow for each element involved in a reaction. For example, the following chemical reaction occurs when methane gas (CH_4) is burned with oxygen:

$$CH_4 + 2O_2 \rightarrow CO_2 + 2H_2O$$

Methane gas burns with oxygen to form carbon dioxide and water vapor; specifically, one molecule of carbon dioxide and two molecules of water. Notice that the reaction begins with one carbon atom (C) and ends with one carbon atom (C). The reaction begins with four hydrogen atoms (H_4) and ends with four hydrogen atoms ($2H_2$ or $2 \times 2 = 4$). The reaction begins with four oxygen atoms ($2O_2 = 2 \times 2 = 4$) and ends with 4 oxygen atoms ($O_2 + 2O = 4$). When the number of atoms of each element is equal on both sides of the equation, we say that the equation is **balanced**.

EXERCISE 5: BALANCED EQUATIONS

Directions: Identify each of the following equations as either balanced (**B**) or unbalanced (**U**).

1. _____ $2H + O \rightarrow H_2O$

2. _____ $2Fe_2O_3 + 3C \rightarrow 2Fe + 3CO_2$

3. _____ $2NaBr + Cl_2 \rightarrow Br_2 + 2NaCl$

Answers are on page 536.

EXERCISE 6: CHEMICAL REACTIONS

Directions: Choose the *best* answer for each of the following questions.

Question 1 refers to the following passage.

A **physical change** is a change that does not produce a new substance. For example, when you saw wood or dissolve salt in water you are not changing the chemical composition of the substances. However, a new substance is formed when a **chemical change** takes place. The result is a change in the chemical composition of a substance. Some common chemical changes include the burning of wood and the rusting of metal on a car.

In an experiment concerning physical and chemical changes, you add 10g of copper sulfate to 100 ml of water. You heat the solution over a low flame and stir. After the solution cools, you place a piece of aluminum foil in the copper sulfate solution. After 24 hours, the solution has changed from deep blue to a very light blue, and the aluminum has acquired a deep copper coating.

1. Which of the following pieces of information would you need to see at the end of the experiment to prove that a chemical change or a new substance had occurred?
   (1) whether the copper sulfate solution had been heated
   (2) whether the solution had been stirred
   (3) whether twenty-four hours had passed
   (4) whether the aluminum had acquired a copper coat
   (5) whether the aluminum was breakable

2. What is the relation of reactants to products of a chemical reaction?
   (1) They always double in mass.
   (2) They must always balance.
   (3) They never equal each other in mass.
   (4) They always need a catalyst.
   (5) They must triple themselves to balance.

3. The chemical reaction that gives soda pop (a carbonated beverage) its fizz results from dissolving a molecule of carbon dioxide into a molecule of water. Which of the following represents the chemical equation for the process?

(1) $CO_3 + H_2O \rightarrow H_2CO_4$
(2) $CO_2 + H_2O \rightarrow H_2CO_3$
(3) $CO + H_2O \rightarrow H_2CO_2$
(4) $CO_2 + H_2O \rightarrow H_2CO_2$
(5) $CO + 2H_2O \rightarrow H_4CO_2$

Answers are on page 536.

Elements in Combination

Compounds are formed when two or more elements combine in a chemical reaction. The resulting product usually has different properties from either of the component elements. Compounds, when formed, can be broken down into simpler substances only by chemical action. For example, water, the most commonly known compound, is composed of two atoms of hydrogen and one atom of oxygen. When water is subjected to extreme temperatures, it can be reduced to its component elements—hydrogen and oxygen—and its liquid characteristic is lost.

Mixtures are substances that are formed when two or more elements or compounds are mixed in different proportions. The resulting product retains the properties of the combining elements. In most mixtures the combining ingredients can be separated easily. For example, gunpowder is a mixture of charcoal (a form of carbon), sulfur, and potassium nitrate (a compound of potassium and nitrogen). When mixed, the three ingredients form gunpowder, a highly explosive substance. These three ingredients can be identified by their different colors in this mixture.

A **solution** is a mixture formed when a solid, liquid, or gaseous substance is dissolved in a liquid. The substance that is dissolved into the liquid is called the **solute**. The liquid in which the substance is dissolved is called the **solvent**. One of the characteristics that distinguishes a solution from a mixture is that a solution is homogeneous—the same throughout. An **aqueous solution** features water as the solvent. A **tincture**, such as the antiseptic tincture of iodine, has alcohol as the solvent. Sometimes a solution is formed when a substance is dissolved in a gas or solid.

When metals are combined in varying proportions, they often form **alloys**. In an alloy, each metal dissolves into the other at high temperatures. Common examples of alloys are brass (copper and zinc), bronze (copper, tin, and other elements), and steel (iron, carbon, and other elements). An **amalgam** is formed when a metal is dissolved into mercury, a liquid metal. Amalgams are used chiefly in making tooth cements and are referred to as silver fillings.

EXERCISE 7: ELEMENTS IN COMBINATION

Directions: Choose the *best* answer to the questions that follow.

1. Table salt—sodium chloride, one of the most common substances occurring in nature—is best classified as which of the following?

   (1) a compound
   (2) a mixture
   (3) a solution
   (4) an alloy
   (5) an amalgam

2. Air is composed of nitrogen (78 percent), oxygen (21 percent), argon (0.93 percent), carbon dioxide (0.03 percent), and other gases (0.04 percent). How may air be best described?

   (1) a compound
   (2) a mixture
   (3) a solution
   (4) an alloy
   (5) an amalgam

Answers are on page 536.

Chemical Bonding

When compounds are made, a bond is formed between two or more elements. A **bond** is a force that holds together two atoms, two ions (electrically charged particles), two molecules, or a combination of these. Bonding may result from either the transfer or the sharing of electrons between atoms.

When electrons are transferred from one atom to another, an **ionic bond** is formed. In the following example, an ionic bond is formed when an electron from a sodium atom is transferred to the outermost shell of a chlorine atom. The result is the common compound table salt.

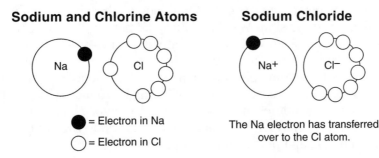

Sodium and Chlorine Atoms

● = Electron in Na
○ = Electron in Cl

Sodium Chloride

The Na electron has transferred over to the Cl atom.

In the preceding example, both sodium and chlorine are electrically neutral (have no charge); however, when the sodium atom loses its electron, it becomes positively charged. Opposite charges attract, forming a bond. Ionic compounds such as salt typically have high melting and boiling points, are flammable, conduct electricity when dissolved in water, and exist as solids at room temperatures.

When two or more atoms of different elements share electrons to form a molecule, a **covalent bond** is formed. In the illustration below, a covalent bond is formed when two atoms of hydrogen are bonded to one atom of oxygen to form the compound water.

Water Molecule

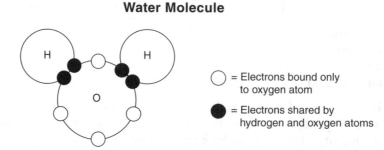

⊖ = Electrons bound only
    to oxygen atom

⬤ = Electrons shared by
    hydrogen and oxygen atoms

In covalent bonding, the outermost shell of the element with the greatest number of electrons is filled to capacity at eight electrons. Once the combining element achieves eight electrons in its outermost ring, it cannot combine with another element. Covalent compounds such as water typically have low melting and boiling points, are nonflammable, have poor conductivity, and exist as gases and liquids.

Polymers have been around since the turn of the 20th century. At that time chemists found that the waste products from organic compounds of phenol and formaldehyde could be treated with heat and high pressure. The resulting material is very hard and is used to make billiard balls and telephones as well as handles on pots and pans. More research with these kinds of organic compounds led to the invention of nylon 66 by two chemists from the Dupont company. Vulcanized rubber that is used to make automobile tires is also the product of experimenting with the bonding of these types of polymer chains.

Another type of synthetic polymer is **polyester** which is used in the making of many types of fabric. Another example of wearable polymers is **acrylic**. Acrylic feels like wool but is less expensive and can be machine washed. The fabric industry cautions that heat from a fire breaks the bonds, and the fragments react with oxygen to continue the burning reaction, possibly adhering to the skin. Warning labels are put on the garments; some fabrics, especially for sleepwear, are treated with flame-retardant material.

Plastics are another chemical invention of bonding. The variety of chemical bonds allows some plastics, such as PET, to be tough and solvent. This plastic, which has a recycling code of 1, can be found in soda bottles and recycled into new bottles or carpeting or sleeping bags. Another type of plastic (PVC) is a tough, flexible plastic used in pipes or vinyl siding and can be recycled into toys and playground equipment.

Recycling Codes for Plastic Products

Recycling code	Type of plastic	Physical properties	Examples	Uses for recycled products
1	polyethylene terephthalate (PET)	tough, rigid; can be a fiber or a plastic; solvent resistant; sinks in water	soda bottles, clothing, electrical insulation, automobile parts	backpacks, sleeping bags, carpet, new bottles, clothing
2	high density polyethylene (HDPE)	rough surface; stiff plastic; resistant to cracking	milk containers, bleach bottles, toys, grocery bags	furniture, toys, trash cans, picnic tables, park benches, fences
3	polyvinyl chloride (PVC)	elastomer or flexible plastic; tough; poor crystallization; unstable to light or heat; sinks in water	pipe, vinyl siding, automobile parts, clear bottles for cooking oil, blister packaging	toys, playground equipment
4	low density polyethylene (LDPE)	moderately crystalline, flexible plastic; solvent resistant; floats on water	shrink wrapping, trash bags, dry-cleaning bags, frozen-food packaging, meat packaging	trash cans, trash bags, compost containers
5	polypropylene (PP)	rigid, very strong; fiber or flexible plastic; light-weight; heat- and stress-resistant	heatproof containers, rope, appliance parts, outdoor carpet, luggage, diapers, automobile parts	brooms, brushes, ice scrapers, battery cable, insulation, rope
6	polystyrene (P/S, PS)	somewhat brittle, rigid plastic; resistant to acids and bases but not organic solvents; sinks in water, unless it is a foam	fast-food containers, toys, videotape reels, electrical insulation, plastic utensils, disposable drinking cups, CD jewel cases	insulated clothing, egg cartons, thermal insulation

EXERCISE 8: CHEMICAL BONDING

Directions: Choose the *best* answer for each of the following questions.

1. In ionic bonding, how are atoms are held together?
   (1) by sharing electrons
   (2) by transferring electrons
   (3) by chemical attraction
   (4) by temperature
   (5) by cohesion

2. Use the Recycling Code Chart to identify the correct code from 1 to 6.
   _____ shrink wrap, trash bags, and meat packaging
   _____ milk containers, toys, and bleach bottles
   _____ diapers, luggage, and appliance parts
   _____ fast food containers, VCR cassettes, and utensils
   _____ pipes, automobile parts, and clear bottles for cooking oil

Answers are on page 536.

Acids, Bases, and Salts

Many compounds that result from ionic and covalent bonding are categorized as acids or bases. An **acid** is a covalent compound that produces hydrogen ions when dissolved in water. Acids have a sour taste. Common acids are acetic acid (the main component of vinegar), citric acid (found in citrus fruits), lactic acid (found in milk), and hydrochloric acid, a component of stomach acid used in digestion.

A **base** is a compound that forms hydroxide ions when dissolved in water. Bases are able to take a proton from an acid or to give up an unshared pair of electrons to an acid. Bases are described as **alkaline** because they dissolve in water and have a slippery feel. Many hydroxides are bases. Household cleaning agents such as ammonia, borax, lye, and detergents are common examples of bases.

When an acid combines with a base, a salt is formed and water released because the metal found in the base replaces the hydrogen contained in the acid. Inorganic acids, bases, and inorganic salts can conduct electricity when dissolved in water. Chemists apply the **litmus test** to a substance to determine whether it is an acid or a base. An acid turns blue litmus paper red, and a base turns red litmus paper blue.

EXERCISE 9: ACIDS, BASES, AND SALTS

Directions: Read the the explanation and scale below. Choose the *best* answer for each question that follows.

The designation pH (potential for hydrogen-ion formation) is a value by which certain substances are classified according to acidity or alkalinity. The pH scale ranges from 0 to 14, with the value 7 representing neutrality. The pH scale is illustrated below.

pH Scale

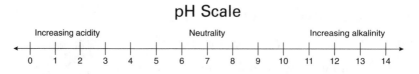

1. According to the pH scale, where would ordinary tap water be found?
   (1) between 0 and 1
   (2) between 3 and 4
   (3) exactly at 7
   (4) exactly at 1
   (5) between 5 and 6

2. Which of the following could be used to prove that a substance is an acid?
   (1) The substance has a pH above 7.
   (2) The substance has a slippery feel.
   (3) It neutralizes a base to form a salt and water.
   (4) When mixed with water, a solid would form.
   (5) The liquid turns red when mixed with water.

Answers are on page 536.

EXERCISE 10: A CAR BATTERY

Directions: Read the passage below and answer the questions that follow.

Acids, bases, and inorganic salts (salts obtained from nonliving things) are effective conductors of electricity. The common car battery demonstrates an electric current generated by the chemical action between an acid and a metal.

In a car battery pure lead (the negative post) and lead dioxide (the positive post) are submerged in sulfuric acid (the conductor). Distilled water is added periodically to maintain the proper level of sulfuric acid. The pure lead loses two electrons when it reacts with the sulfuric acid—the acid changes the lead to lead dioxide. At the same time, the positive post containing lead dioxide gains two electrons and changes the sulfuric acid in which it is submerged into lead sulfate (a salt) and water. The current that makes the car start results from the flow of electrons from the lead dioxide to the lead through the sulfuric acid to the starter switch, all of which makes a complete circuit. A diagram of a car battery is shown below.

Car Battery

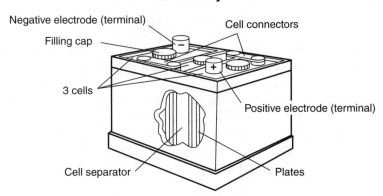

1. An **electrolyte** is an inorganic compound that will conduct an electric current when dissolved in water. What is an electrolyte in the preceding example?

   (1) lead dioxide
   (2) sulfuric acid
   (3) distilled water
   (4) carbon particulates
   (5) carbonic acid

2. A substance is **oxidized** when it loses electrons. In the preceding example, which of the following compounds is oxidized?

   (1) lead
   (2) lead dioxide
   (3) lead sulfate
   (4) water
   (5) sulfuric acid

3. The substances that oxidize and reduce other substances are called **oxidizing agents** and **reducing agents**. According to the reading, in which item are the oxidizing and reducing agents in the correct order?

    (1) lead dioxide and water
    (2) sulfuric acid and lead dioxide
    (3) lead and sulfuric acid
    (4) lead sulfate and lead dioxide
    (5) sulfuric acid and water

4. Which of the following can you conclude to be true when a battery is discharged and can no longer generate a current?

    (1) The sulfuric acid can no longer oxidize the lead.
    (2) The lead dioxide can no longer reduce the sulfuric acid.
    (3) The battery has run out of sulfuric acid.
    (4) The amount of water is too low to generate power.
    (5) The metal casing has corroded.

Answers are on page 536.

Acid Rain

A common example of acid's ability to corrode is seen in the increasing acidity of rainwater. As pollutants such as sulfur and carbon from factories enter the water cycle, new compounds are created. Sulfuric acid in weak concentration as well as carbonic acid come down in the form of precipitation. When these acids come into contact with stone statues or metalwork, corrosion occurs. Old gravestones, marble facades on buildings, and inscriptions that can no longer be read exemplify the disintegration that occurs gradually every time it rains.

Acids in the Human Body

A variety of acids is found in the human body. Your body actually does a remarkable job in controlling its own pH balance. Your blood, for example, needs to remain within the range of 7.35 and 7.45. If the pH of your blood is more acidic, you suffer **acidosis**. If the pH is above 7.45, you are said to have **alkalosis**. The body fights the change in pH by natural chemical balancers called **buffers**. A buffer solution has a weak acid and its conjugate base in equal amounts. The liquid portion of blood is an example of a buffer solution. In some cases, the body may generate too much acid. This is often the case when someone experiences heartburn, which can be temporarily relieved by taking an antacid to neutralize the excess stomach acid.

Reaction Rate, Catalysts, and Equilibrium

Chemical reactions occur at different rates determined by the conditions under which the reactions take place. Sugar dissolves more quickly in hot water than in cold. White phosphorus bursts into flame when exposed to the air. Reactions such as these may be speeded up or slowed down when another substance is introduced.

A **catalyst** is a substance that increases the rate of a chemical reaction but itself remains chemically unchanged. Some catalysts have a negative effect. A negative catalyst slows down the chemical reaction. Negative catalysts, such as the chemicals used in undercoating a car to retard the rusting process, are often inhibitors.

A given set of reactants may react to form more than one product. Often, the by-products react to form the original reactants. When the rate of forward reaction balances the rate of reverse reaction, **chemical equilibrium** occurs. For example, the carbon monoxide in car exhaust systems enters the atmosphere and reacts with oxygen to form carbon dioxide. The carbon dioxide is broken down by sunlight into the original reactant—carbon monoxide. This reaction represents chemical equilibrium because the reaction reverses itself. Chemical reactions such as these create a cycle.

EXERCISE 11: REACTION RATE, CATALYSTS, AND EQUILIBRIUM

Directions: Choose the *best* answers for the following questions.

1. Lipase is an enzyme produced by the liver that helps in the digestion of fats by speeding up the rate at which lipids (fats) are changed into fatty acids and glycerol. According to this description, what can we conclude that an enzyme is?

   (1) a product in a chemical reaction
   (2) a negative catalyst
   (3) a biological catalyst
   (4) a temporary product
   (5) a by-product that is unstable

2. Which of the following processes illustrates chemical equilibrium?

   (1) bonding
   (2) photosynthesis
   (3) respiration
   (4) oxidation
   (5) organic synthesis

Answers are on page 536.

4
PHYSICAL SCIENCE
PHYSICS—THE STUDY OF HOW MATTER BEHAVES

Physics is the branch of science that concerns the forces that cause matter to behave as it does. Physics helps to explain how cellular molecules can move from a lower concentration in an organism to a higher one, how ocean tides occur, and how matter exists in the states of a solid, liquid, or gas. Many of the properties and behaviors of matter can be explained by force and energy. A **force** shows the presence of energy in an environment. **Energy** is the capacity to do work. The area of physics that deals with forces, energy, and their effect on bodies is **mechanics**.

Mechanics

The study of **mechanics** was one of the first sciences developed. Ancient Greek philosopher and scientist **Aristotle** theorized that heavy bodies fall faster than light bodies. This theory was proved false in the early 17th century by Italian scientist and mathematician **Galileo**, who dropped items of different weights from the leaning tower of Pisa. The force acting upon the objects was not fully understood, however, until Englishman **Sir Isaac Newton** formulated laws of gravity and motion that explained how different forces act on objects.

The Force of Gravity

Gravity is the most commonly experienced of all forces in nature. The presence of gravity was first proposed by Newton when he observed the motion of an apple falling from a tree. On the basis of this simple observation, he developed the **Law of Universal Gravitation**, which holds that every body having a mass exerts an attractive force on every other body having a mass in the universe. The strength of the force depends on the masses of the objects and the distance between them. (**Mass** is the measure of the amount of matter in an object.) Thus, the apple's falling illustrates the gravitational pull (attraction) of the larger Earth on the smaller apple. The Law of Universal Gravitation also explains how the planets, attracted by the much larger Sun, remain in their orbits as they revolve around it.

Newton's Three Laws of Motion

The Law of Inertia: A body remains at rest or continues in a state of uniform motion unless a force acts on it. For example, when you drive a car and suddenly jam on the brakes, you continue to move forward. This is because your body's tendency is to remain in the same state of uniform motion (moving forward). The brakes were applied to the car, so its uniform motion was changed.

The Law of Applied Force: A body's change in speed and direction is proportional to the amount of force applied to it. For example, the vanes on a windmill, which move by the force of the wind, will accelerate according to the speed and direction of the wind that drives them.

The Law of Action and Reaction: For every action there is an equal but opposite reaction force. For example, a gun's muzzle kicks backward when a bullet is discharged from it.

EXERCISE 1: LAWS OF FORCE AND MOTION

Directions: Identify the following statements as illustrating (**G**) Newton's Law of Universal Gravitation or applying to (**I**) the Law of Inertia, (**AF**) the Law of Applied Force, or (**AR**) the Law of Action and Reaction.

1. _____ A rocket is propelled upward by the powerful downward discharge of exhaust gases.

2. _____ A bullet fired into the air eventually falls to the ground.

3. _____ A pendulum in a clock, once set in motion, continues to swing, thereby regulating the clock's movement.

4. _____ A jet airplane, upon landing, lowers the flaps on its wings. The flaps create drag, a force that helps the plane to slow down.

Answers are on page 537.

EXERCISE 2: THE FORCE OF GRAVITY

Directions: Read the paragraph below and answer the questions that follow.

An astronaut weighs in before blast-off. He weighs only a fraction of his original weight when he steps on a scale on the moon. Journeying to Jupiter, he finds that his weight has increased several times over his original weight.

1. How may these changes in the astronaut's weight be best explained?
   (1) the amount of force each planetary body exerts as he weighs himself
   (2) the distance from the Sun of the planetary bodies
   (3) changes in the atmospheric pressure on the different heavenly bodies
   (4) the amount of calories consumed during the flight
   (5) the duration of time that elapsed between weigh-ins

2. What do you estimate the weight change for the same astronaut would be if he were to land on Mercury?

Answers are on page 537.

Work, Energy, and Power

According to physics, **work** occurs when a **force** succeeds in moving an object it acts upon. For example, a person who lifts a 50-pound weight one foot off the floor is performing work. For work to be performed, the movement of the object must be in the same direction as the force—in this case vertical. Work may be expressed as any force unit times any distance unit and may be written as follows:

$$W = F \times D$$

The amount of work done is the amount of force multiplied by the distance moved. In the preceding example, 50 foot-pounds of work is done when 50 pounds are lifted one foot:

$$50 \text{ lb} \times 1 \text{ ft} = 50 \text{ ft lb}$$

Energy is required to do work. In the example above, muscular energy is illustrated in the form of a body that is capable of doing work. Energy may be classified as either kinetic or potential energy.

Kinetic energy is energy possessed by a body in motion. The form of energy shown by a moving train is kinetic energy.

Potential energy is energy that is stored or is available for use by a body. For example, coal has potential energy that is released only when it is burned.

Power is the rate at which work is done. Power is generally measured in horsepower, which is equal to 550 foot-pounds per second or 33,000 foot-pounds per minute.

The Law of Conservation of Energy

The **Law of Conservation of Energy** holds that all of the energy of the universe is conserved. The capacity for energy to do work can be changed from one kind to another, but it cannot be lost. This principle can be illustrated in the following example of energy generated from a waterfall:

Water possesses **potential energy**. When water moves rapidly in a downward motion, drawn by the pull of gravity, the potential energy is changed into **kinetic energy**. Kinetic energy from a waterfall can be harnessed to power a turbine, a rotary engine, creating **rotational energy**. This is sufficient to generate **electrical energy**, which in turn is converted into **light** and **heat energy**, which we use in our homes. The initial potential energy has been changed into five different forms.

EXERCISE 3: FORMS OF ENERGY

Directions: Identify the following statements as either demonstrating kinetic energy (**K**) or demonstrating potential energy (**P**).

1. _____ a strong west wind blowing across a region

2. _____ a stick of unlit dynamite

3. _____ a waterfall

Answers are on page 537.

EXERCISE 4: TYPES OF ENERGY

Directions: Read the following definitions of the five types of energy. Then choose the *best* answers for the questions below.

nuclear energy: energy from splitting an atom or fusing atoms

chemical energy: energy from the reaction of two or more substances combining with one another

electrical energy: energy from an electric current

solar energy: energy from the heat of the Sun

steam energy: energy from steam pressure

1. Which form of energy results from the fission of uranium-235 nuclei that is used to generate electrical power?
  (1) nuclear energy
  (2) chemical energy
  (3) electrical energy
  (4) solar energy
  (5) steam energy

2. Which form of energy results from the ignition of a gas and air mixture and powers a car?
  (1) nuclear energy
  (2) chemical energy
  (3) electrical energy
  (4) solar energy
  (5) steam energy

Answers are on page 537.

Simple Machines

A **machine** is a device that transmits or multiplies force. A machine operates on the principle of a little force as being applied through a great distance and a great resistance being overcome through a short distance. A **lever** is a simple machine used to perform work by lifting a great weight. A lever is just a bar that is free to pivot on its support (called a **fulcrum**). Through the use of a lever, for example, a 1,000-pound weight can be lifted with relatively little effort (force).

The Lever—A Simple Machine

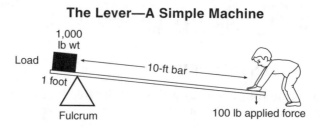

The illustration above shows that it would take 100 pounds of force for a person to lift a 1,000-pound weight positioned 1 foot from the fulcrum when the lever bar is 10 feet long. This may be expressed as follows:

$$\textbf{1,000 lb} \times \textbf{1 ft} = \textbf{100 lb} \times \textbf{10 ft}$$

In this case a relatively small force (100 lb) applied at a great distance from the object (10 ft) is able to overcome great resistance (1,000 lb). According to this principle the greater the distance between the fulcrum and the applied force, the less force required to perform the work.

The wheelbarrow, the crowbar, the pulley, and the inclined plane are simple machines. Complex machines are made up of more than one simple machine.

EXERCISE 5: SIMPLE MACHINES

Directions: Choose the *best* answer for the following question.

1. According to the principle that a little force applied through a great distance can overcome great resistance, which would be most likely to happen if the lever bar in the preceding illustration is increased to 20 feet in length and the weight remained at the end of the bar?
   (1) The effort to lift the weight would increase to 150 pounds of applied force.
   (2) The effort to lift the weight would remain at 100 pounds of applied force.
   (3) The effort would be decreased by half, to 50 pounds of applied force.
   (4) The resistance of the weight would double.
   (5) The resistance of the weight would triple.

Answer is on page 537.

The Nature of Heat and Energy

Today we know that heat is the result of the random motion of molecules. It is nothing more than energy itself. One theory of physics that has contributed greatly to our understanding of the phenomenon of heat is kinetic theory, a basic theory that explains how different states of matter can exist.

The Kinetic Theory of Matter

According to the **Kinetic Theory of Matter**, matter exists in three states—solid, liquid, or gas. A fourth state, **plasma**, is an ionized gas; the Sun is made up of plasma. The form, or phase, of matter is determined by the motion of the molecules within it.

Solids are composed of atoms or molecules in limited motion. These atoms or molecules are in direct contact with one another, allowing little or no space for random movement. The attractive forces of the particles keep the solid intact and give the solid its definite shape and structure.

In **liquids**, individual atoms or molecules are able to move past one another into new positions, giving this form of matter its fluidity. Cohesive forces hold liquids intact.

Gases are substances in which the individual atoms or molecules are in constant random motion. The motion, or kinetic energy, increases along with an increase in temperature. Molecules are unable to hold together, and this property gives gases the ability to flow or spread out to fill the container in which they are placed.

Heat, Temperature, and the States of Matter

The state of matter depends on its heat content. **Temperature** is a measure of heat intensity. The change from one state of matter to another involves the addition or subtraction of a certain amount of heat per gram of substance. For example, at 32 degrees Fahrenheit, water, a liquid, changes to ice, a solid. When the temperature is raised above 32 degrees Fahrenheit, the ice, a solid, changes to water, a liquid. At temperatures at or above 212 degrees Fahrenheit, the boiling point of water, the water changes to steam, a gaseous state. Impurities in water affect its freezing point.

Certain materials expand when their temperatures are raised and shrink when they are lowered. Liquids expand more noticeably than solids, but gases expand even more. The mercury thermometer employs this principle. Temperature can be measured in degrees centigrade or degrees Fahrenheit. On the **centigrade** (or **Celsius**) **scale**, 0 degrees represents the freezing point of water, and 100 degrees is the boiling point. On the **Fahrenheit scale**, 32 degrees represents the freezing point of water, and 212 degrees is the boiling point. Temperature is measured in degrees by thermometer, and heat is measured by the calorie or **British Thermal Unit (BTU)**. A **calorie** is the amount of heat needed to raise one gram of water one degree centigrade. The BTU is the amount of heat required to raise one pound of water 1 degree Fahrenheit.

Heat is transferred by three methods. The first is called **conduction**, the transfer of heat between objects that are in direct contact. You have experienced this whenever you have picked up a hot item, such as a handle on a heated pan. The second method is **convection**. This method depends on the currents of water and air. When you are adding hot water to one end of the bathtub filled with water, convection transfers the heat to the rest of the water. The third method is **radiation**. You can feel waves of heat by putting your hands near a radiator (used to heat many apartments).

EXERCISE 6: KINETIC THEORY OF MATTER

Directions: Identify the following statements as either true (**T**) or false (**F**).

1. _____ There is more rigid molecular structure in a solid than in a gas.

   _____ Molecules in a gas are close together and exhibit little motion.

   _____ Heat is transferred by conduction, convection, or coercion.

2. Which heat transfer method is demonstrated when your hand is positioned directly over the flame of a lighted candle?
   (**1**) convection
   (**2**) conduction
   (**3**) radiation
   (**4**) expansion
   (**5**) coersion

Answers are on page 537.

EXERCISE 7: HEAT AND TEMPERATURE

Directions: Read the passage below and answer the question that follows.

Different materials expand at different degrees of temperature change and in different percentages of their length, volume, or surface. Buckling can occur when a material such as asphalt used for road surfaces reacts to changes in temperature, causing potholes. This is one of the reasons for the widespread use of reinforced concrete (concrete with a steel framework) rather than asphalt on road surfaces and the use of reinforced concrete in high-rise apartment construction.

1. What does the widespread use of reinforced concrete in construction suggest?

   (1) Concrete and steel expand and contract at nearly the same temperatures.

   (2) Reinforced concrete expands at temperatures much higher than ordinary asphalt and does not buckle.

   (3) Reinforced concrete does not expand and contract at all.

   (4) Asphalt can be used only on roadways and never in construction.

   (5) Asphalt is much more expensive and harder to use than concrete.

Answer is on page 537.

The Nature of Waves

A **wave** is a periodic or harmonic disturbance in space or through a medium (water, for instance) by which energy is transmitted. Water, sound, and light all travel in waves. The illumination a lamp provides comes from light waves (a form of electromagnetic waves) while the music emanating from a stereo comes from sound waves. The powers to preserve food and warm it come from electromagnetic waves, and the power that transmits signals to a television set comes from radio waves (another form of electromagnetic waves). The energy that gives a waterbed its soothing motion comes from water waves.

Types of Properties of Waves

Waves transmit energy in different ways, and all phases of matter transmit waves. An example of a solid transmitting wave energy is an earthquake that takes place when rocks are under pressure and snap or slide into new positions. Waves that are felt and seen in water are examples of a liquid transmitting wave energy. Gases also transmit wave energy, as in an explosion, when heat, sound, and light waves are generated. Two basic types of waves exist: longitudinal waves and transverse waves.

longitudinal wave: Particles of the medium move back and forth in the same direction as the wave itself moves. An example of a longitudinal wave is a sound wave that occurs when a tuning fork is tapped, as shown below.

Longitudinal Wave

When a tuning fork is tapped, the prongs move from right to left in a rapid periodic motion. A sound wave is produced, and it moves parallel (right and left) to the moving prong.

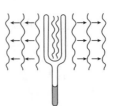

transverse wave: Particles of the medium move at right angles to the direction of the wave's movement. An example of a transverse wave is one that occurs when a pebble is tossed into a still pond. Light travels in transverse waves. An example of a transverse wave is shown below.

Transverse Wave

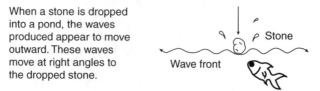

When a stone is dropped into a pond, the waves produced appear to move outward. These waves move at right angles to the dropped stone.

Wave front

Stone

Waves have two components, a crest and a trough. A **crest** is the point of highest displacement in a wave, and the **trough** is the point of lowest displacement. Crests and troughs are easily visible in water waves.

Two specific characteristics of a wave are length and frequency:

- **Wavelength** is defined as the distance between two successive wave crests or two successive wave troughs.

- **Wave frequency** is the number of wave crests that pass a given point per second.

Therefore, the shorter the wavelength, the higher the wave frequency. In fact, a wave's speed equals the wavelength times the wave frequency.

When a source of a wave is in motion, a compression of the wavelength is detected. This can be demonstrated with sound waves. As a train passes while you are standing on the platform, you will notice a distinct drop in the pitch or sound quality. This drop in sound pitch is heard by the observers standing on the side during an automotive race such as the Indianapolis 500. Water waves demonstrate the same compression in the direction of motion. The water waves in the front of a boat are squeezed together, while those at the rear of the boat are far apart. This is referred to as the **Doppler Effect**. Scientists use the Doppler Effect to forcast tornadoes and to detect the motions of stars in our galaxy.

Sound Wave

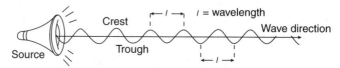

Crest

Trough

Source

l = wavelength

Wave direction

Sound waves, as illustrated above, are longitudinal waves. A musical pitch, or tone, is heard when there is a definite frequency to a wave. The lower the frequency, the lower the tone. For example, the frequency of a bass speaker in a stereo system is lower than a tweeter, or high-frequency speaker, because the low-pitched sound of the bass results from a lower number of vibrations per second.

A sound wave is a wave of compression. It begins at a source—in the example on the previous page, a horn speaker. The speaker vibrates, compressing the air in front of it and, like a spring, pushes it away. As the wave passes, the air molecules are forced together. The sensation of hearing results when these waves strike the eardrum.

Sound waves can travel through solids, liquids, and gases. In fact, the human body can be a medium for sound waves. **Ultrasonic waves**, very high-pitched waves, are used to detect diseases or to show images of unborn fetuses.

EXERCISE 8: WAVE TYPES

Directions: Choose the *best* answers to the questions that follow.

1. In the space provided, write **L** if the example is an example of a longitudinal wave and **T** if it is an example of a transverse wave.

   _____ the noise caused by the detonation of an atomic bomb

   _____ the hum created when an arrow is released from a bow

   _____ waves that appear on the surface of the ocean

2. The Doppler Effect is used for which of the following purposes?
   (1) to find fish in lakes
   (2) to predict storms and tornadoes
   (3) to test wave frequency
   (4) to reflect images to satellites
   (5) to heighten sound in stereos

Answers are on page 537.

EXERCISE 9: PROPERTIES OF WAVES

Directions: Look at the illustration below and choose the *best* answer to the question that follows.

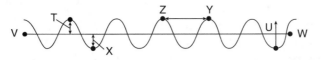

1. According to the illustration above, which points could be used to measure wavelength?
   (1) T and Y
   (2) X and Y
   (3) Z and Y
   (4) V and W
   (5) T, X, and U

Answer is on page 537.

The Nature of Light

Physicists define **light** as a form of electromagnetic energy that stimulates sensitive cells of the retina of the human eye to cause perception of vision. Electromagnetic energy can be expressed in wavelength ranges along a continuum, or spectrum. Light occupies the center of a spectrum that ranges from the low end (**gamma rays**) to the high end (**radio waves**). The other rays that occupy the electromagnetic spectrum are Xrays, ultraviolet rays, and infrared rays. **Ultraviolet rays** are invisible and are chiefly responsible for sunburn and tan. Heat-emitting objects such as the sun or a radiator send out **infrared rays** that can be detected only by certain sensitive instruments.

The Electromagnetic Spectrum

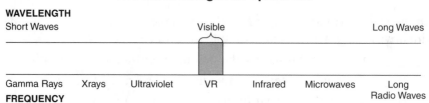

The visible rays of the spectrum are recognized by the human eye as color. In order, these colors are red, orange, yellow, green, blue, indigo (deep blue), and violet. The shortest wavelengths that we can see are those we call violet; the longest ones are those we call red.

Two theories about the nature of light focus on different properties of light. According to the **Wave Theory of Light**, light is a luminous energy emitted by a light source and travels through space as a transverse wave. According to the **Particle Theory of Light**, light energy is both radiated (transmitted) and absorbed as tiny packets, or bundles, and not as continuous waves. Atoms and molecules are able to emit or absorb light energy in specific amounts.

EXERCISE 10: THE PHOTOELECTRIC PRINCIPLE

Directions: Read the passage below and answer the question that follows.

The electric eye, or photoelectric cell, is a mechanism used to open and close a garage door when a beam of light is activated or broken. The principle of the electric eye is based on the photoelectric effect. The photoelectric effect occurs when a beam of light strikes certain metals, causing electrons to be knocked out of the metal, producing an electric current. This is how it happens:

Light falling on the inside of a bulb coated with an active substance causes electrons to be emitted. The electrons are attracted to a positively charged electrode positioned in the center of the bulb as a filament. An electric current results when the electrons (negatively charged particles) are attracted to the positively charged particles of the electrode. It is observed that electrons are knocked loose only when a certain light energy is reached. The current can then be controlled by changes in light intensity. It appears that electrons are able to absorb only a certain amount of light at one time. When light shines on the electric eye, a current is established and the door moves. When the beam of light is broken, the door stops.

1. How does the principle of the electric eye act?
    (1) to support the wave theory of light that light comes only from a luminous source
    (2) to dispute the belief that all light exists only as a continuous wave
    (3) to support the particle theory of light, which states that light energy is transmitted in packets and bundles and not as waves
    (4) to complement the idea that light acts like particles in a wave
    (5) to contradict the idea that light is generated only in a star

Answer is on page 537.

Properties of Light Waves
Following is a summary of the properties of light waves:

reflection: the angular return of a light wave that occurs when it strikes a shiny surface
Example: light bouncing off a mirror

refraction: the apparent bending of light waves as they pass from one medium to another
Example: drinking straw looking broken in a glass of water

diffraction: the bending of light waves according to their wavelengths as they pass near the edge of an obstacle or through a small opening
Example: "rainbow" pattern on an old phonograph record held edgewise toward white light

interference: the altering of brightness of light rays that occurs when they interfere with each other, causing reinforcement and cancellation
Example: holding thumb and finger together and looking through the opening at a bright light

polarization: the restriction of light waves to a particular plane, horizontal or vertical
Example: sunglasses that minimize glare off shiny surfaces

EXERCISE 11: PROPERTIES OF LIGHT WAVES

Directions: Use the information on the previous page to choose the *best* answer for each question below.

1. A coin lying at the bottom of a pool is located at a different point from where the eye perceives it to be. The light rays from the coin bend as they pass from water to air. This demonstrates
   (1) reflection
   (2) refraction
   (3) diffraction
   (4) interference
   (5) polarization

2. Rays of light striking a polished piece of chrome appear to bounce off its surface. This demonstrates
   (1) reflection
   (2) refraction
   (3) diffraction
   (4) interference
   (5) polarization

Answers are on page 537.

The Nature of Electricity

Electricity is another invisible but vital form of energy that we often take for granted. Without electricity, however, our lives would be paralyzed. The more urbanized we become, the more dependent on electricity we are. Nuclear energy, despite its potential hazards, is an important source for generating the electrical power we need. Physicists define electricity as a form of energy that results from the flow of loose electrons—electrons weakly bound to atoms. Electricity is closely related to magnetism; therefore, the attractive force of magnetism must be discussed in order to explain electrical energy.

Magnetism and Electrical Charges

The points of attraction at opposite ends of a magnet are called its **poles**. Magnets have a north and a south pole, also called a positive and a negative pole. The opposite poles of two magnets (a north pole and a south pole) will attract each other. Correspondingly, similar poles (two north or south poles) will repel each other. The space around magnets is called a **magnetic field**. Only a few natural and synthetic materials can be magnetized—iron, steel, nickel, cobalt, and some alloys. A magnet, with its poles and lines of force, is illustrated on the next page.

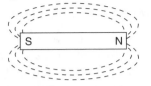

Magnetic Lines of Force

Every magnetic substance contains domains, groups of molecules with attractive forces. Before a substance is magnetized, these domains are arranged randomly so that the field of one domain is canceled out by the field of another. When the substance is magnetized, the domains line up parallel to the lines of force, with all north poles facing in the same direction. This arrangement makes a permanent magnet out of a material in which the domains are too weak to disarrange themselves.

In most elements the atoms possess a slight magnetic field because of their spinning electrons. However, the fields cancel each other out because the atoms rotate and spin in different directions. In a magnet, however, whole groups of atoms line up in one direction and increase one another's magnetic effect rather than cancel it out. These magnetic concentrations are **magnetic domains.**

Unmagnetized and Magnetized Iron Atoms

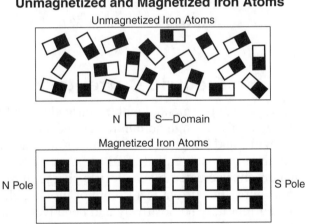

Static Electricity and Magnetism

Static electricity is a stationary electrical charge caused by the friction of two objects, one positively charged and the other negatively charged. Static electricity operates on the same principle as magnetism. The rubbing of the carpet by your shoes causes your body to become electrified. The shock you feel is caused by your negatively charged body being neutralized by the positive charge of the object you touch. Upon contact your body is no longer charged. Static electricity is stored and does not move. The charged object must be brought into contact with another object that has an opposite charge for electrical shock to occur.

EXERCISE 12: ELECTRICITY AND MAGNETISM

Directions: Choose the *best* answer for the questions below.

Earth itself is surrounded by a magnetic field. This may be because of strong electric currents in Earth's core and the rotation of Earth. The north magnetic pole is located in Canada; the south magnetic pole is in nearly the opposite location. The strong magnetic attraction of these poles tends to align the needle of a compass in a northerly–southerly direction.

1. What makes a compass tell direction?
   (1) The whole Earth acts as a magnet.
   (2) The Chinese discovered the magnetic poles.
   (3) The Greeks discovered the magnetic poles.
   (4) Large iron deposits are located in Canada.
   (5) The magnetic attraction of Earth is increasing.

2. Which of the following would be attracted to either pole of a magnet?
   (1) a piece of aluminum
   (2) a piece of brass
   (3) a piece of tin
   (4) an unmagnetized piece of cobalt
   (5) a magnetized piece of cobalt

Answers are on page 537.

Electric Currents

Early scientists who experimented with electric charges found that charges could move easily through certain materials called **conductors** (such as salt solutions, acids, and hot gases). Other materials (such as rubber) found not to conduct charges at all are called **insulators**.

An **electric current** is created by an electric charge in motion. In a solid conductor, such as wire, the current is a stream of moving electrons. In a liquid or gas, the current may be positively and negatively charged atoms—**ions**. An electric current flowing through a solid conductor can be compared to the flow of water through the pipes in your plumbing system. Lights come on instantly when a switch is turned on because the wires are always filled with electrons, just as a water pipe is always filled with water.

Electromagnets

An **electromagnet** is a core of soft magnetic material surrounded by a coil of wire. An electric current is passed through the wire to magnetize the core when a switch is flicked or a button is pushed. The device then has the power to attract iron objects. When the switch is turned off, the attraction is broken. Electromagnets are used in radios and in ordinary doorbells.

EXERCISE 13: CONDUCTORS AND INSULATORS

Directions: Identify the following terms as either a conductor of electricity (**C**) or an insulator (**I**).

1. _____ leather

2. _____ wood

3. _____ salt water

4. _____ plastic

5. _____ copper

Answers are on page 538.

EXERCISE 14: ELECTROMAGNETS

Directions: Choose the *best* answer for the following questions.

1. Why would a radio with a strong electromagnet be placed far away from the navigation instruments on a plane or ship?
   (1) The radio wouldn't work because of electrical interference.
   (2) The radio couldn't be heard clearly because of static.
   (3) The accuracy of the compass would be affected by the magnetic field established by the radio's electromagnet.
   (4) The radio's electromagnet would cause all the navigation instruments to malfunction.
   (5) The radio would draw too much electrical energy, causing the electrical system of the ship or plane to discharge.

2. Identify which of the following are true (**T**) or false (**F**).
   _____ You need an insulator to keep electricity flowing only along wires.
   _____ Electromagnets are used in doorbells.
   _____ When the switch is in the off position, electricity still is flowing through the circuit.

Answers are on page 538.

Creating Electricity

Electricity is created by power companies and sent to our homes by high voltage wires through transformers. Because there is a concern about the limited quantities of fossil fuels, alternative power supplies for electricity are being used.

One system requires the fission of nuclear energy in nuclear power plants. These plants bombard the nuclei of large unstable uranium atoms with neutrons. The large release of heat is used to heat water, which is used to turn a **turbine**, a wire loop connecting two magnets. When the turbine is forced to turn, the electrons are stolen from the magnets and sent through the wire as electricity. This alternative energy has many drawbacks, including the safe disposal of radioactive nuclear waste left over from the reaction.

Another alternative is **solar energy**. Scientists have found that pure silicon (found in sand and one of the most common elements in the crust of the Earth) is electrically excited in the presence of light. You may have experienced this if you own a solar calculator, which will not perform in a dimly lighted area. The sun's energy excites the electrons, which then flow along wires to provide electricity to the attached appliance.

Other alternative energies are limited in availability. One such alternative is **wind power**, captured through the use of windmills. California has wind farms where many large windmills are connected to generate electricity. These new models have arms made of durable synthetic materials. Windmills do not need a strong wind; in fact, strong winds can damage the mechanics. The best condition is a steady wind that maintains a continuous motion of the flywheel.

Hydroelectric power is another source that has to be limited to the already established use of the water flow in the region. Many rivers are used as transportation and cannot be dammed to provide the reservoir of water needed to control the flow of water through the turbine system. Hydroelectric power is a clean, renewable resource.

EXERCISE 15: CREATING ELECTRICITY

Directions: Use the information above to fill in the blanks.

1. Hydroelectric power is not always possible because sometimes rivers are used for _____.

2. Fossil fuels will not be around forever, so we need to explore the use of other energy systems called _____.

3. Windmills do not need strong wind, but they do need _____ wind.

4. Pure silicon has electrons that are excited into motion by _____.

5. A loop or wire that is turned between two magnets and creates electricity is a _____.

Answers are on page 538.

LANGUAGE ARTS, READING

The GED Language Arts, Reading Test consists of prose passages of about 200 to 400 words, poetry passages of about eight to twenty-five lines, and drama excerpts. Each passage is followed by four to eight multiple-choice questions. These questions require you to interpret selections from popular literature, classical literature, and commentaries about literature and the arts. To answer successfully, you will need to understand what you read, apply information to a new situation, analyze elements of style and structure in passages, and synthesize parts of passages into a whole.

How many questions are on the test?

There are 40 multiple-choice questions, and you will be given 65 minutes to complete the test. Each passage is preceded by a **purpose question** that is intended to help you focus your reading of the piece. To get an idea of what the test is like, look at the Posttest at the end of this book.

What's on the test?

The GED Language Arts, Reading Test can be broken down into the content areas it covers and the skills it tests. The following subjects make up the content of the test:

1. Literary Texts (30 items) 75%

    Prose Fiction (45%) from three general time periods:
    Before 1920
    1920–1960
    After 1960
    Poetry (15%)
    Drama (15%)

2. Nonfiction Texts (10 items) 25%

    Informational Text: newspaper or magazine articles, editorials, or speeches
    Literary Nonfiction: biographies, autobiographies, essays, diaries, letters, or reviews
    Critical reviews of fine or performing arts: commentary about films, television, videotapes, photos, artwork, computer images, or charts
    Business Documents: business letters, memos, employee guidelines, company policies, or company programs

Only seven passages will be included in each test form. Each test will have one commentary work about a visual medium, but there will be no graphics. You will not have to recall or have prior knowledge of the text of specific literary works, including titles, dates, or authors. Also remember that you will be tested on your ability to think through certain ideas and concepts. You will be asked to do more than just find a statement or quotation that was given in a passage.

What thinking skills are needed for the test?

Thinking skills that you will be tested on include:

Comprehension (Literal and Inferential)   20%

    Paraphrasing, summarizing, explaining

Application   15%

    Transferring ideas to new situations

Analysis   30–35%

    Drawing conclusions; understanding consequences; making inferences; identifying style and structure; making comparisons and contrasts; using cause and effect

Synthesis   30–35%

    Drawing on the passage as a whole or on several sources; interpreting organizational structure or overall tone, point of view, style, or purpose; making connections

In the Critical Thinking Skills section of this book, the thinking skills above are explained. See pages 31–58.

1
INTERPRETING PROSE FICTION

The fiction passages presented on the Language Arts, Reading Test are taken from either novels or short stories which usually present imaginary people and events that imitate life. Novels and short stories are written in **prose**—ordinary spoken language—and share common literary devices and techniques.

By reading fiction, you can enjoy stories about interesting people and situations and gain a greater understanding of life. Your understanding of literature will also aid you as a moviegoer or as a viewer of television, videotapes, or DVDs. Many aspects of literature can be applied to films and television programs because the script is the basis for any of these.

Think of the author as a type of artist who works with a palette. On the palette the artist mixes colors, just as the author mixes together **characters**, **settings**, and **plots**. The artist works with an overall purpose for his subject matter just as the author conveys **themes**. The artist and the author speak through a particular **point of view** which may be direct or indirect. In the finished product the artist and the author each convey an attitude toward his or her work through a particular **style** shown. The artist achieves an overall result through a painting or other work of art; the fiction author achieves an overall result through a novel or short story.

The Novel and the Short Story

Although many elements in fiction are common to both the novel and the short story, there are basic differences between the two forms. The **novel** is a long, book-length story involving several characters and events in their lives. A skillful novelist brings together characters with their unique personalities, adventures, and struggles; the novelist then combines them into one main plot. The **short story** is much shorter than a novel and usually focuses on fewer characters and only one event or action. By narrowing the focus, the short-story writer achieves a single effect.

Edgar Allan Poe, one of America's earliest and best short-story writers, believed that a short story should be read in one sitting, a much briefer time span than a novel—not many hours, days, or even weeks. A good short-story writer gets to the point and quickly develops believable characters and events. The writer has limited space in which to create a work of art. Think about how the writer presents his or her ideas as well as the meaning behind the ideas themselves.

Although novels and short stories are developed around fictional characters, the events that occur may sometimes be based on fact. This is especially true in historical novels. For example, *The Agony and the Ecstasy,* by Irving Stone, describes events surrounding the life of Italian Renaissance artist and sculptor Michelangelo and his clashes with Pope Julius II. The book is set in the real-life locations of Florence and Rome, Italy, and includes real people of the sixteenth century. Many of the events and the dialogue among characters cannot be known because conversations were not recorded hundreds of years ago.

Two other examples of this historical fiction type are *A Tale of Two Cities,* by Charles Dickens, and *Les Miserables,* by Victor Hugo. The French Revolution is the physical and political setting for both novels; however, the plots and the characters are fiction.

Basic Elements of Fiction

The five basic elements of fiction (setting, characterization, plot, theme, and point of view) are illustrated in the following puzzle. Framing the puzzle is **style**, which includes the author's **language** and **tone**. These elements and other literary terms will be explained in this section. As you progress through this section, this diagram will help you to understand the parts (elements) that make up the whole (novel or short story).

BASIC ELEMENTS OF FICTION
The Novel and the Short Story

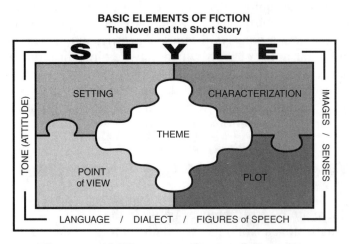

Time and Place as Part of Setting

The **setting** of a short story or novel is the **time** (of day or year), **place** in which the action occurs, and the **atmosphere**, or **mood**. The atmosphere, or mood, includes the weather and conditions of the physical place: dark and dirty if in a dungeon, or colorful and bright if at a carnival. The atmosphere, or mood, also includes the feelings of the characters placed in the setting: discouraged or sad, happy or playful, and so on.

Some authors are very direct about revealing their settings. They state early in a work exactly when and/or where the story is happening:

> "Every day one summer in Larkin's Hill, it rained a little. The rain was a regular thing, and could come about two o'clock in the afternoon."
>
> —Excerpted from *A Curtain of Green* by Eudora Welty

> "Miami was hot and muggy and the land wind that blew from the Everglades brought mosquitoes even in the morning."
>
> —Excerpted from *The Strange Country* by Ernest Hemingway

Inferring Time and Place

In many stories, the time and place are not directly stated. As the reader, you need to read between the lines, or look for clues, to identify a specific time and place. The following exercise will help you practice the skill of inference.

EXERCISE 1: INFERRING TIME AND PLACE

Directions: Read the following paragraph to infer setting. Underline all the clues that suggest time (when the action happens) and place (where the action happens).

WHAT KIND OF WAR IS THIS?

The cold passed reluctantly from the earth, and the retiring fogs revealed an army stretched out on the hills, resting. As the landscape changed from brown to green, the army awakened, and began to tremble with eagerness at the noise of rumors. It cast its eyes upon the roads, which were growing from long troughs of liquid mud to proper thoroughfares. A river, amber-tinted in the shadow of its banks, purled at the army's feet; and at night, when the stream had become of a sorrowful blackness, one could see across it the red, eyelike gleam of hostile camp fires set in the low brows of distant hills.

Once a certain tall soldier developed virtues and went resolutely to wash a shirt. He came flying back from a brook waving his garment bannerlike. He was swelled with a tale he had heard from a reliable friend, who had heard it from a truthful cavalryman, who had heard it from his trustworthy brother, one of the orderlies at division headquarters. He adopted the important air of a herald in red and gold . . .

To his attentive audience he drew a loud and elaborate plan of a very brilliant campaign. When he had finished, the blue-clothed men scattered into small arguing groups between the rows of squat brown huts.

—Excerpted from *The Red Badge of Courage* by Stephen Crane

1. At what time of day does the action take place? What details act as clues?

2. Crane wrote a universal novel, which appeals to all time periods and places, but when does the action more likely take place: in the 1860s or the 1990s? What details act as clues?

3. Where does the action take place? What details act as clues?

Answers are on page 539.

Atmosphere, or Mood, as Part of Setting

An important part of setting is **atmosphere**, or **mood**—the sensations and emotions associated with details of the physical setting. For example, if a story opens with a nighttime setting, a thunderstorm, a castle, and a man approaching the door, the author is creating an atmosphere of mystery or suspense. On the other hand, if a story opens with early morning as the setting and children playing happily in a playground, the atmosphere is lighthearted.

EXERCISE 2: RECOGNIZING ATMOSPHERE, OR MOOD

Directions: Read the passage below and answer the question that follows.

HOW DOES THIS MAN FEEL?

During the whole of a dull, dark, and soundless day in the autumn of the year, when the clouds hung oppressively low in the heavens, I had been passing alone, on horseback, through a singularly dreary tract of country, and at length found myself, as the shades of evening drew on, within view of the melancholy House of Usher. I know not how it was—but, with the first glimpse of the building, a sense of insufferable gloom pervaded my spirit. . . . I looked upon the scene before me—upon the mere house, and the simple landscape features of the domain—upon the bleak walls—upon the vacant eye-like windows—upon a few rank sedges—and upon a few white trunks of decayed trees—with an utter depression of soul. . . .

—Excerpted from "The Fall of the House of Usher" by Edgar Allan Poe

Which descriptive words and phrases does Poe use to create an atmosphere of gloom?

Answers are on page 539.

EXERCISE 3: IDENTIFYING PARTS OF SETTING

Directions: Read the passage below and answer the questions that follow.

HOW DOES THE SEASON AFFECT THE MOOD?

Some of the caddies were poor as sin and lived in one-room houses with a neurasthenic [exhausted, broken down] cow in the front yard, but Dexter Green's father owned the second best grocery store in Black Bear—the best one was "The Hub," patronized by the wealthy people from Sherry Island—and Dexter caddied only for pocket-money.

In the fall when the days became crisp and gray, and the long Minnesota winter shut down like the white lid of a box, Dexter's skis moved over the snow that hid the fairways of the golf course. At these times the country gave him a feeling of profound melancholy—

it offended him that the links should lie in enforced fallowness [inactive period], haunted by ragged sparrows for the long season. It was dreary, too, that on the tees where the gay colors fluttered in summer there were now only the desolate sand-boxes knee-deep in crusted ice. When he crossed the hills the wind blew cold as misery, and if the sun was out he tramped with his eyes squinted up against the hard dimensionless glare.

—Excerpted from "Winter Dreams" in *All the Sad Young Men*
by F. Scott Fitzgerald

1. Is the action taking place in the present, the past, or the future? (What verb tense is used?)

2. In the excerpt, where (place) is Dexter and what is he doing? What details act as clues?

3. How does Fitzgerald describe the same setting (place) in fall, in winter, and in summer?

4. What is the effect of the scenery on Dexter? What atmosphere, or mood, does the author convey through his character?

Answers are on page 539.

Characterization: Who Is in the Story

Characters are the fictional people in a novel or short story. **Characterization** is the method by which a writer creates fictional people who seem lifelike and believable. Writers may use any of these different methods to create character: describing the character and his or her actions, revealing the character's speech patterns, revealing what other characters say about the character, and revealing the character's unspoken thoughts.

EXERCISE 4: INFERRING CHARACTERIZATION

Directions: Read the passage below and answer the questions that follow.

WHAT KIND OF BOY IS HUCK FINN?

You don't know about me, without you have read a book by the name of "The Adventures of Tom Sawyer," but that ain't no matter. That book was made by Mr. Mark Twain, and he told the truth, mainly. There was things which he stretched, but mainly he told the truth. That is nothing. I never seen anybody but lied, one time or another, without it was Aunt Polly, or the widow, or maybe Mary. Aunt Polly— Tom's Aunt Polly, she is—and Mary, and the Widow Douglas, is all told about in that book—which is mostly a true book; with some stretchers, as I said before.

Now the way that the book winds up, is this: Tom and me found the money that the robbers hid in the cave, and it made us rich. We got six thousand dollars apiece—all gold. Well, Judge Thatcher, he took it and put it out at interest, and it fetched us a dollar a day apiece, all the year round—more than a body could tell what to do with. The Widow Douglas, she took me for her son, and allowed she would sivilize [sic] me; but it was rough living in the house all the time, and so when I couldn't stand it no longer, I lit out. I got into my old rags, and my sugar-hogshead again, and was free and satisfied. . . .

—Excerpted from *The Adventures of Huckleberry Finn* by Mark Twain

1. Which description best fits Huck's personality?

    (1) the world's biggest liar

    (2) an uncaring, uninterested youth

    (3) a sad orphan adopted by the Widow

    (4) a somewhat uncivilized boy

    (5) a very educated future judge

2. In this excerpt, from whom do we primarily learn about Huck's character?

    (1) Huck's narrative about himself and others

    (2) Aunt Polly, Mary, and the Widow Douglas

    (3) Huck's unspoken thoughts

    (4) Mark Twain's comments in Tom Sawyer

    (5) Huck shown in action scenes

Answers are on page 539.

Plot: What Happens in the Story

Flashback as an Element of Plot

The events that occur in a story make up the **plot**. The plot events occur in some time order, or sequence. An author may choose to present events out of order. The events begin sometime in the past, then progress in order until, by the end of the story, the characters have returned to the time and place of the opening scene. One such popular technique is called **flashback**. For example, in the 1960 novel *To Kill a Mockingbird*, by Harper Lee, the main character, Scout, starts the narration with "When he was nearly thirteen, my brother Jem got his arm badly broken at the elbow." Then Scout indicates, "When enough years had gone by to enable us to look back on them, we sometimes discussed the events leading to his accident." The story then shifts to years past when their father Atticus practiced law in the fictional town of Maycomb.

Parts of a Plot

The events that make up a fiction plot may be grouped and labeled according to their function in a story: exposition, conflict, climax, and resolution. **Exposition** refers to background information that "sets the stage" for a story. The exposition also introduces setting, characters, and conflict. **Conflict**, or friction between opposing characters or forces, is the basis of every plot. Conflicts are usually stated in this pattern: character or force versus (vs.) character or force.

Most stories and novels are centered around one of the following conflicts:

* individual vs. self—inner struggles characters suffer while trying to decide what to do—change jobs, get divorced, have children, admit the truth about something

* individual vs. another—disagreements between characters

* individual vs. society—struggles against the rules, conventions, or pressures of living with other humans

* individual vs. nature and other forces—struggles against forces beyond a character's control, such as an earthquake or other natural disaster, or an abstraction such as evil

Another element of plot is **climax**, the point of highest intensity in the plot. The climax of a story occurs when the conflict comes to a head. The climax does not always occur at the very end of the story, but it usually occurs in the last part. Mystery stories have very obvious climaxes. All of the clues come together to provide the answer to "Whodunit?" Some good examples of this type are the Sherlock Holmes detective series by Sir Arthur Conan Doyle and the murder mysteries with Belgian detective M. Hercule Poirot or elderly principal detective Ms. Jane Marple by Agatha Christie.

Following the climax, all of the loose ends are tied together, and readers learn the **resolution**, or outcome of the conflict. The resolution of the story is usually its ending.

EXERCISE 5: IDENTIFYING DETAILS OF PLOT (AND CONFLICT)

Directions: Read the following passage composed of selected parts of a short story that show details of plot and conflict. Then answer the questions that follow.

HOW ARE HUSBAND AND WIFE THE "MAGI"?

"Jim, Darling," she cried, "don't look at me that way. I had my hair cut off and sold it because I couldn't have lived through Christmas without giving you a present. It'll grow out again—you won't mind, will you? I just had to do it. . . .

Jim drew a package from his overcoat pocket and threw it on the table. . . .

White fingers and nimble tore at the string and paper. And then an ecstatic scream of joy; and then, alas! A quick feminine change to hysterical tears and wails. . . .

For there lay The Combs—the set of combs, side and back, that Della had worshipped for long in a Broadway window. . . . And now, they were hers, but the tresses that should have adorned the coveted adornments were gone. . . .

Jim had not yet seen his beautiful present. She held it out to him eagerly upon her open palm. The dull precious metal seemed to flash with a reflection of her bright and ardent spirit.

"Isn't it a dandy, Jim? I hunted all over town to find it. You'll have to look at the time a hundred times a day now. Give me your watch. I want to see how it looks on it.

Instead of obeying, Jim tumbled down on the couch and put his hands under the back of his head and smiled.

"Dell," said he, "let's put our Christmas presents away and keep 'em a while. They're too nice to use just at present. I sold the watch to get the money to buy your combs."

—Excerpted from "The Gift of the Magi" by O. Henry

1. One important plot detail that affects the outcome of the story is that Della has her hair cut off. Why did she do this?

   (1) She thought her husband would like her new hairstyle better.
   (2) She had a disease that would be better controlled through shorter hair.
   (3) She sold her hair in order to have money to buy Jim a Christmas present.
   (4) She wanted to present a different image for an anticipated new job.
   (5) She was an actress who was preparing for a role that called for short hair.

2. The author O. Henry is known for ending his short stories ironically, in ways that the reader does not expect. In this case, which of the following details was expected?

   (1) Della sacrificed her hair to buy Jim a Christmas present.
   (2) Jim sacrificed his watch to buy Della a Christmas present.
   (3) Della did not need the combs after her hair was cut short.
   (4) Jim did not need the watch chain after he sold his watch.
   (5) Della and Jim shopped all over town for the perfect gifts.

Answers are on page 539.

Point of View: Who Tells the Story

When you read fiction, ask yourself, "Through whose eyes, or **point of view,** is the story being told?" An author can choose from a variety of ways to tell a story. For example, if you were to write a story about auto racing, you might choose from the following points of view:

- the race car driver wanting to win and picturing the trophy

- the other drivers hoping to win and focusing on their own positions

- the fans or spectators favoring particular drivers and seeking excitement

- the sponsor hoping to increase sales through support of the driver

The point of view from which a story is told is important because the reader has to identify with, or "become," the character. For this reason, sometimes authors tell their story through the eyes of the **main character**—the character whom the action affects most. Only the thoughts of the main character are revealed when the author chooses this point of view.

A writer, having decided who is to tell, or **narrate,** the story, may relate the events in first person or third person. In **first-person narration,** the word *I* is used, and the narrator speaks directly to the reader. In his famous novel *The Adventures of Huckleberry Finn* Mark Twain created Huck Finn as the narrator to tell the story. Huck is the main character, and the story is told through his eyes, using the first-person I method.

In **third-person narration,** the story is told by an outsider—someone who is not involved in the action—and the main character is referred to as *he* or *she.* There are several different approaches to the third-person point of view, depending on how much the author wants readers—and the main characters—to know.

In the short story "The Celebrated Jumping Frog of Calaveras County" Mark Twain quotes the character Smiley who talks about his gifted frog Dan'l Webster, who wanted an education. In the novel *The Old Man and the Sea,* by Ernest Hemingway, the old man Santiago hooks the 18-foot marlin with a simple line. Read the passage below and consider: if a fish could think and talk, what would be the marlin's thoughts as it is being reeled in?

EXERCISE 6: DETERMINING POINT OF VIEW

Directions: Underline each noun or pronoun (*I, me, he, his, himself, you, your,* or *who*) that represents the fisherman. Put brackets [ ] around each noun or pronoun that refers to the fish. The first paragraph is done for you.

HOW MIGHT THE FISH FEEL?

["Fish,"] the old man said. ["Fish,] [you] are going to have to die anyway. Do [you] have to kill me too?"

That way nothing is accomplished, he thought. His mouth was too dry to speak but he could not reach for the water now. I must get him alongside this time, he thought. I am not good for many more turns. Yes, you are, he told himself. You're good for ever.

On the next turn, he nearly had him. But again the fish righted himself and swam slowly away.

You are killing me, fish, the old man thought. But you have a right to. Never have I seen a greater, or more beautiful, or a calmer or more noble thing than you, brother. Come on and kill me. I do not care who kills who.

Now you are getting confused in the head, he thought. You must keep your head clear. Keep your head clear and know how to suffer like a man. Or a fish, he thought.

"Clear up, head," he said in a voice he could hardly hear. "Clear up."

—Excerpted from *The Old Man and the Sea* by Ernest Hemingway

Answers are on page 539.

Theme: What the Story Means

Behind all of the action in a story or movie is the writer's or director's purpose or focus. The main idea, or **theme,** may be an insight into life, a viewpoint about a social issue, a new view of an old problem, or a positive or negative look into human nature.

In successfully written fiction, as in effective films, the theme is rarely stated directly. Instead, it is implied or suggested. The reader or viewer is expected to interpret the meaning from all elements presented. For example, since the early 1980s, many writers and filmmakers have given us stories about problematic, dysfunctional families. Typically family members no longer understand or support each other. Some examples are *The Bridges of Madison County* by Robert J. Waller or *American Beauty* by Alan Ball.

EXERCISE 7: INFERRING THEME

Directions: Read the passage below and choose the *best* answer to each question that follows.

WHAT CONCERNS EDDY, MR. NEWMAN, AND DANNY?

"Eddy, for your courage in facing and breaking your own personal sound barrier, I give you the gift of sound—a collection of tapes for your headphones that represent the best music ever recorded in all styles except disco, which does not qualify as music."

We laughed as he handed Eddy a box about the size of a shoebox. A label was pasted to the lid which listed the songs on each numbered tape. Rhea peeked over Eddy's shoulder and cried with delight, "Oh, all the music in the world."

"Not quite," Mr. Newman said, "but it's a good start. In addition I award you a report card with the 'A' you earned in my course of life, and another well-deserved certificate, a diploma."

He handed Eddy one of the high school's report cards and a diploma, complete with the leather cover and Mrs. Voss's signature. Eddy started to cry. Rhea handed the box of tapes to my Dad, who was closest to her, and hugged Eddy, patting him on the back and saying, "There, there," the way someone had probably taught her in The Home.

Then Mr. Newman turned to me. "Danny, your pain was more than physical, although that was bad enough, and for a few days, we thought we might lose you. Sometimes I wasn't even sure what your assignment was. It didn't really matter because eventually it became a matter of survival. Beyond that, you also graduated. The report cards won't be mailed home until tomorrow; however, I managed to get an early copy printed out by the computer at school. There are quite a few 'D's' here, but I do see one well-earned 'A' in English, no less. At the bottom, a check mark and initials are clearly seen in a space marked 'Requirements completed for graduation.' You already have your diploma. I also have an envelope for you. It contains two reference letters, one by me and one by Mrs. Voss to introduce you to an admissions counselor we both know at the junior college, who can expedite matters for you if you heed our encouragement and look more carefully at your education."

—Excerpted from *The Newman Assignment* by Kurt Haberl

1. Two of the conflicts resolved within this passage involve Eddy, the school custodian, and Danny, a high school senior. Which of the following is not a probable conflict?

   (1) Eddy overcomes his fear of speaking in front of others.
   (2) Danny survives physical injuries from an accident.
   (3) Eddy and Danny each pass the Newman assignment.
   (4) Eddy and his wife Rhea have marital problems.
   (5) Danny overcomes personal and physical difficulties to graduate.

2. The theme of the passage is best stated in which of these ways?

   (1) Barriers can be overcome through effort and sacrifice.
   (2) The purpose of hard work is to win achievement awards.
   (3) Good intentions do not always make up for difficulties.
   (4) The truth will always emerge in the proper time and setting.
   (5) Mental suffering is the way to build personal character.

Answers are on page 540.

Style: Tying All the Elements Together

Style refers to the author's unique use of the language—the choice and arrangement of words. Style includes the author's **tone**, the attitude revealed or displayed toward the subject of the work of fiction or toward the characters. An author's style may contain long, complex sentences, everyday language, or figures of speech. Style is what holds all the elements together.

Types of Styles

Authors who publish many works often become known and appreciated for their styles as well as their themes and characters. Ernest Hemingway, for example, is known for a terse (short, tight) writing style of few words. On the other hand, Charles Dickens is known for a narrative style characterized by long sentences and vivid descriptions. Edgar Allan Poe often used long, complex sentences, the repetition of words, and many dashes, exclamation points, and italics to add emotion and suspense to his stories. In her 1931 novel *The Good Earth,* Pearl S. Buck used a vivid, graphic style to describe the China in which she lived for forty years in the early twentieth century.

Tone and Style: The Author's Attitude

When reading, you must infer the author's tone. The **tone** of a novel or short story is the overall attitude that an author conveys toward his or her subject. When listening to a person speak, you can infer the person's attitude by the sound of his or her voice. The tone tells you whether the person means to be sarcastic, bitter, serious, funny, amazed, sympathetic, or something else. The author conveys the intended tone through use of the dialogue among word choice, characters, sentence structure, figures of speech, and punctuation.

An author's choice of words and phrasing reflects his or her attitude. Write a few words that describe the tone of this passage:

Our first-born was a lovely, intelligent girl whose first real sentence at the age of six months was "Me baby." All things on four legs including lions and tigers were "Doggie." She read valentines sent to her by her preschool classmates and invented names for her baby brother including "Little Daddy" and "Oil Can Harry." As she grew, she developed a love for words and started writing her own poems.

Our second (and last)-born was a boy who as a toddler could spend hours arranging his little Matchbox cars or painting houses at a small easel. If the house scene had a fireplace, he would be sure to draw in every brick. Advice from his preschool teacher was to provide him with art materials but not to try to channel (and possibly "kill") his interest in art. It was very predictable that his art later in life turned into a talent for architectural design.

You might have written *nostalgic, light, retrospective, funny,* or *humorous.* The author is a parent looking back on a daughter and a son whose interests and talents were evident at an early age. The author's tone is not sad or resentful, but full of fond, humorous memories.

To determine the tone of a passage, ask yourself the following questions: What subject is the author describing? How does the author feel about the subject? What language or descriptive details reveal the author's attitude?

EXERCISE 8: DETECTING STYLE AND TONE

Directions: Read the passage below and answer the questions that follow.

WHAT IS THE AUTHOR'S TONE?

"Americans make the best husbands," the American lady said to my wife. I was getting down the bags. "American men are the only men in the world to marry."

"How long ago did you leave Vevey?" asked my wife.

"Two years ago this fall. It's her, you know, that I'm taking the canary to."

"Was the man your daughter was in love with a Swiss?"

"Yes," said the American lady. "He was from a very good family in Vevey. He was going to be an engineer. They met there in Vevey. They used to go on long walks together."

"I know Vevey," said my wife. "We were there on our honeymoon."

"Were you really? That must have been lovely? . . . Where did you stop there?"

"We stayed at the Trois Couronnes," said my wife.

"It's such a fine old hotel," said the American lady.

"Yes," said my wife. "We had a very fine room and in the fall the country was lovely."

"Were you there in the fall?"

"Yes," said my wife.

We were passing three cars that had been in a wreck. They were splintered open and the roofs sagged in.

"Look," I said. "There's been a wreck."

The American lady looked and saw the last car. "I was afraid of just that all night," she said. "I have terrific presentiments about things sometimes. I'll never travel on a *rapide* again at night. There must be other comfortable trains that don't go so fast."

—Excerpted from "A Canary for One" by Ernest Hemingway

1. What is the author's attitude toward the American lady?

She should be

(1) congratulated for her strength
(2) respected for her high ideals
(3) tolerated and sympathized with
(4) imitated for her special graces
(5) exposed for her false values

2. The American lady apparently opposed the marriage of her daughter to a Swiss, but was seemingly taking the canary to her, probably to console her. This probably creates what feeling for the daughter on the part of the reader?

(1) indifference
(2) sympathy
(3) annoyance
(4) gratitude
(5) disbelief

Answers are on page 540.

EXERCISE 9: IDENTIFYING IMAGES AS PART OF OVERALL STYLE

Directions: Read the passage below. Underline all descriptions and images that appeal to your senses of sight and hearing. (Other senses of smell, taste, and touch are not emphasized in this selection.)

WHAT IMAGES DOES THE WRITER CALL TO MIND?

In agony the brakes cried, held: the scene, dizzy with color, rocked with the car, down a little, back up, giddily, helplessly, while dust exploded up on all sides. "Mommy!" Timmy screamed, fascinated by the violence, yet his wail was oddly still and drawn out, and his eyes never once turned to his mother. The little Mexican boy had disappeared in front of the car. Still the red dust arose, the faces at the bus jerked around together, white eyes, white teeth, faces were propelled toward the windows of the bus, empty a second before. "God, God," Annette murmured; she had not yet released the steering wheel, and on it her fingers began to tighten as if they might tear the wheel off, hold it up to defend her and her child, perhaps even to attack.

—Excerpted from "First Views of the Enemy" in
Upon the Sweeping Flood and Other Stories by Joyce Carol Oates

Answers are on page 540.

How to Read Fiction on Your Own

You have learned about the basic elements of fiction illustrated in the puzzle on page 290. In both the novel and the short story, the elements contribute to the whole. While your examination of each element of fiction contributes to your understanding, it is the whole, not its parts, that represents a work of art. Use the tips that follow to guide your reading of literature.

Tips on Reading Fiction
As you read a short story or novel, ask yourself:
• What is the setting (time and place)?
• What is the atmosphere (or mood)?
• Who are the characters?
• Are they named or described?
• Do the characters use special dialogue?
• What is the plot?
• What is the exposition (or background information)?
• Is flashback used?
• What is the conflict?
• What is the climax?
• What is the resolution?
• Are there subplots?
• From whose point of view is the story told?
• Is there first-person, third-person, or author-third person narration?
• What are clues to the theme?
• What is the author's style like?
• What is the author's tone?
• Are there special elements such as dialect or figures of speech?

2
INTERPRETING POETRY

Poetry has served as a means to provoke thought, honor an individual, express emotion, amuse a reader, commemorate an event, evoke a memory, or plead love. **Poetry** is language that expresses ideas and emotions in a tightly controlled and structured way. Simply put, poetry is the best words in their best order. Poetry is compressed. **Imagery** (word pictures that appeal to the five senses) and figures of speech enable the poet to convey ideas in just a few words.

Some poems are written in **rhyme**, the repetition of a sound at the end of two or more words, like *say* and *hay*. **Sounds** and **rhythms**, or the "beat," arouse feelings and evoke thoughts. All of these characteristics of poetry make it a distinct form of literature. On the Language Arts, Reading Test, you will be expected to demonstrate your understanding of a poem's meaning. You should be able to read a poem, spend a few minutes interpreting it, and answer questions about the theme.

Idea and Emotion in Poetry

The following poems are about human relationships. The first poem is a song. The second poem is a sonnet, a 14-line poem that follows a particular form. Both poems express similar emotions and ideas.

EXERCISE 1: UNDERSTANDING IDEA AND EMOTION IN TWO POEMS

Directions: Read each poem aloud and answer the questions that follow.

WHAT ARE THE POETS SAYING AND HOW ARE THEY SAYING IT?

I know not whether thou hast been absent:
I lie down with thee, I rise up with thee,
In my dreams thou art with me.
If my eardrops tremble in my ears,
I know it is thou moving within my heart.

—Aztec Love Song

Sonnet 43

How do I love thee? Let me count the ways.
I love thee to the depth and breadth and height
My soul can reach, when feeling out of sight
For the ends of Being and ideal Grace.
I love thee to the level of every day's
Most quiet need, by sun and candlelight.
I love thee freely, as men strive for Right;
I love thee purely, as they turn from Praise.
I love thee with the passion put to use

In my old griefs, and with my childhood's faith.
I love thee with a love I seemed to lose
With my lost saints—I love thee with the breath,
Smiles, tears, of all my life!—and, if God choose,
I shall but love thee better after death.

—Elizabeth Barrett Browning

1. Which theme is found in both poems?

   (1) separation
   (2) sacrifice
   (3) beauty
   (4) romantic love
   (5) wisdom

2. On the basis of the emotion expressed in these two poems, which one of the following words would best describe the speakers' feelings?

   (1) devoted
   (2) proud
   (3) sad
   (4) amused
   (5) scornful

Answers are on page 540.

Tips on Reading Poetry

- Read the title as a clue to the meaning.
- Read the whole poem to get the general ideas and mood.
- Ask yourself, What is this about? What is the poet saying? What does the poem mean? What is the theme?
- Note the use of any objects or events that might serve as symbols to represent meaning. What feelings and ideas do you associate with those symbols?
- Reread the poem using the punctuation as a guide. (Stop where there's a period or other end mark, not at the end of a line.)
- Notice how lines are grouped together and if lines are repeated. What is the poet stressing by repeating words and lines?
- Notice the language used and unusual word choices, comparisons, imagery, and figures of speech.
- Read the poem aloud so you can hear it, especially if words rhyme.
- To understand the poem's tone and theme, summarize in your own words what the poem is saying.

The Shape of Poetry

The structure and form of poetry distinguish it from other types of literature. Many poets choose a highly structured format, in which they shape their
ideas using rhyme, rhythm, and stanzas. A **stanza** is a group of lines that
work together to express an idea. A new stanza signals that a new idea is
being introduced in a poem. Often, stanzas are separated by a blank space.

The following poem contains two stanzas:

Dreams

STANZA 1
Hold fast to dreams
For if dreams die
Life is a broken-winged bird
That cannot fly.

STANZA 2
Hold fast to dreams
For when dreams go
Life is a barren field
Frozen with snow.

—Langston Hughes

When you sing a song, you may sing a verse, a chorus, the second verse,
the same chorus, the third verse, a chorus, and so on. A **verse** is any piece of
poetry that is arranged in a pattern. Many songs were poems before they
were set to music, and song lyrics often have many of the characteristics of
poetry. The term **free verse** refers to verses without a regular rhythmic pattern and usually without rhyme. Much of today's poetry is free verse.

Capitalization and Punctuation

In poetry a comma or a dash means "pause." A period means "stop." If
the poem contains capitalization and punctuation, it should be read in sentences, not just one line at a time. Sometimes the reader may have to run two
or more lines together. For example, in the poem "Child of the Americas,"
which follows, lines 4 and 5 are read *I am a U.S. Puerto Rican Jew, a product of the ghettos of New York I have never known.*

The use of capital letters in poetry can vary. Sometimes a poet capitalizes
each line. Sometimes a poet capitalizes a word for emphasis.

EXERCISE 2: THE SHAPE OF POETRY

Directions: Read aloud the poem below and answer the questions that follow. Notice the capitalization and punctuation as you read.

WHY DOES THE SPEAKER DESCRIBE HERSELF AS A CHILD?

Child of the Americas

(1)   I am a child of the Americas,
     a light-skinned mestiza of the Caribbean,
     a child of many diaspora,* born into this continent at a crossroads.

     I am a U.S. Puerto Rican Jew,
(5)   a product of the ghettos of New York I have never known.
     An immigrant and the daughter and granddaughter of immigrants.
     I speak English with passion: It's the tool of my consciousness,
     a flashing knife blade of crystal, my tool, my craft.

     I am Caribeña, island grown, Spanish is in my flesh,
(10) ripples from my tongue, lodges in my hips:
     the language of garlic and mangoes,
     the singing in my poetry, the flying gestures of my hands.
     I am Latinoamerica, rooted in the history of my continent:
     I speak from that body.

(15) I am** not african. Africa is in me, but I cannot return.
     I am not taína. Taíno is in me, but there is no way back.
     I am not european. Europe lives in me, but I have no home there.

     I am new. History made me. My first language was spanglish.
     I was born at the crossroads
(20) and I am whole.

diaspora means "migration or scattering of people"
***am** was *an* in the original

                              —Aurora Levins Morales

1. There are three lines in the first stanza. How many sentences are there? (Notice periods.)

_____

2. List at least three details that contribute to the speaker's description of herself as born "at the crossroads" where many ways come to meet together.

    (a)_____

    (b)_____

    (c)_____

3. What do the emotions and ideas expressed in the poem invite a reader to do?

    (1) study American history
    (2) learn another language
    (3) appreciate multiculturalism
    (4) research family background
    (5) plan a family reunion

Answers are on page 540.

The Language of Poetry

Imagery

A poet relies on readers' abilities to create images, or pictures, in their minds from the words on a page. Images may appeal to any senses, enabling readers to experience the emotions and ideas conveyed. For this reason, the poet must choose the perfect word to convey a thought. When a poem appeals to your senses and enables you to imagine a scene, the poem is rich in **imagery**.

Dawn Over the Mountains

(1)   The city is silent,
      Sound drains away,
      Buildings vanish in the light of dawn,
      Cold sunlight comes on the highest peak,
(5)   The thick dust of night
      Clings to the hills,
      The earth opens,
      The river boats are vague,
      The still sky—
(10) The sound of falling leaves.
      A huge doe comes to the garden gate,
      Lost from the herd,
      Seeking its fellows.

                       —Tu Fu

Can you "hear" the silence in line 1 and then the *sound of falling leaves* in line 10? Can you "feel" the *cold sunlight* in line 4 and see *a huge doe . . .* at *the garden gate* in line 11?

Personification

Recall that **personification** is a form of imagery in which human activities or qualities are attributed to an animal or a thing. In other words, a non-human thing comes "alive" as it is given human abilities.

EXERCISE 3: THE LANGUAGE OF POETRY

Directions: Write **imagery** if a line evokes an image or **personification** if it attributes a human quality to an inanimate object.

LINE 1: Midnight, not a sound from the pavement. _____

LINE 2: Has the moon lost her memory? _____

LINE 3: She [the moon] is smiling alone. _____

LINE 4: In the lamp light the withered leaves collect at my feet._____

LINE 5: And the wind begins to moan. _____

—Excerpted from *Cats: The Book of the Musical* by Trevor Nunn

Answers are on page 541.

Simile and Metaphor

A **simile** is a comparison of two unlike things using words such as *like, than,* or *as* to compare two unlike things. Poet Robert Bly uses similes in the following poem, "Poem in Three Parts." What things are being compared with one another? Underline the three similes.

Poem in Three Parts

I

Oh, on an early morning I think I shall live forever!
I am wrapped in my joyful flesh,
As the grass is wrapped in its clouds of green.

II

Rising from a bed, where I dreamt
Of long rides past castles and hot coals,
The sun lies happily on my knees;
I have suffered and survived the night,
Bathed in dark water, like any blade of grass.

III

The strong eaves of the box-elder tree,
Plunging in the wind, call us to disappear
Into the wilds of the universe,
Where we shall sit at the foot of a plant,
And live forever, like the dust.

—Robert Bly

You should have underlined these similes: *I am wrapped in my joyful flesh,/as the grass is wrapped in its clouds of green.; I have suffered and survived the night,/Bathed in dark water, like any blade of grass.;* and *we shall sit at the foot of a plant,/And live forever, like the dust.*

Recall that a **metaphor** is an implied or suggested comparison between two things. A metaphor does not contain *like, than,* or *as.* With a metaphor, one thing is the second thing to which it is being compared.

Note the comparison between hope and a bird in "Hope" by Emily Dickinson. Underline all the words that contribute to the metaphor.

Hope

Hope is the thing with feathers
That perches in the soul,
And sings the tune without the words,
And never stops at all,

And sweetest in the gale is heard;
And sore must be the storm
That could abash the little bird
That kept so many warm.

I've heard it in the chillest land,
And on the strangest sea;
Yet, never, in extremity,
It asked a crumb of me.

—Emily Dickinson

The metaphor of hope as a bird is extended and developed throughout the poem. You should have underlined the following words: *feathers, perches, sings, bird,* and *crumb.*

The Sound of Poetry

Poets rely on many devices to communicate their messages to readers. Most poetry is written to be read aloud. As the poet writes the words, he or she is aware of the sound of the poem. Many poets use "sound words" to enhance the imagery and message of their poetry. Three common poetic devices are **rhyme**, **rhythm**, and **alliteration**.

Nursery rhymes introduce the literature of language to children. **Rhyme** is the repetition, in two or more words, of the stressed vowel sound and of the syllables that follow that sound.

Star light, Star bright, first star I see tonight

Just as word choices produce a desired effect in poetry, so does the beat, or rhythm, of a poem. **Rhythm** is the rise and fall of stressed words and syllables. If the rhythm is regular, or ordered strictly, the poem is said to have **meter**.

The repetition of consonant sounds, usually at the beginning of words, is **alliteration**. *Susie sells seashells down by the seashore* is an example of alliteration. Nursery rhymes contain much alliteration, and advertising slogans and jingles incorporate this technique frequently.

Words that Stand for Sounds

Another device sometimes used in poetry is the choice of a word to imitate a natural sound. **Onomatopoeia** (ahn´-uh-mah´-tuh-pee´-uh) refers to the use of words whose sounds imitate their meanings. Sound-imitating words include *buzz*, *screech*, *boom*, and *crash*. *Whisper* is also a sound word.

EXERCISE 4: THE SOUND OF POETRY

Directions: Read the beginning stanzas from the poem and answer the questions that follow. Notice how the rhyme, the rhythm, and alliteration add to the experience of the poem.

WHAT MIGHT THE RAVEN REPRESENT?

Once upon a midnight dreary, while I pondered weak and weary,
Over many a quaint and curious volume of forgotten lore—
While I nodded, nearly napping, suddenly there came a tapping,
As of someone gently rapping, rapping at my chamber door.
"'Tis some visitor," I muttered, "tapping at my chamber door—
    Only this, and nothing more."

Ah, distinctly I remember it was in the bleak December;
And each separate dying ember wrought its ghost upon the floor.
Eagerly I wished the morrow;—vainly I had sought to borrow
From my books surcease* of sorrow—sorrow for the lost Lenore—
For the rare and radiant maiden whom the angels name Lenore—
    Nameless here for evermore.

surcease means "an end"

—Excerpted from "The Raven" by Edgar Allan Poe

1. List two different examples of alliteration from stanza one or two:

    (a) _____

    (b) _____

2. What effect does the repetition of the word *rapping* have?

    (1) It uses sound to develop the image of persistent knocking.
    (2) It adds to the atmosphere of boredom and isolation.
    (3) It creates a bird-like sound through the use of personification.
    (4) It lightens the mood of the poem through sound.
    (5) It creates alliteration with the poem's title.

Answers are on page 541.

Inferring Mood

Mood is very important in poetry. When a poet creates a poem, the words chosen help present an overall feeling. The mood may be humorous and light, somber and serious, or still something else. Within a poem, the mood sometimes changes. Read the following song from the musical *Cats*. As you read, identify the mood of each part. Circle the word that most accurately describes the mood of the lines.

Memory

Midnight, not a sound from the pavement.	**1.** **(a)** optimistic
Has the moon lost her memory?	**(b)** lonely
She is smiling alone.	**(c)** eager
In the lamp light the withered leaves	
collect at my feet	
And the wind begins to moan.	
Memory. All alone in the moonlight	**2.** **(a)** nostalgic
I can smile at the old days.	**(b)** humorous
I was beautiful then.	**(c)** afraid
I remember the time	
I knew what happiness was,	
Let the memory live again. . . .	
Daylight. I must wait for the sunrise	**3.** **(a)** depressed
I must think of a new life	**(b)** sarcastic
And I mustn't give in.	**(c)** hopeful
When the dawn comes tonight will	
be a memory, too	
And a new day will begin. . . .	
Touch me. It's so easy to leave me	**4.** **(a)** regretful
All alone with the memory	**(b)** content
Of my days in the sun.	**(c)** confused
If you touch me you'll understand what	
happiness is.	
Look, a new day has begun.	

—Excerpted from *Cats*, music by Andrew Lloyd Webber

[Answers: **1. (b)** lonely (moon *smiling alone* and the wind moaning). **2. (a)** nostalgic (cat [narrator] smiling and remembering). **3. (c)** hopeful (*daylight* and *a new day*). **4. (b)** content (*new day has begun*).]

Interpreting and Analyzing Poetry for Meaning

When you interpret a poem, you rephrase it, putting the poem into your own thoughts and words. You may simply change words around to make a statement more understandable, or you may guess at the poet's main purpose. To understand poetry, seek the stated information from the text of the poem, but also use your own experience and knowledge to derive meaning and a fuller appreciation of what you have read.

Read the following stanzas from the poem "My Last Duchess" by Robert Browning. Browning, like most poets, was interested in enabling a reader to see something revealing within a poem. Use the clues from the text, combined with your own assessment of human beings to answer the questions.

That's my last Duchess painted on the wall,
Looking as if she were alive. I call
That piece a wonder, now: Frá Pandolf's hands
worked busily a day, and there she stands,
Will't please you sit and look at her?

She had a heart
A heart—how shall I say?—too soon made glad,
Too easily impressed; she liked whate'er
She looked on, and her looks went everywhere.
Sir, 'twas all one! My favor at her breast,
The dropping of the daylight in the West,
The bough of cherries some officious fool
Broke in the orchard for her, the white mule
She rode with round the terrace—all and each
Would draw from her alike the approving speech,
Or blush, at least. She thanked men,—good! but thanked
My gift of a nine-hundred-years-old name as if she ranked
With anybody's gift.
—and if she let
Herself be lessoned so, nor plainly set
Her wits to yours, forsooth, and made excuse,
—E'en then would be some stooping; and I choose
Never to stoop. Oh sir, she smiled, no doubt,
Whene'er I passed her; but who passed without
Much the same smile? This grew; I gave commands;
Then all smiles stopped together. There she stands
As if alive. Will't please you rise? We'll meet
the company below, then . . .

—Excerpted from "My Last Duchess" by Robert Browning

1. Who is the speaker of the poem?

   (1) Frá Pandolf
   (2) the Duke
   (3) a visitor

2. What kind of person was the Duchess?

   (1) foolish and clumsy
   (2) vain and envious
   (3) kind and friendly

3. In addition to discussing a portrait of the Duchess, how is the character of the speaker portrayed in the poem?

   (1) through what the speaker says about the Duchess
   (2) through what the speaker is wearing
   (3) through what the visitor says to the speaker

[Answers: **1. (2)** The speaker states *That's my last Duchess.* **2. (3)** The poem states *She had a heart . . . too soon made glad and all and each would draw from her alike the approving speech . . .* **3. (1)** What the Duke says about the Duchess reveals a great deal about him.]

Combining Ideas to Develop Meaning

Questions on the Language Arts, Reading Test require you to comprehend, apply, and analyze thoughts in poetry as well as in other literature. Additionally, you will sometimes be asked to consider another source of information in relation to the poem you read. You will be **synthesizing**, combining pieces of information to arrive at an idea.

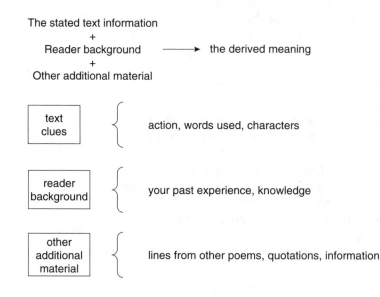

The stated text information
+
Reader background   →   the derived meaning
+
Other additional material

| text clues | { | action, words used, characters |

| reader background | { | your past experience, knowledge |

| other additional material | { | lines from other poems, quotations, information |

The excerpt that follows comes from a poem written by Alfred, Lord Tennyson. The poem is written about the explorer Ulysses, who has traveled for many years across the ocean in his ship.

Old age hath yet his honor and his toil.
Death closes all; but something ere* the end,
Some work of noble note, may yet be done,
Not unbecoming men that strove with Gods.
The lights begin to twinkle from the rocks;
The long day wanes; the slow moon climbs; the deep
Moans round with many voices. Come, my friends.
'Tis not too late to seek a newer world.
Push off, and sitting well in order smite
The sounding furrows; for my purpose holds
To sail beyond the sunset, and the baths
Of all the western stars, until I die.
It may be that the gulfs will wash us down;
It may be we shall touch the Happy Isles,
And see the great Achilles, whom we knew.
Tho' much is taken, much abides; and tho'
We are not now that strength which in old days
Moved earth and heaven, that which we are, we are,—
One equal temper of heroic hearts,
Made weak by time and fate, but strong in will
To strive, to seek, to find, and not to yield.

*ere means "before"

—Excerpted from "Ulysses" by Alfred, Lord Tennyson

Before you try to answer the next two questions:

- Think about the text clues in this excerpt from Tennyson.

- Think about your own knowledge and experience with human beings.

- Think about the meaning of the quotations.

1. Earlier in the poem, the speaker states: "I am a part of all that I have met." In what way is this line consistent with the rest of the poem?

   (1) It adds to the image of a sailing ship.
   (2) It suggests that each individual is incomplete.
   (3) It reminds us of how our experiences shape our lives.
   (4) It adds to the tone of suspense.
   (5) It emphasizes the uncertainty of the future.

2. The poet T. S. Eliot in his poem, "East Coker," states, "Old men ought to be explorers." How does this quotation relate to the poem Ulysses?

   (1) It reaffirms the poem's theme that exploration is lifelong.
   (2) It also suggests that a new world is needed.
   (3) It recreates the fears and fantasies of people.
   (4) It reinforces the idea that youth is wasted on the young.
   (5) It predicts that travel opportunities are limited.

[Answers: **1. (3)** To be *a part of all* encountered suggests experience affects one's development. This is similar to the poem's theme of exploration bringing about experience. **2. (1)** The speaker of the poem states *Old age* *hath yet his honor* and *'Tis not too late to seek. . .*, echoing the idea expressed in the quotation from Eliot's poem.]

EXERCISE 5: INTERPRETING A POEM

Directions: Read the poem and answer the questions that follow.

WHAT DOES NATURE HAVE TO OFFER?

Leisure

(1)   What is this life if, full of care,
We have no time to stand and stare.

No time to stand beneath the boughs
And stare as long as sheep or cows.

(5)   No time to see, when woods we pass,
Where squirrels hide their nuts in grass.

No time to see, in broad daylight,
Streams full of stars, like skies at night.

No time to turn at Beauty's glance,
(10) And watch her feet, how they can dance.

No time to wait till her mouth can
Enrich that smile her eyes began.

A poor life this if, full of care,
We have no time to stand and stare.

—W. H. Davies

1. If the speaker of the poem were hired for a new job, predict what company benefit would have the greatest appeal.
   (1) profit-sharing
   (2) life insurance
   (3) child care
   (4) overtime work
   (5) paid vacation

2. Which piece of advice would the speaker of the poem give, based on the overall attitude the speaker expresses?
   (1) Work hard if you wish to succeed.
   (2) Take time to smell the roses.
   (3) Laugh and the world laughs with you.
   (4) If at first you don't succeed, try again.
   (5) Time flies when you're having fun.

Answers are on page 541.

3
INTERPRETING DRAMA

Drama as a Literary Form

Drama is a form of literature that uses action to tell a story. The story is performed by actors who portray various characters involved in **conflict**, a struggle between opposing forces in a plot. The main character in a drama is called the **protagonist**, and the conflict with which he or she struggles may be external or internal. We encounter drama, not only with plays, movies, and TV, but also every day in our lives and in the lives of those around us.

The requirements for interpreting drama on the Language Arts, Reading Test are similar to the requirements for interpreting prose fiction and poetry. Reading a play differs from reading a novel or short story in some ways. A play is designed to be performed. It is a set of instructions for a stage production. When you are reading a play, you must create the performance by using your imagination to envision the production. It is important to picture the action, characters, and setting in your mind. You need to read carefully to infer setting, characterization, and theme, just as you do when you read prose and poetry.

One of the greatest playwrights of all time is William Shakespeare. An excerpt from his play, *Hamlet,* follows. In the play set several hundred years ago, Hamlet is the Prince of Denmark. Read the dialogue and try to visualize the scene and identify the conflict.

WHAT DOES HAMLET LEARN?

Act I, Scene V

GHOST: My hour is almost come
When I to sulphurous and tormenting flames
Must render up myself.

HAMLET: Alas, poor ghost!

GHOST: Pity me not, but lend thy serious hearing
To what I shall unfold.

HAMLET: Speak, I am bound to hear.

GHOST: So art thou to revenge, when thou shall hear.

HAMLET: What?

GHOST: I am thy father's spirit,
Doomed for a certain term to walk the night,
And for the day confined to fast in fires,
Till the foul crimes done in my days of nature
Are burnt and purged away: but that I am forbid

To tell the secrets of my prison house,
I could a tale unfold whose lightest word
Would harrow up thy soul, freeze thy young blood,
Make thy two eyes like stars start from their spheres,
Thy knotted and combined locks to part,
And each particular* hair to stand on end,
Like quills upon the fretful porcupine.
But this eternal blazon* must not be
To ears of flesh and blood. List, list, oh, list!
If thou didst ever thy dear father love—

HAMLET: Oh, God!

GHOST: Revenge his foul and most unnatural murder.

particular means "individual"
eternal blazon means "description of eternity"

—Excerpted from *Hamlet* by William Shakespeare

Now we can see the start of the conflict Hamlet faces. What should he do? Should he believe his own eyes and ears? Should he trust the ghost is telling the truth? Should he seek revenge for the death of his father? What would you do in his position? To learn about all the other complications, complexities, and considerations involved, you would have to read on in the play.

EXERCISE 1: COMPREHENDING A PLAY

Directions: The previous passage from *Hamlet* could be written in the form of narrative fiction. Fill in the blanks below to complete the narrative.

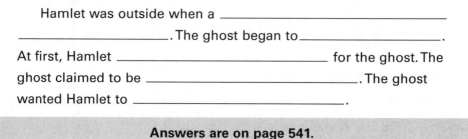

Hamlet was outside when a _____

_____. The ghost began to_____.

At first, Hamlet _____ for the ghost. The

ghost claimed to be _____. The ghost

wanted Hamlet to _____.

Answers are on page 541.

Reading a Play or Script

Dialogue

Drama contains **dialogue**, the exchange of conversation among the characters. Dialogue in a play and the way the lines are said reveal a great deal about the characters. Reading dialogue can sometimes be challenging because a playwright may write the dialogue to imitate speech. The spelling of words may be nonstandard in an attempt to imitate the pronunciation that different people give speech. Some clues are available, however, to help you understand the dialogue that you read.

CLUE #1: **The speakers are identified each time one speaks.** In the scene at the beginning of this section the clues HAMLET and GHOST indicate who is speaking. The names and the use of the colon [:] help to distinguish which character says what.

CLUE #2: **Punctuation marks are used to end a character's speech.** Notice the end marks, especially for questions (?) and exclamations (!). Punctuation is used in drama to show volume of voice and emotion. Dashes (—) and ellipses (. . .) are also used to show pauses. Dashes are used to show a break in thought, while ellipses indicate that there is a pause in the action or that one character is being interrupted by another character.

CLUE #3: **Line spacing between lines of dialogue indicates who is speaking.** A more obvious visual clue that indicates when a different speaker is talking is the white space between lines of dialogue.

Stage Directions

[The scene begins in a nineteenth-century parlor as Catherine, Edward and Victoria's daughter, enters with tea]

CATHERINE: Would you like some tea and . . .

EDWARD: Not now—Can't you see we're talking?

VICTORIA: You're talking—I'm not!

EDWARD: Oh—a little irritable, are we?

VICTORIA: No—just bored—with you . . .

CATHERINE: [Mumbling] I'm leaving. [She exits.]

Stage directions are used to assist the actors and director in interpreting the writer's intentions and purpose and to help the reader follow the imagined actions. In the brief scene above, the stage directions are the introductory words *[The scene begins in a nineteenth-century parlor as Catherine, Edward and Victoria's daughter, enters with tea]* and the directions *[Mumbling]* and *[She exits]*.

In this example notice that the playwright has inserted the directions within the dialogue. In the scene above, the stage directions tell the reader who Catherine is and when she leaves.

EXERCISE 2: INFERRING MOOD FROM DIALOGUE

Directions: Choose the best answer to the questions that follow.

1. Which of the following words best describes the mood of the scene above?
   (1) tense
   (2) happy
   (3) suspenseful
   (4) nostalgic
   (5) humorous

2. What does the use of the dash [—] imply in the dialogue in this scene?

   (1) fast speech
   (2) a brief pause
   (3) rudeness
   (4) humor
   (5) shyness

Answers are on page 541.

Structure of Drama

A play is composed of **acts**—the major divisions of a dramatic work. Acts are composed of scenes. **Scenes** show an action that occurs in one place among characters.

Shakespeare developed and refined the structure of drama as we know it today. He presented his plots in five acts. These acts are subdivided into numbered scenes. The diagram below shows the relationship between the acts and the corresponding elements of a traditional plot.

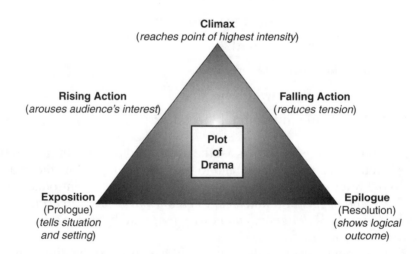

A **prologue** begins classical drama. Because there was no scenery in early drama, the audience needed to know when and where the story was taking place and what circumstances caused the upcoming action. An actor would come on stage and introduce the play by explaining the setting and some of the plot.

The **epilogue** ends classical drama. At the end of the play an actor would come on stage and deliver a summary poem or speech. Although the prologue and epilogue are not as common in drama today, some television dramas and movies use them to help the audience understand the plot.

Elements of Drama

Plot, setting, characterization, and theme are all elements which apply to drama. As you can see from the diagram on page 320, the plot in drama is tightly structured. As in a short story, there is **exposition** that orients the audience to the dramatic situation and setting.

The **rising action** is made up of all of the events that create suspense and arouse the audience's interest. We wonder *What will happen next? What will the main character do?* All of these events and conflicts lead to the **climax**, the point of highest intensity in the play.

The **falling action** may be brief. The conclusion or **resolution** is the logical outcome of the plot. As in fiction, the resolution ties up all of the loose ends of the plot.

From Idea to Production

The ancient Greeks sat in an outdoor theater on a hillside to watch plays; today we turn on our television sets or attend live productions.

To appreciate a play or TV drama fully, it helps to know how drama is created and produced. A play is created by a writer (playwright or dramatist). Usually, it is written to be performed, rather than to communicate directly to readers. It takes the work of many different people with different talents and skills to put on a performance. Producers, directors, costumers, set designers, makeup artists, and many others contribute.

The following diagram illustrates the process by which a play—an idea in the writer's head—becomes the reality of a live production.

Characterization

Characters in plays intended to be brought to life by actors before a live audience are not developed in exactly the same ways as characters in novels and stories. How can you interpret a character? One way is by listening to the character's dialogue and watching his or her facial expressions and mannerisms. Another way to interpret a character is to be aware of the motivation for the character's actions.

Dialogue and Nonverbal Communication

In drama, personalities are revealed by what characters say. In drama more than in fiction, dialogue carries greater responsibility for getting the author's point across. Character is revealed by the actor's **nonverbal communication**—mannerisms, tone of voice, facial expressions, and costumes.

Motivation

A character's behavior is based on his or her **motivation**—the reasons for the character's actions. Actors who perform the roles of characters ask themselves, *What is my motivation? What are my character's reasons for acting this way?*

Below is an excerpt from a play about the developing relationship between a man and woman. They are having a discussion in which much is revealed about their personalities and backgrounds.

EXERCISE 3: UNDERSTANDING CHARACTER

Directions: Read the passage below and answer the questions that follow.

WHAT ARE THE CHARACTERS' PERSONALITIES?

1	BILLIE:	Oh, and you know that little thing you gave me about Napoleon?
	PAUL:	No, what?
	BILLIE:	By Robert G. Ingersoll?
5	PAUL:	Oh, yes.
	BILLIE:	Well, I'm not sure if I get that either.
	PAUL:	No deep meaning there.
	BILLIE:	There must be. He says about how he goes and looks in Napoleon's tomb.
10	PAUL:	Yuh.
	BILLIE:	And he thinks of Napoleon's whole sad life.
	PAUL:	Yuh.

BILLIE:	And then in the end he says he himself would have rather been a happy farmer.
15 PAUL:	(*quoting*). "—and I said I would rather have been a French peasant and worn wooden shoes. I would rather have lived in a hut with a vine growing over the door, and the grapes growing purple in the kisses of the autumn sun. I would rather have been that poor peasant, with my loving wife 20 by my side, knitting as the day died out of the sky—with my children upon my knees and their arms about me—I would rather have been that man and gone down to the tongueless silence of the dreamless dust, than to have been that imperial impersonation of force and murder, known as 'Napoleon 25 the Great.'"
BILLIE:	(*impressed*). How can you remember all that stuff? (*The music, which has by now become part of the background, suddenly changes. A Debussy record comes to a close and a wild Benny Goodman side replaces it. PAUL is startled, 30 so is BILLIE. Then BILLIE rushes over and turns it off.*)
BILLIE:	(PAUL *laughs*.) Once in a while. Just for a change.
PAUL:	Don't try so hard, Billie. Please. You miss the whole point.
BILLIE:	Well, I like to like what's better to like.
35 PAUL:	There's room for all sorts of things in you. The idea of learning is to be bigger, not smaller.
BILLIE:	You think I'm getting bigger?
PAUL:	Yes.
BILLIE:	Glad to hear it. (*She sits at the desk again.*) So he would 40 rather be a happy peasant than be Napoleon. So who wouldn't?
PAUL:	So Harry wouldn't, for one.
BILLIE:	What makes you think not?
PAUL:	Ask him.

—Excerpted from *Born Yesterday* by Garson Kanin

1. On the basis of Paul's character as revealed in the excerpt, what would he most likely do if Billie said she did not understand an artwork she had seen?

(1) Call Billie stupid names.
(2) Show off his knowledge.
(3) Ignore Billie altogether.
(4) Discuss the work with Billie.
(5) Pretend he did not understand the artwork.

2. What purpose do the lines " . . . with a vine growing over the door, and the grapes growing purple in the kisses of the autumn sun" (lines 17–18) have in the passage Paul quotes?

(1) They add to the image of the beauty of a simple life.
(2) They create a sense of wild adventure.
(3) They compare the sun to Napoleon.
(4) They create an atmosphere of foolishness.
(5) They add to a sense of destruction.

3. What does Paul mean when he says to Billie, "The idea of learning is to be bigger, not smaller" (lines 35–36)?

Learning

(1) makes a person act in a big-hearted manner
(2) gives a person a very inflated ego
(3) fills a person with strange thoughts
(4) is valuable if it produces money
(5) enables a person to grow in life

Answers are on page 541.

Tips for Reading Drama

- Read the title as a clue to the meaning.
- Visualize the scene and action in your mind.
- Think about what a character says about others in the play and think about what that speech may reveal about the character speaking.
- Note the stage directions that indicate the characters' movements and emotions.
- Be alert to the use of punctuation as clues to meaningful pauses, interruptions, and silences.
- Use your own knowledge and experience to assess characters and motivation.
- Consider the implications of both the time and place of the setting.

4
INTERPRETING PROSE NONFICTION

If you read a daily or weekly newspaper, you read nonfiction. If you read articles in magazines such as *TV Guide*, *People*, *Newsweek*, *Time*, *Sports Illustrated*, or *Better Homes and Gardens*, you read nonfiction.

Detecting the Author's Purpose

Nonfiction is literature that is based on fact. The nonfiction author writes about actual people, events, and ideas. The author's purpose may be to record, document, examine, analyze, inform, instruct, entertain, or persuade. In this chapter, we will focus on two key questions, as well as other nonfiction concerns:

- What is the author's purpose for writing the piece?

- What details does the author include to support his or her theories?

For example, look at the following passage.

WHAT IS THE AUTHOR POINTING OUT ABOUT MEN AND WOMEN?

Remembering Our Differences

Without the awareness that we are supposed to be different, men and women are at odds with each other. We usually become angry or frustrated with the opposite sex because we have forgotten this important truth. We expect the opposite sex to be more like ourselves. We desire them to "want what we want" and "feel the way we feel."

We mistakenly assume that if our partners love us they will react and behave in certain ways—the ways we react and behave when we love someone. This attitude sets us up to be disappointed again and again and prevents us from taking the necessary time to communicate lovingly about our differences.

Men mistakenly expect women to think, communicate, and react the way men do; women mistakenly expect men to feel, communicate, and respond the way women do. We have forgotten that men and women are supposed to be different. As a result our relationships are filled with unnecessary friction and conflict.

Clearly recognizing and respecting these differences dramatically reduces confusion when dealing with the opposite sex. When you remember that men are from Mars and women are from Venus, everything can be explained.

—Excerpted from *Men Are from Mars, Women Are from Venus*
by John Gray

EXERCISE 1: DETECTING THE AUTHOR'S PURPOSE FOR WRITING

Directions: Place a check mark (✓) before each statement with which the author would likely agree.

1. _____ Men and women expect their spouses or partners to be more like themselves.

2. _____ We are correct in assuming that our partners will behave in a certain way because they love us.

3. _____ We have forgotten that men and women are not supposed to be different.

4. _____ We can reduce confusion in dealing with the opposite sex by recognizing and respecting our differences.

Answers are on page 541.

What is the author's purpose in writing the passage? His purpose is clear. Look particularly at the last line in which he explains the title of the book and introduces the major premise for his book—that men and women are very different. He believes that the way for men and women to learn to get along with each other is to recognize and respect each other's differences.

Types of Nonfiction

Nonfiction prose appears in many forms and covers every conceivable subject. Forms of nonfiction prose include the following: **informational text** (newspaper or magazine articles, editorials, or speeches); **literary nonfiction** (biographies, autobiographies, essays, diaries, journals, letters, and reviews); and **viewing components** (review or commentary about fine and performing arts, including films, television, photos, artwork, computer images, or charts). One more point to remember before we take a closer look, however, is that sometimes these categories overlap. The longer pieces, such as biographies and autobiographies, very likely can include letters, photos, and so on.

Informational Text

Article—Giving You Just the Facts

An **article** is a short nonfiction piece, often appearing in a newspaper or magazine. An article informs and sometimes entertains readers. The writer presents facts, usually in an objective manner. An article should contain the answers to these questions: *Who, What, Where, When, Why,* and/or *How.* A **feature article** is a special nonfiction piece written on a topic that has high reader interest.

EXERCISE 2: READING AN ARTICLE FOR FACTS

Directions: Read the following article with attention to the questions *Who, What, Where, When, Why,* and/or *How.* Then analyze each statement to determine the questions that are answered in each sentence. The first one is done as a sample.

CAN BABIES SPEAK THROUGH SIGN LANGUAGE?

(1) A growing body of research supports [doctoral student and parent Jennifer] Neale's faith in the power of sign language for babies. **(2)** Once considered useful only for the deaf or hard-of-hearing, sign language is becoming a powerful tool to promote early communication for everyone. **(3)** The reason: Professionals say children can communicate with hand signs much sooner than they can master verbal skills. **(4)** "It's a question of how children mature," says Marilyn Daniels, an associate professor of speech communication at Pennsylvania State University and author of a forthcoming book called *Dancing with Word Signing for Hearing Children's Literacy.*

(5) Daniels is one of numerous researchers who encourage families to learn and use basic signs as early as possible. **(6)** Most suggest using American Sign Language (ASL) because it's easy to learn, standardized, and an official language used by the deaf community. **(7)** But others note that even homemade signs can encourage communication at least six months before most children start to form basic words. **(8)** Signing not only increases the parents' bond and interaction with their babies, it helps reduce a major source of tantrums and stress for infants.

—Excerpted from "Look Who's Talking with Their Hands" by Diane Brady,
Business Week, August 14, 2000

Sentence 1: *When:* (not specifically stated, but "A growing body of research" suggests the time period of August 14, 2000, when the article was written.)

Who: doctoral student and parent Jennifer Neale

What: supports research/power of sign language for communicating with babies

Sentence 3: _____

Sentence 4: _____

Sentence 6: _____

Sentence 8: _____

Answers are on page 541.

Make Newspaper and Magazine Nonfiction Reading a Habit

A good way to prepare for the GED Test is to make a habit of reading a major daily newspaper regularly. This enables you to practice your reading and critical thinking skills and allows you to enjoy interesting nonfiction. For further practice and information, another good habit is to read a weekly news magazine or the magazine included with many metropolitan newspapers. As you read your newspaper or magazine, note whether news or feature articles seem sufficiently objective in reporting the facts.

Editorial: Trying to Persuade

An **editorial** is a relatively short piece of nonfiction from a periodical (newspaper or magazine) that is designed to persuade or convince you to believe a certain way or to take a certain action. While an editorial needs to be based on facts, the opinions and views of the publisher are permitted and should be labeled as opinion. While the main editorial for the particular publication is usually in essay form, other editorials may appear as regular **columns** by other publication (or syndicated) staff, **letters to the editor**, **guest editorials** from readers, or **cartoons**.

EXERCISE 3: READING AN EDITORIAL FOR INFORMED OPINION

Directions: In the editorial below, the editor of a metropolitan newspaper comments on a national law. The excerpt includes the first sentence, some background material, and then the concluding sentence of the piece. Answer the questions that follow.

DOES THIS STUDY CHANGE YOUR MIND ABOUT THE BRADY LAW?

Do waiting periods and criminal background checks on prospective handgun buyers deter violent crime?

That question has generated heated debate ever since a federal law requiring both was first proposed more than a decade ago.

A new report published by the *Journal of the American Medical Association* is stoking the controversy again, as authors of the study conclude the Brady Law has failed to significantly decrease handgun homicides since its 1994 enactment.

For one thing, we have never argued that the Brady Law should take sole credit for the declining crime rates of recent years. We concur with the authors of this study on their assertion that many varied factors—including a shift in demographics, aggressive police work, tougher mandatory sentences and a good economy—have contributed.

Factoring those reports into the equation, as well as a separate study linking background checks in California to violent crime reduction in that state, puts Brady's effectiveness in a more positive light. The law's background check requirement remains a reasonable and prudent guard against those who seek handguns with criminal intent.

—Excerpted from "Brady Law Still Makes Sense,"
Daily Herald, August 7, 2000

1. What information does the *Journal of the American Medical Association* study provide about the effectiveness of the Brady Law?

2. What opinion does the editorial reaffirm in its conclusion?

3. Based on the editorial, what action would the newspaper publisher oppose?

Answers are on page 542.

Speech: Telling You as It Is

A **speech** is spoken communication about a topic. A speech is similar to an essay in its organization. The speaker should have an interesting introduction, support for the main idea, and a strong conclusion. Among other things, a speech may entertain, inform, instruct, inspire, or persuade. Notable speeches include Abraham Lincoln's 1863 "Gettysburg Address," John F. Kennedy's 1961 "Inaugural Address," and Martin Luther King, Jr.'s 1963 "I Have a Dream" civil rights speech.

Because speeches are considered to be nonfiction, they can be analyzed by examining tone, style, message, and purpose.

EXERCISE 4: ANALYZING A SPEECH FOR PURPOSE

Directions: Read the famous speech below (with sentences numbered) and answer the questions that follow.

WHAT IS THE OVERALL TONE OF LINCOLN'S SPEECH?

Address at the Dedication of the Gettysburg National Cemetery

(1) Four score and seven [87] years ago our fathers brought forth on this continent, a new nation, conceived in liberty, and dedicated to the proposition that all men are created equal.

(2) Now we are engaged in a great civil war; testing whether that nation, or any nation so conceived and so dedicated, can long endure. **(3)** We are met on a great battlefield of that war. **(4)** We have come to dedicate a portion of that field as a final resting-place for those who here gave their lives that this nation might live. **(5)** It is altogether fitting and proper that we should do this.

(6) But in a larger sense, we cannot dedicate—we cannot consecrate—we cannot hallow—this ground. **(7)** The brave men, living and dead, who struggled here have consecrated it, far above our poor power to add or detract. **(8)** The world will little note, nor long remember, what we say here, but it can never forget what they did here. **(9)** It is for the living, rather, to be dedicated here to the unfinished work which they who fought here have thus far so nobly advanced. **(10)** It is rather for us to be here dedicated to the great task remaining before us—that from these honored dead we take increased devotion to that cause for which they gave the last full measure of devotion; that we here highly resolve that these dead shall not have died in vain; that this nation, under God, shall have a new birth of freedom; and that government of the people, by the people, for the people, shall not perish from the earth.

—Abraham Lincoln

1. Which sentence in the speech is a reference to the ability of the nation to last after the American Civil War?

   (1) Sentence 1
   (2) Sentence 2
   (3) Sentence 3
   (4) Sentence 4
   (5) Sentence 5

2. In sentence 10 what does President Lincoln indicate is the greatest task remaining?

   (1) bury the Civil War dead
   (2) honor those who have died
   (3) change the government
   (4) have a new birth of freedom
   (5) perish from the earth

3. What is *not* a purpose of the speech?

   (1) to dedicate the Gettysburg National Cemetery
   (2) to rebuke the South for its Civil War actions
   (3) to honor those who gave their lives in battle
   (4) to dedicate a portion of the field as a final resting place
   (5) to inspire all the American people to persevere

Answers are on page 542.

Literary Nonfiction

Biography: Revealing Details about People

Biography is a popular form of nonfiction. A **biography** is a factual book or sketch that records the life of an individual. Biographies are written about historical figures, politicians, sports figures, current and past celebrities, and others.

Biographers report major events in a person's life and interpret their meaning. A biography often is meant to entertain as well as to educate; you can certainly learn from the experiences of others. Typically, biographies are written as a tribute after someone's death, but other biographies are written about people who are still alive.

Most major writers and literary figures are subjects of biographies because critics and readers want to know more about the personal lives of writers and how those events relate to their writings. Also, biographies often are written about famous entertainers.

Many times, nonfiction authors interview their sources, then summarize the interview in their own words. In his 1998 collection of biographical sketches, *The Greatest Generation,* author Tom Brokaw relates the stories of many ordinary as well as famous persons of the World War II generation.

EXERCISE 5: FINDING THE NOTABLE IN A BIOGRAPHY

Directions: Read the biographical sketch below of Magaret Ray Ringenberg and answer the questions that follow.

WHAT CAREER OPTIONS WERE OPEN TO WOMEN IN THE 1940s?

In 1940 she [Margaret Ray Ringenberg] started taking lessons at the local airfield and earned her license by the time she was twenty-one, just in time for the Army Air Force to recruit her for the WASPs [Women's Air Force Service Pilots]. "I was flabbergasted," she remembers. "What an opportunity. My father said, 'I didn't get to serve and I don't have any boys, so I guess you'll have to do it.'"

After six months of rigorous training in a wide variety of military aircraft in Sweetwater, Texas, Maggie was sent to Wilmington, Delaware, the 2nd Ferrying Division, assigned to testing and transporting the planes used to train young men for combat flying. . .

In the mid-fifties she discovered a new dimension to her flying: the Powder Puff Derby, a cross-country air race for women pilots. For the next twenty years, she was a competitor in the Derby, later named the Classic Air Race. She won it in 1988 and finished second six times. That was a warm-up for her big race.

In 1994 Margaret Ringenberg, the former farm girl who fell in love with flying at the age of seven and learned in the WASPs that she could hold her own against the best of the best, decided to compete in a race around the world. Twenty-four days in a small, twin-engine plane, a Cessna 340, more than a hundred hours in the air. She was seventy-two years old at the time, the oldest entrant.

—Excerpted from "Margaret Ray Ringenberg" in *The Greatest Generation*
by Tom Brokaw

1. What is the best evidence in the biographical sketch for the premise that Margaret viewed flying seriously all her life?
   (1) In the 1950s she entered the women's Powder Puff Derby, a cross-country race.
   (2) She fell in love with flying when she was only seven years of age.
   (3) She tested and transported planes for training for combat flying.
   (4) She responded to the Army Air Force when it recruited her for the WASPs.
   (5) She competed in a race around the world in 1994 at age seventy-two.

2. If Margaret Ray Ringenberg were to speak to elementary school children today, what career advice would she likely give them?
   (1) Use the wisdom of your parents to select a future career field.
   (2) Follow your mind and heart as to your career interests and choices.
   (3) Find role models of the same gender to bolster your confidence.
   (4) Follow in traditional career choices so as not to upset parents.
   (5) Do not openly show your talents if you expect to be accepted.

Answers are on page 542.

Not all biographical works document the lives of famous or distinguished individuals. In *Slats Grobnik and Some Other Friends,* Chicago journalist Mike Royko reprinted newspaper columns from 1966 to 1973 and told stories about Slats, "a neighborhood truant raised in a second-floor flat above a tavern with the El tracks in back."

Authors may use interviews to record oral histories and to create biographies. In *Hard Times,* Studs Terkel recorded facts and impressions about the lives of many different "common people" who were affected by the Great Depression of the 1930s. Similarly, Studs Terkel produced "an oral history of World War II" in the 1984 biography, *The Good War.*

Autobiography: Telling about Yourself

Only you can write your autobiography, the story of your own life. An **autobiography** is a self-biography. Many writers of autobiographies are not professional writers but notable individuals telling their own stories. Autobiographies are also known as **memoirs**. An example of a memoir is *Ever the Winds of Chance,* in which well-known American poet Carl Sandburg chronicles his years as a college student and young adult.

Some notable autobiographies include *Life on the Mississippi* by Mark Twain, recounting the author's journey on the river; *The Diary of Anne Frank,* a diary of a young Jewish girl who hid from the Nazis during World War II; *Out of Africa,* the autobiography of Karen Blixen (Isak Dinesen), which was the basis for the film of the same title; and *The Autobiography of Malcolm X,* which served as the basis for Spike Lee's film about Malcolm X.

Like authors of fiction, authors of nonfiction exhibit particular styles. Autobiographies, especially, tend to be written in a less formal style because the writers are revealing the personal details of their lives. In *My Story*, Geraldine A. Ferraro, the first woman to be nominated as a candidate by a major political party for vice president of the United States, talked about her experience in Congress. She talked about her need to be "tough" and her frustration regarding women's issues.

Essay: Presenting One Person's View

An **essay** is a nonfiction work in which an author presents a personal viewpoint on a subject. Let's look at a passage by an ordinary person whose essay was published in a national news magazine.

WHAT ARE THE RESPONSIBILITIES OF PARENTS?

You've heard the calls. I've heard the calls. I've taken them, too—which is one reason that my phone isn't on all the time.

But there's another reason, too. I believe we well-meaning parents need to get comfortable with the fact that we cannot and should not orchestrate every moment in our children's lives for them. Partly because the effort turns out to be futile, but more importantly because it prevents our kids from learning life skills they need to succeed in the real world. There are times they need to ad lib. There are times they need to wait. There are even times they need to turn to someone else—another family member, a teacher, a neighbor—and ask for help.

—Excerpted from "My Turn: Parents Shouldn't Be On Call All the Time" by Nicole Wise, *Newsweek,* August 7, 2000

Traditionally, an essay is a formal piece of writing, an expository piece that exposes and analyzes a subject. Essays embrace a variety of tones, styles, language, and themes. An essay is a *written* communication of an opinion or a point of view.

The well-known formal essay, "On the Duty of Civil Disobedience" by Henry David Thoreau, was written after Thoreau was jailed for refusing to pay a poll tax that he viewed as support for the Mexican War. The essay is personal in that Thoreau used it to explain his views; it was serious in tone, and the vocabulary was somewhat different from that of today's prose. The ideas put forth in this excerpt of the long essay were shared by the Nazi-resisters of the 1930s and 1940s, civil rights leaders of the 1960s and 1970s, and others.

Diaries, Journals, and Letters

Both **diaries** and **journals** are daily records of personal activities, events, travels, or reflections. You may keep records for yourself or for your children or grandchildren. Should you ever write your autobiography, you may refer to your diaries or journals as sources of material.

In the passage below, an author returns to her birthplace in another country 5,000 miles away some 45 years after she left as a child. Because it's an excerpt from a travel journal, it includes incomplete sentences.

SATURDAY, JULY 15

Continued to walk the streets of Alta Villa. Saw old people with nothing else to do but sit outside on chairs. An old nun was delighted to see us. Strangers (to us) greeted and kissed us and remembered my parents. Memories never cease here. Paramount are relationships: "son of," "daughter of," "sister of," "brother of," "cousin of," etc. Had some home-made ice-cream at Teresa's house.

Continued walking and had *deja vu* feeling again. Hills, fig plants, flowers, etc. Felt that I was close to drop-off point. Could this be where I fell down the hill chasing after Jack and Marie? I was told that Dad's farm was in the vicinity and that while the hill didn't lead to the Mediterranean, it once had led to a river, now dry. So I could have been rolling toward the river then. Dad saved me, and I lost one shoe. Could I *really* remember from about age two, or do I remember a story told over and over to me?

Ralph Waldo Emerson referred to his journals as his savings banks in which he deposited his thoughts. Below is an entry from one of his journals. Later, he "withdrew" those thoughts to write some of his famous speeches, essays, and poems.

EXERCISE 6: INTERPRETING A DIARY OR JOURNAL

Directions: Read the passage below and answer the questions that follow.

WHAT IS EMERSON'S ATTITUDE TOWARD LIFE?

Society everywhere is in conspiracy against the manhood of every one of its members. . . . The virtue in most request is conformity. Self-reliance is its aversion. It loves not realities and creators, but names and customs.

Whoso would be a man, must be a nonconformist. He who would gather immortal palms must not be hindered by the name of goodness, but must explore if it be goodness. Nothing is at last sacred but the integrity of your own mind.

—Excerpted from "Self-Reliance" by Ralph Waldo Emerson

1. As Emerson looked around the society of his time, he saw that conformity was everywhere. Which of the following concepts would have best described the *opposite* behavior that Emerson advocated?

   (1) conspiracy
   (2) agreement
   (3) authority
   (4) fraternity
   (5) individuality

2. Based on the passage, with which of the following statements about conformity might Emerson agree?

   (1) When in doubt, it is best to follow the crowd.
   (2) Leadership is finding a parade and getting in front.
   (3) You are the most reliable judge of what's best for you.
   (4) It is best to agree with others for the sake of harmony.
   (5) Those who don't challenge authority do best.

Answers are on page 542.

Viewing Component

The **viewing component** of the Language Arts, Reading Test will include critical reviews or published commentary of fine and performing arts, including films, television programs, photography, artwork, computer images, or charts. **Commentary** is a form of nonfiction in which the writer comments about any of the visual forms listed. A person who writes commentary—a **critic**—evaluates a nonfiction form and assesses the work's strengths and weaknesses.

The Style and Language of Commentary

Because a reviewer (or critic) is both describing and analyzing a visual form, the style and language of commentary often is highly descriptive. As the reader of commentary, you must be able to analyze style (including tone) to evaluate the reviewer's judgment about the visual form. A reviewer may write general commentary about nonfiction in a newspaper or magazine column that appears regularly.

A review deals with a specific work. The reviewer reacts to one book, film, or work of art. However, criticism may discuss trends or characteristics of a whole type of art. To understand criticism, you must be able to read on two levels. First, you must understand facts about both the visual form and its creator. Then, you have to understand the critic's opinions. As you read, look for statements of facts and opinion. Remember that most reviews are persuasive essays.

Tips for Reading Nonfiction Commentary

When you read nonfiction commentary, ask yourself these questions:

1. What facts about the work itself does the critic include?

2. What does the critic say about the author, the author's abilities, and the author's background?

3. What does the critic like about the visual form? What does the critic dislike about the visual form? Look for words that communicate the critic's feelings about the form.

4. What statements are based on facts about the visual form? What statements are based on the critic's opinion or personal reaction to the visual form?

5. Does the critic recommend the visual form? Does the critic recognize the value of the visual form?

6. What is the critic's style? How does he or she present the message?

EXERCISE 7: INTERPRETING ARTISTIC COMMENTARY

Directions: Read the commentary about the famous American painting shown below and answer the questions that follow.

HOW DOES THE AUTHOR FEEL ABOUT THE PAINTING?

—Grant Wood, American, 1891–1942, American Gothic, 1930, oil on beaverboard, 74.3 x 62.4 cm, Friends of American Art Collection.
All rights reserved by The Art Institute of Chicago and VAGA, New York, NY, 1930.934. ©The Art Institute of Chicago. All rights reserved.

A geography of the imagination would extend the shores of the Mediterranean all the way to Iowa.

Eldon, Iowa—where in 1929 Grant Wood sketched a farmhouse as the background for a double portrait of his sister Nan and his dentist, Dr. B. H. McKeeby, who donned overalls for the occasion and held a rake. Forces that arose three millennia ago in the Mediterranean changed the rake to a pitchfork, as we shall see.

Let us look at this painting to which we are blinded by familiarity and parody. In the remotest distance against this perfect blue of a fine harvest sky, there is the Gothic spire of a country church, as if to seal the Protestant sobriety and industry of the subjects. Next there are trees, seven of them, as along the porch of Solomon's temple, symbols of prudence and wisdom.

Next, still reading from background to foreground, is the house that gives the primary meaning of the title, *American Gothic*, a style of architecture. It is an example of a revolution in domestic building that made possible the rapid rise of American cities after the Civil War and dotted the prairies with decent, neat farmhouses. It is what was first called in derision a balloon-frame house, so easy to build that a father and his son could put it up. It is an elegant geometry of light timber posts and rafters requiring no deep foundation, and is nailed together. Technically, it is, like the clothes of the farmer and his wife, a mail-order house, as the design comes out of a pattern, this one from those of Alexander Davis and Andrew Downing, the architects who modified details of the Gothic Revival for American farmhouses . . .

—Excerpted from "On Grant Wood, American Gothic, 1930" by Guy Davenport in *Transforming Vision*, selected and introduced by Edward Hirsch

1. In the first line reviewer Guy Davenport introduces his commentary regarding the painting with, "A geography of the imagination would extend the shores of the Mediterranean all the way to Iowa."

   The effect of this line is to

   (1) question whether the painting is American or European (Mediterranean)
   (2) establish the influence of Mediterranean art on American art
   (3) provide a lesson to compare American and European geography
   (4) introduce the subject of soil and ocean shores conservation
   (5) show that the shores of Iowa are similar to those of the Mediterranean

2. The reviewer says, "Let us look at this painting to which we are blinded by familiarity and parody." Parody means to imitate something for the purposes of comic effect or ridicule. What is the reviewer asking the reader to do?

    (1) find anything and everything to criticize about the painting
    (2) compose a literary or a musical comedy of the painting
    (3) go beyond our usual or common understanding of the painting
    (4) learn so much about the painting that one could describe it blind-folded
    (5) look at the painting only under controlled indoor, darker lighting

3. The artist draws the subjects in the painting and the reviewer describes them as having "Protestant sobriety and industry." What conclusion can you reach about what the subjects are like?

    (1) rich, exciting, and mysterious
    (2) happy, carefree, and irresponsible
    (3) educated, professional, and opinionated
    (4) loose, careless, and unthinking
    (5) serious, steady, and hardworking

Answers are on page 542.

Business Documents

The final type of nonfiction that will be included on the Language Arts, Reading Test is **business documents**. Documents may be contracts or lease agreements, written work requirements or guidelines for conduct (employee handbooks, policy or procedural manuals, pamphlets, or memoranda), or other forms.

Let's focus on documents one could find in the workplace. These include **handbooks** or **procedure manuals**, **policies** (or rules of conduct), and **programs**. These business documents address the following topics:

- **Handbooks or Procedure Manuals:** classification levels, work schedules, compensation and salary schedules, benefits programs, payroll deductions, health and safety conduct, travel reimbursement, medical needs, leaves of absence with and without pay, review and evaluation, disciplinary or dismissal measures, grievance, or termination

- **Policies:** equal opportunity employment, standards of conduct/ethics, attendance and tardiness, communications, vacation and holiday, promotion or transfer, recruitment for employment of other individuals, substance abuse, drug and alcohol testing, smoking, sexual harassment, discounts, or environment

- **Programs:** orientation or employee development, insurance, educational assistance, employee assistance (counseling), substance abuse prevention, retirement, or recycling

MATHEMATICS

What kind of test is the GED Mathematics Test?

The GED Mathematics Test consists of questions based on mathematical problems people encounter in everyday life as individuals, family members, workers, and citizens. All of the questions will be based on information presented in words, diagrams, charts, graphs, or pictures. The math problems will test not only your ability to do arithmetic, algebra, and geometry operations but also your ability to apply problem-solving skills. To be successful, you will need to

- understand what the question is asking

- organize data and identify information necessary to solve the problem

- select a problem-solving strategy using appropriate mathematical operations

- set up the problem, estimate, and then compute the exact answer

- check the reasonableness of the answer

How many questions are on the Test? What does it look like?

The GED Mathematics Test is presented in two separate booklets: Part I permits the use of a **calculator**; Part II does not. You will have to complete both parts of the Test to earn a score. There are 50 problems, and you will be given 90 minutes to complete the Test. Some of the problems will not require any computation. Instead, on 25% of the Test you will have to identify the correct way to **set up a problem** to solve it. Some of the questions will appear in item sets. In these problems you will use information from multiple sources such as a circle graph, bar graph, or table and text to answer as many as two or three questions.

The question format may be **multiple-choice** items or **alternate-format** items. On multiple-choice items you will be asked to select from a list of answers. In alternate-format items no possible responses are provided. Alternate formats may include

- entering a number (whole, decimal, or fraction—not mixed) on a standard grid

- entering an ordered pair representing a point on the coordinate plane grid

To get an idea of what the Test is like, look at the Posttest at the end of this book. This Posttest is based on the real GED Test.

What's on the Test?

The GED Mathematics Test can be broken down into the content areas it covers and the skills it tests. The Test covers the following content areas:

Number Sense and Operations	20–30%
Data, Statistics, and Probability	20–30%
Algebra, Functions, and Patterns	20–30%
Measurement and Geometry	20–30%

In each of these content areas the problems will test your ability to follow mathematical procedures (15–25% of the test), demonstrate an understanding of concepts (25–35% of the test), and/or apply problem-solving skills (approximately 50% of the test).

What math resources can I use on the Test?

In Part I a calculator will be provided for your use; in Part II no calculator will be permitted. All testing centers will distribute the same calculator: the Casio *fx*-260 SOLAR. It is important that you become familiar with the calculator and practice using it for problem solving. Instructions for using the calculator will be attached to the GED Test.

A formula page with a list of common formulas is provided with all Test forms to help you solve problems. You should become familiar with the formulas on the page, learn how to select the appropriate formula for a problem, and practice evaluating a formula using given values. The formula page is on page 456.

A mathematician's best "friends" are paper and pencil. At the Test, you will be given scratch paper to use. If you organize your work on the paper, you will be able to easily review problems later and find information that might help you with other problems. You should also use scratch paper and pencil as you work through this textbook to take notes and/or practice skills.

1
<u>NUMBER SENSE</u>

In mathematics there are rules and procedures that guide every operation. This is an important part of number sense. There are special rules for the use of symbols—such as parentheses, exponents, and radicals—and for the order of all operations performed. Good problem solving will require you to use your number sense and mathematical knowledge effectively.

Powers

When a number is multiplied by itself, we say that it is **squared.** We show that with a small "2" placed to the upper right of the number. For example, $7^2 = 7 \times 7 = 49$. This means seven squared is 7 times 7, which is 49.

In the expression 7^2, the two is called the **power** or **exponent,** and the seven is called the **base.** It is best to think of the exponent as an instruction. The exponent tells you what to do with the base. When the exponent is two, the base is squared, and we multiply the base by itself.

Examples $10^2 = 10 \times 10 = 100$ $(\frac{1}{3})^2 = \frac{1}{3} \times \frac{1}{3} = \frac{1}{9}$

Sometimes the exponent is a number other than 2. The exponent tells how many times to multiply the base by itself. For example:

$3^4 = 3 \times 3 \times 3 \times 3 = 81$

$10^6 = 10 \times 10 \times 10 \times 10 \times 10 \times 10 = 1,000,000$

$(\frac{2}{3})^3 = \frac{2}{3} \times \frac{2}{3} \times \frac{2}{3} = \frac{8}{27}$

Special Rules About Powers
1. The number 1 to any power is 1. $1^5 = 1 \times 1 \times 1 \times 1 \times 1 = 1$
2. Any number to the first power is that number. $6^1 = 6$
3. Any number to the zero power is 1. $14^0 = 1$

When you multiply a number by itself, you get a **perfect square.** For instance, $6^2 = 36$; so 36 is a perfect square. Some perfect squares that are helpful to know are listed here.

$1^2 = 1$	$6^2 = 36$	$11^2 = 121$	$20^2 = 400$
$2^2 = 4$	$7^2 = 49$	$12^2 = 144$	$30^2 = 900$
$3^2 = 9$	$8^2 = 64$	$13^2 = 169$	$40^2 = 1600$
$4^2 = 16$	$9^2 = 81$	$14^2 = 196$	$50^2 = 2500$
$5^2 = 25$	$10^2 = 100$	$15^2 = 225$	$100^2 = 10,000$

Square Roots

The operation opposite of squaring a number is finding the **square root** of a number. The symbol for square root is the **radical symbol, $\sqrt{\ }$**. For instance, $5^2 = 25$, so $\sqrt{25} = 5$. $\sqrt{25}$ is read, "the square root of 25." Being familiar with perfect squares makes many square roots easy to recall. For instance, $\sqrt{100} = 10$ because $10^2 = 100$.

If you need to find the square root of a number that is not a perfect square, you can do one of three things: simplify the square root, approximate the square root, or use a calculator.

Example 1   Simplify a square root by writing the number as a product of numbers using perfect squares if possible.

$\sqrt{75}$ can be expressed as $= \sqrt{25 \times 3} = \sqrt{25} \times \sqrt{3} = 5\sqrt{3}$. You choose 25 and 3 because 25 is a perfect square and you can find its square root.

Example 2   Approximate the square root of a number by looking at the perfect square closest to the number to make an estimated guess at the answer.

$\sqrt{75}$ is between $\sqrt{64}$ and $\sqrt{81}$.

$\sqrt{64} = 8$ and $\sqrt{81} = 9$ so

$\sqrt{75} \approx 8.7 \leftarrow$ ($\sqrt{75}$ is between 8 and 9 but closer to 9, so we estimate about 8.7.)

CALCULATOR: TO FIND POWERS AND ROOTS

Your calculator can be used to perform powers and roots. Become familiar with these keys on your calculator and how to use them.

Keys: x^2 squares the numbers

x^y raises the number to the power indicated

SHIFT   accesses key operations indicated above the key

$\sqrt{\ }$ finds the square root of the number

EXERCISE 1: POWERS AND ROOTS

Directions: Evaluate the powers below. Use your calculator to check your answer.

1. 8^2 **2.** 1^7 **3.** 4^0 **4.** 10^3 **5.** 5^4

Evaluate the square roots below. When finding the square root of a perfect square, give the exact answer. When finding a square root that is not a perfect square, give either an approximate answer or a simplified answer. Use your calculator to check your answers.

6. $\sqrt{1}$ **7.** $\sqrt{144}$ **8.** $\sqrt{28}$ **9.** $\sqrt{400}$ **10.** $\sqrt{0}$

Answers are on page 543.

Parentheses

Parentheses are powerful symbols in mathematics problem solving. As you know, parentheses can be used to indicate multiplication. For example, $5(3) = 15$. Parentheses can also be used as a grouping symbol to organize a problem. For instance, $5(3 + 6) = 45$. Before you multiply by 5, you should add 3 and 6 because they are grouped together inside the parentheses. Use parentheses anytime you want to **emphasize an operation** and want that operation to **precede other operations**.

Order of Operations

Accurate calculations depend on careful use of addition, subtraction, multiplication, and division. These operations must be performed in a certain order when there are two or more operations in the same problem. The rules that describe that order are called the **order of operations**. All operations should be performed moving from the left to the right. Be sure to start at the beginning for every problem. Do not skip a step unless there is no operation to do at that level.

Order of Operations
First, do all the work grouped inside parentheses or above a fraction bar.
Second, evaluate powers and square roots.
Third, multiply and divide as indicated from left to right.
Last, add and subtract as indicated from left to right.

Example 1   Calculate $3(5 + 7)$.

First, add the numbers inside the parentheses. $3(5 + 7) =$

Then multiply 3×12 to get 36. $3 \times 12 = \mathbf{36}$

Example 2   Calculate $\frac{5 + 7 + 6}{3}$.

First, add the numbers grouped above the fraction bar. $\frac{5 + 7 + 6}{3} =$

Then divide by 3 to get 6. $\frac{18}{3} = \mathbf{6}$

Example 3   Calculate $3 \times 5 + 2 \times 10$.

First, notice there are no parentheses. Then multiply 3×5 and 2×10.

$$3 \times 5 + 2 \times 10 =$$

Last, add $15 + 20$ to get 35.

$$15 + 20 = \mathbf{35}$$

Example 4   Calculate 4×5^2.

First, notice there are no parentheses. Then raise 5 to the second power.

$$4 \times 5^2 =$$

Last, multiply 4×25 to get 100.

$$4 \times 25 = \mathbf{100}$$

CALCULATOR: ORDER OF OPERATIONS

The calculator that you will use on the GED Test has the order of operations programmed in it. If a problem has more than one operation, the calculator will follow the order of operations to arrive at the answer. Be sure to key in the problem correctly.

Keys: [(open parentheses

)]   close parentheses

To evaluate a numerical expression on a calculator, key in the numbers, symbols, and operations as they occur. Use the *open parentheses* and *close parentheses* keys to indicate an operation that is to be calculated first. If a number precedes the parentheses, it indicates that you are to multiply the amount in the parentheses by the number. For example:

$5(3 + 8)$ means $5 \times (3 + 8)$ <u>You must key in the multiplication sign</u>.

EXERCISE 2: ORDER OF OPERATIONS

Directions: Evaluate each numerical expression below without using a calculator. Be sure to follow the order of operations rules. Then use a calculator to check your answers.

1. $2 + 6 \times 4 + 8$
2. $\dfrac{6 + 9}{3}$
3. $8 \times 3 + 6 \times 4$
4. $4 \times (8 - 3)$

5. $7 - 5 + 3 - 5$
6. $6 + 21 \div 3 - 5$
7. $15 - 3 + 2^3$
8. $4(5 + 3)^2$

Answers are on page 543.

Setup Problems

Some problems on the GED Test will require you to identify the correct setup to solve them. These setup problems do not require you to perform the calculations. You are being tested on your ability to demonstrate how you can use numbers, operations, and mathematical processes to solve problems.

To set up a problem, represent the mathematical relations using numbers and operation symbols. This relationship is called an **arithmetic expression.** There are rules that must be followed when writing an arithmetic expression involving more than one arithmetic operation.

Writing Arithmetic Expressions
1. Write an arithmetic expression using numbers and operation symbols following the rules of operations and identifying the individual steps in the multistep problem.
2. Use parentheses or the fraction bar to separate one part of an arithmetic expression from another.
3. Follow the order of operations rules to indicate the order in which the arithmetic expression should be solved. (See page 343.)

Example   If Becky can walk a mile in 20 minutes, how far can she walk in 3 hours?

Question:	How far does she walk in 3 hours?
Information:	One mile in 20 minutes; 3 hours; 60 minutes in one hour
Operations:	Step 1: To get the total minutes— multiply 3×60 Step 2: To get the number of miles— divide by 20
Setup and Estimation:	$\dfrac{3 \times 60}{20}$ This is the arithmetic expression that sets up the problem.
Computation:	$3 \times 60 = 180$, $180/20 = $ **9 miles**
Is the answer reasonable?	Yes, because one mile in 20 minutes would be 3 miles per hour $\times$ 3 hours $= 9$.

EXERCISE 3: ARITHMETIC EXPRESSIONS

Directions: In each of the following problems, select the arithmetic expression that represents the appropriate setup to solve the problem.

1. In 2001 Harper College charged $55 per credit hour. Find the total bill for a student who takes 15 credit hours and pays a $75 activity fee.
   (1) $55 + 75 + 15$
   (2) $75 + 15 \times 55$
   (3) $(75 + 55) \times 15$
   (4) $75 \times 55 \times 15$
   (5) $55 \times 15 - 75$

2. Angela used her 75¢-off coupon to buy a roll of film for her camera. If the film was priced at $3.98 and tax was 31¢, how much change did she receive if she paid with a $5 bill?

(1) $5.00 - (3.98 + .31 - .75)$
(2) $5.00 - 3.98 - .31 - .75$
(3) $3.98 + .31 + .75 - 5.00$
(4) $3.98 + .31 - .75 - 5.00$
(5) $5.00 + 3.98 + .31 + .75$

3. As a waiter Jorge was responsible for four tables. If his customers left tips of $5, $7, $3, and $9, what was the average tip per table?

(1) $5 + 7 + 3 + 9$
(2) $4 \times (5 + 7 + 3 + 9)$
(3) $\dfrac{5 + 7 + 3 + 9}{4}$
(4) $5 + 7 + 3 + 9 \div 4$
(5) $4 \div (5 + 7 + 3 + 9)$

Answers are on page 543.

EXERCISE 4: WORD PROBLEMS

Directions: Solve each problem. Check your work using your calculator.

1. A garment factory completed an order for 500 pairs of pants and was paid $5500. If the factory received $9130 for a second order for pants at the same price, how many pairs of pants were in the second order?

(1) 363
(2) 500
(3) 830
(4) 913
(5) 3630

2. A charity organization collected $348,284 in a recent fund-raising drive. Of the amount collected, some was put aside to pay expenses. The remaining money was divided equally among six local charities. What amount did each charity receive?

(1) $ 58,041
(2) $ 58,047
(3) $ 58,053
(4) $348,284
(5) Not enough information is given.

Questions 3–4 refer to the information in the table below.

The local school district has experienced a recent increase in enrollment. The table compares enrollment figures between 1992 and 2002 for its five schools.

High School Student Enrollment

Year	Lincoln	Mead	Sandburg	Austin	Edison
1992	1420	1650	1847	1296	1318
2002	1686	1982	2234	1648	1846

3. What was the total increase in enrollment in the district during the ten-year period?

(1) 1865
(2) 2865
(3) 7531
(4) 9396
(5) Not enough information is given.

4. What was the average increase in enrollment per school in the district?

(1)　373
(2) 1865
(3) 1879
(4) 7531
(5) 9396

5. Four technicians for Transcom must produce 1298 parts in a week's time. The first one produces 350 parts, the second produces 375 parts, and the third produces 417 parts. Which expression shows how many parts remain for the fourth technician to make?

(1) $1298 \div 4$
(2) $350 + 375 + 417$
(3) $1298 - (350 + 375 + 417)$
(4) $(350 + 375 + 417) - 1298$
(5) $(350 + 37 + 417) \div 3$

6. Gary bought a new sport-utility vehicle. The price was $19,700 including an AM/FM CD/cassette radio and automatic transmission. The car dealer gave him a $500 rebate for the purchase of the new car, and Gary made a down payment of $3150. What would be the expression for his monthly payments if he takes 60 months to pay the remaining balance?

(1) $19700 + 3150 + 500 \div 60$
(2) $60 \div (19700 + 3150 + 500)$
(3) $\dfrac{19700 - (3150 + 500)}{60}$
(4) $\dfrac{19700 - 3150 + 500}{60}$
(5) $60 \times (19700 + 3150 + 500)$

Answers are on page 543.

Formulas

Letters of the alphabet often are used to represent numbers that you need to find. For instance, you may remember the distance formula $d = rt$. The letters d, r, and t are used to represent numbers for distance, rate, and time. Letters used this way are called **unknowns** or **variables.** This use of letters helps us express general relationships about numbers.

Formulas are a way of showing these general relationships. Some common formulas that help us are the area of a circle ($A = \pi r^2$), the perimeter of a rectangle ($P = 2l + 2w$), and the Pythagorean theorem ($a^2 + b^2 = c^2$). The GED Mathematics Test will include a formula page that will help you solve some problems on the Test. As you read a particular problem, you will have to decide which formula will help you solve it. You should become familiar with the formula page on page 456 and practice using it as you solve problems.

Evaluating Formulas

When you replace letters with numbers in a formula, you **substitute** numbers for letters. When you perform mathematical operations on the substituted values, you are **evaluating** a formula. When you evaluate a formula, be sure to follow the **order of operations**. (See page 343.)

Example 1   The formula for the perimeter of (distance around) a rectangle is $P = 2l + 2w$. Find the perimeter of a rectangle if the length is 6 and the width is 5.

STEP 1   Substitute in the formula. $P = 2l + 2w$
                                                 $P = 2(6) + 2(5)$

STEP 2   Multiply first. $P = 12 + 10$

STEP 3   Add. $P = \mathbf{22}$

Example 2   Find the volume of a rectangular box whose length is 7 inches, width is 5 inches, and height is 3 inches. Use the formula for volume $V = lwh$ (see the formula on page 456).

STEP 1   Find the formula for volume. $V = lwh$

STEP 2   Substitute the values given. $V = (7)(5)(3)$

STEP 3   Multiply as indicated by the parentheses. $V = \mathbf{105\ cubic\ inches}$

EXERCISE 5: EVALUATING FORMULAS

Directions: Select the appropriate formula from formula page 456. Substitute the values given and evaluate the formula. The units for your answers are given in parentheses following the problem.

1. Find the area of the square.
   (The answer will be in square inches.)

   12 inches

2. Find the volume of the cube.
   (The answer will be in cubic inches.)

   5 inches

3. Find the area of a triangle where the base (*b*) is 12 centimeters and the height (*h*) is 9 centimeters. (The answer will be in square centimeters.)

   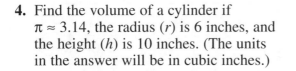

   9 centimeters

   12 centimeters

4. Find the volume of a cylinder if π ≈ 3.14, the radius (*r*) is 6 inches, and the height (*h*) is 10 inches. (The units in the answer will be in cubic inches.)

   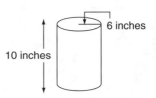

   6 inches

   10 inches

Answers are on page 543.

2
DECIMAL NUMBERS
AND OPERATIONS

Every day we use familiar decimal numbers. A person's normal temperature is 98.6°. A cup of coffee and bagel with cream cheese is $3.25. The odometer on the car reads 12,356.8 miles. You will review place values, reading decimals, rounding decimals, comparing and ordering decimals, and performing decimal operations.

Using Decimals

In our number system, you use ten digits (0, 1, 2, 3, 4, 5, 6, 7, 8, 9) to write every number. The place that a digit occupies in a number tells us the value of the digit. This means that each digit has a **place value.**

You can use the place value chart below to read numbers. The whole numbers are to the left of the **decimal point.** The decimals, which are parts of a whole, are to the right of the decimal point. The places to the right of the decimal point are called **decimal places.** Decimal places represent fractional values whose parts are tenths, hundredths, thousandths, and so on. Note that the names of the decimal places end in *th.*

Billions	Hundred Millions	Ten Millions	Millions	Hundred Thousands	Ten Thousands	Thousands	Hundreds	Tens	Ones	AND	Tenths	Hundredths	Thousandths	Ten Thousandths	Hundred Thousandths	Millionths
							3	2	6	.	7	5				

> **TIP** The decimal point separates the whole-number places from the decimal places. The point is read as "and."

The number 326.75 has two decimal places (tenths and hundredths), but *only* the last decimal place is named when the number is read. The number is read as "326 *and* 75 hundredths."

$$326.75 = 326 \text{ and } \frac{75}{100}$$

326 *and* 75 hundredths

Reading Decimals
1. Read the whole part first.
2. Say "and" for the decimal point.
3. Read the decimal part.
4. Say the place value of the last digit.
• If there is no whole number, start at step 3. For instance, .008 is read as "8 thousandths."

Zeros in Decimals

The zero is very important in writing and reading decimal numbers. To see how important zeros are, read the names of each of the decimals below.

.5 (5 tenths)   .05 (5 hundredths)   .005 (5 thousandths)

You can see that the only digits used to write these numbers are 0 and 5. The actual value of the number depends on the place value of each digit. The zeros in the numbers hold the number 5 in a specific decimal place.

EXERCISE 1: READING AND WRITING DECIMALS

Directions: In problems 1–3, select the number that matches the written value. Remember that the word *and* stands for the decimal point.

1. five hundredths
   (1) 500   (2) .05   (3) .5   (4) .50   (5) .500

2. six and two tenths
   (1) 6.2   (2) .62   (3) 62.0   (4) .062   (5) .602

3. four hundred thirty and six thousandths
   (1) 436,000   (2) .436   (3) 430.006   (4) 400.036   (5) 430.06

In problems 4–6, write the numbers in the row across the top. Then fill in the grid sections that correspond to your answer. Remember to select the decimal point as necessary.

4. seven tenths

5. six and thirty-two thousandths

6. sixty-five ten-thousandths

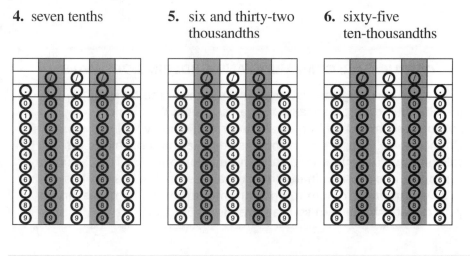

Answers are on page 543.

Comparing and Ordering Decimals

Sometimes you need to compare decimals to see which one is larger. Decimal numbers can be rewritten with attached zeros to make it easier to compare numbers that have the same number of decimal places. Attaching zeros to the right of the last decimal digit does not change the value of the number. For example, $12 can also be written as $12.00. Likewise, 12.5, 12.50, and 12.500 all have the same value.

To compare .14 and .126, attach a zero to .14 to make it .140. Now both .126 and .140 are expressed in thousandths and have the same number of decimal places.

.14 = .140
.126 = .126

You can now see that 126 thousandths is smaller than 140 thousandths because 126 is less than 140.

Example   Put 4.8, 4.12, 4.2, and 4.1003 in order from the smallest to the largest.

STEP 1   Attach zeros so that each number has the same number of decimal places. Then number the mixed decimals in order from the smallest to the largest.

4.8	= 4.8000	4th
4.12	= 4.1200	2nd
4.2	= 4.2000	3rd
4.1003	= 4.1003	1st

STEP 2   Using your ranking system, put the original numbers in order from smallest to largest.

1st	4.1003
2nd	4.12
3rd	4.2
4th	4.8

CALCULATOR: COMPARING AND ORDERING DECIMALS

Zeros following the last digit to the right of the decimal point are eliminated automatically on the calculator. You can enter numbers such as 4.50 into a calculator and display will show 4.50. On the other hand, if 4.50 is the answer to a math problem, the calculator will eliminate the zero and display only 4.5. The calculator is programmed to eliminate unnecessary zeros. If 4.5 is the answer to an arithmetic problem referring to money, it will be necessary for you to reattach the zero so that it reads $4.50.

EXERCISE 2: COMPARING DECIMALS

Directions: Solve the following problems.

1. Select the larger number in each pair.
   (a) .005; .05   **(b)** 4.1; 4.01   **(c)** .7; .68   **(d)** .5; .51   **(e)** 1.033; 1.03

2. Arrange each set of numbers in order of size with the *largest* number first.
  (a) 1.95; 2.105; 2.15   **(b)** .0035; .0503; .005   **(c)** 6.4; 6; 6.07; 6.607

3. Put these weights in order from the *lightest* to the *heaviest*.
  14.3 lb   14.03 lb   14.003 lb   14.3033 lb

Answers are on page 543.

Rounding Decimals

You might solve a problem involving money and get $25.128 for the answer. Since money is expressed in hundredths and not thousandths, you must round off the answer to dollars and cents.

Example   Round off $25.128 to the nearest cent.

STEP 1	Underline the place value to which you are rounding.	$25.1<u>2</u>8
STEP 2	Identify the digit to the right of the place to which you are rounding.	$25.12<u>8</u>
STEP 3	If the digit to the right of the underlined number	$25.1<u>2</u>8
	(a) **is 5 or more,** increase the digit in the place to which you are rounding by 1 and drop the digits to the right	+1 <hr> **$25.13**
	(b) **is less than 5,** keep the same digit in the place to which you are rounding and drop the digits to the right	

EXERCISE 3: ROUNDING DECIMALS

Directions: Solve the following problems.

1. On the state income tax form, numbers are rounded to the nearest dollar. Round $1826.53 to the nearest dollar amount.

2. The 8% sales tax on an $16.99 item is $1.3592. Round this amount to the nearest cent.

3. The value of π is 3.14159. Round off this value to the nearest hundredth. (This Greek symbol pronounced "pie" is used in geometric measurement.)

Answers are on page 543.

Scientific Notation

Our number system is based on multiples of ten. **Scientific notation** uses this idea of a base of 10 to give us a shortened method of writing extremely large or extremely small numbers. We can express multiples of 10 using powers of ten. To designate decimal values such as .1, .01, .001, we use negative powers of ten. A negative exponent is used to indicate the **reciprocal** value. The reciprocal of 10 is $\frac{1}{10}$.

So $10^{-1} = \frac{1}{10^1} = .1$.

Let's look at some powers of ten using positive and negative exponents.

$10^0 = 1$ $10^{-1} = \frac{1}{10} = .1$

$10^1 = 10$ $10^{-2} = \frac{1}{10^2} = \frac{1}{100} = .01$

$10^2 = 100$ $10^{-3} = \frac{1}{10^3} = \frac{1}{1000} = .001$

$10^3 = 1000$

$10^4 = 10,000$

Writing a Number in Scientific Notation
1. Represent the number as a number between 1 and 10.
2. Write a multiplication sign and represent the number's value to the correct power of 10.
Use scientific notation to write numbers in shortened form. Simply count the number of positions that the decimal point must be moved to determine which power of 10 to use. The power of 10 is positive for whole numbers and negative for decimals.

Example   Express 86,200,000 in scientific notation.

STEP 1   Represent the number as a mixed $86,200,000 = 8.62 \times 10^?$
decimal between 1 and 10. Insert the
decimal point between 8 and 62 to
get 8.62.

STEP 2   Count the number of places the decimal $86,200,000 = \mathbf{8.62 \times 10^7}$
point moved to get from 86,200,000
to 8.62. Since the point moved 7 places   7 places
to the left, the power of 10 is 7.

EXERCISE 4: SCIENTIFIC NOTATION

Directions: Express each of the numbers below in scientific notation.

1. .0082   **2.** 38,200   **3.** .58

Each number below is written in scientific notation. Find the actual value.

4. 1.624×10^3 **5.** 3.12×10^{-1} **6.** 8.24×10^0

Answers are on page 544.

Adding and Subtracting Decimals

Adding and Subtracting Decimals
1. Line up the decimal points.
2. Be sure that the whole numbers are to the left of the decimal point.
3. Add or subtract the numbers.
4. Bring the decimal point straight down in the answer.

Example 1   Add 4.5 and 38.68.

Read this space as a zero. ⟶   Line up the decimal points.

$$
\begin{array}{r}
4.50 \\
+\ 38.68 \\
\hline
43.18
\end{array}
$$

4.50 ← Attach a zero to help you keep the columns lined up.

➤ **TIP**   You may attach zeros following the decimal point or following the last digit *after* the decimal point. This will help you keep the place value columns lined up but won't change the value of the numbers.

Example 2   Jake gave the cashier a $20 bill to pay the $7.48 lunch check. How much change did Jake get back?

$$
\begin{array}{r}
\$20.00 \\
-7.48 \\
\end{array}
$$
Remember to attach a decimal point and zeros.
$$
\begin{array}{r}
\overset{1\,9\ \ 9\,1}{\$20.00} \\
-7.48 \\
\hline
\$12.52
\end{array}
$$

➤ **TIP**   When you subtract decimals, fill in zeros to get enough decimal places.

EXERCISE 5: ADDING AND SUBTRACTING DECIMALS

Directions: Solve each problem. Grid your answers for the problems indicated. Use your calculator to check your answers.

1. Add 5.9, 2.46, 6, 3.07, and .48.   **2.** Subtract 5.2 from 43.

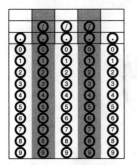   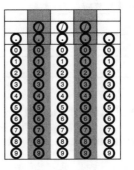

3. Find the distance around the field shown. All distances are in meters.

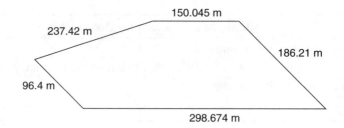

150.045 m

237.42 m

186.21 m

96.4 m

298.674 m

4. Can you balance a checkbook? At the beginning of the week, your balance was $472.24. During the week, you wrote checks for $42.87, $5.93, $20, $17.48, and $38.40. What is your new balance?

5. At the start of a trip, your mileage meter read 25,176.3; at the end of the trip, it read 28,054.1. How far did you travel?

6. A piece of wood is 46.75 centimeters long. If you trim .5 centimeters off the end, how many centimeters long is the remaining piece?
- **(1)** 41.75
- **(2)** 46.25
- **(3)** 46.7
- **(4)** 46.8
- **(5)** 47.25

Part of a service order is shown below. Use the service order information and your calculator to answer questions 7 and 8.

Lake Marine Service		Date: 8/12		NAME: Kim Yang
Qty.	Part	Amount	Labor	Charge
1	Gear lube	$17.50	Winterize	$70
1	Grease	4.95	Weld skeg	$90
1	Oil	6.00	Repair ladder	no charge
1	Gas	16.25		
3	Antifreeze	6.75		
Total Parts			**Total Labor**	$160
			Total Parts	
			Tax	$3.66
			Invoice Total	

7. Find the total cost of the parts.

8. What is the invoice total for Mr. Yang's boat?

Answers are on page 544.

Multiplying Decimals

Decimals are multiplied the same way as whole numbers, and then the decimal point is placed in the answer. These are the rules for multiplying decimals.

Multiplying Decimals
1. Multiply the two numbers as whole numbers, ignoring the decimal points.
2. Find the total number of decimal places in the numbers being multiplied.
3. Count the total number of decimal places in the answer. Starting at the right, move to the left the same number of places, and put the decimal point there.

Example 1   Multiply 3.2 and 4.05.

$$
\begin{array}{r}
4.05 \quad \longleftarrow \text{ 2 decimal places} \\
\times\,3.2 \quad \longleftarrow \text{ 1 decimal place} \\
\hline
810 \\
12\ 15 \\
\hline
\mathbf{12.960}
\end{array}
$$

Count and move to the left a total of 3 decimal places.

The final answer is **12.96** because you can drop the unnecessary zero.

Example 2   28 × .06

$$
\begin{array}{r}
28 \quad \longleftarrow \text{ no decimal places} \\
\times .06 \quad \longleftarrow \text{ 2 decimal places} \\
\hline
\mathbf{1.68}
\end{array}
$$

Count and move left a total of 2 decimal places.

➤ **TIP**   Sometimes you have to put zeros at the beginning of the answer to have enough decimal places.

Example 3   .043 × .0056

$$
\begin{array}{r}
.0056 \quad \longleftarrow \text{ 4 decimal places} \\
\times .043 \quad \longleftarrow \text{ 3 decimal places} \\
\hline
168 \\
224 \\
\hline
2408 \\
\mathbf{.0002408}
\end{array}
$$

You need a total of 7 decimal places. Attach 3 zeros at the beginning of the number and then the decimal point.

EXERCISE 6: MULTIPLYING DECIMALS

Directions: Multiply as indicated. Check your answers using your calculator.

1. 0.85 × .06   **2.** $6.50 × .085   **3.** $128 × .07

4. Monica pays $7.85 each month for newspaper home delivery. Which expression shows how much she pays for the newspaper over a year's time?

(1) $7.85 \times 4 \times 12$
(2) $(7.85 + 4) \times 12$
(3) 7.85×12
(4) 7.85×52
(5) 7.85×365

Answers are on page 544.

Dividing Decimals

Split $45.75 equally among five people. How many $.59 hamburgers can you buy for $8? There are two basic types of decimal division: (1) division of decimals by whole numbers and (2) division of decimals by decimals.

Dividing by a Whole Number

Dividing Decimals by Whole Numbers
1. Divide by the number that follows the division sign ($\div$).
2. Divide as though both numbers were whole numbers. Keep numbers aligned properly.
3. Place the decimal point in the answer directly above the decimal point in the dividend.

Example 1   Dividing a decimal by a whole number: $36.48 \div 4$

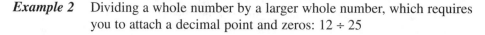

Place the decimal point directly above the decimal point in the dividend.

$$
\begin{array}{r}
9.12 \\
4\overline{)36.48} \\
-36 \\
\hline
04 \\
-4 \\
\hline
08 \\
-8 \\
\hline
0
\end{array}
$$

Example 2   Dividing a whole number by a larger whole number, which requires you to attach a decimal point and zeros: $12 \div 25$

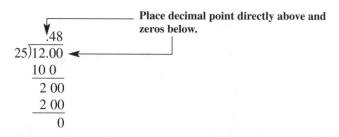

Place decimal point directly above and zeros below.

$$
\begin{array}{r}
.48 \\
25\overline{)12.00} \\
10\ 0 \\
\hline
2\ 00 \\
2\ 00 \\
\hline
0
\end{array}
$$

Example 3   Dividing by a whole number that doesn't divide into the first number after the decimal point, requiring you to put in a zero placeholder before continuing your division: $.35 \div 7$

Put in the zero after the decimal point because the point started the answer.

$$7\overline{).35}^{.05}$$

Dividing by a Decimal

Dividing Decimal Numbers by Decimal Numbers
1. Move the decimal point in the divisor all the way to the right.
2. Move the decimal point in the dividend the same number of places to the right.
3. Place the decimal point in the answer directly above the decimal point in the dividend.
4. Divide as though both numbers are whole numbers.

Example 1 $4.864 \div .32$

Move the decimal point two places to the right.

Place the decimal point directly above the new decimal point in the dividend.

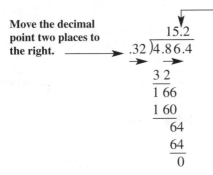

$$
\begin{array}{r}
15.2 \\
.32\,\overline{)4.86.4} \\
3\,2 \\
\hline
1\,66 \\
1\,60 \\
\hline
64 \\
64 \\
\hline
0
\end{array}
$$

Example 2 $25 \div .125$

Move the decimal point three places to the right.

Add three zeros and move the decimal point three places to the right.

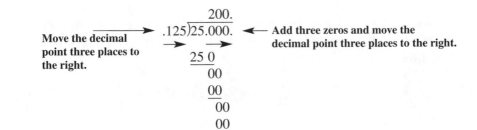

$$
\begin{array}{r}
200. \\
.125\,\overline{)25.000.} \\
25\,0 \\
\hline
00 \\
00 \\
\hline
00 \\
00
\end{array}
$$

EXERCISE 7: DIVIDING DECIMALS

Directions: Solve each division problem. Check your answers using your calculator. (In division problems, be sure to enter the divisor after the division symbol.)

1. Divide 6.005 by .05.　　**2.** .012 ÷ 3　　**3.** 4.75 ÷ 2.5

4. How many $1.25 items can you buy for $20?

Answers are on page 544.

Multiplying and Dividing by Multiples of 10

The easy way to multiply or divide by multiples of ten (10, 100, 1000, and so on) is simply to move the decimal point. When you multiply, you move the decimal point to the right. When you divide, you move the point to the left. In either case, the decimal point moves as many places as there are zeros in the multiple of ten. (As the examples show, you add zeros when necessary.)

Example 1　.13 × 1000 = 130.
　　　　　　　⟶
3 zeros move the decimal point 3 places to the right in multiplication.

Example 2　9.5 ÷ 100 = .095
　　　　　　　⟵
2 zeros move the decimal point 2 places to the left in division.

EXERCISE 8: MULTIPLYING AND DIVIDING DECIMALS BY MULTIPLES OF 10

Directions: Use the shortcuts to multiply and divide the decimals below. Use your calculator to check your answers.

1. .472 × 10,000　　**2.** .617 ÷ 10　　**3.** 456.12 ÷ 100　　**4.** 57 ÷ 1000

5. Finishing Touch Decorators can paint 1.5 rooms in an hour. Working 10 hours each day, how many days will it take them to paint a 75-room building?

Answers are on page 544.

Estimating for Problem Solving

Estimation is a handy tool to use in solving decimal problems. If a problem involves decimals, reread the problem and replace the mixed decimals with whole numbers. This will help you see how to solve the problem. After choosing the correct operations to use, work the problem with the original decimal numbers if an exact answer is necessary.

Example   What is the cost of 12.8 gallons of gasoline at $1.89 per gallon?

Estimation: What is the cost of 13 gallons of gasoline at $2 per gallon? Using whole numbers helps you see that you should multiply 2 × 13, which equals 26. Your answer in the original problem should be about **$26.** The exact answer is 24.192, which rounds to $24.19.

EXERCISE 9: ESTIMATING

Directions: Estimate the answers to the following problems. Use your calculator to find the exact answers.

1. Dino drove his truck the following distances during the week: Monday, 4.8 miles; Tuesday, 12.3 miles; Wednesday, 74.5 miles; Thursday, 10 miles; and Friday, 8.1 miles. Approximately how far did he travel?

2. Connie had $50 in her purse. She spent $24.75 on cosmetics and $2.50 on a magazine. After these purchases, approximately how much did she have left in her purse?

Answers are on page 544.

EXERCISE 10: DECIMAL WORD PROBLEMS

Directions: Use estimation to help you solve the problems. Sometimes you may need to find the exact amount. Check your work with a calculator.

1. Mr. Stansky earns a part-time salary of $425 every four weeks. During the past four weeks he also received commissions of $485.75, $399.87, $642.15, and $724.52. What was his total income for the past 4-week period?
   (1) $ 535.46
   (2) $ 669.32
   (3) $ 2252.29
   (4) $ 2256.42
   (5) $ 2677.29

2. On a bicycle road trip, Otis rode 2492 miles in 140 hours. What was his average speed in miles per hour?
   (1)   1.78
   (2)   17.8
   (3)   178
   (4)   1780
   (5) 34,888

Questions 3 and 4 are based on the table below.

As an assistant accountant for a computer company, you must calculate each employee's gross earnings, total of deductions, and net pay by using the following table.

Employee Earnings

Employee Number	247	351	178
Regular Pay	307.20	368.80	338
Overtime Pay	69.12	96.81	114.03
Gross Earnings			
Social Security Tax (FICA)	26.34	32.60	31.64
Federal Income Tax (FIT)	56.45	83.81	81.37
Total of Deductions			
Net Pay			

3. Find the net pay for employee 178 after deductions are taken out.
   (1) $113.01
   (2) $339.02
   (3) $452.03
   (4) $565.04
   (5) Not enough information is given.

4. How much did employee 247 make per hour to earn his regular pay for a 40-hour work week?
   (1) $ 4.44
   (2) $ 7.68
   (3) $ 8.45
   (4) $ 9.22
   (5) $ 9.41

5. A new sedan can be bought for $3500 down and monthly payments of $345.81 for 48 months. To the nearest dollar, what is the total cost of the sedan?
   (1) $ 3,846
   (2) $ 13,099
   (3) $ 16,599
   (4) $ 20,099
   (5) Not enough information is given.

Answers are on page 544.

3
FRACTIONS AND OPERATIONS

Understanding Fractions

Fractions represent parts of a whole that has been divided into equal sections. The top number, called the **numerator,** tells how many parts of the whole you have. The bottom number, called the **denominator,** tells into how many total sections the whole has been divided.

$\dfrac{5}{8}$ ◄──────── numerator—parts of the whole you have

◄──────── denominator—total number of sections in the whole

➤ TIP   There are three meanings for fractions. $\frac{5}{8}$ means

| 5 out of 8 parts | 5 items compared to 8 | 5 divided by 8 |

There are many types of fractions that you will use in your work.

Proper fraction: The numerator is smaller than the denominator. $\dfrac{1}{2}, \dfrac{2}{5}, \dfrac{1}{7}, \dfrac{3}{9}$

Improper fraction: The numerator is the same as or larger than the denominator. $\dfrac{5}{5}, \dfrac{5}{4}, \dfrac{3}{2}, \dfrac{7}{3}$

Mixed number: Combines a whole number and a proper fraction. $2\dfrac{1}{3}, 3\dfrac{1}{4}, 6\dfrac{1}{5}$

Like fractions: Fractions have the same denominator. $\dfrac{1}{8}, \dfrac{3}{8}, \dfrac{6}{8}, \dfrac{9}{8}$

Unlike fractions: Fractions have different denominators. $\dfrac{1}{4}, \dfrac{7}{8}, \dfrac{3}{5}, \dfrac{9}{2}$

EXERCISE 1: TYPES OF FRACTIONS

Directions: Match the letter from the second column that best describes the following groups of fractions.

1. _____ $1\frac{3}{4}, 7\frac{1}{5}, 2\frac{1}{8}$ **a.** improper fractions

2. _____ $\frac{9}{3}, \frac{10}{5}, \frac{4}{2}, \frac{6}{6}$ **b.** unlike fractions

3. _____ $\frac{1}{2}, \frac{5}{4}, \frac{2}{5}, \frac{3}{7}$ **c.** mixed numbers

Answers are on page 545.

Raising and Reducing Fractions

To use fractions effectively, you must be able to rename fractions conveniently. In some cases you will want to **raise a fraction to higher terms**, or in other cases to **reduce a fraction to lower terms**. In either case, you are changing both the numerator and the denominator of the fraction to find an **equivalent fraction**—a fraction that has the same value. For example, a half-dollar has the same value as two quarters. As equivalent fractions, these can be written as $\frac{1}{2} = \frac{2}{4}$.

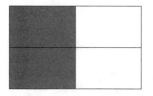

This rectangle has been divided into four equal sections. Two of the four sections, or $\frac{2}{4}$ of the rectangle, are shaded. Notice that $\frac{2}{4}$ is equivalent to half the rectangle. So we say that $\frac{2}{4} = \frac{1}{2}$.

To Raise a Fraction to Higher Terms
Multiply both the numerator and the denominator by the same number. You will obtain an equivalent fraction.

Example 1 $\frac{5 \times 2}{8 \times 2} = \frac{10}{16}$

To Reduce a Fraction to Lower Terms
Divide both the numerator and the denominator by the same number. You will obtain an equivalent fraction.
Hint: Look for a number that divides evenly into both the numerator and the denominator.

Example 2 $\frac{10 \div 2}{16 \div 2} = \frac{5}{8}$

A fraction is in the **lowest terms** if there is no whole number that will divide evenly into both the numerator and denominator. For example, $\frac{3}{8}$ is already in lowest terms because there is not a whole number other than 1 that divides evenly into 3 and 8. Fraction answers should always be reduced to lowest terms.

CALCULATOR: TO ENTER AND REDUCE FRACTIONS

Your calculator can be used to reduce fractions and to change fractions to decimals.

Keys: a b/c   enters and displays fractions and mixed numbers and changes fractions to decimals

Process	Key In:	Display	Example: $4\frac{6}{8}$
Step 1	AC to clear display	0.	0.
Step 2	whole number	whole number	4.
Step 3	a b/c key	number and fraction symbol	4⌐.
Step 4	numerator	number, fraction symbol, and numerator	4⌐6.
Step 5	a b/c key	number, fraction symbol, numerator, and fraction symbol	4⌐6⌐.
Step 6	denominator	number, fraction symbol, numerator, fraction symbol, and denominator	4⌐6⌐8.
Step 7	=	reduced mixed number	4⌐3⌐4.
Step 8	a b/c key	decimal equivalent	4.75

EXERCISE 2: RAISING AND REDUCING FRACTIONS

Directions: Solve each problem.

Raise each fraction to higher terms as indicated by the new denominator.

1. $\dfrac{3 \times 3}{8 \times 3} = \dfrac{}{24}$ **2.** $\dfrac{3}{7} = \dfrac{}{21}$ **3.** $\dfrac{2}{5} = \dfrac{}{30}$

Reduce each fraction to lower terms as indicated by the new denominator.

4. $\dfrac{12 \div 4}{16 \div 4} = \dfrac{}{4}$ **5.** $\dfrac{24}{36} = \dfrac{}{3}$ **6.** $\dfrac{30}{42} = \dfrac{}{7}$

Reduce each fraction to lower terms. Enter the answers to problems 7–8 on the grid provided. Use the / for the fraction bar.

7. $\frac{9}{27}$　　　　　　　　　　　　　　**8.** $\frac{25}{30}$

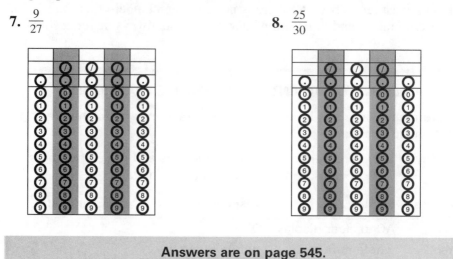

Answers are on page 545.

Relating Fractions and Decimals

In many arithmetic problems, you will work with both fractions and decimals. Each fraction can be expressed as a decimal and vice versa. You can think of decimals as fractions with denominators in multiples of 10: 10, 100, 1000, and so on.

For example:

One decimal place is tenths:　　　　　　　　　　$.3 = \frac{3}{10}$

Two decimal places is hundredths:　　　　　　　　$.03 = \frac{3}{100}$

Three decimal places is thousandths:　　　　　　　$.003 = \frac{3}{1000}$

Changing a Decimal to a Fraction
1. Put the number (with the decimal point removed) in the numerator of the fraction.
2. Make the denominator the value of the last place value in the decimal.

Example 1　Change .75 to a fraction.

　　STEP 1　Write the number 75 without a decimal point $\frac{75}{}$ as a numerator.

　　STEP 2　Write 100, the value of the last decimal place, $\frac{75}{100}$ **This can be reduced to $\frac{3}{4}$.** as a denominator.

Example 2　Change .039 to a fraction.

　　　　$.039 = \frac{39}{1000}$ ◄——— **number without decimal point**
　　　　　　　　　　　 ◄——— **Three decimal places are thousandths.**

Changing a Fraction to a Decimal

1. Divide the numerator by the denominator to two decimal places.

$$\frac{3}{4} = 4\overline{)3.00} \quad \begin{array}{r} .75 \\ \hline \end{array}$$

$$\begin{array}{r} 2\,8 \\ \hline 20 \\ 20 \\ \hline \end{array}$$

2. If after two decimal places there is still a remainder, you may do one of two things.

Example 1 Divide again if the divisor will divide evenly.

$$\frac{5}{8} = 8\overline{)5.000} \quad \begin{array}{r} .625 \\ \hline \end{array}$$

$$\begin{array}{r} 4\,8 \\ \hline 20 \\ 16 \\ \hline 40 \\ 40 \\ \hline \end{array}$$

Example 2 Make a fractional remainder.

$$\frac{2}{3} = 3\overline{)2.00} \quad \begin{array}{r} .66\frac{2}{3} \\ \hline \end{array}$$

$$\begin{array}{r} 1\,8 \\ \hline 20 \\ 18 \\ \hline 2 \\ \end{array}$$

➤ **TIP** Example 2 is a repeating decimal. After two decimal places, you can bring up the remainder to be a part of a fraction. If necessary, you can round off decimals; for example, $.66\frac{2}{3} = .67$.

➤ **TIP** Some fractions are repeating decimals. For example, $\frac{2}{3} = 0.3333333$ repeating can be rounded off to .33 or changed to $.33\frac{1}{3}$ exactly.

(Use long division by hand and bring the remainder up as the numerator over the divisor in fraction form.)

EXERCISE 3: CHANGING BETWEEN FRACTIONS AND DECIMALS

Directions: Solve each problem. Use your calculator to check your work.

Change the following decimals to fractions. Reduce if necessary.

1. .450   **2.** .07   **3.** 3.1

Change the following fractions to decimals. Write a fractional remainder after two decimal places. Check your answers with your calculator.

4. $\frac{1}{5}$ **5.** $\frac{4}{9}$ **6.** $\frac{5}{4}$

Answers are on page 545.

Relating Mixed Numbers and Improper Fractions

In your work with fractions, you will have to change mixed numbers to improper fractions and change improper fractions to mixed numbers.

Changing a Mixed Number to an Improper Fraction
1. Multiply the whole number by the denominator.
2. Add that value to the numerator of the fraction.
3. Write the sum over the original denominator.

Example 1   Change $3\frac{7}{8}$ to an improper fraction.

STEP 1   Multiply the whole number by the denominator. $3 \times 8 = 24$

STEP 2   Add that value to the numerator of the fraction. $24 + 7 = 31$

STEP 3   Write the sum over the original denominator. $\frac{31}{8}$

So $3\frac{7}{8} = \frac{31}{8}$.

Changing an Improper Fraction to a Mixed Number
1. Divide the numerator by the denominator to get the whole-number part of the answer.
2. Put the remainder over the denominator to get the fractional part of the mixed number.

Example 2   Change $\frac{11}{5}$ to a mixed number.

STEP 1   Divide the numerator by the denominator.

$$\frac{11}{5} = 5\overline{)11} \begin{array}{c} 2 \\ \underline{10} \\ 1 \end{array}$$

STEP 2   Put the remainder over the denominator.   The answer is $2\frac{1}{5}$.

EXERCISE 4: CHANGING IMPROPER FRACTIONS AND MIXED NUMBERS

Directions: Solve each problem. Use your calculator to check your work.

Change the following to improper fractions.

1. $1\frac{5}{9}$ **2.** $3\frac{2}{5}$ **3.** $4\frac{1}{8}$

Change the following to whole or mixed numbers.

4. $\frac{17}{7}$ **5.** $\frac{9}{9}$ **6.** $\frac{3}{2}$

Answers are on page 545.

Comparing Numbers

On the GED Test, you will sometimes have to compare whole numbers, fractions, and decimals. In mathematics you can use a number line to help you "see" the relationships among numbers.

The Number Line

The number line is similar to a ruler except that it has no beginning or end. Indicate this by putting arrows at both ends of the line. You can say that all numbers are represented on this line even though it would be impossible to label all of them. Note that the numbers get larger as you go to the right on the line. Whole numbers as well as mixed numbers can be represented on the number line.

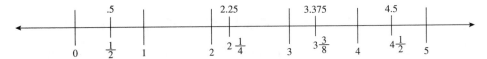

As the illustration shows, the same points can indicate either fractions or decimals. For example, $2\frac{1}{4}$ has the same value as 2.25.

You can use the number line to compare numbers and show their order. If you are given two numbers, then one of three statements must be true.

1. The two numbers are equal.

2. The first is larger than the second.

3. The first is smaller than the second.

There are symbols to indicate these relationships.

Symbol	Meaning	Example
=	is equal to	4 = 4
>	is greater than	7 > 3
<	is less than	3 < 7

➤ **TIP** The arrow always points to the smaller number.

Comparing Decimals

When you compare decimals, make sure you have the same number of decimal places in each number. Attach as many zeros as needed after the last number in the decimal. Remember that attaching zeros to the end of a decimal number does not change its value.

Example   Compare .064 and .06.

.064 has 3 decimal places.   .064

.06 has 2 decimal places.
(Attach a zero to get three decimal places.)   .060

Now both numbers are expressed in thousandths.
Because 64 > 60, **.064 > .06.**

Comparing Fractions

To compare fractions accurately, both fractions need to have the same denominator. This is called the **common denominator.** For instance, we know that $\frac{11}{16}$ is greater than $\frac{3}{16}$ because 11 is greater than 3. If the fractions that you are comparing have different denominators, you must find a common denominator and raise the fractions to higher terms.

To Find a Common Denominator
Consider the larger denominator. Does the other denominator divide into it evenly?
If the answer is **yes:**
1. The larger denominator is the common denominator.
2. Raise the other fraction to higher terms to match the common denominator.

Example   Compare $\frac{1}{4}$ and $\frac{3}{8}$.

8 is the larger denominator.

8 is evenly divisible by 4.

Thus, 8 is the common denominator.

Raise to higher terms: $\frac{1}{4} \times \frac{2}{2} = \frac{2}{8}$

We know that $\frac{2}{8} < \frac{3}{8}$.

So $\frac{1}{4} < \frac{3}{8}$.

If the answer is **no:**
1. Find the multiple of the larger denominator that is evenly divisible by the other denominator.
2. The multiple will be the common denominator.
3. Raise both fractions to higher terms to match the common denominator.

Example   Compare $\frac{2}{3}$ and $\frac{3}{4}$.

4 is the larger denominator.

4 is *not* evenly divisible by 3.

The multiples of 4 are 4, 8, 12, 16, and so on. <u>12 is the multiple that is evenly divisible by 3</u>.

Raise both fractions to 12ths.

$$\frac{2}{3} \times \frac{4}{4} = \frac{8}{12} \qquad \frac{3}{4} \times \frac{3}{3} = \frac{9}{12}$$

We know that $\frac{8}{12} < \frac{9}{12}$.

So $\frac{2}{3} < \frac{3}{4}$.

Comparing Fractions and Decimals

We can compare fractions and decimals by first changing the decimal to a fraction or the fraction to a decimal. The calculator can help you quickly change a fraction to a decimal by dividing the denominator into the numerator.

Example   Compare $\frac{7}{8}$ and .75.

STEP 1	Change $\frac{7}{8}$ to a decimal.	$\frac{7}{8} = 8\overline{)7.000}^{.875}$
STEP 2	Write .75 with 3 decimal places.	.75 = .750
STEP 3	Compare .875 and .750.	.875 > .750
STEP 4	Conclusion:	$\frac{7}{8} > .75$

EXERCISE 5: COMPARING NUMBERS

Directions: Compare the numbers as indicated. Use your calculator as needed.

Select the larger number in each pair of numbers below.

1. $\frac{7}{8}$ or $\frac{3}{5}$ **2.** $\frac{2}{3}$ or $\frac{4}{9}$ **3.** $\frac{3}{10}$ or $\frac{3}{4}$

Insert the appropriate symbol ($<$, $>$, or $=$) between each pair of numbers below.

4. 3 ☐ 8   **5.** $\frac{3}{8}$ ☐ $\frac{1}{8}$ **6.** $2\frac{3}{8}$ ☐ $\frac{5}{2}$ **7.** $\frac{5}{6}$ ☐ $\frac{8}{9}$

8. .3 ☐ $\frac{1}{4}$ **9.** $\frac{9}{9}$ ☐ $\frac{2}{2}$ **10.** .4 ☐ .27   **11.** $\frac{3}{5}$ ☐ .6

Answers are on page 545.

Operations with Fractions

Adding and Subtracting Fractions

When you are asked to add or subtract fractions or mixed numbers, you must be sure that the fractions have common denominators. If they don't, rewrite the fractions with common denominators before adding or subtracting.

To Add Fractions
1. Be sure all fractions have common denominators.
2. Add the numerators.
3. Put the total over the common denominator.
4. Reduce the answer to the lowest terms.

Example 1 Add $\frac{1}{10}$ and $\frac{3}{5}$.

    STEP 1   Find the common denominator and equivalent fractions.

    STEP 2   Add the numerators.

$$\frac{1}{10} = \frac{1}{10}$$
$$+\frac{3 \times 2}{5 \times 2} = \frac{6}{10}$$
$$\frac{7}{10}$$

Example 2 $\frac{2}{3} + \frac{1}{6} + \frac{3}{4}$

    STEP 1   Find the common denominator for all numbers.

    STEP 2   Add the numerators and put them over the denominator.

    STEP 3   Change the improper fraction to a mixed number.

$$\frac{2}{3} = \frac{8}{12}$$
$$\frac{1}{6} = \frac{2}{12}$$
$$+\frac{3}{4} = \frac{9}{12}$$
$$\frac{19}{12} = 1\frac{7}{12}$$

CALCULATOR: ADDING AND SUBTRACTING FRACTIONS

Check your work by adding the fractions on your calculator. When you add three or more fractions, enter the first fraction, then the plus sign, then the second fraction, then another plus sign, then the last fraction, followed by the equal sign. The calculator keeps a running sum and always reduces the final answer.

You follow the same method for adding mixed numbers. Add the fractions first, in case you need to combine your fraction total with the whole numbers.

To Add Mixed Numbers
1. Be sure fractional parts have common denominators.
2. Add the fractional parts. Simplify to a mixed number, if necessary.
3. Add the whole numbers.
4. Be sure your answer is in lowest terms.

Example 3   Alfonso bought $1\frac{3}{4}$ pounds of chicken and $6\frac{2}{3}$ pounds of ground beef for the picnic. How much did he buy altogether?

STEP 1   Find the common denominator: 12.

STEP 2   Add the fractions.

STEP 3   Simplify the improper fraction $\frac{17}{12}$ to the mixed number $1\frac{5}{12}$.

STEP 4   Add the whole numbers.

$$1\frac{3}{4} = 1\frac{9}{12}$$
$$+ \ 6\frac{2}{3} = 6\frac{8}{12}$$
$$7\frac{17}{12} = 7 + 1\frac{5}{12} = \mathbf{8\frac{5}{12}}$$

STEP 5   Add $1\frac{5}{12}$ to 7 to get $8\frac{5}{12}$.

The process of subtracting fractions is similar to adding fractions.

To Subtract Fractions
1. Be sure the fractions have common denominators.
2. Subtract the numerators.
3. Put the difference over the common denominator.
4. Be sure your answer is in lowest terms.

Example 4 $\frac{11}{12} - \frac{3}{8}$

$$\frac{11}{12} = \frac{22}{24}$$
$$- \ \frac{3}{8} = \frac{9}{24}$$
$$\frac{13}{24}$$

Sometimes there is an extra step when you subtract mixed numbers. You may have to regroup a whole number to a fraction before you can subtract a fraction that is too large.

➤ **TIP**   To rewrite 1 borrowed from the whole number when you regroup, use the denominator of the fraction subtracted.

Example 5 $1 - \frac{3}{8}$

(Replace the 1 with $\frac{8}{8}$.)

$$
\begin{aligned}
1 &= \frac{8}{8} \\
-\frac{3}{8} &= -\frac{3}{8} \\
\hline
&\quad \frac{5}{8}
\end{aligned}
$$

To Subtract Mixed Numbers
1. Be sure the fractions have common denominators.
2. Subtract the numerators. If you have to regroup 1 borrowed from a whole number, convert it to an improper fraction with the same denominator and add it to the original fraction if there is one.
3. Subtract the whole numbers.

Example 5   The jockey needs to lose $9\frac{1}{4}$ pounds. He has already lost $5\frac{3}{4}$ pounds. How much does he have left to lose?

STEP 1   Notice that you can't take $\frac{3}{4}$ from $\frac{1}{4}$.

STEP 2   Subtract 1 whole from 9, leaving 8.

STEP 3   Regroup 1 whole as $\frac{4}{4}$ and add that to $\frac{1}{4}$ to get $\frac{5}{4}$.

STEP 4   Subtract the fractions and whole numbers.

$$
\begin{aligned}
9\frac{1}{4} &= 8\frac{4}{4} + \frac{1}{4} = 8\frac{5}{4} \\
-5\frac{3}{4} &= \qquad\quad -5\frac{3}{4} \\
\hline
&\qquad\quad 3\frac{2}{4} = 3\frac{1}{2} \text{ pounds}
\end{aligned}
$$

STEP 5   Reduce the fraction.

EXERCISE 6: ADDING AND SUBTRACTING FRACTIONS

Directions: Solve each problem. Check each answer with your calculator.

1. $\frac{1}{10} + \frac{7}{10}$ 2. $\frac{3}{8} + \frac{1}{12}$ 3. $4\frac{1}{5} + 3\frac{2}{7}$ 4. $3\frac{7}{8} + 2\frac{5}{6} + 3\frac{1}{3}$

5. $\frac{5}{8} - \frac{1}{2}$ 6. $\frac{11}{16} - \frac{5}{16}$ 7. $25\frac{1}{6} - 11\frac{1}{2}$ 8. $10 - 4\frac{2}{3}$

Answers are on page 545.

Multiplying Fractions

There is no need for common denominators when you multiply and divide fractions. You will multiply straight across, multiplying numerator by numerator and denominator by denominator. You can reduce before you multiply.

To Multiply Fractions
1. Reduce numerators and denominators by canceling before you multiply.
2. Multiply straight across.
3. Be sure your answer is reduced to lowest terms.

Example 1 $\frac{6}{15} \times \frac{5}{12}$

STEP 1 The 15 and 5 can be divided by 5.

STEP 2 The 6 and 12 can be divided by 6.

STEP 3 Multiply straight across.

$$\frac{6}{15} \times \frac{5}{12}$$

$$\frac{6}{15} \times \frac{5}{12}$$

$$\frac{1}{3} \times \frac{1}{2} = \frac{1}{6}$$

You can also cancel with three fractions. Sometimes you have to "jump" over the middle number.

Example 2 $\frac{3}{8} \times \frac{4}{7} \times \frac{5}{9}$

STEP 1 Divide both the 3 and 9 by 3.
Divide both the 4 and 8 by 4.

STEP 2 Multiply straight across.

$$\frac{3}{8} \times \frac{4}{7} \times \frac{5}{9}$$

$$\frac{1}{2} \times \frac{1}{7} \times \frac{5}{3} = \frac{5}{42}$$

To Multiply Mixed Numbers
1. Change mixed numbers to improper fractions.
2. Reduce numerators and denominators divisible by the same number.
3. Multiply straight across.
4. Be sure your answer is reduced to lowest terms.

Example 3 Holly usually jogs $2\frac{1}{3}$ miles daily. She jogged the full distance on 3 days and $\frac{1}{2}$ the distance on another day. How many miles did she jog in all?

STEP 1 Change all mixed numbers to improper fractions.

$$2\frac{1}{3} \times 3\frac{1}{2} = \frac{7}{3} \times \frac{7}{2}$$

STEP 2 Multiply and change the improper fraction back to mixed numbers.

$$\frac{7}{3} \times \frac{7}{2} = \frac{49}{6} = 8\frac{1}{6}$$

EXERCISE 7: MULTIPLYING FRACTIONS

Directions: Solve each problem. Check your answers using the calculator. Grid the answers to problems 1–2. Use / for the fraction bar.

1. $\dfrac{6}{15} \times \dfrac{5}{12}$

2. $\dfrac{3}{8} \times \dfrac{2}{15} \times \dfrac{6}{7}$

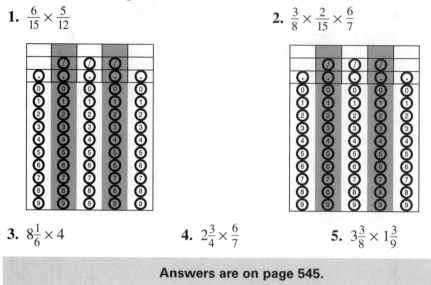

3. $8\dfrac{1}{6} \times 4$

4. $2\dfrac{3}{4} \times \dfrac{6}{7}$

5. $3\dfrac{3}{8} \times 1\dfrac{3}{9}$

> **Answers are on page 545.**

Dividing Fractions

Division is the opposite operation of multiplication. For instance, when we divide a number by 2, we are actually multiplying by $\dfrac{1}{2}$.

The fraction $\dfrac{1}{2}$ is called the **reciprocal** of 2. Two numbers whose product is 1 are reciprocals. Because $5 \times \dfrac{1}{5} = 1$, the numbers 5 and $\dfrac{1}{5}$ are reciprocals. To find the reciprocal of a number, you invert it, which means you exchange the numerator and denominator.

To Divide Fractions or Mixed Numbers
1. Change mixed numbers to improper fractions.
2. Multiply the first fraction by the reciprocal of the second.
3. Change any improper fractions back to mixed numbers.

To divide a fraction, follow the method shown below.

Example 1   Divide $\dfrac{7}{8}$ by $\dfrac{3}{4}$.

STEP 1   Multiply the first fraction by the reciprocal of the second.

$$\frac{7}{8} \div \frac{3}{4} = \frac{7}{8} \times \frac{4}{3}$$

STEP 2   Multiply across and change the improper fraction to a mixed number.

$$\frac{7}{\underset{2}{8}} \times \frac{\overset{1}{4}}{3} = \frac{7}{6} = 1\frac{1}{6}$$

To divide a mixed number, first change any mixed numbers to improper fractions.

Example 2 $4\frac{2}{3} \div 1\frac{1}{2}$

STEP 1   Change both mixed numbers to improper fractions.

$$4\frac{2}{3} \div 1\frac{1}{2} = \frac{14}{3} \div \frac{3}{2}$$

STEP 2   Multiply the first fraction by the reciprocal of the second fraction. Then change the improper fraction back to a mixed number.

$$\frac{14}{3} \times \frac{2}{3} = \frac{28}{9} = \mathbf{3\frac{1}{9}}$$

EXERCISE 8: DIVIDING FRACTIONS

Directions: Solve each problem. Check your work using the calculator.

1. $\frac{4}{10} \div \frac{2}{3}$ **2.** $\frac{2}{5} \div 4$ **3.** $3\frac{2}{3} \div 1\frac{1}{2}$ **4.** $9 \div 2\frac{1}{2}$

Answers are on page 545.

Simplifying Fraction Problems

The best way to simplify fraction word problems is to **restate** the problem using whole numbers.

Example 1   An upholstery cleaner schedules $1\frac{1}{2}$-hour appointments for each couch to be cleaned. How many couches can he clean in a $7\frac{1}{2}$-hour work day?

Restated: An upholstery cleaner schedules 2-hour appointments for each couch to be cleaned. How many couches can he clean in an 8-hour workday?

Solution: After restating the problem it's obvious that this is a division problem to see how many 2-hour segments are in an 8-hour day. Solve the problem using the original numbers.

$$7\frac{1}{2} \div 1\frac{1}{2} = \frac{15}{2} \div \frac{3}{2} = \frac{\overset{5}{\cancel{15}}}{\underset{1}{\cancel{2}}} \times \frac{\overset{1}{\cancel{2}}}{\underset{1}{\cancel{3}}} = 5$$

Be sure that the number following the division symbol is the number that represents the type of segments you are dividing by. In this example you are dividing by $1\frac{1}{2}$-hour segments.

The cleaner will clean **5 couches.**

➤ **TIP**   A frequently used key word in fraction problems is "of." **This always indicates multiplication.** For example, a problem may ask you to find $\frac{3}{4}$ *of* \$24.

Multiply: $24 \times \frac{3}{4} = \frac{\overset{6}{\cancel{24}}}{1} \times \frac{3}{\underset{1}{\cancel{4}}} = 18.$ So $\frac{3}{4}$ *of* \$24 is **\$18.**

Item Sets

An **item set** refers to information given in a paragraph or two or in an illustration. Then several questions based on that information (usually 3 to 5
questions) will follow.

> ➤ **TIP**   The key to solving questions based on item sets is choosing only the
> information needed to answer that particular question.

EXERCISE 9: ITEM SETS

Directions: Solve each problem. Use your calculator to check each answer.

Questions 1–2 are based on the information below.

> Fidel wants to build bookshelves in his den. He needs 8 shelves,
> each $5\frac{1}{4}$ feet long. He must buy the lumber for the shelves in 6-foot
> lengths and then cut the $5\frac{1}{4}$-foot pieces from those lengths. The cost
> of the lumber is 98 cents per linear foot.

1. How much will the lumber cost for all of the shelves?
   (1) $5.88   **(2)** $7.84   **(3)** $47.04   **(4)** $252   **(5)** $470.40

2. The cost of varnishing all of the shelves will amount to an additional $12.
   Fidel can buy pre-varnished $5\frac{1}{4}$-foot length shelves for $13.95 each.
   How much will he save if he does the cutting and varnishing himself?

   (1) $52.56   **(2)** $59.04   **(3)** $73.24   **(4)** $83.70   **(5)** $111.60

Questions 3–4 are based on the diagram below.

> The owner of a campground is planning to add two new roads,
> Birch Trail and Pine Way. The campground area is $\frac{7}{8}$ miles deep and
> $\frac{3}{4}$ mile wide.

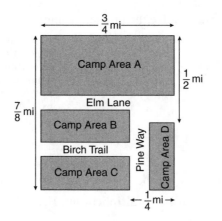

3. What is the total length of the two new roads?

(1) $\frac{1}{8}$ mile **(2)** $\frac{5}{12}$ mile **(3)** $\frac{7}{8}$ mile **(4)** $1\frac{1}{4}$ miles **(5)** $1\frac{5}{8}$ miles

4. How wide is Elm Lane?

(1) $\frac{1}{16}$ mile **(2)** $\frac{1}{8}$ mile **(3)** $\frac{3}{16}$ mile **(4)** $\frac{1}{4}$ mile

(5) Not enough information is given.

Questions 5–6 are based on the information below.

Mike Maloney gets paid an hourly wage for the first 40 hours he works. He gets $1\frac{1}{2}$ times his hourly wage for any overtime hours past the original 40 hours. The chart below shows his time sheet for the second week in April.

Week	Name	Employee #	Hourly Rate	Hours
4/8 – 4/14	Mike Maloney	08395	$12.72	$43\frac{1}{4}$

5. What is Mike's total pay for the third week in April?

(1) $508.80 **(2)** $550.14 **(3)** $570.81 **(4)** $825.21
(5) Not enough information is given.

6. Which expression represents Mike's total pay for the second week in April?

(1) $(40 \times 12.72) + (3\frac{1}{4} \times 12.72)$

(2) $40 \times 1\frac{1}{2} \times 3\frac{1}{4} \times 12.72$

(3) $(12.72 \times 40) + (1\frac{1}{2} \times 12.72 \times 3\frac{1}{4})$

(4) $12.72 \times 1\frac{1}{2} \times 43\frac{1}{4}$

(5) Not enough information is given.

Answers are on page 545.

4
<u>NUMBER RELATIONSHIPS</u>

In this section you will expand your understanding of number relationships by looking at **signed numbers,** which include all positive numbers, zero, and all negative numbers.

Number Line

The **number line** shown below represents all of the real numbers that you use. You use **negative numbers** (numbers less than zero), **zero,** and **positive numbers** (numbers greater than zero).

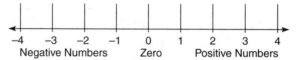

Positive numbers may have a plus sign in front of them, like +7, or no sign in front, like 7. Negative numbers have a minus sign in front of them, like –2 (read as "negative 2"). The graph of a signed number is a dot on the number line. On the number line below, you see the graph of –3.5, –1, and 3.

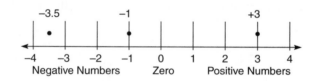

CALCULATOR: POSITIVE AND NEGATIVE NUMBERS

You can enter both positive and negative numbers on your calculator. To enter a positive number, you simply enter the digit. You do not need to enter the + sign. To enter a negative number, you first enter the digit and then use the +/– key to make the number negative.

Key: +/–   indicates a negative number

Process	Key In:	Display	Example: –5
Step 1	AC to clear the display	0.	0.
Step 2	digits	digits	5.
Step 3	negative symbol	negative number	–5.

You can use the number line to show the relationship among signed numbers. A number to the right of another number is greater than (>) the other number. A number to the left of another number is less than (<) the other number.

> ➢ **TIP** Remember that the symbols > and < always point to the smaller number.

Example 1 −2.5 > − 4 because −2.5 is to the right of −4.

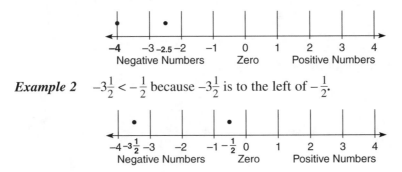

Example 2 $-3\frac{1}{2} < -\frac{1}{2}$ because $-3\frac{1}{2}$ is to the left of $-\frac{1}{2}$.

EXERCISE 1: NUMBER LINE

Directions: Use the > and < symbols to identify the relationships between the numbers graphed below.

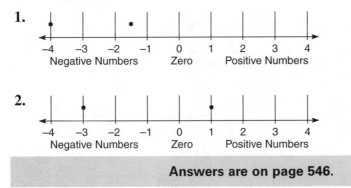

Answers are on page 546.

Absolute Value

The **absolute value** is the distance on the number line between zero and the number. Since distance is always a positive value, the absolute value of a number is always positive or zero. The symbol for absolute value is | |.

| 7 | = 7 **The absolute value of 7 is 7.**

| −7 | = 7 **The absolute value of −7 is 7.**

> ➢ **TIP** The absolute value of a positive number is the same positive number. The absolute value of a negative number is the same number without the negative sign. The absolute value of zero is zero.

EXERCISE 2: SIGNED NUMBERS

Directions: Solve each problem. For questions 1–3, represent the quantities with either positive or negative numbers.

1. a loss of $12

2. a credit of $75 on your credit card

3. a stock rise of 4.5 points

For questions 4–7, place the correct symbol, < or >, between the pairs of numbers.

4. 7   11   **5.** –9   –4   **6.** –6   2.4   **7.** $-\frac{1}{4}$ $-\frac{1}{2}$

For questions 8–10, find the absolute values.

8. $|9|$ **9.** $\left|-\frac{1}{2}\right|$ **10.** $\left|2\frac{3}{4}\right|$

Answers are on page 546.

Operations with Signed Numbers

Signed numbers can be added, subtracted, multiplied, and divided.

Combining Signed Numbers

Combining Signed Numbers
1. If the numbers being combined are all positive or all negative, ADD THE NUMBERS AND KEEP THE SAME SIGN.

Example 1 $8 + 7 = 15$ (both positive and the result is positive)

Example 2 $-8 - 7 = -15$ (both negative and the result is negative)

2. If the numbers being combined are opposite in sign, SUBTRACT THE NUMBERS AND USE THE SIGN FROM THE NUMBER WITH THE LARGER ABSOLUTE VALUE.

Example 3 $-8 + 7 = -1$
          sign of larger number

Example 4 $-7 + 8 = +1$ (or just 1)
          sign of larger number

The next example contains some positive and some negative numbers. Use both rules to come up with the answer.

Example $-6 + 1 + 14 - 2 - 8 + 6 - 9$

STEP 1   Combine the positive numbers. $1 + 14 + 6 = 21$

STEP 2   Combine the negative numbers. $-6 - 2 - 8 - 9 = -25$

STEP 3   Find the difference between 21 and 25,
         which is four. $25 - 21 = 4$

STEP 4   Take the negative sign because $|-25| > |21|$. $-25 + 21 = -4$

➤ **TIP**   Notice that -25 indicates that there are more negatives than the 21 positives, so the answer has to be negative.

EXERCISE 3: COMBINING SIGNED NUMBERS

Directions: Solve each problem. Check your answers with a calculator.

1. $6 - 8$ **2.** $-9 - 8$ **3.** $-3 - 2$ **4.** $-127 + 94$

5. $-12 + 6 + 3$ **6.** $-5 - 7 - 1 - 6$ **7.** $5.2 - 6.7 + 5.3$ **8.** $-4.5 - 3.2$

Answers are on page 546.

Eliminating Double Signs

Sometimes you encounter a number that has two signs in front of it. You always want to **eliminate** double signs. There are two rules for doing this.

Eliminating Double Signs
1. If the double signs are the same, replace them with a + sign.

Example 1 $+(+3) = +3$
Example 2 $-(-8) = +8$
Example 3 $-4 - (-12) \quad = \quad -4 + 12 = +8$
                 Same double signs   Replace with + sign

(Note: a double negative changes the following number to a positive.)

2. If the double signs are opposite, replace them with a − sign.

Example 4 $+(-4) = -4$
Example 5 $-(+2) = -2$
Example 6 $5 + (-7) = 5 - 7 = -2$
Opposite double signs   Replace with − sign

EXERCISE 4: ELIMINATING DOUBLE SIGNS

Directions: Solve each problem. Check your answers using a calculator.

1. $-6 + (-2) - (-9)$

2. A running back on a football team makes the following yardage on six plays: $+23, -4, +8, +3, -6$, and -2. What is his total gain or loss?

3. At Arlington Park Racetrack, Larry had $140 to begin the day. On the first race, he won $56; on the second race, he lost $14; on the third race, he lost $32; on the fourth race, he lost $18; on the fifth race, he won $26. How much money did he have at the end of the 5 races?

Answers are on page 546.

Multiplying and Dividing Signed Numbers

Multiplying and Dividing Signed Numbers
1. When you are multiplying or dividing two numbers with the same sign, the answer is positive.

Example 1 $8 \times 7 = 56$ Both positive, the answer is positive.

Example 2 $(-26) \div (-2) = 13$ Both negative, the answer is positive.

2. When you are multiplying or dividing two numbers with opposite signs, the answer is negative.

Example 3 $8(-7) = -56$ Opposite in sign, the answer is negative.

Example 4 $\dfrac{12}{-48} = -\dfrac{1}{4}$ Opposite in sign, the answer is negative.

> **TIP**   When multiplying a string of signed numbers, count the number of negative signs to determine whether the answer is positive or negative.
> *If there is an *even* number of negative signs, the answer will be *positive*.
> *If there is an *odd* number of negative signs, the answer will be *negative*.

Example 5 $(-3)(-2)(-1)(-5) = \mathbf{30}$ (4 negative signs; 4 is even, answer is positive)

Example 6 $(-1)(-5)(-4) = \mathbf{-20}$ (3 negative signs; 3 is odd, answer is negative)

EXERCISE 5: MULTIPLYING AND DIVIDING SIGNED NUMBERS

Directions: Solve each problem. Check your answer with a calculator.

1. 12(–12) **2.** –15(–15) **3.** (–6)(–7)(–2)

4. –8(5)(0) **5.** –25 ÷ 5 **6.** $\frac{-48}{-16}$ **7.** $\frac{7}{-14}$

8. A-One Sales bought 9 cell phones at a cost of $246 each. How much does the company owe for the phones? (Express the answer as a negative number.)

Answers are on page 546.

EXERCISE 6: USING SIGNED NUMBERS IN PROBLEM SOLVING

Directions: Use your understanding of signed numbers to solve each problem below.

1. When Heather got her paycheck, she immediately sat down to pay her bills. Her take-home pay was $575. She also received a bonus check from her employer for $125 and a tax refund of $46. Her bills included an insurance payment for $98, cleaning bill for $26, long distance phone charges of $38, and car payment of $310. If she also put $50 in her savings plan, which expression below shows how much spending money she had left?

(1) 575 + 125 – 46 – 98 – 26 – 38 – 310 – 50
(2) 575 + 125 + 46 –98 – 26 – 38 – 310 + 50
(3) 575 – 125 – 46 + 98 + 26 + 38 + 310 – 50
(4) 575 + 125 + 46 – (98 + 26 + 38 + 310 + 50)
(5) Not enough information is given.

For question 2, use the following information.

Foods that Add Calories		Activities that Burn Off Calories	
1 slice of cheesecake	+475 calories	1 set of tennis	–200 calories
1 chocolate sundae	+560 calories	1 hour of swimming	–480 calories
1 soda pop (12 oz)	+105 calories	1 mile of walking	–172 calories
1 orange juice (8 oz)	+96 calories	1 hour of dancing	–264 calories
1 apple (medium)	+70 calories	1 hour cross-country skiing	–430 calories
3 chocolate chip cookies	+160 calories		

2. This afternoon, Mark had a chocolate sundae before playing three sets of tennis. After tennis, he had a glass of orange juice and six cookies. How many calories has he burned or gained during the afternoon?

(1) –40 **(2)** +216 **(3)** +376 **(4)** +616 **(5)** +1416

Answers are on page 546.

5
STATISTICS AND DATA ANALYSIS

To set up a relationship, you begin with numerical information called **data.** When the data is collected and organized, it is called **statistics.** You can put the data into mathematical formats. In this chapter you will develop skills with **data analysis** formats, including **ratio**, **rate**, **proportion**, and **probability**. Further, you'll study methods of data analysis such as **range**, **measures of central tendency**, and data organization using **tables**, **charts**, and **graphs**.

Ratio and Rate

A **ratio** is a mathematical way of comparing two quantities. Some everyday uses of ratio are "Six out of every eight students in my class watched the World Series," and "I drove 55 miles per hour on the expressway, and people were speeding by me."

If the ratio compares two quantities with different units that cannot be converted to a common unit, it is called a **rate.** For example, 55 *miles* per *hour* is a rate. Whether you call the comparison a ratio or a rate, it can be written as a fraction, as a comparison using the word *to,* or as a comparison using a colon. You can set up a ratio whenever you are comparing two numbers.

> ➤ **TIP**   If you write a ratio as a fraction, reduce it but do not change to a mixed number. Improper fractions are acceptable. For instance, $\frac{3}{2}$ is preferred to $1\frac{1}{2}$ and $\frac{5}{1}$ is preferred to 5.

Example 1   Write a ratio for "six out of eight students."

The ratio is **6 to 8** or **6:8** or $\frac{6}{8}$. ($\frac{6}{8}$ can be reduced to $\frac{3}{4}$)

Example 2   Write a rate for "55 miles per hour."

The rate is   **55 miles to 1 hour** or **55:1** or $\frac{55}{1}$.

> ➤ **TIP**   The word *per* often tells you to set up a ratio. The ratio in Example 2 is a rate because it compares two different units: miles to hours.

EXERCISE 1: RATIO AND RATE

Directions: Write each comparison as a ratio or a rate in fraction form.

1. 3 miles to 12 miles

2. 3 pounds of meat for 4 people

3. 300 miles on 15 gallons of gas

4. $56 earned in 7 hours

Answers are on page 546.

EXERCISE 2: APPLICATIONS OF RATIO

Directions: The real value of ratio is its application to real-life problem solving. Solve each problem.

Questions 1–2 are based on the information in the table below. Write each ratio as a fraction to compare the expenses.

Painter's Weekly Work Expenses

Tools	Supplies	Transportation	Telephone	TOTAL
$25	$120	$40	$15	$200

1. Compare the cost of supplies to total expenses.

2. Find the ratio of supplies to tools.

3. A company has assets of $6,800,000 and liabilities of $1,700,000. What is the company's ratio of liabilities to assets?

4. You own 300 shares of Consolidated Technologies stock and receive a dividend of $729. What is the dividend per share?

5. In a tennis club of 750 members, 500 members are men. What is the ratio of female members to total membership?

Answers are on page 546.

Proportion

A **proportion** is a statement that two ratios (fractions) are equal. The statement $\frac{7}{8} = \frac{14}{16}$ is an example of a proportion. In other words, it means "7 is to 8 as 14 is to 16." In a proportion you find that when you multiply the diagonal numbers, the results are equal. You can say that in a proportion the cross products are always equal.

Example 1 $\frac{7}{8} >\!\!=\!\!< \frac{14}{16}$

$7 \times 16 = 112$ and $8 \times 14 = 112$ show that the cross products are equal. Notice that if the product 112 is divided by one factor, the result is the other factor. For instance, $112 \div 7 = 16$ because $7 \times 16 = 112$.

➤ **TIP**   When setting up a proportion, be sure to set up both fractions in the same order. The relationship between the numerator and the denominator on the left side of the equal sign should be reflected in the same order on the right side of the equal sign. It helps to write unit labels by each number as a reminder to keep both sides of the proportion in the same order.

To Solve a Proportion
1. Set up a proportion, making sure that the fraction on the left side of the equal sign is set up in the same order as the fraction on the right side.
2. Set up the method of solution by setting the missing value equal to the cross product of the diagonal of the two given numbers divided by the remaining number.
3. Solve by multiplying the cross product and then dividing.

Example 2 $\frac{5}{6} = \frac{n}{42}$

STEP 1   Set up the proportion. $\frac{5}{6} = \frac{n}{42}$

STEP 2   Set up the solution. $n = \frac{5 \times 42}{6}$

STEP 3   Calculate the answer. $n = \frac{210}{6} = 35$

$n = \mathbf{35}$

EXERCISE 3: SOLVING PROPORTIONS

Directions: Solve the following proportions for the missing element symbol in each.

1. $\frac{2}{5} = \frac{m}{10}$ **2.** $\frac{x}{7} = \frac{3}{21}$ **3.** $\frac{5}{y} = \frac{15}{20}$ **4.** $\frac{n}{12} = \frac{30}{24}$

Answers are on page 546.

Application of Proportion

In this section you will consider problems involving cost, mixtures, rates, ratio, and scale. In later sections, you will continue to use proportion to solve problems involving measurement, percent, and geometric relationships.

Example A baseball player hits 10 home runs in the first 45 games. If he continues at the same rate, how many home runs can he expect to hit during the 162-game season?

STEP 1 Set up the proportion. Be sure to set up both sides of the equals sign in the same order.

$$\frac{10 \text{ HRs}}{45 \text{ games}} = \frac{H}{162 \text{ games}}$$

$$H = \frac{10 \times 162}{45}$$

STEP 2 Set up the solution.

$$H = \frac{1620}{45} = 36$$

STEP 3 Calculate the answer.

$$H = \textbf{36 home runs in 162 games}$$

EXERCISE 4: APPLICATION OF PROPORTION

Directions: Solve each problem. Choose the best answer for each problem.

1. At Wilkins Department Store the ratio of managers to sales clerks is 2:9. If Wilkins currently has 189 sales clerks, how many managers are there?

    (1) 11   **(2)** 42   **(3)** 200   **(4)** 378   **(5)** 1701

2. On the scale drawing at the right, $\frac{1}{8}$ inch = 1 foot. If the length of a room on the scale drawing is $2\frac{1}{4}$ inches, how many feet long is the actual room?

    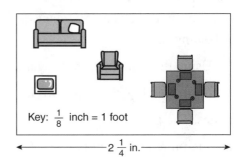

    Key: $\frac{1}{8}$ inch = 1 foot

    $2\frac{1}{4}$ in.

    (1) $2\frac{1}{8}$ **(2)** $2\frac{3}{8}$ **(3)** 9   **(4)** $16\frac{1}{4}$ **(5)** 18

3. A picture 4 inches wide and 6 inches tall must be enlarged to a width of 10 inches. What will be the height of the enlargement?

    (1) 12 inches **(2)** 14 inches **(3)** 15 inches **(4)** 16 inches **(5)** 20 inches

Answers are on page 546.

Probability

Probability can be called the language of chance. The weather reporter says there is a 40% chance of rain today, but you still don't know if it's going to rain or not. **Probability** is a practical mathematical tool used in developing mortality rates for insurance companies, constructing polls to assess public opinion during elections, and evaluating statistical data in scientific experiments.

You can use a game spinner to illustrate probability. Assume that the spinner is perfectly balanced and there is an even chance it will stop on any color. Each spin of the wheel is an **event**. The color it stops at is an **outcome**.

There are four possible outcomes when you spin this wheel: red, blue, green, and pink. A **favorable outcome** occurs when you spin the wheel and get the color you want. The probability a particular event will occur is the ratio of the number of favorable outcomes to the number of possible outcomes of that event.

Using the spinning wheel, the probability of stopping at red would be $\frac{1}{4}$. There is one favorable outcome (red) out of a total of four possible outcomes (red, blue, green, and pink). Since $\frac{1}{4}$ can also be written as 25%, you can say there is a 25% chance of landing on red.

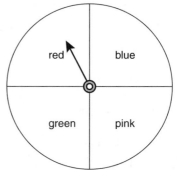

Using the spinning wheel again, find the probability of landing on *either* red *or* green. Now there are two favorable outcomes out of four possible outcomes. The probability is $\frac{2}{4}$, which reduces to $\frac{1}{2}$. Thus, the probability of landing on red or green is $\frac{1}{2}$, or 50%.

Probability of 0 or 1

A probability of 0 or 0% means an event will not take place. Using the same spinning wheel, the probability of landing on purple is 0 because the number of favorable outcomes of purple on this wheel is 0.

A probability of 1 or 100% means an event is *certain* to happen. You can use the spinning wheel to find the probability of landing on red, green, blue, or pink. The number of favorable outcomes is 4, and the number of possible outcomes is 4. There is 100% certainty that the spinner will land on red, green, blue, or pink.

EXERCISE 5: PROBABILITY

Directions: Solve each problem. Remember to use your calculator to check your calculations.

Questions 1–2 are based on the following information.

A deck of playing cards has 52 cards divided evenly into 4 suits of 13 cards each. There are two red suits (hearts and diamonds) and two black suits (spades and clubs). Each suit has an ace, king, queen, jack, 10, 9, 8, 7, 6, 5, 4, 3, and 2.

1. From the same deck of cards what is the probability of drawing a heart? Give your answer as a percent.

2. In a deck of playing cards what is the probability of drawing a king? Give your answer as a fraction.

For question 3–5, consider the roll of a single die. A single die has six faces as shown.

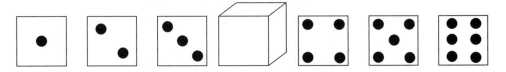

3. What is the probability of *not* rolling a 5?
   (1) $\frac{1}{6}$ **(2)** $\frac{1}{5}$ **(3)** $\frac{1}{3}$ **(4)** $\frac{1}{2}$ **(5)** $\frac{5}{6}$

4. What is the probability of rolling either a 3 or a 4?
   (1) $16\frac{2}{3}\%$ (2) 25%   (3) 30%   (4) $33\frac{1}{3}\%$ (5) 40%

5. What is the probability of rolling an even number?
   (1) $16\frac{2}{3}\%$ **(2)** 20%   **(3)** 30%   **(4)** $33\frac{1}{3}\%$ **(5)** 50%

6. What is the probability that your social security number will end in 8?
   (1) $\frac{1}{12}$ **(2)** $\frac{1}{10}$ **(3)** $\frac{1}{8}$ **(4)** $\frac{4}{5}$ **(5)** Not enough information is given.

7. You flip a coin nine times, and each time it lands on heads. What is the probability that it will land on heads the tenth time you flip it?
   (1) $\frac{1}{9}$ **(2)** $\frac{1}{10}$ **(3)** $\frac{1}{2}$ **(4)** $\frac{9}{10}$ **(5)** Not enough information is given.

8. In every shipment of clay pots, a number of them will be broken. In a recent shipment, 240 out of 960 were cracked. At the same rate, what is the probability of getting pots that are *not* cracked?
   (1) $\frac{1}{24}$ **(2)** $\frac{1}{4}$ **(3)** $\frac{1}{2}$ **(4)** $\frac{3}{4}$ **(5)** Not enough information is given.

Answers are on page 546.

Dependent Probability

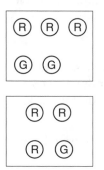

Suppose a box contains two green balls and three red balls. If one ball is drawn from the box, the probability of drawing a green ball is $\frac{2}{5}$ and the probability of drawing a red ball is $\frac{3}{5}$. If you do not replace the ball drawn, there are now only four balls in the box. The probability for the drawing of the next ball now depends on which ball you drew the first time. This situation is called **dependent probability.**

1st Possibility: You drew a green ball.

If you drew a green ball on the first draw, the box now contains one green ball and three red balls. In this situation, the probability of next drawing a green ball is now $\frac{1}{4}$ and the probability of drawing a red ball is $\frac{3}{4}$.

2nd Possibility: You drew a red ball.

If you drew a red ball on the first draw, the box now contains two green balls and two red balls. The probability of drawing a green ball is now $\frac{2}{4} = \frac{1}{2}$, and the probability of drawing a red ball is now $\frac{2}{4} = \frac{1}{2}$.

> **TIP**   A second draw depends on the first draw. If the first draw is not replaced, the total number of possibilities is reduced by one.

EXERCISE 6: DEPENDENT PROBABILITY

Directions: Solve each problem.

Questions 1–2 are based on the following situation. Express your answers as fractions. Draw a picture if necessary to help you find the probabilities.

Two cards are drawn in succession from a deck of 52 playing cards without the first card being replaced.

1. What is the probability that the second card drawn is an ace if the first card drawn was not an ace?

2. Suppose the first card drawn is a spade and not replaced. What is the probability that the second card drawn is a spade?

Questions 3–4 are based on the following situation. Express your answers as fractions.

A committee is to be chosen at random from a group of seven men and three women. The names of the ten people are placed on slips of paper and put in a hat.

3. If the first name drawn is a man's, what is the probability that the second name drawn will also be a man's?

4. What is the probability that the third name drawn will be a woman's if the first two draws were also women's names?

Question 5 is based on the following situation. Express your answer as a fraction.

A change purse contains 3 nickels, 4 dimes, and 2 quarters.

5. If the first coin taken from the purse was a nickel, what is the probability that the next coin will be a quarter?

Answers are on page 546.

Measures of Central Tendency

There are three common ways of looking at the center of a set of data. The **mean** is the *average* of a set of data. To find the average, you add the data and then divide by the number of items. The **median** of a set of data is found by arranging the numbers from smallest to largest and then choosing the *middle* number in the arrangement. That middle number is the median. The **mode** of a set of data is the *most frequent* item in the set.

Example To get information on the number of evening diners at his Shamrock Inn, Michael O'Shay accumulated the following information for the first 17 days of March. What is the range in the number of diners? What are the mean, median, and mode of the number of diners? Which measure best represents the most common number of diners daily? How would you describe the business at the Inn?

Friday, March 1	48	Sunday, March 10	30
Saturday, March 2	53	Monday, March 11	21
Sunday, March 3	37	Tuesday, March 12	39
Monday, March 4	21	Wednesday, March 13	21
Tuesday, March 5	32	Thursday, March 14	42
Wednesday, March 6	38	Friday, March 15	46
Thursday, March 7	45	Saturday, March 16	86
Friday, March 8	28	Sunday, March 17	117
Saturday, March 9	44		

The **range** is the difference between the lowest and the highest number: $117 - 21 = 96$. The range between the lowest and highest number of diners is **96**.

The **average** is the total divided by the number of dates:
$748 \div 17 = 44$. There is an average of **44 diners per day.**

The **median** is the middle of the numbers arranged from lowest to highest. The median is **39 diners.** Half the dates the number of diners is less than 39, and half the dates the number of diners is more than 39.

The **mode** is the number of diners most frequently repeated. The mode is **21 diners.** On three dates there were 21 diners each night. The pattern suggests that this most often happens on Monday.

EXERCISE 7: MEASURES OF CENTRAL TENDENCY

Directions: Solve each problem. Use your calculator to perform the calculations.

Questions 1–4 are based on the information below. Round your answer to the nearest whole number.

On May 24, 2000, seven of the most widely-held stocks in the stock market were listed with their closing price per share and volume (number of shares traded that day).

Stock	Price per Share	Volume
AT&T	$34.81	16,959,000
Cisco Systems	$50.55	64,840,400
Compaq	$26.50	13,411,500
GE	$49.50	11,384,500
Intel	$109.88	24,695,600
Lucent	$54.56	9,819,900
Microsoft	$63.19	28,274,700

1. What is the range in stock prices for the most widely-held stocks?

2. What is the mean price per share of these stocks? What is the median price per share of these stocks?

3. According to the volume of shares traded this day, what is the mode for the prices per share?

4. If you owned 100 shares of the most expensive stock and 100 shares of the least expensive stock, how much money in total would you have invested in the two stocks? What would be the average price per share of stock that you own?

Answers are on page 546.

Charts, Tables, and Schedules

To use charts, tables, and schedules effectively, here are some strategies you should remember.

- Read the title and headings to clearly understand how the information is organized.

- Survey the rows and columns to gain an overall understanding of the number patterns.

- Read the numbers carefully and notice if they contain fractions, decimals, or percents.

- Notice the labels on the numbers; do they represent money, measures, sizes, or time?

Charts are used to organize and display data for comparison. On the GED Test you may be asked to select information from a chart and then use that information to solve the problem.

Tables are lists of figures and values in orderly sequences. The numbers presented in **rows** read across and numbers in **columns** read up and down. Examples of tables that you may have used include a multiplication table, an income tax table, or a sales tax table.

Schedules present organized information pertaining to events and time. Schedules can influence your life. You may check a train schedule to plan your transportation to work or read a loan repayment schedule to plan your family budget.

EXERCISE 8: CHARTS, TABLES, AND SCHEDULES

Directions: Solve each problem.

Questions 1–3 are based on the following chart that compares the U.S. population in 1990 and in 2000.

U.S. Population (times one thousand)

Race	1990 Population	2000 Population	% Change
Caucasian	188,315	196,659	4%
African American	29,304	33,476	14%
Hispanic	22,379	32,440	45%
Asian/Pacific Islander	6,996	10,504	50%
American Indian, Eskimo, Aleutian Islander	1,797	2,050	14%
TOTAL	**248,791**	**275,129**	**11%**

1. How much did the Hispanic population increase from 1990 to 2000?

2. What is the approximate ratio of the African-American population in 2000 to the total population in 2000?

    (1) $\frac{1}{8}$ **(2)** $\frac{1}{3}$ **(3)** $\frac{1}{6}$ **(4)** $\frac{1}{14}$ **(5)** $\frac{11}{14}$

3. Which group showed the highest percent rate of change?

    (1) Caucasian   **(2)** African American

    (3) Hispanic   **(4)** Asian/Pacific Islander

    (5) American Indian, Eskimo, Aleutian Islander

Answers are on page 547.

Graphs

Graphs are useful tools for organizing and displaying large amounts of information by putting the data in a visually effective format. Tables, charts, and schedules generally present exact data. On the other hand, graphs often present data that has been rounded off to simplify the presentation of the information.

You may have to estimate a value when it is not at the mark for a distinct value. It is called **interpolation** to estimate the value between two given values. It is called **extrapolation** to estimate a value outside the given values. For both interpolation and extrapolation you will need to use ratios to find the answer. For example, consider the enrollment bar graph shown below.

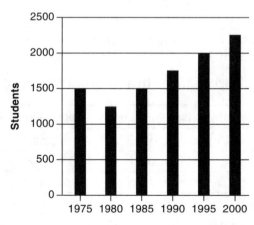

School Enrollments

Example 1   What was the approximate enrollment in 1993?

    1993 is $\frac{3}{5}$ of the five years between 1990 to 1995. So $\frac{3}{5}$ of the 250 students between 1750 and 2000 is $\frac{3}{5} \times 250 = 150$. Finally, $1750 + 150 = 1900$. By **interpolation**, in 1993 the enrollment was **1900 students**.

Example 2   What do you predict the enrollment will be in 2005?

The graph shows that enrollments have been rising about 250 students every five years since 1980. By **extrapolation**, enrollment in 2005 will be **2500 students**.

Circle Graphs

The circle in a **circle graph** represents a whole quantity. For instance, a circle could represent the whole population of the United States or an entire family income. Each circle is then subdivided into sections that represent parts of the whole.

The circle represents all of the business expenses of Kacimi Design Company, a family business. If you add all the sections, the total is 100%.

Kacimi Design Company Business Expenses

Bar Graphs

A **bar graph** is an excellent way of comparing amounts. The bars on the graph can run horizontally (across) or vertically (up and down).

The horizontal bar graph below shows the distance five experimental cars traveled on one gallon of gas. You can see that Car Z had the best gas mileage and that Car T traveled 30 miles on one gallon of gas. Car X went the shortest distance on a gallon of gas.

Notice that you have to estimate the values for Car X and Car Z because the bars do not end on distinct values. If you perform calculations using the estimates, your answers will be approximate. In many cases, the approximate answer will be sufficient.

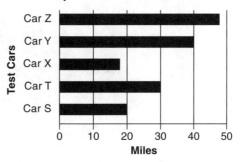

Line Graphs

Line graphs are used to show trends or patterns. On a line graph, each point relates two values. One is the value on the vertical (up and down) axis at the left side, and the other is the value on the horizontal (left to right) axis at the bottom.

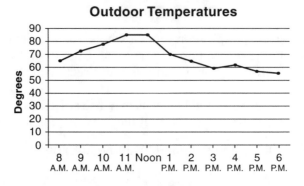

Outdoor Temperatures

On some graphs you can use **correlation** to describe the relationship between the values on the horizontal axis and the values on the vertical axis. The horizontal values and the vertical values can have a **positive correlation** when both values increase or both decrease at the same time. A **negative correlation** exists when one value increases at the same time the other value decreases.

EXERCISE 9: MIXED GRAPH PRACTICE

Directions: Solve each problem.

Questions 1–3 are based on the circle graph below.

Gross pay represents earnings. Net pay is take-home pay. FICA is Federal Insurance Contribution Act, or Social Security.

Distribution of Gross Pay

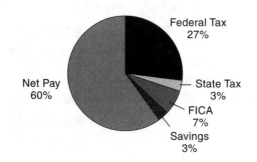

1. What is the ratio of savings to earnings?

2. If you wanted to have take-home pay of $24,000, how much would your actual earnings have to be?

3. One year, Bill earned $40,000. The deductions from his paycheck were federal tax, FICA, and state tax. What was his yearly take-home pay?

Questions 4–6 refer to the bar graph below.

Tall Buildings

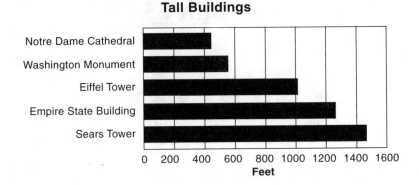

4. If a 107-foot TV antenna were erected at the top of the Sears Tower, what would be the total height of the tower?

5. The height of Notre Dame Cathedral is approximately what percent of the height of the Sears Tower?

6. What is the median height of these five structures?

Questions 7–9 refer to the line graph below.

Concert Attendance 2001

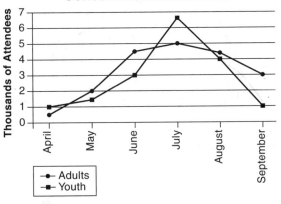

7. If adult tickets were $12.50 and youth tickets were $8.50, what were the receipts for the concerts held in August?

8. As summer turns to fall, what is the correlation between the time of year and attendance in general?

9. What was the average monthly concert attendance for both adults and youth combined?

Answers are on page 547.

6
PERCENTS

What Are Percents?

Percents, like decimals and fractions, are parts of a whole. A percent is a part of a whole that has been divided into 100 equal pieces. **Percent** means "per hundred."

The symbol for percent is %. For example, $50\% = .50 = \frac{50}{100}$.

In problem solving you may need to change percents to equivalent decimals or fractions or vice versa. The following chart shows the relationship among some common percents, fractions, and decimals.

Percent	Fraction	Decimal	Percent	Fraction	Decimal
1%	$\frac{1}{100}$	.01	50%	$\frac{50}{100} = \frac{1}{2}$	.50
5%	$\frac{5}{100} = \frac{1}{20}$	.05	$66\frac{2}{3}\%$	$\frac{66\frac{2}{3}}{100} = \frac{2}{3}$	$.66\frac{2}{3}$
10%	$\frac{10}{100} = \frac{1}{10}$	.10	75%	$\frac{75}{100} = \frac{3}{4}$	.75
25%	$\frac{25}{100} = \frac{1}{4}$	.25	100%	$\frac{100}{100} = 1$	1.00
$33\frac{1}{3}\%$	$\frac{33\frac{1}{3}}{100} = \frac{1}{3}$	$.33\frac{1}{3}$			

➤ **TIP**   Since 100% is one whole, anything less than 100% is less than one whole. For example, 75% of a quantity is a part of that quantity.

Interchanging Percents, Fractions, and Decimals

Problem solving may require changing back and forth from fractions to decimals to percents. To change a percent to a fraction or decimal, multiply the number by one hundredth.

The % symbol means "$\times \frac{1}{100}$" or "$\times .01$."

Changing Percents to Fractions or Decimals
1. To change a percent to a fraction, multiply the number by $\frac{1}{100}$.

Example $13\% = 13 \times \frac{1}{100} = \frac{13}{1} \times \frac{1}{100} = \frac{13}{100}$

2. To change a percent to a decimal, multiply the number by .01.

Example $13\% = 13 \times .01 = .13$

> **TIP**   Multiplying by .01 moves the decimal point 2 places to the left.

$13\% = 13.\% = .13$

100% represents the whole thing. For example, 100% of 25 is 25.

200% is more than one whole. For example, 200% is the same as 2 times a whole. Thus, 200% of 25 is 50. Anything over 100% is more than one whole.

$\frac{3}{4}\%$ and .75% are less than 1%. $\frac{3}{4}\%$ means "three quarters of one percent," and .75% means "seventy-five hundredths of one percent," not 75 percent.

> **TIP**   Any proper fraction or decimal followed by % means "less than 1%."

In some problems you are given a fraction or a decimal, and you need to change it to a percent. You can do this by dividing by one-hundredth.

Changing Fractions and Decimals to Percents
1. To change a fraction to a percent, divide by $\frac{1}{100}$ and attach a % symbol. (Remember dividing by $\frac{1}{100}$ is the same as multiplying by its reciprocal 100.)

Example 1   Change $\frac{7}{8}$ to a percent.

$$\frac{7}{8} \div \frac{1}{100} = \frac{7}{\underset{2}{8}} \times \frac{\overset{25}{100}}{1} = \frac{175}{2} = 87\frac{1}{2} \quad \text{So } \frac{7}{8} = 87\frac{1}{2}\%.$$

2. To change a decimal to a percent, divide by .01 and attach a % symbol. (Remember dividing by .01 moves the decimal point two places to the right.)

Example 2   Change .3 to a percent.

$.3 \div .01 = .30 \div .01 = 30 \quad \text{So } .3 = 30\%.$

Example 3   Change 2.04 to an equivalent percent.

$2.04 \div .01 = 2.04 \div .01 = 204 \quad \text{So } 2.04 = 204\%.$

EXERCISE 1: INTERCHANGING PERCENTS, FRACTIONS, AND DECIMALS

Directions: Change each percent to an equivalent fraction and to an equivalent decimal.

1. 87%   **2.** 2%   **3.** $16\frac{2}{3}\%$ **4.** 300%   **5.** 125%

6. .5%   **7.** 9.9%   **8.** $\frac{1}{2}$%   **9.** 75%   **10.** 5%

Change the following numbers to equivalent percents.

11. .0025   **12.** $\frac{3}{8}$ **13.** 4.5   **14.** .625   **15.** $2\frac{1}{4}$

Answers are on page 547.

Solving Percent Problems

A percent word problem can be solved by setting up a proportion that shows that the relationship between the part and the whole is the same as the relationship of a percent part to 100%. The proportion below shows how to set up a problem like this.

$$\frac{\text{PART}}{\text{WHOLE}} = \frac{\% \text{ PART}}{100 \ (\% \text{WHOLE})}$$

In the example above, the proportion would look like this.

Part $\longrightarrow$ $\dfrac{15}{60} = \dfrac{25\%}{100\%}$ $\longleftarrow$ Percent Part

Whole $\longrightarrow$ $\qquad\qquad$ Percent Whole (always 100%)

To solve a percent word problem, you must read the problem carefully and first decide if the number you are looking for is the **part**, the **whole**, or the **percent part**. Remember the percent whole is always 100%. You can always use a proportion to find the missing number.

If you are looking for the part, you may use an alternative method to help you find it. You may multiply the whole by a decimal equivalent of the percent. Examples of both methods will be given below. However, to find the whole or the percent part, it is usually most reliable to use a proportion to solve the problem.

Solving a Percent Problem
1. Decide if you are looking for the part, the whole, or the percent part. Label the missing value with N.
2. If you are looking for the part, you may choose to solve the problem one of two ways: (1) Multiply the whole by the decimal equivalent of the percent part. *Or*   (2) Set up the proportion $\dfrac{N}{\text{WHOLE}} = \dfrac{\%\text{PART}}{100\ (\%\text{WHOLE})}$ and solve for *N*.
3. If you are looking for the whole, set up the following proportion and solve for *N*. $\dfrac{\text{PART}}{N} = \dfrac{\%\text{PART}}{100\ (\%\text{WHOLE})}$
4. If you are looking for the % part, set up the following proportion and solve for *N*. $\dfrac{\text{PART}}{\text{WHOLE}} = \dfrac{N}{100\ (\%\text{WHOLE})}$
5. To solve for *N*, multiply diagonally and divide by the third number.

To illustrate the use of this method in solving percent problems, work through the following three examples.

Example 1   Find 40% of 120.

Solution: You are looking for the **part** of 120.

Method 1

40% of 120 means .40 x 120

Change 40% to .40

Multiply $.40 \times 120 = 48.00 = $ **48**

So 40% of 120 is **48**.

Method 2

Set up the proportion.

$\frac{N}{120} = \frac{40}{100}$

$N = \frac{40 \times 120}{100} = \frac{4800}{100} = $ **48**

So 40% of 120 is **48**.

Example 2   18 is what percent of 72?

Solution: You are looking for the **percent part**.

Set up the proportion: $\frac{18}{72} = \frac{N}{100}$

Set up the method of solution for N: $N = \frac{18 \times 100}{72} = \frac{1800}{72} = $ **25**

So 18 is **25%** of 72.

Example 3   60 is 120% of what number?

Solution: You are looking for the **whole**.

Set up the proportion: $\frac{60}{N} = \frac{120}{100}$

Set up the method of solution for N: $N = \frac{60 \times 100}{120} = \frac{6000}{120} = $ **50**

So 60 is 120% of **50**.

Notice that the part (60) is larger than the whole (50). This is because the percent is 120%, which is more than 100%.

EXERCISE 2: PERCENT PROBLEMS

Directions: In each problem decide which you are looking for: part, whole, or percent. Then solve the problem. Use your calculator to check your work.

1. Find 4% of 30.

2. What is 200% of 45?

3. 10 is 2.5% of what number?

4. 210 is what percent of 600?

5. 16% of what number is 18?

6. What percent of $340 is $30.60?

Answers are on page 547.

Percent Problem Solving

Percent word problems require careful reading to identify what the question is asking. For example, the question might be "What is the final sale price for an item discounted 20%?" To find the final sale price, you will first have to determine 20% of the original price and then subtract that amount from the original price.

The following examples are typical percent problems.

Example 1   To pass her science test, Amy must get 75% of the problems correct. Out of the 80 questions on the test, how many may she miss and still pass?

STEP 1   Find 75% of 80 problems. $.75 \times 80 = 60$ problems

This means Amy needs to get 60 problems correct to pass the test.

STEP 1   Subtract 60 problems from 80 problems. $80 - 60 = \textbf{20 problems}$

She can miss 20 problems and still pass the test.

Example 2   A car depreciates 20% the first year it is owned. Elena's car cost $12,480 originally. What was the car worth after the first year?

STEP 1   Find 20% of $12,480. $.20 \times \$12,480 = \$2,496$

The amount of depreciation is $2,496.

STEP 2   Subtract $2,496 from $12,480. $\$12,480 - \$2,496 = \textbf{\$9,984}$

Depreciation reduces the value of the car from $12,480 to $9,984.

EXERCISE 3: PERCENT WORD PROBLEMS

Directions: Solve each problem.

1. On her test Rachel got 8 wrong out of 40 questions. What percent did she get *right*?

2. Employees at Taylor's Music Mart get a 20% discount on all purchases. If Brandon buys three CDs at $9.99 each, what will he have to pay after his employee discount?

Questions 3–4 refer to the following information. Enter each answer in the corresponding number grid.

Each month Jesse takes home $2100. He puts 12% of this amount into his savings account. He pays $420 monthly for rent.

3. How much money does Jesse save each month?

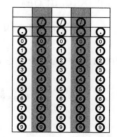

4. Jesse's employer has offered him a 5% raise for next year. At that rate, what will be his annual take-home pay next year?

Answers are on page 547.

Interest Problems

Interest is the amount earned on an investment or the cost to be paid for a loan. If you borrow or invest money, you will be dealing with an **interest rate** that is expressed as a percent. The original amount of money that is borrowed or invested is called the **principal.** Interest rates are calculated on an annual basis.

To find interest, multiply the *principal* times the *interest rate* (expressed as a decimal). If a loan is longer or shorter than one year, multiply the amount of interest by the length of time in years or fraction of a year.

The length of **time** of a loan must always be expressed in terms of years. If the time is given in months, change the time to a fraction of a year by comparing the given number of months to 12 months.

For example, 9 months = $\frac{9 \text{ months}}{12 \text{ months}} = \frac{3}{4}$ year.

If the time is given in days, change it to a fraction of a year by comparing the given number of days to 360 (approximate number of days in a year).

For example, 120 days = $\frac{120 \text{ days}}{360 \text{ days}} = \frac{1}{3}$ year.

Example 1   Find the amount of interest you pay on a $850 credit card balance at 18%. Determine how much you would pay in interest if you carry that balance for the following lengths of time: a) 1 year, b) 2 years, c) 120 days, or d) 6 months.

STEP 1 $850 × 18% = $850 × .18 = **$153 interest for one year**.

STEP 2   Multiply by the time expressed in years or fractions of a year.

     a) For 2 years, multiply $153 × 2 years = **$306 in interest for the two years**.

     b) For 120 days, change 120 days to $\frac{1}{3}$ year. Multiply $153 × $\frac{1}{3}$ = **$51 interest for 120 days**.

     c) For 6 months, change 6 months to $\frac{1}{2}$ year. Multiply $153 × $\frac{1}{2}$ = **$76.50 interest for 6 months**.

Solving Interest Problems
1. To find the interest earned on an investment or paid on a loan, multiply the principal times the decimal equivalent of the interest rate times the length of time expressed in years. *interest = principal × rate × time*

Example 2 Find the interest earned on $250 invested at 5% for 2 years.

interest = $250 × .05 × 2 = **$25**

The interest earned in 2 years is $25.

2. To find the total amount of the loan or investment, add the principal to the interest.

Example 3 Find the total amount repaid on a $500 loan borrowed at 9% for 3 years.

interest = $500 × .09 × 3 = $135.

principal + interest = $500 + $135 = **$635**

The total amount repaid is $635.

3. To find the rate of interest for a year, set up a percent proportion and solve the proportion.

Example 4 The yearly interest paid on a $1500 loan is $120. What is the annual rate of interest?

$$\frac{\$120 \ (\text{part/interest})}{\$1500 \ (\text{whole/principal})} = \frac{N \ (\%\text{part/rate})}{100 \ (\%\text{whole})} \quad N = \frac{\$120 \times 100}{\$1500} = 8$$

The annual interest rate is 8%.

4. To find the principal, set up a percent proportion and solve the proportion.

Example 5 Find the principal investment if 12% interest earned on the investment is $576.

$$\frac{\$576 \ (\text{part/interest})}{N \ (\text{whole/principal})} = \frac{12 \ (\%\text{part})}{100 \ (\%\text{whole})} \quad N = \frac{\$576 \times 100}{12} = \$4800$$

The principal invested is $4800.

➤ **TIP** The formula for interest can be found on formula page 456. The formula is *interest = principal × rate × time*.

EXERCISE 4: INTEREST PROBLEMS

Directions: Solve each problem.

1. Margaret borrowed $18,000 for 90 days at an annual rate of 12% to buy inventory for her gift shop. How much interest did she pay?

   (1) $24   **(2)** $540   **(3)** $1,500   **(4)** $2,160   **(5)** $216,000

2. You borrowed $6000 and paid $480 in interest. Which expression shows how to find the percent of interest?

   (1) $\frac{6000 \times 100}{480}$ **(2)** $\frac{480 \times 100}{6000}$ **(3)** $\frac{480 \times 6000}{100}$ **(4)** $\frac{480 - 100}{6000}$ **(5)** $\frac{6000}{480}$

3. Chris borrowed some money for one year at a rate of 8%. If he paid $360 in interest that year, how much did he borrow?

   (1) $28.80   **(2)** $288.   **(3)** $2,880   **(4)** $4,500   **(5)** $36,000

Questions 4 is based on the problem below.

   Darryl has saved $25,000, which he plans to use in building a summer cottage by a lake. The lot he wants costs $15,000. The builder estimates that it will cost $65,000 to build the cottage and an extra $5,000 to cover expenses for permits and insurance. Darryl will use his savings and take out a loan for the remaining amount to pay for everything.

5. At 10.5%, how much interest will he owe on the amount he borrows at the end of two years?

   (1) $8,400   **(2)** $8,925   **(3)** $12,600   **(4)** $23,100   **(5)** $682,500

Answers are on page 548.

7
ALGEBRA

The Language of Algebra

Algebra, an extension of arithmetic, is an organized system of rules that help to solve problems. Algebra uses letters of the alphabet to represent unknown quantities. These letters are called **variables.** These letters are variable because they change value from problem to problem. The letters can be capital letters, lowercase letters, or even Greek letters. Some examples are x, t, n, B, R, and ϕ. **Constants** are fixed values. The value of a constant is known and does not change from problem to problem. Examples of constants are 8, 75, 0, π, and $\sqrt{3}$.

In algebra you work with the four operations of addition, subtraction, multiplication, and division. Whenever a number and a variable are multiplied together, the number part is called the **coefficient** of the variable. In the expression $7x$, the coefficient of x is 7. The variable x is multiplied by 7.

Algebraic Expressions

An **algebraic term** can be a constant, a variable, or the multiplication or division of numbers with variables. Some examples of terms are 4, y, $3n$, or $\frac{x}{2}$.

An **algebraic expression** is any combination of numbers, variables, grouping symbols, and operations. In an algebraic expression, terms are separated by + and – signs. The sign before the term belongs to the term. For example, $5 - 3y$, $a + 4$, and $\frac{m}{4} + 2$ are all algebraic expressions.

$$\underset{\text{1st term} \quad\quad\quad \text{2nd term}}{5 - 3y} \qquad \underset{\text{1st term} \quad\quad\quad \text{2nd term}}{a + 4} \qquad \underset{\text{1st term} \quad\quad\quad \text{2nd term}}{\frac{m}{4} + 2}$$

$5 - 3y$ is an algebraic expression that has two terms: 5 and $-3y$.

$a + 4$ is an algebraic expression that has two terms: a and $+4$.

$\frac{m}{4} + 2$ is an algebraic expression that has two terms: $\frac{m}{4}$ and $+2$.

EXERCISE 1: TERMS

Directions: Name the terms in the following expressions.

1. $8x + 7y - 6$ **2.** $2x^2 - \frac{3}{x}$ **3.** $8ab + 12$

Answers are on page 548.

Evaluating Algebraic Expressions

An algebraic expression has no value until the variables in the expression have been replaced with numbers. To **evaluate** an expression, replace every variable with a given value for the variable. Then evaluate the resulting numerical expression. Remember to follow the rules for the order of operations and the rules for signed numbers.

Evaluate the algebraic expressions for the given values of the variables.

Example 1 Evaluate $t^2 - t + 3$ when t is 4.
$t^2 - t + 3 = (4)^2 - 4 + 3 = 16 - 4 + 3 = \mathbf{15}$

Example 2 Evaluate $7 + 4(8 - x)$ when x is –2.
$7 + 4(8 - x) = 7 + 4(8 - (-2)) = 7 + 4(8 + 2) = 7 + 4(10) = 7 + 40 = \mathbf{47}$

In Example 2 you must do the work inside the parentheses first. $8 - (-2)$ means $8 + 2$ following the rules for signed numbers.

EXERCISE 2: EVALUATING ALGEBRAIC EXPRESSIONS

Directions: Evaluate the following expressions for the given values.

1. $x^2 - 3x + 2$, when x is 5

2. The formula for distance is $d = rt,$ where r is the rate, t is the time, and d is the distance. Find the distance if the rate is 60 miles per hour and the time is 2.5 hours.

3. The formula for the perimeter of a rectangle is $2(l + w)$ where l is the length and w is the width of the rectangle. Find the perimeter of the rectangle if the length is 15 inches and the width is 7 inches.

Answers are on page 548.

Equations

An **equation** states that one expression is equal to another expression. For example, the equation $x + 7 = 10$ sets the expression $x + 7$ equal to the expression 10. In the equation $x + 3 = 2x - 9$, the expression $x + 3$ is set equal to the expression $2x - 9$.

It is important to recognize the difference between an expression and an equation. An equation always has an **equal sign**.

An equation may be true or false depending on the replacement value for the variables. The equation $x + 7 = 10$ says that some number x added to 7 equals 10, so you know that $x = 3$ is the **solution** of the equation. The solution is the value of the variable that makes the statement true. You **solve** an equation when you find the solution for the variable. On the GED Mathematics Test, you may have to translate a word problem into an equation. You may also write and interpret your own equations.

Example   Solve the equation $2x + 5 = 17$.

This expression means that a number multiplied by 2 and added to 5 equals 17. The number is **6** because $2(6) + 5 = 17$.

EXERCISE 3: EQUATIONS

Directions: Write in words what each equation means. Use the words *a number* for any variable.

1. $5 + 7y = 19$ **2.** $a - 5 = 23$ **3.** $\frac{y}{8} = 9$

Answers are on page 548.

Solving One-Step Equations

Among the most important uses of algebra are solving equations and using equations to solve word problems.

Eyeballing the Solution

Solving an equation means finding the value of the variable that makes the equation true. If you can look at the equation and see the answer, you are "eyeballing" the equation. For example, $x - 4 = 10$ is an equation. What value of x will make this true? You would choose $x = 14$ because you know that $14 - 4 = 10$.

EXERCISE 4: EYEBALLING

Directions: Solve the following equations by "eyeballing" them.

1. $p - 5 = 8$ **2.** $5a = 10$ **3.** $t + 3 = 8$ **4.** $\frac{36}{n} = 9$

Answers are on page 548.

Algebraic Solutions

Let's look at algebraic methods of solving one-step equations. Before you start solving equations, you must understand a couple of mathematical ideas.

First, an equation is a perfect balance between what is on the left side of the equal sign and what is on the right side of the equal sign. If you make any changes on the left side, you must make the same changes on the right side. For instance, if you add 7 to the left side, you must add 7 to the right side for the two sides to remain equal. Then you know the result will be true.

Second, your goal in solving an equation is to get the variable all by itself on one side of the equation. Concentrate on the variable. In the equation $x + 3 = 10$, concentrate on the x. Notice that the x is being added to 3. This will tell you how to solve the equation.

To solve an equation, perform the opposite operation (called the **inverse operation**). Addition and subtraction are opposites, and multiplication and division are opposites. In the equation $x + 3 = 10$, you see that 3 is being added to x, so subtract three from both sides to get x all by itself.

Example 1 $x + 3 = 10$

STEP 1	Look at x. 3 is added to it.	$x + 3 = 10$
STEP 2	Subtract 3 from both sides.	$x + 3 - 3 = 10 - 3$
		$x + 0 = 7$
STEP 3	Solve the equation.	$x = 7$

Solving an Equation
1. Keep the equation in balance.
2. Concentrate on the variable.
3. Perform the opposite operations.
4. Isolate the variable on one side of the equation.

Example 2 $7x = 21$

STEP 1	Look at x. It is multiplied by 7.	$7x = 21$
STEP 2	Divide by 7 on both sides of the equation.	$\frac{7x}{7} = \frac{21}{7}$
		$1x = 3$
STEP 3	Solve the equation.	$x = 3$

Check the answers to each problem by substituting the answer in the original equation.

Substitute 3 for x. This is a true statement, $\quad 7(3) = 21$

so $x = 3$ is the solution for $7x = 21$. $\quad\quad 21 = 21$

EXERCISE 5: ONE-STEP EQUATIONS

Directions: Solve for x. Check your answers.

1. $x + 6 = 15$ **2.** $x - 3 = 12$ **3.** $\frac{x}{4} = 16$ **4.** $\frac{1}{2}x = 14$

Answers are on page 548.

Solving Algebra Word Problems

To use algebra to solve mathematical problems, you have to translate the problem into algebraic language. Let a variable represent the unknown quantity. The letters x, y, and z are most often used as variables. A few English phrases are used repeatedly in algebra problems. Some examples are *increased by, reduced by, product of, quotient of,* or *square root of.*

Translating Expressions
1. Assign a variable to the unknown quantity.
2. Use that variable to write an expression for any other unknown quantity.
3. Identify the phrases that indicate the mathematical operation.
4. Use the operation to write the expression. (Use parentheses to group an operation with two numbers to be calculated first when a second operation is to be performed on the result.)

Translate: The square of a number decreased by the number.
Let x be the number.
The square of a number is x^2.
Decreased by means to subtract.
Write $x^2 - x$.

EXERCISE 6: TRANSLATING ENGLISH TO ALGEBRA

Directions: Translate the English phrases to algebraic expressions using x and y to stand for the unknown numbers.

1. the product of fourteen and a number

2. the difference between two numbers divided by 3

3. the sum of a number squared and another number squared

4. a number cubed divided by 4

5. five times a number divided by twice the same number

Answers are on page 548.

Translating Equations

You can now practice translating an entire sentence into an algebraic equation. Remember, an equation has three parts: left-side expression, equal sign, and right-side expression.

Translating Equations
1. Assign a variable to the unknown quantity.
2. Write two expressions for the values.
3. Use an equal sign between the expressions.

Example 1   Twice a number reduced by six is equal to 9.

$$2x - 6 = 9$$

Example 2   To promote holiday sales, a magazine offers one-year subscriptions for $15 and additional gift subscriptions for $12 each. With a one-year subscription, how many gift subscriptions can you get if you have $75 to spend altogether?

Let x represent the number of $12 gift subscriptions. Then 12 times x is the cost of the additional subscriptions. The basic statement is original subscription price plus additional subscription cost is 75.

$15 + 12x = 75$

EXERCISE 7: TRANSLATING SENTENCES TO EQUATIONS

Directions: Translate each sentence to an equivalent algebraic equation.

1. Two less than a number is 40.

2. Three times a number increased by 1 is 25.

3. Eighteen more than twice a number is 22.

4. A number divided by 4 yields a quotient of 18.

In questions 5–6, select the equation that could be used to find the unknown in the problem.

5. A man has x dollars. After paying a bill of $48, he has $75 left.
   (1) $x + 48 = 75$ **(2)** $48 - x = 75$ **(3)** $x - 48 = 75$ **(4)** $75 - 48 = x$

6. A plumber charges $25 for a house call plus $32 per hour for the time worked. If the charge is $84, how many hours, h, did he work?
   (1) $32 + h + 25 = 84$ **(2)** $32h = 84$ **(3)** $25 + 32h = 84$ **(4)** $\frac{h}{32} + 25 = 84$

Answers are on page 548.

Solving One-Step Algebra Word Problems

This next exercise combines practice in translating, setting up, and solving one-step algebra problems. Look at an example before you begin the exercise.

Example   Sue has money, and Tom has $\frac{2}{3}$ as much money as Sue. If Tom has $48, how much does Sue have?

STEP 1   Translate and set up the equation. Let x represent Sue's money. Then $\frac{2}{3}x$ represents Tom's money. So $\frac{2}{3}x = 48$.

STEP 2   Solve the equation. Multiply both sides by $\frac{3}{2}$.

$$\frac{2}{3}x = 48$$

$$\frac{3}{2} \times \frac{2}{3}x = 48 \times \frac{3}{2}$$

$$x = 48 \cdot \frac{3}{2} = 72 \quad \text{So Sue has } \textbf{\$72.}$$

EXERCISE 8: SOLVING ONE-STEP ALGEBRA WORD PROBLEMS

Directions: Solve each problem.

1. Baseballs cost $3.25 each. How many baseballs can you buy for $52?

2. Steve invested $\frac{3}{4}$ of his year-end bonus. If he invested $1875, how much is his bonus?

3. After Roy gained 14 pounds, he weighed 172 pounds. What was his original weight?

4. By purchasing a fleet of cars for its salespeople, Tower Manufacturing gets a discount of $1620 on each car purchased. This is 9% of the regular price. Find the regular price.

Answers are on page 548.

Simplifying Algebraic Expressions

Many algebraic expressions contain two or more terms. For instance, $2x - 7$ has two terms, and $3x - 9y + 7x$ has three terms. To simplify an algebraic expression, combine like terms and remove all symbols of grouping such as parentheses ( ) and brackets [ ].

Simplifying by Combining Like Terms

Like terms are terms that contain the same variables to the same power. Examples of like terms are $4x\ 7x\ 12x$ and $2xy\ xy\ 17xy$ and $9x^2\ 4x^2\ x^2$. Examples of **unlike terms** are $3x\ 4y\ -2\ 2xy$ and $3x\ 4y\ 3x^2$. You can combine like terms to simplify an expression.

> *Example 1* $7y^2 - 5y^2 = \mathbf{2y^2}$ (You can also subtract coefficients.)

> *Example 2* $2x - 3y - 5y + 2 + 4x - 6 = \mathbf{6x - 8y - 4}$
> (Combine the x terms, combine the y terms, and combine the numbers.)

EXERCISE 9: COMBINING LIKE TERMS

Directions: Simplify the following expressions by combining like terms.

1. $3x^2 + 14 + 7x + 2x^2 - 5$ 2. $7y - 4y$ 3. $4a + 3b - 2a - 3b + a$

4. $8x - 3 + 5x$ 5. $5xy + 7x - 3y - x + 4xy$

Answers are on page 548.

Removing Grouping Symbols

Simplifying Grouping Symbols

To simplify an expression containing grouping symbols, use one of the following procedures.

1. Remove the parentheses and distribute the multiplication over every term in the parentheses.

Example 1 $3(2x - 4) = 3(2x) + 3(-4) = \mathbf{6x - 12}$

Example 2 $-3(4x - 1) = -3(4x) + -3(-1) = \mathbf{-12x + 3}$

2. Remove the parentheses and distribute the negative sign over every term in the parentheses, following the rules for double signs.

Example 3 $3x - (6x - 4) = 3x - (6x) - (-4) = \mathbf{3x - 6x + 4}$

   or $\mathbf{-3x + 4}$ after combining like terms

3. Remove the parentheses but do not change the signs on any terms if there is a plus sign or no sign in front of the parentheses.

Example 4 $6x + (2x - 7) = \mathbf{6x + 2x - 7}$

   or $\mathbf{8x - 7}$ after combining like terms

EXERCISE 10: SIMPLIFYING GROUPING SYMBOLS

Directions: Simplify the following expressions by removing grouping symbols.

1. $4(7x - 8)$ **2.** $-2(x - 1)$ **3.** $3(2x + 4 - 3y)$

4. $x - 2(9 + 6x)$ **5.** $4x - (2 - x)$

Answers are on page 549.

Solving Multistep Equations

Solving Equations Step by Step

1. Simplify expressions on both sides of the equation.
2. Get all the variables on the left side of the equation using addition or subtraction from the right side of the equation.
3. Concentrate on the variable, *undo addition and subtraction* using the opposite operation.
4. To isolate the variable, *undo multiplication and division* using the opposite operation.

Example $3(x - 2) + 18 = 6 + 2(x + 6)$

STEP 1   Simplify the expressions. $3x - 6 + 18 = 6 + 2x + 12$
                                           $3x + 12 = 2x + 18$

STEP 2   Move the variable to the left side. $3x - 2x + 12 = 2x - 2x + 18$
                                           $x + 12 = 18$

STEP 3   Undo addition using the $x + 12 - 12 = 18 - 12$
         opposite operation. $x = 6$

EXERCISE 11: SOLVING MULTISTEP EQUATIONS

Directions: Solve the following equations.

1. $3x + 9 = 15$ **2.** $2(5x - 11) + 12x = 0$ **3.** $\frac{4x}{3} - 14 = 14$

Answers are on page 549.

Solving Multistep Problems

To set up a multistep problem, you have to translate from English to algebra. Remember to check your answer to see if it satisfies the original problem.

Example   Tony worked 35 hours last week and only a few hours this week. He makes $15 per hour, and his paycheck for the two weeks is $795 before deductions. How many hours did he work this week?

STEP 1   Let x be the number of hours he worked this week.

STEP 2   Let $x + 35$ be the total number of hours worked during both weeks.

         $15(x + 35)$ is the expression for money paid at $15 per hour.

STEP 3   Write the equation: $15(x + 35) = 795$

STEP 4   Solve the equation. $15(x + 35) = 795$

                             $15x + 525 = 795$

                             $15x + 525 - 525 = 795 - 525$

                             $15x = 270$

                             $\frac{15x}{15} = \frac{270}{15}$

                             $x = 18$

Tony worked 18 hours this week.

EXERCISE 12: SETTING UP AND SOLVING MULTISTEP EQUATIONS

Directions: Solve each problem.

Questions 1 and 2 are based on the following information.

> The distance around a triangle is 56 inches. If one side is 24 inches and the other two sides have the same measure, find the length, *x*, of one of these two sides.

1. Which equation best describes the problem above?

   (1) $x + 24 = 56$ **(2)** $2x + 56 = 24$ **(3)** $2x - 24 = 56$
   (4) $2x + 24 = 56$ **(5)** $x - 24 = 56$

2. What is the length of one of the two equal sides?

   (1) 16   **(2)** 32   **(3)** 40   **(4)** 80   **(5)** 160

Questions 3 and 4 are based on the following information.

> Twice as many adult tickets as children's tickets were sold for a soccer game. Also 38 tickets were given free of charge to contest winners. The attendance at the game was 8324 people. How many tickets of each type were sold?

3. Which equation best describes the problem above? Let *x* be the number of children's tickets sold.

   (1) $x + 2x + 38 = 8324$ **(2)** $2x + x = 8324$ **(3)** $2(x + 2) - 38 = 8324$
   (4) $2(x - 2) = 8324$ **(5)** Not enough information is given.

4. How many adult tickets were sold?

   (1) 2762   **(2)** 2775   **(3)** 4143   **(4)** 4181   **(5)** 5524

Answers are on page 549.

Inequalities

The relationship between two amounts is not always equal, so you cannot always use an equation to solve a problem. If the relationship is not equal, you can use **inequalities** such as < (**is less than**) or > (**is greater than**) to solve the problem. For example, $x + 3 > 10$ is an algebraic inequality. What value of *x* would make this a true statement? Several values of *x* would make this statement true. The letter *x* could be 8 because $8 + 3 > 10$. The letter *x* could also be 25 because $25 + 3 > 10$. In fact, *x* could be any number greater than 7. The solution is $x > 7$.

When you solve any inequality, the set of possible solutions is often infinite. You must be aware of the boundary of the solution. In this case the boundary is 7; *x* cannot be 7 or less than 7, but it can be any number greater than 7.

Solving Inequalities

Rule for Multiplying and Dividing an Inequality by a Negative
When you multiply or divide both sides of an inequality by a negative number, it changes the direction of the inequality sign.

For example you know that $8 < 12$.	$8 < 12$
If you multiply both sides by -2, you get $8(-2)$, which is -16, and $12(-2)$, which is -24. Notice that the arrow changed direction from *less than* to *greater than*.	$8(-2) > 12(-2)$
You know that -16 is greater than -24.	$-16 > -24$

You may see the signs $\leq$ meaning **is less than or equal to** and $\geq$ meaning **is greater than or equal to.** So if an answer is $x \geq 3$, this means that the answer is 3 or a number greater than 3.

Solving Inequalities
1. Keep the inequality in balance. Whatever operation you perform on one side of the inequality, perform on the other.
2. Concentrate on the variable. Your goal is to get the variable on one side of the inequality.
3. Perform the opposite operation. First, do addition or subtraction; then do multiplication or division.
4. Remember to change the direction of the inequality sign when you multiply or divide by a negative number.

Example $-4x < 12$

Divide both sides by -4. Notice that you are dividing by a negative number, so change the direction of the inequality sign.

$$-4x > 12$$
$$\frac{-4x}{-4} > \frac{12}{-4}$$

Check: Choose any number greater than -3. For instance, if you choose 0, then $-4(0)$ is 0 and that is greater than -3. Your answer that $x > -3$ makes sense.

$$x > -3$$

EXERCISE 13: ONE-STEP INEQUALITIES

Directions: Choose either (a) or (b) to represent the relationship that makes the most sense.

1. If x represents the items in your grocery cart in the express line, then
   (a) $x \geq 10$ (b) $x \leq 10$

Solve each of the following inequalities for x. Check your answers.

2. $x - 3 > -5$ 3. $5 + x < 7$ 4. $\frac{x}{-3} < 12$ 5. $x - 7 \leq 0$ 6. $-5x > -20$

Answers are on page 549.

Coordinate Graphing

Graphs can also be used to represent an equation. To understand the graph of an equation, you must first learn how points are plotted on a grid. The grid is called a **rectangular coordinate plane.** A horizontal number line called the *x*-**axis** and a vertical number line called the *y*-**axis** intersect at the **origin.**

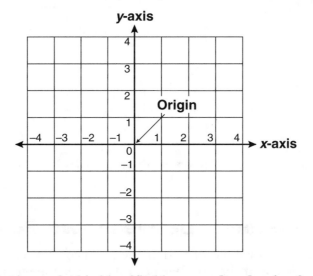

Each point that is graphed is identified by an **ordered pair** of numbers *(x, y).* The first number is called the *x*-**coordinate,** and the second is called the *y*-**coordinate.** The order of the coordinates is very important. The *x*-coordinate is always given first , and the *y*-coordinate is always second.

Plotting a Point with the Coordinates (*x, y*)
1. Start at the origin (0, 0).
2. If *x* is positive, move x units to the right. If *x* is negative, move x units to the left. If *x* is 0, make no move.
3. If *y* is positive, move y units upward. If *y* is negative, move y units downward. If *y* is 0, make no move.
4. Place a point at the location and label the ordered pair (*x, y*).

Example Plot the point (–3, 2).

Start at the origin.

x is –3 → move 3 units left.

y is 2 → move 2 units up.

Place a point at that location.

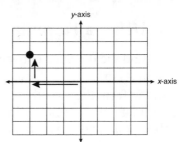

EXERCISE 14: ORDERED PAIRS

Directions: Plot the following points on the coordinate plane. Label each point A, B, C, and so on.

1. A (–3, 4)

2. B (–2, –3)

3. C (1, –1)

4. D (3, 0)

5. E (2, 2)

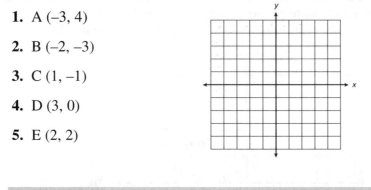

Answers are on page 549.

Distance Between Two Points

There are two methods of finding the distance between two points on a graph. You can **count the number of units** between the points when the two points are on the same horizontal line or the same vertical line. The second method is to **use the formula for the distance between two points**. (Note: This will always be on the formula page, which is page 456.) You can use this method to find the distance between any two points, whether or not they are on the same horizontal or vertical line.

Counting

To find the distance between point B and point A, count the units from B to A. The distance is 4 units.

To find the distance between point B and point E, count the units from B to E. The distance is 6 units.

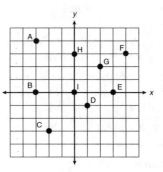

Using a Formula

To find the distance between any two points, you can use the **distance formula** $d = \sqrt{(x_2 - x_1)^2 + (y_2 - y_1)^2}$ for the points (x_2, y_2) and (x_1, y_1).

In the formula, x_1 is the x-coordinate of one graphed point and x_2 is the x-coordinate of the other point. Similarly, y_1 is the y-coordinate of the first graphed point and y_2 is the y-coordinate of the other point. For example, in the points (4, 2) and (3, –3), $x_1 = 4$ and $x_2 = 3$, $y_1 = 2$ and $y_2 = -3$.

Example   Use the graph on page 420 along with the counting method to find the distance from point C to point F.

Let point C be $(x_1, y_1) = (-2, -3)$.

Let point F be $(x_2, y_2) = (4, 3)$.

So $x_1 = -2$ and $x_2 = 4$; $y_1 = -3$ and $y_2 = 3$.

$d = \sqrt{(x_2 - x_1)^2 + (y_2 - y_1)^2}$

$d = \sqrt{(4 - -2)^2 + (3 - -3)^2}$

$d = \sqrt{(6)^2 + (6)^2}$

$d = \sqrt{36 + 36}$

$d = \sqrt{72}$ (Use your calculator to find the square root.)

$d = \mathbf{8.49}$

EXERCISE 15: DISTANCE BETWEEN TWO POINTS

Directions: Use the graph to find the distance between the following points. Use either the counting method or the formula method.

1. H to F

2. I to F

3. D to G

4. A to D

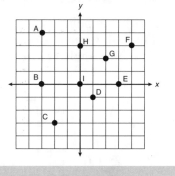

Answers are on page 549.

The Graph of a Line

An equation that shows the relationship between x and y to the first power is called a **linear equation**. The graph of the equation is the set of all points determined by the equation. These points all fall in a straight **line**. Notice the word *linear* contains the word *line*.

For example, $y = x + 4$ is a linear equation. To obtain a set of points that follow the rule of the equation, you must substitute values of x into the equation to get the corresponding values of y. You can arbitrarily select *any* three values for x and substitute them.

Suppose you choose 0, 1, and 2 as values to substitute for *x*.
For ***x* = 0,** $y = x + 4$ becomes $y = 0 + 4 = 4$. So when $x = 0$, then $y = 4$.
This gives you the ordered pair **(0, 4).**
For ***x* = 1,** $y = x + 4$ becomes $y = 1 + 4 = 5$. So when $x = 1$, then $y = 5$.
This gives you the ordered pair **(1, 5).**
For ***x* = 2,** $y = x + 4$ becomes $y = 2 + 4 = 6$. So when $x = 2$, then $y = 6$.
This gives you the ordered pair **(2, 6).**

If you plot the ordered pairs on a coordinate graph and draw the line that connects them, you have the line that represents all ordered pairs that satisfy the equation $y = x + 4$.

The graph shows the points and the line.

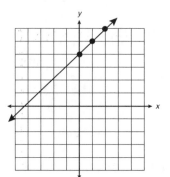

Intercepts

An intercept is a coordinate point located on an axis. A line crosses the *y*-axis at a point called the **y-intercept** and crosses the *x*-axis at a point called the **x-intercept.** Look at the example below.

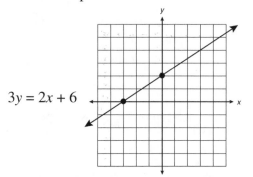

$$3y = 2x + 6$$

The graph of the line for the equation $3y = 2x + 6$ crosses the *x*-axis at the *x*-intercept (–3, 0) and crosses the *y*-axis at the *y*-intercept (0, 2).

Finding Intercepts
1. To find the *x*-intercept of a line, substitute 0 for *y* in the equation and solve for *x*.

Example 1 In the equation $\qquad\qquad\qquad$ $y = x + 2$
Substitute 0 for *y*. $\qquad\qquad\qquad$ $0 = x + 2$
Solve for *x*. $\qquad\qquad\qquad\qquad$ $0 - 2 = x + 2 - 2$
$\qquad\qquad\qquad\qquad\qquad\qquad\qquad$ $-2 = x$

The *x*-intercept is (–2, 0). Notice that *y* in the ordered pair is 0.

2. To find the *y*-intercept of a line, substitute 0 for *x* in the equation and solve for *y*.

Example 2 In the equation $\qquad\qquad\qquad\qquad y = x + 2$

Substitute 0 for *x*. $\qquad\qquad\qquad y = 0 + 2$

Solve for *y*. $\qquad\qquad\qquad\qquad y = 2$

The *y*-intercept is (0, 2). Notice that *x* in the ordered pair is 0.

EXERCISE 16: INTERCEPTS

Directions: Find the coordinates of the *x*-intercepts and *y*-intercepts in the equations below.

1. $y = 2x - 6$ $\qquad$ **2.** $y = x + 5$

Answers are on page 550.

The Slope of a Line

An equation whose graph is a straight line has a special number associated with the line. This number is called the **slope** of the line. The slope is actually the **ratio** of the change in *y*-values to the change in *x*-values as we go from point to point on the line.

The formula for the slope of a line is given on formula page 456. For two general points (x_2, y_2) and (x_1, y_1), the **slope** is $\frac{y_2 - y_1}{x_2 - x_1}$.

Finding the Slope of a Line
1. Choose two points on the line.
2. Subtract the *y*-coordinates to find the change in *y*.
3. Subtract the *x*-coordinates to find the change in *x*.
4. Write the slope as the ratio $\frac{\text{change in } y}{\text{change in } x}$.
5. Reduce the ratio.

Example 1 Find the slope of the line that contains the points (2, 1) and (–2, –1).

Subtract the *y*-coordinates to find the change in *y*: $1 - (-1) = 1 + 1 = 2$

Subtract the *x*-coordinates to find the change in *x*: $2 - (-2) = 2 + 2 = 4$

$\text{Slope} = \frac{\text{change in } y}{\text{change in } x} = \frac{2}{4} = \frac{1}{2}$

The line has a positive slope, which means it slants upward. As you move from point to point on the line, you move one unit up for every two units to the right.

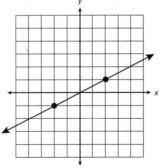

Example 2   Find the slope of the line graphed below.

Let $(x_2, y_2) = (0, 4)$ and $(x_1, y_1) = (2, -2)$

$$\text{Slope} = \frac{\text{change in } y}{\text{change in } x} = \frac{4-(-2)}{0-2} = \frac{6}{-2}$$

$$= -\frac{3}{1} = -3$$

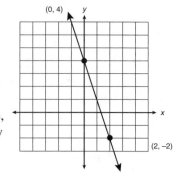

The line has a negative slope, which means it slants downward. As you move from point to point on the line, you move three units down for every one unit to the right.

➤ **TIP**   • If the slope of a line is a positive number, the line slants upward from left to right. If the slope of the line is a negative number, the line slants downward from left to right.

• A line parallel to the *x*-axis has a slope of zero. A line parallel to the *y*-axis has no slope.

EXERCISE 17: THE SLOPE OF A LINE

Directions: Find the value of the slope of each line.

1. (0, 0) and (3, 4)

2. (−1, −2) and (−2, −1)

For questions 3–4, find the slope of the graphed lines.

3.   **4.**

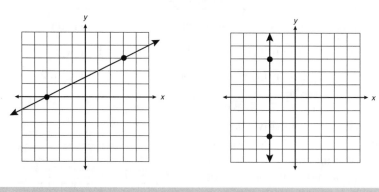

Answers are on page 550.

Multiplying Algebraic Expressions

Algebraic expressions can be multiplied together. An algebraic expression may consist of a number (coefficient), a letter (variable), and/or an exponent. When you multiply variables with exponents, you can add the exponents if the variables are the same. For example, x^2, x^3, and x^5 all have the same base variable, x. So $x^2 \cdot x^3 \cdot x^5 = x^{2+3+5} = x^{10}$. However, since x^2 and y^3 have different bases, you can't add the exponents. Therefore, $x^2 \cdot y^3 = x^2y^3$.

Multiplying Variable with Exponents
1. Keep the base.
2. Add the exponents on like bases.

Examples $x^2 \cdot x^3 = x^{2+3} = x^5$ $x^2y^3 \cdot x^4y^5 = x^{2+4} \cdot y^{3+5} = x^6y^8$

One Term Times One Term
1. Multiply the coefficients.
2. Multiply the variables. Keep the same base and add the exponents.

Example $-3y^2 \cdot 5xy = -3 \cdot 5 \cdot x \cdot y^2 \cdot y^1 = -15xy^3$

One Term Times an Expression of Two or More Terms
Distribute the multiplication over the expression by multiplying each term.

Example $5x(2x + 3) = 5x \cdot 2x + 5x \cdot 3 = 10x^2 + 15x$

Multiplying a Two-Term Expression Times a Two-Term Expression
1. Multiply each term in the first expression times each term in the second expression. (This is often called the **FOIL** method—standing for *F*irst term times the first term, *O*uter term times outer term, *I*nner term times inner term, and *L*ast term times last term.)
2. Combine like terms and simplify the result, if possible.

Example $(x + 4)(x + 3) = x^2 + 3x + 4x + 12 = x^2 + 7x + 12$

EXERCISE 18: MULTIPLYING ALGEBRAIC EXPRESSIONS

Directions: Multiply as indicated.

1. $7xy(-4x)$ **2.** $(-6ab^2)(3a^2)$ **3.** $3y(2y^2 - 4y - 7)$ **4.** $(x - 4)(x - 1)$

Answers are on page 550.

Factoring

Some problems require factoring algebraic expression. To **factor** means to find and separate numbers that have been multiplied. For example, there are two ways to multiply to get the number 15: $3 \times 5 = 15$ and $15 \times 1 = 15$. You can say that 1, 3, 5, and 15 are factors of 15. The factors are the numbers that were multiplied.

Factoring is the process of looking for the factors in a multiplication problem. This process can be used to solve some types of equations and to simplify some expressions. Algebraic expressions can be the answer to a multiplication problem. You must determine what expressions were multiplied to get the given expression.

Finding the Greatest Common Factor

The expression $2x + 10$ has two terms, $2x$ and 10. To factor $2x + 10$, look for the largest number that is a factor of both $2x$ and 10. Since $2x = 2 \cdot x$ and $10 = 2 \cdot 5$, you will notice that 2 is the **greatest common factor** of both terms. You write $2x + 10 = 2(x + 5)$ in **factored form.**

Example 1   Factor $7x^2 + 14x$.

    STEP 1   Look for the common factors. $7x^2 + 14x$

                7 and x are common factors in $\underline{7} \cdot \underline{x} \cdot x + 2 \cdot \underline{7} \cdot \underline{x}$
                both terms.

    STEP 2   Write the common factors in front   **$7x(x + 2)$**
                of the parentheses which contain
                the rest of the expression.

                To check this factored expression, multiply $7x$ by $x + 2$ to be sure the result is $7x^2 + 14x$.

                $7x(x + 2) = 7x \cdot x + 7x \cdot 2 = 7x^2 + 14x$

Example 2   Factor $65y^3 - 35y^2 + 15y$.

    STEP 1   Look for the common factors. $65y^3 - 35y^2 + 15y$

                5 and y are common factors in $\underline{5y} \cdot 13y^2 - \underline{5y} \cdot 7y + \underline{5y} \cdot 3$
                all three terms.

    STEP 2   Write the common factors in front   **$5y(13y^2 - 7y + 3)$**
                of the parentheses which contain
                the rest of the expression.

EXERCISE 19: THE GREATEST COMMON FACTOR

Directions: Write each expression in factored form.

1. $100a^4 - 16a^2$ **2.** $121p^5 - 33p^4$ **3.** $9x^3y^2 + 36\,x^2y^3$

4. $4x^4 + 25x^3 - 20x^2$ **5.** $9x^3 - 9x$ **6.** $6xy^2 + 12x^2y$

Answers are on page 550.

Factoring by Grouping

In an expression of four or more terms, you can use the method of **factoring by grouping** to factor the expression. You generally separate the four terms of the expression into pairs of terms. Then you factor out the common factor from each pair. If possible, factor the common factor from the results.

Factoring by Grouping
1. Separate the four terms into pairs that have common factors.
2. Factor out the common factor from each pair of terms.
3. Put the common factor in front of the other factors.

Example $x^2 + 5x + 2x + 10$

STEP 1   Separate into pairs of terms. $(x^2 + 5x) + (2x + 10)$

STEP 2   Factor each pair. $x(x + 5) + 2(x + 5)$

STEP 3   Put the common factor $(x + 5)$ in
front and the remaining parts of $(x + 5)(x + 2)$
the terms in the second parentheses.

EXERCISE 20: FACTORING BY GROUPING

Directions: Use grouping to factor these expressions with four terms.

1. $x^2 + 4x + 3x + 12$ **2.** $8y^2 + 6yz + 12yz + 9z^2$

Answers are on page 550.

Factoring to Reverse FOIL

An expression, which has two or three terms, begins with an x^2 term, and ends with a constant, may be factored by reversing the FOIL method of multiplying. To begin, look at the factors and the sign of the constant term. Choose the factors and appropriate signs that will combine to make the coefficient of the middle x term. Then write the factors in parentheses using x and the factors and appropriate signs. Look at the following examples to better understand this process.

Example 1 $x^2 + 7x + 10$

STEP 1   Note that $x^2 = x \cdot x$. $x^2 + 7x + 10$

STEP 2   Factor the constant term. $+10 = 1 \cdot 10$ or $(-1)(-10)$

Since the coefficient of the middle x term is +7, choose the factors 2 and 5, which combine to 7.   or $2 \cdot 5$ or $(-2)(-5)$

STEP 3   Write the answer using parentheses beginning with x followed by the numerical factors.   **$(x + 2)(x + 5)$**

To check your answer, you can use the FOIL method to multiply the factors. $(x + 2)(x + 5) = x^2 + 7x + 10$

Example 2 $x^2 - 25$

STEP 1   Note that $x^2 = x \cdot x$. $x^2 - 25$

STEP 2   Factor the constant term. $-25 = (-1)(25)$ or $(1)(-25)$

Since there is no x term and the middle coefficient is 0, choose the factors 5 and –5, which combine to zero.   or $(5)(-5)$

STEP 3   Write the answer using parentheses beginning with x followed by the numerical factors.   **$(x + 5)(x - 5)$**

To check your answer, you can use the FOIL method to multiply the factors. $(x + 5)(x - 5) = x^2 - 25$

EXERCISE 21: FACTORING TO REVERSE FOIL

Directions: Factor each expression below.

1. $x^2 - 7x - 8$ **2.** $x^2 + 2x - 15$ **3.** $x^2 - 6x + 8$

Answers are on page 550.

8
<u>MEASUREMENT</u>

Standard Measurement

The units of measurement below are the **standard units of measure** used most often in the United States.

Units of Length
12 inches (in.) = 1 foot (ft)
3 feet = 36 inches = 1 yard (yd)
5280 feet = 1760 yards = 1 mile (mi)

Units of Weight
16 ounces (oz) = 1 pound (lb)
2000 pounds = 1 ton (T)

Units of Capacity
8 ounces (oz) = 1 cup (c)
2 cups = 16 ounces = 1 pint (pt)
2 pints = 4 cups = 32 ounces = 1 quart (qt)
4 quarts = 8 pints = 16 cups = 128 ounces = 1 gallon (gal)

Units of Time
60 seconds (sec) = 1 minute (min)
60 minutes = 1 hour (hr)
24 hours (hr) = 1 day
7 days = 1 week
52 weeks = 1 year (yr)
12 months = 1 year
365 days = 1 year

Converting Units

When solving measurement problems, it is often convenient to change the units of measure. This is called making a **conversion.** There are two types of conversions: from a large unit to a smaller unit or from a small unit to a larger unit.

To **convert** from one unit of measure to another unit of measure, you multiply or divide by a **conversion factor.** A conversion factor is the ratio that describes the relationship between the large and small unit. For example, because 12 inches equals 1 foot, the conversion factor is $\frac{12 \text{ inches}}{1 \text{ foot}}$. You would multiply or divide by $\frac{12 \text{ inches}}{1 \text{ foot}}$ to convert between inches and feet.

Converting Units of Measure

1. To change a LARGE UNIT to a smaller unit: multiply by the conversion factor. (This is because it takes <u>more</u> small units to be equivalent.)

$$\text{LARGE UNIT} \xrightarrow[\div]{\times} \text{SMALL UNIT}$$

2. To change a small unit to a LARGER UNIT: divide by the conversion factor. (This is because it takes <u>fewer</u> large units to be equivalent.)

Example 1 Change $2\frac{1}{2}$ tons to pounds.

Because you are changing from a large unit (ton) to a smaller unit (pounds), multiply. The conversion factor is $\frac{2000 \text{ pounds}}{1 \text{ ton}}$ because there are 2000 pounds in a ton. $\frac{2000 \text{ pounds}}{1 \text{ ton}} \times 2\frac{1}{2}$ tons = 5000 pounds. So $2\frac{1}{2}$ tons is equivalent to **5000 pounds.**

Example 2 Change 48 ounces to pints.

Because you are changing from a small unit (ounces) to a larger unit (pints), divide. The conversion factor is $\frac{16 \text{ ounces}}{1 \text{ pint}}$ because there are 16 ounces in a pint. 48 ounces $\div \frac{16 \text{ ounces}}{1 \text{ pint}} = 3$ pints. So 48 ounces is equivalent to **3 pints.**

EXERCISE 1: CONVERSIONS

Directions: Convert the measurements in the following problems.

1. 40 ounces = _____ pounds

2. 2 quarts = _____ ounces

3. 2 days = _____ minutes

4. 3 pints = _____ quarts

5. One shrub is to be placed every 15 feet along an expressway. How many shrubs are to be planted along a 2-mile stretch of the expressway?

Answers are on page 550.

Basic Operations with Measurements

1. Add, subtract, or multiply like units.

2. Regroup units when necessary.

3. Write the answer in simplest form.

Example   Subtract 2 yards 2 feet from 6 yards 1 foot.

$$\begin{array}{r} \overset{5}{\cancel{6}}\text{ yd} \overset{4}{\cancel{1}}\text{ ft} \\ -2\text{ yd } 2\text{ ft} \\ \hline \mathbf{3\text{ yd } 2\text{ ft}} \end{array}$$

From 6 yards, regroup 1 yard to 3 feet. Add 3 feet to 1 foot. Then subtract feet from feet and yards from yards.

1. For division only, divide into the larger unit first.
2. Convert the remainder to the smallest unit.
3. Add the converted remainder to the existing smaller unit, if any.
4. Then divide into the smaller units.
5. Write the answer in simplest form.

Example   Divide 2 quarts 5 ounces by 3.

$$\begin{array}{r} \underline{0\text{ qt } 23\text{ oz}} = \mathbf{1\text{ pt } 7\text{ oz}} \\ 3\overline{)2\text{ qt } 5\text{ oz}} \\ \underline{-0\text{ qt}} \\ 2\text{ qt} = 64\text{ oz} \\ \hline \\ 69\text{ oz} \\ \underline{-69\text{ oz}} \\ 0 \end{array}$$

← **3 will not go into 2 quarts. Change 2 quarts to 64 ounces.**

← **Add 64 ounces to 5 ounces. Then divide by 3.**

EXERCISE 2: BASIC OPERATIONS WITH MEASUREMENTS

Directions: Be sure the answer to these problems is in simplest form.

1. 1 hour 20 minutes + 3 hours

2. 5.3 inches × 7

3. 22 feet 6 inches ÷ 3

4. What is the difference in weight of two boxes of cereal, one weighing 1 pound 4 ounces and the other weighing 13 ounces?

5. Each of 45 delegates to the convention will be given a badge made of a 4-inch piece of ribbon. At 65 cents per yard, how much will the ribbon cost to make the badges?

   (1) $1.80   **(2)** $2.40   **(3)** $3.25   **(4)** $3.60   **(5)** $6.50

6. Shane has a part-time job at the local hardware store. He earns $9 per hour. Last week he worked the following times: Monday, $2\frac{1}{2}$ hours; Wednesday, 3 hours; Friday, 4 hours 45 minutes; Saturday 7 hours 15 minutes; and Sunday, 4 hours. How much was he paid last week?

   (1) $20   **(2)** $21.50   **(3)** $180   **(4)** $193.50   **(5)** $198

Answers are on page 550.

The Metric System

The **metric system** is an international **decimal** measuring system used to simplify trade and commerce among countries. The basic units of measure are

Length: meter (m) a few inches longer than our standard yard
1 meter = a little more than 39 inches
1 yard = 36 inches

Weight: gram (g) a very small unit of weight; there are about 30 grams in one ounce
1 gram = 1 kernel of unpopped popcorn
1 ounce = 30 kernels of unpopped popcorn

Liquid Capacity: liter (L) a little bit bigger than a quart

Units of measure are derived from the basic units: meter, gram, and liter. Prefixes are attached to the basic unit to indicate of the amount of each unit.

For example, the prefix *centi* means one-hundredth ($\frac{1}{100}$); therefore, one *centi*meter is one-hundredth of a meter, one *centi*gram is one-hundredth of a gram, and one *centi*liter is one-hundredth of a liter.

The following six prefixes can be used with every unit:

kilo (k)	hecto (h)	deka (dk)	UNIT	deci (d)	centi (c)	milli (m)
1000	100	10		$\frac{1}{10}$	$\frac{1}{100}$	$\frac{1}{1000}$

Examples   1 kilometer = 1 km = 1000 meters

1 centimeter = 1 cm = $\frac{1}{100}$ meter = .01 meter

1 kilogram = 1 kg = 1000 grams

1 milliliter = 1 mL = $\frac{1}{1000}$ liter = .001 liter

5 km = 5000 meters

5 cm = $\frac{5}{100}$ meter = .05 meter

12 kg = 12,000 grams

19 mL = $\frac{19}{1000}$ milliliters = .019 liter

The most common relationships used in metric measures are shown in the chart below.

Length	Weight	Capacity
1 km = 1000 m	1 kg = 1000 g	1 kL = 1000 L
1 m = .001 km	1 g = .001 kg	1 L = .001 kL
1 m = 100 cm	1 g = 1000 mg	1 L = 100 cL
1 cm = .01 m	1 mg = .001 g	1 cL = .01 L
1 m = 1000 mm		1 L = 1000 mL
1 mm = .001 m		1 mL = .001 L

EXERCISE 3: THE METRIC SYSTEM

Directions: Fill in the blanks with the word that makes the sentence true.

1. The metric measure most closely related to a quart is _____.

2. If a dosage of a prescription drug is 20 mg, then that amount is _____ than a gram.

3. If a mile is 1760 yards, then a kilometer is _____ than a mile.

4. If a kilogram is a little more than 2 pounds, then a 150-pound person weighs about _____ kilograms.

5. The metric system is a decimal system, and that means that the prefixes are multiples of _____.

Answers are on page 550.

Conversion in the Metric System

Conversions between units in the metric system move the decimal point to the right or left because the conversion factor is always 10 or a power of 10. As with standard measurement, when you change from a large unit to a smaller unit you multiply, and when you change from a small unit to a larger unit you divide.

To Change Metric Units
1. List the prefixes from largest to smallest.
2. Put a mark at the starting prefix.
3. Count the moves from the first prefix right or left to the new prefix.
4. In the number, move the decimal point the same number of places in the same direction.

Example   Change 420 meters to kilometers.

STEP 1   Recognize that changing meters to kilometers is going from small units to larger units and that you will move the decimal point to the left.

STEP 2   Beginning at the UNIT (for meters), you will see a move three prefixes to the left.

k h dk unit d c m

STEP 3   Move the decimal point from the end of 420 to the left three places.   420.

Place the decimal point before the 4.   .420

Your answer is 420 meters = **.420 kilometers.**

EXERCISE 4: METRIC MEASUREMENT

Directions: Convert to the units shown.

1. 1 kiloliter 47 liters to liters

2. Find the length in meters of the gearshaft illustrated below.

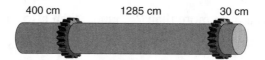

400 cm   1285 cm   30 cm

3. The recommended dosage of vitamin C is 857 milligrams per day. How many grams of vitamin C will Max take in one week if he takes the recommended dosage?

4. The speed limit sign in Canada reads 80 kilometers per hour and the speed limit sign in the United States reads 55 miles per hour. If 1 kilometer = .621 mile, which country allows the motorist to drive at a faster speed?

5. Which expression can be used to find the cost of .75 kilogram of cheese at the price of $6.40 per kilogram?
    (1) $\frac{\$6.40}{.75}$ **(2)** $.75 \times \$6.40$ **(3)** $\frac{\$6.40}{2}$ **(4)** $.75 + \$6.40$ **(5)** $\$6.40 - .75$

Answers are on page 550.

Problem Solving with Money

Look at a few problems that require calculations involving money. To do these calculations, you use the formula $c = nr$.

To find the total cost c, multiply the number of units n by the cost per unit r. For example, you buy 4 tires at $98 each. To find the total cost of the tires, multiply $4 \times \$98 = \$392$.

Example   Margaret bought the following groceries on May 15: $1\frac{1}{2}$ dozen apples at $2.69 per dozen, 2 dozen eggs at $.94 per dozen, 2 boxes of bran flakes at $3.15 each, 1 pound of margarine at $1.58 per pound, and 3 cans of soup at $.79 per can. How much change did Margaret receive from a twenty-dollar bill?

STEP 1   Use the formula $c = nr$ to find the
total cost of each item.

Apples: Multiply $1.5 \times 2.69 = 4.035$, which rounds to	$4.04
Eggs: Multiply $2 \times .94$	$1.88
Bran flakes: 2×3.15	$6.30
Margarine: 1×1.58	$1.58
Soup: $3 \times .79$	+ $2.37

STEP 2   Add to find the total cost of all items. $16.17

STEP 3   Subtract the total cost from $20. $20.00 − 16.17 = $ 3.83

The change Margaret received was **$3.83**.

➤ TIP   Always round money to the hundredths place. In general, you round upward. For instance, suppose you want one item and the price is 3 items for $1.24. If you divide $1.24 by 3, you get about $.413. The actual price you would pay would be $.42 because money always rounds upward.

EXERCISE 5: MONEY PROBLEMS

Directions: Solve each problem.

1. You need 78 feet of molding to finish decorating the family room. What is the cost of the molding if each 1-yard length costs $1.98?

   (1) $26   **(2)** $51.48   **(3)** $154.45   **(4)** $234   **(5)** $463.32

2. Better Bran cereal costs $2.79 for a 1-pound 9-ounce box; Wheatos cereal in a 12-ounce box costs $2.49; Friendly Flakes costs $3.19 for a 1-pound 13-ounce box; and Sugar Snaps is $2.39 for 1 pound 4 ounces. Which cereal is the most economical purchase?

   (1) Better Bran   **(2)** Wheatos   **(3)** Friendly Flakes
   (4) Sugar Snaps   **(5)** They are all the same.

3. A prescription for cold relief costs $8.64 for 36 capsules. The generic equivalent costs $6.48 for 36 capsules. How much money do you save per dose using the generic medicine if each dose is 2 capsules?

(1) $.06   **(2)** $.12   **(3)** $.18   **(4)** $.24   **(5)** $2.16

Answers are on page 551.

Time Problems

Many jobs require you to punch in on a time clock when you arrive at work and punch out when you leave. The time card will record a starting time and an ending time so an employer can calculate wages.

A.M. means "hours between midnight and noon."
P.M. means "hours between noon and midnight."

Numbers to the left
of the colon are hours.   **3:30**   Numbers to the right
of the colon are minutes.

How to Calculate Time
1. Count the number of morning hours.
2. Count the number of afternoon hours.
3. Add the morning and afternoon hours together.
4. Change the number of extra minutes to a fraction of an hour.
5. Simplify your answer.

Example   Lucy worked from 8 A.M. to 6:30 P.M. If she gets paid $10 per hour straight time and $15 per hour overtime, how much did she make that day?

1. Calculate the work hours.

From 8 A.M. to noon is 4 hours.

From noon to 6 P.M. is 6 hours.

$6:30 - 6:00 = :30 = \frac{1}{2}$ hour

Total $= 10\frac{1}{2}$ hours

2. Calculate the overtime hours. $10\frac{1}{2}$ hours $- 8$ hours $= 2\frac{1}{2}$ hours

3. Calculate the pay.

8 hours at $10 per hour $=$ $8 \times \$10 = \$ 80$

$2\frac{1}{2}$ hours at $15 per hour $=$ $2\frac{1}{2} \times \$15 = \underline{\$ 37.50}$

$117.50 total pay

Time is an important factor in the calculation of distance. You can use the distance formula $d = rt$ to solve problems. If you know rate and time, you can find the distance d by multiplying the rate r by the time t traveled. This formula is found on formula page 456.

For instance, if you travel 6 hours at 55 miles per hour, you can find the distance traveled by using the formula $d = rt$. Let r be 55 and t be 6; then $d = rt = 55 \times 6 = 330$. The distance traveled is **330 miles.**

On the other hand, you often know the distance to be traveled but have to figure out the length of time required for a trip. Suppose you must travel 726 miles and the legal speed limit is 55 mph.

Use the formula $d = rt$.	$d = rt$
Let $d = 726$ and $r = 55$.	$726 = 55t$
Solve the equation for t.	$\dfrac{726}{55} = \dfrac{55}{55}t$
The trip will take $13\frac{1}{5}$ **hours.**	$13\frac{1}{5} = t$

EXERCISE 6: TIME PROBLEMS

Directions: Solve each problem.

1. The sign on the parking meter states, "12 minutes for a nickel; maximum deposit 75 cents." How many *hours* can you legally park for the maximum deposit?

   (1) $1\frac{1}{4}$ **(2)** 3   **(3)** $6\frac{1}{4}$ **(4)** $7\frac{1}{2}$ **(5)** 15

2. In his retirement, Roger works part-time at a restaurant during the lunch shift from 10 A.M. to 2:30 P.M. Monday through Friday. He earns $12 per hour. Which expression shows how much he earns in four weeks?

   (1) $4\frac{1}{2} + 12 + 5 + 4$ **(2)** $(4\frac{1}{2} \times 12) + (5 \times 4)$ **(3)** $4\frac{1}{2} \times 12 \times 5 \times 4$

   (4) $4\frac{1}{2}(12 + 5 + 4)$ **(5)** $4\frac{1}{2} \times 12$

Questions 3–4 refer to the time card below.

Name: Mark Musselman	SS#: 000-45-0000			
Date **5/20**	**5/21**	**5/2**	**5/23**	**5/24**
From 8:00 A.M.	8:00 A.M.	8:00 A.M.	8:00 A.M.	8:00 A.M.
To 4:00 P.M.	5:30 P.M.	4:00 P.M.	4:00 P.M.	4:30 P.M.
Total Regular Hours	@ $12.85 per hour			
Overtime Hours over 40	@ $18.00 per hour			

3. According to his time card, Mark Musselman worked the week of 5/20 to 5/24. How many overtime hours did he work that week?

   (1) 0   **(2)** $\frac{1}{2}$ **(3)** $1\frac{1}{2}$ **(4)** 2   **(5)** $2\frac{1}{2}$

4. What is Mark's full pay before deductions?

   (1) $36   **(2)** $514   **(3)** $550   **(4)** $539.70   **(5)** $756

Answers are on page 551.

Reading and Interpreting
Scales and Meters

Reading Scales and Meters
1. Read the labels and keys carefully.
2. If instructions are included, refer to the scale or meter as you read them.
3. Write down the information you get as you read the scale or meter.
4. Ignore extra information that is not needed for the problem.

Scale Drawings

A map is a drawing of land area. When a map is drawn to **scale,** it is drawn in proportion to the land it represents. A **key** is given so you may calculate distances on the map. A key has the information about the ratio for that particular drawing. You can use the scale to set up a proportion to find a distance. Look at the local map below. Notice the scale of miles near the top of the map.

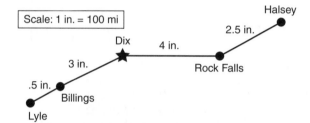

Example   To go by road from Lyle to Halsey, you must go through Billings, Dix, and Rock Falls. How much farther is it from Lyle to Halsey than from Billings to Rock Falls?

STEP 1   Calculate the distance in inches from Lyle to Halsey. $.5 + 3 + 4 + 2.5 = 10$ inches

STEP 2   Calculate the distance from Billings to Rock Falls. $3 + 4 = 7$ inches

STEP 3   Subtract to find the difference. $10 - 7 = 3$ inches

STEP 4   Set up a proportion. $\dfrac{1 \text{ in.}}{100 \text{ mi}} = \dfrac{3 \text{ in.}}{n}$

STEP 5   Solve the proportion. $n = \dfrac{3 \times 100}{1} = 300$

It is **300 miles farther** from Lyle to Halsey.

Reading Meters

Meters are devices used to measure time, speed, distance, and energy used. You might recognize some meters such as a speedometer, barometer, or thermometer. Appliances such as refrigerators, fans, TVs, and dishwashers require electricity. An **electric meter** is the instrument that measures the amount of electricity used in kilowatt-hours (kWh). The numbers above the dial indicate one complete round around the dial. Notice that the numbers may go in different directions around the dial.

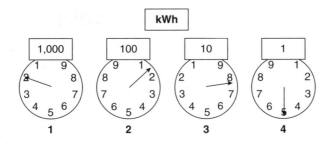

Example How many kilowatt-hours are shown on the meter above?

Start reading the dials with the left dial. If the pointer is between two numbers, read the *smaller* of the two numbers.

Dial (1) is 2, so 2 × 1000	= 2000
Dial (2) is 1, so 1 × 100	= 100
Dial (3) is 7, so 7 × 10	= 70
Dial (4) is 5, so 5 × 1	= 5
Total kWh used:	= **2175**

EXERCISE 7: SCALES AND METERS

Directions: Solve each problem.

1. The scale on a map is 1 inch = 180 miles. How many inches apart on this map are two cities if the distance between them is 450 miles?

   (1) 1 **(2)** $1\frac{1}{2}$ **(3)** 2 **(4)** $2\frac{1}{2}$ **(5)** $3\frac{1}{2}$

2. Scott needs to figure his gas bill for 173 units at \$.3065 per unit. His bill includes a \$2.00 customer charge and a \$19.16 distribution charge. In addition, he must pay a 5% utility tax on a total of the above charges. What is his total bill?

   (1) \$3.71 **(2)** \$53.02 **(3)** \$74.19 **(4)** \$77.89 **(5)** \$203.87

Answers are on page 551.

9
GEOMETRY

Geometry is the study of shapes and the relationships among them. The geometry that you are required to know for the GED Mathematics Test is fundamental and practical.

Figures and Shapes

Term	Definition	Example
Point	location in space	
Line	infinite collection of points lined up straight	
Horizontal line	across	
Vertical line	up and down	
Diagonal line	slanted	
Angle	two lines intersect (*RS* and *ST*)	
Vertex	point of intersection (*S*)	
Rays	two sides which continue indefinitely	
Degrees	measure angles	360° is a full circle
Right angle	90° angle; often used in construction	
Parallel lines	lines running in the same direction, always at an equal distance apart	
Intersecting lines	lines crossing at one point	

Term	Definition	Example
Perpendicular lines	lines intersecting at right angles	
Plane	a flat surface	
Polygon	any closed geometric figure with straight sides	
Triangle	polygon with three sides and three angles; sum of the three angles of any triangle is 180°	
Equilateral triangle	three sides are equal and three angles are equal	
Isosceles triangle	two sides are equal	
Right triangle	triangle with a right angle	
Quadrilateral	any polygon with four sides and four angles	
Parallelogram	quadrilateral with opposite sides parallel and equal and four angles	
Rectangle	quadrilateral with opposite sides parallel and equal and four right angles	
Square	quadrilateral with all four sides equal, opposite sides parallel, and four right angles	
Trapezoid	quadrilateral with four sides; only one pair of sides parallel	
Pentagon	polygon with five sides and five angles	
Octagon	polygon with eight sides and eight angles	
Circle	set of points all the same distance from a center point	
Radius	distance from the center to any point on the circle	
Diameter	straight line that goes through the center of the circle and has its endpoints on the circle; twice as long as the radius	

Term	Definition	Example
Rectangular solid	three-dimensional figure whose faces are rectangles; faces are four sides, bottom, and top of the box; all corners are right angles; described by its length, width, and height	
Cube	solid figure whose six faces are squares; all corners are right angles; lengths of all edges equal	edge
Cylinder	solid figure whose top and bottom bases are circles; sides are perpendicular to the bases; described by its radius and height	
Sphere	geometric figure shaped like a ball; described by the radius of the circle cut through the center of the sphere; distance around the circle is circumference of sphere	

EXERCISE 1: GEOMETRY FIGURES AND SHAPES

Directions: Match the geometry vocabulary to the following descriptions.

1. _____ Point of intersection of the sides of an angle   A. equilateral
2. _____ Degrees in a full circle   B. face
3. _____ A polygon with four equal sides   C. parallel
4. _____ Sum of the angles of a triangle   D. perpendicular
5. _____ Lines running in the same direction, not intersecting   E. radius
6. _____ Distance from the center to the circle   F. square
7. _____ Side of a rectangular solid   G. vertex
8. _____ Measure of a right angle   H. 90°
9. _____ Lines intersecting at right angles   J. 180°
10. _____ Triangle with all sides equal   K. 360°

Answers are on page 551.

Measurement of Figures

Perimeter

Perimeter is the distance around a figure. Measuring for a fence around a yard, putting a baseboard around a room, or setting up a baseball diamond are uses of perimeter. You will find formulas for perimeter on the formula page of the GED Mathematics Test.

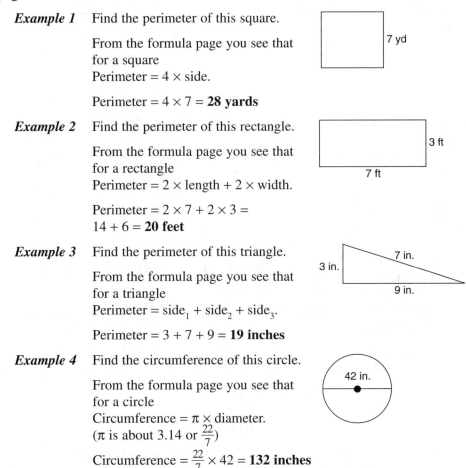

Example 1 Find the perimeter of this square.

From the formula page you see that for a square
Perimeter = 4 × side.

Perimeter = 4 × 7 = **28 yards**

Example 2 Find the perimeter of this rectangle.

From the formula page you see that for a rectangle
Perimeter = 2 × length + 2 × width.

Perimeter = 2 × 7 + 2 × 3 =
14 + 6 = **20 feet**

Example 3 Find the perimeter of this triangle.

From the formula page you see that for a triangle
Perimeter = side$_1$ + side$_2$ + side$_3$.

Perimeter = 3 + 7 + 9 = **19 inches**

Example 4 Find the circumference of this circle.

From the formula page you see that for a circle
Circumference = π × diameter.
(π is about 3.14 or $\frac{22}{7}$)

Circumference = $\frac{22}{7}$ × 42 = **132 inches**

EXERCISE 2: PERIMETER

Directions: Solve each problem. Use formula page 456 as needed.

1. A baseball diamond is a square with distances between the bases as shown. How far will the batter run if he hits a home run?

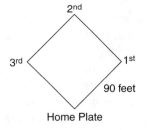

2. How much binding is needed around a triangular sail for the toy sailboat shown at the right?

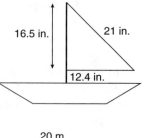

16.5 in.   21 in.

12.4 in.

3. Find the perimeter of the figure at the right.

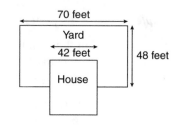

20 m

4.2 m

10.8 m

15.3 m

4. How many feet of fencing are needed to fence the yard at the right? (Hint: Do not put fencing around the house.)

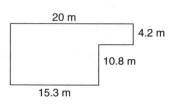

70 feet

Yard

42 feet   48 feet

House

5. Find the perimeter of the ice-skating rink with the given dimensions. (Hint: Think of the rink as made up of 2 half-circles at the top and bottom of the rectangle.)

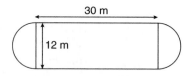

30 m

12 m

Answers are on page 551.

Area

Area is the amount of surface over a certain region. It can be used to describe the size of farmland, floor space, or a tabletop. Area is measured in **square units** such as **square inches** or **square feet.** Imagine a square that has one-inch sides. This is a square inch.

1 inch

When you are asked to find the area in square inches, you are actually finding the number of squares one inch by one inch that could fit on the surface you are measuring. For example, the rectangle to the right contains 8 square inches.

2

4 inches

Remember that the formula page of the GED Test will provide the formulas for the area of the square, the rectangle, the triangle, the parallelogram, the trapezoid, and circle.

The **area of a square** = side². The area equals the side times the side. Given a square with a side of 7 inches, the area equals 7 in. × 7 in. = 49 square inches.

The **area of a rectangle** = length × width. The area equals the length times the width.

Example 1 How much surface area is the rectangular top of a desk 3 feet by 5 feet?

From the formula page for a rectangle
Area = length times width.
3 ft × 5 ft = **15 square feet, or 15 ft²**

The **area of a triangle** $= \frac{1}{2} \times$ base × height.
To find the area of a triangle, multiply the base by the height and find $\frac{1}{2}$ of that amount.

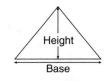

Example 2 Find the area of a triangle with a base of 6 inches and height of 9 inches.

From the formula page for a triangle

Area $= \frac{1}{2} \times$ base × height.

$\frac{1}{2} \times 6 \times 9 = \frac{1}{2} \times 54 = $ **27 square inches, or 27 in.²**

The **area of a circle** $= \pi \times$ radius², where π is approximately 3.14 or $\frac{22}{7}$.

Example 3 Find the area of a circle whose diameter is 12 inches.

First find the radius by dividing the diameter 12 by 2.   12 ÷ 2 = 6

From the formula page for a circle

Area $= \pi \times$ radius².

$3.14 \times 6^2 = 3.14 \times 36 = $ **113.04 sq in.**

EXERCISE 3: AREA

Directions: Solve each problem. For questions 1–2, find the area of the figures.

1.

2.

3. At $1.75 per square foot, find the rental cost for an office 20 feet by 15 feet.

4. How many square feet is the largest circular rug that can be put on a floor of a room 10 feet by 12 feet?

Questions 5–6 are based on the following information and diagram.

  The diagram below shows the backyard at the Singer house. In the yard are an 18-foot diameter swimming pool, an 8-foot square garden, and a 10-foot by 20-foot patio deck. The rest of the yard is covered with grass.

5. What percentage (to the nearest 1 percent) of the yard is covered by the pool?

6. How many square yards (to the nearest hundredth) of outdoor carpeting are needed to cover the patio?

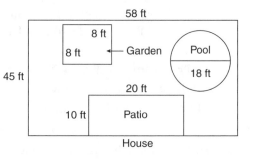

Answers are on page 551.

Volume

  Volume is the amount of space contained in a solid, three-dimensional figure. Examples of solids are shown below.

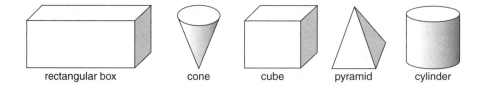

rectangular box cone cube pyramid cylinder

  Volume is measured in **cubic units,** such as cubic feet, cubic inches, or cubic yards. For example, a cubic inch is a cube with edges each one inch long. The **volume of a cube** = edge³. A die and a square box are examples of cubes. Each edge of the cube has the same length. Thus, the volume of a cube is equal to the edge cubed, or edge times edge times edge.

  The formula page of the GED Mathematics Test gives formulas for the volume of a rectangular container, a cone, a cube, a square pyramid, and a cylinder.

  Example 1 Find the volume of the cube at the right.

    Volume = edge³

    $2^3 = 2 \times 2 \times 2 = $ **8 cu in.**

2 in.

The **volume of a rectangular container** is length $\times$ width $\times$ height.

Example 2   What is the volume of the container
at the right?

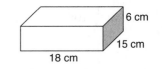

Volume = length $\times$ width $\times$ height

$18 \times 15 \times 6 = \textbf{1620 cm}^3$

The **volume of a cylinder** $= \pi \times$ (radius of the base)^2 $\times$ height of the cylinder. π is approximately equal to 3.14.

Example 3   Find the volume of the container
at the right.

Volume = $\pi \times$ radius^2 $\times$ height

$3.14\,(3)^2(5) = \textbf{141.3 cu in.}$

The **volume of a square pyramid** $= \frac{1}{3} \times$ (base edge)^2 $\times$ height.

Example 4   Find the volume of the pyramid
at the right.

Volume $= \frac{1}{3} \times$ edge^2 $\times$ height

$\frac{1}{3} \times 4^2 \times 6 = \textbf{32 cu in.}$

The **volume of a cone** $= \frac{1}{3} \times \pi \times$ radius^2 $\times$ height. π is approximately equal to 3.14.

Example 5   Find the volume of the cone
at the right.

Volume $= \frac{1}{3} \times \pi \times$ radius^2 $\times$ height

$\frac{1}{3} \times 3.14 \times 2^2 \times 9 = \textbf{37.68 cu in.}$

EXERCISE 4: VOLUME

Directions: Solve each problem.

1. Find the volume of a freezer chest that is 6 feet long, 4 feet deep, and
   3 feet wide.

2. The highway department stores sand in a
   cone-shaped structure as shown. How many
   cubic yards of sand can be stored in the
   storage building with a diameter of 45 feet
   and height of 15 feet? (There are 27 cu ft in
   one cu yd.)

3. A crystal in the shape of a square pyramid is used as a paperweight.
   What is the volume of the crystal if the edge of the base is 4 centimeters
   and the crystal is 9 centimeters tall?

4. The farmer's silo has the dimensions shown at the right. What is the volume of the silo?

(Use $\frac{22}{7}$ for π.)

28 ft

42 ft

Answers are on page 552.

Special Pairs of Angles

There are special angular relationships that can be used to find the measure of angles whose measure is not known.

Complementary angles are two angles whose sum is 90°. That means the two angles together make a right angle. A 60° angle and a 30° angle are **complements** of each other because their sum is 90°.

Example 1   What is the complement of a 53° angle?

Solution: 90° − 53° = **37°**

A **37° angle** is the complement of a 53° angle.

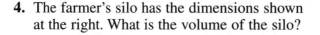

?

53°

Supplementary angles are two angles whose sum is 180°. When the two angles are placed side by side, their sides form a straight line. A 110° angle is the **supplement** of a 70° angle because their sum is 180°.

Example 2   What is the supplement of a 30° angle?

Solution: = 180° − 30° = 150°

A **150° angle** is supplementary to a 30° angle.

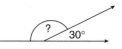

?   30°

Vertical angles are formed when two lines intersect. The pair of angles opposite each other are equal. In the picture at the right, ∠*ABC* and ∠*DBE* are vertical angles. Therefore, ∠*ABC* = ∠*DBE*. In addition, ∠*ABD* and ∠*CBE* are vertical angles, so ∠*ABD* = ∠*CBE*. Sometimes, as in Example 3, you may be given a pair of intersecting lines and the measurement of one angle. From that one angle, you can find the measure of the other angles.

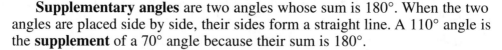

A   C
       B
D   E

Example 3   Find the measure of ∠*HFJ*.

Solution: ∠*EFG* and ∠*HFJ* are vertical angles. Therefore, they are equal. ∠*HFJ* = **130°**

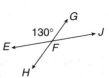

130°   G
E   J
    F
H

Example 4   Find the measure of ∠*GFJ*.

>Solution: Notice that ∠*GFJ* is supplementary to ∠*EFG*. Together, they are on a straight line that equals 180°.
>
>180° − 130° = 50°, so ∠*GFJ* = **50°.**

Corresponding angles are formed when you have angles placed in the same relative position in a figure. When parallel lines are cut by a third line called a **transversal,** corresponding angles are formed.

For example, in the picture at the right, angles *a* and *e* are corresponding because they are above lines *l* and *m*, respectively, and they are to the left of the transversal *t*. Other pairs of corresponding angles are *c* and *g*, *b* and *f*, and *d* and *h*. Corresponding angles are equal. So ∠*a* = ∠*e*, ∠*c* = ∠*g*, ∠*b* = ∠*f*, and ∠*d* = ∠*h*.

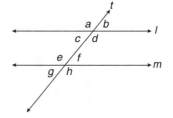

Example 5   In the drawing above, if ∠*a* = 100°, find the measure of ∠*h*.

>Solution: ∠*a* = ∠*e* because they are corresponding angles. So ∠*e* = 100°. Then ∠*e* = ∠*h* because they are vertical angles. Therefore, ∠*h* = **100°.**

Sometimes, angles are merely parts of a picture in a problem.

Example 6   Find the measure of the angle indicated.

>The angle formed by the ladder and the ground is a supplementary angle with the 45° angle. To find the missing angle, subtract 45° from 180°.
>
>Solution: 180° − 45° = **135°**

EXERCISE 5: PAIRS OF ANGLES

Directions: Solve each problem.

Use the picture at the right to answer questions 1–3.

1. Find the measure of ∠*b*.

2. Find the measure of ∠*g*.

3. Find the measure of ∠*e*.

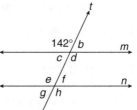

4. A carpenter is putting an oak chair rail around a dining room wall. He wants to make sure it fits nicely and looks straight. What is the measure of the angle that will supplement 75° to make a straight, snug fit?

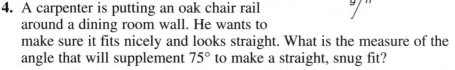

Answers are on page 552.

Problem Solving Using Triangular Relationships

Triangles are the basis of land measurement. Triangles are used in science, navigation, and building construction. There are also important uses for triangles in maps, scale drawings, and architectural plans.

The three angles of every triangle add up to 180°. Use this fact to find the measure of the third angle of a triangle when the measure of the first two angles is known, as in the following example.

> ***Example*** Find $\angle C$ in the triangle at the right.
>
> STEP 1   Add the two known angles.
> $40° + 100° = 140°$
>
> STEP 2   Then subtract the sum from 180°.
> $180° - 140° = 40°$ $\angle C = \mathbf{40°}$

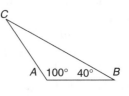

EXERCISE 6: ANGLES IN TRIANGLES

Directions: Find the measurement of the missing angle in each of the following triangles.

1. $\triangle ABC$ is an equilateral triangle. What is the measure of $\angle C$?

2. $\triangle RST$ is an isosceles triangle. Because two sides are equal, the two base angles are equal. If the two equal angles are each 65°, what is the measure of the third angle?

3. Find $\angle B$.

4. Find $\angle Q$.

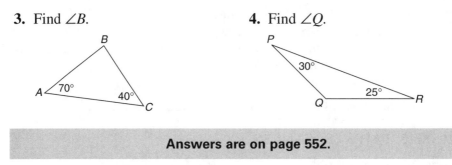

Answers are on page 552.

The Pythagorean Theorem

Although the **Pythagorean theorem** was developed by the Greek mathematician Pythagoras in about 500 B.C., it is still used today. Since the rule applies only to right triangles, the triangle has to include a 90° angle. In a right triangle, the side opposite the right angle is called the **hypotenuse**, and the other two sides are called the **legs** of the triangle.

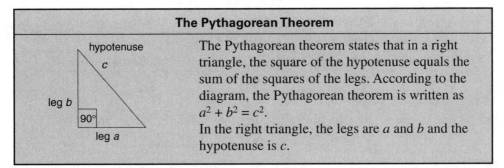

The Pythagorean Theorem
The Pythagorean theorem states that in a right triangle, the square of the hypotenuse equals the sum of the squares of the legs. According to the diagram, the Pythagorean theorem is written as $a^2 + b^2 = c^2$. In the right triangle, the legs are a and b and the hypotenuse is c.

Example 1   Find the length of the hypotenuse of a right triangle with legs 6 inches and 8 inches.

STEP 1   Draw a right triangle and label its sides.

STEP 2   Using the Pythagorean theorem, substitute the numbers for legs a and b in the formula.

$$a^2 + b^2 = c^2$$
$$8^2 + 6^2 = c^2$$

STEP 3   Square the numbers.

$$64 + 36 = c^2$$

STEP 4   Add the numbers when looking for the hypotenuse.

$$100 = c^2$$

STEP 5   Take the square root to find c.

$$c = \sqrt{100} = \textbf{10 in.}$$

To find a leg rather than the hypotenuse, you subtract instead of add before taking the square root.

Example 2   The hypotenuse of a right triangle is 13 feet. If one leg is 12 feet, what is the length of the other leg?

STEP 1   Draw a right triangle and label its sides.

STEP 2   Using the Pythagorean theorem, substitute the numbers for leg b and hypotenuse c in the formula.

$$a^2 + b^2 = c^2$$
$$a^2 + 12^2 = 13^2$$

STEP 3   Square the numbers.

$$a^2 + 144 = 169$$

STEP 4   Subtract the numbers when looking for a leg.

$$a^2 = 169 - 144 = 25$$

STEP 5   Take the square root to find a.

$$a = \sqrt{25} = \textbf{5 ft}$$

Solving Pythagorean Theorem Problems
1. Sketch the information in the problem and label the parts.
2. Note the triangular shape; identify the right angle and the hypotenuse.
3. Substitute the values into the formula $a^2 + b^2 = c^2$.
4. Square the values.
5. Add if you are looking for the hypotenuse, or subtract if you are looking for a leg.
6. Take the square root.

EXERCISE 7: THE PYTHAGOREAN THEOREM

Directions: Solve each problem.

1. Find the length of the missing side in the right triangle whose legs are a and b and whose hypotenuse is c. $a = 10$, $b = 24$

2. The screen on Alberto's TV has the measurements shown. Find the measure of the diagonal for Alberto's TV.

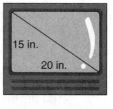

15 in.

20 in.

3. At summer camp, the swimming course runs across a small lake. To determine the length of the course, the camp counselors measure the two "dry" legs of a right triangle. What is the length in meters of the swimming course l?

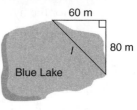

60 m

80 m

l

Blue Lake

   (1) 75   **(2)** 90   **(3)** 100   **(4)** 120   **(5)** 144

4. A television antenna is 24 feet tall and is held in place by *three* guy wires (braces) fastened at the top of the antenna and to hooks 7 feet from the base of the tower. If the antenna is installed on a flat roof, how many feet of guy wire are used?

   (1) 40   **(2)** 50   **(3)** 60   **(4)** 65   **(5)** 75

Answers are on page 552.

Similar Triangles

Similar triangles are figures that have the same shape. We often use similar figures to find hard-to-measure lengths, such as the distance across a lake or the height of a building. **Similar triangles** are two triangles whose **corresponding angles** are equal and whose **corresponding sides** are in proportion.

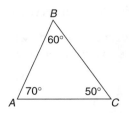

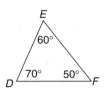

Look at △*ABC* and △*DEF*. They are similar triangles because they have the same shape. You see that corresponding angles are equal. ∠*A* = ∠*D*, ∠*B* = ∠*E*, and ∠*C* = ∠*F*. Although the two triangles are not the same size, their sides are in proportion. You write this relationship as

$$\frac{\text{side } AB}{\text{side } DE} = \frac{\text{side } BC}{\text{side } EF} = \frac{\text{side } AC}{\text{side } DF}.$$

Solving Similar Triangles Problems
1. Look for two triangles that have the same shape. Be sure the triangles are similar. Corresponding angles must be equal.
2. Redraw the triangles if necessary to show the corresponding sides and angles.
3. Set up and solve a proportion to find the missing length.

Example 1 On a sunny day, the village inspector used similar triangles to find the height of a flagpole without climbing it. She found that her 6-foot-tall coworker cast a 10-foot shadow at the same time the flagpole cast a 40-foot shadow. How tall is the flagpole?

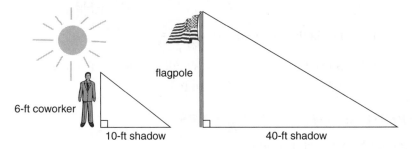

STEP 1 Notice that the coworker and the flagpole are at right angles to the ground. Set up a proportion. $\frac{\text{flagpole}}{\text{coworker}} = \frac{\text{flagpole shadow}}{\text{coworker shadow}}$

STEP 2 Fill in the numbers from the problem. Let *f* stand for flagpole. $\frac{f}{6} = \frac{40}{10}$

STEP 3 Solve the proportion for *f* by cross multiplying and then dividing. $f = \frac{6 \times 40}{10} = \frac{240}{10} = \textbf{24 ft}$

Another type of problem involving similar triangles is a surveying problem.

Example 2   The figure below shows a method of measuring the width of a river. If measurements are taken along the riverbank as shown, how wide is the river?

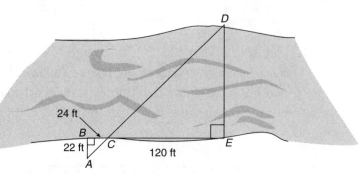

STEP 1   Look to see if there are two similar triangles. $\angle B = \angle E$ because they are both right angles, and both angles at point C are the same because they are vertical angles. Since two pairs of angles are the same, the triangles must be similar.

STEP 2   Redraw the small triangle by turning it in the same direction as the large triangle. Label the sides.

STEP 3   Set up a proportion with the sides of the triangles.

$$\frac{\text{side } AB}{\text{side } DE} = \frac{\text{side } CB}{\text{side } CE}$$

STEP 4   Fill in the values known. $\frac{22}{DE} = \frac{24}{120}$

STEP 5   Solve for side DE by cross multiplying and dividing.
$DE = \frac{120 \times 22}{24} = \frac{2640}{24} = \textbf{110 ft}$

EXERCISE 8: SIMILAR TRIANGLES

Directions: Solve each problem.

1. An oak tree along a parkway casts an 18-foot shadow at the same time an 8-foot traffic light casts a 12-foot shadow. Find the height of the tree.

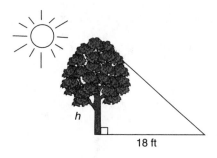

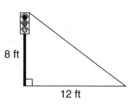

2. Suppose we need to find the distance *d* across a pond but are unable to swim to the other side and measure the distance directly. We can still find the distance. Find a marker on one side of the pond. On the other side of the pond, place a stake in the ground directly across from the marker. Measure a given distance *c* on a line perpendicular to the line determined by the marker and the stake. Then form two triangles as in the sketch below.

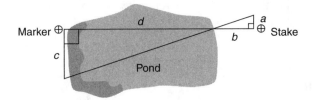

(a) With these measures, what would you do first to determine the distance, *d*?

(b) Find the distance across the pond if *a* = 2 feet, *b* = 6 feet, and *c* = 50 feet.

3. To find the height of a tower, Melissa held a yardstick perpendicular to the ground. She measured the shadow cast by the tower and the shadow cast by the yardstick. The tower's shadow was 42 feet, and the yardstick's shadow was 4 feet. How tall is the tower?

Answers are on page 552.

FORMULAS

AREA of a:

square	Area = side^2
rectangle	Area = length × width
parallelogram	Area = base × height
triangle	Area = $\frac{1}{2}$ × base × height
trapezoid	Area = $\frac{1}{2}$ × (base$_1$ + base$_2$) × height
circle	Area = π × radius^2; π is approximately equal to 3.14.

PERIMETER of a:

square	Perimeter = 4 × side
rectangle	Perimeter = 2 × length + 2 × width
triangle	Perimeter = side$_1$ + side$_2$ + side$_3$

CIRCUMFERENCE of a circle

Circumference = π × diameter; π is approximately equal to 3.14.

VOLUME of a:

cube	Volume = edge^3
rectangular solid	Volume = length × width × height
square pyramid	Volume = $\frac{1}{3}$ × (base edge)^2 × height
cylinder	Volume = π × radius^2 × height; π is approximately equal to 3.14.
cone	Volume = $\frac{1}{3}$ × π × radius^2 × height; π is approximately equal to 3.14.

COORDINATE GEOMETRY

distance between points = $\sqrt{(x_2 - x_1)^2 + (y_2 - y_1)^2}$; (x_1, y_1) and (x_2, y_2) are two points in a plane.

slope of a line = $\frac{y_2 - y_1}{x_2 - x_1}$; (x_1, y_1) and (x_2, y_2) are two points on the line.

PYTHAGOREAN RELATIONSHIP

$a^2 + b^2 = c^2$; a and b are legs and c the hypotenuse of a right triangle.

MEASURES OF CENTRAL TENDENCY

mean = $\frac{x_1 + x_2 + \ldots + x_n}{n}$ where the x's are the values for which a mean is desired, and n is the total number of values for x.

median = the middle value of an odd number of _ordered_ scores, and halfway between the two middle values of an even number of _ordered_ scores.

SIMPLE INTEREST

interest = principal × rate × time

DISTANCE

distance = rate × time

TOTAL COST

total cost = (number of units) × (price per unit)

POSTTESTS

How do I use the Posttests?

You have been moving closer to your goal—passing the actual GED Tests—by completing the instructional material in the five test areas: Language Arts, Writing; Social Studies; Science; Language Arts, Reading; and Mathematics. Now it's time to measure your readiness for the GED Tests. These tests, which are half-length, are similar to the actual GED Tests in terms of content areas, format, level of thinking skills, and percentages found on the real tests. After you have completed the Posttests, you will be better able to determine whether you are ready to take the GED Test and, if not, what areas you need to review. Evaluation Charts are included to help you judge your performance. We recommend the following approach to the Posttests.

1. Take only one Posttest at a time. Try to finish the test within the allotted time so that you can see how you will do on the actual GED Tests. If you are not done within that time period, mark where you were when the time was up and finish the test. You need to finish the entire Posttest so that you can make use of the Evaluation Charts.

2. Check the answers in the Answer Keys and fill in the Evaluation Charts. The charts follow each Answer Key. Be sure to read the explanations for all of the questions that you missed.

3. Refer to the review pages given in the Evaluation Charts if you still need work in certain areas.

4. Although these are Posttests, you should give them your best effort. If an item seems difficult, mark it and come back later. Always answer every question—even if you have to make an "educated guess." Sometimes you may know more than you think. Also, blanks count as wrong answers on the actual GED Tests, so it's always wise to answer every question as best you can.

Good luck on the Posttests and on the GED!

Time Allowed for Each Test	
Language Arts, Writing	
Part I: Editing	38 minutes
Part II: Essay	45 minutes
Social Studies	35 minutes
Science	40 minutes
Language Arts, Reading	33 minutes
Mathematics	
Part I	23 minutes
Part II	23 minutes

LANGUAGE ARTS, WRITING POSTTEST

Part I: Editing

Directions: The following items are based on documents of several paragraphs marked by letters. Each paragraph contains numbered sentences. Most sentences contain errors, but a few may be correct as written. Read the documents and then answer the questions based on them. For each item, choose the answer that would result in the best rewriting of the sentence or sentences. The best answer must be consistent with the meaning and tone of the rest of the document.

Answer each of the 25 questions as carefully as possible, choosing the best of five answer choices and blackening in the grid. You should take approximately 38 minutes to complete this test.

When you have finished the test, check your answers using page 553. Use the Evaluation Chart on page 554 to determine whether or not you are ready to take the actual GED Test and, if not, in what areas you need more work.

LANGUAGE ARTS, WRITING POSTTEST ANSWER GRID

1 ① ② ③ ④ ⑤   14 ① ② ③ ④ ⑤

2 ① ② ③ ④ ⑤   15 ① ② ③ ④ ⑤

3 ① ② ③ ④ ⑤   16 ① ② ③ ④ ⑤

4 ① ② ③ ④ ⑤   17 ① ② ③ ④ ⑤

5 ① ② ③ ④ ⑤   18 ① ② ③ ④ ⑤

6 ① ② ③ ④ ⑤   19 ① ② ③ ④ ⑤

7 ① ② ③ ④ ⑤   20 ① ② ③ ④ ⑤

8 ① ② ③ ④ ⑤   21 ① ② ③ ④ ⑤

9 ① ② ③ ④ ⑤   22 ① ② ③ ④ ⑤

10 ① ② ③ ④ ⑤   23 ① ② ③ ④ ⑤

11 ① ② ③ ④ ⑤   24 ① ② ③ ④ ⑤

12 ① ② ③ ④ ⑤   25 ① ② ③ ④ ⑤

13 ① ② ③ ④ ⑤

Choose the best answer to each question that follows.

Questions 1–6 refer to the following document.

ALLERGIES

(A)

(1) More people than ever report suffering from seasonal allergies and millions more suffer all year. (2) Although no cure is currently available, some simple practices within the home can help. (3) The library is a helpful place to find information about allergies.

(B)

(4) Certain housekeeping practices can reduce the effect of allergies. (5) Work to control and decrease dust in your home. (6) Clean hard furniture to avoid circulating dust with a damp cloth into the air. (7) Blinds, shades, fans, and draperies also needs attention. (8) Be especially attentive to cleaning in the bedroom. (9) Remember that you probably spend at least eight hours of every day there, so wash bed linens and blankets weakly in hot water temperatures of at least 130 degrees. (10) Don't hang sheets outside to dry because pollens and molds may gather on them.

(C)

(11) Kill mold and mildew in the kitchen and bathrooms by using a disinfectant weekly in those rooms. (12) Have a regular plan that you follow for cleaning in each of the rooms in your home.

Source: "Cleaning House Can Reduce Impact of Allergens in the Air." *Daily Herald*, October 29, 2000

1. Sentence 2: **Although no cure is currently <u>available, some</u> simple practices within the home can help.**

   Which is the best way to write the underlined portion of the text? If the original is the best way, choose option (1).

   (1) available, some
   (2) available some
   (3) available, but some
   (4) available. Some
   (5) available with some

2. Sentence 3: **The library is a helpful place to find information about allergies.**

   What revision should be made to sentence 3?

   (1) move sentence 3 to the beginning of paragraph A
   (2) move sentence 3 to follow sentence 1
   (3) move sentence 3 to follow sentence 8
   (4) remove sentence 3
   (5) no revision is necessary

3. Sentence 6: **Clean hard furniture <u>to avoid circulating dust with a damp cloth</u> into the air.**

   Which is the best way to write the underlined portion of the text? If the original is the best way, choose option (1).

   (1) to avoid circulating dust with a damp cloth
   (2) avoiding circulating dust with a damp cloth
   (3) with a damp cloth to avoid circulating dust
   (4) to circulate dust with a damp cloth
   (5) and avoid circulating dust with a damp cloth

4. Sentence 7: **Blinds, shades, fans, and draperies <u>also needs</u> attention.**

Which is the best way to write the underlined portion of the text? If the original is the best way, choose option (1).

(1) also needs
(2) also needing
(3) have needed also
(4) also need
(5) also are needing

5. Sentence 9: **Remember that you probably spend at least eight hours of every day there, so wash bed linens and blankets weakly in hot water temperatures of at least 130 degrees.**

What correction should be made to sentence 9?

(1) change <u>there</u> to <u>they're</u>
(2) replace <u>so</u> with <u>for</u>
(3) insert a comma after <u>linens</u>
(4) change <u>weakly</u> to <u>weekly</u>
(5) change <u>degrees</u> to <u>Degrees</u>

6. Sentence 11: **Kill mold and mildew in the kitchen and bathrooms by using a disinfectant weekly in those rooms.**

Which revision would improve the text, "Allergies"?

(1) move sentence 11 to follow sentence 8
(2) remove sentence 11
(3) combine paragraphs B and C into one paragraph
(4) move sentence 11 to follow sentence 12
(5) move sentence 11 to follow sentence 3

Questions 7–12 refer to the following document.

HOLIDAYS

(A)

(1) Whether the day is identified by a turkey, a Santa Claus, or a red heart, a holiday commemorates a special time for celebration. **(2)** Indeed, holidays can certainly provide some wonderful experiences that can long be remembered. **(3)** However, sometimes expectations of holiday celebrations exceeding reality, causing a general feeling of disappointment.

(B)

(4) As preparations for holiday celebrations begin well in advance of the actual day, very often, our expectations rise. **(5)** All around us, we see decorations displayed, we hear people talk about plans, foods, and activities. **(6)** Media may inundate us with ads, shows, articles, and music. **(7)** The creation of some false impressions may be created in our minds by stereotypes of family gatherings and friendships. **(8)** As a result, the perfect holiday exists more in our minds than in our homes.

(C)

(9) To have an enjoyable, if not perfect, holiday, a couple of suggestions can help. **(10)** First of all it is extremely valuable to maintain a sense of humor. **(11)** Secondly, we should prepare ourselves to enjoy the day for what it brings. **(12)** If we let go of the image of the ideal, we'll relax and have a better time. **(13)** There is no set way in which anyone has to celebrate a holiday. **(14)** Humor can relieve awkward moments or tensions and smooth ruffled feelings.

7. Sentence 3: **However, sometimes expectations of holiday celebrations <u>exceeding reality</u>, causing a general feeling of disappointment.**

Which is the best way to write the underlined portion of the text? If the original is the best way, choose option (1).

(1) exceeding reality
(2) exceed reality
(3) exceeds reality
(4) in exceeding reality
(5) excessive reality

8. Sentence 5: **All around us, we see decorations <u>displayed, we</u> hear people talk about plans, foods, and activities.**

Which is the best way to write the underlined portion of the text? If the original is the best way, choose option (1).

(1) displayed, we
(2) displayed we
(3) displayed, hearing
(4) displayed, but we
(5) displayed and

9. Sentence 7: **The creation of some false impressions may be created in our minds by stereotypes of family gatherings and friendships.**

The most effective revision of sentence 7 would include which group of words?

(1) may create some
(2) stereotyping minds of
(3) since family gatherings
(4) despite the false
(5) being false to

10. Sentence 10: **First of all it is extremely valuable to maintain a sense of humor.**

What correction should be made to sentence 10?

(1) insert a comma after <u>all</u>
(2) change <u>is</u> to <u>are</u>
(3) change <u>to maintain</u> to <u>too maintain</u>
(4) replace <u>a</u> with <u>the</u>
(5) no correction is necessary

11. Sentence 13: **There is no set way in which anyone has to celebrate a holiday.**

If you rewrote sentence 13 beginning with <u>No one,</u> the next word should be

(1) holiday
(2) there
(3) does
(4) celebrate
(5) has

12. Sentence 14: **Humor can relieve awkward moments or tensions and smooth ruffled feelings.**

What revision should be made to sentence 14?

(1) move sentence 14 to follow sentence 9
(2) move sentence 14 to follow sentence 10
(3) begin a new paragraph with sentence 14
(4) remove sentence 14
(5) no revision is necessary

Questions 13–18 refer to the following document.

Director of Customer Service
Packemin Airlines
100 W. Sorree Drive
Dallas, TX

Dear Mr. Wescott:

(A)

(1) For many years, I have been pleased with your airlines service. **(2)** However, last week when I was booked on a direct flight from Dallas to Pittsburgh, a combination of errors, problems, and I received some poor service, caused me severe inconvenience. **(3)** As a result, I believe I am entitled to some compensation from your company. **(4)** I am sure that you will agree to the validity of my complaint, and I will be waiting to hear from you.

(B)

(5) The first problem began at the gate when I was told that mechanical problems had grounded the plane. **(6)** Your representative assured me that I would be booked on another flight leaving in four hours. **(7)** However, that flight flew first to Denver and would require a change of planes to fly on to Pittsburgh. **(8)** Reluctantly, I agreed to the change and flew to Denver.

(C)

(9) When I arrived in Denver, however, I was told that the connecting flight had been cancelled. **(10)** Your service representative suggested that if I agreed to fly to Los Angeles, your company would then fly me first-class on another plane to Pittsburgh. **(11)** Having little other choice, I waited another five hours, then boarded the plane to Los Angeles.

(D)

(12) When I arrived in Los Angeles, however, your service representative tells me that because of a strike, no planes were flying until further notice. **(13)** After spending the rest of the night on an airport bench, limited service was restored. **(14)** I was put in an economy class seat on an indirect flight to Pittsburgh with a stop over in Seattle. **(15)** Once I reached Seattle, however, all passengers and me were told that weather conditions in Pittsburgh had prompted the cancellation of all flights to that area.

(E)

(16) Exhausted and defeated, I managed to fly home to Dallas where I was told that the location of my luggage was completely unknown because of mechanical failure of equipment, strike, weather, and computer error. **(17)** Attached is copies of my boarding passes.

13. Sentence 1: **For many years, I have been pleased with your airlines service.**

What correction should be made to sentence 1?

(1) change <u>years</u> to <u>year's</u>
(2) change <u>have been</u> to <u>will be</u>
(3) insert a comma after <u>pleased</u>
(4) change <u>your</u> to <u>you're</u>
(5) change <u>airlines</u> to <u>airline's</u>

14. Sentence 2: **However, last week when I was booked on a direct flight from Dallas to Pittsburgh, a combination of errors, problems, and <u>I received some poor service,</u> caused me severe inconvenience.**

Which is the best way to write the underlined portion of the text? If the original is the best way, choose option (1).

(1) I received some poor service,
(2) I received, some poor service
(3) that poor service I received,
(4) after receiving poor service,
(5) poor service

15. Sentence 12: **When I arrived in Los Angeles, however, your service representative tells me that because of a strike, no planes were flying until further notice.**

What correction should be made to sentence 12?

(1) remove the comma after <u>Los Angeles</u>
(2) change <u>tells</u> to <u>told</u>
(3) replace <u>because of</u> with <u>due to</u>
(4) change <u>strike</u> to <u>Strike</u>
(5) change <u>were</u> to <u>are</u>

16. Sentence 13: **After spending the rest of the night on an airport <u>bench, limited</u> service was restored.**

Which is the best way to write the underlined portion of the text? If the original is the best way, choose option (1).

(1) bench, limited
(2) bench, some limited
(3) bench that limited
(4) bench, I learned limited
(5) bench, finally limited

17. Sentence 15: **Once I reached Seattle, however, <u>all passengers and me were</u> told that weather conditions in Pittsburgh had prompted the cancellation of all flights to that area.**

Which is the best way to write the underlined portion of the text? If the original is the best way, choose option (1).

(1) all passengers and me were
(2) everybody there were
(3) all passengers and I were
(4) airline representatives
(5) I was

18. Sentence 17: **<u>Attached is</u> copies of my boarding passes.**

Which is the best way to write the underlined portion of the text? If the original is the best way, choose option (1).

(1) Attached is
(2) Attached are
(3) Attaching to
(4) Attached were
(5) Attached being

Questions 19–25 refer to the following document.

MICROWAVE OVENS

(A)

(1) Many people own and operate microwave ovens but are not really aware of exactly how a microwave oven cooks their food. (2) A magnetron tube in the oven converts electrical energy to microwave energy and directs that energy to a fanlike stirrer. (3) The stirrer evenly channels into the oven the short radio waves they penetrate food and cause the molecules in the food to vibrate. (4) This vibration, or friction, creates the heat that cooks the food. (5) Glass, paper, and most types of china are used in microwave cooking because the microwaves can pass through these containers, but the microwaves do not pass through metal. (6) The microwaves penetrate the food to a depth of about one inch. (7) The interior of the food receives the heat which spreads as the cooking process continues on. (8) When the microwaves stop, the friction action continues, slows, and it stops.

(B)

(9) Most microwave ovens have settings such as warm, defrost, simmer, medium high, and high so that a person can choose the speed at which their food cooks. (10) The amount of time that is necessary for food to cook is dependent on the amount of food someone is cooking. (11) One hot dog may cook in one minute while four hot dogs take about two minutes. (12) Microwave ovens vary in features and size, but owners can safely and effectively use this household appliance by following instructions carefully.

19. Sentence 3: **The stirrer evenly channels into the oven the short radio <u>waves they</u> penetrate food and cause the molecules in the food to vibrate.**

Which is the best way to write the underlined portion of the text? If the original is the best way, choose option (1).

(1) waves they
(2) waves and, they
(3) waves that
(4) waves, they
(5) waves these

20. Sentence 4: **This vibration, or <u>friction, creates</u> the heat that cooks the food.**

Which is the best way to write the underlined portion of the text? If the original is the best way, choose option (1).

(1) friction, creates
(2) friction create
(3) friction that creates
(4) friction have created
(5) friction are creating

21. Sentence 7: **The interior of the food receives the heat which spreads as the cooking process continues on.**

If you rewrote sentence 7 beginning with
<u>As cooking continues,</u>
the next word should be

(1) spreading
(2) on food
(3) which spreads
(4) the heat
(5) process is

22. Sentence 8: **When the microwaves stop, the friction action continues, slows, <u>and it stops.</u>**

Which is the best way to write the underlined portion of the text? If the original is the best way, choose option (1).

(1) and it stops.
(2) and stopped.
(3) and they stop.
(4) and stopping.
(5) and stops.

23. What sentence below would be most effective at the beginning of paragraph B?

(1) Any person using a microwave oven needs to know some basic information to operate it.
(2) Technology has been responsible for the invention and use of many home products we use today.
(3) Cooking in a traditional oven is a different process from cooking in a microwave.
(4) The cost of microwave ovens has decreased even as the quality of the product has increased.
(5) Many people do not really like to cook food in microwave ovens.

24. Sentence 9: **Most microwave ovens have settings such as warm, defrost, simmer, medium high, and high so that a person can choose the speed at which <u>their food cooks.</u>**

Which is the best way to write the underlined portion of the text? If the original is the best way, choose option (1).

(1) their food cooks.
(2) the food cooks.
(3) their food will cook.
(4) their food cooked.
(5) your food cooks.

25. Sentence 10: **The amount of time that is necessary for food to cook is dependent on the amount of food someone is cooking.**

The most effective revision of sentence 10 would begin with which group of words?

(1) Although the amount
(2) Being necessary in cooking
(3) The time needed
(4) Depending on time
(5) The right amount

Part II: The Essay

Directions: This part of the test is designed to find out how well you write. The test has one question that asks you to present an opinion and explain your ideas. Your essay should be long enough to develop the topic adequately. In preparing your essay, you should take the following steps:

1. Read the directions and topic carefully.

2. Think about your ideas and plan your essay before you write.

3. Use scratch paper to make notes of your ideas.

4. Write your essay in ink on two other pages of paper.

5. After finishing your writing, read your paper carefully and make appropriate changes.

Topic

Has technology greatly affected your life, or is your life largely unaffected by technology?

In your essay, state your opinion and give examples supporting it.

Information on evaluating your essay is on page 554.

SOCIAL STUDIES
POSTTEST

Directions: This Social Studies Posttest will give you an opportunity to evaluate your readiness for the actual GED Social Studies Test. This test contains 25 questions. Some of the questions are based on short reading passages, and some of them require you to interpret a graph, chart or table, map, or an editorial cartoon. You should take approximately 35 minutes to complete this test.

When you have finished the test, check your answers using pages 555 and 556. Use the Evaluation Chart on page 557 to determine whether or not you are ready to take the GED Social Studies Test and, if not, in what areas you need more work.

SOCIAL STUDIES POSTTEST ANSWER GRID

1 ① ② ③ ④ ⑤   14 ① ② ③ ④ ⑤

2 ① ② ③ ④ ⑤   15 ① ② ③ ④ ⑤

3 ① ② ③ ④ ⑤   16 ① ② ③ ④ ⑤

4 ① ② ③ ④ ⑤   17 ① ② ③ ④ ⑤

5 ① ② ③ ④ ⑤   18 ① ② ③ ④ ⑤

6 ① ② ③ ④ ⑤   19 ① ② ③ ④ ⑤

7 ① ② ③ ④ ⑤   20 ① ② ③ ④ ⑤

8 ① ② ③ ④ ⑤   21 ① ② ③ ④ ⑤

9 ① ② ③ ④ ⑤   22 ① ② ③ ④ ⑤

10 ① ② ③ ④ ⑤   23 ① ② ③ ④ ⑤

11 ① ② ③ ④ ⑤   24 ① ② ③ ④ ⑤

12 ① ② ③ ④ ⑤   25 ① ② ③ ④ ⑤

13 ① ② ③ ④ ⑤

Question 1 is based on the following cartoon.

Reprinted with permission from
The Detroit News

1. Which of the following is a correct interpretation of this cartoon?

    (1) The budget will not be balanced if the economy "crashes."
    (2) The budget is balanced because the economy is stable.
    (3) The budget is balanced because the economy is weak.
    (4) The budget will remain balanced under all economic conditions.
    (5) The budget will not be balanced if the economy is strong.

Question 2 is based on the following excerpt.

WE, THEREFORE, the Representatives of the UNITED STATES of AMERICA in General Congress, Assembled, appealing to the Supreme Judge of the world for the rectitude of our intentions, do, in the Name, and by Authority of the good People of these Colonies, solemnly publish and declare, That these United Colonies are, and of Right ought to be, FREE AND INDEPENDENT STATES . . .

2. This statement was proclaimed by members of which group?

    (1) Constitutional Convention
    (2) Boston Tea Party participants
    (3) Articles of Confederation writers
    (4) Second Continental Congress
    (5) First House of Representatives

Question 3 is based on the following graph.

Aging U.S. Population

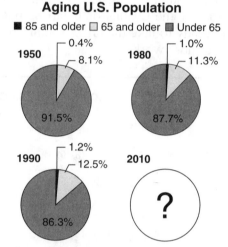

Source: Bureau of the Census,
U.S. Department of Commerce

3. Which adult population statistical prediction for 2010 would be likely, given the information in the circle graphs?

    (1) 1 percent over 85 years of age and 31 percent 65 and older
    (2) 2 percent over 85 years of age and 30 percent 65 and older
    (3) 0.5 percent over 85 years of age and 12 percent 65 and older
    (4) 2 percent over 85 years of age and 10 percent 65 and older
    (5) 2 percent over 85 years of age and 15 percent 65 and older

Question 4 refers to the following chart.

Constitutional Powers: Three Branches of Government

Legislative	Executive	Judicial
• Passes bills into laws	• Serves as Commander-in-Chief of Army, Navy, and militia	• Settles controversies among states and citizens
• Lays and collects taxes	• Makes treaties with other nations with Senate consent	• Determines the constitutionality of laws
• Regulates commerce among states and with other foreign nations	• Appoints ambassadors, judges of the Supreme Court, and Cabinet officers	• Determines original and appellate jurisdiction of the Supreme Court
• Coins money; establishes values and standards	• Enforces laws of Congress	• Interprets the laws
• Declares war		• Determines the constitutionality of the president's actions
• Raises and supports armies		
• Provides for a militia		

4. Considering the powers of the legislative branch, evaluate and select the reason that the writers of the Constitution of the United States might have given the power to declare war to Congress and not to the executive branch.

   (1) Congress best represents the people and should finalize the decision to declare war.
   (2) The president shouldn't be involved in any affair regarding military decisions.
   (3) Congress should make all decisions involving problems between the states.
   (4) The president's being the supreme commander of the armed forces creates a conflict of interest.
   (5) The president of the United States has enough information to declare war.

5. Liberals believe that the problems of the country should be solved by a strong federal government. They support funding social programs, limiting military spending, and negotiating as the basis for American foreign policy. Which one of the following federal programs would liberals in America be likely to oppose?

   (1) guaranteed government loans to college students
   (2) a national health insurance program
   (3) stricter pollution laws
   (4) the Star Wars space defense system
   (5) job training for the disabled

Question 6 refers to the following passage.

Archaeologists study past societies through the analysis of artifacts found buried at old dwelling sites. These artifacts could include weapons, tools, pottery, or personal items. Anthropologists study human remains and fossils to determine the physical nature and possible behaviors of ancient people. Scientists study remains throughout the world to try to understand past cultures. In some cases, as in Egypt, an artifact like the Rosetta Stone provides enough information to help archaeologists decipher written language that tells of ancient lifestyles. Because of the Rosetta Stone, we can read the hieroglyphics of ancient Egypt and understand this extinct civilization.

6. Which of the following discoveries was most likely made by an anthropologist?
   (1) artifacts from the Titanic, which sank on its maiden voyage
   (2) skeletal remains from the Yucatán Peninsula in Mexico
   (3) farming tools used by the Hopi Indians in New Mexico
   (4) spears and shields used by the Vikings in Northern Scotland
   (5) murals in caves drawn by the Anasazi Indians in Arizona

Question 7 is based on the following graph.

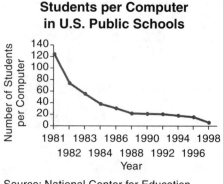

Students per Computer in U.S. Public Schools

Source: National Center for Education Statistics, U.S. Dept. of Education; National Education Association

7. Which of the following statements best supports the data provided in the line graph?
   (1) More students are wealthier and can afford the newest technology.
   (2) Fewer students are sharing computers in the public schools.
   (3) The United States has prioritized spending on computers with tax dollars.
   (4) Schools have used more budgeted income for buying computers.
   (5) More students have computers in their classrooms because of corporate donations.

Questions 8 and 9 are based on the following amendments to the Constitution of the United States.

(16)

The Congress shall have power to lay and collect taxes on incomes, from whatever source derived, without apportionment among the several states, and without regard to any census or enumeration.

(24)

The right of citizens of the United States to vote in any primary or other election for President or Vice President, for electors for President or Vice President, or for Senator or Representative in Congress, shall not be denied or abridged by the United States or any state by reason of failure to pay any poll tax or other tax.

8. Which of the following statements is best supported by the text?
   (1) Congress can only issue new tax laws after each census.
   (2) The American people vote on income tax laws every four years.
   (3) Almost half of the money in the federal budget comes from personal income tax.
   (4) The House of Representatives and the Senate have the power to collect taxes.
   (5) Tax laws in the United States can never be changed.

9. What conclusion can be drawn from reading Amendment 24?
   (1) Individual states should have the right to issue poll taxes.
   (2) No state can take away a person's right to vote because of failure to pay a poll tax.
   (3) Congress has the power to create a special tax for voters who are new citizens of the United States.
   (4) All citizens had to pay a poll tax after the creation of this amendment.
   (5) A poll tax was created to finance campaign expenses.

Question 10 refers to this graph.

World Infant Mortality Rates for 1999

Country	Infant Deaths per 1,000 Live Births
U.S.A.	6.33
Brazil	35.37
Russia	23
South Africa	51
Germany	5.14

Source: National Center for Health Statistics, U.S. Dept. of Health and Human Services

10. Based on this bar graph, what conclusion can you draw?
   (1) Southern hemisphere countries (Brazil and South Africa) had higher infant mortality rates.
   (2) Northern hemisphere countries (U.S.A., Russia, and Germany) had higher infant mortality rates.
   (3) Countries with advanced technology had lower infant mortality rates.
   (4) Countries with higher populations had greater infant mortality rates.
   (5) Countries with smaller populations had greater infant mortality rates.

Question 11 is based on the following passage.

Vice President Andrew Johnson succeeded Lincoln as president after Lincoln's assassination. Johnson was from Tennessee and was the only Southern senator not to join the Confederacy when war broke out. Lincoln had trusted him totally, but many in Congress did not. In spite of Johnson's refusal to join the Confederacy, his every action appeared to be suspiciously pro-South to them.

11. Which of the following actions by Andrew Johnson does *not* support these congressmen's opinion of him?

(1) his issue of a proclamation forgiving most Confederates

(2) his demand that Confederate states ratify the Thirteenth Amendment abolishing slavery

(3) his veto of the civil rights bill that guaranteed rights to freed slaves

(4) his veto of the Freedman's Bureau bill that had been approved without the input of the southern states

(5) his opposition to the Fourteenth Amendment that toughened the stand of Congress against former Confederate loyalists

12. How does a presidential primary election differ from a general election?

(1) A presidential primary is usually of local interest only.

(2) A person does not have to be a registered voter to vote in a primary.

(3) A primary election does not determine who will be the president of the United States.

(4) A primary election determines the number of electoral college votes a particular candidate gets.

(5) A primary election must have only two opposing candidates on the ballot.

13. The United States has put quotas (limits) on the number of automobiles that foreign countries can export to America. Which of the following is a belief that helps to justify the quotas?

(1) American manufacturers must be protected from unfair competition.

(2) Exporting automobiles should not cost more than exporting other products.

(3) Foreign manufacturers deserve to meet their own business needs.

(4) The dollar amount of trade between other car-manufacturing countries is too low.

(5) There should be no demand for foreign cars by American consumers.

Question 14 is based on the map below.

14. How would this map be most useful?

(1) identifying political boundaries
(2) developing a highway map
(3) identifying topographical formations
(4) recognizing historical landmarks
(5) identifying population centers

Question 15 is based on the graph below.

Top 5 Countries with the Highest Military Expenditures

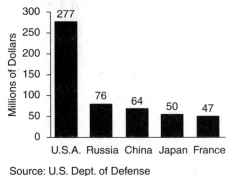

Source: U.S. Dept. of Defense

15. What conclusion can be drawn from the bar graph?

(1) The United States spends over three times as much in military expenditures as Russia.
(2) The countries of central Europe spend over $200 million on maintaining an army.
(3) The United States is the most advanced in its military technology.
(4) Japan and Russia spend the same amount of money on military expenditures.
(5) The United States spends the least amount on military expenditures.

Question 16 is based on the following definitions.

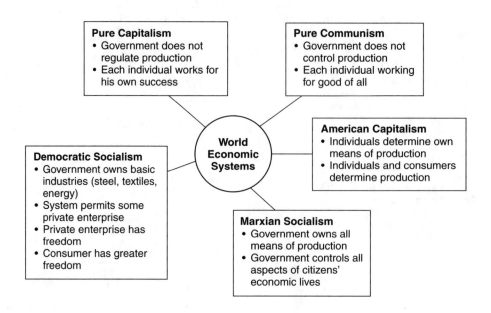

Pure Capitalism
- Government does not regulate production
- Each individual works for his own success

Pure Communism
- Government does not control production
- Each individual working for good of all

Democratic Socialism
- Government owns basic industries (steel, textiles, energy)
- System permits some private enterprise
- Private enterprise has freedom
- Consumer has greater freedom

World Economic Systems

American Capitalism
- Individuals determine own means of production
- Individuals and consumers determine production

Marxian Socialism
- Government owns all means of production
- Government controls all aspects of citizens' economic lives

16. An economic system is designed to meet the needs of the people by establishing production priorities and allocating the limited resources. In which one of the following economic systems would there be the most coordinated use of production facilities while still permitting individual consumer choice?

(1) pure communism
(2) Marxian socialism
(3) democratic socialism
(4) American capitalism
(5) pure capitalism

17. Biologist Charles Darwin believed that the species that was best able to adapt would continue to exist—survival of the fittest. Under which of the following situations would his theory apply?

(1) Franklin Roosevelt's New Deal and government-funded work programs
(2) Teddy Roosevelt's progressivism and regulation of big business activities
(3) Herbert Hoover's conservatism and noninterference in the affairs of business
(4) Dwight Eisenhower's policies of moderation in defense spending
(5) Lyndon Johnson's Great Society and generous spending for social programs

Question 18 is based on the following excerpt.

In 1679 the Habeas Corpus Act in England made it illegal for a person to be retained in prison without a trial. It also ruled that an individual could not be imprisoned twice for the same crime. The writers of the Constitution of the United States also included the rights granted in the Habeas Corpus Act in Article I of the Constitution.

18. What resolution does the need for a Habeas Corpus Act support?

Every individual must

(1) serve as a member of a jury if summoned

(2) pay an excessive bail if arrested

(3) be protected from arbitrary arrest

(4) accept decisions made by the appellate court

(5) be protected from cruel and unusual punishment if arrested

19. In 1972 eighteen-year-olds were given the right to vote. This occurrence is an example of which of the following methods to effect changes in our system of government?

(1) a United States Court decision

(2) a law enacted by both houses of Congress

(3) an amendment to the United States Constitution

(4) an executive order from the President of the United States

(5) a consensus of the legislatures in the fifty states

Question 20 is based on the following cartoon.

"Great news! The shareholders have approved your heart bypass!"

Bruce Beattie, Copley News Service

20. What is the main idea of the cartoon?

(1) Corporate shareholders influence health care expenditures in America.

(2) Only elderly patients have HMOs in the United States.

(3) Doctors are benefiting financially from corporate health care.

(4) Americans in general are concerned about the cost of health care.

(5) Corporate health care managers are not covering major health problems.

Question 21 is based on the following excerpt.

Ellis Island is a symbol of America's immigrant heritage. For more than six decades—1892 to 1954—the immigrant depot processed the greatest tide of incoming humanity in the nation's history. Some twelve million people landed here; today their descendents account for almost 40% of the country's population. Opened on January 1, 1892, Ellis Island ushered in a new era of immigration with each newcomer's eligibility to land now determined by federal law. The government established a special bureau to process the record numbers that were arriving at the end of the 19th century. Fleeing hardships such as poverty, religious persecution, or political unrest in their homelands, they journeyed to the United States in search of freedom and opportunity. More than 70% landed in New York, the country's largest port. First and second class passengers were processed on board ship, but third or steerage class were ferried to Ellis Island where they underwent medical and legal examinations in the main building.

—Excerpted from "Ellis Island," National Monument New York, U.S. Department of the Interior National Park Service by Brian Feeney

21. Which of the following is a clear implication of the passage?
   (1) All immigrants were detained at Ellis Island.
   (2) Ellis Island was the gateway to America for many immigrants.
   (3) Most of the immigrants that arrived at Ellis Island were from the Middle East.
   (4) The government did not need to open an immigration center on Ellis Island.
   (5) All passengers underwent legal examinations on Ellis Island.

22. The fact that the U.S. Constitution can be amended is the basis for what belief of the Founding Fathers?
   (1) They made legislative mistakes in the original writing.
   (2) They acknowledged their lack of writing skills in framing the constitution.
   (3) They accounted for any further changes in values and needs of the American people.
   (4) They included this power as required by the Supreme Court.
   (5) They considered all possible circumstances in the original Constitution.

Question 23 is based on the following excerpt.

... millions of other women were experiencing their own unique odysseys at home as a result of the gender climate changes brought on by the demand for men in fighting jobs. In fact, there were 350,000 women in uniform and estimated 6.5 million at work in war-related jobs on the home front. Harder to measure but equally important were the contributions of the women who stayed home, raised the children, taught school, clerked in schools and banks, kept the fabric of society together. At night they went to bed wondering if their sons or husbands were safe in those far-off places where they were fighting for their lives every day. All these experiences—for the women in uniform, for those assembling airplanes or ships, for the women who kept families and communities together—shaped that generation of women as much as combat shaped the men of their time. . . .

—Excerpted from
"Women in Uniform and Out" in
The Greatest Generation by
Tom Brokaw

23. The following quotations are also from Tom Brokaw's book, *The Greatest Generation*. Which does *not* support the author's opinion as stated in the passage?
   (1) "A full-blown spirit of patriotism was in every heart." Marion Rivers Nittel
   (2) "You had to do your part." Alison Ely Campbell
   (3) "Everyone should learn the meaning of that famous little four-letter word—Work." Bob Bush
   (4) "The one time the Nation got together was WWII. We stood as one. We spoke as one. We clenched our fists as one." Daniel Inouye
   (5) "We were trained so well I didn't believe anything could kill us." Leonard Lovell

24. What argument would the presidents of the Union Pacific and the Central Pacific railroads have used to justify expenses incurred throughout the creation of the transcontinental railroad?

   The transcontinental railroad would allow for
   (1) affordable travel for all Americans
   (2) improved relations with Native Americans
   (3) industrial growth throughout the United States
   (4) increased job security for all railroad employees
   (5) pleasant working conditions for immigrant railroad laborers

Question 25 is based on the following map.

Modern Middle East

25. What conclusion can you draw
about the distribution of oil-
producing areas in the Middle
East?

(1) The distribution of crude oil
is not uniform throughout the
Middle East.
(2) The amount of oil available
is dependent upon the size of
the country.
(3) The major oil-producing
areas are all located on the
coast of the Black Sea.
(4) The Middle East produces
more oil than the United
States.
(5) The amount of oil produced
is not determined by the size
of the country.

SCIENCE
POSTTEST

Directions: The Science Posttest consists of 25 multiple-choice questions. The questions are based on graphs, maps, tables, diagrams, editorial cartoons, and reading passages. Answer each question as carefully as possible, choosing the best of five answer choices and blackening in the grid. You should take approximately 40 minutes to complete this test.

When you have finished the test, check your answers using pages 557 and 558. Use the Evaluation Chart on page 558 to determine whether or not you are ready to take the GED Science Test and, if not, in what areas you need more work.

SCIENCE POSTTEST ANSWER GRID

1 ① ② ③ ④ ⑤   14 ① ② ③ ④ ⑤

2 ① ② ③ ④ ⑤   15 ① ② ③ ④ ⑤

3 ① ② ③ ④ ⑤   16 ① ② ③ ④ ⑤

4 ① ② ③ ④ ⑤   17 ① ② ③ ④ ⑤

5 ① ② ③ ④ ⑤   18 ① ② ③ ④ ⑤

6 ① ② ③ ④ ⑤   19 ① ② ③ ④ ⑤

7 ① ② ③ ④ ⑤   20 ① ② ③ ④ ⑤

8 ① ② ③ ④ ⑤   21 ① ② ③ ④ ⑤

9 ① ② ③ ④ ⑤   22 ① ② ③ ④ ⑤

10 ① ② ③ ④ ⑤   23 ① ② ③ ④ ⑤

11 ① ② ③ ④ ⑤   24 ① ② ③ ④ ⑤

12 ① ② ③ ④ ⑤   25 ① ② ③ ④ ⑤

13 ① ② ③ ④ ⑤

Question 1 refers to the following cartoon.

Malcom Mayes/Artizans.com

1. Which of the following environmental concerns does *not* support the main idea of this cartoon that people are observing unusual weather patterns?
   (1) an increase in carbon dioxide in the air
   (2) overpopulation around the world
   (3) forest fires in western states
   (4) overharvesting of seafood species
   (5) burning of fossil fuels around the world

2. As many as twenty-five persons can benefit from a single organ and tissue donor. Thousands of people are in need of an organ or tissue transplant, and anyone, regardless of age, race, or gender can be a donor. Organs that can't be placed are often used for research on a variety of diseases and conditions. Which of the following body parts is a tissue that could be used in a transplant?
   (1) heart
   (2) kidney
   (3) cornea
   (4) pancreas
   (5) lungs

Question 3 is based on the following passage.

Fat can be defined loosely as a source for energy storage in the human body. The human anatomy is designed to carry food reserves to ensure the body's survival when food becomes scarce. However, in our slim-conscious society, many people go to great lengths to keep fat from accumulating on their bodies, sometimes with harmful effects.

Fat is more efficient in storing energy than carbohydrates for several reasons. First, fat is a highly concentrated energy source. Second, fat weighs less than the same energy amount of carbohydrates. Third, fat is much more efficient to carry as an energy source because it does not hold water as do carbohydrates. For example, an average 70-kilogram human male normally has about 11 kilograms of fat in his body. This fat represents enough stored energy to keep him alive for a month without eating. The same amount of energy stored as starch would double his body weight.

3. Which view does the passage support?
   (1) Being obese is healthier than being underweight.
   (2) Reserves of fat serve no purpose in the human body.
   (3) Excessive dieting can be detrimental to one's health.
   (4) Fats lead to high levels of cholesterol.
   (5) One heavy meal each day suffices for usual intake.

Question 4 is based on the following information.

One way in which organisms are classified is by how they obtain their food for energy use. Listed and defined below are five categories that describe the food habits of organisms.

herbivore—feeds directly on plant matter

carnivore—feeds on the flesh of other organisms

omnivore—includes both plant and animal matter in its diet

parasite—obtains its nourishment by attaching itself to another organism, called a host

decomposer—usually lives in soil and obtains food by breaking down the wastes and remains of other organisms

4. Based on the information above, what would be the relationship between a flea and its canine or feline victim?

   (1) prey-predator
   (2) organism-decomposer
   (3) parasite-host
   (4) herbivore-carnivore
   (5) omnivore-carnivore

Question 5 is based on the following information.

The brain has five basic regions:

cerebellum—coordinates body movement

brain stem—responsible for basic life functions such as blood pressure and breathing

thalamus—a Grand Central relay station for incoming data from all the senses except smell

hypothalamus—a regulator of hunger, thirst, sleep, sexuality, and emotions

cerebrum—our gray matter, home to thought, vision, language memory, emotions. It's divided into hemispheres. If you're right-handed, odds are the right hemisphere is where you make sense of music, images, space, emotions. Your left hemisphere is apt to focus on math, language, speech. In left-handed people, tasks are usually reversed

5. What conclusion can you draw from the information provided about the brain?

   (1) An injury to the brain stem may result in sensory dysfunction.
   (2) Eating disorders do not involve testing on any regions of the brain.
   (3) All regions of the brain are essential for normal human function.
   (4) The brain uses a higher percentage of oxygen than any other organ.
   (5) The cerebrum is the most essential region of the brain.

Question 6 is based on the following diagram.

Pea Plants

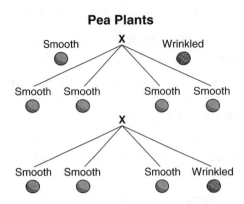

6. Based on the information above, what would a geneticist say about the example of the pea plants?
   (1) It has no relationship to human transmission of traits.
   (2) It is true only in the plant world.
   (3) It helps show transmission of traits from parents to offspring.
   (4) It is too dated to have application in today's world.
   (5) It is based purely on chance.

Question 7 is based on the diagram and the information below.

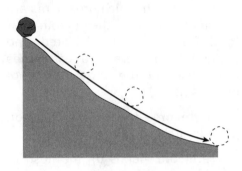

Mechanical energy is classified in two ways: energy waiting to be used and energy causing action. When an object is at rest at a place from which it can move, it is said to have **potential energy**. One example is the rock illustrated in the diagram; the higher the rock sits on the hill, the greater the potential energy. Other examples are an idling car, a ball in one's hand, or a cocked pistol.

Kinetic energy is the energy of motion. Once an object is upset from its position and set into motion, the potential energy is converted to kinetic energy. Examples are depressing the accelerator of a car, throwing a ball, or firing a pistol.

7. In the diagram, what is the rock in the resting position at the top of the hill said to have?
   (1) mechanical force
   (2) mechanical advantage
   (3) no energy
   (4) kinetic energy
   (5) potential energy

Question 8 is based on the following passage.

The orderly pattern of the atoms in a crystal influences many properties apart from its external appearance. One of these properties is cleavage. *Cleavage* refers to the ability of a crystal to split in a certain direction along its surface. The direction of the cleavage is always parallel to a possible crystal face. Cleavage planes are dependent on the atomic structure, and they pass between sheets of atoms in well-defined directions.

How easily a mineral cleaves and the effect of the cleavage vary from one mineral to another. A crystal whose cleavage results in exceptionally smooth surfaces is said to show eminent cleavage; other types of cleavages are classified as distinct or poor. All crystalline gemstones undergo cleavage before they can be mounted in a setting. This cutting process may also be easy or difficult. A diamond cleaves easily despite its great hardness and may be cut into many different forms.

8. According to the passage, what can we conclude about cleavage?

    (1) All crystals demonstrate good cleavage.
    (2) Some crystals with poor cleavage may not be used for gemstones.
    (3) Eminent cleavage is inherent in all crystals of the quartz family.
    (4) Cleavage of diamonds is a random property and differs from stone to stone.
    (5) Cleavage improvement depends on the location of mineral excavation.

Question 9 is based on the following graph.

New AIDS Cases

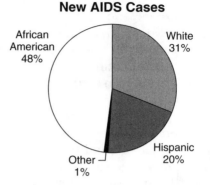

Source: Centers for Disease Control

9. According to statistics from the Centers for Disease Control, the number of deaths by AIDS has dropped; however, the slowing decline concerns experts. Considering the data about new AIDS cases provided in the circle graph, what conclusion can be drawn about the AIDS epidemic in 2000?

    (1) All races are equally affected by the AIDS epidemic.
    (2) AIDS medications are powerful and extremely successful.
    (3) Many people are still misinformed about the severity of AIDS.
    (4) More children and teenagers are affected by AIDS than adults.
    (5) Most people are not concerned about AIDS.

Question 10 is based on the following passage.

Off the coast of Chile and Peru, ocean currents and winds cause a rising of cold, nutrient-laden water. This enrichment of the ocean's surface layer results in an abundant plankton crop, which in turn supports large fish and seabird populations.

El Niño is the name for a set of oceanographic conditions that occurs every five to eight years, causing disturbances in Earth's biological and weather systems. El Niño occurs when trade winds that drive the currents weaken and fail. In the ocean, the supply of nutrients is cut off, and rather sterile warm water kills off the plankton. The fish and seabirds starve.

Dramatic changes also take place in the world's weather. As the trade winds subside, the wind patterns around the globe are disrupted. For example, the normally cool European continent may experience prolonged periods of torrid temperatures as its normal wind patterns change. El Niño's effects may be felt for as long as two years at a time.

10. According to the passage, El Niño occurs with failed trade winds. Thus, a conclusion that can be drawn is that a resumption of trade winds off the coast of South America is likely to result in what phenomena?

(1) a major anchovy and tuna migration

(2) an end to El Niño conditions

(3) an increase in weather disruptions

(4) a continuation in high European temperatures

(5) a condition known as *El Aguaje*

Question 11 is based on the following graph.

Evaluation of the Water Condition in the United States Watersheds, 2000

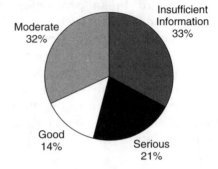

Source: U.S. EPA *World Almanac 2000*

11. A watershed is an area of land that catches precipitation and drains to rivers and lakes. Which of the following conclusions can be drawn about the quality of water in the watersheds of the United States in 2000?

(1) The EPA (Environmental Protection Agency) need not be concerned.

(2) More than half of the water in the watersheds is dangerously polluted.

(3) Contaminated water in watersheds is a serious problem around the world.

(4) Polluted run-off affects over 50% of the water in varying degrees.

(5) It is very difficult to analyze water in watersheds.

Question 12 is based on the following table.

Wind Chill Index (and its Effect on Skin)							
Wind Speed MPH	Degrees in Fahrenheit						
	35	30	25	15	10	5	0
5	33	27	21	12	7	0	–5
10	22	16	10	–3	–9	–15	–22
15	16	9	2	–11	–18	–25	–31
20	12	4	–3	–17	–24	–31	–39
25	8	1	–7	–22	–29	–36	–44
30	6	–2	–10	–25	–33	–41	–49
35	4	–4	–12	–27	–35	–43	–52
40	3	–5	–13	–29	–37	–45	–53
45	2	–6	–14	–30	–38	–46	–54

Source: National Weather Source, NOAA, U.S. Department of Commerce
World Almanac 2000

12. Temperature and wind combine to cause heat loss. Hypothermia occurs when the body temperature falls more than 4°F below normal. Death can occur if hypothermia persists for over three hours. According to the table above, in which of the following temperature and wind combinations would the body temperature be the lowest and a person most at risk for developing hypothermia?

(1) windspeed of 5 mph and a temperature of 5°F
(2) windspeed of 10 mph and a temperature of 15°F
(3) windspeed of 25 mph and a temperature of 35°F
(4) windspeed of 30 mph and a temperature of 15°F
(5) windspeed of 35 mph and a temperature of 30°F

Question 13 is based on the following passage.

Nuclear scientists have determined that a fourth state of matter exists: **plasma**. The state of plasma is reached when matter acquires a temperature so high that some of the molecules and atoms are broken down into ions and electrons. Stellar and interstellar matter mostly occur as forms of plasma.

On Earth, plasma exists in the ionosphere, in flames, and in chemical and nuclear explosions. Matter in a controlled thermonuclear reactor also exists in a plasma state. Plasma is most like a gas. However, it differs from un-ionized gas in that it is a good conductor of electricity and heat. Scientists hope to understand the occurrence of plasma in nature and to harness it as an inexpensive energy source.

13. Based on the passage, how can the cost of developing thermonuclear power with plasma be defended?

(1) It is applicable to all technologies.
(2) A plasma power source can be used without special equipment.
(3) It can provide an inexpensive power source.
(4) It is almost perfected already.
(5) Current nuclear power is too dangerous.

Question 14 is based on the following illustration.

pH Scale

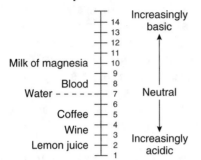

14. According to the scale above, how would a substance that registers 2.5 on the pH scale be categorized?

(1) base
(2) neutral substance
(3) alkali
(4) acid
(5) hydroxide

Question 15 is based on the following passage.

Although water is the most common hydrogen-oxygen compound, hydrogen and oxygen form another compound called **hydrogen peroxide**, H_2O_2. Hydrogen peroxide was first obtained by treating barium peroxide with an acid. Very small quantities of hydrogen peroxide are present in dew, rain, and snow because of the action of ultraviolet light on oxygen and water vapor.

Hydrogen peroxide has many different applications, depending upon its concentration. A 3 percent solution is used in the home as a mild antiseptic and germicide. A 30 percent solution is used in industry as a bleaching agent because of the permanency of the whiteness it produces. Concentrations of 90 percent are used as oxidizing agents in rockets and high explosives.

15. According to the information in the passage, what can we predict that adding water to an industrial-strength hydrogen peroxide solution will result in?

(1) an explosion
(2) a new substance
(3) an antiseptic
(4) a rocket fuel
(5) a bleaching agent

Question 16 is based on the following definitions.

reflection—angular return of a light wave

refraction—apparent bending of light waves through different media

diffraction—bending of light waves near an obstacle

interference—altering of brightness of light waves

polarization—restriction of light waves to one plane

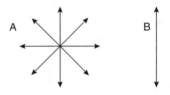

16. A certain type of lens changes the direction of light rays from A to B. What property does this illustrate?

(1) deflection
(2) diffraction
(3) reflection
(4) refraction
(5) polarization

17. Bob discovered that he had high blood pressure, which was the result of years of poor eating habits. Bob's physician gave him a diet to follow that would help to lower his blood pressure naturally but not create a mineral deficiency. Which of the following statements is irrelevant to Bob's understanding of his diet?

(1) Low-fat dairy products, green leafy vegetables, and tofu are good sources of calcium.

(2) Lean red meat, whole-grain cereals, and beans are valuable sources of iron.

(3) A daily vitamin and mineral supplement is more important than a well-balanced diet.

(4) Whole-wheat breads fortified with iron and calcium are better than white breads.

(5) The restriction of sodium-rich foods reduces the risk of heart disease.

Question 18 is based on the following information.

RICE Routine for First Aid (rest, ice, compression, and elevation)
Rest—Rest the injured part of your body to reduce further swelling and bleeding. Avoid moving the injured part.
Ice—Apply an ice pack to the injured area for twenty to thirty minutes every two to three hours for the first forty-eight hours after an injury. This will help relieve pain and minimize bruising and swelling.
Compression—Wear a compressed bandage for at least two days to help reduce bleeding and swelling.
Elevation—Raise the injured part of your body (above your heart when possible) to help reduce swelling.

Source: American Medical Association

18. The RICE routine for first aid would be helpful for which of the following soft-tissue injuries?

(1) broken leg
(2) strained muscle
(3) dislocated shoulder
(4) detached retina
(5) herniated disk

19. Tissue engineering is the ability to grow cells in a laboratory. These cells are collected from an animal, a donor organ, or a patient's body and grown in liquid nutrients that allow them to divide and multiply. This science explores the possibility of replacing or repairing human body parts. How is the term *engineering* as used in this process applied?

By the use of

(1) science and mathematics to produce a material
(2) biology, medicine, and engineering to produce a material
(3) mathematics and engineering to produce a material
(4) history, mathematics, and biology to produce a material
(5) chemistry, mathematics, and engineering to produce a material

Question 20 is based on the following passage.

Quasars are recent additions to our body of knowledge about the physical universe. *Quasars* (quasi-stellar objects) are astronomical objects that are starlike in appearance and emit nonthermal radiation, usually more ultraviolet and infrared radiation than stars.

Quasars were first discovered in the early 1960s when telescopes picked up mysterious radio-wave emission sources that, at the time, could not be explained. Since then, thousands of radio-emitting and radio-quiet quasars have been located.

One interesting feature of quasars is that their energy output can change by great amounts in a short period of time. To date, scientists have not been able to account for these energy changes.

20. What belief does the information in the passage support?

(1) We really know nothing about our physical universe.

(2) Scientists hold the key to all knowledge about outer space.

(3) Scientists are baffled by new discoveries in outer space.

(4) We often make significant discoveries by accident.

(5) We will someday know everything about our physical universe.

Question 21 is based on the following passage.

Chemists have determined that elements with atomic numbers greater than 92 are all radioactive. In general, their half-lives are much shorter than the age of the universe. This means that they no longer exist in nature and have all been artificially produced by scientists in nuclear reactions.

Elements 93 through 105 in the periodic table have been created and named, and scientists have claimed discovery of elements 106 and 107. The *transuranium elements*, as they are called, become less stable as the atomic number and mass increase. For example, element number 93, neptunium, has a half-life of two million years, while element number 104, kurchatovium, has a half-life of seventy seconds.

21. Based on the information in the passage, which of the following relationships appears to be true for elements 93 through 105?

(1) The greater the atomic number, the higher the half-life.

(2) The greater the atomic number, the lower the half-life.

(3) The greater the radioactivity, the greater the half-life.

(4) The greater the half-life, the greater the radioactivity.

(5) The greater the atomic number, the greater the element stability.

Question 22 is based on the following graph.

Water Use in the United States

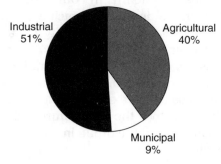

Industrial 51%

Agricultural 40%

Municipal 9%

Source: *Chemcon: Chemistry in the Community*

22. Ninety-seven percent of the world's water supply is difficult, if not impossible, to obtain or to use because it is in the oceans or in the form of glaciers and ice caps. Scientists are exploring methods of conserving and protecting the rest of Earth's water supply for the growing population. According to the information provided, which of the following activities most directly affects the water supply?

   (1) drinking and cooking
   (2) irrigating field crops
   (3) flushing toilets and bathing
   (4) growing all types of food
   (5) producing energy and manufacturing

Question 23 is based on the following definitions.

Plants can *propagate*, or reproduce themselves, by one of five different methods. Listed and described below are five parts of plants out of which new plants are known to grow.

bud—a protuberance of a plant that can be cut off and planted, resulting in a new plant

runner—a horizontal plant offshoot that runs above or below ground and that can develop root systems to start new plants

bulb—an underground fleshy bud that multiplies and whose leaves store food; bulbs can be separated to grow a new plant

seed—a grain or ripened ovule of a mature plant that, when planted in moist soil, sprouts a new plant

stem cutting—a section of a plant that, when placed in a moist environment, develops roots and grows into a new plant

23. New peonies, perennial plants that produce showy flowers, can be propagated from the parent plant by dividing corms that grow underground. This reproductive form described most closely resembles which of the following?

   (1) bud
   (2) runner
   (3) bulb
   (4) seed
   (5) stem cutting

Question 24 is based on the following passage.

Insectivorous (insect-eating) plants are among the most fascinating members of the plant kingdom. They combine the characteristics of a plant with those of an animal. These plants have highly specialized leaves that capture and digest insects. The proteins of the digested insect supply the plant with nitrogen, which is usually unavailable in the poor soils in which these plants grow.

The Venus's-flytrap of North and South Carolina is an example of an insectivorous plant. The leaves of this plant are hinged along the middle and swing upward and inward. An insect landing on the leaf triggers a sensitive motor mechanism that closes the leaf blades. The captured insect is then slowly digested by enzymes secreted by cells in the leaves.

24. According to the passage, what is the probable effect of growing insectivorous plants in richer soils?

(1) Plants grow to a much larger size.
(2) Plants are unable to take larger insects.
(3) Plants are able to obtain nitrogen from sources other than insects.
(4) Plants bloom in more frequent cycles.
(5) Plants grow with deeper roots.

Question 25 is based on the following passage.

Cancer is one of the leading causes of death in our society. Cancer is a disease in which a cell in the body loses its sensitivity to factors which regulate cell growth and division. The cell begins to multiply without restriction, creating a growing mass called a tumor, which interferes with the structure and functioning of the organ in which it is located.

Frequently, cancer cells become metastatic, meaning that they travel, settling in a number of places and giving rise to secondary tumors. Much of medical research is devoted to finding ways of preventing, controlling, and curing cancer.

25. Because of the metastatic trait of cancer cells, how can we judge a cancer treatment to be effective?

(1) if the entire body has been proven free of tumors over a period of time
(2) if the highest possible levels of treatment have been used
(3) if the original-source tumor has been identified
(4) if no new cancer cells are found in two weeks
(5) if the complete tumor is removed

LANGUAGE ARTS, READING
<u>POSTTEST</u>

Directions: The Language Arts, Reading Posttest will give you the opportunity to evaluate your readiness for the actual GED Language Arts, Reading Test. This test contains 20 questions based on excerpts from fiction (novels and short stories), poetry, drama, and nonfiction prose. You should take approximately 33 minutes to complete this test.

When you have finished the test, check your answers using pages 559 and 560. Use the Evaluation Chart on page 560 to determine whether or not you are ready to take the GED Language Arts, Reading Test and, if not, in what areas you need more work.

LANGUAGE ARTS, READING POSTTEST ANSWER GRID

1 ① ② ③ ④ ⑤   11 ① ② ③ ④ ⑤

2 ① ② ③ ④ ⑤   12 ① ② ③ ④ ⑤

3 ① ② ③ ④ ⑤   13 ① ② ③ ④ ⑤

4 ① ② ③ ④ ⑤   14 ① ② ③ ④ ⑤

5 ① ② ③ ④ ⑤   15 ① ② ③ ④ ⑤

6 ① ② ③ ④ ⑤   16 ① ② ③ ④ ⑤

7 ① ② ③ ④ ⑤   17 ① ② ③ ④ ⑤

8 ① ② ③ ④ ⑤   18 ① ② ③ ④ ⑤

9 ① ② ③ ④ ⑤   19 ① ② ③ ④ ⑤

10 ① ② ③ ④ ⑤   20 ① ② ③ ④ ⑤

Questions 1–3 are based on the following poem.

WHAT DOES THE SPEAKER WISH?

My Heart Leaps Up

1 My heart leaps up when I behold
      A rainbow in the sky;
So was it when my life began;
So is it now I am a man;
5   So be it when I shall grow old,
      Or let me die!
The Child is father of the Man;
And I could wish my days to be
Bound each to each by natural piety.

    —by William Wordsworth

1. Which would be the most effective substitution for "rainbow" in the poem?

  (1) star
  (2) skyscraper
  (3) pyramid
  (4) celebrity
  (5) statue

2. What idea is suggested by the line "The Child is father of the Man" (line 7)?

  (1) Children often control their parents.
  (2) Unnatural results come from disorder.
  (3) Fathers must be responsive to children.
  (4) Experiences in childhood shape adults.
  (5) Youth sometimes knows much wisdom.

3. The overall purpose of the poem is to direct attention to which of the following?

  (1) the wonders of nature
  (2) the life span of man
  (3) the changes from pollution
  (4) the passing of childhood
  (5) the past to the future

Questions 4–6 are based on the following play excerpt.

IS MORTIMER A ROMANTIC MAN?

Act One

MORTIMER See that statute* there. That's a horundinida carnina.

MARTHA Oh, no, dear—that's
5 Emma B. Stout ascending to heaven.

MORTIMER No, no,—standing on Mrs. Stout's left ear. That bird—that's a red-crested swal-
10 low. I've only seen one of those before in my life.

ABBY (*crosses around above table and pushes chair R. into table*). I don't know how you can
15 be thinking about a bird now— what with Elaine and the engagement and everything.

MORTIMER It's a vanishing species. (*He turns away from
20 window.*) Thoreau was very fond of them. (*As he crosses to desk to look through various drawers and papers.*) By the way, I left a large envelope around here last
25 week. It was one of the chapters of my book on Thoreau. Have you seen it?

MARTHA (*pushing armchair into table*). Well, if you left it here
30 it must be here somewhere.

ABBY (*crossing to D. L. of MORTIMER*). When are you going to be married? What are your plans? There must be something
35 more you can tell us about Elaine.

MORTIMER Elaine? Oh, yes, Elaine thought it was brilliant.

40 (*He crosses to sideboard, looks through cupboards and drawers.*)

MARTHA What was, dear?

MORTIMER My chapter on Thoreau. (*He finds a bundle of papers [script] in R. drawer and*
45 *takes them to table and looks through them.*)

ABBY (*at C.*). Well, when Elaine comes back I think we ought to have a little celebration.
50 We must drink to your happiness. Martha, isn't there some of that Lady Baltimore cake left?

(*During last few speeches MARTHA has picked up pail from*
55 *sideboard and her cape, hat and gloves from table in U. L. corner.*)

MARTHA (*crossing D. L.*). Oh, yes!

ABBY And I'll open a bottle of
60 wine.

MARTHA (*as she exits to kitchen*). Oh, and to think it happened in this room!

MORTIMER (*has finished*
65 *looking through papers, is gazing around room*). Now where could I have put that?

ABBY Well, with your fiancée sitting beside you tonight, I do
70 hope that play will be something you can enjoy for once. It may be something romantic. What's the name of it?

MORTIMER "Murder Will Out."

75 ABBY Oh dear! (*She disappears into kitchen as MORTIMER goes on talking.*)

*Mortimer means *statue*

—Excerpted from *Arsenic and Old Lace*
by Joseph Kesselring

4. What is Martha referring to when she says, "Oh, and to think it happened in this room!"(lines 62–63)?
   (1) the proposal of marriage
   (2) the sighting of a statue
   (3) a plan for a celebration
   (4) the writing of a book
   (5) a speech of Thoreau's

5. Which of the following best describes Abby's feeling about Mortimer's marriage?
   (1) uncomfortable
   (2) embarrassed
   (3) excited
   (4) amused
   (5) fearful

6. Which of the following words best describes the overall tone of this passage?
   (1) thoughtful
   (2) angry
   (3) determined
   (4) bored
   (5) light-hearted

Questions 7–10 are based on the following passage.

WHAT POSITIVE CHARACTERISTICS AND LIMITATIONS DID THE AUTHOR GIVE TO CHANCE?

Chance walked though the rooms, which seemed empty; the heavily curtained windows barely admitted the daylight. Slowly he looked at the large pieces of furniture shrouded in old linen covers, and at the veiled mirrors. The words that the Old Man had spoken to him the first time had wormed their way into his memory like firm roots. Chance was an orphan, and it was the Old Man himself who had sheltered him in the house ever since Chance was a child. Chance's mother had died when he was born. No one, not even the Old Man, would tell him who his father was. While some could learn to read and write, Chance would never be able to manage this. Nor would he ever be able to understand much of what others were saying to him or around him. Chance was to work in the garden, where he would care for plants and grasses and trees which grew there peacefully. He would be as one of them: quiet, openhearted in the sunshine and heavy when it rained. His name was Chance because he had been born by chance. He had no family.

Although his mother had been very pretty, her mind had been as damaged as his; the soft soil of his brain, the ground from which all his thoughts shot up, had been ruined forever. Therefore, he could not look for a place in the life led by people outside the house or the garden gate. Chance must limit his life to his quarters and to the garden; he must not enter other parts of the household or walk out into the street. His food would always be brought to his room by Louise, who would be the only person to see Chance and talk to him. No one else was allowed to enter Chance's room. Only the Old Man himself might walk and sit in the garden. Chance would do exactly what he was told or else he would be sent to a special home for the insane where, the Old Man said, he would be locked in a cell and forgotten.

Chance did what he was told. So did black Louise.

—Excerpted from *Being There* by Jerzy Kosinski

7. Which of the following paragraph details does not support the conclusion that Chance is very limited in his abilities?

   (1) While some could learn to read and write, Chance would never be able to manage this.
   (2) Nor would he ever be able to understand much of what others were saying . . . around him.
   (3) Chance was to work in the garden, where he would care for plants and grasses and trees. . .
   (4) . . . her mind had been as damaged as his; the soft soil of his brain. . . had been ruined forever.
   (5) . . . he must not enter other parts of the household or walk out into the street.

8. From details in the passage, what type of person may Chance be compared to?

(1) an insane adult
(2) an unhappy teenager
(3) a controlling master
(4) an ungrateful son
(5) an obedient child

9. What is the overall purpose of the passage from this novel?

(1) compare and contrast the characters of the Old Man and Chance
(2) provide a background description of Chance and his life
(3) explain the heredity (similar disabilities) of Chance's mother
(4) promote the health benefits of peaceful gardening
(5) point out the problems of raising orphans in one's home

10. Later in the novel the reader learns that the Old Man dies, that Chance packs his suitcase and leaves through the gate for the first time. Chance is struck by a limousine carrying the wife of a dying rich man. From then on, he comes to have power and influence. From what the reader knows already about Chance, what is the reader's probable reaction to the change in Chance's lifestyle and stature?

(1) jealousy
(2) hostility
(3) amusement
(4) surprise
(5) indifference

Questions 11–15 are based on the following passage.

HOW DOES IT FEEL FOR THE NARRATOR (AND OTHERS) OUTSIDE HER MOTHER'S INNER CIRCLE?

Passage One

Mama and the Ya-Yas were always using different plays on my mother's name. If Teensy walked into a party that lacked pizzazz, she might announce, "This party needs to be Vivi-fied." Sometimes they declared things to be "Re-Vivi-fication projects," like the time Mama and Necie redesigned the uniforms of my Girl Scout troop.

When I was young, I thought my mother was so internationally well known that the English language had invented words just for her. As a child, I would turn to the skinny "V" section of Webster's and study the many words that referred to Mama. There was "vivid," which meant "full of life; bright; intense." And "vivify," which meant "to give life or to make more lively." There were "vivace," "viva," "vivacious," "vivacity," "vivarium," and "viva voce." Mama was the source of all these words. She was also the reason for the phrase "Vive le roi" (which she told us meant "Long live Vivi the Queen!"). All these definitions had to do with life, like Mama herself.

Passage Two

It was not until I was in second or third grade that my friend M'lain Chauvin told me that Mama had nothing to do with those words in the dictionary. We got into a fight about it and Sister Henry Ruth intervened. When the nun confirmed M'lain's claim, I was heartbroken at first. It changed my whole perception of reality. It began the unraveling of unquestioned belief that the world revolved around Mama. But along with my disappointment came a profound relief, although I could not admit it at the time.

I thought my mother was a star for so many years that when I found out she wasn't, I was stupefied. Had she once been a star and her bright burning had dimmed? Maybe because she had us? Or had Mama never been a star to begin with? Somewhere guilt developed whenever I seemed to eclipse Mama in any little way. Even winning a spelling bee made me worry, because I never trusted that I could shine without obliterating her.

I did not understand then that my mother lived in a world that could nor or would not acknowledge her radiance, her pull on the earth—at least not as much as she needed. So she made up her own solar system with the other Ya-Yas and lived in its orbit as fully as she could.

My father was not included in this orbit, not really. All the Ya-Ya husbands existed in a separate universe from the Ya-Yas and us kids.

—Excerpted from *Divine Secrets of the Ya-Ya Sisterhood* by Rebecca Wells

11. Which of the following is *not* evidence of Mama's persona (appearance or role) as a "star"?

(1) The English language had invented words just for her.

(2) She was the reason for the phrase, "Long live Vivi the Queen!"

(3) Sometimes they declared things to be "Re-Vivi-fication projects."

(4) It began the unraveling of the unquestioned belief that the world revolved around Mama.

(5) So she made up her own solar system with the other Ya-Yas.

12. If the details about Mama in this passage were in a science book, in what section would you most likely find them?

(1) atomic structure (chemistry)

(2) genetics and heredity (biology)

(3) reflection and refraction (physics)

(4) geologic time (geology)

(5) stars and solar systems (astronomy)

13. The author uses details to describe the narrator's actions and feelings when she was in the second or third grade. What effect does this have on the reader?

(1) to establish sympathy for the narrator

(2) to create greater admiration for Mama

(3) to enhance the importance of the narrator's father

(4) to develop understanding for Sister Henry Ruth

(5) to explain rivalry between "Aunts" Teensy and Necie

14. From which point of view is the story told?

(1) the Ya-Ya member, Necie

(2) the husband of a Ya-Ya

(3) the daughter of a Ya-Ya

(4) Vivi, one of the Ya-Yas

(5) M'lain Chauvin, a friend

15. What is the overall purpose of the passages from this novel?

(1) to give an English language lesson on "V" words

(2) to explore a daughter's feelings about her mother

(3) to explain how a human "star" can rise and fall

(4) to compare and contrast personalities of the Ya-Yas

(5) to examine the relationship between the narrator's parents

Questions 16–20 are based on the following article.

WHAT HAS MADE UP THE ESSENTIAL ELEMENTS OF FILM COMEDY IN THE PAST?

Passage One

There are no lasting formulas to comedy, but I've found a few theories over the years. Comedy is like bass fishing. Everyone is an expert, the fish is smarter than all of them, and the flashiest, shiniest lures never work. Always, the audience will make its own discoveries. The mere whiff of someone working overtime, straining for a laugh, is the biggest laugh killer of all.

With a tip of the hat to manic geniuses like the Marx Brothers and Jim Carrey, who manage to make their intricate and bizarre humor look spontaneous, the great moments of comedy tend to be stolen moments. The joke you never expected. Director Ernst Lubitsch was an early master of this, building elegantly hilarious jokes, one on top of the other, until his audience was charmed and satisfied. In "Ninotchka" (1939), a sterling example of the "Lubitsch touch," watch what comedic mileage he gets out of a hat. Greta Garbo portrays an unbending Russian envoy who has come to Paris to supervise the sale of some jewels for the benefit of the socialist republic. Upon arriving at her needlessly upscale hotel, she is already in a bad mood. She sees a window display featuring a flamboyant [elaborate] hat. The chapeau strikes her as a frivolous display of capitalism, and she comments darkly to her Bolshevik [communist] accomplices: "How can such a civilization survive which permits their women to put such things on their heads? It won't be long now, comrades."

Passage Two

Today Lubitsch would do it not unlike modern film-comedy masters like James L. Brooks, Mike Nichols, or Woody Allen. If only for the sparkling exchanges of dialogue that mark their work, each of them has long been in the big-screen comedy hall of fame. But the timeless images of their films often come not in the banter but in the devastating dialogue-free moments like Jane Craig's (Holly Hunter) daily cathartic [tension releasing] cry in "Broadcast News."

—Excerpted from "Leave 'em Laughing,"
Newsweek Extra, Summer 1998

16. The author of the article states that "the great moments of comedy tend to be stolen moments." What is he saying about the best of comedy?

It is

(1) mysterious
(2) enjoyable
(3) hilarious
(4) touching
(5) unexpected

17. How would early master director Ernst Lubitsch direct a modern film-comedy?

He would probably

(1) mix comedy and tragedy for a new type of comedy
(2) follow the comedic pattern of current master directors
(3) include a great deal of dialogue among characters
(4) focus on a great deal of slapstick (physical comedy)
(5) use a great deal of outrageous costumes and props

18. Which of the following comparisons is not made when the author discusses theories of comedy?

(1) the expert bass fisherman, fish, and lures and comedy

(2) Ernst Lubitsch's and modern comedy directors' techniques

(3) sparkling dialogue and hall of fame quality of comedy

(4) great moments of comedy and spontaneous humor

(5) the Marx Brothers' and Mike Nichols's types of comedy

19. What is the effect of the author's use of the supporting detail in the example in which Greta Garbo goes to Paris to sell jewels for the socialist republic and focuses on a flamboyant hat?

(1) The hat becomes a symbol of socialism in Russia.

(2) The hat creates great sympathy for the theme of capitalism.

(3) The hat reveals a very dark side of the Russian envoy's character.

(4) The hat allows for the building of one joke on top of another.

(5) The hat explains the film narrator's third-person point of view.

20. Later in the *Newsweek* article on comedy, the author writes, "In the quest for fast-moving global entertainment, these days studios often trim these quiet moments. Move things along! The audience is ahead of you!" In light of the previous passages quoted, what is the probable result?

(1) displeasure by the audience in not wanting to move too quickly

(2) great film success as measured by box office receipts

(3) savings to the studios in making shorter films that cost less

(4) recognized genius by those who write critical film reviews

(5) improvement of acting techniques of comedic film stars

MATHEMATICS POSTTEST

Directions: This Posttest will give you the opportunity to evaluate your readiness for the actual GED Mathematics Test. The Mathematics Posttest, which is half the length of the GED Test, consists of two parts: Part I (calculator allowed) has 12 questions, and Part II (no calculator allowed) has 13 questions. Part I and Part II have a combined score of 25 points. Each part should take approximately 22–23 minutes, for a total test time of 45 minutes. Remember to use the calculator only during Part I. You may use the formula page (located on page 456) throughout both Parts I and II.

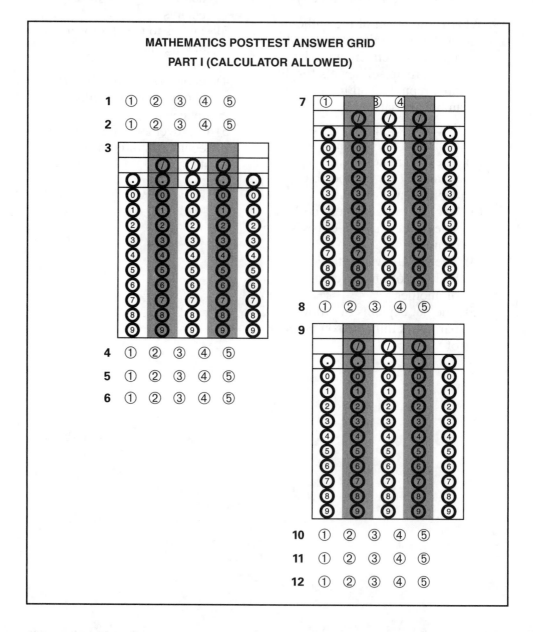

Part I

Directions: Solve each problem. You may use your calculator and formula page 456 as needed.

Questions 1–2 refer to the following information.

To help decide how much to charge for its services, Custom Computers management compiled the following employee data.

Number of Employees	Weekly Wages Each Employee Earned
19	$360
18	$400
8	$480
5	$600

1. Which expression below represents the average wages the company pays per employee each week?
   (1) $\dfrac{360 + 400 + 480 + 600}{4}$

   (2) $\dfrac{19(360) + 18(400) + 8(480) + 5(600)}{19 + 18 + 8 + 5}$

   (3) $\dfrac{19(360) \times 18(400) \times 8(480) \times 5(600)}{19 + 18 + 8 + 5}$

   (4) $(19 + 18 + 8 + 5)(360 + 400 + 480 + 600)$

   (5) $4(360 + 400 + 480 + 600)$

2. If Custom Computers gives a 4% raise to all employees, how much will this add to the weekly payroll?
   (1) $ 83.52
   (2) $ 835.20
   (3) $ 8,352
   (4) $ 20,880
   (5) $ 21,715.20

3. Ahmed borrowed $450 from his credit union to buy a copier. If the interest rate is 9.9% and he takes the loan for a year, what will be his monthly payment to the nearest penny to repay the loan plus interest?

Mark your answer in the circles in the grid on your answer sheet.

Question 4 refers to the following information.

Juan worked as a waiter on Saturday nights to supplement his income. He kept a list of the tips he received for 8 weeks and the number of hours he worked each Saturday night.

Week	Tips	Hours
1	$98	6
2	$75.25	6
3	$84	5
4	$92	6
5	$60	4
6	$86.50	6
7	$90.60	6
8	$77	5

4. What was the median amount of Juan's weekly tips?
   (1) $ 60
   (2) $ 85.25
   (3) $ 92
   (4) $ 84
   (5) $663

5. Temperatures in degrees Celsius (C) may be changed to degrees Fahrenheit (F) by using the formula $F = 1.8C + 32°$. Find the temperature in degrees Fahrenheit when C equals 25°.
   (1)   45°
   (2)   57°
   (3)   58.8°
   (4)   77°
   (5)   102.6°

6. The weekly investment report shows each company's stocks with its high bid, low bid, closing bid prices, and the net change from last week's closing bid. What is the average net change for all five companies listed?

Company			
High	**Low**	**Close**	**Change**
U.S. Investments			
23.16	22.91	23.61	+.38
Global Growth			
15.13	14.77	15.13	+.14
Select Services			
22.01	21.94	21.97	−.09
United Funds			
14.56	14.29	14.56	+.09
American Mutual			
17.36	16.94	17.26	+.08

(1) .02
(2) .06
(3) .6
(4) .12
(5) 1.2

7. If 27 out of 30 people passed a driving test, what percent failed?

Mark your answer in the circles in the grid on your answer sheet.

Question 8 refers to the following information.

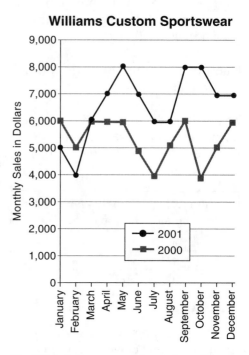

Williams Custom Sportswear

8. Which statement best describes the graph?

(1) Average sales were higher in 2001.
(2) Average monthly sales were about the same in both years.
(3) Average monthly sales doubled in 2001.
(4) Average sales were higher in 2000.
(5) Sales were always higher in the summer than in the rest of the year.

9. Find the height of the 32-inch TV screen shown below. Round your answer to the nearest tenth of an inch.

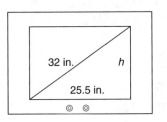

Mark your answer in the circles in the grid on your answer sheet.

10. If the cube and rectangular box have the same volume, which equation can you use to find the height (h) of the box?

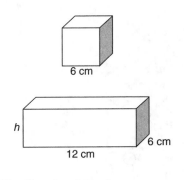

(1) $6^3 = 6 \times 12 \times h$
(2) $6^2 = 6 \times 12 \times h$
(3) $6^3 = 6 + 12 + h$
(4) $6 = (6 + 12)h$
(5) $h = 6 \times 6 \times 12$

11. Find the difference between the volume of the cylinder and the volume of the rectangular box below. Use $\frac{22}{7}$ for π.

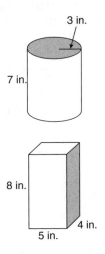

(1)   28 cu in.
(2)   38 cu in.
(3)   94 cu in.
(4) 160 cu in.
(5) 198 cu in.

12. If a ream of paper (500 sheets) is 2.125 inches thick, how thick is one sheet of paper? Give your answer in scientific notation.

(1) 1.0625×10^3
(2) 42.5×10^3
(3) 4.25×10^3
(4) 4.25×10^{-3}
(5) 4.25×10^{-2}

Directions: You may *not* use a calculator while taking Part II of the test, but you may use the formulas on page 456.

When you have finished the test, check your answers using pages 561 and 562. Use the Evaluation Chart on page 562 to determine whether or not you are ready to take the actual GED Test and, if not, in what areas you need more work.

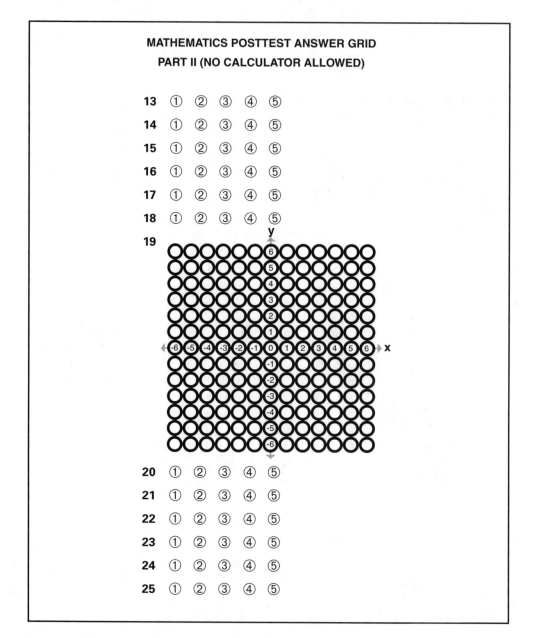

MATHEMATICS POSTTEST ANSWER GRID

PART II (NO CALCULATOR ALLOWED)

13 ① ② ③ ④ ⑤
14 ① ② ③ ④ ⑤
15 ① ② ③ ④ ⑤
16 ① ② ③ ④ ⑤
17 ① ② ③ ④ ⑤
18 ① ② ③ ④ ⑤
19

20 ① ② ③ ④ ⑤
21 ① ② ③ ④ ⑤
22 ① ② ③ ④ ⑤
23 ① ② ③ ④ ⑤
24 ① ② ③ ④ ⑤
25 ① ② ③ ④ ⑤

Part II

Directions: Solve each problem. Do *not* use a calculator. Use formula page 456 as needed.

13. Arrange the following numbers in order from the *smallest* value to the *greatest:*
1^5, 2^3, 4^1, and 6

(1) 6, 4^1, 1^5, 2^3
(2) 1^5, 4^1, 6, 2^3
(3) 1^5, 2^3, 4^1, 6
(4) 6, 4^1, 2^3, 1^5
(5) 2^3, 4^1, 6, 1^5

14. Many calculators express very large or very small numbers in scientific notation. If the number 4.32×10^4 appears in the display of a calculator, what is the value of this number?

(1) .0432
(2) 4.0032
(3) 432
(4) 43,200
(5) 4,320,000

Question 15 refers to the following information.

An adult education class of 30 students had the following characteristics.

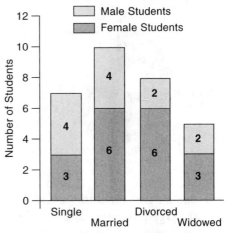

Adult Student Marital Status

15. What is the probability that a student selected at random from this class is married?

(1) $\frac{1}{3}$

(2) $\frac{1}{5}$

(3) $\frac{2}{3}$

(4) $\frac{2}{15}$

(5) $\frac{1}{2}$

16. The force of gravity is 6 times greater on the earth than it is on the moon. What is the weight of a 150-pound man on the moon?

(1) 25 pounds
(2) 144 pounds
(3) 156 pounds
(4) 900 pounds
(5) Not enough information is given.

Question 17 refers to the following information.

In 2001 the Barnes family total income was $45,000. This circle graph describes how the Barnes family distributed their income to cover their expenses and savings.

19. In the figure below find the coordinates of the midpoint of the line segment.

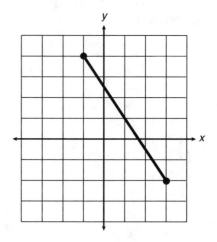

Mark your answer on the coordinate plane grid on your answer sheet.

17. Housing costs include home mortgage payments and utilities. How much were the housing costs in 2001 for the Barnes family?

(1) $ 1,551
(2) $ 4,050
(3) $ 9,000
(4) $13,050
(5) $15,517

18. In the expression $x + 2 > 13$, which of the following could be the value of x?

(1) 2
(2) 9
(3) 11
(4) 13
(5) Not enough information is given.

20. Jane got a good deal on her new coat. She bought her coat on sale as shown and then used her coupon to further reduce the price. Which expression below shows how much she paid for the coat originally selling for $126?

(1) (.75)(.90)(126)
(2) (.25)(.10)(126)
(3) .25(126) − .10(126)
(4) 126 − .25(.10)
(5) 126 − .25(126) − .10(126)

21. Find the measure of ∠*x* in the triangle below.

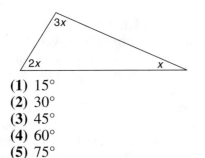

- **(1)** 15°
- **(2)** 30°
- **(3)** 45°
- **(4)** 60°
- **(5)** 75°

22. Which expression below represents the cost of one roll of paper towels if the price is 3 rolls for $*t* and you get a 75¢ rebate?

- **(1)** $\frac{t}{3} - .75$
- **(2)** $3t + .75$
- **(3)** $3t - .75$
- **(4)** $\frac{t}{3} + .75$
- **(5)** $\frac{t - .75}{3}$

23. How many square inches larger is the area of Δ*ABC* than Δ*CDE* shown in the figure?

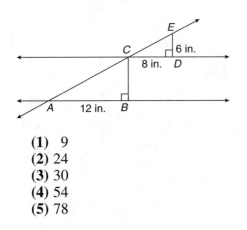

- **(1)** 9
- **(2)** 24
- **(3)** 30
- **(4)** 54
- **(5)** 78

24. Which statement best describes the relationship between lines *M* and *N*?

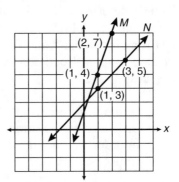

- **(1)** Line *M* and line *N* both have positive slopes.
- **(2)** Line *M* and line *N* both have negative slopes.
- **(3)** Line *M* has a positive slope, and line *N* has a negative slope.
- **(4)** Line *M* has a negative slope, and line *N* has a positive slope.
- **(5)** There is not enough information to calculate the slopes of line *N* and line *M*.

25. What is the area of the parallelogram shown in the diagram?

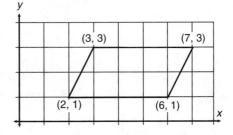

- **(1)** 8 sq units
- **(2)** 12 sq units
- **(3)** 18 sq units
- **(4)** 42 sq units
- **(5)** Not enough information is given.

GED READINESS CHART

To help determine if you are ready for the actual GED Test, use the conversion charts below. Count the number of correct answers on your Posttest for each subject and find that number in the left-hand column for the appropriate subject. Read across to find the GED standard score in the right-hand column.

The minimum score requirement for each test is 410. The average score requirement for all five tests is 450. Standard scores that are at or below the minimum indicate that more study is needed before taking the GED Test. However, in order to meet the average score on the GED Test, several of the test scores must be higher than 450.

SOCIAL STUDIES		SCIENCE		LA, READING		MATHEMATICS	
Correct Answers	Standard Score	Correct Answers	Standard Score	Correct Answers	Standard Score	Correct Answers	Standard Score
25	800	25	800	20	800	25	800
24	710	24	700	19	670	24	720
23	640	23	630	18	580	23	640
22	590	22	600	17	520	22	590
21	560	21	530	16	490	21	550
20	540	20	500	15	460	20	520
19	520	19	480	14	450	19	500
18	500	18	460	13	430	18	490
17	490	17	450	12	420	17	470
16	470	16	440	11	410	16	460
15	460	15	430	10	390	15	450
14	450	14	420	9	380	14	440
13	430	13	410	8	370	13	430
12	420	12	400	7	350	12	420
11	410	11	390	6	330	11	410
10	390	10	380			10	400
9	380	9	370			9	390
8	360	8	360			8	380
7	340					7	360

For the most recent statistical information regarding the conversion charts and their accuracy, visit our website at www.mhcontemporary.com.

To determine the Language Arts, Writing standard score, use the conversion chart below. Count the number of correct answers on the Posttest for Part I and find that number in the left-hand column. Then find the averaged essay score across the top of the chart. Read across and down to find the combined GED standard score. Remember that you must score 2 or above on the essay to pass the Language Arts, Writing Test.

LANGUAGE ARTS, WRITING					
Correct	Averaged Essay Score				
Answers	2	2.5	3	3.5	4
25	630	670	710	750	800
24	560	600	630	670	720
23	510	540	580	620	670
22	480	520	550	600	640
21	470	500	540	580	630
20	460	490	530	560	620
19	450	480	520	550	610
18	440	470	510	540	600
17	430	460	500	530	590
16	420	450	490	530	580
15	410	440	480	520	570
14	400	440	470	510	570
13	390	430	470	500	560
12	380	430	460	500	560
11	370	420	460	490	550
10		420	450	490	550
9		410	450	480	540
8		410	440	480	530
7		400	440	470	520
6		390	430	460	520
5		380	420	450	510
4		370	410	440	500
3			380	410	470
2			340	380	410
1			300	340	390

For the most recent statistical information regarding the conversion charts and their accuracy, visit our website at www.mhcontemporary.com.

ANSWER KEY
PRETEST:
LANGUAGE ARTS, WRITING

PART I: EDITING

1. **(5)** Sentence 7 is a fragment that should be attached to sentence 6.

2. **(2)** The sentence is improved by omitting unnecessary words: *One disadvantage to these batteries is that they require frequent recharging.*

3. **(4)** Paragraphs C and D should be combined into one paragraph because both explain the three kinds of primary-cell batteries.

4. **(5)** The paragraph needs a topic sentence to provide a focus.

5. **(4)** *Smoke alarms* are one kind of gadget, not two separate items. The comma should not separate *smoke* from *alarms*.

6. **(4)** The sentence is irrelevant and does not belong in the paragraph.

7. **(2)** In the original sentence, the modifier is misplaced so that *you* rather than *a form* appears attached to this memo.

8. **(5)** The pronoun *them* should be changed to *it* to agree in number with the noun *form*.

9. **(4)** Improve the original sentence by reducing wordiness: *You may elect to change to direct deposit at any time in the next six months.*

10. **(4)** Two independent sentences cannot be joined with only a comma.

11. **(5)** The sentence needs a parallel construction so that *a fire has started* matches *the smoke alarm sounds*.

12. **(1)** A new idea about fire extinguishers is begun with sentence 10, so a new paragraph should be started.

13. **(4)** The verb *serve* must agree with the subject *smoke alarms and fire extinguishers*, and the verb must appear in the present tense to fit the meaning of the passage.

Use the answer key above to check your answers to the Pretest. Then find the item number of each question you missed and circle it on the chart below to determine the writing content areas in which you need more practice.

Language Arts, Writing Pretest Evaluation Chart

Content Area	Item #	Review Chapter
Subject/Verb Agreement	13	1
Pronoun Use	8	1
Sentence Fragments	1	2
Run-ons, Comma Splices, Sentence Combining	10	2
Independent/Dependent Clauses, Effective Sentence Structure	2, 9	2
Dangling or Misplaced Modification	7	2
Parallel Structure	11	2
Capitalization, Punctuation	5	3
Paragraph Composition	4	4
Text Division	3, 12	4
Paragraph Unity and Coherence	6	4

Part II: The Essay

If possible, give your essay to an instructor to evaluate. If, however, you are unable to show your work to someone else, use the five questions in the Essay Evaluation Checklist to help evaluate your writing. The more questions you can answer with a strong yes, the better your chances are for achieving a passing or high score.

Essay Evaluation Checklist

Yes	No	
		1. Does the essay answer the question asked?
		2. Does the main point of the essay stand out clearly?
		3. Does each paragraph contain specific examples and details that develop and explain the main point?
		4. Are the ideas organized clearly into paragraphs and complete sentences?
		5. Is the essay easy to read, or do problems in grammar, usage, punctuation, spelling, or word choice interfere?

Important Note

On the actual GED Language Arts, Writing Test, you will be given one score, which is a composite of your scores from Part I and Part II of the test. This score is determined by grading your essay holistically, giving it a score, and then combining this score with your score from Part I in a proportion determined by the GED Testing Service.

ANSWER KEY
PRETEST:
SOCIAL STUDIES

1. **Comprehension (2)** Not all Americans supported the Civil Rights Act. The Civil Rights Act was to protect the rights of any minority group. Congress drafted the Civil Rights Act which was passed in both the House and the Senate but was not a unanimous decision.

2. **Evaluation (4)** The phrase from Dr. King's speech, "I Have a Dream . . ." told the listeners that even though the Emancipation Proclamation had been in effect for a long time, in practice it was still a dream, not a reality. The Constitution and the Declaration of Independence did not directly address the issue of slavery and equality of minority groups.

3. **Analysis (3)** The United States government owns 79.8% of all the land in Nevada. Much of this land is used for military testing. This testing could include target bombing by the Air Force as well as bomb detonation, including underground nuclear weapons testing.

4. **Comprehension (2)** The circle graphs give information about federally owned acreage in only three states. No information is given about the population of any states. No information is specific to the use of the land in any of these states.

5. **Analysis (5)** Although there is no educational requirement to earn larger incomes, studies show that those with a college education have a greater likelihood of earning a higher salary. Many companies will financially assist their workforce in gaining higher education degrees.

6. **Evaluation (3)** High school counselors often cite the statistics concerning career success and the earning of a high school diploma. Often, those that did not finish high school seek the diploma through local school districts, community colleges, adult education centers, and other means.

7. **Evaluation (2)** George Washington states in his farewell address that the European nations have a different set of priorities and interests. He suggests it would be unwise to complicate our own priorities and get caught up with the ever-changing conflicts that arise in Europe.

8. **Application (4)** America has developed a sense of responsibility for other nations that are in a struggle with foreign powers. Often these struggles are over issues that Americans feel a moral need to support. These issues include democratic principles and human rights. This type of assistance is possible due in part to the large size (land and population) and power (financial and military) that the United States has achieved. Many times the foreign country in the struggle will ask for help from the United States.

9. **Analysis (3)** Although many women have voiced a concern that the choice of a career as a homemaker does not have the same level of respect as it did throughout history, studies show that most women in the workforce believe they are working for financial reasons. Career women have often mentioned that the selection of day care options and larger choices of career opportunities also increase the attraction in participating in the workforce outside the home.

10. **Analysis (1)** After World War II many young men returned to the United States as heroes. The government encouraged the return to civilian life by giving some financial incentives to get an education and a job. The large number of men also returned to domestic living in the United States got married and started families. This, in turn, had other effects on the growth of our country. Soon the expansion of suburban areas was needed to house the new families. Many families became more mobile in their attempt to increase job opportunities and advancement.

11. **Application (3)** While some people have had success in investing in the stock market, analysts always stress that a savings plan is the best way to ensure financial security. College degrees may allow someone to get a job that pays better than a job that does not require a degree. These higher paying jobs, however, do not necessarily ensure a saving plan. Those who

open their own businesses are at financial risk that the businesses may fail.

12. **Analysis (3)** The crash of the stock market has been blamed on financial panic. With so much of the nation's money held in investments, there was not enough money in the banks to hand to the people who wanted to withdraw their cash. This, in turn, caused many banks to fail. As Americans lost confidence in the economic strength of our nation, the stock market experienced record losses. This had a devastating effect throughout the world, casting many nations as well as the United States into a deep financial depression.

13. **Evaluation (4)** At the time of the crash of the stock market, many Americans were interested in making a lot of money in a short time through investments. If people had had a more conservative attitude, they might not have overextended the lending of money to make more profits for their banks.

Social Studies Pretest Evaluation Chart

Use the answer key above to check your answers to the Pretest. Then find the item number of each question you missed and circle it on the chart below to determine the Social Studies content areas in which you need more practice.

Skill Area/ Content Area	Comprehension	Application	Analysis	Evaluation
World History			12	13
U.S. History	1		10	2
Civics and Government		8	9	7
Economics		11	5	6
Geography	4		3	

ANSWER KEY
PRETEST:
SCIENCE

1. **Evaluation (3)** The author is expressing an opinion about second-hand smoke. The other choices do not address this concern about smoking.

2. **Application (3)** A common cause of a heart attack is a blood clot, which restricts the blood supply to the heart. According to the passage, an aspirin can thin the blood and reduce clotting.

3. **Analysis (4)** The table indicates that a person with blood type AB can act as a donor only to a person with blood type AB.

4. **Analysis (3)** Diluted hydrochloric acid is found in the stomach's gastric juices, but undiluted hydrochloric acid is harmful when humans are exposed to it.

5. **Evaluation (4)** There is no rain in the forecast for Florida. The other choices are not true based on the information provided.

6. **Application (4)** Kidney stones are the only condition that is not caused by a problem in cellular division.

7. **Comprehension (2)** The Appalachian Mountains are lower than the Rocky Mountains; therefore, the Appalachian Mountains are older.

8. **Analysis (2)** The predictions for dental protection will hopefully prevent cavities and gum disease; therefore, fewer painful procedures will be needed.

9. **Evaluation (2)** Sound waves must travel at a constant speed through the sea in order for the principle under which a Fathometer works to be valid.

10. **Comprehension (3)** The metals silver, copper, aluminum, and iron have the highest heat conduction coefficients; therefore, they are the best conductors among the materials listed.

11. **Application (4)** One of the goals of the International Space Station involves the study of Earth's environment, which would include atmospheric conditions. The other choices would not need to be studied in the station.

12. **Application (5)** The gravitational pull is not important in the study of the distance of stars according to the passage.

13. **Evaluation (2)** Professor Samuel Katz would probably include the positive results such as the elimination of smallpox and the reduction of other serious diseases.

Science Pretest Evaluation Chart

Use the answer key above to check your answers to the Pretest. Then find the item number of each question you missed and circle it on the chart below to determine the Science content areas in which you need more practice.

Skill Area/ Content Area	Comprehension	Application	Analysis	Evaluation
Life Sciences (Biology)		6	3, 8	1, 13
Earth and Space Science	7	11, 12	5	
Physical Sciences (Chemistry and Physics)	10	2	4	9

ANSWER KEY
PRETEST:
LANGUAGE ARTS, READING

1. **Application (3)** Theresa is very taken with the sentiments in the letter and compares the writer to David and others she had dated. There is no evidence that she plans any punitive action such as exposing the writer (choice 1), that Garrett copied someone else's work (choice 4), or that the paper is trying to hire him (choice 5). As a reporter she very briefly thinks of other possibilities such as making lonely women cry (choice 2).

2. **Analysis (1)** Approximately half the passage is dialogue between Deanna and Theresa, and the other half are Theresa's private thoughts revealed by the author. There is no evidence of fact and opinion (choice 2), formal hypotheses and conclusions (choice 3), or time order—chronology (choice 4). There is no mention of a narrator (choice 5).

3. **Synthesis (1)** Theresa muses at length about the man who wrote the letter, and she obviously wants to meet him. She doesn't really care to search for other bottles (choice 2). If she really wanted a scoop for her paper (choice 3), she wouldn't have to think so long about finding the man. David (choice 4) is only mentioned in passing in terms of his lack of writing ability, and she is not seriously deciding between working at her current job or working for Hallmark (choice 5).

4. **Analysis (1)** The speaker cannot instantly decide as evidenced by "long I stood," showing uncertainty about the decision.

5. **Comprehension (5)** To be telling something "with a sigh" indicates that the speaker feels regret.

6. **Synthesis (3)** In the poem, the two roads that confront the speaker represent a choice in life. The speaker must choose one way to go knowing that another interesting possibility exists. Nevertheless, the speaker in the line "I doubted if I should ever come back" acknowledges that the chance of returning is unlikely. The theme of the poem suggests that life offers possibilities but rarely second chances.

7. **Analysis (1)** Joan's relationship with the king's court is compared. She has shown up the court advisers by successfully helping the king attain power when the advisors were unable to do so. Her success does not make them fond of her.

8. **Synthesis (4)** For anyone to win enough power to crown a king is amazing. For a woman to do so through military means during the play's time setting is even more extraordinary.

9. **Comprehension (1)** The clues to oppression are the fact that "many Jewish friends are being taken away by the dozen," "being treated. . . without a shred of decency," "not nearly enough lavatories [bathrooms]," and "no separate accommodation." Choices 2, 3, and 4 are incorrect because they depict positive treatment. Choice 5 is less positive than the other three choices but still not harsh enough.

10. **Synthesis (5)** The items mentioned in choices 1, 2, 3, and 4 (boy friends, teachers, parents, and sweets and money) are not necessarily a sign of maturity or lack of maturity. Choice 5 shows a growth in maturity because the life she enjoyed in 1942 was "unreal" in comparison to the life she knew two years later in 1944. She says, "It was quite a different Anne who enjoyed that heavenly existence from the Anne who has grown wise within these walls."

Language Arts, Reading Pretest Evaluation Chart

Use the answer key on the previous page to check your answers to the Pretest. Then find the item number of each question you missed and circle it on the chart below to determine the reading content areas in which you need more practice.

Skill Area/ Content Area	Comprehension	Application	Analysis	Evaluation
Fiction		1	2	3
Poetry	5		4	6
Drama			7	8
Nonfiction	9		10	

ANSWER KEY
PRETEST:
MATHEMATICS

1. 1.93

$$1.43$$
$$+.5$$
$$\overline{1.93}$$

2. $3\frac{1}{6}$ yards

If she used $\frac{3}{4}$ of the material, then she has $\frac{1}{4}$ of it left. So

$$\frac{1}{4} \times 12\frac{2}{3} = \frac{1}{4} \times \frac{38}{3} = \frac{38}{12} = 3\frac{2}{12} = 3\frac{1}{6} \text{ yd}$$

3. 120 tons

$$\frac{30 \text{ feet}}{100 \text{ tons}} = \frac{36 \text{ feet}}{x}$$
$$x = \frac{36 \times 100}{30} = \frac{3600}{30} = 120$$

4. $252

$$\frac{x}{\$350} = \frac{72}{100}$$
$$x = \frac{\$350 \times 72}{100} = \frac{\$25,200}{100} = \$252$$
$$or \ \$350 \times .72 = \$252$$

5. $462.80

Find Nick's hours, including overtime.
$$8 + 8\frac{3}{4} + 8\frac{1}{2} + 9\frac{1}{2} + 8\frac{1}{4} = 43$$
This is 40 hours regular and 3 hours overtime. Find Nick's total pay.

$$40 \times \$10.40 = \$416.00$$
$$+ \ 3 \times \$15.60 = \$ \ 46.80$$
$$\overline{\$462.80}$$

6. 3.14(6)

The formula for circumference is
$$C = \pi d.$$

$$d = 2 \times radius = 2 \times 3 = 6$$
$$C = \pi d = 3.14(6)$$

7. 200% increase

Year 5 – Year 3 = 450 – 150 = 300
$$\frac{300 \text{ increase}}{150 \text{ year } 3} = \frac{N\%}{100\%}$$
$$N = \frac{100 \times 300}{150} = \frac{30000}{150} = 200$$

8. 72 cu ft

$$V = length \times width \times height$$
$$= 8 \times 6 \times 1\frac{1}{2} \qquad (18 \text{ in.} = 1\frac{1}{2} \text{ ft})$$
$$= 72 \text{ cu ft}$$

9. 75°

Since the two angles are corresponding angles, they are equal.

10. $x = 4$

$$4x - 9 = 7$$
$$4x - 9 + 9 = 7 + 9$$
$$4x = 16$$
$$\frac{4x}{4} = \frac{16}{4}$$
$$x = 4$$

11. –5

$$-4 + (-3) - (-2)$$
$$-4 - 3 + 2$$
$$-7 + 2 = -5$$

12. −13°

Find the total.

$-19 -12 -18 -10 -13 -12 -7 = -91$

$-91 \div 7 = -13°$

13. 3 quarters, 4 dimes, 7 nickels

Let x = quarters, $x + 1$ = dimes, and $x + 1 + 3$ = nickels. Then

$$x + x + 1 + x + 1 + 3 = 14$$
$$3x + 5 = 14$$
$$3x + 5 - 5 = 14 - 5$$
$$3x = 9$$
$$x = 3$$

$x = 3$ quarters, $x + 1 = 4$ dimes, and $x + 1 + 3 = 7$ nickels

14. about 4.5 or $2\sqrt{5}$

$$d = \sqrt{(x_2 - x_1)^2 + (y_2 - y_1)^2}$$
$$d = \sqrt{(5 - 1)^2 + (4 - 2)^2}$$
$$d = \sqrt{4^2 + 2^2} = \sqrt{16 + 4} = \sqrt{20} =$$
$$\sqrt{4 \times 5} = 2\sqrt{5} = \text{about } 4.5$$

(If you use your calculator to find the square root, 4.47.)

15. 70°

Because side ab and side bc are each 6 inches, the triangle is isosceles. Then the measure of $\angle c$ is 55°, like $\angle a$.

To find $\angle b$,
$180° - 2(55°) = 180° - 110° = 70°$.

Mathematics Pretest Evaluation Chart

After you have used the answer key to check the Pretest, find the item number of each question you missed and circle it on the chart below. These are the mathematics content areas in which you need more practice.

Skill Area/Content Area	Item Number	Review Chapter
Decimals	1	2
Fractions	2	3
Ratio and Proportion	3	5
Percent	4	6
Measurement	5	8
Data Analysis	7, 12	5
Geometry	6, 8, 9, 15	9
Algebra	10, 11, 13, 14	7

ANSWER KEY
CRITICAL THINKING SKILLS

LEVEL TWO–COMPREHENSION

Exercise 1: Summarizing the Main Idea (page 36)

Possible summary of message is as follows:

Christopher, Mom called from Paris! Very upset but everyone's OK. Can't use your credit cards. Lost wallet on train—a young boy and girl stole and jumped off. All four went back but kids gone. Went to clerk for help. Went to report it to the police—hard to find. Nice officer took report. Lost French francs but reported credit cards stolen. Closed those accounts but thieves charged over $800. Your family not liable. A few days before new cards issued and sent. Need something, use my card. Pay me later.

LEVEL THREE–APPLICATION

Exercise 2: Applying Appropriate Definitions or Principles (page 38)

1. **(1)** The passage describes an easygoing look at friends and friendships.

2. **(4)** The passage describes the sinking of a ship and loss of lives.

3. **(3)** The passage describes an improbable plot.

Exercise 3: Using Application in Science (page 39)

1. **(3)** The passage states that the lymphatic system helps fight infection.

2. **(5)** According to the passage, muscles belong to the muscular system.

3. **(4)** The passage states that the digestive system processes and distributes nutrients from food.

LEVEL FOUR–ANALYSIS

Exercise 4: Recognizing Facts, Opinions, and Hypotheses (page 43)

1. O   2. F   3. H   4. F

Exercise 5: Determining Adequacy of Facts (page 44)

1. CS (Credible Source)

2. NS (No Support)

3. F (Fact)

Exercise 6: Distinguishing Conclusions from Supporting Statements (page 45)

1. **Choice (5)** contains the conclusion from Sentence 11 that despite the comfort, reassurance, cuddling, and words of encouragement that are given to infants and small children, *it is not possible to "spoil" a child before the age of two or three.*

2. **Choice (4)** is a secondary conclusion because it arrives at the conclusion of *practices that seem to produce the most secure children.*

3. **Choice (1)** includes the link between the word *dependence* and a derivation of the same word: *dependable.*

Exercise 7: Drawing Conclusions through Inductive Reasoning (page 46)

1. A study was conducted of 461 children with persistent middle ear infections.

2. The study looked at those who had had surgery (adenoids and tonsils out) and those who had not.

3. Ear infections were reduced to an average of 1.4 per year for those who had surgery from 2.1 per year for those who did not have surgery.

4. Children who had adenoids and/or tonsils out did not do much better than those who had not had surgery.

5. Medical treatment followed by ear tubes should be tried first before resorting to surgery.

Exercise 8: Drawing Conclusions through Deductive Reasoning (page 47)

1. *Yes.* An embolism results from the blockage (obstruction) of a blood vessel; if the embolism is found in an artery of the brain, it can lead to a stroke.

2. *No.* A tumor is not a rupture or an obstruction of an artery of the bran.

3. *Yes*. An aneurysm is a blood-filled swelling of a vessel (artery). The rupture of an aneurysm can lead to a stroke.

Exercise 9: Identifying Comparison and Contrast Patterns (page 49)

1. Which first ladies belonged to the Democratic Party?

   Jacqueline Lee Bouvier Kennedy, Claudia Taylor Johnson, Rosalynn Smith Carter, or Hillary Rodham Clinton

2. Which first ladies belonged to the Republican Party?

   Patricia Ryan Nixon, Elizabeth Bloomer Ford, Nancy Davis Reagan, Barbara Pierce Bush

3. Volunteer Service

   Pat Nixon and Barbara Bush

4. Promotion of the Performing Arts

   Pat Nixon, Rosalynn Carter, or Hillary Clinton

5. Campaign Against Alcohol or Drug Dependency

   Betty Ford and Nancy Reagan

Contrast the causes that were different by naming the first lady associated with each cause.

1. Rosalynn Carter
2. Barbara Bush
3. Betty Ford
4. Hillary Clinton

Exercise 10: Identifying Cause-and-Effect Relationships (page 51)

1. Effect: Many seniors took advantage of the development.

2. Cause: the construction of thousands of new homes

3. Cause: building of stores, pharmacies, theaters, restaurants, and so on

LEVEL FIVE–SYNTHESIS

Exercise 11: Using Synthesis

Part A (page 54)
a. 1   b. 3   c. 4   d. 5   e. 7

Part B (page 55)
1. Kent reveals that Covey "has gone on to become a counselor to political leaders, chief executives and ordinary people the world over" and that Covey has become vice chairman of "a global professional-services company and publishers of the Franklin Planner products."

2. Kent apparently admires Covey and his book. Kent says "Covey is as self-effacing as ever." He also says that Covey "worries about having become, in effect, a guru." In other words, Kent recognizes that Covey is an established authority on the subject of "highly effective people" but that Covey does not seek the acclaim or status of a "guru."

LEVEL SIX–EVALUATION

Exercise 12: Evaluating Objective and Subjective Criteria (page 56)

1. Objective
2. Objective
3. Subjective: note the use of the word *should*
4. Subjective: note the use of the word *must*

Exercise 13: Understanding the Roles of Values and Beliefs (page 57)

1. promised land of freedom
2. parental right or authority to raise a child
3. material things, fun
4. government or law or rulings

ANSWER KEY
LANGUAGE ARTS, WRITING

CHAPTER 1:
BASIC ENGLISH USAGE

Exercise 1: Possessive Nouns (page 64)

Corrections are in **bold** type.

1. Years ago, Australians bought weasels to hunt rabbits, but instead the weasels attacked the **Australians'** chickens.

2. Today in the United States, animals such as dogs, birds, and cats are popular **children's** pets.

3. **Japan's** scientists have been investigating to see if cows and worms can predict earthquakes.

Exercise 2: The Simple Tenses (page 67)

Verb	Time Clue
1. drinks	Every morning
2. tried	a few hours ago
3. will vote	next presidential election

Exercise 3: The Continuous Tenses (page 68)

Verb	Time Clue
1. were walking	yesterday
2. will be beginning	One week from today
3. is shining	right now

Exercise 4: The Perfect Tenses (page 69)

Verb	Time Clue
1. will have left	By 6:00 A.M. tomorrow morning
3. has saved	So far
4. have had	yet
6. had performed	Up until the development

GED Practice Exercise 5: Verbs (page 70)

1. (4) The verb needs to be in present tense to match the time clue today.

2. (2) The verb should be past perfect because the action occurred before another past action.

3. (5) The verb should be in past tense because the action was completed in the past.

4. (1) The verb should be in present perfect because the action began in the past but is still continuing into the present.

Exercise 6: Subject-Verb Agreement (page 73)

Subject	Verb
1. employees and the boss	were
2. boss	was
3. crackers	come
4. a serving spoon and butter knife	are
5. problems	seem

Exercise 7: Pronoun Forms (page 75)

1. **He** drove to work with **them.**

2. **Their** shirts cost the same as **her** hat.

3. The invitation said that children were invited, so I brought **mine.**

4. Yesterday Mike and **his** family left to go camping.

Exercise 8: Possessive Pronouns and Contractions (page 76)

1. The earth is mostly water so only about 30% of **its** surface is land.

2. Seven of the planets in our solar system have moons, and all **their** moons have names.

3. If you think **you're** uncomfortable on a hot day in summer, just consider that the temperature in the center of the sun is about 27,000,000 degrees F.

4. Stephen Hawking, **whose** contributions to science include knowledge about black holes and the evolution of the universe, may be one of the greatest physicists of the twentieth century.

Exercise 9: Identifying Antecedents (page 77)

Pronouns	Antecedent
1. His	farmer
2. that	bill

3. who   spokesperson
4. she   spokesperson
5. it   bill
6. their   people

Exercise 10: Agreement in Number (page 78)

Corrections are in **bold** type.

Each company has certain expectations of **its** employees. . . . Employees, in turn, have certain expectations about a company and **its** treatment of personnel. . . .

Exercise 11: Clarifying Antecedents (page 79)

The following sentences are possible revisions. The words in **bold** type replace the confusing pronoun or pronouns. Remember that your sentences can be different from those given here and still be correct. When checking your work, be sure that you have replaced all vague pronouns.

1. Wendy gave Bonnie the keys to **Wendy's** car.
2. The man followed Mr. Reynolds in **the man's** new car.
3. We heard on the news that **medical researchers** are trying to find a cure for diabetes.
4. Obesity and malnutrition are growing concerns in the United States. **These conditions** continue to be a threat to the health of many people.
5. C

Exercise 12: Agreement in Person (page 80)

Corrections are in **bold** type.

One survey report states that 66 percent of us just want some time for ourselves. In general, we are working more than ever, so **we** have less and less free time. Two strategies **we** can use to save some of that valuable time are helpful. We need to learn to combine **our** errands, and we need to buy time rather than things.

Exercise 13: Usage (page 80)

1. **(2)** The verb must agree with the compound subject *work disputes, social disagreements, and family problems.*
2. **(1)** Pronouns should not shift in a passage. The voice should be consistent.

The writer is speaking directly to the reader.

3. **(3)** The verb *talk* must be used in present tense to be consistent with the rest of the sentence.
4. **(5)** The verb tense must be consistent. The sentence states advice and fact and requires present or present continuous tense.
5. **(3)** The pronoun *it* is a vague reference. What is important must be stated.
6. **(3)** The verb must agree with the singular subject *code.*

CHAPTER 2: SENTENCE STRUCTURE

Exercise 1: Rewriting Fragments (page 83)

Corrected sentences are in **bold** type. Remember, your revised sentences can be different and still be correct.

The most successful people are often those who are willing to experience failure **without letting it stop them. . . . For example, the deaths of his mother and fiancée were very difficult for him.** . . .

Exercise 2: Run-ons and Comma Splices (page 84)

The sentences in **bold** type show possible ways to correct the run-ons and comma splices in this paragraph. They have been separated into two sentences or combined using a comma with *and, but, or, for, nor, so,* or *yet.*

We tend to take our feet for granted, but **they are actually quite remarkable. . . . Women suffer from foot problems about four times as often as men do. Some of those problems are directly related to the wearing of high heels. We do need to care for our feet, for they will be used to carry us thousands of miles during our lifetimes.**

Exercise 3: Conjunctions (page 85)

The correct conjunction and punctuation are in **bold** type. More than one conjunction may be correct in some sentences.

1. The first compact microwave ovens came out in the 1960s, **but** they didn't become widely used until the 1980s.
2. People ate with their hands for centuries, **but** a big change finally occurred in the

1100s when people used forks, knives, and spoons.

3. It seems silly to say we will dial a telephone number, **for** push button phones are used everywhere.

Exercise 4: Using Commas Correctly (page 86)

Remember, a comma is needed when two complete sentences are joined by a coordinating conjunction such as *and* or *but*. If you use a comma, make sure the sentences you join have both a subject and a predicate.

1. Jessica won the first game, and Elizabeth asked for a rematch.

2. They started a second game, but they were interrupted by the doorbell.

3. Games are inexpensive and entertaining, so they are popular to play.

4. A game such as chess has been played for hundreds of years, so it is very well known in the world.

Exercise 5: Dependent Clauses (page 87)

Remember, your answers can be different from those in **bold** type and still be correct.

1. Books were made more cheaply and quickly **after** Gutenberg invented moveable type to use in printing in 1450.

2. **Before** the invention of a process to produce paper in China, the Chinese used clay or wood blocks to make books in the 10th century.

3. In early Egypt, scribes would write needed documents on scrolls in a library **where** the documents were stored in jars.

4. **Although** information is stored electronically in the modern world, a lot of paper is still used.

Exercise 6: Passive or Active Voice (page 88)

1. **P** The man was bitten by the dog.

2. **A** The dog bit the man.

3. **P** Last week the driver was given a ticket.

4. **A** Last week a police officer gave the driver a ticket.

Exercise 7: Structure and Usage (page 90)

1. **(2)** The verb *is* must agree with the subject of the sentence, *one*.

2. **(4)** The meaning of the original can be preserved, and the sentence can be improved by changing the passive voice to the active voice: *Another disturbing estimate claimed that more than one third of elementary and high school students read below grade level.*

3. **(5)** The sentences are most effectively combined using a comma and the conjunction *but*.

4. **(1)** The meaning of the original can be preserved, and the sentence can be improved by omitting useless words: *Newspapers, magazines, and books help build skills and establish the habit of reading.*

Exercise 8: Dangling and Misplaced Modifiers (page 92)

The modifying phrase in each of the following sentences is in **bold** type and is in the correct place—nearest to the word it modifies.

1. **As the sun slowly sank beneath the horizon,** we watched the sunset.

2. On Saturday at the bookstore, he bought an instruction book **for training dogs.**

3. A cold drink tasted refreshing **after she had been working outside in the heat for several hours.**

4. **After we had been listening to the music for an hour,** the radio program was interrupted by a weather bulletin.

5. Our neighbors took their dog **that had fleas** to the groomer.

Exercise 9: Parallel Structure (page 93)

1. (a)　　2. (b)　　3. (b)　　4. (a)

CHAPTER 3: MECHANICS

Exercise 1: Capitalization Rules (page 95)

The corrected words in each of the following sentences are in **bold** type.

1. Our friends went to a **concert** last **Monday** on Labor **Day** and listened to music from an opera called *The Magic Flute* by **Mozart.**

2. Not only did Thomas Jefferson write the **Declaration** of **Independence** for the **country,** but he also served as a **governor** of Virginia.

3. If you take **Interstate** 80 and travel **west**, you will see many **national parks** such as **Yellowstone** or Great Teton which have been preserved because of the efforts of John Rockefeller.

4. The ceiling of the **Sistine Chapel** in **Rome** contains a painting 133 feet long and 45 feet wide that was painted by **Michelangelo** for **Pope** Paul III.

Exercise 2: Using Commas (page 97)

Commas are added after the words in **bold** type.

To: All Employees
From: Personnel

    The new insurance plan will go into effect in the next **month,** so all company employees need to attend an information session. After hearing the **information,** each employee **must,** of **course,** select a plan option. **In addition,** each employee will need to indicate whether family members are to be covered. An employee may opt for coverage for a **spouse, dependents,** or just the employee. Registration for an information session can be completed by dialing extension 608. Six sessions have **been scheduled,** and each will last approximately one hour. If there are any immediate **questions,** please call the director of personnel at extension 442.

Exercise 3: Punctuation Review (page 98)

Corrections are added to the words in **bold** type.

1. We can learn a lot from other **people's** experiences and ideas.

2. Charles **Kingsley said** that people shouldn't ever go to sleep at night without having added to another person's happiness that day.

3. If you look in the **library,** you will find many great writers' books.

4. Many famous **artists'** masterpieces hang in the Louvre in Paris.

CHAPTER 4: ORGANIZATION

Exercise 1: Topic Sentences (page 99)

The topic is underlined, and the controlling idea is in **bold** type.

1. A linguist is **more interested in describing how language is used rather than in prescribing how it should be used.**

2. The movie we saw last weekend was the **worst we had seen in years.**

3. Some studies suggest that belief in a treatment or medicine may be **more important than previously believed.**

Exercise 2: Effective Topic Sentences (page 100)

1. **(b)** Classical sonatas are relaxing after a stressful day at work.

2. **(a)** The leaves of some ordinary garden-variety plants are actually quite toxic.

3. **(b)** The health risks, the costs, and the smell make smoking undesirable.

Exercise 3: Topic Sentences in Paragraphs (page 100)

The topic sentence for each paragraph is indicated.

1. **The topic sentence is implied.** It would be something like this: *Shopping at the store seems very unpleasant to me.*

2. She realized upon hearing that noise that she had a problem; water had flooded the basement.

Exercise 4: Text Division (page 102)

The text for each passage is organized into two paragraphs below. The first sentence of each paragraph is indicated.

1. Who is the greatest writer in English? . . .

    Before Shakespeare, the most famous writer of English literature was Geoffrey Chaucer. . . .

2. Many great scientific advances occurred in the 20th century. . . .

    Many notable scientific achievements occurred before the 20th century as well.

Exercise 5: Organizing Text (page 103)

The text should be organized into three paragraphs.

    It's important to store food carefully to maintain the quality and safety. Improperly stored food can cause health problems. Furthermore, food that is not stored properly will not taste very good.

    Eggs are very perishable and require careful storage practices. Buy refrigerated grade A or AA eggs with uncracked, clean shells, and keep them refrigerated at 40 degrees or lower. Do not store eggs in the door of the refrigerator. Egg dishes can be left at room temperature for a maximum of two hours. These guidelines for egg storage will help ensure safety and quality.

Ice cream is another example of a food that benefits from proper storage. Keep ice cream stored at 0 degrees or lower. Once a carton of ice cream has been opened and used, put plastic wrap over the surface of the remaining ice cream before putting the carton's lid on and storing in the freezer. The plastic wrap will help prevent a skin from forming and help control the formation of ice crystals. Be careful to wrap other foods in the freezer tightly so that the odors do not taint the ice cream. A little effort can ensure some good results.

Exercise 6: Irrelevant Sentences (page 105)

The irrelevant sentences are as follows:

That was even before the development of computers. People were also afraid of other diseases as well.

Exercise 7: Transitional Expressions

Part A (page 106)

Some suggested answers are given in **bold** type. More than one choice is possible.

1. Mexico City is a very large city. **In fact,** it is the largest city in the world.

2. Modern doctors scrub and sterilize their equipment and hands. **Thus,** fewer people die from infections after operations.

3. My neighbor was a careless driver who was always in a hurry. **As a result,** one day he received a ticket.

Part B (page 106)

The sentences may be completed in various ways. A possible answer in **bold** type is given for each.

1. Judy ate a cheeseburger, salad, baked potato, taco, and ice cream cone for lunch. As a result, **she didn't want any dinner.**

2. As we get older, we grow more experienced. Furthermore, **we become more patient.**

3. We would love to travel to many places in the world. For example, **we really wish we could go to Europe.**

Exercise 8: Writing Errors (page 107)

1. **(3)** The sentence is irrelevant and does not support the paragraph's main idea.

2. **(5)** The meaning of the original can be preserved, and the sentence can be improved by omitting unnecessary words and using the active voice: *In 1999, the mint began issuing the first state quarters.*

3. **(3)** Correct the fragment by replacing *being* with the verb *is*.

4. **(4)** Correct the dangling modification by placing *the mint* after the modifying phrase *In addition to minting the state quarters.*

5. **(2)** Combine paragraphs B and C because both support the same topic sentence.

CHAPTER 5: PREPARING FOR THE GED ESSAY

Exercise 6: Types of Writing (page 115)

The two types of writing used in the passage are narration and description.

Exercise 7: Identifying Supporting Reasons (page 118)

1. reason given

2. no reason given

3. reason given

Exercise 9: Thesis Statements (page 120)

1. **(b)** A universal health care plan is needed in the U.S.

2. **(b)** Three major events that influenced my life were moving to another state, marrying the one I love, and becoming a parent.

Exercise 11: Essay Analysis (page 122)

The first problem is that the essay does not have a clear focus or thesis statement. The second problem is that the essay rambles and lists ideas rather than developing them. The writer should have selected two or three strategies for dealing with stress and developed each with supporting examples and reasons.

A possible thesis statement for this essay might read: *In order to cope with stress, I read, walk, or talk with a friend.* Then the essay could develop those three strategies: *read, walk, talk.*

Exercise 12: Scoring and Evaluating Essays (page 124)

The scores below were assigned by the GED Testing Service. Each score is accompanied by an explanation and evaluation of the essay.

Essay A: **Score 2.** In this essay, the prompt is addressed and a main idea immediately established. However, the long single paragraph reads as transcribed thought rather than planned writing and makes it difficult for a reader to follow the writer's ideas. The writer's focus on changing his or her attitude toward other people and life shifts at one point toward a discussion of life as a game. Other than the game metaphor, idea development is limited to insistent repetition of the need to change attitudes. Sentences that run together make reading difficult, and noticeable phrase repetition detracts from the essay. There are few errors in Edited American English, but the absence of appropriate commas impairs readability. Word choices are frequently inappropriate, marked by an intrusion of slang into an otherwise conventional voice.

Essay B: **Score 4.** In a clearly focused discussion, the writer focuses on the need to "stop being such a procrastinator." The reader moves smoothly and logically through a sequence of well-structured sentences describing parts of the psychological puzzle of procrastination. In a clearly organized plan, each paragraph grows progressively more intent on self-discipline so that the reader can appreciate the emotional growth sought by the writer. Ideas are developed with specific relevant examples and some humorous asides—"the angels in heaven above start biting their nails." The writer's choice of words is precise, varied, analytical, and intimate. The essay exhibits consistent control of the conventions of Edited American English throughout.

Source: GED Testing Service

ANSWER KEY
<u>SOCIAL STUDIES</u>

CHAPTER 1: WORLD HISTORY

Exercise 1: Early Humanity (page 129)

1. **Application (3)** Fossil remains are not made by humans. All of the other choices are items that are made by people and are, therefore, artifacts.

2. **Application (1)** Currency and members of society that were called money lenders were not established until a much later time. The other choices have a connection to the roles that early man started in the first societies.

Exercise 2: Early Civilization (page 131)

1. **Analysis (3)** Even though the Egyptians did not have an alphabet of letters as languages have today, the symbols they used did allow for them to record events and conditions of their society.

2. **Analysis (1)** There has not been any information that the Egyptians were a warring group. They did enslave the lower classes and trade in slavery, but the growth of their civilization came more from successes in farming and commerce. There is no recorded history of the Egyptians declaring war on neighboring tribes. All the other choices are supported in the text.

Exercise 3: Civilizations Begin to Interact (page 132)

1. **Comprehension (2)** The Romans were far more interested in aggressive military strength. It was this military priority that allowed the Romans to conquer the Greeks.

2. **Application (4)** Aggressive contact sports would more likely be an activity that exemplifies Roman ideology. The other choices could be activities that improve the mind or the body.

Exercise 4: The Middle Ages and the Feudal System (page 134)

1. **Comprehension (5)** The nobles wanted the peasants to work their land and pay taxes. The peasants were led to believe that it was in their best interest to be protected by the lord, but in reality there was not much the nobles could do other than keep in good standing with the ruler to ask for assistance if there was an invasion.

2. **Analysis (2)** The Magna Carta was a charter to confirm the freedom the Church of England had from the King's rule.

Exercise 5: The Renaissance (page 135)

1. **Analysis (4)** The reference to the best poetry is an opinion statement. Many scholars of poetry would argue that each period had its own poetry style, which added to the variety of poetic verse, but it is a personal opinion as to which style a reader prefers.

2. **Analysis (3)** Western Europe had to stabilize politically and economically before painting, literature, and sculpture could flourish.

Exercise 6: The Reformation Divides Christianity (page 136)

1. **Analysis (2)** The Reformation is the name of the period of time when Martin Luther brought up criticisms about the Roman Catholic Church, which led to the new Christian belief system called Protestantism (from its protest against the Catholic Church).

2. **Comprehension (2)** Mary Tudor ordered the deaths of many people who would not accept the Catholic Church.

Exercise 7: The Enlightenment (page 137)

1. **Analysis (5)** The invention of the microscope allowed scientists to see bacteria and microbes that caused diseases.

Exercise 8: The Industrial Revolution (page 138)

1. **(F)** The telegraph and telephone allowed long-distance communication.

2. **(T)**

3. **(F)** Marx thought that the industrialists were forcing workers to be poor.

Exercise 9: World War I (page 140)

Comprehension

1. Russia was not allied to Germany; it was allied to France.

2. England was not allied to Germany; it joined the war to protect Belgium.

3. Belgium was not allied to Germany; it tried to remain neutral but was invaded by Germany as the German army advanced on France.

4. Hungary was allied to Germany. At the time the Austria-Hungarian Empire also included modern day Slovakia and the Czech Republic. Italy also supported Germany.

Exercise 10: The Russian Revolution and the Rise of Communism (page 140)

1. **(4)** With the desperation caused by meager resources, poverty, food shortages, and other poor conditions, the people lost faith in the rule of the czars and accepted communism.

2. c; b; a

Exercise 11: World War II (page 142)

Comprehension

1. Propaganda

2. genocide

3. Germany; Japan

4. Hiroshima; Nagasaki

CHAPTER 2: U.S. HISTORY

Exercise 1: A New Nation Is Born (page 143)

1. **Analysis (4)** The map shows the country from which each of the explorers started his journey. It shows that representatives from many nations visited America.

2. **Comprehension (5)** The map shows the paths each explorer took and the area of North America where each explorer landed.

Exercise 2: The Original Thirteen English Colonies (page 145)

1. **Comprehension (5)** Two places on the map are labeled MA (Massachusetts), but one has ME (Maine) written in it. This indicates that Maine was originally a part of Massachusetts.

2. **Evaluation (3)** The map shows the area west of the thirteen colonies to be disputed

by France and Britain. Therefore, the map indicates that France still had interest in the New World. The other choices, whether true or untrue, cannot be supported by the information in the map.

Exercise 3: The Declaration of Independence (page 146)

1. **Comprehension (3)** The passage states that the colonists were outraged by the taxes imposed by the Townshend Acts and protested them by dumping tea into Boston Harbor.

2. **Analysis (2)** The main idea of the Declaration of Independence was to state that people had rights and freedoms referred to as *inalienable*. This means that the people of the colonies wanted to exercise this freedom to govern themselves and not be governed by a king across the Atlantic Ocean.

Exercise 4: The Revolutionary War (page 147)

Analysis

1. **Cause** The Intolerable Acts sought to further establish the authority of the king.

2. **Effect** The document led to the Revolutionary War.

3. **Effect** This led to the Declaration of Independence.

4. **Cause** The British Army was defeated.

Exercise 5: The Beginnings of American Government (page 148)

1. **Analysis (5)** The founding fathers made the central government weak on purpose to avoid repeating the abuses the colonies had suffered under the king. Maintaining state sovereignty was one way to do this.

2. **Comprehension (1)** The founding fathers needed to review and change the Articles of Confederation because they had not specified enough of the responsibilities for the federal government. The king's power had nothing to do with it.

Exercise 6: The U.S. Constitution and Federalism (page 149)

1. **Analysis (2)** The population determines how many people represent that region in the House of Representatives. If the slave population was counted as full individuals, then the House of Representatives would have had more Southerners, and they would have had a majority vote. The South

did not want to give slaves full rights because they would challenge the white governments in the South.

2. **Application (1)** According to the passage, Anti-Federalists were largely farmers who favored individual liberties and feared authoritative control by a central government.

Exercise 7: Jacksonian Democracy and the Mexican War (page 152)

1. **Analysis (2)** Because he believed that all people, not just those with property, should have a voice in government, Jackson's attitude can be described as populist.

2. **Comprehension (4)** The map shows the boundaries of the newest land acquisitions. In some cases the land was purchased, acquired by deed, or annexed.

Exercise 8: Prelude to War (page 153)

1. **Application (3)** Popular sovereignty permitted the people to approve or disapprove of a legislative action; therefore, of the choices given, popular sovereignty is the most similar to a referendum.

2. **Evaluation (5)** When the Supreme Court ruled that Dred Scott could be returned to his master, it was upholding the practice of treating slaves as personal property.

Exercise 9: Secession (page 154)

Comprehension

1. **b** Virginia split in two over the issue of secession, with the western part (now known as West Virginia) loyal to the Union.

2. **c** Texas seceded from the Union despite the fact that only the eastern part of the state voted to do so.

3. **a** Kentucky was a border state that remained with the Union despite being a slave state.

Exercise 10: The Civil War (page 155)

1. **Analysis (5)** The passage says, "As a result, the Union army's ranks grew by 180,000 former slaves who fought against the South." This was a considerable contribution to the Union's forces.

Exercise 11: Growth of Big Business and Urbanization (page 157)

1. **Comprehension (5)** Half of the 2000 U.S. Census population of 275 million is 137.5 million. In 1940 the U.S reached 131 million (57 million rural and 74 million urban population); this is close to the 137.5 million figure.

2. **Comprehension (3)** The chart shows a slow but steady increase in rural population until 1930.

Exercise 12: Labor and Progressivism (page 158)

1. **Application (4)** Agreement by oil companies on a minimum price to set for gasoline is an example of price-fixing, an act outlawed by the Sherman Anti-Trust Act.

2. **Comprehension (3)** The passage says that government-sanctioned monopolies like public utilities are allowed to exist in order to save resources.

Exercise 13: The United States as a World Power (page 159)

1. **Analysis (3)** The Philippines were ceded to the United States under the terms of the treaty that ended the Spanish-American War; therefore, the U.S. establishment of military bases there is a result of the policy of expanding American control over other areas.

2. **Analysis (4)** The most likely explanation for America's isolationist position from the end of the Civil War until the Spanish-American War is that the country was preoccupied with healing its wounds and rebuilding the South after the Civil War.

Exercise 14: The New Deal (page 162)

Application

1. c   2. a   3. d   4. b

Exercise 15: World War II (page 163)

1. **Application (5)** Dark green military fatigues are not an example of technology. The clothing chosen in any war is designed to camouflage the soldier to make him blend into the natural surroundings.

2. **Analysis (3)** The passage says that World War II began in Europe in 1939, but the United States did not join the war until after Japan attacked Pearl Harbor.

Exercise 16: The Korean Conflict (page 164)

1. **Analysis (4)** The belief that the U.S. government should not commit soldiers to an undeclared war represents opinion, not a fact.
2. **Comprehension (5)** The passage states that when North Korean troops crossed the border, President Truman committed U.S. troops, effectively beginning the war.

Exercise 17: The Eisenhower Years (page 165)

1. **Application (2)** At both the Salem witch trials and the McCarthy hearings, accusations were made with almost no evidence, but simply being accused was enough to make people think someone was guilty.
2. **Analysis (3)** *The Brown v. Topeka Board of Education* decision is significant today because it ruled that "separate but equal" educational facilities could no longer exist. This serves as the legal basis for school busing to achieve desegregation.

Exercise 18: The Kennedy Administration (page 166)

1. **Application (3)** The Soviet attempt to establish a missile base in Cuba may be interpreted as a direct violation of the principles of the Monroe Doctrine, which opposed foreign interference in the affairs of the Western Hemisphere.
2. **Analysis (4)** From reading the passage, it may be assumed that Cuba, a Communist nation, was an ally of the Soviet Union.

Exercise 19: Détente and Watergate (page 167)

Comprehension

1. Opinion
2. Opinion
3. Fact
4. Fact

Exercise 20: Ending the Twentieth Century (page 167)

1. **Comprehension (4)** None of the presidents listed had to deal with an economic depression.
2. **Comprehension (3)** From 1989 through 1993 many of the Soviet Union counties reestablished themselves as independent nations.

CHAPTER 3: CIVICS AND GOVERNMENT

Exercise 1: Political Systems (page 169)

Application

1. **(3)** Hitler had absolute authority to govern his country.
2. **(5)** Queen Elizabeth II inherited her position of government in England.
3. **(5)** The president of the United States is elected by the people through a system of representation by electors from each state.

Exercise 2: Legislative Representation (page 171)

Analysis

1. **(3)** Since the number of representatives a state has is based on its population, you can infer that New Jersey, in spite of its small size, is densely populated.
2. **(5)** Because the number of a state's representatives is based on its population, and because Arizona is gaining residents at the expense of states in the Northeast, the number of representatives for both Arizona and northeastern states will need to be adjusted.

Exercise 3: The Legislative Branch (page 172)

Application

1. **E** The power to impose economic sanctions is not stated in the Constitution; therefore, the elastic clause applies.
2. **C** The power to approve treaties is stated in the Constitution.
3. **C** The power to approve presidential appointments is stated in the Constitution.

Exercise 4: Presidential Powers (page 173)

Evaluation Answers marked should be **(1)** serves as commander in chief, **(2)** grants reprieves and pardons, and **(3)** appoints Supreme Court Judges.

Exercise 5: The Executive Branch (page 173)

1. **(3) Analysis** If the years an individual president can serve are limited, new policy ideas can be instituted because of a change in political party and/or candidate.

Exercise 6: The Judicial Branch (page 174)

Comprehension

1. **(4)** The practice of deciding on the constitutionality of a law (which the Supreme Court does) is called the power of judicial review.

2. **(4)** The quotation both defines the role of the Supreme Court and affirms that the Court is the final authority on the Constitution's meaning.

Exercise 7: System of Checks and Balances (page 175)

Comprehension

1. **(a)** executive **(b)** judicial
2. **(a)** legislative **(b)** executive
3. **(a)** judicial **(b)** legislative
4. **(a)** executive **(b)** legislative

Exercise 8: The Enactment of a Law (page 175)

Evaluation

1. **(2)** This choice is supported by the part of the chart that shows that a bill must go to a conference committee for compromise.

2. **(1)** In the chart, specific procedures are outlined for allowing a vetoed bill to become law.

Exercise 9: Powers of State Government (page 177)

Application

1. B 2. F 3. F 4. S

Exercise 10: Political Parties (page 179)

Application

1. **R** Republicans generally favor stronger state and local authority.

2. **D** Democrats generally endorse the efforts of labor unions.

3. **D** Democrats support government expenditures for the disadvantaged and minorities.

Exercise 11: The Electoral Process and Voting (page 180)

Comprehension

1. c 2. b 3. a

Exercise 12: Voter Rules (page 180)

Analysis

1. opinion 2. fact 3. fact 4. opinion

CHAPTER 4: ECONOMICS

Exercise 1: Factors of Production (page 182)

Application

1. **N** Gemstones are found in nature.

2. **C** Computers and printers are equipment used to provide a service.

3. **L** Carpenters who build shopping malls are laborers.

Exercise 2: Economic Systems and Governments (page 183)

Comprehension

1. **(1)** This quotation reflects the capitalist feature of government noninterference in business.

2. **(4)** Because capitalism and communism occupy the extremes of the continuum, you can conclude that they are opposites.

3. **(3)** An aspect of a U.S. dairy manufacturer's operations (capitalist system) is dictated by a government agency's requirement (a feature of a socialist system).

Exercise 3: Supply, Demand, and Equilibrium (page 186)

1. **Comprehension (3)** The point where the line intersects is at $300.

2. **Analysis (3)** With a greater supply brought about by the entrance of Asian economies into the market and a low demand for digital cameras, the supply would exceed demand, resulting in a surplus.

Exercise 4: Economic Growth (page 187)

1. **Comprehension (3)** Unemployment is a factor that may lead to a recession or depression; it is not a stage in the business cycle.

2. **Analysis (2)** A depression is a severe decline in business, which usually affects the majority of citizens in a country.

Exercise 5: Money and Monetary Policy (page 190)

1. Fact 2. Opinion 3. Fact

Exercise 6: Government and Fiscal Policy (page 191)

Comprehension

1. **increase; lowering** To stimulate the economy during a recession, the

government should increase government spending while lowering taxes. The actions put more money into circulation and into the hands of consumers.

2. **decrease; raising; increasing** Inflation is an increase in the amount of money in circulation. To reduce inflation, the Fed reduces the amount of money in circulation by raising the discount rate. This makes it more costly for banks to borrow from the Fed. By increasing the reserve ratio, the Fed reduces the amount of money a bank can lend.

3. **budget deficit** When operating at a budget deficit, the government is spending more money than it takes in.

CHAPTER 5: GEOGRAPHY

Exercise 1: Styles of Maps (page 194)

1. **Analysis (4)** When a spherical shape is flattened, as on a map, the surface will be stretched or distorted in some places.

2. **Comprehension (4)** Political maps show boundaries of political areas like countries or states or provinces.

3. **Comprehension (1)** Topographical maps have contour lines that indicate elevation. Many lines show a dramatic increase of elevation that would indicate a mountain.

Exercise 2: Measuring Distances (page 195)

Comprehension

1. The student needs to measure and calculate based on scale. (approximately 850 or 900 miles)

2. Los Angeles has a much larger dot; therefore, it has a larger population.

3. To go from Colorado to California you would travel west.

Exercise 3: Latitude and Longitude (page 197)

Comprehension

1. **(5)** Central Africa   2. **(4)** South Africa

Exercise 4: Time Zones (page 198)

1. **Application (2)** Los Angeles falls within the pacific time zone, which is three hours earlier than the eastern time zone in which Philadelphia falls.

2. **Analysis (5)** Northwest Indiana is economically tied to the Chicago metropolitan area; therefore, for economic reasons northwest Indiana is in the same time zone as Chicago.

Exercise 5: U.S. Topography (page 200)

1. **Analysis (3)** Denver has the highest elevation of those cities listed. It is nicknamed the mile-high city because its elevation is close to one mile above sea level.

Exercise 6: Climate (page 201)

1. **Analysis (1)** The passage states that the higher elevations usually have lower temperatures.

2. **Application (2)** Air is colder at higher elevations, so there is more likely to be precipitation in the mountains than the plains.

Exercise 7: Population Distribution (page 201)

1. **Analysis (5)** Rapid waterways do not affect the population of the area. Waterways have often been a source of transportation, but the speed of flow is not important. Cold temperatures and high elevations would prevent a large population from settling in that area. Grassy valleys and cultivated plains would draw a larger population.

2. **Application (4)** The mountains of West Virginia would not allow for an even distribution of population.

ANSWER KEY
SCIENCE

CHAPTER 1:
LIFE SCIENCE: BIOLOGY

Exercise 1: Cell Structure (page 207)

Comprehension
1. c   2. a   3. b   4 d

Exercise 2: Cells (page 207)

1. **Comprehension (4)** The other choices do not identify the main idea. They serve as details to support the main idea that the cell is complex, with organized subsystems.

2. **Comprehension (5)** Chloroplasts are important in the food-making process for plants. Because animal cells cannot make their own food, we can infer that they must obtain nutrients elsewhere.

3. **Application (5)** Because chloroplasts create energy, they can be thought of as the power plant of the plant cell.

Exercise 3: Cells and Active Transport (page 208)

Comprehension
1. high/low   2. low/high

Exercise 4: Diffusion and Osmosis (page 208)

1. **Analysis (3)** Diffusion is the passage of molecules from an area of higher concentration to an area of lower concentration. This process allows for an even distribution of substances throughout the cells of the body.

2. **Analysis (1)** In osmosis, water moves from an area of higher concentration of water to an area of lower concentration of water. The salt water has a lower concentration of water, so the water will leave the cell in an attempt to equalize the percentage of water outside as well as inside the cell. The cell will lose water.

Exercise 5: Mitosis (page 210)

Comprehension
1. a   2. b   3. d   4. c

Exercise 6: Meiosis (page 212)

Comprehension
4, 1, 3, 2

Exercise 7: Cell Division (page 212)

1. **Application (3)** Because of the exchange and recombination of chromosomal material, the method of reproduction that allows for the most variety is sexual reproduction.

2. **Analysis (3)** Because cancerous cells spread to invade healthy cells, we can conclude that cancer cells divide more unpredictably than normal cells.

Exercise 8: Cloning (page 214)

Comprehension
1. False
2. False
3. False
4. True
5. True

Exercise 9: Organ Systems (page 215)

Application
1. d   2. e   3. f   4. b   5. a   6. c

Exercise 10: The Nervous System (page 217)

Application
1. a. cerebellum
    b. spinal cord
    c. medulla oblongata
    d. cerebrum

2. (False) The spinal cord is responsible for the reflex condition.
    (True)
    (True)
    (False) There are two hemispheres of the brain.

Exercise 11: The Circulatory and Respiratory Systems (page 218)

1. **Comprehension (2)** The alveoli are the small sacs in the lungs that are responsible for the actual exchange of oxygen and carbon dioxide.

2. H Heart, V Vessels, V Vessels, H Heart, V Vessels

Exercise 12: The Digestive and Excretory Systems (page 219)

Comprehension

1. b 2. d 3. e 4. a 5. c

Exercise 13: The Skeletal and Muscular Systems (page 220)

Comprehension

1. skeletal, smooth, cardiac

2. osteoporosis

3. marrow

4. 206

5. Ligaments

Exercise 14: The Nitrogen Cycle (page 221)

1. **Analysis (1)** The only case that shows a mutually beneficial relationship between two different organisms is that of bacteria that live in the stomachs of hoofed animals and at the same time help the animal to digest food.

2. **Application (4)** Soybeans are legumes that are important in the nitrogen-fixing process. The introduction of soybeans into the crop-rotation process improves the possibility of replenishing the supply of nitrogen.

Exercise 15: Photosynthesis (page 223)

1. **Comprehension**

   True, False, True

2. **Analysis (1)** Green pigment indicates the presence of chlorophyll. The areas of the coleus leaf that were green originally contained starch, which is produced through photosynthesis. Therefore, the starch turns brown when iodine is applied.

Exercise 16: Cellular Respiration (page 224)

1. **Comprehension (1)** Glucose molecules must be present for cellular respiration to occur. Because glucose molecules are the end product of photosynthesis in plants, you can infer that photosynthesis must precede cellular respiration.

2. **Application (4)** The more active a person is, the more energy he or she expends and the more carbon dioxide he or she exhales. Physically active people would have higher rates of cellular respiration than non-physically active people.

3. **Evaluation (2)** The other choices are unrelated.

Exercise 17: Classification of Organisms (page 225)

1. **Application (1)** Streptococcus is a single-celled organism of the bacteria family and fits in the kingdom Monera.

2. **Application (3)** Mold lacks chlorophyll and obtains food from another organism. It is classified in the kingdom Fungi.

Exercise 18: Evolution and Natural Selection (page 226)

1. **Application (3)** According to the passage, certain forms of life adapted to meet the demands of the environment. The fact that the duckbill platypus is found only in and around Australia supports the hypothesis that the platypus developed independently in a closed environment during the early history of mammals.

2. **Comprehension (1)** This is the best answer because the other choices are not true.

3. **Evaluation (1)** Of the choices listed, the migration pattern of a bird is a behavioral adaptation, not a physical one.

Exercise 19: Ecology and Ecosystems (page 228)

Application

1. grass for grazing

2. cattle, deer

3. mountain lion

Analysis

4. The destruction of the **mountain lion** led to the increase of grazing by **deer** and **cattle**, which led to **stripping** the grasses of the land and its eventual **erosion** by heavy rains.

CHAPTER 2: EARTH AND SPACE SCIENCE

Exercise 1: Stars and Galaxies (page 231)

Comprehension

1. 3, 4, 1, 2

2. **False** They would become black holes.

   True Red giants are the first visible sign we have of star death.

   False An Open universe would mean no stopping of expansion because of lack of gravity.

False The Sun is eight light minutes away; all other stars are much farther away.

Exercise 2: The Sun and the Solar System (page 232)

1. b, d, a, c

2. **False** Mars has dust storms; Jupiter has a gaseous surface.

   True The canals turned out to be possibly old river beds from earlier, warmer conditions.

   True The wind bands travel in the opposite direction, giving the planet a stripped look.

   True The sun is thought to be about five billion years old, halfway through its life cycle.

   False While the planet is covered in clouds, the vapor in the clouds is sulfuric acid, not rain (H_2O).

Exercise 3: Space Travel (page 233)

Analysis

1. 5, 1, 4, 2, 3

2. land like an airplane

   mutual efforts from many countries

   Skylab and Mir

   National Aeronautics and Space Administration

Exercise 4: The Planets (page 234)

Application

1. Earth, Mars

2. Mercury

3. Venus

Exercise 5: Plate Tectonics (page 236)

Comprehension

1. (2) In the passage, the occurrence of earthquakes, volcanoes, and mountains is explained by the theory of plate tectonics.

2. (4) Glaciers carve out glacier valleys and are not caused by plate tectonics.

Exercise 6: Continental Drift (page 237)

1. **Analysis** (3) This is the best choice because it takes into account both the theory of plate tectonics and the behavior of sea turtles.

Exercise 7: Earthquakes (page 238)

Evaluation

1. (3) The map shows the potential for the occurrence of the most moderate and major earthquake damage as being in the western United States. Choice (5) is an opinion statement.

2. **True**

   True

   False Not all earthquakes occur along the plate boundaries. The New Madrid earthquake zone in Missouri is the middle of the North American Plate.

   True

Exercise 8: Measuring Geologic Time (page 240)

1. **Comprehension** (5) The text states that sedimentary rocks are deposited near Earth's surface and that metamorphic rock is located just below igneous rock.

2. **Analysis** (5) The trilobite rocks are likely to be older than the coral because the greater the depth at which fossils are found, the older they are likely to be.

Exercise 9: Minerals and Rocks (page 241)

1. **Analysis** (3) Potassium, which makes up 1.85 percent of Earth's crust, is the only element that occupies three times more space than does silicon.

2. **Analysis** (5) The fact that oxygen combines with most of Earth's elements explains why it constitutes such a great part of Earth's crust.

Exercise 10: The Changing Earth (page 242)

1. gravity, wind, glaciers, running water

2. **Application** (5) Planting more seeds than necessary is a procedure most farmers follow to increase their chances of a bountiful harvest and has nothing to do with preventing erosion.

Exercise 11: The Beginning of the Oceans (page 244)

1. **Evaluation** (4) According to the text, many scientists believe that oceans were formed by the release of water bound up in Earth's interior.

2. **Comprehension** (2) Drinking water is purified from fresh water lakes and rivers.

Exercise 12: Ocean Tides (page 245)

1. **Analysis (4)** According to the illustration, the Moon is in a direct line with the Sun; therefore, Earth receives the combined gravity from the Sun and the Moon. This occurs during the new phase.

2. **Application (2)** The opposite condition of syzygy occurs when the Sun and the Moon are at their farthest distances from Earth. This means the least amount of gravity is affecting the tides, and the tidal difference is the lowest measured.

Exercise 13: Layers of Earth's Atmosphere (page 247)

1. **Comprehension (4)** The ionosphere extends from 30 miles to 300 miles in Earth's atmosphere. Noctilucent clouds are found at heights above 50 miles.

2. **Comprehension (3)** "D" radio waves are found at the same level as noctilucent clouds—in the lower ionosphere.

3. **Comprehension (1)** Clouds (located in the troposphere) shown at the same level as Mt. Everest's peak suggest that it may be occasionally hidden by clouds.

Exercise 14: The Water Cycle (page 248)

Analysis

1. B 2. D 3. A 4. C

Exercise 15: Humidity (page 249)

1. **Analysis (3)** According to the passage, warm air holds more moisture than cold air; therefore, when the temperature drops, the cold air cannot hold the amount of moisture that the warmer air held. At that temperature, the saturation point would be exceeded and the excess humidity would be released as rain.

2. **Analysis (3)** At a given time, water vapor in the air is constant. Cold air can hold less than warm air; and when air is heated, it has a greater capacity to hold moisture. If that moisture is not added to the air, the humidity level goes down.

Exercise 16: Air Masses, Fronts, and Weather (page 251)

1. **Comprehension (2)** According to the passage, warm fronts bring low-lying clouds, steady winds, and drizzling rain.

2. **Evaluation (5)** The reading covers all of the properties affecting fronts except the direction in which the air mass moves.

3. T (tornado)

   B (both)

   H (hurricane)

   T (tornado)

CHAPTER 3: PHYSICAL SCIENCE: CHEMISTRY

Exercise 1: Atomic Structure (page 253)

Comprehension

1. d 2. e 3. f 4. b 5. c 6. a

Exercise 2: Nuclear Energy (page 255)

1. **Application (4)** The passage states that fusion involves the uniting of two nuclei of a chemical element at high temperatures and pressures to form a new element. Hydrogen, the lightest element, is the only element listed whose nuclei when fused can form the second lightest element—helium.

2. **Application (1)** The passage states that fission involves the splitting of the nucleus of a heavy element. Plutonium is not a gas and, therefore, is the only heavy element listed.

Analysis

3. **False** That occurred at Chernobyl.

   False There are risks with any storage.

   True The control rods cover the fuel rods and prevent unchained reaction.

Exercise 3: Isotopic Elements (page 256)

1. **Application (3)** According to the chart, lithium's atomic mass is 6.94. Of all the elements shown, it would be the most likely to have an isotope of 6. If two lithium isotopes are fused, the atomic mass of the new element would be 12—the atomic mass of carbon.

2. **Application (1)** According to the passage, an isotope is a form of an element whose number of neutrons in its nucleus varies. The only element represented that is capable of doubling or tripling its mass to achieve a final mass of 2 or 3 would be hydrogen.

3. **Analysis** Opinion, Fact, Fact, Opinion, Fact

Exercise 4: Elements and Periodicity (page 258)

1. **Application (4)** The passage states that as the atomic number increases for elements in a column, similar chemical properties occur regularly and to a greater degree. The only physical property of which gold would have a higher degree is malleability because it is a soft and workable metal.

2. **Evaluation (3)** The fact that radon is found in the ground suggests that it is denser and weighs more than the others. It also has a higher atomic number, meaning that its weight and density are greater than those of other elements in its family.

Exercise 5: Balanced Equations (page 261)

Comprehension

1. B (balanced). The reaction begins and ends with two atoms of hydrogen (H) and one atom of oxygen (O).

2. U (unbalanced). The Fe (iron) does not balance out. The right side of the equation needs to read: $4Fe+3CO_2$.

3. B (balanced). All the elements are balanced at 2.

Exercise 6: Chemical Reactions (page 261)

1. **Evaluation (4)** The fact that there is a copper coating on the aluminum is the only evidence cited that can prove that a chemical change has taken place.

2. **Comprehension (2)** According to the passage, a chemical equation is balanced when it follows the Law of Conservation of Matter, which states that matter can neither be created nor destroyed in a chemical reaction.

3. **Analysis (2)** None of the others is a balanced equation indicating one molecule of carbon dioxide (CO_2) and one molecule of water (H_2O). Choice (4) started with carbon dioxide and water, but the equation does not balance.

Exercise 7: Elements in Combination (page 263)

1. **Application (1)** Salt is a compound composed of elements sodium and chlorine and has properties different from each.

2. **Application (2)** Air is a mixture of at least four gases. Each gas retains its own distinct properties.

Exercise 8: Chemical Bonding (page 265)

1. **Comprehension (2)** The passage says that ionic bonding is achieved by the transfer of electrons.

2. **Application** 4, 2, 5, 6, 3

Exercise 9: Acids, Bases and Salts (page 266)

1. **Analysis (3)** Water is neither acidic nor alkaline; therefore, it would be neutral on the pH scale.

2. **Evaluation (3)** A substance is an acid if it neutralizes a base to form a salt.

Exercise 10: A Car Battery (page 267)

1. **Application (2)** In the example, sulfuric acid, a conductor of electricity, is dissolved in water.

2. **Application (1)** The passage says that the lead loses two electrons when it reacts with sulfuric acid; therefore, lead is oxidized.

3. **Application (2)** Sulfuric acid is an oxidizing agent because it causes the lead in the battery to lose electrons. The lead dioxide is a reducing agent because it causes the sulfuric acid to gain electrons.

4. **Analysis (2)** A battery is completely discharged when the sulfuric acid is no longer capable of oxidizing lead and the lead dioxide is no longer able to reduce the sulfuric acid. The oxidation-reduction process that causes an electric current to flow cannot occur, and the battery is dead.

Exercise 11: Reaction Rate, Catalysts, and Equilibrium (page 269)

1. **Analysis (3)** A catalyst is an agent that speeds up a chemical reaction but that is not affected by the reaction itself. Lipase speeds up the rate at which fats are changed into fatty acids. Because lipase is found in the body, it may be described as a biological catalyst.

2. **Application (5)** According to the passage, chemical equilibrium occurs when the rate of forward reaction balances the rate of reverse reaction. In photosynthesis, plants take in water and carbon dioxide from the air to make starch with the light energy from the sun. The by-product of oxygen is released. The reverse of the process is respiration, the taking in of oxygen and combining of it with starch to form carbon dioxide and water, which plants then use for photosynthesis. Thus, the forward

reaction of photosynthesis is balanced by the reverse reaction of respiration, resulting in chemical equilibrium.

CHAPTER 4:
PHYSICAL SCIENCE: PHYSICS

Exercise 1: Laws of Force and Motion (page 271)

Application

1. AR   2. G   3. I   4. AF

Exercise 2: The Force of Gravity (page 271)

1. **Application (1)** Weight is the function of the attractive force between two objects. According to the passage, the strength of the force depends on the masses of the objects. Since Jupiter is larger than Earth, the attractive force must be greater, so the astronaut would weigh more on Jupiter.

2. **Application** The astronaut's weight would be less on Mercury since that planet has less mass.

Exercise 3: Forms of Energy (page 273)

Application

1. K   2. P   3. K

Exercise 4: Types of Energy (page 273)

1. **Application (1)** Nuclear energy results from the splitting of an atom of a heavy chemical element such as U-235.

2. **Application (2)** Gas and air are mixtures. When they are ignited, the chemical process of combustion occurs.

Exercise 5: Simple Machines (page 274)

1. **Analysis (3)** According to the passage, the greater the distance between the fulcrum and the applied force, the less the force required to perform the work. If the distance is increased to 20 feet, then the effort would be halved.

Exercise 6: Kinetic Theory of Matter (page 276)

Comprehension

1. True, False, False

2. **Application (1)** Convection is described as heat transferred by currents of gases and liquids. Warm air rising off a candle flame demonstrates convection.

Exercise 7: Heat and Temperature (page 276)

1. **Analysis (1)** Because concrete and steel both expand at about the same temperatures, they are ideal to use for roadways. Since concrete expands at a higher temperature, choice (2) is false.

Exercise 8: Wave Types (page 279)

Application

1. L (longitudinal wave)

   L (longitudinal wave)

   T (transverse wave)

2. **Application (2)** The Doppler Effect has become an important part of forecasting weather, especially when there are circulating wind patterns as you would see with a tornado, hurricane, or any low-pressure center.

Exercise 9: Properties of Waves (page 279)

1. **Comprehension (3)** The passage states that the wavelength is the distance between two successive wave crests or troughs. Points Z and Y are two successive wave crests.

Exercise 10: The Photoelectric Principle (page 280)

1. **Evaluation (2)** The passage states that an active substance emits electrons when light falls on it. Light intensity determines the strength of the current generated by the emission of electrons. This suggests that light energy is transmitted in packets or bundles and disputes the belief that light exists only as a continuous wave.

Exercise 11: Properties of Light Waves (page 282)

1. **Application (2)** Refraction is the bending of light waves as they pass from one medium to another—in this case, from water to air.

2. **Application (1)** Reflection is the return of a light wave when it strikes a shiny or very flat surface.

Exercise 12: Electricity and Magnetism (page 284)

1. **Analysis (1)** According to the text, the strong magnetic attraction coming from Earth's core tends to align the needle of the compass in a north-south direction.

2. **Application** (5) A magnetized object will attract either end of an unmagnetized object made of iron, steel, nickel, or cobalt but will attract only the opposite pole of another magnetized object. Aluminum, brass, and tin cannot be attracted.

Exercise 13: Conductors and Insulators (page 285)

Application

1. I (insulator)

2. I (insulator)

3. C (conductor)

4. I (insulator)

5. C (conductor)

Exercise 14: Electromagnets (page 285)

1. **Analysis** (3) The radio's electromagnet should not be placed near the compass because it would affect the magnetic reading from the North Pole.

2. **True** An insulator prevents the electricity from leaving the wire.

   True The electromagnet allows the doorbell to make a circuit when pressed.

   False The circuit is broken when the switch is in the off position.

Exercise 15: Creating Electricity (page 286)

Comprehension

1. transportation

2. alternative energies

3. steady

4. light

5. turbine

ANSWER KEY
LANGUAGE ARTS, READING

CHAPTER 1: INTERPRETING PROSE FICTION

Exercise 1: Inferring Time and Place (page 291)

1. The action takes place in early morning. Clues *are retiring fogs, an army stretched out . . . resting, and the army awakened.*

2. Clues as to the time period are subtle, but you can assume that the action took place in the 1860s because the method of communication seems very informal and "word-of-mouth." There are no official orders and no instruments of technology such as telephones, walkie-talkies, or e-mail. Present are *blue-clothed men*, an indication of soldiers of the Northern Army during the Civil War.

3. The action takes place on a site of a battlefield in the hills. Clues are *army stretched out on the hills, a river, hostile camp fires, distant hills, a brook*, and *rows of squat brown huts.*

Exercise 2: Recognizing Atmosphere (page 292)

Details that create an atmosphere of gloom include: a description of the day (*dull, dark*, and *soundless*), the tract of country (*clouds hung oppressively low* and *dreary*), and the House of Usher (*melancholy, bleak walls*, and *decayed trees*). These elements affect the character who had been riding alone on horseback so that *a sense of insufferable gloom pervaded [his] spirit* and who feels *an utter depression of soul.*

Exercise 3: Identifying Parts of Setting (page 292)

1. This part of the action takes place in the past because the past tense of verbs is used: *were, owned, patronized, became, moved, gave, offended, haunted, was, crossed, tramped*, and *squinted.*

2. Dexter is walking or skiing through the fairways of a golf course that *lie in enforced fallowness* because it is off-season. There are *desolate sandboxes knee-deep in crusted ice.*

3. In fall, *the days became crisp and gray.* In winter, *Dexter's skis moved over the snow that hid the fairways*, the links were *haunted by ragged sparrows for the long season*, and *the wind blew cold as misery.* In summer, there were *tees where the gay colors fluttered.*

4. The scenery *gave him a feeling of profound melancholy* [sadness or depression].

Exercise 4: Inferring Characterization (page 293)

1. **(4)** Although Huck misspells the word, he is afraid that the Widow Douglas would *civilize* him. Huck refers to the author Mark Twain as mainly telling the truth (with some "stretchers") in the book *Tom Sawyer*, but Huck is not saying that he himself was a liar. Thus, Choice 1, the world's biggest liar is not true. There is no evidence for choices 2, 3, or 5.

2. **(1)** Huck starts out by saying to the reader, *You don't know about me*, then proceeds to relate the narrative about himself and about Tom Sawyer, Aunt Polly, Mary, and the Widow Douglas.

Exercise 5: Identifying Details of Plot (and Conflict) (page 295)

1. **(3)** She sacrificed by selling her hair in order to have money to buy Jim a Christmas present.

2. **(5)** It is true that Della shopped all over town for the perfect gift, but Jim bought the combs in the store where Della had previously noticed them. Moreover, this detail does not compare with the irony that each gave up a prized possession in order to buy the other a gift. In so doing, the gift each gave the other was no longer practical.

Exercise 6: Determining Point of View (page 297)

Nouns or pronouns in the passage that refer to the old man are underlined. Nouns or pronouns that refer to the fish are shown in brackets [ ].

["Fish,"] the <u>old man</u> said. ["Fish,] [you] are going to have to die anyway. Do [you] have to kill <u>me</u> too?"

That way nothing is accomplished, <u>he</u> thought. <u>His</u> mouth was too dry to speak but <u>he</u> could not reach for the water now. <u>I</u> must get [him] alongside this time, <u>he</u> thought. <u>I</u> am not good for many more turns. Yes, <u>you</u> are, <u>he</u> told <u>himself</u>. <u>You're</u> good for ever.

On the next turn, <u>he</u> nearly had [him]. But again the [fish] righted [himself] and swam slowly away.

[You] are killing <u>me,</u> [fish,] the <u>old man</u> thought. But [you] have a right to. Never have <u>I</u> seen a greater, or more beautiful, or a calmer or more noble thing than [you], [brother]. Come on and kill <u>me.</u> <u>I</u> do not care [who] kills <u>who.</u>

Now <u>you</u> are getting confused in the head, <u>he</u> thought. <u>You</u> must keep <u>your</u> head clear. Keep <u>your</u> head clear and know how to suffer like <u>a man</u>. Or a [fish], <u>he</u> thought.

"Clear up, head," <u>he</u> said in a voice <u>he</u> could hardly hear. "Clear up."

In terms of how the fish might feel if it could think or talk, possibly the fish would feel some "kinship" with the man who describes the fish as beautiful, calm, and noble and who calls him "brother." The fish might empathize with the man who is doing what he must do, that is to fish. This may be the case even though for the man to be successful in fishing means that the fish will be caught and die. The fish might also admire the man for his courage and suffering.

Exercise 7: Inferring Theme (page 298)

1. **(4)** There is no evidence in the text that Eddy and Rhea are having marital problems.

2. **(1)** Both Danny and Eddy overcome barriers through effort and sacrifice. Danny graduates from high school in spite of an assistant principal who always blames him unfairly, a father who is verbally abusive, and other boys who cause the auto accident that nearly kills Danny. Eddy, who lacks general ability and fears speaking, gives an excellent speech at graduation.

Exercise 8: Detecting Style and Tone (page 301)

1. **(5)** A woman such as the American should be exposed for her false values because she was overlooking the fact that her daughter was in love; instead, she made light conversation about train travel, the country, the season of the year, and a hotel.

2. **(2)** The reader feels sympathy for a young woman who cannot marry the man of her choice because of her mother's influence and, perhaps, control.

Exercise 9: Identifying Images as Part of Overall Style (page 302)

This passage is heavy in descriptions and images that appeal to your sense of sight and are <u>underlined</u>; those that appeal to your sense of hearing are in **boldface**.

In agony the **brakes cried,** held: the scene, <u>dizzy with color,</u> rocked with the <u>car,</u> down a little, back up, giddily, helplessly, while <u>dust exploded</u> up on all sides. "Mommy!" Timmy **screamed,** fascinated by the violence, yet his **wail** was oddly still and drawn out, and <u>his eyes</u> never once turned to his mother. The <u>little Mexican boy</u> had <u>disappeared</u> in <u>front of the car</u>. Still the <u>red dust arose,</u> the faces at the bus jerked around together, <u>white eyes, white teeth, faces</u> were propelled toward the <u>windows of the bus,</u> empty a second before. "God, God," Annette **murmured;** she had not yet released the <u>steering wheel</u>, and on it her <u>fingers began to tighten</u> as if they might tear the wheel off, hold it up to defend <u>her and her child,</u> perhaps even to attack.

CHAPTER 2: INTERPRETING POETRY

Exercise 1: Understanding Idea and Emotion in Two Poems (page 304)

1. **(4)** Romantic love is mentioned in both poems; it is referred to repeatedly in Sonnet 43.

2. **(1)** The speakers in both poems express love consistently, proclaiming constant devotion toward the loved one.

Exercise 2: The Shape of Poetry (page 307)

1. There is one sentence; a period ends it.

2. The first stanza states the speaker is *a child of the Americas, mestiza of the Caribbean, and a child of many diaspora."* In the second stanza, she describes herself as *a U.S. Puerto Rican Jew, a product of the ghettos, an immigrant.* The third stanza states she's *Caribeña Latino-american.* In the fourth stanza, she claims *Africa is in me, Taino is in me,* and *Europe lives in me.*

3. (3) The citing of many cultures joining together and the sense of pride and wholeness expressed by the speaker suggest an appreciation of multiculturalism.

Exercise 3: The Language of Poetry (page 309)

Line 1: imagery

Line 2: personification

Line 3: personification

Line 4: imagery

Line 5: personification

Exercise 4: The Sound of Poetry

(page 311)

1. Examples in stanza 1 are w*eak and weary, quaint and curious, nodded, nearly napping.* Examples in stanza 2 are *surcease of sorrow, lost Lenore,* and *rare and radiant.*

2. (1) Repeating the word *rapping* with its short a vowel sound is suggestive of knocking.

Exercise 5: Interpreting a Poem (page 316)

1. (5) The speaker longs for leisure time to enjoy life and consequently would be attracted by vacation time.

2. (2) Throughout the poem, the speaker emphasizes the joys of stopping to notice animals, woods, streams, and skies—all embodiments of Beauty. Enjoy life while the opportunity exists.

CHAPTER 3: INTERPRETING DRAMA

Exercise 1: Comprehending a Play (page 318)

(Exact wording may vary)

Hamlet was outside when a <u>ghost appeared</u>. The ghost began to <u>speak</u>. At first, Hamlet <u>felt sorry</u> for the ghost. The ghost claimed to be <u>the spirit of Hamlet's father</u>.

The ghost wanted Hamlet to <u>revenge the murder of Hamlet's father.</u>

Exercise 2: Inferring Mood from Dialogue (page 319)

1. (1) The rudeness of Edward toward Catherine, Victoria's responses to Edward, and Catherine's abrupt departure all indicate that the mood of the scene is tense.

2. (2) The use of the long dash [—] indicates a brief pause or break in thought: *Not now—; You're talking—;* and *Oh—.*

Exercise 3: Understanding Character (page 322)

1. (4) Paul attempts to explain and discuss the significance of the reading passage to Billie. In the same way, he would explain and discuss an artwork with her.

2. (1) The lines provide pleasant images and metaphor, recommending the simple life and its beauty.

3. (5) The phrase *to be bigger* suggests growth. Learning helps a person grow.

CHAPTER 4: INTERPRETING PROSE NONFICTION

Exercise 1: Detecting the Author's Purpose for Writing (page 326)

The author would agree with statements 1 and 4.

In statement 2, we are not correct in assuming that our partners will behave in a certain way.

In statement 3, we have forgotten that men and women are supposed to be different.

Exercise 2: Reading an Article for Facts (page 327)

Sentence 3: *Why:* Professionals say children can communicate with hand signs much sooner than they can master verbal skills.

Sentence 4: *How:* "It's a question of how children mature"

Who: Marilyn Daniels, an associate professor of speech communication and author of a forthcoming book . . .

Where: at Pennsylvania State University

Sentence 6: *What:* Most suggest using American Sign Language (ASL)

Why: because it's easy to learn, standardized, and an official language used by the deaf community

Sentence 8: *What:* Signing not only increases the parents' bond and interaction with their babies, it helps reduce a major source of tantrums and stress for infants.

Exercise 3: Reading an Editorial for Informed Opinion (page 328)

1. The study concludes that the *Brady Law has failed to significantly decrease handgun homicides since its 1994 enactment . .*

2. The editorial affirms the publisher's belief that *the law's background check requirement remains a reasonable and prudent guard against those who seek handguns with criminal intent.*

3. The newspaper would not favor a repeal (abandonment or recall) of the Brady Law.

Exercise 4: Analyzing a Speech for Purpose (page 329)

1. **(2)** Sentence 2: "testing whether that nation . . . can long endure."

2. **(4)** It is necessary, of course, to bury the dead (Choice 1) and honor the dead (Choice 2), but the real challenge after the Civil War is for the nation to "have a new birth of freedom." President Lincoln does not say anything about changing the government (Choice 3). He says the government "shall not perish from the earth," so this makes Choice 5 incorrect.

3. **(2)** *Rebuke* means to reprimand, and there was no evidence of criticism of the South in the speech.

Exercise 5: Finding the Notable in a Biography (page 331)

1. **(5)** All statements in Choices 1, 2, 3, 4, and 5 are true, but only Choice 5 shows participation in flying at the age of seventy-two. This is the best evidence of a serious interest in flying all her life.

2. **(2)** As a female pilot in World War II, Ringenberg certainly demonstrated her willingness to enter a nontraditional field. She selected her career herself, so she did follow her own mind and heart.

Exercise 6: Interpreting a Diary or Journal (page 334)

1. **(5)** As is evident by the title "Self-Reliance," Emerson believed in the power of the individual, rather than in the group or in greater society. Choices 1, 2, and 4 do not express Emerson's beliefs because they all involve working with others. Choice 3 does not express his beliefs because the person in authority would be dictating action to the individual.

2. **(3)** Emerson felt that the individual was the most reliable source by saying, *Nothing is at last sacred but the integrity of your own mind.* He would not have agreed with following the crowd (Choice 1), agreeing just for the sake of harmony (Choice 4), or not challenging authority (Choice 5). The passage does not deal with the concept of leadership (Choice 2).

Exercise 7: Interpreting Artistic Commentary (page 336)

1. **(2)** In using the metaphor *a geography of the imagination,* the reviewer is asking the reader to make the "journey" in time and history from architecture in the Mediterranean area of Europe to farm country in Iowa. The effect, thus, is to show that this example of American art and architecture was influenced by Europe. Choice 1 is false, and Choices 3, 4, and 5 are too literal in focusing on geography and conservation.

2. **(3)** If we are "blinded by familiarity and parody," we are not looking carefully at the painting because we know it so well and perhaps because the painting has sometimes been criticized as too common in subject. Thus, the reviewer is asking us to take a more careful look at the painting to understand it better. There is no support in the text for the other choices.

3. **(5)** *Sobriety* is a characteristic that means serious, steady, and earnest. *Industry* is the characteristic of being hard working (and productive). The other choices are not reasonable conclusions.

ANSWER KEY
MATHEMATICS

CHAPTER 1: NUMBER SENSE

Exercise 1: Powers and Roots (page 342)
1. **64** $8 \times 8 = 64$
2. **1** $1 \times 1 \times 1 \times 1 \times 1 \times 1 \times 1 = 1$
3. **1**   A number to zero power is 1.
4. **1000** $10 \times 10 \times 10 = 1000$
5. **625** $5 \times 5 \times 5 \times 5 = 625$
6. **1** $1 = 1^2$
7. **12** $144 = 12^2$
8. **5.3 or $2\sqrt{7}$** $\sqrt{28}$ is a little more than $\sqrt{25} = 5$, so 5.3 is a good estimate. $\sqrt{28} = \sqrt{4 \times 7} = 2\sqrt{7}$
9. **20** $400 = 20^2$
10. **0** $0 = 0^2$

Exercise 2: Order of Operations (page 344)
1. **34** $2 + 6 \times 4 + 8 = 2 + 24 + 8 = 26 + 8 = 34$
2. **5** $\frac{6+9}{3} = \frac{15}{3} = 5$
3. **48** $8 \times 3 + 6 \times 4 = 24 + 24 = 48$
4. **20** $4 \times (8 - 3) = 4 \times 5 = 20$
5. **0** $7 - 5 + 3 - 5 = 2 + 3 - 5 = 5 - 5 = 0$
6. **8** $6 + 21 \div 3 - 5 = 6 + 7 - 5 = 13 - 5 = 8$
7. **20** $15 - 3 + 2^3 = 15 - 3 + 8 = 12 + 8 = 20$
8. **256** $4(5 + 3)^2 = 4(8)^2 = 4(64) = 256$

Exercise 3: Arithmetic Expressions (page 345)
1. **(2) $75 + 15 \times 55$**

   15 hrs @ \$55 + \$75 = $15 \times 55 + 75$
2. **(1) $5.00 - (3.98 + .31 - .75)$**

   Add price + tax and subtract the coupon; then subtract that amount from \$5.
3. **(3) $\frac{5 + 7 + 3 + 9}{4}$**

   To find the average, find the total and then divide by 4.

Exercise 4: Word Problems (page 346)
1. **(3) 830** $5500 \div 500 = 11$

   $9130 \div 11 = 830$
2. **(5) Not enough information is given.**

   Information not given: amount used for expenses

3. **(1) 1865**

   $266 + 332 + 387 + 352 + 528 = 1865$
4. **(1) 373** $1865 \div 5 = 373$
5. **(3) $1298 - (350 + 375 + 417)$**
6. **(3)** $\frac{19700 - (3150 + 500)}{60}$

Exercise 5: Evaluating Formulas (page 349)
1. **144 sq in.**   Area of a square = side^2 = $12^2 = 144$ sq in.
2. **125 cu in.**   Volume of a cube = edge^3 = $5^3 = 125$ cu in.
3. **54 sq cm**   Area of a triangle $= \frac{1}{2} \times$ base $\times$ height $= \frac{1}{2} \times 12 \times 9 = 54$
4. **1130.4 cu in.**   Volume of a cylinder = $\pi \times$ radius$^2 \times$ height $= 3.14 \times 6^2 \times 10 = 1130.4$ cu in.

CHAPTER 2: DECIMAL NUMBERS AND OPERATIONS

Exercise 1: Reading and Writing Decimals (page 351)
1. **(2) .05**
2. **(1) 6.2**
3. **(3) 430.006**
4. **.7**
5. **6.032**
6. **.0065**

Exercise 2: Comparing Decimals (page 352)
1. (a) **.05**   (b) **4.1**   (c) **.7**
   (d) **.51**   (e) **1.033**
2. (a) **2.15, 2.105, 1.95**
   (b) **.0503, .005, .0035**
   (c) **6.607, 6.4, 6.07, 6**
3. **14.003 lb, 14.03 lb, 14.3 lb, 14.3033 lb**

Exercise 3: Rounding Decimals (page 353)
1. **\$1827**
2. **\$1.36**
3. **3.14**

Exercise 4: Scientific Notation (page 354)
1. 8.2×10^{-3}
2. 3.82×10^4
3. 5.8×10^{-1}
4. 1624
5. .312
6. 8.24

Exercise 5: Adding and Subtracting Decimals (page 355)

1. 17.91
$$\begin{array}{r} 5.9 \\ 2.46 \\ 6 \\ 3.07 \\ + .48 \\ \hline 17.91 \end{array}$$

2. 37.8
$$\begin{array}{r} 43.0 \\ - 5.2 \\ \hline 37.8 \end{array}$$

3. 968.749
$$\begin{array}{r} 237.42 \\ 96.4 \\ 298.674 \\ 186.21 \\ + 150.045 \\ \hline 968.749 \end{array}$$

4. $347.56
$$\begin{array}{r} 42.87 \\ 5.93 \\ 20 \\ 17.48 \\ 38.40 \\ \hline 124.68 \end{array} \qquad \begin{array}{r} 472.24 \\ -124.68 \\ \hline 347.56 \end{array}$$

5. 2877.8 mi
$$\begin{array}{r} 28054.1 \\ -25176.3 \\ \hline 2877.8 \end{array}$$

6. (2) 46.25
$$\begin{array}{r} 46.75 \\ - .50 \\ \hline 46.25 \end{array}$$

7. $51.45 $17.50 + 4.95 + 6 + 16.25 + 6.75 = 51.45$

8. $215.11 $160 + 51.45 + 3.66 = 215.11$

Exercise 6: Multiplying Decimals (page 357)

1. .051
$$\begin{array}{r} .85 \\ \times .06 \\ \hline .0510 \end{array}$$

2. .5525
$$\begin{array}{r} 6.50 \\ \times .085 \\ \hline 3250 \\ 52000 \\ \hline .55250 \end{array}$$

3. $8.96
$$\begin{array}{r} \$128 \\ \times .07 \\ \hline 8.96 \end{array}$$

4. (3) 7.85×12

Exercise 7: Dividing Decimals (page 360)

1. 120.1
$$.05\overline{)6.005} \quad 120.1$$

2. .004
$$3\overline{)0.012} \quad .004$$

3. 1.9
$$2.5\overline{)4.75} \quad 1.9$$

4. 16
$$1.25\overline{)20.00} \quad 16$$

Exercise 8: Multiplying and Dividing Decimals by Multiples of 10 (page 360)
1. 4720
2. .0617
3. 4.5612
4. .057
5. 5 days
$1.5 \times 10 = 15$
$75 \div 15 = 5$

Exercise 9: Estimating (page 361)
1. Estimate: $5 + 12 + 75 + 10 + 8 = 110$
   Exact: $4.8 + 12.3 + 74.5 + 10 + 8.1 = 109.7$

2. Estimate: $25 + 3 = 28, 50 - 28 = 22$
   Exact: $24.75 + 2.50 = 27.25, 50 - 27.25 = 22.75$

Exercise 10: Decimal Word Problems (page 361)
1. (5) $2677.29
   Estimate: $400 + 500 + 400 + 600 + 700 = $2600
   Exact: $425 + 485.75 + 399.87 + 642.15 + 724.52 = 2677.29$

2. (2) 17.8
   Estimate: $2500 \div 125 = 20$
   Exact: $2492 \div 140 + 17.8$

3. (2) $339.02
   Estimate: gross pay = $350 + 100 = 450$, deductions = $30 + 80 = 110$, net pay = $450 - 110 = 340$
   Exact: gross pay = $338 + 114.03 = 452.03$, deductions = $31.64 + 81.37 = 113.01$, net pay = $452.03 - 113.01 = 339.02$

4. (2) $7.68
   Estimate: $320 \div 40 = 8$
   Exact: $307.20 \div 40 = 7.68$

5. (4) $20,099

Estimate: $3500 + 50 \times 300 = 3500 + 15000 = 18500$

Exact: $3500 + 48 \times 345.81 = 20,098.88 \approx 20,099$

CHAPTER 3: FRACTIONS AND OPERATIONS

Exercise 1: Types of Fractions (page 364)
1. c   2. a   3. b

Exercise 2: Raising and Reducing Fractions (page 365)
1. 9   2. 9   3. 12   4. 3
5. 2   6. 5   7. $\frac{1}{3}$ 8. $\frac{5}{6}$

Exercise 3: Changing Between Fractions and Decimals (page 367)
1. $\frac{450}{1000} = \frac{9}{20}$

2. $\frac{7}{100}$

3. $3\frac{1}{10}$

4. .2 $5\overline{)1.0}^{\,.2}$

5. $.44\frac{4}{9}$ $9\overline{)4.00}^{\,.44\frac{4}{9}}$

6. 1.25 $4\overline{)5.00}^{\,1.25}$

Exercise 4: Changing Improper Fractions and Mixed Numbers (page 368)
1. $\frac{14}{9}$ 2. $\frac{17}{5}$ 3. $\frac{33}{8}$ 4. $2\frac{3}{7}$
5. 1   6. $1\frac{1}{2}$

Exercise 5: Comparing Numbers (page 371)
1. $\frac{7}{8}$ 2. $\frac{2}{3}$ 3. $\frac{3}{4}$ 4. <
5. >   6. <   7. <   8. >
9. =   10. >   11. =

Exercise 6: Adding and Subtracting Fractions (page 374)
1. $\frac{4}{5}$ $\frac{1}{10} + \frac{7}{10} = \frac{8}{10} = \frac{4}{5}$

2. $\frac{11}{24}$ $\frac{3}{8} + \frac{1}{12} = \frac{9}{24} + \frac{2}{24} = \frac{11}{24}$

3. $7\frac{17}{35}$ $4\frac{1}{5} + 3\frac{2}{7} = 4\frac{7}{35} + 3\frac{10}{35} = 7\frac{17}{35}$

4. $10\frac{1}{24}$ $3\frac{7}{8} + 2\frac{5}{6} + 3\frac{1}{3} = 3\frac{21}{24} + 2\frac{20}{24} + 3\frac{8}{24} = 8\frac{49}{24} = 10\frac{1}{24}$

5. $\frac{1}{8}$ $\frac{5}{8} - \frac{1}{2} = \frac{5}{8} - \frac{4}{8} = \frac{1}{8}$

6. $\frac{3}{8}$ $\frac{11}{16} - \frac{5}{16} = \frac{6}{16} = \frac{3}{8}$

7. $13\frac{2}{3}$ $25\frac{1}{6} - 11\frac{1}{2} = 25\frac{1}{6} - 11\frac{3}{6} = 24\frac{7}{6} - 11\frac{3}{6} = 13\frac{4}{6} = 13\frac{2}{3}$

8. $5\frac{1}{3}$ $10 - 4\frac{2}{3} = 9\frac{3}{3} - 4\frac{2}{3} = 5\frac{1}{3}$

Exercise 7: Multiplying Fractions (page 376)
1. $\frac{1}{6}$ $\frac{6}{15} \times \frac{5}{12} = \frac{30}{180} = \frac{1}{6}$

2. $\frac{3}{70}$ $\frac{3}{8} \times \frac{2}{15} \times \frac{6}{7} = \frac{36}{840} = \frac{3}{70}$

3. $32\frac{2}{3}$ $8\frac{1}{6} \times 4 = \frac{49}{6} \times \frac{4}{1} = \frac{196}{6} = \frac{98}{3} = 32\frac{2}{3}$

4. $2\frac{5}{14}$ $2\frac{3}{4} \times \frac{6}{7} = \frac{11}{4} \times \frac{6}{7} = \frac{66}{28} = \frac{33}{14} = 2\frac{5}{14}$

5. $4\frac{1}{2}$ $3\frac{3}{8} \times 1\frac{3}{9} = \frac{27}{8} \times \frac{12}{9} = \frac{324}{72} = 4\frac{36}{72} = 4\frac{1}{2}$

Exercise 8: Dividing Fractions (page 377)
1. $\frac{3}{5}$ $\frac{4}{10} \div \frac{2}{3} = \frac{4}{10} \times \frac{3}{2} = \frac{12}{20} = \frac{3}{5}$

2. $\frac{1}{10}$ $\frac{2}{5} \div 4 = \frac{2}{5} \times \frac{1}{4} = \frac{2}{20} = \frac{1}{10}$

3. $2\frac{4}{9}$ $3\frac{2}{3} \div 1\frac{1}{2} = \frac{11}{3} \div \frac{3}{2} = \frac{11}{3} \times \frac{2}{3} = \frac{22}{9} = 2\frac{4}{9}$

4. $3\frac{3}{5}$ $9 \div 2\frac{1}{2} = \frac{9}{1} \div \frac{5}{2} = \frac{9}{1} \times \frac{2}{5} = \frac{18}{5} = 3\frac{3}{5}$

Exercise 9: Item Sets (page 378)
1. **(3) $47.04**

$6 \times .98 = 5.88$, $8 \times 5.88 = 47.04$

2. **(1) $52.56**

$8 \times 13.95 = 111.60$
$47.04 + 12 = 59.04$
$111.60 - 59.04 = 52.56$

3. **(3) $\frac{7}{8}$ mi**

$\frac{3}{4} - \frac{1}{4} = \frac{2}{4}$

$\frac{2}{4} + \frac{3}{8} = \frac{7}{8}$

4. **(5) Not enough information is given.**

5. **(5) Not enough information is given.**

The chart is for the second week in April, not the third.

6. **(3) $(12.72 \times 40) + (1\frac{1}{2} \times 12.72 \times 3\frac{1}{4})$**

CHAPTER 4: NUMBER RELATIONSHIPS

Exercise 1: Number Line (page 381)

1. $-4 < -1\frac{1}{2}$ or $-1\frac{1}{2} > -4$
2. $-3 < 1$ or $1 > -3$

Exercise 2: Signed Numbers (page 382)

1. -12 2. $+75$ 3. $+4.5$ 4. $<$

5. $<$ 6. $<$ 7. $>$ 8. 9

9. $\frac{1}{2}$ 10. $2\frac{3}{4}$

Exercise 3: Combining Signed Numbers (page 383)

1. -2 2. -17 3. -5 4. -33

5. -3 6. -19 7. 3.8 8. -7.7

Exercise 4: Eliminating Double Signs (page 384)

1. 1 2. 22 3. $\$158$

Exercise 5: Multiplying and Dividing Signed Numbers (page 385)

1. -144 2. 225 3. -84 4. 0

5. -5 6. 3 7. $-\frac{1}{2}$ 8. $-\$2214$

Exercise 6: Using Signed Numbers in Problem Solving (page 385)

1. (4) $575 + 125 + 46 - (98 + 26 + 38 + 310 + 50)$
2. (3) $+376$

CHAPTER 5: STATISTICS AND DATA ANALYSIS

Exercise 1: Ratio and Rate (page 387)

1. $\frac{1}{4}$ 2. $\frac{20}{1}$ 3. $\frac{8}{1}$

Exercise 2: Applications of Ratio (page 387)

1. $\frac{3}{5}$ $\dfrac{120\ \text{supplies}}{200\ \text{total}} = \dfrac{3}{5}$

2. $\frac{24}{5}$ $\dfrac{\$120\ \text{supplies}}{\$25} = \dfrac{24}{5}$

3. $\frac{1}{4}$ $\dfrac{\$1{,}700{,}000\ \text{liabilities}}{\$6{,}800{,}000\ \text{assets}} = \dfrac{1}{4}$

4. $\$2.43$ $\$729 \div 300 = \$2.43$

5. $\frac{1}{3}$ $\dfrac{250\ \text{females}}{750\ \text{members}} = \dfrac{1}{3}$

Exercise 3: Solving Proportions (page 388)

1. 4 $m = \dfrac{2 \times 10}{5} = \dfrac{20}{5} = 4$

2. 1 $x = \dfrac{3 \times 7}{21} = \dfrac{21}{21} = 1$

3. $6\frac{2}{3}$ $y = \dfrac{5 \times 20}{15} = \dfrac{100}{15} = 6\frac{2}{3}$

4. 15 $n = \dfrac{30 \times 12}{24} = \dfrac{360}{24} = 15$

Exercise 4: Application of Proportion (page 389)

1. (2) 42 $\dfrac{2\ \text{managers}}{9\ \text{sales clerks}} = \dfrac{N\ \text{managers}}{189\ \text{sales clerks}}$

   $N = \dfrac{2 \times 189}{9} = 42$

2. (5) 18 $2\frac{1}{4} \div \frac{1}{8} = 18$

3. (3) 15 inches $\dfrac{4}{6} = \dfrac{10}{x}$

   $x = \dfrac{6 \times 10}{4} = 15$

Exercise 5: Probability (page 391)

1. 25% $\dfrac{13}{52} = \dfrac{1}{4} = 25\%$

2. $\frac{1}{13}$ $\dfrac{4}{52} = \dfrac{1}{13}$

3. (5) $\frac{5}{6}$

4. (4) $33\frac{1}{3}\%$ $\dfrac{2}{6} = \dfrac{1}{3} = 33\frac{1}{3}\%$

5. (5) 50% $\dfrac{3}{6} = \dfrac{1}{2} = 50\%$

6. (2) $\frac{1}{10}$

7. (3) $\frac{1}{2}$

8. (4) $\frac{3}{4}$ $960 - 240 = 720$ not broken

   $\dfrac{720}{960} = \dfrac{3}{4}$

Exercise 6: Dependent Probability (page 392)

1. $\frac{4}{51}$

2. $\frac{4}{17}$ $\dfrac{12}{51} = \dfrac{4}{17}$

3. $\frac{2}{3}$ $\dfrac{6}{9} = \dfrac{2}{3}$

4. $\frac{1}{8}$

5. $\frac{1}{4}$ $\dfrac{2}{8} = \dfrac{1}{4}$

Exercise 7: Measures of Central Tendency (page 394)

1. $\$83.38$

   $\$109.88 - 26.50 = \$83.38$

2. **Mean = \$55.57**

   Median = \$50.55

   Mean = $(34.81 + 50.55 + 26.50 + 49.50 + 109.88 + 54.56 + 63.19) \div 7 = 55.57$

   Median: 50.55 is the middle value because there are three stocks less expensive and three stocks more expensive.

3. **Cisco Systems (50.55) is the mode** because it had the highest volume.

4. **Total investment would be \$13,638. The average price per share would be \$68.19.**

   $100 \times 109.88 + 100 \times 26.50 = 13638$

   $13638 \div 200 = 68.19$

Exercise 8: Charts, Tables, and Schedules (page 395)

1. **10,061** $32,440 - 22,379 = 10,061$

2. **(1) $\frac{1}{8}$** $\frac{30000}{280000} = \frac{1}{8}$

3. **(4) Asian/Pacific Islander**

   Asian/Pacific Islander % change = 50%

Exercise 9: Mixed Graph Practice (page 398)

1. **$\frac{3}{100}$** 3% means 3 per hundred.

2. **\$40,000** $\frac{24000}{N} = \frac{60}{100}$

   $N = \frac{24000 \times 100}{60} = 40000$

3. **\$25,200** $.27 + .03 + .07 = .37$

   $1.00 - .37 = .63$

   $.63 \times 40000 = 25,200$

4. **appx. 1557 ft** $1450 + 107 = 1557$

5. **31%** $\frac{450}{1450} = \frac{N}{100}$

   $N = \frac{450 \times 100}{1450} = 31.03$

6. **1000 ft**

   The middle value is the Eiffel Tower at 1000 ft.

7. **\$90,250**

   $4000 \times 8.50 + 4500 \times 12.50 = 90250$

8. **attendance declines**

9. **$6083\frac{1}{3}$**

   $(500 + 1000 + 1500 + 2000 + 3000 + 4500 + 5000 + 6500 + 4000 + 4500 + 3000 + 1000) \div 6 = 6083\frac{1}{3}$

CHAPTER 6: PERCENTS

Exercise 1: Interchanging Percents, Fractions, and Decimals (page 401)

1. **87%** $\frac{87}{100}$ .87

2. **2%** $\frac{2}{100} = \frac{1}{50}$ .02

3. **$16\frac{2}{3}\%$** $\frac{50}{3} \times \frac{1}{100} = \frac{1}{6}$ $.16\frac{2}{3}$

4. **300%** $\frac{300}{100} = 3$ 3.00

5. **125%** $\frac{125}{100} = \frac{5}{4}$ 1.25

6. **.5%** $\frac{5}{10} \times \frac{1}{100} = \frac{1}{200}$ .005

7. **9.9%** $9\frac{9}{10} \times \frac{1}{100} = \frac{99}{1000}$ .099

8. **$\frac{1}{2}\%$** $\frac{1}{2} \times \frac{1}{100} = \frac{1}{200}$

   $.5 \times .01 =$ .005

9. **75%** $\frac{75}{100} = \frac{3}{4}$ .75

10. **5%** $\frac{5}{100} = \frac{1}{20}$ .05

11. **.25%** $.0025 \div .01 =$ .25

12. **37.5%** $3 \div 8 = .375 =$ 37.5%

13. **450%** $4.5 \div .01 =$ 450

14. **62.5%** $.625 \div .01 =$ 62.5

15. **225%** $2.25 \div .01 =$ 225

Exercise 2: Percent Problems (page 403)

1. **1.2** $.04 \times 30 = 1.2$

2. **90** $45 \times 2.00 = 90$

3. **400** $\frac{10}{N} = \frac{2.5}{100}$

   $N = \frac{10 \times 100}{2.5} = 400$

4. **35%** $\frac{210}{600} = \frac{N}{100}$

   $N = \frac{210 \times 100}{600} = 35$

5. **112.5** $\frac{18}{N} = \frac{16}{100}$

   $N = \frac{18 \times 100}{16} = 112.5$

6. **9%** $\frac{30.60}{340} = \frac{N}{100}$

   $N = \frac{30.60 \times 100}{340} = 9$

Exercise 3: Percent Word Problems (page 404)

1. **80%** $\frac{32}{40} = \frac{N}{100}$

   $N = \frac{32 \times 100}{40} = 80$

2. **\$23.98** $.80 \times 3 \times 9.99 = 23.98$

3. **\$252** $.12 \times 2100 = 252$

4. **\$26,460** $12 \times 1.05 \times 2100 = 26460$

Exercise 4: Interest Problems (page 407)

1. (2) **\$540**

   90 days is $\frac{1}{4}$ of a year, so $i = prt = 18000 \times .12 \times \frac{1}{4} = 540$.

2. (2) $\frac{480 \times 100}{6000}$

   $$\frac{480}{6000} = \frac{N}{100}$$

   $$N = \frac{480 \times 100}{6000}$$

3. (4) **\$4,500**

   $$\frac{360}{N} = \frac{8}{100}$$

   $$N = \frac{360 \times 100}{8} = 4500$$

4. (3) **\$12,600**

   $15,000 + 65,000 + 5,000 - 25,000 = 60,000$

   $i = prt = 60,000 \times .105 \times 2 = 12600$

CHAPTER 7: ALGEBRA

Exercise 1: Terms (page 408)

1. $8x$, $7y$, and -6

2. $2x^2$ and $-\frac{3}{x}$

3. $8ab$ and 12

Exercise 2: Evaluating Algebraic Expressions (page 409)

1. **12**

   $x^2 - 3x + 2 = 5^2 - 3 \times 5 + 2 = 25 - 15 + 2 = 12$

2. **150 miles**

   $d = rt = 60 \times 2.5 = 150$

3. **44 inches**

   $P = 2(l + w) = 2(15 + 7) = 2 \times 22 = 44$

Exercise 3: Equations (page 410)

1. 5 plus 7 times a number is 19.

2. A number less 5 is 23.

3. A number divided by 8 is 9.

Exercise 4: Eyeballing (page 410)

1. 13   2. 2

3. 5   4. 4

Exercise 5: One-Step Equations (page 411)

1. **9** $x + 6 = 15$

   $x + 6 - 6 = 15 - 6$

   $x = 9$

2. **15** $x - 3 = 12$

   $x = 12 + 3 = 15$

3. **64** $\frac{x}{4} = 16$

   $x = 16 \times 4 = 64$

4. **28** $\frac{1}{2}x = 14$

   $x = 14 \times 2 = 28$

Exercise 6: Translating English to Algebra (page 412)

1. $14x$

2. $\frac{x - y}{3}$

3. $x^2 + y^2$

4. $\frac{x^3}{4}$

5. $\frac{5x}{2x}$

Exercise 7: Translating Sentences to Equations (page 413)

1. $x - 2 = 40$

2. $3x + 1 = 25$

3. $2x + 18 = 22$

4. $\frac{x}{4} = 18$

5. (3) $x - 48 = 75$

6. (3) $25 + 32h = 84$

Exercise 8: Solving One-Step Algebra Word Problems (page 414)

1. **16** $3.25x = 52$

2. **\$2500** $\frac{3}{4}x = 1875$

3. **158 lbs** $x + 14 = 172$

4. **\$18,000** $.09x = 1620$

Exercise 9: Combining Like Terms (page 414)

1. $5x^2 + 7x + 9$

2. $3y$

3. $3a$

4. $13x - 3$

5. $9xy + 6x - 3y$

Exercise 10: Simplifying Grouping Symbols (page 415)

1. $28x - 32$
2. $-2x + 2$
3. $6x + 12 - 9y$
4. $-11x - 18$
5. $5x - 2$

Exercise 11: Solving Multistep Equations (page 416)

1. $x = 2$

$$3x + 9 = 15$$
$$3x = 15 - 9 = 6$$
$$x = \frac{6}{3} = 2$$

2. $x = 1$

$$2(5x - 11) + 12x = 0$$
$$10x - 22 + 12x = 0$$
$$22x - 22 = 0$$
$$22x = 22$$
$$x = \frac{22}{22} = 1$$

3. $x = 21$

$$\frac{4x}{3} - 14 = 14$$
$$\frac{4x}{3} = 28$$
$$4x = 84$$
$$x = \frac{84}{4} = 21$$

Exercise 12: Setting Up and Solving Multistep Equations (page 417)

1. (4) $2x + 24 = 56$
2. (1) 16

$$2x + 24 = 56$$
$$2x = 56 - 24 = 32$$
$$x = \frac{32}{2} = 16$$

3. (1) $x + 2x + 38 = 8324$
4. (5) 5524

$$x + 2x + 38 = 8324$$
$$3x + 38 = 8324$$
$$3x = 8324 - 38 = 8286$$
$$x = \frac{8286}{3} = 2762$$
$$2x = 2(2762) = 5524$$

Exercise 13: One-Step Inequalities (page 418)

1. (b) $x \leq 10$
2. $x > -2$
3. $x < 2$
4. $x > -36$
5. $x \leq 7$
6. $x < 4$

Exercise 14: Ordered Pairs (page 420)

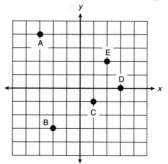

Exercise 15: Distance Between Two Points (page 421)

1. 4 units
2. 5 units

$$d = \sqrt{(x_2 - x_1)^2 + (y_2 - y_1)^2}$$
$$d = \sqrt{(4 - 0)^2 + (3 - 0)^2}$$
$$d = \sqrt{16 + 9} = \sqrt{25} = 5$$

3. 3.2 units

$$d = \sqrt{(x_2 - x_1)^2 + (y_2 - y_1)^2}$$
$$d = \sqrt{(2 - 1)^2 + (2 - -1)^2}$$
$$d = \sqrt{1 + 9} = \sqrt{10} = 3.16 = 3.2$$

4. 6.4 units

$$d = \sqrt{(x_2 - x_1)^2 + (y_2 - y_1)^2}$$
$$d = \sqrt{(-3 - 1)^2 + (4 - -1)^2}$$
$$d = \sqrt{16 + 25} = \sqrt{41} = 6.4$$

Exercise 16: Intercepts (page 423)

1. x-intercept $(3, 0)$ $0 = 2x - 6$

$6 = 2x$

$3 = x$

    y-intercept $(0, -6)$ $y = (2)0 - 6$

$y = -6$

2. x-intercept $(-5, 0)$ $0 = x + 5$

$-5 = x$

    y-intercept $(0, 5)$ $y = 0 + 5$

$y = 5$

Exercise 17: The Slope of a Line (page 424)

1. slope $= \dfrac{\text{change in y}}{\text{change in x}} = \dfrac{4 - 0}{3 - 0} = \dfrac{4}{3}$

2. slope $= \dfrac{-2 - -1}{-1 - -2} = \dfrac{-1}{1} = -1$

3. slope $= \dfrac{3 - 0}{3 - -3} = \dfrac{3}{6} = \dfrac{1}{2}$

4. no slope (vertical line)

Exercise 18: Multiplying Algebraic Expressions (page 425)

1. $-28x^2y$

2. $-18a^3b^2$

3. $6y^3 - 12y^2 - 21y$

4. $x^2 - 5x + 4$

Exercise 19: The Greatest Common Factor (page 427)

1. $4a^2(25a^2 - 4)$

2. $11p^4(11p - 3)$

3. $9x^2y^2(x + 4y)$

4. $x^2(4x^2 + 25x - 20)$

5. $9x(x^2 - 1)$

6. $6xy(y + 2x)$

Exercise 20: Factoring by Grouping (page 427)

1. $x(x + 4) + 3(x + 4) = (x + 4)(x + 3)$

2. $2y(4y + 3z) + 3z(4y + 3z) =$
$(4y + 3z)(2y + 3z)$

Exercise 21: Factoring to Reverse FOIL (page 428)

1. $(x - 8)(x + 1)$

2. $(x + 5)(x - 3)$

3. $(x - 4)(x - 2)$

CHAPTER 8: MEASUREMENT

Exercise 1: Conversions (page 430)

1. **2.5 lb** $40 \text{ oz} \times \dfrac{1 \text{ lb}}{16 \text{ oz}} = 2.5 \text{ lbs}$

2. **64 oz** $2 \text{ qts} \times \dfrac{32 \text{ oz}}{1 \text{ qt}} = 64 \text{ oz}$

3. **2880 min** $2 \text{ days} \times \dfrac{24 \text{ hrs}}{1 \text{ day}} \times \dfrac{60 \text{ min}}{1 \text{ hr}} =$
2880 min

4. **1.5 qt** $3 \text{ pts} \times \dfrac{1 \text{ qt}}{2 \text{ pts}} = 1.5 \text{ qt}$

5. **704 shrubs**
$2 \times 5280 \text{ ft} = 10560 \text{ ft}, \ 10560 \div 15 = 704$

Exercise 2: Basic Operations with Measurements (page 431)

1. **4 hours 20 minutes**

1 hour 20 minutes

$+$ 3 hours

4 hours 20 minutes

2. **37.1 inches**

5.3 inches $\times$ 7 = 37.1 inches

3. **7 feet 6 inches**

        7 feet 6 inches
$3\overline{)22 \text{ feet 6 inches}}$

    21 feet
      1 foot = 12 inches
            18 inches

4. **7 ounces**

1 pound 4 ounces = 20 ounces

20 ounces − 13 ounces = 7 ounces

5. **(3) $3.25**

45×4 inches = 180 inches

180 inches $\times \dfrac{1 \text{ yard}}{36 \text{ inches}} = 5$ yards

$5 \times \$.65 = \$3.25$

6. **(4) $193.50**

$2\dfrac{1}{2} + 3 + 4\dfrac{3}{4} + 7\dfrac{1}{4} + 4 = 21\dfrac{1}{2}$ hours

$21\dfrac{1}{2} \times \$9 = \$193.50$

Exercise 3: The Metric System (page 433)

1. liter   2. less   3. shorter

4. 75   5. 10

Exercise 4: Metric Measurement (page 434)

1. **1,047 liters**

1 kiloliter = 1000 liters

1000 + 47 = 1047 liters

2. **17.15 meters**

400 cm + 1285 cm + 30 cm = 1715 cm =
17.15 m

3. **5.999 grams**

857 milligrams $\times$ 7 = 5999 milligrams = 5.999 grams

4. **U.S.**

80 km = 80 $\times$ .621 mi = 49.68 mi

55 mph > 49.68 mph

5. **(2) .75 $\times$ \$6.40**

Exercise 5: Money Problems (page 435)

1. **(2) \$51.48**

78 ÷ 3 $\times$ \$1.98 = \$51.48

2. **(3) Friendly Flakes**

Better Bran = \$2.79 ÷ 25 oz = \$.1116/oz

Wheatos = \$2.49 ÷ 12 oz = \$.21/oz

Friendly Flakes = \$3.19 ÷ 29 oz = \$.11/oz

Sugar Snaps= \$2.39 ÷ 20 oz = \$.1195/oz

3. **(2) \$.12**   36 ÷ 2 = 18

\$8.64 ÷ 18 − \$6.48 ÷ 18 = .12

Exercise 6: Time Problems (page 437)

1. **(2) 3**

$.75 \div \$.05 \times 12$ minutes $\div \frac{60\ \text{minutes}}{1\ \text{hour}} =$
3 hours

2. **(3) $4\frac{1}{2} \times 12 \times 5 \times 4$**

3. **(4) 2**

On 5/21 he worked $1\frac{1}{2}$ hours overtime, and on 5/24 he worked $\frac{1}{2}$ hour overtime for a total of 2 hours overtime.

4. **(3) \$550**

40 $\times$ \$12.85 + 2 $\times$ \$18 = \$550

Exercise 7: Scales and Meters (page 439)

1. **(4) $2\frac{1}{2}$**

$\frac{1\ \text{inch}}{180\ \text{miles}} = \frac{N\ \text{inches}}{450\ \text{miles}}$

$N = \frac{1 \times 450}{180} = 2\frac{1}{2}$

2. **(4) \$77.89**

$(173 \times \$.3065 + \$2.00 + \$19.16) \times$
$1.05 = \$77.893725 = \$ 77.89$

CHAPTER 9: GEOMETRY

Exercise 1: Geometry Figures and Shapes (page 442)

1. **G. vertex**

2. **K. 360°**

3. **F. square**

4. **J. 180°**

5. **C. parallel**

6. **E. radius**

7. **B. face**

8. **H. 90°**

9. **D. perpendicular**

10. **A. equilateral**

Exercise 2: Perimeter (page 443)

1. **360 feet**   4 $\times$ 90 feet = 360 feet

2. **49.9 inches**

Perimeter of a triangle = side_1 + side_2 + side_3 = 16.5 + 21 + 12.4 = 49.9 inches

3. **70 m**

20 + 4.2 + 4.7 + 10.8 + 15.3 + 15 = 70

4. **194 feet**

70 + 2 $\times$ 48 + 70 − 42 = 194

5. **97.68 m**

$2 \times 30 + \pi \times 12 = 97.68$

Exercise 3: Area (page 445)

1. **$\frac{11}{14}$ sq in. or .785 sq in.**

Area of a circle = $\pi \times \text{radius}^2$ =
$\frac{22}{7} \times (\frac{1}{2})^2 = \frac{11}{14}$ or $3.14 \times (\frac{1}{2})^2 = .785$

2. **75.09 sq in.**

Area of rectangle = length $\times$ width =
10 $\times$ 4.7 = 47

Area of square = $\text{side}^2 = 5.3^2 = 28.09$

47 + 28.09 = 75.09

3. **\$525**

20 ft $\times$ 15 ft $\times$ \$1.75/sq ft = \$525

4. **78.5 sq ft**

The diameter of the largest circle that will fit is 10 feet. So the radius is 5 feet. Using the formula for the area of a circle, $\pi \times \text{radius}^2 = 3.14 \times 5^2 = 78.5$

5. **10%**

area of pool = $3.14 \times 9^2 = 254.34$

area of yard = 58 $\times$ 45 = 2610

$\frac{254.34}{2610} = \frac{N\%}{100\%}$

$N = \frac{254.34 \times 100}{2610} = 9.7 \approx 10$

6. **22.22 sq yd**

area of patio = 200 sq ft

200 sq ft ÷ 9 sq ft/sq yd = 22.22 sq yd

Exercise 4: Volume (page 447)

1. **72 cu ft**

   Volume of a rectangular container = length × width × height = $6 \times 4 \times 3$ = 72 cu ft

2. **294.375 cu yd**

   Volume of a cone = $\frac{1}{3} \times \pi \times$ radius^2 × height = $\frac{1}{3} \times 3.14 \times 22.5^2 \times 15 = 7948.125$
   7948.125 cu ft ÷ 27 cu ft/cu yd = 294.375

3. **48 cu cm**

   Volume of a square pyramid = $\frac{1}{3} \times$ edge^2 × height = $\frac{1}{3} \times 4^2 \times 9 = 48$

4. **25,872 cu ft**

   Volume of a cylinder = $\pi \times$ radius^2 × height = $\frac{22}{7} \times 14^2 \times 42 = 25872$

Exercise 5: Pairs of Angles (page 449)

1. **38°**

   $\angle b$ and 142° are supplementary angles, so 180°–142° = 38°.

2. **38°**

   $\angle g$ and $\angle f$ are vertical angles, so they are equal and both equal to 38°.

3. **142°**

   $\angle e$ corresponds to 142°, so it is equal to 142°.

4. **105°**

   If two angles combine to form a straight line, they are supplementary and must add up to 180°.

   180° − 75° = 105°

Exercise 6: Angles in Triangles (page 450)

1. **60°**

   The three equal angles of an equilateral triangle add up to 180°, so each must be 60°.

2. **50°**

   65° + 65° = 130° so 180° − 130° = 50°

3. **70°**   180° − 70° − 40° = 70°

4. **125°**   180° − 30° − 25° = 125°

Exercise 7: The Pythagorean Theorem (page 452)

1. **26**

   $a^2 + b^2 = c^2$
   $10^2 + 24^2 = c^2$
   $100 + 576 = 676$
   $c = \sqrt{676} = 26$

2. **25**

   $a^2 + b^2 = c^2$
   $15^2 + 20^2 = c^2$
   $225 + 400 = 625$
   $c = \sqrt{625} = 25$

3. **(3) 100**

   $a^2 + b^2 = c^2$
   $60^2 + 80^2 = c^2$
   $3600 + 6400 = 10000$
   $c = \sqrt{10000} = 100$

4. **(5) 75**

   $a^2 + b^2 = c^2$
   $7^2 + 24^2 = c^2$
   $49 + 576 = 625$
   $c = \sqrt{625} = 25$
   3 wires × 25 = 75

Exercise 8: Similar Triangles (page 454)

1. **12 ft** $\frac{h}{18} = \frac{8}{12}$

   $h = \frac{8 \times 18}{12} = 12$

2. **(a) Find the land measures and set up a proportion.**

   (b) 150 ft $\frac{2}{6} = \frac{50}{d}$

   $d = \frac{6 \times 50}{2} = 150$

3. **31.5 ft** $\frac{h}{42} = \frac{3}{4}$

   $h = \frac{3 \times 42}{4} = 31.5$

ANSWER KEY
POSTTEST:
LANGUAGE ARTS, WRITING

Part I: Editing

1. **(1)** No correction is necessary.

2. **(4)** The sentence is irrelevant to the paragraph topic about home practices affecting allergies.

3. **(3)** Structure the sentence so that the modifying phrase *with a damp cloth* follows *furniture* and provides clear meaning.

4. **(4)** The verb *need* agrees with the subject *Blinds, shades, fans, and draperies*.

5. **(4)** Change the spelling of *weakly* to *weekly* to obtain the meaning needed for the sentence to make sense.

6. **(3)** Paragraph C, which continues support for the main idea about using housekeeping practices to reduce allergens, should be combined with paragraph B.

7. **(2)** The sentence needs an appropriate verb to avoid being a fragment.

8. **(5)** Correct the comma splice by using *and* to join the two verbs *see* and *hear*.

9. **(1)** Using the active rather than passive voice improves the sentence: *Stereotypes of family gatherings and friendships may create some false impressions.*

10. **(1)** Use a comma after an introductory part to a sentence.

11. **(5)** Reduce wordiness and create a more effective sentence with this revision: *No one has to celebrate a holiday in any set way.*

12. **(2)** Sentence 14 provides additional explanation for sentence 10.

13. **(5)** The possessive noun *airlines* needs an apostrophe and should be changed to *airline's*.

14. **(5)** Make the sentence parallel by using *poor service* to fit with *errors* and *problems*.

15. **(2)** The verb *tells* should be changed to the past tense *told* to remain consistent with the sentence and the rest of the letter.

16. **(4)** A subject must be added to the independent clause so that *service* does not spend the night on a bench.

17. **(5)** A subject pronoun and an appropriate verb are needed.

18. **(2)** The verb *are* is needed to agree with the subject *copies*.

19. **(3)** The run-on sentence can be corrected by subordinating the second sentence so that it is dependent on the first.

20. **(1)** No correction is necessary.

21. **(4)** The sentence can be revised to be more easily understood and less wordy with this version: *As cooking continues, the heat spreads to the interior of the food.*

22. **(5)** The series of actions in the sentence should be parallel.

23. **(1)** An appropriate topic sentence for the paragraph identifies the main idea of basic information needed for a person using a microwave.

24. **(2)** The pronoun *their* is plural, but the antecedent *a person* is singular.

25. **(3)** A shorter, more effective version of the sentence would read this way: *The time needed to cook the food depends on the amount of food cooked.*

Language Arts, Writing Posttest Evaluation Chart

Use the Answer Key on the previous page to check your answers to the Posttest. Then find the item number of each question you missed and circle it on the chart below to determine the writing content areas in which you need more practice.

Content Area	Item #	Review Chapters
Nouns	13	1
Verbs	4, 15	1
Subject/Verb Agreement	18	1
Pronoun Use	17, 24	1
Sentence Fragments, Run-ons, Comma Splices	7, 8, 19	2
Independent/Dependent Clauses	1, 9, 11	2
Effective Sentence Structure	21, 25	2
Dangling or Misplaced Modification	3, 16	2
Parallel Structure	14, 22	2
Capitalization, Punctuation, Spelling	5, 10, 20	3
Paragraph Composition/Text Division	6, 23	4
Paragraph Unity and Coherence	2, 12	4

Part II: The Essay

If possible, give your essay to an instructor to evaluate. If, however, you are unable to show your work to someone else, use the five questions in the Essay Evaluation Checklist to help evaluate your writing.

Essay Evaluation Checklist

Yes	No	
		1. Does the essay answer the question asked?
		2. Does the main point of the essay stand out clearly?
		3. Does each paragraph contain specific examples and details that develop and explain the main point?
		4. Are the ideas organized clearly into paragraphs and complete sentences?
		5. Is the essay easy to read, or do problems in grammar usage, punctuation, spelling, or word choice interfere?

Important Note

On the actual GED Language Arts, Writing Test, you will be given one score, which is a composite of your scores from Part I and Part II of the Test. This score is determined by grading your essay holistically, giving it a score, then combining this score with your score from Part I in a proportion determined by the GED Testing Service.

ANSWER KEY
POSTTEST :
SOCIAL STUDIES

1. **Comprehension (1)** By representing the budget as a boat that is positioned over a wave, the cartoonist is making a statement about the changeable nature of the economy. The budget could be said to be in a stable position that is only temporary. The cartoonist wants to alert people to the fact that the economy is very changeable and that the budget needs to be carefully watched as the economy changes.

2. **Comprehension (4)** The Second Continental Congress, made up of representatives from the original thirteen colonies, is giving a declaration of its intention to decree independence from England. After that time, a convention of representatives was gathered to create a constitution that the new independent government could use as an outline in the formation of the laws of this new country. The House of Representative was not created until after the Constitution called for the three separate branches of government.

3. **Application (5)** The change for both groups seems to be a slow increase. This would mean that an increase to 2 percent for those over 85 years of age is likely as well as an increase for the age group of 65 years and older. It would seem more likely that the increase for the 65 and older age group might be more realistically 15 percent, given growth in the past. It is not likely that the statistics for the 65 and older age group would jump up to 30 percent.

4. **Evaluation (1)** Because the people of a state elect the members of Congress (House of Representatives and the Senate), this branch can best determine the sentiments of the people of this nation and would represent their opinions about declaring war better than a single president.

5. **Application (4)** If liberals are for limited military spending, then the Star Wars defense program would not be something they would financially support.

6. **Analysis (2)** The information in the paragraph mentions that the anthropologist studies human skeletal remains while the archaeologist studies the artifacts. In this case the remains on the Yucatán Peninsula would be the discovery that would involve the anthropologist.

7. **Analysis (2)** The graph tells us that there are fewer people per computer in the public schools than there were in the past. It does not indicate why the ratio has changed. There is no information regarding finances or technology.

8. **Analysis (4)** The amendments listed do not address the census and tax laws. Amendment 16 states that Congress has the power to lay and collect taxes on income.

9. **Analysis (2)** The ability to vote and to participate in the government of the United States is deemed a right granted to every citizen. The right to vote is not dependent on current financial status.

10. **Analysis (1)** This is the only logical conclusion that can be inferred from the information presented on the graph. While some other choices may be true, you cannot determine this from looking at the graph.

11. **Evaluation (2)** By demanding that the Confederate states ratify the Thirteenth Amendment, President Johnson is showing what is considered to be a strong pro-North attitude. The other responses support a pro-South attitude.

12. **Comprehension (3)** The president of the United States is determined only by a general election. The primary election determines what candidate a political party chooses to run in the general election.

13. **Evaluation (1)** The government has a responsibility first to the industries that support the economy of our own nation. In many cases, foreign automobile manufacturers have built plants in the United States. By building the foreign cars here and using American laborers, foreign companies have decreased the concern that

the selling of foreign cars in the United States competes too much with American corporations.

14. **Application (1)** This map indicates political regions in Mexico as well as southern states in the United States and Central American country borders.

15. **Analysis (1)** The United States spends 277 million dollars in military expenditures, and this is clearly more than three times the 76 million that Russia spends on its military.

16. **Application (3)** Democratic socialism controls the main resource industries, while allowing some private enterprise. The consumer has greater freedom under this economic system than other socialist systems.

17. **Application (3)** Under the theory that the strongest survive, governments would not create the social support systems mentioned in choices 1 and 5. Moderation in spending (choice 4) also limits the ability to create a very strong military. If there is a belief in noninterference in business, then the stronger business will be successful. This is possibly at the cost of smaller businesses, which is in keeping with the philosophy expressed by Darwin.

18. **Analysis (3)** Any citizen accused of a crime gets an opportunity to face the accuser and be informed of the crime for which he/she is accused before being held by police.

19. **Analysis (3)** Constitutional changes throughout the years have allowed women to vote. Later changes allowed those who are eighteen years old to vote, thereby giving them a voice in their country's government.

20. **Analysis (1)** HMOs have been accused of placing the monetary benefits of health care above the medical needs of the patient. Since the HMOs are at the mercy of their stockholders to show profits, expenditures may be limited to allow for greater profits.

21. **Comprehension (2)** Ellis Island was the gateway to the United States for many immigrants, but it was only one of several ports of entry. Not all immigrants had to be processed on the island; those passengers in first or second class were processed on board the ship. Those processed on Ellis Island came from a great variety of foreign lands.

22. **Evaluation (3)** The creators of the Constitution realized they could not foresee all the possible situations that might challenge their new democratic country. They created a system that would allow for these adjustments but required that changes would oblige a large percentage of the representative government to agree to the Constitutional amendments.

23. **Evaluation (5)** All the other responses were similar in their support of teamwork and a cooperative united American spirit that kept the country together while the United States sent troops to fight overseas in World War II.

24. **Evaluation (3)** Businesses in the West were unsatisfied with transporting raw materials and products by shipping around the southern tip of South America or through Panama. A railway system that connected the two sides of the nation was an eventual necessity for a country with a growing economy. It wasn't until much later that railways were used as a form of travel for enjoyment.

25. **Analysis (1)** The deposits of oil are determined by processes of nature and are not impacted by political borders. The deposits are not given any production values and cannot be compared to deposits found elsewhere.

Social Studies Posttest Evaluation Chart

Use the answer key on the previous pages to check your answers to the Posttest. Then find the item number of each question you missed and circle it on the chart below to determine the social studies content areas in which you need more practice.

Skill Area/ Content Area	Comprehension	Application	Analysis	Evaluation
World History		16, 17	6, 10	
U.S. History	2, 13		8, 9	11, 23, 24
Civics and Government	12	4	18, 19	5, 22
Economics	1		7, 15, 20	21
Geography		3, 14	25	

ANSWER KEY
POSTTEST :
<u>SCIENCE</u>

1. **Comprehension (4)** Although the overharvesting of seafood species is an environmental concern, it is not a cause or result of unusual weather patterns.

2. **Application (3)** The cornea is considered a tissue that could be donated to restore eyesight. The other choices are organs.

3. **Evaluation (3)** The passage supports the view that excessive dieting can be dangerous to one's health, and many people are very concerned about their body fat.

4. **Application (3)** The flea lives on the dog's or cat's blood; therefore, the relationship would be described as parasite-host.

5. **Analysis (3)** According to the data provided, the conclusion is that all regions of the brain are vital.

6. **Evaluation (3)** By studying heredity in pea plants, geneticists have learned how plants and animals transmit traits to their offspring.

7. **Comprehension (5)** The rock is not in motion, so it has potential energy.

8. **Analysis (2)** A conclusion from the passage is that a crystal must have good cleavage in order to be cut into a gemstone.

9. **Analysis (3)** The data on the circle graph prove that many people are still contracting AIDS; therefore, it can be assumed that all people need to be educated on the severity of the disease.

10. **Analysis (2)** A resumption of the trade winds would reverse the condition that caused El Niño.

11. **Analysis (4)** Pollution seriously affected 21% of the water and moderately affected another 32%. This means that over 50% was affected at some level.

12. **Application (4)** The wind chill would be most severe at −25 degrees Fahrenheit.

13. **Evaluation (3)** The cost can be defended because the passage states that scientists hope to harness plasma as an inexpensive energy source.

14. **Application (4)** An acid registers below 7 on the pH scale.

15. **Comprehension (3)** We can predict that diluting an industrial hydrogen peroxide solution with water will reduce it to a concentration suitable for use as an antiseptic.

16. **Application (5)** Polarization of light rays is the restriction of reflected rays to one plane.

17. **Evaluation (3)** Healthy foods provide important minerals and vitamins naturally and economically and are a better choice for changing eating habits.

18. **Application (2)** A strained muscle is the only soft-tissue injury listed.

19. **Comprehension (2)** Tissue engineering involves the knowledge of life processes (biology), disease (medicine), and science and mathematical principles (engineering).

20. **Evaluation (4)** According to the passage, quasars were discovered when astronomers picked up mysterious wave emissions from planetary objects. This fact supports the belief that the discovery of quasars was an accident.

21. **Evaluation (2)** According to the information in the passage, the true relationship is that the transuranium elements become less stable as their atomic numbers increase. This means that the greater the atomic number, the lower the half-life.

22. **Application (5)** According to the circle graph, industry uses more than half (51%) of the water supply.

23. **Application (3)** A corm is similar to a bulb, which grows underground and stores food for the plant's usage. Corms and bulbs multiply and can be divided to start new plants.

24. **Analysis (3)** From the information given, the only choice that can be made is that plants may become less dependent on insects for nitrogen.

25. **Evaluation (1)** Since cancer can spread so widely, only long-term scans of the body that indicate an absence of cancer can indicate that the cancer has been cured.

Science Posttest Evaluation Chart

Use the answer key above to check your answers to the Posttest. Then find the item number of each question you missed and circle it on the chart below to determine the science content areas in which you need more practice.

Skill Area/ Content Area	Comprehension	Application	Analysis	Evaluation
Life Sciences (Biology)	19	2, 4, 18, 22, 23	5, 9, 24	3, 6, 21, 25
Earth & Space Science	1	12	10, 11	20
Physical Sciences (Chemistry and Physics)	7, 15	14, 16	8	13, 17

ANSWER KEY
POSTTEST :
LANGUAGE ARTS, READING

1. **Application (1)** A star would be the most effective substitution because, like a rainbow, it is a natural object unlike the other choices.

2. **Analysis (4)** The experience of childhood guides and produces, or "fathers," a man. Therefore, the child becomes the father of the man.

3. **Synthesis (1)** The image of nature, "a rainbow in the sky", and the speaker's response, "My heart leaps up," affirm the value of nature. The tie to nature is also recognized in the words "wish my days to be/Bound each to each by natural piety." The combination of these directs the reader to the wonders of nature.

4. **Comprehension (1)** References to the engagement of Mortimer and Elaine are made repeatedly throughout lines 16–63.

5. **Analysis (3)** Abby expresses her excitement and interest by asking Mortimer several questions about Elaine and the engagement. Abby also proposes having a celebration.

6. **Synthesis (5)** The tone of the passage is light-hearted because the language "That's a horundinida carnina," and the dialogue, "that's Emma B. Stout ascending to heaven," create an expectation of fun.

7. **Analysis (3)** Choice 3 states that Chance is to care for plants, trees, and grasses; gardening itself is no indication that anyone, including Chance, has very limited capabilities. Choices 1, 2, 4, and 5 are all statements supported by the text.

8. **Analysis (5)** Chance is most like an obedient child because all his life he has always done "exactly as he was told" by the Old Man. He has never questioned that he could never venture outside the garden or speak to anyone else. There is no support for the other choices, especially that of an unhappy teenager (choice 2) who is likely to rebel.

9. **Synthesis (2)** Most of the supporting details describe Chance and his life since childhood, which form the overall purpose of the passage. Choices 1 and 3 minimally describe the Old Man and Chance's mother, but these characters are not the central focus. There is no explanation of health benefits of gardening (choice 4) or problems of raising orphans (choice 5).

10. **Synthesis (4)** The reader has come to know that Chance is a man of limited ability, little knowledge of the world, and sheltered experience; therefore, the reader should have a reaction of surprise that he adopts a new lifestyle that includes influence and power. There is no reason for the reader to react with jealousy, hostility, amusement, or indifference.

11. **Comprehension (4)** This is the option that uses the phrase *unraveling of unquestioned belief that the world revolved around Mama.* A star attracts a great deal of attention and expects others to be drawn to her. Choices 1, 2, 3, and 5 all contain clues of special attention or "star" status: invented words, queen, projects, and her own solar system.

12. **Application (5)** The details that lead to the astronomy section are references to "star," "pull on the earth," "orbit," "solar system," and "separate universe." There are no details as references to the other sciences—chemistry, biology, physics, or geology (choices 1, 2, 3, and 4).

13. **Analysis (1)** The author's details have the effect of causing the reader to feel sympathy for the narrator because she has a mother who must be the center of attention and a father who seems to be fairly uninvolved. Choices 2, 3, 4, and 5 are not true statements.

14. **Synthesis (3)** The point of view from which the story is told is that of the daughter of a Ya-Ya. There are many references to "Mama" and to "my mother." The daughter is not named in these passages.

15. **Synthesis (2)** The overall purpose of the passages from the novel is to explore a daughter's feelings about her mother both in the past and in the present. The narrator mentions developing guilt if she were to "eclipse Mama in any little way," even "winning a spelling bee." The intent of the passages is not to be a lexicon of words (choice 1). The passages do not give much attention to explaining how a human "star" can rise and fall (choice 3) or to comparing and contrasting personalities of the Ya-Yas (choice 4). The narrator's father is mentioned in only one line, so there is no examining of the relationship between the narrator's parents (choice 5).

16. **Comprehension (5)** In Passage One, the next line after the sentence with "stolen moments" is "The joke you never expected." Also, further support for this view is found in the first paragraph: "Always, the audience will make its own discoveries." Certainly, comedy can be described in the ways indicated by the other choices; however, those do not explain "stolen moments."

17. **Application (2)** In Passage Two, the author states, "Today Lubitsch would do it not unlike modern film-comedy masters like James L. Brooks, Mike Nichols, or Woody Allen."

18. **Analysis (3)** In Passage Two, the author states, "But the timeless images of their films often come not in the banter but in the devastating dialogue-free moments . . . " This is the only false comparison.

19. **Analysis (4)** In Passage One, the author states, "Director Ernst Lubitsch was an early master of this, building elegantly hilarious jokes, one on top of the other, until his audience was charmed and satisfied." The hat allows for the building of jokes.

20. **Synthesis (1)** We can expect that the audience would be displeased at being rushed because of these author's comments: "the audience will make its own discoveries," ". . . stolen moments. The joke you never expected," and "dialogue-free moments."

Language Arts, Reading Posttest Evaluation Chart

Use the answer key above to check your answers to the Posttest. Then find the item number of each question you missed and circle it on the chart below to determine the reading content areas in which you need more practice.

Skill Area/ Content Area	Comprehension	Application	Analysis	Evaluation
Fiction	11	12	7, 8, 13	9, 10, 14, 15
Poetry		1	2	3
Drama	4		5	6
Nonfiction	16	17	18, 19	20

ANSWER KEY
POSTTEST :
MATHEMATICS

Part I

1. (2) $\dfrac{19(360) + 18(400) + 8(480) + 5(600)}{19 + 18 + 8 + 5}$

First find the total wages paid by multiplying the number of employees times the weekly wages each employee earned for each category. Then add those amounts. Finally divide by the sum of the employees.

2. (2) $835.20

$19(360) + 18(400) + 8(480) + 5(600) = 20880$

$20880 \times 4\% = 20880 \times .04 = 835.20$

3. 41.21

$\$450 \times 9.9\% = 450 \times .099 = \$44.55$

$450 + 44.55 = 494.55$

$494.55 \div 12 = \$41.21$

4. (2) $85.25

Put the numbers in order and select the middle value.

$60, 75.25, 77, 84, \Uparrow 86.50, 90.60, 92, 98$

$(84 + 86.50) \div 2 = 85.25$

5. (4) 77°

$F = 1.8C + 32 = 1.8 \times 25 + 32 = 45 + 32 = 77$

6. (4) .12

$\dfrac{.38 + .14 - .09 + .09 + .08}{5} = \dfrac{.60}{5} = .12$

7. 10

$30 - 27 = 3$ failed

$\dfrac{3}{30} = \dfrac{N}{100} \quad N = \dfrac{3 \times 100}{30} = 10$

8. (1) Average sales were higher in 2001.

9. 19.3 in.

Use the Pythagorean relationship.

$a^2 + b^2 = c^2$

$25.5^2 + h^2 = 32^2$

$650.25 + h^2 = 1024$

$h^2 = 373.75$

$h = \sqrt{373.75} = 19.3$

10. (1) $6^3 = 6 \times 12 \times h$

Volume of a cube = edge^3 = 6^3

Volume of a rectangular box =

length $\times$ width $\times$ height = $6 \times 12 \times h$

So $6^3 = 6 \times 12 \times h$

11. (2) 38 cu in.

Volume of a cylinder =

$\pi \times$ radius$^2 \times$ height =

$\dfrac{22}{7} \times 3^2 \times 7 = 198$ cu in.

Volume of a rectangular box =

length $\times$ width $\times$ height =

$5 \times 4 \times 8 = 160$ cu in.

$198 - 160 = 38$ cu in.

12. (4) 4.25×10^{-3}

$2.125 \div 500 = .00425 = 4.25 \times 10^{-3}$

Part II

13. (2) $1^5, 4^1, 6, 2^3$

$1^5 = 1, 4^1 = 4, 6 = 6, 2^3 = 8$

14. (4) 43,200

$4.32 \times 10^4 = 43200$

Move the decimal point 4 places to the right.

15. (1) $\dfrac{1}{3}$

$\dfrac{10 \text{ married}}{30 \text{ total}} = \dfrac{1}{3}$

16. (1) 25 pounds

$\dfrac{150}{6} = 25$

17. (4) $13,050

$20\% + 9\% = 29\% = .29$

$\$45,000 \times .29 = \$13,050$

18. (4) 13

$x + 2 > 13$

When $x = 13$, then $13 + 2 = 15$, and 15 is greater than 13.

19.

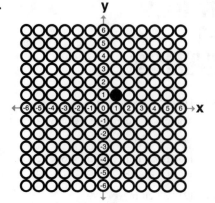

20. **(1)** **(.75)(.90)(126)**

$100\% - 25\% = 75\% = .75$

$100\% - 10\% = 90\% = .90$

For coat sale, pay 75% of $126.

Using coupon, pay 90% of the 75% of $126 = (.75)(.90)(126).

21. **(2)** **30°**

$$x + 2x + 3x = 180°$$
$$6x = 180°$$
$$x = 30°$$

22. **(1)** $\frac{t}{3} - .75$

$\frac{t}{3}$ = cost of one roll

Then subtract the 75¢ rebate.

23. **(3)** **30**

Area $\triangle CDE = \frac{1}{2} \times 6 \times 8 = 24$ sq in.

Since $\triangle ABC$ is similar to $\triangle CDE$, the sides are in proportion.

$$\frac{12}{8} = \frac{CB}{6}$$

$$CB = \frac{6 \times 12}{8} = \frac{72}{8} = 9$$

Area $\triangle ABC = \frac{1}{2} \times 9 \times 12 = 54$ sq in.

$\triangle ABC - \triangle CDE = 54 - 24 = 30$

24. **(1)** **Line M and line N both have positive slopes.**

Use the slope of a line formula $\frac{y_2 - y_1}{x_2 - x_1}$.

Slope of line $M = \frac{7-4}{2-1} = \frac{3}{1} = 3$

Slope of line $N = \frac{5-3}{3-1} = \frac{2}{2} = 1$

Both slopes are positive numbers.

25. **(1)** **8 sq units**

Area of a parallelogram = base × height = $4 \times 2 = 8$ sq units

Mathematics Posttest Evaluation Chart

Use the answer key above to check the Posttest. Then find the item number of each problem you missed and circle it on the evaluation chart to determine the mathematics skills and content areas in which you need more practice.

Skill Area/Content Area	Item Number	Review Chapters
Number Operations and Number Sense	Part I: 1, 2, 3 Part II: 13, 14, 16	1, 2, 3, 6
Data Analysis, Statistics, and Probability	Part I: 4, 6, 7, 8 Part II: 15, 17, 20	5
Measurement and Geometry	Part I: 9, 11 Part II: 21, 23, 25	8, 9
Algebra, Functions, and Patterns	Part I: 5, 10, 12 Part II: 18, 19, 22, 24	7

INDEX

Trapezoid, 441
Trench (geology), 236
Triangles, 441, 450–455
    equilateral, 441
    isosceles, 441
    Pythagorean theorem and, 450–452
    right, 441
    similar, 452–454
Truman, Harry, 162

U

Ultraviolet rays, 280
United Nations, 162
United States. *See also* Congress (U.S.);
        Constitution (U.S.); Supreme Court
    government, 147, 169–180
    history, 143–168
    political system, 177–180
Universe, 229
Unknowns, 348
Unlike fractions, 363
Urbanization, 156

V

Values, 56
Variables, 348, 408
Verbs, 64–70
    base, 65
    function of, 65
    helping, 65
    irregular, 66–67
    linking, 64–65
    regular, 65
    subject-verb agreement, 71–73
    tenses, 67–70
Verse, 306
Vertical angles, 448
Vespucci, Amerigo, 135, 143
Veto, 174
Vietnam War, 166
Viewing components, 326, 335
Voice (grammar)
    active, 87–88
    passive, 87–88
Volcano, 236
Volume, 446–447

W

Wars. See specific wars
Washington, George, 150
Water cycle, 248
Watergate scandal, 167
Wave Theory of Light, 280
Waves, 277–279
Weathering, 242
Wilson, Woodrow, 160

Wind power, 286
Women, suffrage for, 160
Word problems
    in algebra, 411–413
    estimating for, 360
    interest and, 405–406
    with money, 435
    multistep equations, 416–417
    percent problems, 402–403, 404
    signed numbers in, 385
    with time, 436
    triangular relationships in, 450
Wordiness, 88
Work, 272
World history, 129–142
World War I, 139, 160
World War II, 141, 162
Writing
    descriptive, 116
    GED test essay, 109–126
    informative, 116–117
    narrative, 115
    persuasive, 117
    printing press and, 134
    product, 109
    types, 114–117
Writing process, 109–114, 119
Writing product, essay, 119–122

Z

Zero, 380
    in decimals, 351